Charles D. Ellis is the author of fourteen books, including *Winning the Loser's Game*, *Capital* and the biography *Joe Wilson*. For thirty years he was managing partner of Greenwich Associates, the international strategy consulting firm he founded that serves virtually all the leading financial service organizations around the world. A past trustee of Yale University and chair of its investment committee, he is a trustee of the Robert Wood Johnson Foundation, director of Vanguard, and chair of the Whitehead Institute of Biomedical Research and consults on investing with major institutions in Asia, Europe and North America.

THE
PARTNERSHIP

THE MAKING OF
GOLDMAN SACHS

CHARLES D. ELLIS

PENGUIN BOOKS

PENGUIN BOOKS

Published by the Penguin Group
Penguin Books Ltd, 80 Strand, London WC2R ORL, England
Penguin Group (USA) Inc., 375 Hudson Street, New York, New York 10014, USA
Penguin Group (Canada), 90 Eglinton Avenue East, Suite 700, Toronto, Ontario, Canada M4P 2Y3
(a division of Pearson Penguin Canada Inc.)
Penguin Ireland, 25 St Stephen's Green, Dublin 2, Ireland (a division of Penguin Books Ltd)
Penguin Group (Australia), 250 Camberwell Road, Camberwell, Victoria 3124, Australia
(a division of Pearson Australia Group Pty Ltd)
Penguin Books India Pvt Ltd, 11 Community Centre, Panchsheel Park, New Delhi – 110 017, India
Penguin Group (NZ), 67 Apollo Drive, Rosedale, North Shore 0632, New Zealand
(a division of Pearson New Zealand Ltd)
Penguin Books (South Africa) (Pty) Ltd, 24 Sturdee Avenue, Rosebank, Johannesburg 2196, South Africa
Penguin Books Ltd, Registered Offices: 80 Strand, London WC2R ORL, England

www.penguin.com

First published in the United States of America by The Penguin Press,
a member of Penguin Group (USA) Inc. 2008
First published in Great Britain by Allen Lane 2008
Published in Penguin Books with a new chapter 2009
1

www.greenpenguin.co.uk

TO MY GRANDCHILDREN
JADE, MORGAN, CHARLES, AND RAY

CONTENTS

INTRODUCTION

T his book was almost never written—several different times. In the winter of 1963 at Harvard Business School, I was, like all my classmates, looking for a job. My attention was drawn to a three-by-five piece of yellow paper posted at eye level on a bulletin board in Baker Library. In the upper left corner was printed "Correspondence Opportunities" and typed to the right was the name "Goldman Sachs." As a Boston securities lawyer, my dad had a high regard for the firm, so I read the brief description of the job with interest but was stopped by the salary: $5,800.

My then wife had just graduated from Wellesley with three distinctions: she was Phi Beta Kappa, the soprano soloist, and had covered her costs with a scholarship and loans. I was determined to pay off those loans, so I figured I'd need to earn at least $6,000. With no thought of the possibility of earning a bonus or a raise, I naively "knew" I could not make it on $5,800. So Goldman Sachs was not for me. If I had joined the firm, like everyone else who has made a career with Goldman Sachs I would never have written an insider's study of Goldman Sachs.*

---

* John Whitehead and Robert Rubin have both included a few stories about the firm in their books but have certainly not tried to provide a complete picture. Lisa Endlich, a fine writer but with limited access to the full range of

In the early 1970s, while promising future partners that we would develop our fledgling consultancy, Greenwich Associates, into a truly superior professional firm, I had to laugh at myself: "You dummy! You make the promise, but you don't even know what a truly superior professional firm is all about or how to get there. You've never even worked for one. You'd better learn quickly."

From then on, at every opportunity I asked my friends and acquaintances in law, consulting, investing, and banking which firms they thought were the best in their field and what characteristics made them the best. Over and over again, well past the bounds of persistence, I probed those same questions. Inevitably, a pattern emerged.

A truly great professional firm has certain characteristics: The most capable professionals agree it is the best firm to work for and that it recruits and keeps the best people. The most discriminating and significant clients agree that the firm consistently delivers the best service value. And the great firms are, sometimes grudgingly, recognized by competitors as the real leaders in their field over many years. On occasion, challenger firms rise to prominence—usually on the strength of one exciting and compelling service capability—but do not sustain excellence.

Many factors that contribute to sustained excellence vary from profession to profession, but certain factors are important in every great firm: long-serving and devoted "servant leaders"; meritocracy in compensation and authority; disproportionate devotion to client service; distinctively high professional and ethical standards; a strong culture that always reinforces professional standards of excellence; and long-term values, policies, concepts, and behavior consistently trumping near-term "opportunities." Each great organization is a "one-firm firm" with consistent values, practices, and culture across geographies, across very different lines of business, and over many years. All the great firms have constructive "paranoia"—always on the alert for and anxious about challenging competitors. However, they seldom try to learn much from competitors: they see themselves as unique. But like Olympic athletes who excel in different events, they are also very much the same.

---

partners, wrote a thoughtful and wide-ranging study centered on the development of the firm in the 1980s and 1990s. Bob Lenzner, a gifted writer for *Forbes* who had worked in arbitrage at Goldman Sachs a generation ago, started a book but set it aside, saying he didn't want to lose his friends at the firm.

Armed with Greenwich Associates' extensive proprietary research and working closely as a strategy consultant with all the major securities firms, I was in a unique position to make comparisons between competing firms on the dozens of salient criteria on which they were evaluated by their own clients market by market, year after year. Over time, I became convinced that my explorations were producing important discoveries that would be of interest to others who are fascinated by excellence, who retain professional firms for important services, or who will spend their working careers in professional firms. One discovery surprised me: In each profession, one single firm is usually recognized as "the best of us" by the professional practitioners—Capital Group in investing, McKinsey in consulting, Cravath in law (nicely rivaled by Davis Polk or Skadden Arps), and Mayo Clinic in medicine (nicely rivaled by Johns Hopkins). And Goldman Sachs in securities.

Ten or twenty years ago, many people in the securities business would have argued that other firms were as good or better, but no longer. (Much further back, few would have ever chosen Goldman Sachs.) For many years, it has seemed clear to me that Goldman Sachs had unusual strengths going for it. Compared to its competitors, the firm recruited more intriguing people who cared more about their firm. Their shared commitments, or "culture," were stronger and more explicit. And the leaders of the firm at every level were more rigorous, more thoughtful, and far more determined to improve in every way over the longer term. They took a longer-horizon view *and* were more alert to details. They knew more about and cared more about their people. They worked much harder and were more modest. They knew more *and* were hungrier to learn. Their focus was always on finding ways to do better and be better. Their aspirations were not on what they wanted to be, but on what they wanted to do.

Goldman Sachs has, in the last sixty years, gone from being a marginal Eastern U.S. commercial-paper dealer, with fewer than three hundred employees and a clientele largely dependent on one improbable investment banker, to a global juggernaut. It has recruited better people than any other financial service firm, adapted to or created change faster and more forcefully, attracted more important clients, developed leadership in more businesses, spawned more centimillionaires, and set the standard of excellence on Wall Street and around the world. Goldman Sachs today is the most powerful and most dynamic organization in the history of finance.

Being liked is not a business priority for Goldman Sachs—respect leads to more business and more profits. Investment banking, bond dealing, risk arbitrage, foreign exchange, prime brokerage, private equity, real estate, commodities, hedge funds, and derivatives are not nice businesses. They are brutally competitive and can be rough. Winning, for those who really care, is worth all the strain. The financial rewards to the best can be spectacular. The drive to win those large financial rewards can be comparably spectacular.

When everything is going well and everyone is prospering, we cheer the achievers and are fascinated by the glitter and glamour. But the cheering stops and we look for "Who did this?" when financial markets plummet and the economy is thrown into crisis, when major companies falter or fail, when many people lose their jobs and many more worry about losing theirs, and when the government has to incur huge debts to rescue organizations that are seen by the public as central participants in the creation of the disaster they are experiencing so personally. In the topsy-turvy world of public perceptions, Goldman Sachs got flipped in late 2008 and 2009 from being one of the most admired financial organizations in the world with a long tradition of leadership in philanthropy and public service to being questioned as a potentially malign conspiracy with far too much influence.

Suspicion, anger, distrust, hostility, indignation, and a gaggle of rude epithets were thrown at Wall Street and its major firms and their leaders as people all over the world realized the magnitude of harm and destruction coming from the awful experience so gently termed "the global financial crisis." At the very center of that perfect storm was Goldman Sachs.

The search for the cause of an economic collapse can convert quickly into a search for villains and conspiracies. In 2008 and 2009, a whole new dimension was added to the challenge of leadership at Goldman Sachs. After a century of carefully avoiding visibility and publicity as a very private firm, the firm had gone public and, given its prominence, was suddenly a high-profile factor in the unfamiliar world of politics and mass media. Public opinion and the media, which had been giddily celebrating the successes and gawking at the paychecks, swiftly turned against "the banks" and "Wall Street"—and Goldman Sachs—just as Sidney Weinberg had warned could happen half a century ago.

Conspiracy theorists seemed to enjoy pointing out how many people from Goldman Sachs were in influential government positions and how important to

Goldman Sachs various decisions were: letting Lehman Brothers—a major competitor—go bankrupt; bailing out AIG—a major counterparty; and investing $10 billion of federal money in Goldman Sachs.

On one level, Goldman Sachs has recently been paying a substantial "penalty of leadership," particularly in the popular press where just a few years ago it had been showered with persistent adulation. The change in perception has certainly been unpleasant for the people of Goldman Sachs, who believe deeply that their firm is the best and strongest investment bank and is established today in its strongest ever competitive position.

Of the thirty thousand people of Goldman Sachs, fewer than half of one percent are even mentioned in this book, but the great story of Goldman Sachs is really their story—and that of the many thousands who joined the firm before them and enabled it to become today's Goldman Sachs. Goldman Sachs is a partnership. The legal fact that after more than a hundred years it became a public corporation may matter to lawyers and investors, but the dominating reality is that Goldman Sachs is a true partnership in the way people at the firm work together, in the way alumni feel about the firm and each other, and in the powerful spiritual bonds that command their attention and commitment.

This biography of Goldman Sachs explains how and why Goldman Sachs has risen from the near-terminal disaster of Goldman Sachs Trading Corporation in 1929 to global leadership in finance in 2009. The story of Goldman Sachs— and the people who made it—is a fascinating adventure story and represents the broader story of America's rise to global power and the continuing challenges of earning the respect and trust of others.

Charles D. Ellis
New Haven, Connecticut
May 2009

1

BEGINNINGS

On November 16, 1907, an unremarkable event took place that would have remarkable importance for Goldman Sachs: Looking for a job, sixteen-year-old Sidney Weinberg headed back to Wall Street. The territory was familiar. Young Weinberg had worked there briefly as a "flower and feather horse," delivering millinery goods for two dollars a week, and one summer as a runner for three odd-lot brokerage houses[1]—until each of these employers found out he held two other identical jobs and all three firms promptly fired him.

Earlier in 1907 Weinberg had learned from a pal on the Brooklyn-to-Manhattan ferry that there was a panic on Wall Street, which Weinberg later admitted "meant no more to me than if you said it was raining." The panic caused a run on the Trust Company of America, so Weinberg could make even more money—up to five dollars a day—by standing in the long queue of anxious depositors who lined up to withdraw their balances and, when he got close to the bank's door, selling his place in the line to a late-arriving, desperate depositor. Quickly getting back in line to work his way up to the door, he did the same thing all over again. Pocketing all the money he could, Weinberg skipped school, but after having played hooky for a full week, he was not allowed to return to school at PS 13. So now he needed a real job.

His father, Pincus Weinberg, was a struggling, Polish-born wholesale liquor dealer and sometime bootlegger who, having been widowed with eleven children, had recently remarried. His new wife did not want the third-eldest child—that fresh kid—around the house, so Sidney was pushed out to fend for himself. As a seventh-grade dropout, he had only one apparent advantage—a general letter of introduction signed by one of his teachers, saying: "To whom it may concern: It gives me great pleasure to testify to the business ability of the bearer, Sidney Weinberg. He is happy when he is busy, and is always ready and willing to oblige. We believe he will give satisfaction to anyone who may need his services."

Short—his legs were only twenty-six inches long—and with a speaking voice that was heavily larded with a thick Brooklyn Jewish accent in which girls were "goils," oil was "erl," and turmoil was "toi-merl," Weinberg went looking for a job—*any* job. Deciding to try lower Manhattan's financial district, he concentrated on the tall buildings. As he later explained his first triumph on Wall Street, "Looking for an indoor job, I walked into 43 Exchange Place, a nice-looking, tall building, at eight o'clock one morning and took the elevator to the twenty-third floor. Starting from the top, I stuck my head in every office and asked as politely as I could, 'Want a boy?' By six o'clock, I had worked my way down to the third floor and still had no job. Goldman Sachs was on that floor and it was closing up for the day. The cashier told me there was no work, but to come back. Next morning, I came back at eight o'clock and started right where I had left off."

Brazenly, Weinberg said he had been *asked* to come back. "The cashier, Mr. Morrissey, turned to the hall porter: 'Jarvis, do you need an assistant?' Jarvis was willing, so they hired me at $5 a week as assistant to Jarvis the janitor." His new job included the lowly task of cleaning out cuspidors.* Lowly, but a start.

Weinberg did not stay long at the starting line. Told to take an eight-foot

---

* Until his death at seventy-seven in 1969, Weinberg kept in his office the brass spittoon he allegedly polished for Jarvis in his first job. He also kept a bag he bought as a naive young man at Niagara Falls from a smooth-talking con man who said, "You look like a great young man. Do you know that down at the bottom of those falls are diamonds and nobody's been able to get them, but I can, and I have some of them in this little bag here, and I'm willing to sell it to you." "Well, how much do you want for it?" "One buck," said the man. "I haven't got a dollar. I've only got fifty cents left." "Well, you're such a promising young man I'll sell it to you for fifty cents." Weinberg bought the bag for fifty cents and soon learned there was nothing in it but an ordinary pebble. He kept that pebble all his life as a reminder to never be a sucker again.

flagpole uptown on the trolley—"Ever try to carry a flagpole on a trolley car? It's one hell of a *job!*"—Weinberg arrived at Paul Sachs's door, where he was met not by a butler, but by Mr. Sachs himself, a son of Goldman Sachs's first junior partner. Demonstrating his lifelong knack for becoming friendly with men in high positions who could help him, Weinberg so impressed Sachs with his energy and brightness that Sachs invited the likable teenager to stay for dinner—with, of course, the servants. Weinberg soon became head of the mail room and prepared a complete plan for its reorganization that again brought him to the attention of Paul Sachs, who would become Weinberg's "rabbi" among the partners of his new employer.

Sachs decided to send Weinberg to Browne's Business College in Brooklyn for a course in penmanship and to learn something about the math of Wall Street.[2] Sachs paid the $50 tuition, advised Weinberg to clean up his rough language, told him how to advance within Goldman Sachs, and continued to watch over and watch out for him. "Until he took me in hand, I was an awful kid—tough and raw. Paul Sachs gave me another $25 to pay for a course at NYU. He didn't tell me what course to take. I had never heard of New York University, but I sought it out. Lots of courses didn't interest me. One course was called Investment Banking. I knew the firm was in the investment banking business, so I took that course. I think it did me a lot of good."

Weinberg took one other course to complete his education: "Some time later, they were considering promoting me to the foreign department. I went to Columbia University and took a course in foreign exchange." He also developed his office skills. "At that time, the firm used mimeographed sheets offering commercial paper. I became proficient at making copies and won the $100 prize as the fastest operator of National Business Equipment mimeograph machines at the New York Business Show in 1911."

Irreverent then as later, brash young Weinberg was clearly on the make: "I had expensive tastes and used to sit behind one of those big desks after the bosses went home and smoke fifty-cent cigars that belonged to one of the men I later became partners with." When too slow a series of promotions at the firm left him frustrated, Weinberg quit in 1917 to enlist as a seaman in the U.S. Navy. Nearsighted, short, and scrappy, he cajoled his recruiting officer into inducting him as an assistant cook, a rating for which he affected great pride in later years, even though he actually transferred after a few weeks to Naval Intelligence at Norfolk, Virginia.[3]

A friend[4] told of Weinberg's being the guest of honor at J. P. Morgan's luncheon table, where the following exchange occurred: "Mr. Weinberg, I presume you served in the last war?"

"Yes, sir, I was in the war—in the navy."

"What were you in the navy?"

"Cook, Second Class."

Morgan was delighted.

Though inconsequential by Wall Street standards, the firm that Sidney Weinberg joined in 1907—and later helped to rescue from a disaster, and eventually propelled almost to Wall Street's top tier—was already nearly four decades old when Weinberg arrived. The financial colossus got its start as the inconspicuous business of a single immigrant with no staff and almost no capital. Marcus Goldman, the son of a peasant cattle drover, was twenty-seven when he left the village of Burbrebae near Schweinfurt in Bavaria during the turmoil of Europe's conservative counterrevolutions of 1848. Having decided like millions of others to leave Europe, he had taught school for several years to save enough money to pay for his six-week crossing of the stormy Atlantic Ocean as part of the first major Jewish migration to America.

The Kuhns, the Lehmans, the Loebs, the Seligmans, and others—the families that called themselves "our crowd"—were already establishing the German Jewish banking community that became powerful as the United States industrialized. But with no connections to that crowd, Goldman began working as an itinerant merchant peddler in New Jersey. There he met and married Bertha Goldman, no relation, the eighteen-year-old daughter of a locksmith and jeweler from Darmstadt in northern Germany. They settled in Philadelphia and moved to New York in 1869.

Interest rates were high following the Civil War, and Goldman developed a small business in mercantile paper—similar to today's commercial paper—in amounts ranging upward from $2,500. Commercial banks had few if any branches and expected customers to come to them, so this left an opportunity for entrepreneurs like Goldman to get to know the merchants, evaluate their creditworthiness, and act as an intermediary between small borrowers and institutional lenders. Goldman conducted most of his business among the wholesale jewelers on Maiden Lane in lower Manhattan and in the nearby "swamp" area where leather merchants congregated on John Street. Both groups were doing their business with minimal capital, so money lending or "note shaving" was a profitable opportunity for someone as diligent as Goldman. He either bought the merchants' promissory paper at a price discounted at 8 percent to 9 percent per annum or worked on a consignment fee of half of 1 percent, which could produce a much higher return if turnover was rapid.

"It was a small business done in a small way, but with accuracy and exactitude."[5] Collecting the paper he purchased during the morning inside the interior band of his high silk hat, Goldman would take a horse-drawn cab up Broadway to the crossing of Chambers and John streets to visit the commercial banks where he hoped to resell the paper at a small profit. Over a century and a half of persistent entrepreneurship, his tiny proprietorship would evolve and grow into the world's leading securities organization, but in 1870, forty-nine-year-old Marcus Goldman was still an outsider at the lower end of the financial food chain. By the end of that year, however, he had developed enough business to employ a part-time bookkeeper and an office boy. Dressed in a Prince Albert frock coat and tall silk hat, he presented himself rather grandly as "Marcus Goldman, Banker and Broker."

In 1882, thirteen years into his career as a sole proprietor, Goldman's annual profits, which were not taxed, approximated fifty thousand dollars. Perhaps beginning to feel flush, he took thirty-one-year-old Samuel Sachs—the husband of his youngest daughter, Louisa Goldman—as his junior partner and renamed the firm M. Goldman and Sachs.

Marcus and Bertha Goldman enjoyed a particularly warm and close friendship with Sam's parents, Joseph and Sophia Sachs.[6] The Sachses' eldest son, Julius, had married the Goldmans' daughter Rosa in a match approved by both mothers. The two mothers agreed that another Sachs-Goldman marriage would be desirable, and Sam Sachs, who had begun work at fifteen as a bookkeeper, soon married Louisa Goldman.

Marcus Goldman advanced Sam Sachs fifteen thousand dollars so he could liquidate his small dry goods business in an orderly way and make his capital commitment to the partnership. The loan was to be repaid over three years in three promissory notes of five thousand dollars each. By the time Sam and Louisa's third son was born, Sam had repaid Marcus two of the three notes, and Marcus, in his old-fashioned German script, wrote formally to his son-in-law to say that, in recognition of Sam's energy and ability as a partner, and in honor of little Walter's arrival, he was forgiving Sam the final payment. Thus, Walter Sachs was able to say many years later, "It appeared that on the very first day of my entrance into this world I concluded my first business deal for Goldman Sachs."[7]

Louisa Goldman Sachs, a sentimental sort, always kept her father's letter, along with the canceled note, in the little strongbox where she also kept, tied in faded bows, her little boys' silky blond ringlets and, dated and labeled, all their baby teeth.

The name of the firm became Goldman, Sachs & Co. in 1888. During the firm's first fifty years, all partners were members of a few intermarrying families, and its business affairs were always conducted by consensus. By the 1890s Goldman Sachs was already the nation's largest dealer in commercial paper. Sales doubled from $31 million in 1890 to $67 million in 1894; two years later the firm joined the New York Stock Exchange. To expand beyond New York City, Henry Goldman began making regular trips to such business centers as Chicago, St. Louis, St. Paul, and Kansas City[8] and to financial centers including Providence, Hartford, Boston, and Philadelphia.

In 1897 Sam Sachs, hoping to expand the business and bearing a letter of introduction from England's leading coffee merchant, Herman Sielcken, went to London and called at 20 Fenchurch Street on Kleinwort, Sons & Co. The Kleinworts, whose business had originated in Cuba in 1792, had transferred their operations to London in 1830 to engage in merchant banking, and seventy years later were important merchant bankers there, accepting checks and other so-called bills of exchange from around the world and, with their well-established creditworthiness, enjoying the best rates in the city. To Herman and Alexander Kleinwort, who were looking for a more aggressive American correspondent than the one they had at the time,[9] Sam Sachs explained Goldman Sachs's business in New York and the attractive possibilities for both foreign exchange and arbitrage between the markets in New York and London.

Although Sachs's proposition was clearly interesting, the Kleinworts, given their sterling reputation, were understandably cautious about doing business with a firm they did not know. They inquired through August Belmont, the leading Jewish banker in New York City and N. M. Rothschild's New York agent, about the acumen, integrity, and zeal of the firm. Hearing no evil, Kleinwort, Sons & Co. accepted Goldman Sachs's proposal for a joint undertaking, and it ran successfully for many years without a written contract.

The business friendship was not always as easily matched by a social friendship. The Kleinworts soon began a custom of entertaining the Sachses at their country home, but were amused by the unsophisticated Americans and learned to be careful about which of their wealthy and cultured English friends they entertained at home while the Sachses were visiting. Walter Sachs recalled reaching out during a visit when he was fifteen to shake hands and saying, "How do you do, sir?"—to the Kleinworts' butler. As a young trainee, Walter Sachs would again blunder, passing on to Alexander Kleinwort that he had heard a concern expressed in the City about the amount of Goldman Sachs–Kleinwort paper on the market. The great man listened in granite silence. Only weeks later was Sachs advised privately of his transgression: In a breach of business etiquette, he had nearly implied the slight possibility of the impossible—that anyone would ever doubt or question Mr. Kleinwort's impeccable credit standing.

Correspondent relationships were opened with banks on the Continent. Goldman Sachs limited activities to self-liquidating transactions to avoid risking capital, and profits in the foreign department rose to five hundred thousand dollars in 1906.[10] Profits were largely made through arbitraging the money rates in New York against those in London, where they were substantially lower even after the joint operation's commission of 0.5 percent for ninety-day paper. With its credit established in Europe's financial markets, Goldman Sachs extended the money-market activities, at least in small amounts, to South America and into the Far East.

Marcus Goldman remained a partner until his death in 1909. Sam and Harry Sachs continued to build the firm's most important business: commercial paper. Harry Sachs later admonished his son: "Never neglect this specialty." Meanwhile, Henry Goldman, who was as boldly expansionist as Sam Sachs was meticulous and conservative, sought to develop a domestic securities business by selling railroad bonds to savings banks in New York and New England.

In the mid-1890s, the firm had occupied two rooms on the second floor at 9 Pine Street,* with a staff of nearly twenty working from 8:30 a.m. to 5 p.m.

each day of a six-day week. It moved in 1897 to 31 Nassau Street. To build the commercial-paper business, Goldman Sachs opened its first branch office in Chicago in 1900, and a one-man office was soon operating in Boston. Thanks mainly to the rapidly expanding commercial-paper business, capital reached one million dollars in 1904, when the firm moved again to the more spacious quarters on Exchange Place.

Goldman Sachs was prospering, and its partners, led by Henry Goldman, had a new ambition: to expand into investment banking.

G oldman Sachs was unable to break into what was the major part of the securities business in the early twentieth century—underwriting the new bond and stock issues of the rapidly expanding, cash-hungry railroads. J.P. Morgan, Kuhn Loeb, and Speyer & Company operated an effective underwriting oligopoly, and these dominant investment banking firms warned Henry Goldman that they would do whatever it took to prevent his firm's getting any part of this large and lucrative business. Goldman was not intimidated; he was angry and keen to fight his way in, but he couldn't find an opening. His only choice was to retreat and look for other opportunities. That proved fortunate: If the oligopolists had opened the door a crack, Goldman Sachs would have struggled for years to build up a share of a business that had already peaked and was entering a long, long decline—eventually leading to multiple bankruptcies.

The attempted expansion into railroad bonds led to what was long remembered as "that unfortunate Alton deal"[11] in which the firm agreed to take ten million dollars of a bond issue by a Midwest railroad. Expecting to earn a 0.5 percent syndication fee, the firm instead suffered a considerable loss when interest rates suddenly rose before Goldman Sachs and the other members of the underwriting syndicate had sold their allocations to investors.

As so often in Goldman Sachs's history, specific gains and losses led to strategic entrepreneurial decisions. Locked out of underwriting the major railroads, Henry Goldman turned to the then unsavory business of "industrial" financing. Most industrial companies were still rather small proprietorships; only a few of the

---

* Having moved from 30 Pine Street. In 1928, at least partly for sentimental reasons, the firm built a twenty-one-story building at 30 Pine.

larger enterprises were looking for more capital than their owners and commercial banks could provide. Goldman Sachs began near the bottom with manufacturers of cigars. The firm owed at least part of the opportunity in financing cigar manufacturers, and later retailers, to religion. Two leading financiers—J. P. Morgan and George F. Baker of what is now Citigroup—would not deal with "Jewish companies" but left these companies for "Jewish firms" like Goldman Sachs.

After the turn of the century, the partners of the family firm, led by Henry Goldman, were increasingly committed to growth and expansion. In 1906 an opportunity came in the form of a company recently established by the merger of three cigar-making companies into United Cigar (later renamed General Cigar).[12] Goldman Sachs had dealt in the constituent companies' commercial paper for several years as they financed inventories, and United's chief executive, Jake Wertheim, was a friend of Henry Goldman's.[13] Wertheim and Goldman were both keen to do business, but the public securities markets, both debt and equity, had always been carefully based on the balance sheets and the capital assets of the corporations being financed—which is why railroads were such important clients. To expand, United Cigar needed long-term capital. Its business economics were like a "mercantile" or trading organization's—good earnings, but little in capital assets. In discussions with United's half dozen shareholders, Henry Goldman showed his creativity in finance: He developed the pathbreaking concept that mercantile companies, such as wholesalers and retailers—having meager assets to serve as collateral for mortgage loans, the traditional foundation for any public financing of corporations—deserved and could obtain a market value for their business franchise with consumers: their earning power.

Fortunately, a friendship led simultaneously to a timely expansion of resources. Henry Goldman introduced his pal Philip Lehman and the firm of Lehman Brothers, then an Alabama cotton and coffee merchant, into the discussions with United Cigar. Philip Lehman, one of five ambitious brothers, was able and competitive. "At anything he did, Philip had to win," said a member of his family.[14] Philip Lehman was determined to see Lehman Brothers venture into the New York City business of underwriting securities and often discussed the opportunities with Henry Goldman. Sam Sachs's summer place in Elberon, New Jersey, was back to back with Lehman's, so it was easy to discuss business and make deals over the shared back fence.

The wealthy Lehmans were looking for new opportunities to invest for growth, and with their substantial capital they could be valuable partners in underwriting securities. The process of underwriting and distributing securities—buying them from the issuing corporations and reselling them to investors—lacked the established industry structure and the swift, well-organized procedures that would later develop. Selling the securities of an unfamiliar company could take a long time—three months was not at all unusual—so the underwriter's reputation and capital were of great importance in supporting the sale. In a rapidly expanding firm-to-firm partnership, the Goldmans provided the clients and the Lehmans provided the capital. Their sharing arrangement would continue until 1926.

The sale of United Cigar's common shares, "of necessity a prolonged affair,"[15] eventually succeeded. The investment bankers agreed to purchase forty-five thousand shares of the company's preferred stock plus thirty thousand shares of common stock for a total of $4.5 million. After several months of continuous selling efforts, the securities were sold to investors for $5.6 million, a 24 percent markup. In addition, Goldman Sachs kept 7,500 shares as part of its compensation, adding another three hundred thousand dollars to the firm's profits. More important, this innovative financing—based on earnings instead of assets—opened up new opportunities for Goldman Sachs. A successful debt underwriting followed, for Worthington Pump.

Another major financing—and the start of a very important relationship—developed from taking up a conventional family responsibility. Before the turn of the century, Samuel Sachs's sister, Emelia Hammerslough,[16] and her husband had reluctantly taken in a boarder from Germany because he was a distant relative, despite their not caring much for him; he seemed crude and uncultured. The boarder was Julius Rosenwald, who soon went west and linked up with his brother-in-law, Aaron Nusbaum, who invited him to join in purchasing a one-third interest in Sears Roebuck. (Rosenwald had done business with Sears and evidently used sums owed him by Sears as part of his investment.) In 1901, Rosenwald bought out Nusbaum's interest for $1,250,000 and went on with Sears to build the mail-order business that eventually made Sears Roebuck a major American company, but back in 1897, with net worth less than $250,000, they first needed working capital to finance inventories of merchandise purchased in New York City.

Apparently Rosenwald never knew how restrained his welcome at the Sachs home had been, but he did know that Emelia's brother Sam's firm could raise money and was looking for business. Rosenwald, as Sears's treasurer, following Nusbaum's practice, turned naturally to Goldman Sachs to sell Sears Roebuck's commercial paper. Goldman Sachs arranged a seventy-five-million-dollar commercial-paper financing and was soon linked to an explosively growing retailing client with voracious needs for financing.

Less than ten years later, after substantial growth and with great expectations, Sears and Rosenwald decided they needed five million dollars in long-term capital to build a major mail-order plant in Chicago. Rosenwald turned again to Sam Sachs's firm, hoping it could arrange a loan, but Henry Goldman countered with a bigger and better proposition: a public stock offering for ten million dollars to be underwritten jointly by Lehman Brothers and Goldman Sachs.

Since there had never before been a public flotation of securities for a mail-order company, there was no way to know in advance how investors might respond. The stock issue was clearly daring. Once again the entrepreneurial innovator, Henry Goldman proposed using the United Cigar "formula": Preferred stock would be supported by hard net assets, while the earning power of Sears Roebuck's customer acceptance—its goodwill franchise—would be the basis for a simultaneous issue of common stock. The Sears Roebuck underwriting, with many shares placed in Europe through Kleinwort, was eventually a substantial success for investors, but completion took an agonizing nine months—three *times* the ninety days needed to complete the United Cigar underwriting.

By 1910 Goldman Sachs had three senior and three junior partners. Sears's stock had already doubled—and went on to double again. To watch out for their investors' interests and because, in those days, the bankers were better known to investors than the companies they underwrote, Henry Goldman and Philip Lehman joined the boards of directors of both Sears Roebuck and United Cigar. This watchdog role led later to Walter Sachs's succeeding Henry Goldman as a Sears Roebuck director—and to his being succeeded by Sidney Weinberg in what had become known in-house as a firm tradition.

Goldman Sachs and Lehman Brothers not only found a fast-growing client in Sears Roebuck, they jointly launched a substantial business in financing retailers and up-and-coming industrial companies. Lehman Brothers and Goldman Sachs jointly underwrote the initial public offerings of May Department Stores, Underwood Typewriter, Studebaker, B.F. Goodrich, Brown Shoe, Cluett Peabody, Continental Can, Jewel Tea, S.H. Kress, and F.W. Woolworth. In 1909, with Sears Roebuck's market value up over 250 percent, Goldman Sachs organized a nine-million-dollar syndicate to buy out Richard Sears's personal ownership.

Walter Sachs, fresh out of Harvard College, where he was elected to the *Crimson* with Franklin D. Roosevelt, joined the firm in 1907—the same year Sidney Weinberg became an assistant janitor. Sachs started as a commercial paper salesman, covering accounts in Hartford and Philadelphia. A few years later he was in Chicago, opening an account with J. Ogden Armour at Armour & Co. Because Goldman Sachs could offer access to the lower-cost London money market through its Kleinwort connection, the initial Armour account was large: five hundred thousand dollars.*

Henry Goldman and Philip Lehman developed an unusual collaborative arrangement: Lehman Brothers and Goldman Sachs would each continue with its own business specialty—commodities for Lehman Brothers and commercial paper for Goldman Sachs—while the two friends' firms conducted a joint venture in securities underwriting, splitting profits fifty-fifty. The capital required was eventually too much for the two Americans firms, so they organized a three-handed syndicate with Kleinwort & Sons, which had much more capital.[17]

Goldman Sachs's business with F.W. Woolworth & Co. illustrated Henry Goldman's drive. After being refused by another underwriter who found it "unfitting" to be identified as the underwriter of the common stock of a mere five-and-dime store chain, Frank Woolworth approached Goldman Sachs. Dynamic and imaginative, Woolworth had expanded his company by acquiring other companies and now wanted to continue expanding by branching. An aggressive financing plan was developed that still caused some awe in recollection. Walter Sachs observed many years later: "Our firm was bolder and more imaginative [than others]; and bolder still was the capitalization. To justify this capitalization required a degree of optimism almost beyond the dictates of conservatism."[18]

---

* Half a century later, Goldman Sachs would successfully reverse the transatlantic flow of funds, doing substantial business with major British companies because it could then raise working capital via commercial paper at cheaper rates in America than the rates charged on loans by the British banks—and, still benefiting from Kleinwort's stature, could place substantial portions of stock and bond underwritings with investors in Europe.

Sachs was not exaggerating. Woolworth's sales were sixty million dollars and its net assets fifteen million dollars. Preferred stock of fifteen million dollars was issued against 100 percent of the assets, and common stock of fifty million dollars was issued against goodwill based on projections that sales would rise rapidly and lift earnings to $5.4 million—with expectations for more growth generously added in.

Fortunately, investors were enthusiastic. Woolworth's preferred and common shares both went quickly to a premium over the issuing price. Offered at fifty-five dollars, the common stock went to eighty dollars on the first day of trading. The preferred stock was eventually retired in 1923 at $125 a share.

With successes like Sears and Woolworth, Goldman Sachs advanced rapidly from just a Jewish outsider that struggled to complete its underwritings to a firm increasingly recognized as innovative, effective, and highly profitable to itself and to investors. On April 24, 1913, a year after the successful Woolworth offering, completion of the truly monumental Woolworth building in lower Manhattan— to this day one of the most handsome skyscrapers—was celebrated at a dinner. Frank Woolworth was flanked at the banquet table by Cass Gilbert, his architect, and Sam Sachs, his banker. Woolworth introduced Sachs and Gilbert, saying, "These are the two men who made this building possible."

Until his retirement from Goldman Sachs, Arthur Sachs was a director of Woolworth, but to the firm's surprise, Woolworth did not elect a successor director from the firm. For forty years Goldman Sachs did no business with Woolworth. Still, Walter Sachs and after him Stanley Miller continued to solicit Woolworth's business. Finally, in the sixties, this led to Goldman Sachs's issuing Woolworth's commercial paper and arranging the purchase of Kinney Shoe Co. from Brown Shoe. These transactions caused Walter Sachs to observe: "I know of no situation which exemplifies better the importance of nursing an old relationship."[19] Others might question the value of forty years of solicitations for just one transaction—particularly a transaction that might have been accomplished without the considerable cumulative cost of the forty years of solicitations—but during Sachs's years of leadership, client service was particularly important because new clients were hard to come by. Still, Goldman Sachs and Lehman Brothers gained a reputation as underwriters of good companies—particularly in retailing—whose stocks performed well. Partners began to say proudly these companies bore the two firms' "hallmark."

Around the time of the Woolworth offering, Goldman Sachs took on its first full-time new-business solicitor: Colonel Ned Arden Flood, a "colorful individual, elegant in appearance, smooth in manner. Flood dressed in the height of fashion, spats and all, and invariably carried a cane."[20] Never an employee of the firm, Flood received a percentage of the profits on deals completed through his introductions. He did so well at bringing new accounts to the firm—including Studebaker and Cluett Peabody—that he retired after half a dozen years.[21] After Flood, soliciting new business was left to younger partners and the managers of the firm's branch offices. Surely it was neither a bold nor an imaginative effort. In that era—and among the leading Wall Street firms for another half century—corporations were not solicited by competitors. It simply was not done.

"Those were the days," Walter Sachs later observed, "when the course of business seemed to move uninterruptedly and serenely forward."[22] But the serene family world of Goldman Sachs—two of Henry Goldman's sisters were married to Sachs brothers, and all partners in the firm were members of the two families—was disrupted by an argument over foreign affairs at a dinner at the Hotel Astor. It divided the families and broke up the firm. And this estrangement led to splitting up the joint-account arrangement that had been so successful between Goldman Sachs and Lehman Brothers.

In August 1914 Germany declared war on Russia and a day later on France and England. When Walter Sachs returned from England shortly after the outbreak of war, expecting his partners to be strongly pro-Allies—as he had assured the Kleinworts he and all his partners would surely be—he was dismayed to find Henry Goldman proudly and intensely expressing views highly sympathetic to Germany and making pro-German speeches. When his partners and sisters begged Goldman to modify or at least conceal his feelings, he refused. His public utterances became more frequent and startling. Henry Goldman admired the Prussianism that others deplored, and quoted Nietzsche to anyone who would listen.

The rift between Goldman and Sachs came to a head in 1915 when J.P. Morgan offered for public subscription a five-hundred-million-dollar Anglo-French loan. Almost all the leading houses on Wall Street were participating, but Henry

Goldman objected, so the firm could not join in. As Walter Sachs later explained, "The firm had an age-old rule that participation in any business could only be accepted if all the partners were unanimous in their desire to accept." Chagrined, the two Sachs brothers went to J. Pierpont Morgan's office, where each man subscribed personally for $125,000 of the loan.

Even America's 1917 entry into the war did not stop Henry Goldman's "utterances and tirades."[23] Nor did Howard Sachs's service overseas with the Twenty-Sixth Division, nor Paul Sachs's service in the field with the Red Cross, nor the Liberty Bond sales by other members of the firm. Nor did the Kleinworts' warning that Goldman Sachs would be blacklisted in the City of London, nor the Bank of England's forbidding Kleinwort to do any foreign exchange business with Goldman Sachs. The split within the firm rapidly worsened. Finally Henry Goldman realized he was out of step with his partners and after thirty-five years with the firm resigned from Goldman Sachs the day the firm began selling Liberty Bonds for the United States government. Goldman kept his office at the firm for a while, but "in the heated atmosphere of wartime, his very presence in the office created difficulties,"[24] so he moved uptown. Henry Goldman's departure left the firm severely shorthanded, because he had been key to all its lucrative industrial financings.

In leaving, Henry Goldman withdrew his substantial capital, which created an enormous financial problem for the firm and left its underwriting business without his dynamic, thrusting leadership.* The rupture also left Goldman Sachs under the pall of being considered a "German firm," which hurt business. Henry Goldman and Samuel Sachs would never speak again.[25] Their personal hostilities continued into the next generation, and to this day there are hardly any Goldmans who are on speaking terms with any Sachses.

A fter the Great War, Sidney Weinberg returned to Goldman Sachs, but his old job was gone and he was told if he wanted a job, he'd have to create one.

---

* Goldman left the firm a very rich man, with successful investments in Sears Roebuck and May Department Stores. In the early 1930s he traveled to his beloved Germany with the idea of settling there permanently as a demonstration of his national loyalty. He collected paintings by Rubens, Van Dyck, and Rembrandt, bought a Stradivarius for twelve-year-old Yehudi Menuhin, and gave Albert Einstein a yacht, which was confiscated by the Nazis. With Hitler rising to power, Goldman was seized and searched and was subjected to "many other humiliations," according to his family. He returned to New York in 1936, defeated and disillusioned.

He did—as a bond trader. In 1920 he married Helen Livingston, a lovely, cultured amateur pianist and the daughter of a dress manufacturer. He soon became a recognized authority within the firm on pricing, making recommendations based on his sense of the market. Weinberg also built up the over-the-counter stock-trading business. In April 1925 he bought a seat on the New York Stock Exchange for $104,000.[26] Proudly, Weinberg stressed that the money came from his own earnings: "None of it was from trading. I never traded. I'm an investment banker. I don't shoot craps. If I had been a speculator and taken advantage of what I know, I would have made five times as much money."

He became a partner of Goldman Sachs in 1927—only the second from outside the two founding families. "The people I worked with were always boosting me, and I was made a partner ahead of many people who were senior to me. They told me this was due to my personality, ability to work hard, and good health—plus integrity and character." He became the principal assistant to senior partner Waddill Catchings. As assistant treasurer of Goldman Sachs Trading Corporation, Weinberg developed his knowledge and understanding of each of Trading's various investments. In the ensuing crisis, this knowledge would catapult him into much larger responsibilities and authority within the firm.

2

DISASTER

GOLDMAN SACHS
TRADING CORPORATION

W hile Henry Goldman and Philip Lehman's friendship brought their firms together in a long series of transactions—they comanaged 114 underwritings for fifty-six issuers—the two firms continued to be rivals that never fully trusted each other. Goldman Sachs partners believed that since they brought in a majority of the business, the original fifty-fifty agreement should be modified. Lehman partners thought Goldman Sachs was being greedy.

Partly in hopes of overcoming this problem, partners of Lehman Brothers and Goldman Sachs developed a routine in the 1920s of having lunch together each day at Delmonico's, an ornate Wall Street restaurant that specialized in rich German food. One day, only halfway through the meal, one of the Goldman Sachs partners jumped up from the table, exclaiming with alarm: "I forgot to lock the safe!"

"No need to worry," laconically responded a Lehman man, glancing around at his partners. "We're all here."

With Henry Goldman's departure, the close relationship between Goldman Sachs and Lehman Brothers, which had originated with and developed through and depended upon the friendship between Philip Lehman and Henry Gold-man, was destined to change. More and more differences arose. Arguments were increasingly frequent, particularly on the division of profits. Why, the Leh-mans demanded, did Goldman Sachs take all the credit, with its name showing at the top of the advertisements, for ventures for which Lehman had supplied the money? Goldman Sachs, in turn, asked why the Lehmans expected half the profits on deals originated and managed by Goldman Sachs. The arguments fre-quently degenerated into name-calling. As one banker has said, "They were both too ambitious to stay married."

But there was more to it than that. In the long run, the split actually benefited both firms—Lehman Brothers most of all. It forced the Lehmans to take off their coats, roll up their sleeves, and go out and get into investment banking on their own, without depending on the crutch of Goldman Sachs. "Lehman Brothers always had a lot of money, but that's different from being aggressive to get busi-ness," said a Goldman Sachs partner many years later. "After the dispute, they became real go-getters." At the same time, the split challenged Goldman Sachs to build up its own capital.

During the later 1920s, a series of conferences was held to redefine the busi-ness relationship. The "change in the generations" had included Waddill Catch-ings's coming to power at Goldman Sachs and Robert "Bobby" Lehman, Paul Mazur, and John Hancock at Lehman Brothers. Sidney Weinberg was among those impatient with the Lehman relationship and wanted to end it. A formal memorandum of separation was prepared that listed sixty corporations that the two firms had jointly underwritten. Each of the sixty was allocated to the firm with the primary interest: Goldman Sachs got forty-one, Lehman Brothers got nineteen. Each firm agreed not to solicit the other firm's clients.[1]

The Lehmans continued Philip's policy of underwriting issues that seemed too undignified for other investment bankers to handle. Among these were early stock offerings in airlines, electronics, motion pictures, and liquor companies, all of which helped Lehman Brothers become what *Fortune* would call "one of the biggest profit makers—many believe the biggest—in the business." The Leh-mans liked to describe themselves as merchants of money, intermediaries between men who wanted to produce goods and men looking for something to do with their surplus funds.[2]

Replacing the capital that Lehman Brothers had supplied turned out to be a challenge caused by Henry Goldman's departure that Goldman Sachs could handle well. But replacing Henry Goldman was a challenge that the firm would not handle well—although the dire results took years to unfold.

Goldman's departure left the firm without an entrepreneurial leader in underwriting, the main business of the leading firms in Wall Street and the standard by which industry stature was and still is measured. Despite its success in the retailing industries, Goldman Sachs was still relatively unimportant. The Sachs family was now clearly in control, but no employee of the firm was capable of providing the bold, effective leadership Goldman Sachs would clearly need to recover its prewar momentum in investment banking.

The search for a successor to Goldman led the partners in 1918 to invite Waddill Catchings to join the firm and head up underwriting. Catchings, who grew up in Mississippi, seemed just the man. A close friend of Arthur Sachs's at Harvard, he went on to Harvard Law School and joined Goldman Sachs's future law firm, Sullivan & Cromwell. There he attracted the attention of James Wallace, president of the Central Trust Company, who invited Catchings on successive occasions to head reorganized companies: Millikan Brothers, Central Foundry, and Sloss Sheffield Steel & Iron. This gave Catchings substantial industrial experience. During the war years, he was part of the organization set up by J.P. Morgan & Co. under Edward R. Stettinius to purchase war supplies for the Allies, so in the final year of the war Catchings was able to become quite familiar with Goldman Sachs, its clients, and its activities. His training and experience seemed to suit him ideally for his major role at the firm. On top of all that, Catchings was one of the most talented, charming, handsome, well-educated, and upwardly mobile people in Wall Street.

Yet Catchings would in just ten years very nearly destroy the firm, proving once again that articulate optimists encouraged by early successes and armed with financial leverage can become hugely destructive.

"Waddill Catchings was very tall, quite handsome, and had great charisma," said Albert Gordon, the long-serving leader of Kidder Peabody, who began his career at Goldman Sachs. "More important, he not only was a lawyer, a partner of Sullivan & Cromwell, but had had real experience in industrial management. He also had great charm and a generous way with employees. For example, he had scheduled the two of us to go together to Pittsburgh to call on an important prospective client corporation, but when he heard of my plans to go duck hunting that same weekend, he simply called the CEO and explained that that tentative date would be inconvenient and suggested an alternate date. That's the way he was."[3] Proudly self-confident, sure of his standing, he was easing into arrogance.

Catchings wrote a series of books with an easy, engaging prose style that expounded optimistically on the promising economic prospects for America. In one visionary and best-selling volume, cheerfully titled *The Road to Plenty*,[4] he exuberantly explained: "If business is to be kept zooming, production must be kept at high speed whatever the circumstances." Naively, he believed that the business cycle no longer threatened and that America's economic prospects were truly limitless. Convinced that his Harvard professors had been far too theoretical about long-run economics while real people cared much more about short-run results, Catchings saw himself as just the person to take the middle way and integrate up-to-date theory and real-world practice. He intended to establish himself as a national thought leader and was gaining the public attention he sought.

Meanwhile, confidence was running high among the partners of Goldman Sachs, and with Catchings's dynamic leadership in underwriting, the firm was once again clearly moving ahead and entering an active period of industrial financing. Goldman Sachs's first underwriting after the war was an issue for Endicott Johnson, the shoe maker, in 1919. The postwar boom in business, "which grew with astounding rapidity" through the twenties, led to an era of mergers in which the firm played an increasingly important part.[5]

With his successes, Catchings became increasingly self-confident and insisted on a larger and larger ownership share in the firm. By 1929 he held the largest single percentage in the partnership and was clearly the leader of Goldman Sachs.

However, Philip Lehman, the leader of Lehman Brothers, was not favorably impressed. He felt Catchings lacked balance and was too aggressive and optimistic. But Lehman's doubts didn't faze Catchings's partners. Neither did the cautions of Catchings's Harvard classmate Arthur Sachs. The partners of Goldman

Sachs, determined to make up for the loss of Henry Goldman, had been looking for a real go-getter, and Catchings was the man of the hour.[6]

The exciting "New Era" of economic growth accelerating through the 1920s brought increasing public recognition of America's stature in the world, exciting new technologies, and a booming stock market with wider and wider participation by individual investors. Before investing in stocks became widely accessible, individual investors' principal investment opportunities had been confined primarily to railroad bonds and mortgages on single-family homes. Catchings got more and more interested in the trading side of the firm's business. He organized several successful pooled trading accounts, installed a stock ticker in his office, and encouraged expansion in foreign exchange. The nation's giddy overconfidence was best represented by a wonderfully optimistic 1928 article in a popular magazine, written by the chief financial officer of General Motors Corporation, John J. Raskob. With the encouraging title "Everybody Ought to Be Rich," it presented a "simple plan of moderate, prudent" borrowing on margin to buy more and more fully into the steadily rising stock market. (Eventually, however, Raskob himself sold all but three thousand of his 150,000 shares of GM.)

In this heady environment, Catchings's charismatic presentation of his optimistic views and his penchant for bold action would lead the firm into a major public commitment and a massive public failure. With enthusiasm, Catchings advocated creating a modern "corporation of corporations"—a holding company or investment trust similar to those being established by other securities firms. In his vision, a truly dynamic business organization would move out of markets or products with declining profitability and move into markets and products that were new and dynamic. The one great objective for investor-owners was profits—maximum profits on their invested capital—with products or markets merely the means to achieve that end. So the truly modern business leader would run a pure investment trust—and concentrate on redeploying capital to maximize profits.

Organized as holding companies, the investment trusts were promoted as companies whose business was investing in, controlling, and managing other companies. Often, but not always, these holding companies were concentrated in a single business, particularly insurance or banking (such as A. P. Giannini's Transamerica, which was an outgrowth of his original Bank of Italy, later named

Bank of America) or utilities (such as the empire constructed by Samuel Insull). The benefits, in management, innovation, and financing, of corporate consolidation were being demonstrated over and over again by the increased profitability of such merger-created corporations as General Motors, General Electric, General Foods, and International Harvester.

Catchings saw no reason to confine his futuristic vision to just one industry. Why not create companies that would use these exciting modern techniques of finance and management *and* be free to go into any industry where opportunity was particularly great and promising—where experts in modern management and finance could make the greatest gains for investors!

Investment trusts were designed to capitalize on the continuing growth opportunities for American business, which many assumed were inevitable. And not unlike the conglomerates of the 1960s, they specialized in "financial engineering" as they concentrated on maximizing profits to shareholders. Often using borrowed money and increasingly elaborate "senior" financing—such as preferred stock, convertible debt, convertible preferred stock, or debt with warrants attached to buy equity—the trusts raised capital to buy a controlling interest in operating companies. They gained control of other corporations that, in turn, controlled still other corporations as subsidiaries. The layers of corporations controlling corporations that controlled still other corporations and the opportunities for financial leverage seemed nearly endless. The remarkable extent of corporate pyramiding by investment trusts was illustrated by one retailer, Metropolitan Chain Stores, whose dividends went through eight tiers of holding companies; the cash dividends paid out to common-stock investors were what little remained after paying the required dividends and interest expenses of all the layers of senior securities.[7] The idea of creating investment trusts seemed to open new horizons for financial creativity to capitalize on the New Era in American industry.

Seeing the remarkable profitability of other firms' ventures with investment trusts, the partners of Goldman Sachs got more and more enthusiastic. As Walter Sachs later ruefully noted, "All would have been well had the firm confined its activities strictly to the type of business which had been done over the years." Al Gordon recalled, "Catchings got quite concerned about the booming speculation on margin in the late 1920s and for a while was almost bearish. Then, with most unfortunate timing, Catchings became convinced that he could see and project all the great growth that was ahead for this country. He became quite bullish at the worst possible time... in the spring of 1929."

As plans developed, the scale of the proposed investment trust was rapidly expanded. From a moderate twenty-five-million-dollar initial plan, the proposed size of the trust was doubled to fifty million dollars, and then doubled again to one hundred million dollars (about $1.2 billion in today's dollars). A salient indicator of the ascending prominence of the "trust concept" within the firm was the name it was given: Goldman Sachs Trading Corporation. As originators, partners of the firm bought 10 percent of the original offering, and that ten million dollars represented nearly half the firm's total capital. The rest of the offering, even though the trust had not yet begun operations, was heavily oversubscribed by the investing public, and the firm made a quick profit of over three million dollars on its initial stake, lifting expectations still higher. In addition to its stock ownership, Goldman Sachs would be paid 20 percent of the trust's net income for its management.[8] Immediately after the initial public offering, the price of shares in Goldman Sachs Trading leaped up—in just two months, the stock jumped from its $104 offering price to $226 per share, twice its book value in shares and cash.

Flush with success and eager to expand, Catchings arranged a merger with another investment trust, Financial & Industrial Corporation, which controlled Manufacturers Trust Company and a group of insurance companies. This doubled the assets of Goldman Sachs Trading to $244 million just three months after the original issue.

Walter Sachs described the growth of Goldman Sachs Trading as meteoric. The trust went rapidly on to control companies with total assets over $1.5 billion. As Sachs put it, "Rising markets in investment trust shares during 1929, to which the shares of Goldman Sachs Trading were no exception, led to grandiose ideas involving further bank acquisitions."[9] Goldman Sachs Trading gained dominant ownership positions in banks in New York, Philadelphia, Chicago, Los Angeles, and San Francisco, as well as in insurance and industrial companies.[10]

With serene confidence in continuing success, Catchings and Goldman Sachs were caught up in the elation of the time and went boldly on to add further leverage—at the worst possible time. Despite its high price, Goldman Sachs Trading repurchased fifty-seven million dollars' worth of its own shares. Joining forces with Harrison Williams, who was expanding his utilities empire, Goldman Sachs

Trading in the summer of 1929 launched two new subsidiary trusts bearing the picturesque names Shenandoah and Blue Ridge and through them invested in such holding companies as Central States Electric, North American Company, and American Cities Power & Light. In addition to fifty million dollars of preferred stock, Shenandoah sold one million shares of common stock to the public at $17.80. Four million shares were taken at only $12.50 by the promoters: Goldman Sachs Trading Corporation and Central States Electric Company.[11] Both hands were in the cookie jar, but euphoric investors didn't care. Shenandoah shares, seven times oversubscribed, closed the first day of trading at thirty-six dollars. Shenandoah was both oversubscribed and overleveraged with $42.5 million of convertible preferred stock providing over one-third of its total capital. (Like debt, preferred stock is senior to common stock, and its dividends, like bond interest, must be paid before common dividends.) One month later, Blue Ridge was launched. In leverage, it went even further: fifty-eight million dollars of preferred stock or 44 percent of $131 million in total capital. Together these preferred issues had annual dividend commitments of nearly six million dollars. Goldman Sachs Trading owned 40 percent of Shenandoah, and the partners of Goldman Sachs must have felt euphoria worthy of the first man to invent a perpetual motion machine.

Partners of Goldman Sachs put considerable pressure on associates in the firm to invest in the new investment trusts at double the amount each had taken in Goldman Sachs Trading. When a young associate declined the "invitation" being made to all employees to subscribe to the Shenandoah issue, Sidney Weinberg, by then Catchings's number two at Goldman Sachs Trading, sternly scolded the recalcitrant: "This won't help you here."[12]

Goldman Sachs Trading Corporation and its two new subsidiaries greatly expanded Goldman Sachs's reach. With total capital of less than twenty-five million dollars, the firm effectively controlled five hundred million dollars in investments—approximately six billion dollars in today's dollars. This was wonderfully convenient for an active, deal-minded Wall Street firm. Goldman Sachs Trading controlled banks and insurance companies that the firm could encourage to buy the newly issued corporate securities that Goldman Sachs was underwriting, while the controlled corporations generated investment banking business for the firm. All this was in addition to the substantial profits from originating the three investment trusts and any gains on the shares held by the firm.

But as Walter Sachs later observed, "The entire structure had become top-heavy and too extensive for easy and intelligent management." Goldman Sachs Trading's portfolio was far too concentrated: If any of its major holdings cut or stopped paying dividends, the trust would become a house of cards. And that is what happened when American Trust Company of San Francisco—then nearly 50 percent of Goldman Sachs Trading's total portfolio—stopped paying dividends in July 1929. North American, a utility holding company controlled by Shenandoah and Blue Ridge, never paid a dividend.

In early 1929, Goldman Sachs Trading had bought thirty thousand shares of Guardian Group shares at $130, versus a market price of $120. Trading soon made a good profit. But Guardian wanted to be independent, so its directors asked Sidney Weinberg to sell the shares back. Correctly expecting the share price to keep rising, Weinberg indignantly refused. But by October 1929, when the market price had fallen from a high of three hundred dollars to $220, another approach by Guardian got an agreement from Weinberg, who was trying to raise cash, to sell twenty-five thousand shares at $184. Weinberg got the better deal: When Guardian attempted to resell those shares, it could unload only seven thousand. In November, to save embarrassment, Guardian directors, including Edsel Ford—one of the company's original sponsors, who had put up $1.2 million—bought the balance of the shares at $184 even though the market value had by then dropped to just $120.[13]

Walter and Arthur Sachs were traveling in Europe during the summer of 1929. In Italy they learned of the deals Catchings was doing on his own, and Walter Sachs got worried. On his return to New York, he went straight to Catchings's apartment in the Plaza Hotel to urge greater caution. But Catchings, still caught up in the bull-market euphoria, was unmoved. "The trouble with you, Walter," he said, "is that you've no imagination."[14]

The Dow Jones Industrial Average had begun 1929 at exactly 300, fluctuated over the next five months between 300 and 320, and then soared in both price and trading volume. It peaked at 381 on September 3: thirty times 1929 earnings per share, over four times book value, and yielding only 2.5 percent in dividends—astounding numbers in those days. Euphoria was easy to find—National City

Bank of New York stock traded at 120 times earnings, and several companies, including International Nickel, sold at ten times book value. New common stock issues jumped from an average annual volume of five hundred million dollars to ten times as much in 1929—$5.1 billion, dominated by the investment trusts.

By October 23, the Dow had fallen back down almost to its January level of 305. The 20 percent decline in less than two months provoked widespread margin calls, and selling seemed sure to accelerate. On Thursday, October 24, the New York Stock Exchange required all 1,100 members be on the floor for the 10 a.m. opening.[15] Prices fell quickly, and in just half an hour the ticker tape was sixteen minutes late. By one o'clock the tape was ninety-two minutes late. The 3:30 closing prices were not reported until 7:35 that evening. Trading volume was a record 12,894,650 shares—three times the normal volume. Then margin calls and European selling, combined with urgent selling by brokers whose short-term loans were being called, ignited heavy selling on the day still called Black Friday, as 16.4 million shares traded—another record—and major stocks dropped 20 percent to 30 percent. (Prices temporarily turned around on November 14 and rose 25 percent over just five days—and then added another 6 percent. The Dow closed the year at 248.)

With the October stock market crash, Goldman Sachs Trading Corporation, which had seemed so sure to be a great success, quickly turned into an astounding failure. Trading's shares took their first big plunge from $326—on their way to just $1.75, or less than 2 percent of their original value and less than 1 percent of their market high. While all the investment trusts suffered, Goldman Sachs Trading—because it was so large and so highly leveraged and because Catchings had optimistically made overly concentrated investments—became one of the largest, swiftest, and most complete investment disasters of the twentieth century. And since the investing public saw no real difference between Goldman Sachs and Goldman Sachs Trading Corporation, the harm done to the firm and its reputation was comparably horrific.

I n the crucial period, as the crash gathered momentum, Waddill Catchings was not at Goldman Sachs: He had left New York for the far West, partly to see to Goldman Sachs Trading's western investments firsthand, and partly to divorce his wife. In early 1930, as the stock market appeared to improve, Catchings called from California to tell Weinberg, who was working closely with him, of the "splendid" opportunities he saw for further investment on the Pacific Coast. At the time, Goldman Sachs Trading had debts and forward commitments of twenty million dollars. Stubbornly bullish, Catchings proposed issuing fifty million dollars of two-year convertible notes to fund the existing debt and provide funds for bold action: "With the remaining $30 million, Taylor out here can make a world of money."*

Sidney Weinberg and Walter Sachs agreed that such a note issue would be folly and decisively rejected Catchings's proposal. They were thinking differently now about Catchings. Walter Sachs spoke to his brother Arthur the next day, saying apologetically, "You have been right about Catchings and I have been wrong. I am afraid that he will never learn." Walter Sachs then went to Chicago to meet Catchings for several hours at the University Club. "I told him in no uncertain terms that in the future he could not carry on without the complete approval of the entire partnership."[16] Sachs was too late.

Necessarily, a program of quiet liquidations to pay off debts was begun, even with the difficulties of a falling market and the illiquidity of most of Goldman Sachs Trading's investments. Catchings came back to New York City, where, at Weinberg's initiative, he was obliged by the other partners to resign as president of Goldman Sachs Trading Corporation in May, to quit as a director of companies in which it was invested, and to withdraw from the Goldman Sachs partnership at the end of 1930.[17] In one last hurrah, Catchings organized a stock market pool of speculators to invest in Chrysler. Between October 1929 and July 1930 it lost $1.6 million.[18]

Under Sidney Weinberg's direction, Goldman Sachs Trading Corporation was steadily wound down and eventually taken over by Floyd Odlum's Atlas Corporation, which bought shares of various trusts at major discounts from their net asset values. Atlas acquired eighteen trusts by late 1932, increasing its per-share book value even as others were plunging—and trading on the stock market at a premium over book value while others sold at a discount. The financial cost to Goldman Sachs was punishing. In an enormous double whammy, the firm not

---

* Frank Taylor, who had been affiliated with Tucker, Hunter, Dulin & Co., a Pacific Coast investment house that had become a subsidiary of Goldman Sachs Trading.

only lost the chance to make the great fortune it had so recently and confidently expected, but it also suffered huge losses, taking its accumulated capital down to the level it had passed thirty long years before and eliminating the fruits of all the labors of an entire generation.[19] The venture cost Goldman Sachs, which never sold a share of its own original stake in Goldman Sachs Trading Corporation, more than twelve million dollars. Recognizing the destructive impact of these losses on their younger partners, the Sachses announced that their family would cover partners' losses. As the Depression settled in, employees were asked what minimum salary they needed to live on—and were paid just that sum and no more.[20]

For Walter Sachs, now serving as president of Goldman Sachs Trading Corporation, it must have been painful to go before one after another group of irate stockholders and appear in court to defend against shareholder suits.* Catchings got a termination payout of $250,000, and his capital account deficit was absorbed by the other partners. He moved to California, wrote another book—*Do Economists Understand Business?*—and produced various radio programs. Walter Sachs observed of Catchings: "Most men can stand adversity; very few men can stand success. He was not one of them. He ... had had no money. He suddenly thought himself to be a rich man. He *was* a rich man on paper. In that very year—it all happened in twelve months—he just went haywire. We weren't smart enough, perhaps—or perhaps we were too greedy, too—but we didn't stop it in time."[21]

By 1931 the losses of Goldman Sachs Trading exceeded by far the losses of other investment trusts.[22] Of the $172.5 million lost by fourteen leading trusts, Goldman Sachs Trading accounted for $121.4 million, or 70 percent. In distant second place on this dishonor roll was Lehman Corporation, which lost just under $8 million.

With 70 percent of its assets tied up in Shenandoah and American Trust Company, both paying no dividends, Goldman Sachs Trading's revenues plunged from five million dollars in 1930 to just five hundred thousand dollars in 1932. It couldn't pay six million dollars of dividends on the preferred stock, nor the one million dollars in debt interest.

For the proud Sachs family, the failure of Goldman Sachs Trading Corporation became a very public humiliation. In 1932, Eddie Cantor, the popular

---

* Sidney Weinberg took his son Jim to court in Foley Square on the day when Judge Milton Pollack threw out the last lawsuit linked to Goldman Sachs Trading—in 1968.

comedian and one of forty-two thousand individual investors in Goldman Sachs Trading Corporation, sued Goldman Sachs for one hundred million dollars while regularly including in his vaudeville routine bitter jokes about the firm. One: "They told me to buy the stock for my old age . . . and it worked *perfectly*. . . . Within six months, I felt like a *very* old man!"

The Sachs family's stress and anguish were exacerbated when the trust's third-largest investment—Manufacturers Trust Company, a major lender to the Jewish garment industry—cut its dividend and a run on the bank began. The best solution for the bank was to join the New York Clearing House, whose members guaranteed each other's deposits. But the price of admission was high: separation from Goldman Sachs Trading and the installation of a non-Jew as CEO.[23] The crude message clearly reflected anti-Jewish prejudice, which Goldman Sachs would experience for many years.

For the Sachses, the hardest part was the harm done to their family firm's reputation, to which they had devoted so much time, effort, and attention. In the last years of his father's life, when Walter Sachs called on the man who had seen the firm grow over fifty years from tiny beginnings, "He was interested in only one aspect: how the name was regarded." Sam Sachs would die in 1934, at eighty-four.

Goldman Sachs Trading canceled its management contract with Goldman Sachs near the market bottom in April 1933 and changed its name to Pacific Eastern Corporation. That September, Floyd Odlum bought an additional 501,000 shares, gaining over 50 percent control of a mixed bag of small stocks that had not participated fully in the market recovery.[24]

Because he knew the companies previously served by Waddill Catchings, Weinberg was selected as a director for, among others, Sears Roebuck, Continental Can, National Dairy, B.F. Goodrich, and General Foods. At the same time, Weinberg led the painful process of reconstructing the firm's position on the Street.

It could have been worse. Goldman Sachs nearly lost the man who was destined to be its decisive leader. A decade after Henry Goldman had resigned because he supported the Kaiser, Sidney Weinberg went to him. Weinberg explained that he did not think the Sachses were particularly bright and said, "I want to work for you, because you've got the brains." Henry Goldman declined, saying: "My career is ending. You stay with Goldman Sachs."

THE LONG ROAD BACK

Goldman Sachs was fighting for its life all through the Depression and World War II and was profitable in only half of the sixteen years from the 1929 crash to the end of the war. Most partners owed the firm money because their partnership income was less than the moderate "draws" that their families needed to get along.[1] There was little need for Wall Street services, particularly services from a midsize Jewish firm with few distinctive capabilities and a prominent negative reputation from the failure of Trading.[2] In the early thirties, the firm neither led nor co-led any underwritings, and in 1935 it did only three debt placements that totaled less than fifteen million dollars. This period was later described euphemistically by Walter Sachs as a time of "defensive action" as the partners worked to unravel the many problems caused by Goldman Sachs Trading Corporation and "fought valiantly to retain the firm's corporate relations." Sachs always called it "Trading Corp."—apparently reluctant to use the firm's name when identifying the great failure.

The Sachs family was vital to the rescue of Goldman Sachs in an essential but unusual way: They stepped aside. Howard and Walter Sachs knew that, having become accustomed to genteel affluence, dignity, culture, and refined tastes, they were not the right people for the gritty job that had to be done. They couldn't do it. So they took secondary roles for themselves and gave Weinberg the power to lead the firm, knowing he was smarter and tougher than they were and could do what had to be done. Arthur Sachs, living abroad with his French second wife, agreed with them; he retired and eventually withdrew his capital. Weinberg himself had no alternatives either, particularly when the Sachs family agreed to underwrite and forgive well over one million dollars of his share of the operating losses.

Jim Weinberg, Sidney's older son, gives the Sachs family great credit for sustaining the firm: "Over the twenty years from 1927 to 1947, Goldman Sachs made $7 million—and lost $14 million. The Sachs family were extraordinarily important to the firm for many, many years and in many ways, but surely the most important was their stamina and persistence over twenty long years of staying with the firm, covering the losses of others, and never compromising on any of the firm values they believed in."

Where the Sachses were genteel, cultured, and had refined tastes, Weinberg was smart, tenacious, and aggressive. "We had learned to live by the street code: you do everything right—and nothing wrong," explained Weinberg, who had scars on his back from knife fights as a newspaper boy. "We would never retreat for anything or from anybody." Al Gordon, later senior partner of Kidder Peabody, recalled an instance of Weinberg's aggressiveness in the 1920s that still rankled more than seventy years later. Goldman Sachs and Lehman Brothers were preparing to underwrite what was then an unusually large bond issue—fifty million dollars—for National Dairy Products. Gordon, having met Sumner Pike of Continental Insurance on behalf of Goldman Sachs, became convinced that the market was underestimating National Dairy's creditworthiness, so, on his own initiative and based on his own analysis, he urged Pike to invest in the National Dairy bonds. Appreciative, Pike insisted that the lucrative order for two million dollars of bonds go entirely to Goldman Sachs, even though a Lehman Brothers partner was on Continental's board of directors. Continental's order—the largest placed by any investor in that bond issue and the largest order Goldman Sachs had ever gotten—produced a seventy-thousand-dollar commission (over eight hundred thousand dollars in today's dollars). Gordon naturally thought the credit was rightfully all his, but Weinberg, as the partner in charge of distribution, took full credit for himself. It would not be their only confrontation.

"He was a trader and built the firm's over-the-counter business," recalls Gordon. "Salomon Brothers, Asiel, and Goldman Sachs were the recognized trading firms in the 1920s. Weinberg was very competitive and ran Goldman Sachs with an iron hand. He wanted me to work for him, but I shifted to commercial paper and the new business department. From time to time thereafter, he would try to get me to come back into his area, but I wouldn't go. He had much too dominating a way of operating."

Weinberg knew the markets and had a quick mind for numbers, people, and markets. To price a Sears bond issue, Stanley Miller, a persistent number cruncher, worked out an enormous spreadsheet with all the conceivable interest rates along one side and years to maturity along another side. He'd labored all night, pulling the long handle of one of the huge NCR adding machines to get each possible combination. As Miller was unrolling his masterpiece, Weinberg simply announced that the bonds would be issued at par with a 4⅜ percent coupon—and he was exactly right for the market.

Weinberg had an extraordinary capacity to appraise people, and on one occasion it saved him some real money.[3] Richard Whitney, then chairman of the NYSE but soon to be jailed for serious fraud,[4] had gotten in the habit of stopping stock exchange members to make surprising requests for large personal loans, often several hundred thousand dollars at a time and always without collateral. Widely recognized as the House of Morgan's broker and the brother of George Whitney, one of J.P. Morgan's senior partners, Whitney was tall, impeccably dressed, and imperious. In what might have seemed a great compliment (if he hadn't shown his disdain for Weinberg by calling him "Weinstein"), Whitney once asked Weinberg to lend him the relatively small sum of fifty thousand dollars. Weinberg said he'd think it over and, returning to his office, called Whitney to say he would not make the loan. Asked by a colleague why he hadn't refused Whitney right away, Weinberg said, almost sheepishly, "I wanted to be a little more gentlemanly."[5]

Weinberg could be strikingly generous, as E. J. Kahn Jr. noted in his 1956 New Yorker profile: "On learning that a former business rival of his had run into hard times, Weinberg called on the fellow and, after satisfying himself of the reality of his plight, summarily arranged to provide him with a hundred dollars a week for the rest of his life." As B.F. Goodrich's board of directors was meeting in Akron in 1931, a run started on the local banks, threatening hardship for Goodrich and its thousands of employees. Weinberg offered to see what could be done and spent the next ten days examining the banks' books. Convinced that they could make it if they got enough help, he called New York and persuaded some bankers there to put up the money. "The doors of Akron's banks stayed open, the funds of Goodrich and its employees remained intact, and Weinberg came back to New York, another little job out of the way."[6]

Goldman Sachs was in a period of acute "internal management transition" and anxiously hoping for a business recovery. As Ernest Loveman, then one of Goldman Sachs's five partners, cheerfully said, "We have to have a good future because we can't get any lower than we are now." From that "can't get any worse" base, Weinberg led in consolidating the firm's position on Wall Street in what *Fortune* described in 1937 as "one of the most remarkable investment banking comebacks of the decade."[7] The firm decided to expand, and as Walter Sachs described the results: "We carried on with a sharply expanding business for the ensuing twenty-five years,"[8] though profits remained elusive until the mid-1940s.

Weinberg increasingly clearly ran the firm, and it soon became known as Sidney Weinberg's firm. Even though Goldman Sachs was a family firm, he was tough on the Sachses. To make it clear to everyone that the Sachses were *not* in charge, he put a round table in the partners' dining room so no Sachs could ever sit at the head of the table. Weinberg moved up fast and was continuously aggressive. His percentage participation in the Goldman Sachs partnership began in 1927 at 9.5 percent, but grew to 30 percent by 1937. Sullivan & Cromwell rewrote the partnership agreement so that a small trust owned the rights to the name Goldman Sachs; when the other two trustees died, Weinberg personally controlled the name. Weinberg's stated secret of success: "Love of hard work, no fear of tackling anything—and liking every minute of it." He didn't mention intimidation, but others certainly would.

Troubled times can uncover opportunities as well as problems, and Goldman Sachs experienced both. When Weinberg went around to call on the senior people at other firms, several refused to see him because his firm was not important or because of the failure of Goldman Sachs Trading Corporation. Opportunities came in commercial paper where, as others struggled, the firm expanded through the acquisition in 1932 of its main rival, Hathaway & Company, which gave the firm strength in the Midwest.[9] And a few years later, when Boston's Weil McKay & Company split in two, the McKay brothers brought their Southern textile accounts into the firm. With economic recovery, the market for commercial paper would expand substantially beyond commercial banks to include other kinds of financial institutions and industrial corporations. While "the business is done on a rather close margin of profit,"[10] the volume became so large that it could be relied on as a regular source of profit and, far more important for the firm's future, as an opening-wedge line of business with many corporations.

In 1935 a new crisis for Sidney Weinberg hit the front pages of the newspapers: McKesson & Robbins—on whose board Weinberg sat, supposedly looking out for investors' interests as an independent, "outside" professional director—was suddenly bankrupt, after several years of reporting substantial and apparently steady progress. The failure was no accident: It was part of a major accounting fraud. Originally a Bridgeport, Connecticut, manufacturer of pharmaceuticals, McKesson & Robbins was controlled by a man called F. Donald Coster, whom Weinberg had met on a vacation. Coster, cruising near Nantucket, where the Weinbergs rented a house each summer, invited Weinberg to come aboard his 134-foot yacht. As the Weinbergs rowed out, the yacht captain waved off their small, decrepit rowboat—until Coster came to their rescue.

Coster had conceived the idea of acquiring drug wholesalers across the country to create a nationwide drug manufacturing and distributing organization. Having persuaded accountants at Price Waterhouse to accept an inventory "verification"—done by Coster and other McKesson officials—which purported to show that the company had, supposedly in a large warehouse in Canada, a large inventory of crude drugs that it did not have,[11] the company reported hugely overstated "earnings."

McKesson's bankruptcy came as a stunning surprise, but it should have been no surprise at all. As it unfolded that Coster was an impostor whose real name was Philip Musica, that name triggered an old memory. A check of the credit files showed that Walter Sachs's father had, many years before, red-penciled the comment that Goldman Sachs should not do business with Musica, who had been accused of irregularities by U.S. Customs.[12] In addition, Walter Sachs had, several years before, refused "Coster's" request that Goldman Sachs sell several million dollars in notes to finance McKesson's continued expansion. A rueful Weinberg said, "All I know is that the figures of the crude drug department showed that it was doing a splendid and profitable business." His self-appraisal: "I just wasn't very bright." During an emergency meeting of the McKesson directors, news came that Musica had committed suicide. Weinberg didn't miss a beat: "Let's fire him for his sins anyway!"[13]

Apparently Weinberg learned his lesson. According to George Doty, later a partner of Goldman Sachs, "Sidney could and would smell a rat a mile away. Sidney Weinberg's fondest word was *integrity*. He virtually worshipped that word, and what it meant for him"—honesty and putting customers' interests first. "Mistakes were quite forgivable, but dishonesty was unpardonable. He was a looming presence and Mr. Integrity. If ever a question of ethics came up, it would be described as a 'Sidney Weinberg question.'"

"The real culture of Goldman Sachs traces back to Sidney Weinberg," says Al Feld, who worked at the firm for more than fifty years. "Tough as nails, he held the firm on the straight and narrow path of very high ethics—and true fellowship throughout. Goldman Sachs was a total meritocracy. Mr. Weinberg tolerated none of the politics or infighting that hurt so many of the other firms. And the key to there being no political games was the omnipotence of Sidney Weinberg, who was tough and endowed with tremendous energy."

One use of that power was to keep payouts to partners low, forcing them to build up equity in the firm. "Sidney Weinberg set the policy on tough capital retention," says partner Peter Sacerdote. "It was good for the firm because it made everyone focus always on what was best for Goldman Sachs as a whole firm. And it was good for the individual partner because it kept you financially modest. You couldn't get into fancy spending habits because you didn't have the money to spend."

Hard as he worked at rebuilding Goldman Sachs, Weinberg was also seriously engaged in reforming Wall Street—and in national politics and as a director of many major corporations. When the New York Stock Exchange was reorganized in the early thirties, Weinberg played an important behind-the-scenes role as a member of an insurgent group, persuading Carl Conway of Continental Can and Thomas McInnerny of National Dairy to head the crucial committee on reorganization, known popularly as the Conway Committee. Weinberg became a member of the NYSE Board of Governors. When he declined to run for a second two-year term in 1940, he successfully advocated the election of William McChesney Martin Jr. (later the longest-serving chairman of the Federal Reserve) as the first paid president of the New York Stock Exchange. After the Second World War, he orchestrated the election of Keith Funston, whom he had earlier recruited to the War Production Board.

Having tasted politics in 1932 by working for Franklin D. Roosevelt as a member of the Democratic Party's National Campaign Finance Committee, where he raised more money than any other member,[14] Weinberg launched a long series of relationships with occupants of the White House that would continue for more than thirty-five years. Almost everybody on Wall Street voted against FDR, and many distrusted him or literally hated him. For Weinberg this was an opportunity to go the other way and reach out to be helpful to the president, and he took it. In 1933 the president had him organizing the Business Advisory and Planning Council, through which corporate executives could present their views to the government with an assured hearing. And suddenly, there he was—a Jew from a Jewish firm of no great stature on Wall Street—extending as valuable an invitation as a business executive could have: to be one of the corporate executives who would meet with the top people in government and speak on behalf of the American business community.

The council became the bridge between business and government during the New Deal, helping coordinate business and government relations, clearing up misunderstandings, and restoring confidence. Weinberg not only decided who got invitations, he made sure he was the only investment banker in the group, making him the classic fox in the chicken coop. With an engaging personality and a great gift for gab, he was a star of the show and was soon known to everybody. He knew exactly how to capitalize on all these contacts. With his subsequent War Production Board service, he soon became the number one go-to man between corporate America and the U.S. government.

President Roosevelt paid Weinberg a singularly handsome tribute, considering the source, by conferring on him the nickname "The Politician." In recognition of his ability to handle touchy problems smoothly and effectively, FDR also offered him a number of federal appointments—including cabinet positions—and nearly proposed him for the new Stock Market Board, the pre-decessor to the Securities and Exchange Commission.[15] As reported at the time, "What the brokers have feared is that it may be extremely difficult to get men of sufficient experience in business and finance to serve on the Commission because of the small $10,000 salary and the requirement that Commissioners have no other business interests. Among the possible nominees, including T. J. Watson of IBM and General Robert E. Wood of Sears Roebuck, Mr. Weinberg is regarded as having the most thorough knowledge of the stock market."[16] In 1938 he was informally offered the post of ambassador to the Soviet Union.[17] The Russians had already been sounded out and had accepted Weinberg, but when he realized that anti-Semitism was gathering momentum there, he graciously begged off, mischievously saying: "I don't speak Russian. Who the hell could I talk to over there?"[18] The president wrote Weinberg a letter of regret, which he kept on dis-play in his office with the rest of what he fondly called "my mementos."

In 1939 Weinberg got another assignment: conducting an exhaustive study of investment banking for FDR, with particular attention to the wholesale and retail distribution of securities.[19] Again and again, Weinberg said that "govern-ment service is the highest form of citizenship,"[20] and as World War II began, he joined up full time. "I'll never take a job in government in peacetime, but I'll take any job in time of war."

Weinberg was active in forming the Industry Advisory Committee in 1941, initially as assistant director of purchases under Donald Nelson, a former exec-utive vice president of Sears Roebuck who headed the War Production Board. Weinberg's main job for Nelson was to get the very best executive talent he could for the war effort. (Another task was arranging the presence of attractive young women—the Miss Indianas and Miss Ohios for whom Nelson had such an enor-mous appetite that the FBI worried that the Germans might figure it out and plant some of their female spies in Nelson's bedchamber.) Weinberg also became acquainted with young Henry Ford during this period, earned his trust, and established what would become a most important friendship.

He advanced to be chief of the Bureau of Clearances, where he was paid the classic wartime patriot's one dollar a year. On January 26, 1942, Weinberg was made assistant to the chairman of the War Production Board, where General Motors's Charles E. Wilson observed: "His wide and influential friendships were invaluable in inducing outstanding men to come to Washington to work with us." That put it politely. Weinberg, as usual, put the matter far more directly. To get the numerous top-flight young executives he needed, Weinberg called on practically every giant corporation in America, met one-on-one with the CEO, and explained his mission clearly and forcefully: "Our nation is in grave danger. America needs an enormous number of talented executive leaders to organize a *massive* war production effort. The President has sent me here to get your help in identifying your very best young men. We need the smartest young stars you've got. And don't you even *think* of passing off older men or second-raters. I'm asking the same thing of every major company in the country, and I'll be watching *very* closely how well your men do compared to the best young men from all the other corporations. God forbid the people you pick are less than the best because God, President Roosevelt, and I would *never, ever* forgive you."

Affectionately called "the body snatcher" by FDR because his CEO meetings proved so very effective, Weinberg rapidly accumulated an extraordinary advantage for an investment banker: He got to know large numbers of America's best young executives and to see firsthand how effective each one really was, what work he was best at, and with whom he worked particularly well. After the war, hundreds of these same executives went back to run their companies, and many decided to make Sidney Weinberg their investment banker. Many more, when they became CEOs, were looking for suggestions as to who would be effective directors—and they usually wanted other CEOs. Weinberg knew more young CEOs than anyone else and was perceptive about which people would work well or not so well with each other person or group. He became a high-volume, high-level matchmaker who was discreet, got things done quietly and effectively, and was remarkably successful. More than anything else, the power and stature Weinberg accumulated during the war years—plus his remarkable one-to-one relationships with America's top executive talent and his encyclopedic knowledge of the skills and personalities of many top executives—boosted the stature of Sidney Weinberg.

Naturally appreciative, many of the men he placed in top-executive positions became clients of Goldman Sachs or, more precisely, clients of Sidney Weinberg, whose firm was Goldman Sachs. Numerous executives wanted Weinberg himself to be one of their directors, a role he performed particularly well. Over time, his detailed knowledge of specific companies led to his being elected a director of such corporations as Sears Roebuck, Continental Can, National Diary, B.F. Goodrich, and General Foods. (In 1953 the Department of Justice sued to require Weinberg to stop serving on the boards of both B.F. Goodrich and Sears Roebuck because both were so prominent in automobile tires.) In preparing for board meetings, Weinberg had an assistant, Nat Bowen, study all the facts and figures and the minutes of all previous discussions—with everything relevant to each item on the agenda kept in a small, coded notebook for handy reference—and then thoroughly brief him just before each meeting. With such complete preparation, Weinberg easily distinguished himself as a director by asking unusually penetrating questions during meetings. Weinberg wanted to know everything and would travel to see individual plants so he could take the company apart to see how it ticked. He became recognized as one of the first professional "outside" directors, serving as the representative of the public shareholders. In a departure from the then current convention, Weinberg asserted that directors' responsibilities were to the shareholders of the company they were supposed to direct and so they must be privy to all significant corporate information. He wrote an article for the *Harvard Business Review* outlining a series of recommendations on boards of directors that were then considered novel, but have since been largely adopted. His reputation soared, and Weinberg's capabilities as a director are fairly credited with cementing Goldman Sachs's relationships with many major corporations—invaluable in the investment banking business.

Weinberg had an extraordinary capacity to inspire trust, and with his effervescent personality was unusually well liked by people of all stations in life. At a General Foods board of directors meeting, always a formal and dignified affair, a long presentation was being made that was overloaded with dull, detailed statistics. Number after number was read off. When the droning presenter finally paused for breath, Weinberg jumped up, waving his papers in mock triumph, to call out "Bingo!"[21]

Called "the boy wonder" in his early years, Weinberg was widely known in his later years as "Mr. Wall Street." His offhand explanation, "I'm just a Brooklyn boy from PS 13 and I know a lot of business people," was cited as an extraordinary understatement of the reason for his great success by *BusinessWeek*, which explained that his bluntness was accepted because he was always objective, had no personal rancor, and "startles you with extra kindness."[22] Cocky and tart-tongued, Weinberg had an amazing ability to get along with anyone and relate to anybody.

Weinberg would not only tease corporate executives with a temerity almost unique in a man of his status, he would frequently twit the corporations themselves. Shortly after he was elected a director of General Electric, he was called upon by Philip D. Reed, GE's chairman of the board, to address a group of company officials at a banquet at the Waldorf-Astoria. In presenting Weinberg, Reed said that he was sure this new director would have some interesting and penetrating remarks to make about GE and that he hoped Mr. Weinberg felt, as he felt, that GE was the greatest outfit in the greatest industry in the greatest country in the world. Weinberg got to his feet. "I'll string along with your chairman about this being the greatest country," he began. "And I guess I'll even buy that part about the electrical industry. But as to GE's being the greatest business in the field, why, I'm damned if I'll commit myself until I've had a look-see."[23] Then he sat down to vigorous applause, provoked by both his brevity and his brashness.

In 1946 General Electric had mapped an expansion program of several hundred million dollars, but president Charles E. Wilson (known as Electric Charlie to differentiate him from GM's Engine Charlie) was not sure how his board would react. His worries vanished when director Weinberg supported the plans with hard facts and figures. Said Wilson: "Sidney had done his homework, and that was all I needed."[24]

Weinberg could be shatteringly frank, but his irreverent wit could deflate his listeners somehow without offending them. "Sidney is the only man I know who could ever say to me in the middle of a board meeting, as he did once, 'I don't think you're very bright,' and somehow give me the feeling that I'd been paid a compliment," said Charles Mortimer, chairman of General Foods. Such abrupt candor in formal board meetings was captivating. Weinberg knew he was different: "I've no family background and no blue blood. When I bleed, it's red as hell! That's the trouble with Wall Street. It's stuffy. There's so much tradition down here that people don't have a good time." Receiving an honorary degree from Trinity College, he cheerfully observed that he was the only Jew with an honorary degree from an Episcopal college and that for twenty-three years he had been a trustee of Presbyterian Hospital. After a long General Foods board of directors meeting, Weinberg agreed to stay over at Charles Mortimer's home in the exclusive Greenwich compound of Belle Haven. At the guardhouse, the car window was lowered and a deep voice from the rear seat intoned, "Mor-ti-mer." After the car was waved on, a rasping voice piped up, "What would the guard have said if he'd heard: 'Wine-boig'!?"

When Scott Paper's CEO, a Philadelphia Main Liner, put on a lavish black-tie dinner to celebrate his own sixtieth birthday and rose to toast his guests, he introduced Weinberg as "my very great friend." The puckish reply from Weinberg, who was always looking for business, delighted the crowd: "If we're such very good friends, why aren't we your company's investment bankers?" Irreverence won the day again for Weinberg when the head of Lehman Brothers brought his father, Governor Herbert Lehman, who had been a revered financier, to impress a company's board of directors. Tipped in advance by telephone, Weinberg hurried to the meeting and quickly turned the situation to his own advantage: "I'm sorry, gentlemen, *my* father is dead. But I have an uncle over in Brooklyn who is a tailor and who *looks* like him, and if that would mean anything to you, I'd be glad to bring him over!" When the directors stopped laughing, Goldman Sachs got the mandate for the underwriting.

General Robert E. Wood, the very formal and commanding chief executive of Sears Roebuck—as well as an outspoken anti-Semite and America Firster—once called on the offices of Goldman Sachs. At any other firm, a visit by General Wood would have been a Very Important Occasion marked with pomp and circumstance, but not at Sidney Weinberg's Goldman Sachs. As soon as Weinberg saw him, he called out cheerfully, "C'mon in, General!" Far from offended, Wood loved Weinberg and his irreverent ways. On another occasion, Weinberg turned to Wood and deadpanned: "You're so old, you won't live long. So why don't you leave all your money ... to *me?*"

"Mr. Weinberg had a remarkable talent for spotting superior companies that would succeed and grow over many years—companies like 3M and GE," says partner Bob Menschel. "He had great taste and selectivity. He felt particularly close to the Morgan bank and he always expected of you what J.P. Morgan wanted—a first-class business done in a first-class way. He was very clear that if you lower the standards you set for the clients you'd accept and work for, your best clients will know—and they will leave." Weinberg's comment on doing business with second-tier companies as clients was typically blunt: "If you lie down with dogs, you'll wake up with fleas."

Throughout his career, Weinberg's irrepressible sense of humor centered on practical jokes. As a beginner at the firm, he had enjoyed placing tacks on seats where other low-level employees would sit down. On one occasion, he put an advertisement in the newspaper stating that a new Broadway musical would be produced by Sam Sachs and that chorus-line applicants should come to Sachs's Wall Street office for an interview. This produced a string of pretty young dancers that embarrassed the elderly Sachs—and delighted others in the office.

I n the nation's capital, Weinberg's pranks expanded to an appropriately grander scale. Paul Cabot, a patrician, Harvard-educated Boston Brahmin, and Sidney Weinberg, the drop-out Jew from Brooklyn, had hit it off as soon as they met in the 1920s. Cabot was as shrewd and blunt as Weinberg and, like Weinberg, a dedicated practical joker. They soon developed a truly great friendship.

Cabot was both "to the manor born" and famous for his direct manner. Serving as a director of J.P. Morgan along with General Motors's great leader Alfred P. Sloan, Cabot once asked Sloan how things were coming along at GM. Mr. Sloan began carefully describing the smooth but complex workings of the corporation's committee system, when Cabot cut in: "What we all want to know is this: when are you going to make some real *dough?*" Cabot was managing partner of State Street Research & Management, treasurer of Harvard University, and the very successful overseer of Harvard's endowment who declared that each school or department must finance itself rather than relying on the central university, saying famously, "every tub on its own bottom." Despite the "impossibility" of controlling a university faculty, he made that dictum stick.

During the thirties, Weinberg arranged to put Cabot on the boards of several major corporations, including Ford, B.F. Goodrich, National Dairy, and Continental Can, so when Weinberg urged him to come down to Washington as a wartime dollar-a-year man, Cabot was ready.

Weinberg decided to teach Cabot a lesson to remember by putting him in charge of a raucous bunch of scrap dealers, expecting he would soon have Cabot in full retreat, humbly asking for help. Not so. Cabot quickly took firm control of the scrap dealers. They worked so well together that at the end of the war, the dealers gave Cabot a solid gold tray with their signatures on it. Cabot knew that he had gotten that particular job because it suited Weinberg's sense of humor to put his friend, the Boston blue blood, in with a crude and rough bunch—another practical joke, but nothing like his next one.

The Hopkins Institute, notorious as the largest of the many busy brothels operating in the nation's capital during the early war years, was finally raided and closed down by the District of Columbia police. A few weeks later, learning that Mr. and Mrs. Cabot would soon move their home from Boston to Washington, where they planned to stay for the duration, Weinberg suddenly had a great idea: With the nation at war, telephone service was, of course, tightly restricted, so if and when a telephone number was finally assigned to a customer, it was virtually impossible to get that number changed to another listing. This reality would be Weinberg's fulcrum, and the reputation of the Hopkins Institute would be his Archimedes' lever.

Printing up a stack of handsome four-by-six cards proudly announcing the "Grand Reopening" of the Hopkins Institute in response to strong public demand, Weinberg hired several smartly dressed young men to go down to Union Station and hand out the happy announcements to soldiers, sailors, or civilian travelers—anyone they thought might be a good prospect for the Institute's fabled services. Hundreds of cards were given out, all asking interested patrons to call a special number for directions to the Institute's secret new address—and all giving the Cabots' newly assigned telephone number. The calls began coming into the Cabots' home about four in the afternoon, increased steadily to a peak near midnight, and then gradually declined into the early morning. The calls from insistent, often inebriated, "customers" came in night after night—for weeks and weeks.

With this beginning, the personal war between the two jokesters was on. It would last long after the shooting war was over. Weinberg and Cabot, both armed with clever imaginations, were constantly looking for ways to pull pranks on each other. After many weeks in sweltering Washington, Cabot somehow got tickets to fly to Boston for a weekend with his family. Weinberg, affecting great urgency, said the director of the Office of War Production, William S. Knudsen, had called an emergency meeting to reorganize the whole war production operation. Knowing they could never be rebooked, Weinberg told Cabot he'd better cancel his tickets. Fortunately, a pal had tipped Cabot that it was all a joke, so Cabot kept his tickets but told Weinberg he had given them up. Panicking, Weinberg called airline after airline, trying to get tickets—*any* tickets. No luck at all. Desperate, Weinberg decided to pretend he was Knudsen and called Cabot, who had never met Knudsen, to say the meeting was called off. Weinberg hoped that maybe Cabot could get himself reinstated with the airlines. Cabot, of course, still had the treasured tickets in his pocket and was delighted to see Weinberg squirm. When the call came in, Cabot told his secretary to say he was too busy. Cabot's secretary said, "Mr. Knudsen insists," so Cabot picked up the phone, certain that it was Weinberg. In what had to be Weinberg pretending a Swedish accent, Cabot was requested to come around to Knudsen's office. Certain he had all the cards, Cabot snapped: "For God's sakes, go piss up a wall!" Unfortunately, Knudsen himself had happened to call moments before Weinberg got through. Suddenly realizing it really *was* Director Knudsen, Cabot dashed to his office to apologize. Luckily, Knudsen knew of Weinberg's jokes, so they had a good laugh together—and Cabot flew home to Boston for the weekend.

"He had a fantastic nose for who was honest and who was not quite so good," said Cabot of his friend. "Plus he had that great sense of humor."[25] The peak of Weinberg's irreverence during World War II may have been achieved when Admiral Darlan, the senior Vichy French naval officer and a politically powerful, haughty, and ambitious man known to have Nazi sympathies, was at the White House being courted with attentive protocol by the Allies for political reasons. When it was time to leave, Weinberg reached into his pocket as he came to the front door, pulled out a quarter, and handed it to the resplendently uniformed admiral, saying, "Here, boy, get me a cab."

Cabot introduced Weinberg to his patrician friends and they got along famously, often sailing on summer cruises in the cold waters off Maine. Despite his navy service, Weinberg knew nothing about sailing and never learned how to swim. On one occasion, obliged by his companions to jump into the cold water— because all hands were required to wash at least once each day—Weinberg prudently tied one end of a long rope to the mast and the other around his waist before he climbed carefully down the boat's ladder into the sea. Cabot, quickly untying the line from the mast, joyfully tossed it into the water where Weinberg, in a bulky life preserver, struggled to stay afloat.

Cabot and Weinberg both loved dirty jokes, which they delighted in telling each other in their regular telephone calls. In their later years, both were losing their hearing, and Cabot's proper Bostonian secretary was so offended when overhearing Cabot's end of those scatological calls that she insisted Cabot close the door when Weinberg's calls came in. To accommodate her request, but knowing such offending calls came in quite often, Cabot found a clever solution: a foot pedal under his desk that would automatically close the door.

Cabot had occasion to learn that Weinberg, while widely respected and very well liked, was not free from other people's prejudice. One morning the acting president of Manhattan's exclusive club, the Brook, went to the dining room table where Cabot was eating his breakfast to inform him that it had been "inappropriate to do what he had done the night before." Cabot had dined with two guests; one was Sidney Weinberg. A man with no time for fools, Cabot sensed what was up, but decided to play innocent: "Did we speak in too-loud voices?"

"Oh, no, it wasn't that. It was the *individuals* at your table."

"What's your exact meaning?"

"You know we don't accept Jews at the Brook."

"Well, I've read the by-laws and there's nothing on the subject there." Cabot's voice changed to a firmer tone: "If that's the way this club is to be run, you can stick your club you know where. You will have my resignation this very morning."

At other times, prejudice was shown more innocently if just as obviously. Once Morgan Stanley's senior partner, Perry Hall, called Weinberg to tell him some wonderful news: "We've just made our first Jewish partner!" "Oh, Perry," retorted Weinberg without a pause, "that's *nothing*. We've had them here for *years*!"

After the war, Weinberg resigned from government service, explaining cheerfully: "There was less and less real work for me to do. In the winter, I was reading important papers until eight p.m. Last spring, I'd be finished by three. When I was done by ten a.m., I knew it was time to resign in Washington and return to New York."

But he stayed active as a Democratic fund-raiser. Weinberg did detour from the New and Fair Deals in 1940 to back Wendell Willkie, because he believed two terms was a proper limit for presidents, and in 1952 to play a key role in the election campaign via Businessmen for Eisenhower. As many other major figures did when Weinberg's name came up, Ike said: "He's a close personal friend of mine." Weinberg's fund-raising technique—mostly personal solicitation with his rasping Brooklyn voice—was abrupt and effective. According to his friend John Hay "Jock" Whitney, the financier and newspaper and radio proprietor, "Sidney is the best money-getter I've ever seen. He'll go to one of his innumerable board meetings—General Foods, General Electric, or General Whatnot—and make no bones about telling everybody there what he wants. Then he'll say, 'Come on boys: where is it?—and up it comes." Weinberg went on to successfully recommend to Eisenhower the following appointments: George Humphrey, who became treasury secretary; Charles Wilson of General Motors, who was made secretary of defense; and Robert Stevens, who was appointed secretary of the army. Later on, Weinberg also played a key role in organizing the Communications Satellite Corporation (Comsat) for John F. Kennedy and then served on the Committee for Johnson-Humphrey. In 1964 he helped form a Johnson for President group and later recommended John Connor and Henry H. Fowler to the president; Connor became secretary of commerce and Fowler secretary of the Treasury.

During Hubert Humphrey's 1968 campaign against Richard Nixon, L. Jay Tenenbaum, a Goldman Sachs partner, got a rare call from Weinberg, who asked: "L. Jay, what are the odds on the [stock exchange] floor in the Humphrey-Nixon election?" Tenenbaum said he would find out and called Bunny Lasker, a floor specialist, who said the odds were seven to five for Nixon. "Don't cuff it," said Tenenbaum: "Sidney Weinberg wants to know." Lasker replied bluntly: "I offer $70,000 to Sidney Weinberg's $50,000!" Weinberg couldn't believe it: "Doesn't he know that George Ball has just come out for Humphrey?" Tenenbaum couldn't resist making up a quick reply: "Lasker says he knows Humphrey has Ball—and when he has *two* balls, he'll have a shot at the White House." Immediately,

Tenenbaum called Lasker to say, "Protect me on this, Bunny," but Lasker was laughing and saying, "I've gotta tell RN!"

"With his strong Brooklyn accent," recalls John Whitehead, Goldman Sachs's cohead from 1976 to 1984, "Sidney couldn't possibly masquerade as a Harvard man, so he made fun of the Harvard aura." He got pawnshops all over Brooklyn to sell him any Phi Beta Kappa keys that came in, kept them on a wire in his desk drawer, and, if he had a stuffed shirt going on and on for too long about something, would pull the wire full of PBK keys out of his drawer and say admiringly, "Gee, you're so awfully smart, you should have one of these." He observed, "One scientist accused me of shaking the bedrock of Phi Beta Kappa until I reminded him that *I* wasn't the one who had hocked his key." Weinberg helped organize a "counter Phi Beta Kappa" called Kappa Beta Phi, had keys made up, and proudly wore one on his watch chain. The group inducted new members at annual ceremonies featuring racy skits and nude women.

Weinberg's engagingly outrageous chutzpah prevailed on the day the firm was sued for one hundred million dollars by Eddie Cantor, the Broadway entertainer and major stockholder in Goldman Sachs Trading Corporation. The suit got front-page coverage in the *New York Times* on the day Weinberg and all the other big shots on Wall Street took the evening train to Washington for the annual meeting of the Investment Bankers Association. With such a public embarrassment, other bankers might have gone into hiding. Not Sidney Weinberg. He worked his way through every car on the train, making a joke out of the disaster by facetiously urging each of the other firms to join in a general syndication of the lawsuit.

Weinberg never forgot his Brooklyn background and its lessons in thrift. He rode the subway, cheerfully reminding others that he was saving five dollars every week: "You can learn a lot more looking around at the people and the ads on the subway than you can by watching the back of a chauffeur's head in a limousine." Savings came in other ways too. The heir to a large retailing fortune once spent a night in Scarsdale with the Weinbergs and retired early. After Weinberg and his wife, whose only servant was a cook, had emptied the ashtrays and picked up the glasses, they noticed that their guest had put his suit and shoes outside his bedroom door. Amused, Weinberg took the suit and shoes down to the kitchen, cleaned the shoes, brushed the suit, and put them back. The following day, as the guest was leaving, he handed Weinberg a five-dollar bill and asked him to pass it along to the butler who had taken such excellent care of his things. Weinberg thanked him gravely and pocketed the money.

As much as he always exuded self-confidence, in some ways Weinberg was uncertain about himself. He knew he had little education and would write out a letter he wanted to send to a client—always with a very wide nub on his pen and always on a yellow pad of paper—and then say to one of his Harvard-trained associates, "Please read this. Is it okay?" As partner Jim Marcus recalls, "You might offer a suggestion or two—for which he'd always be appreciative—but it really wasn't easy to find corrections." Marcus adds, "Sidney was fun, and he had a big temper that usually erupted only because he was so frustrated when he couldn't get something done that he wanted to do."

One device that was apparently beyond Weinberg, quick study that he otherwise was, was the slide rule. John Whitehead recalls, "Sidney would call me into his office and ask me to close the door so we could be alone. Then he'd open the desk drawer where he had a very large, fancy slide rule someone had given to him and say, 'Now, John, just show me once again how this thing works.' So I'd go around behind where he was sitting, reach around his shoulders to the slide rule, and explain, 'You put the one here over the two here and then slide the plastic with the vertical line on it over this two and read below the line here, where it says four.' You could sense his frustration swelling as he looked down at all the numbers and saw complexity and felt confusion. And then he would burst out with, 'Damn it all, I *know* that two times two is four! What use is this!' And he'd slam the drawer shut for another year or so. We *never* got any farther."

Loyalty was a central value to Weinberg. He ate, drove, wore, and used the products produced by "his" companies—cheese had to be Kraft, coffee had to be Maxwell House, cars were Fords, etc.—and when a young executive wanted to leave General Foods for a career at Goldman Sachs, it first had to be approved by one of General Foods's directors, Sidney Weinberg. "He was," John Whitehead recalls, "very protective—indeed possessive—about his clients. The only time I remember his becoming really angry at me was when Henry Ford, finding that

Sidney was out of the office, switched to me to leave a message. When I passed the message on to Sidney, he made it clear that he did not want me ever again talking to Henry. I could talk to anyone else at Ford, but conversations with Henry were to be his alone. I was upset at the time, and the edict disappeared as time passed, but I noted that, as with so many famous people, there was still with him a basic underlying insecurity."

Weinberg was deeply upset when the Department of Justice, "unmindful of the great service that the leading banking houses had made in time of peace and war to the country's economy,"[26] initiated an antitrust suit in 1949 against seventeen leading banking houses and the Investment Bankers Association for colluding to fix prices. Weinberg was convinced that his beloved firm was seriously threatened by the government's action, and he was determined to fight. Still, it was better to be included than, as almost happened, to be left out.[27] Weinberg was distressed that the firm was far down the list of the industry's hallowed pecking order: Goldman Sachs ranked only seventeenth of the seventeen. Weinberg knew that rival investment banking firms were sure to bring that sign of insignificance to the attention of the corporate executives that Weinberg was striving to win over as clients.

When the investment banks won the lawsuit in October 1953, Goldman Sachs received a compliment in Judge Harold Medina's final decision, which ran to four hundred printed pages: "Goldman Sachs pursued throughout the entire period, from the turn of the century down to the date of the filing of the complaint, a competitive policy which was in every sense of the term aggressive. Goldman Sachs even transcended the bounds of reasonable competitive effort in its endeavor to get every piece of business it could possibly secure, within the limits of its personnel and its resources." Despite this complimentary finding, the lawsuit cost the firm dearly: $7.5 million in legal expenses. But it was worth it to be included.

While the firm was, just barely, a member of the club, it clearly had a long, long way to go. Weinberg had no intention of remaining just a member of the club: He was determined to be important. "All the prestige clients of Goldman Sachs were not *firm* clients, they were the *personal* clients of Sidney Weinberg," says Al Feld, "and those core clients were crucial. For example, what got the firm into other firms' syndicates was our ability to trade positions in *their* syndicates for positions in *our* syndicates—which were really Mr. Weinberg's syndicates.

Mr. Weinberg's business was *his* business, and he brooked no interference. He was rough and knew how to be tough with others. He once gave an ultimatum that no one else could have given to the Sears Roebuck board of directors. He was not pleased with the way Lehman Brothers had been conducting itself and put the matter bluntly: 'Either they go or I go!' Lehman Brothers went."

During his era—from 1930 to 1969—Weinberg exercised control over Goldman Sachs by force of will and personality; by his standing within the firm; by his stature in the outside world, particularly in Washington; because he was by far the largest-percentage partner; and because he alone decided who would become a partner and once every two years he alone decided the percentage participations of all the other partners. (One year, partner Stanley Miller looked at the list and couldn't find his name. It wasn't there. So Weinberg gave Miller a piece of his own participation.) A further reason for Weinberg's dominance was that he was a director of so many corporations[28]—over time, serving on forty boards of major corporations or their subsidiaries and bringing vast business to the firm. "Sidney Weinberg was so clearly Mr. Goldman Sachs," recalls partner Ray Young, "that it was not surprising that when a bellhop was delivering a telegram addressed simply to 'Goldman Sachs at the Waldorf-Astoria,' he took it right to Weinberg's table because, after all, he was Mr. Goldman Sachs."[29]

"Mr. Weinberg felt very strongly about making no noise in the press," recalls Bob Menschel. "He did not want to create our own competition and was very strict about never talking about what we were doing. 'If you think it's to help the firm's business,' he'd say, 'you're just kidding yourself. The people who really want to know what you can do will figure it out. If it's for your own ego, go ahead. But remember: The press that praises you when you're up is the same press that kicks you when you're down.'" Weinberg's appraisal was not just an opinion. As Menschel recalls, "One indiscretion and you'd get a real reaming. Two and out you'd go. Fired."

Weinberg developed a reputation as a whiz at reconciling groups with different, even contradictory objectives. Recalls Al Gordon, "Sidney Weinberg was remarkably effective at bringing people together—very different people from very different backgrounds—so they would talk and cooperate." Weinberg became famous for his "evangelical talks," persuading people to do what they would otherwise be unwilling even to consider. In discussions of complicated problems, he could almost always cut to the core, come up with *the* common-sense decision, and promptly act on it.

One exercise in "evangelism" enabled Owens-Corning Fiberglas Corporation to bring off what was at the time described as "one of the most successful public stock offerings in corporation history."[30] Corning and Owens-Illinois, as the principal shareholders, together owned 84.5 percent of OCF but were prohibited under an antitrust ruling from putting any more money into OCF and didn't want to sell any shares. The shares were not listed because the NYSE was insisting that the public had to hold at least 50 percent of the shares for any stock to be listed. As problem solver, Sidney Weinberg had a particular personal advantage: He knew all three corporate CEOs and Keith Funston, the president of the NYSE, so he was able to negotiate a solution acceptable to all four parties. The exchange reduced its public ownership requirement to 20 percent, and the two parent companies sold enough shares to meet this revised minimum required for listing.

Another time, when a group meeting with him were wringing their hands over a series of minor settlement problems with Morgan Guaranty Trust, he picked up the phone and told his secretary to get Henry Clay Alexander, then mighty Morgan's CEO. The two organizations had business relationships, but Mr. Alexander was considered far too senior to be bothered with such minor matters as trading settlements.

"You *can't* call Mr. Alexander about a small matter like this!" protested Weinberg's associate.

"Why not?" replied Weinberg. "If your friends won't tell you when you're making a mistake, who will?" The settlement problems were resolved.

Weinberg's personal habits were notably plain. His Scarsdale house was the same twelve-room frame structure he and Helen had moved into in 1923, three years after their marriage and four years before he became a partner of Goldman Sachs.[31] In the fifties Weinberg bought a piece of *The Pajama Game* at the urging of one of his friends, Floyd Odlum, president of the Atlas Corporation, and it was such a hit that he gave the impression of wishing he hadn't. Holding his latest check from the investment at arm's length, he observed ruefully to a visitor, "Money! Keeps coming in all the time and hardly means anything at all." As he explained, he was too busy to make as much for himself as he could have.[32] He wasn't kidding. At his death, Weinberg's personal fortune would amount to little more than five million dollars.

Sidney Weinberg was—and clearly knew he was—far more important as an individual than Goldman Sachs was as a firm, and that was just fine with him. "Sidney Weinberg—Mr. Weinberg, as we all called him—had a tremendous, commanding personality and was an amazing producer of business," recalls Al Feld. "Many of the corporate executives he served so effectively came to feel they needed Sidney Weinberg to achieve their most important corporate and personal objectives, and that's why he and Goldman Sachs got their investment banking business. Otherwise, how could anyone explain why Henry Ford II, who could have picked anyone and any firm, selected Sidney Weinberg and Goldman Sachs to mastermind what was to be the underwriting of the century?"

4

✒

FORD

THE LARGEST IPO

Goldman Sachs's most important transaction and the firm's relationship with its most important client for many years originated in a very personal way. The young CEO of the largest privately owned business in the world had a special friendship with Goldman Sachs's senior partner. That relationship was improbable: They were different in age, religion, wealth, social standing, and personal values. But they had both been in Washington during the war, and one of them, Sidney Weinberg, knew everyone from political and military leaders to showgirls, and he knew how to make connections.

The Ford Motor Company was built as an increasingly gigantic proprietorship by Henry Ford, a notorious anti-Semite who would never have been willing to rely on a Jewish financier. After Henry Ford's death, his son Edsel became CEO—but when Edsel died six months later, the title passed to his thirty-five-year-old son, Henry Ford II.

Young Henry's principal distinction to that date may have been getting dismissed from Yale not only for having his term papers written by a commercial agency, but also for being so casual about academic standards as to have carelessly left the agency's invoice inside a paper's cover. At Yale, Ford bought suits of clothes a dozen at a time, had them delivered to his dormitory room, and, when told the closet was already full, said: "Just take out as many as you put in—and do whatever you want with them." Arguably, the best thing young Ford did before becoming CEO was to make friends at the War Production Board with a man who was twenty-five years older and really knew his way around: Sidney Weinberg.

When young Henry suddenly became CEO, the Ford Motor Company was in serious trouble—converting from wartime truck and tank production to making passenger cars; breaking the power of a thug named Harry Bennett, who effectively controlled the River Rouge factory operations with goons carrying guns until he was forced out with the help of the former head of the FBI in Detroit; and establishing a management team that was up to the enormous postwar tasks and responsibilities of reorganizing a sprawling, mismanaged proprietorship into an effective corporate giant. Ford addressed the third challenge in part by hiring in Tex Thornton's Air Force Whiz Kids—including Robert McNamara, who later became Ford's president and then JFK's secretary of defense. In addition, Ford got invaluable help from FDR's "body snatcher," Sidney Weinberg, who helped recruit—with large incentive pay packages—Ernie Breech, the former chairman of Bendix, as president; Bill Gussett as general counsel; Ted Yntema as chief financial officer; and a cluster of young executives who would make Ford Motor Company a leader in corporate financial management—and Sidney Weinberg a real influence at Ford.

One day John Whitehead, who was then working as an assistant to Weinberg, asked: "Do you think Ford will ever go public?"

"No," said Weinberg, "but taking Ford public would certainly be a great coup." Little did either know that their brief exchange would soon lead to one of the most important transactions on Wall Street.

Ford was a *very* private company, and everything financial was kept secret. But Whitehead began to think that there must be some financial information somewhere, and he started searching for it. Sure enough, the Commonwealth of Massachusetts had a law requiring any company doing business there to register—and file a balance sheet at the state Department of Commerce so people could get basic information about any company with which they might do business. Since Ford did business in the Commonwealth and could get no exception to the rule, Ford had to file.

Whitehead took the train to Boston, searched the files, and located Ford's single-page filing. It was the Ford Motor Company's balance sheet. Weinberg and Whitehead took a long look. Ford was not just big. It was *huge* in assets and had few liabilities. Indeed, it was the largest privately owned company in the world. However, as Weinberg and Whitehead would later find out when the Ford family—not the corporation—gave them a look at the financials, large as it was, Ford Motor Company was not profitable.

The Ford family had been shocked to learn that old Mr. Ford had decided just before his death to save on estate taxes by creating the Ford Foundation, funded with 88 percent of Ford Motor Company's common stock. With 2 percent owned by Ford directors, officers, and employees, only 10 percent would pass on to family members—but this 10 percent would hold 100 percent of the voting rights, so the family still had complete control.

The Ford Foundation finance committee—chaired by yet another of Weinberg's many close friends, Charles E. Wilson, chairman of General Electric—was in an untenable situation: Ford stock paid no dividends, so the foundation could not make grants. Equally important, the trustees sensibly believed that prudence required them to diversify the foundation's endowment, so they were determined to sell a large block of Ford stock in a public offering and have Ford listed on the New York Stock Exchange. The exchange, however, required all listed stocks to have voting rights and pay dividends—which the family opposed. Family members were all on the Ford payroll at handsome salaries, so they had no need for even more income through dividends. In addition to these strong differences, the Internal Revenue Service would have to agree to make a special private ruling that the benefits—presumably paid in additional shares—that the family would receive in exchange for giving up absolute voting control would not be subject to taxation. Otherwise the family would never agree. As both sides would soon learn, there was one more potential conflict: Both the foundation and the family intended to retain the same expert adviser—Sidney Weinberg.

Weinberg may have been the smallest important man on Wall Street physically, but it did not matter: He was at the height of his personal powers and stature.

Goldman Sachs may have been a small, second-tier firm with little experience in managing underwriting syndicates, but it did not matter: It was Sidney Weinberg's firm. The issue was whether Weinberg would represent the Ford Foundation or the Ford family.

The foundation's finance committee had thought it wise to retain an expert adviser for an operation that was so large and complex. Over the years, Charles E. Wilson had become acquainted with practically all the shrewdest money men in the country, and there was no question in his mind about which one of them he wanted as the foundation's adviser: "I want Sidney Weinberg." When Wilson told young Henry Ford, who was also the chairman of the foundation, that he planned to enlist Weinberg as his adviser, Ford promptly blocked that idea: "You can't have him. Sidney is financial adviser to the family." The family got Weinberg, and the foundation got three other advisers.

As E. J. Kahn observed in his *New Yorker* profile of Weinberg:

> That both of the principal parties involved in the nation's most impressive stock offering wanted the services of the same individual was no surprise to people familiar with the individual—Sidney James Weinberg, a 65-year-old oracle whose counsel has long been one of the financial community's most avidly sought commodities. As the senior partner of the venerable and powerful investment banking firm of Goldman, Sachs & Co.; as a director, over the years, of more big corporations than any other American; and as an adviser to whom not only the country's industrialists but its presidents listen attentively, Weinberg, though largely unknown to the man in any street but Wall, is among the nation's most influential citizens . . . as a power behind the throne.[1]

Ford offered Weinberg the job on October 1, 1953. Weinberg immediately accepted without knowing how much of his time or how long it would take to complete. As things turned out, it took about half his working time for two straight years. "The big problem was to get all hands to agree on how much stock the Fords should get for transferring a part of their voting rights to the shares the foundation wanted to sell. Although others naturally had a hand in the proceedings, the immense chore of reorganizing the Ford Motor Company's entire financial setup was left pretty much up to him."[2]

Over the next two years, Weinberg and Whitehead, with help from Shearman & Sterling, developed fifty-six different and very complex reorganization plans—all in absolute secrecy. To ensure strict security, Weinberg dictated no letters, notes, or memoranda on the subject. Anything he absolutely needed in writing was written out in longhand—using a promotional pen received from National Dairy showing "Sealtest" in bold letters—and Ford was never discussed by name: It was always "X."

To avoid attracting attention, meetings were held in various inconspicuous locations or at the magnificent home of Edsel Ford's formidable widow, now remarried to Ernest Kanzler, a Ford executive who had headed the War Production Board in World War II. Mrs. Kanzler chaired the meetings with her children Henry, Benson, Bill, and Josephine attending. The meetings were strictly private. To avoid public recognition of the frequency of Weinberg's visits, travel was usually by private plane. When Henry Ford went to Europe for a holiday, Weinberg gave him a code sheet for deciphering cables. The company was "Agnes"; Henry Ford was "Alice"; his brothers were "Ann" and "Audrey"; the family's lawyer was "Meg"; the foundation was "Grace"; and Weinberg was "Edith." Whitehead and Ford's messages read a lot like *Little Women*, though both enjoyed playing with double entendres in how the names were used.

In 1955 Weinberg and Whitehead were given something remarkable to look at—an *absolute* secret. It was a full-scale annual report for Ford Motor Company with color pictures, full text, and all the financials, including detailed footnotes.[3] This was all for practice and to make sure the detailed data required by the SEC could be collected and reported accurately and quickly after years of closely guarded secrecy. In anticipation of possibly going public, every aspect of that mock annual report was designed to equal the annual report of archrival General Motors. Only one copy was ever taken outside the Ford headquarters building— the copy entrusted to Sidney Weinberg.

On the way to one of those rigorously clandestine family meetings, Weinberg nearly ruined everything. Landing fifteen minutes earlier than expected one morning at the general aviation terminal at Detroit's airport, Weinberg and

Whitehead had to wait for the limousine sent to fetch them to headquarters, so they paused at a newsstand to buy a local newspaper. Weinberg put down the zippered leather portfolio in which he carried Ford's supersensitive private documents, including the corporation's full and audited financial statements, while he reached into his pocket for the coins to pay for the newspaper, never pausing in his item-by-item review with Whitehead of what must be accomplished during the day ahead as they went into the café for a cup of coffee. When the limousine driver sent to meet them came to the table, apologizing for their having to wait, Weinberg, anxious to be punctual, quickly paid the bill and got into the car, all the while continuing the item-by-item review with Whitehead as they drove to their meeting at Ford headquarters in Dearborn. Suddenly, Weinberg stopped talking. He looked horrified and turned immediately to Whitehead and almost shouted: "John! *John!!* Where in hell did you put my portfolio?"

Weinberg knew Whitehead didn't have it: He knew he had lost those papers himself. "But," recalls Whitehead, "it was in his nature to be aggressive like that. That was Sidney." Weinberg, of course, insisted that the car turn around and drive all the way back to the airport where the two men jumped out and ran to the café and the newsstand, desperately hoping to find that essential portfolio. If anyone found that envelope and opened it and Ford's sensitive financials got disclosed, all their work over the past two years—all Weinberg's work over the past *forty* years—would be threatened. Fortunately, there it was, right where Weinberg had left it. Seeing the two men so out of breath, the news vendor observed laconically: "If you fellas hasn't come soon for those papers, I'd've tossed 'em away."

Almost losing those precious documents was a close call, but the secret that Ford and Weinberg were up to something was kept until Weinberg met with Henry Ford and several other members of the family at Palm Beach in March 1955. After working all one day, Weinberg and Ford decided to relax at a large charity ball, where their cover was pierced by a society columnist who noticed the pair when Ford guided Weinberg to the table of the Duke and Duchess of Windsor. As Weinberg later observed, "How could you keep anything confidential under *those* conditions?"

The Ford offering was certain to be the defining underwriting of the postwar era in Wall Street. Every investment banker wanted a major role. Weinberg shrewdly positioned himself to control participation in the syndicate even though the foundation was the actual seller and well-respected Blyth & Co. the nominal lead underwriter.[4]

Most important, Weinberg carefully arranged everything so that he would personally be understood to be making all the key selections of the specific firms to be given the lucrative and prestigious positions as the principal underwriters. He had wanted fewer underwriters, but Ford wanted more, so in a compromise Weinberg determined that seven was the appropriate number of lead underwriters—an elite group including, of course, Goldman Sachs.* Nearly one hundred other firms filled out the enormous syndicate. While some of the leading firms might have argued that seven lead underwriters were really too many, they knew all too well that if they ever complained, Weinberg, being Weinberg, would make certain that their firm—whichever firm it might be—would be taken out of the lucrative underwriting altogether.

Every major underwriter soon understood that Sidney Weinberg intended to achieve two simultaneous objectives: first, to put together the strongest possible syndicate so the Ford family and the Ford Foundation would get the best possible price, and second, to ensure a major advance in the stature of Goldman Sachs among underwriters. As he chose each of the lead underwriters for one of the coveted, lucrative slots, Weinberg made sure its leaders knew where this opportunity came from and understood what reciprocal business would be expected in the years to come.

After one of the many grueling days, followed by an evening of difficult negotiations, it was finally time to leave Ford headquarters. As it happened, Henry Ford and Sidney Weinberg were both headed to New York City's LaGuardia Airport, so Ford offered Weinberg and Whitehead a ride in his private plane. "Should I order a car to meet you, Mr. Ford?" asked the pilot. Ford asked, "Going to Manhattan, Sidney?" Weinberg was going to the Sherry-Netherland, while Ford was going to the Regency. Their hotels were close, so they could share a cab. Trying to be helpful, Whitehead offered, "I have a car at the airport. I'll be going through Manhattan on my way to New Jersey and can easily drop you both

* John Whitehead kept a photo of the then heads of all seven lead underwriters—with himself substituting for Weinberg. He also kept the full-page "tombstone" newspaper advertisement for the Ford offering, which included the names of all the many firms in the syndicate. Over the next several decades, as firms failed, merged, or changed names, Whitehead carefully drew a red line through their names on a clear plastic sheet he would pull down over the ad, until only a few firms' names were left. One of the few was Goldman Sachs.

off." As Whitehead drove his car up to the Butler Aviation private-plane build-ing, Ford gasped, "My God! You can't ask *me* to ride in a goddamn *Chevy!* What will people say?"

"John," exclaimed Weinberg, "what have you *done*? This is worse than awful. This is the end of the world!"

Then Ford turned on Weinberg. "Sidney, don't you pay your people enough so they can afford a really *good* car?"

It was too late to change plans: They would have to make the best of it. Embarrassed and determined not to get caught, Ford instructed Whitehead, "If you have shades on this car, pull 'em down!" and tugged his coat collar up as he slid down, hoping to hide from view. When they got to Manhattan, Ford told Whitehead, "Let me out on the corner two blocks away from my hotel and I'll walk to the front door—and send a bellboy back to get the bags."

Nevertheless, the story was soon passed around Detroit that Henry Ford had been riding around New York City in a Chevrolet.

The Ford offering in January 1956 was a personal and professional triumph for Weinberg and a business triumph for Goldman Sachs. Weinberg's final plan rewarded the Ford family with a huge increase in shareholdings—tax free. At the time, Ford's was the largest IPO ever: 10.2 million shares at $64.50 per share for nearly seven hundred million dollars (over five billion in today's dollars). The offering dwarfed all previous underwritings and attracted five hundred thousand individual investors. The *New York Times* carried the story with Sidney Wein-berg's photograph—on the front page, above the fold.

When Henry Ford had asked Weinberg at the outset what his fee would be, Weinberg had declined to get specific; he offered to work for a dollar a year until everything was over and then let the family decide what his efforts were really worth. Far more than the actual fee, Weinberg always said he appreciated an affectionate, handwritten letter he received from Ford, which says, along with other flattering things, "Without you, it could not have been accomplished." Weinberg had the letter framed and hung in his office, where he would proudly direct visitors' attention to it, saying: "That's the big payoff as far as I'm con-cerned." He was speaking more literally than his guests knew. The fee finally paid was estimated at the time to be as high as a million dollars. The actual fee was nowhere near that amount: For two years' work and a dazzling success, the indispensable man was paid only $250,000. Deeply disappointed, Sidney Weinberg never mentioned the amount.

In fact, the fee was not really important in the overall picture. Weinberg soon became a director of the Ford Motor Company—and took his pal Paul Cabot onto the board with him—and for nearly half a century Ford would be Goldman Sachs's most prestigious investment banking client. Even more important, Sidney Weinberg used the Ford Motor Company underwriting to leapfrog his firm's standing on Wall Street into the top tier of underwriters, strongly positioned as a major firm that others had to treat well. The continuing stream of Ford financings expected over the following decades could be shared and traded with others to keep Goldman Sachs in that top tier.

Though a major success for Weinberg and his firm, the Ford underwriting was a dud for many investors. Offered at $64.50, the shares jumped to seventy dollars by the end of the first day's trading, a clear, clean underwriting triumph. But then, over several months, the price drifted down into the forties. The problems, both the initial sharp price rise and the subsequent fall, were due to Ford's insistence on allocating over 10 percent of the shares to Ford dealers. In the initial excitement around the IPO, many dealers rushed to buy still more shares. Later, remembering that they had huge bank debts to finance their inventories of cars, most dealers felt obliged to sell—and as the price fell, other dealers rushed to sell their shares too. Believing it was always in an issuer's long-term interests for investors to make a profit, Weinberg insisted, when Ford subsequently borrowed one hundred million dollars in bonds, that the yield be set slightly *above* the market, saying that Ford could not afford to have another poor performer in the aftermarket.

Not long after the record Ford equity underwriting, Weinberg did a record bond underwriting—a $350 million issue for Sears Roebuck. It was then the largest public debt offering ever made. The issue was floated in a bond market that was so soft that professionals at other firms had doubted it could sell at all, but the issue was a success. Right after the Sears bonds came a three-hundred-million-dollar bond issue for General Electric, comanaged with Morgan Stanley. Goldman Sachs was moving up in the ranks and was arguably now one of Wall Street's Top Ten.

Ford was for many years certainly the firm's most important client in prestige, but not in business volume. After the IPO, Ford did no long-term financing because young Henry Ford relied entirely on Sidney Weinberg for financial advice and Weinberg was sure that interest rates would decline, so he flatly opposed using any new long-term debt. Any borrowing would have to be done with commercial paper. Unfortunately, Weinberg was wrong about interest rates. His control of Ford finance so angered Ed Lundy, Ford's brilliant CFO, that when Weinberg died, most Ford executives wanted to get rid of Goldman Sachs. Gus Levy, John Whitehead, and Don Gant, the partner covering the Ford account for many years under Weinberg, were warned that they would have to compete for any future business, and that they would begin that competition several yards behind the starting line. While Gant was successful at rebuilding the relationship, Ford was so successful in the fifties and sixties that financing, and the services of Goldman Sachs, were seldom needed.

Underwriting wasn't the only area in which Sidney Weinberg set the pace for Goldman Sachs. He was also an active innovator in giving merger advice. As John Whitehead recalls with admiration: "The first time Goldman Sachs charged a fee for M&A advice was, to all of us in the firm at the time, stunning. Naturally, it was Sidney Weinberg who brought in the business. Through his remarkable network he knew both Jerry Lambert and William Warner, and that enabled him to bring them together in a merger as Warner Lambert Pharmaceuticals. The fee was quite impressive. In those days, most investment bankers got paid only for underwriting stocks and bonds, and didn't charge *anything* for advisory work on mergers and acquisitions. But for this particular merger, Sidney Weinberg did indeed charge a fee: one million dollars!"

Weinberg's million-dollar fee was a harbinger of the high mergers-and-acquisitions fees and the profusion of Wall Street–initiated mergers that lay ahead. But Weinberg was not a champion of corporate mergers. When two Midwest retailers, Hudson and Dayton, wanted to merge in 1969, Goldman Sachs worked on the merger in a most unusual way. Weinberg and partner Bob Horton represented Hudson, while John Whitehead represented Dayton. At one point Weinberg asked, "Why does Dayton want to grow so fast? What good will that do them?" Whitehead just rolled his eyes. M&A was about to become a major part of Wall Street's business and a strategic catapult for Goldman Sachs. Weinberg was clearly from a different era.

5

~

TRANSITION YEARS

T he Ford offering, spectacular personal triumph that it was for Sidney Weinberg, might have turned out to be an isolated event with little long-term impact on Goldman Sachs's competitive position. That was not acceptable to Weinberg. Always looking for openings and quick to see how openings could be exploited, he was determined to see his firm move up in the ranks of investment banking.

In addition to his business-attracting personal stature and notoriety, Weinberg's main business contribution was crucial: He was a director of over two dozen major corporations where he could make sure Goldman Sachs got the business. As the lead underwriter for those companies, Goldman Sachs could then swap participations in the syndicates it organized for lucrative participations in the syndicates of the other leading underwriters.

Weinberg's successes were always the result of his direct action on specific subjects with specific individuals, almost always corporate CEOs. "The structure of the firm was determined by *clients*," explains John Whitehead. "Since Sidney Weinberg controlled most of the clients, he controlled the firm." John Weinberg recalled: "He was very definitely *the* senior partner. And, boy, was he the boss! I can hear him now saying at a partners' meeting, 'I've listened and heard all you've said. I've considered it very carefully. I will tell you now that democracy has gone far enough.' And then he'd announce his final decision."

Like all the great Wall Street leaders of his era, Weinberg had no interest in internal operations. He and his peers were no more concerned with organizational management than the members of great social clubs are with housekeeping. Weinberg would advise his son John: "Don't waste your time on internal operations of the organization. If they have important problems, they'll bring them to you." As John recalled, "He didn't enjoy management of the firm; he liked investment banking. So he had other people manage the firm."

One exception Weinberg made was recruiting. He looked for outstanding talent on two levels. At the top, hoping to find a leader who could carry on his own work of building up Goldman Sachs in investment banking, and certainly not able to believe that anyone then at the firm could fill his shoes, he recruited Charles Saltzman and Stanley Miller as potential successors. Miller had experience in Wall Street and was well connected in New York City and with business leaders across the country. Saltzman, also well connected socially, had been a Rhodes Scholar, a general in the army, and assistant secretary of defense under George Marshall. However talented, neither man was ever accepted as Goldman Sachs's leader by the other partners. That was probably just as well, since it left an opening that would eventually be memorably filled by Gus Levy, who spearheaded the growth of Goldman Sachs's trading business in the forties, fifties, and sixties.

At the entry level, Weinberg took a special interest in recruiting MBAs from Harvard, particularly to be associates in investment banking. That's how John Whitehead came to join Goldman Sachs in 1947.

Whitehead, born in Evanston, Illinois, on April 2, 1922, grew up in Montclair, New Jersey, where his father had worked as a New Jersey Telephone lineman before transferring into personnel. After high school, John went to Haverford College, where he took a course with Edmund Stennis. Stennis had left his wealthy, cultured family in Germany because of Hitler; when he landed in Haverford, Pennsylvania, the president of the college invited him to teach. He and young Whitehead developed a special bond. As Whitehead recalls, "Stennis certainly opened my eyes to Europe and a wider world and was an important factor in my confidence that Goldman Sachs must expand internationally." Whitehead worked his way through Haverford; served three years in the navy during World War II attached to an attack transport that participated in the invasions of Normandy, southern France, Iwo Jima, and Okinawa;[1] and then earned an MBA (with distinction) at Harvard Business School. The navy had earlier assigned him to the business school as a wartime instructor, so Whitehead had the unique experience of resigning from the faculty to become a student at the school.

After graduating in 1947, Whitehead joined Goldman Sachs as one of just three hundred employees for what he expected would be only a transitional position in a family firm: "I thought of working on Wall Street as a form of postgraduate training and as a way to get a broad exposure to American business and learn from seeing many companies before eventually taking up a career in corporate management." Declining an offer from DuPont's finance department, Whitehead accepted the only investment banking job offer he got and the only offer made that year by Goldman Sachs.[2] "Candidly, I'd heard almost nothing about the firm." The salary was $3,600 a year.

In the late 1950s, Goldman Sachs was Sidney Weinberg's firm and John Whitehead was Sidney Weinberg's man. "Working for and under Sidney Weinberg," explains Whitehead, "I had the day-to-day responsibility for the Ford equity offering. I was selected as a good assistant: young, quiet, and not yet a partner. Then not long after the Ford equity issue, I found myself working on General Electric's three-hundred-million-dollar bond offering. At the time, it was the largest industrial *bond* offering in history. Those were exciting days."

Whitehead's first impression of Goldman Sachs's office at 30 Pine Street was disappointment. "Goldman, Sachs & Co." was in large gold letters by the entrance of the narrow twelve-story building that was squeezed between a much higher office tower and a tavern. But the building was not owned by Goldman Sachs. It was owned by the N and L Realty Company. The *N* was for "Nellie Sachs" and the *L* for "Louisa Goldman Sachs," the deceased mothers of the two Sachs senior partners, Howard and Walter. While the dark mahogany partners' offices on the seventeenth floor were suitably impressive, Whitehead was assigned to a metal desk squeezed with six others into a converted squash court incongruously located on the twentieth floor. While most of the other occupants were college graduates, none had been to business school. The squash court, ventilated by a small "porthole" window that could only be opened with a long pole, got cold in winter and hot in summer. "Regardless of the temperature," recalls Whitehead, "we were expected to keep our suit jackets on year-round." Suits were woolen: That was the Goldman Sachs way.

"I complied for most of that first year, but when I started to roast in midsummer, I thought I might branch out sartorially, and I bought myself a lightweight seersucker suit that I thought very handsome. The next morning, I felt quite snappy as I passed through the Goldman Sachs entrance and down the hall to the elevator and stepped aboard the car to ascend to my sweltering squash court office. But before the doors could close, Walter Sachs entered just behind me. The son of the cofounder, he was one of the great eminences at the firm. Short, stocky, with a distinguished white beard, he inspired a certain awe, if not dread, and I started to feel miserable as he surveyed me in my seersucker suit that morning. Walter Sachs was the sort of person that other people remembered, but he did not always remember them. Although we'd been introduced a few times in the previous months, the great man clearly had no idea who I was. 'Young man,' he addressed me anonymously in a withering tone. 'Do you work at Goldman Sachs?'

" 'Yes sir, I do,' I replied proudly. He scowled, and his visage turned black.

" 'In that case, I would recommend that you go home right now and change out of your pajamas.' "

Despite this sartorial gaffe, Whitehead made early progress in his career. Unusually foresighted and more than willing to work unrelentingly to achieve his objectives, Whitehead was soon rising within the firm and even more rapidly in the esteem of Sidney Weinberg.

After several years at Goldman Sachs, however, Whitehead began to worry about his progress and his prospects for a major career if he stayed there. In 1954 Goldman Sachs sold only one underwriting deal in the entire year. Business was so very slow that partner Myles Cruickshank installed a wastepaper basket in one corner of the squash court so the young investment bankers could compete at *something*—tossing coins into that basket—to keep their interest up. Then things began to improve.

Still, it seemed to Whitehead that the firm was too dependent on just one man, a man clearly at or past the peak of his career and getting older. Even though

Sidney Weinberg may have been the best business getter on Wall Street, Whitehead worried: "Sidney brought in business, and our group of bright young men handled it, but I didn't think that an investment banking firm could grow and succeed with its source of revenues so concentrated in one single person."

While Whitehead worried about his future at Goldman Sachs, he received, from time to time over the years, offers to join other firms. Early in 1956, J.H. Whitney & Co. offered him a partnership in an exciting new enterprise in venture capital for which Jock Whitney put up 100 percent of the capital and agreed to split all the profits fifty-fifty with the staff. "Goldman Sachs had no employee-review process at that time, so if you were young and hopeful, you couldn't help wondering about your standing. I'd been at Goldman Sachs for eight years and no one had even *mentioned* my being a partner, so I was seriously interested in J.H. Whitney's approach."

When Whitehead went to tell Weinberg that, much as he loved working for him at Goldman Sachs, he had received a very special offer to become a partner at J.H. Whitney, Weinberg replied in quite absolute terms that this was not to be: "Oh, no, John, you cannot and will not do that. You are needed here—at Goldman Sachs." Weinberg promptly reached for the telephone, called Mr. Whitney, and spoke directly: "Jock, your firm has made an offer to John Whitehead. Now, Jock, we need John. He's doing important work for Goldman Sachs—and for me. You really must not take him: We need him here. He's one of our best young men and valuable to me. I cannot spare him, so I ask you now to withdraw your offer, Jock." Whitney deferred to Weinberg, and that was the end of that. At year-end, Whitehead made partner at Goldman Sachs.

To build up capital in the firm, Weinberg had established a capital-retention policy that kept everyone focused on what was best for the firm—Goldman Sachs retained most of each partner's yearly earned income. As a result, anyone who became a partner in Goldman Sachs usually experienced a drop in spendable income.

L. Jay Tenenbaum had become a partner in 1959, with his initial participation set at 1.5 percent. He was soon the firm's number two salesman, behind only one colleague, Jerry McNamara, and on his way to becoming one of the leading partners of Goldman Sachs. But thanks to the strict capital-retention policy, Tenenbaum's spendable income was just forty thousand dollars—no princely sum for a successful man with family expenses and a need to "keep up" in New York City. Indeed, Tenenbaum was borrowing spending money from his father so he and his family could get along. Tenenbaum's situation was comparable to the other hardworking and ambitious younger partners: For most of them, finances were tight at home and aspirations were high at work, where the key factor in total compensation was their share of participation in the firm's success. So when participations were reviewed every two years, the personal stakes were high.

By 1962, apart from his sales prowess Tenenbaum was increasingly important in the firm's very profitable arbitrage business. Weinberg spoke gravely to his young partner: "L. Jay, you have had two good years. You and the four other members of your class of partners have made a fine contribution to the firm. I've decided to recognize that fine contribution by raising all of you in percentage participation. I'm increasing your percentages from one point five percent to two percent!" Clearly expecting an expression of jubilation and gratitude, Weinberg leaned back in his chair and said to Tenenbaum, "Now, young man, how do you feel about *that*?"

After a split second's silence, the reply came quickly and directly: "Mr. Weinberg, we are *not* equals. Either I'm better than the others and do more for Goldman Sachs, or I'm not as good. But we're not in one 'class'; we are not equals."

Tenenbaum had just "put 'em up"—one on one—with the man who had the power to determine his destiny at Goldman Sachs. After a long pause during which neither man broke eye contact, Weinberg closed the discussion—but signaled recognition of the central point: "You keep your nose clean for the next two years and do a good job for Goldman Sachs, and then we'll see about that."

When Weinberg decided in 1968 that a young investment banker, Mike Coles, should become a partner, he called him. When Coles picked up the phone, Weinberg said, "Sidney Weinberg," but he pronounced it "Wine-boig" and he had a mannerism of raising his tone on the last syllable, which made his self-announcement sound more like a question.

Coles didn't have any reason to expect a call from Sidney Weinberg: Mr. Weinberg had never called or spoken to him before. So, quite understandably, he thought it must be a call *for* Sidney Weinberg and hastened to explain in his courtly way that no, he was not Mr. Weinberg—to which his caller responded in exasperation, "I *know* you're not Sidney Wine-boig" and hung up in frustration.

Fortunately for Coles, Weinberg called again: "Is this Michael Coles?"

"Yes."

"I want you to be my partner."

By this time, Coles, thinking the whole thing must be some sort of practical joke, was not going to bite. He had been with the firm for only seven years and knew it traditionally took ten years to make partner, so it took more than a few minutes to get everything sorted out. As Coles later ruefully observed, "What a way to begin the most important phone call in your career!"

Coles and John Jamison, who later earned a big fee for Goldman Sachs when Procter & Gamble acquired Clorox, were both "Weinberg's boys," so when room was made in the partnership for both of them, Gus Levy was able to get one of his "boys" in too: Robert Rubin.

Weinberg was particularly highly regarded for his ability to get things done in a uniquely quiet but effective way, sometimes concealing aggressiveness that stretched the limits of hardball. An investment banker who was there gave this example:

After making a lot of money going public with his own company, a corporate raider noticed that Baldwin United was selling at a very cheap price. So he took a big position and was going to offer to buy the rest of the stock at a price well above the market. Since the founding family's stock was held in a trust at a bank, the raider knew the bank trustee would be under terrific pressure to accept such an offer and sell the stock.

Takeover defense is something Goldman Sachs specialized in, so the firm was asked to help. Nobody was sure what to do, so Weinberg was asked for suggestions. At first, he was not sure either. A little later, he told a young banker to call a particular guy. A meeting was arranged at Gage & Tolner's restaurant in Brooklyn.

Weinberg's man, wearing a black suit, black shirt, and a black string tie, came to the table and sat down, saying, "The only reason I'm here is I owe Weinberg." After a brief explanation, the man in black said he would see what he could do. Nobody heard from him for a week, then two weeks. Finally he called to say, "We've got him. It'll cost a hundred dollars—fifty dollars for a photographer and fifty dollars for the bell-boy. He's got a cutie holed up in a midtown hotel."

A week later, the man in black called on the corporate raider and respectfully said to him, "You believe in this free country and so do I. *Anybody* can buy *anything* in this wonderful free country." Then he started spreading the pictures from the hotel on the man's desk, and said, "You can buy *almost* anything. But don't do Baldwin or these could show up in the *New York Post*." Then he excused himself and left. Nothing happened to Baldwin United, and nothing was printed in the newspapers.

"Sidney Weinberg had great willingness to confront a tough issue straight on. You didn't have to watch his hands when he was dealing the cards," recalls George Doty. "He always took it to the edge in his negotiations. One example was when I'd prepared an estate plan for him. He said Coopers & Lybrand's fee was too high. I said it was the normal fee and that the work had been very well done. Looking right at me, eyeball to eyeball, he said, 'I'll pay whatever fee you say is right. But if you insist I pay that fee, I'll never again do business with you or your firm.' I quietly insisted; he quietly paid—and we never discussed the matter again, quietly doing our business together as we always had."

Weinberg always understood power. After he made Gus Levy managing partner in 1969, he moved his own office uptown to the Seagram Building to give Levy room to manage the firm. But he kept to himself the ultimate power to decide on partnership percentages, the single greatest power in any partnership.

The relationship between Levy and Weinberg was clearly defined by Weinberg at the annual partners' dinner at "21" Club in Midtown Manhattan. After dinner, Levy rose to speak on behalf of all the partners with appropriately respectful humility: "Mr. Weinberg, even though your office is now uptown and we're downtown so we don't see you at the office anymore, we all want you to know that you are *always* in our thoughts and *always* in our hearts and we are so glad you are active and well and we just want you to know that never a day goes by without our thinking of you and how much we respect you. Wherever you are and wherever you go, Goldman Sachs is always with you—and you are always with Goldman Sachs."

Warm applause confirmed that Levy was speaking for all the partners. Weinberg stood to respond. "Those are very nice thoughts, Gus, and I'm glad you feel as you say you do." But then his manner changed from accommodating to commanding: "But don't you ever forget this, Gus. No matter where I am, *I* am the senior partner of Goldman Sachs and *I* run this firm!" With that, Weinberg sat down. The entire room was silent and the silence confirmed the obvious reality: Gus Levy still reported to Sidney Weinberg.

By the late 1960s, Sidney Weinberg had done his work. Weinberg told his wife, "If I die tomorrow, I don't want anyone to mourn for me because every day I lived was a little better than the day before." He had saved Goldman Sachs in the thirties, established its stature in the forties and fifties through his government service and corporate directorships, and carved in stone a series of core policies: capital retention, competitiveness, integrity, disdain for publicity or pretension, and toughness. But the business of Goldman Sachs had changed greatly and forever, and he had become an older man who had lost touch.

The hundredth anniversary year of Goldman Sachs was 1969. In anticipation, the annual partners' Christmas party in 1968 was moved from "21," where they traditionally went each year, to a larger place so wives could be invited for the first time. That was also the occasion for Weinberg to introduce an important new partner. Henry Fowler, the former secretary of the treasury who long ago had been an important staff member of the War Production Board, would serve as chairman of Goldman Sachs International.

After Weinberg finished his usual welcoming remarks, Trudye Fowler went up to the head of the table and asked if she could say a few words. Weinberg passed the mike to her and she began, "A year ago, we were the guests of the president and Mrs. Johnson at the White House for a dinner for America's leading men and women—and that was quite a thrill. Tonight is an even greater thrill and an even more important occasion because tonight the *wives* of the partners of Goldman Sachs are all included for the very first time. This is so wonderful and says so much about our firm." Turning with an admiring smile to Weinberg, she concluded, "So I say to you, Sidney Weinberg: congratulations!"

Weinberg took the microphone back to say, "Thank you, Trudye, for those truly touching words. I'm so touched. Tomorrow, I'll recommend to the management committee that inviting the wives be made a new tradition...and that the wives all be invited to come back for the Christmas dinner...on our two hundredth anniversary."

For decades Weinberg had held that directors should retire at seventy to make room for younger men, a view he would later brush aside with this assertion: "I'm not like those guys—some in wheelchairs—who fall asleep at meetings. I'm not like that!"[3] Weinberg continued as a Ford director until his death at seventy-seven in 1969.

6

GUS LEVY

Born and raised in New Orleans, Gustave Lehmann Levy never lost the soft Louisiana slur in his speech. He was the only son of Sigmund Levy, a crate manufacturer who died in 1923 when Gus was twelve, and Bella Lehmann Levy. As a teenager, Gus moved for a while to Paris with his mother and two sisters; he enrolled at the American School but said he spent most of his time "just bumming around." Back in Louisiana, he dropped out of Tulane University after a few months and went to New York City, where he got a room at the 92nd Street YMHA and a job as an assistant trader in arbitrage at Newborg & Company.[1] After work he sometimes went uptown to dance at the Casino in Central Park.

In 1933, on the recommendation of a friend, Gus Levy moved to Goldman Sachs at $1,500 a year—first trading in foreign bonds and then in arbitrage, where he was an understudy of Edgar Baruc, who wore celluloid collars and had a small, waxed mustache.[2] Baruc was a friend of the Sachs family but never became a partner because the Sachses didn't want the stigma of having as a partner of Goldman Sachs anyone who had once been with any firm that had failed. Because of his past link to a bankruptcy, Baruc technically reported to Levy. They worked together as a team under Walter Sachs's supervision and, with a "wealth of ideas, added substantial profits to what would have been otherwise very lean years."[3]

Gus Levy was destined to become by the late sixties and early seventies the most powerful man on Wall Street: the chairman of the New York Stock Exchange, the head of Mount Sinai Hospital, a power in the Republican Party, the "best" director of numerous corporations, the center of action in New York City philanthropic fund-raising, the go-to man at the market center of conglomerate finance, and the unquestioned leader of Goldman Sachs. But power and stature were far ahead of Levy when he first joined Goldman Sachs, a firm still suffering the ignominy of Goldman Sachs Trading Corporation.

Levy liked to say he was "one of the few guys who didn't lose any money in the stock market crash—because I didn't have any money to lose." He moved out of the 92nd Street Y owing two dollars. (He later became a major contributor to its parent organization, the Federation of Jewish Philanthropies, saying, "They gave me friendship and confidence in myself when I needed it badly.") By the end of the thirties, Levy had already made his first million dollars. Despite a distinctive lisp that complicated the bayou drawl, he drew on his aptitude for math, extraordinary memory, ability to connect with many, many people, and capacity for long hours of highly concentrated hard work to become stronger and stronger within Goldman Sachs during the firm's rebuilding years.

With world war coming, Levy, six feet tall and slim, was determined to get into action right away, telling his wife, Janet, simply, "I'm goin' in."[4] Through a Wall Street friend, I. W. "Tubby" Burnham, a pilot in the Civil Air Patrol, Levy had become a mission observer with responsibility for navigation and communications in 1941. Entering the army as a private in 1942, he went to Officer Candidate School, saw action in France with the Eighth Air Corps, rose to the rank of major, and mustered out as a lieutenant colonel. After he rejoined the firm as a partner in 1945, Levy and Baruc expanded Goldman Sachs's arbitrage operations and "built one of the most active over-the-counter trading departments on Wall Street."[5]

Levy built his early career in arbitrage, analyzing and trading the complex securities created by the breakup of public utility holding companies and later the reorganization of various railroads. America's railroads, while temporarily enriched by the enormous volume of freight and passenger traffic required during wartime, were expected to fall back into serious long-term difficulty in the widely anticipated postwar depression.

Under the 1937 Public Utility Holding Company Act, designed to permit the restructuring and then the reemergence of debt-ridden holding companies like Samuel Insull's collapsed utilities empire, holding companies were allowed to keep only those operating companies whose service territories were contiguous. The more distant properties had to be divested. Trading in the securities of the newly independent operating companies would be allowed on a "when and if issued" basis in anticipation of final SEC approval of each holding company's plan of reorganization. So as the holding companies were broken up, investors needed to evaluate each operating company separately to determine its most likely market valuation.

Both investors and utility companies needed shrewd risk arbitrageurs willing to commit significant capital to making markets in those "when issued" securities. Arbitrage involved accumulating long positions or selling short in relatively large amounts and often in illiquid securities. This market need represented Levy's opportunity. He had access to capital and, as a trader, he was in the business of buying whatever existing security was being exchanged for new securities and then trading the new securities on a when-issued basis—profiting from the spread and changes in the spread between the whole and the component parts. This arbitrage trading provided rigorous training in gathering disparate bits of information with which to estimate and anticipate the actions others *might* take in that soft gray area in which an expression of "no interest" could, if properly nurtured and stimulated at just the right time in just the right way, be converted into a buy or sell transaction—sometimes even a significant transaction.

Valuation uncertainties surrounding the newly issued, unseasoned utility and railroad securities—which were rife with legal and credit complexities— provided an ideal environment for an astute, disciplined arbitrage operation like Levy's. "Gus was very smart, and an innovator," said his contemporary, Al Feld. "He built a good business because he recognized the opportunity in all the when-issued paper that came out of the big railroad and public utility financings of the 1940s. And he built a reputation for making good markets—in size. And if he had to take a loss, he took it."

Levy took charge when Baruc died suddenly in 1953, and continued to develop a "remarkably efficient and hard-hitting organization."[6] Whenever operating losses were incurred for two or three months in a row, the Sachses would call for a financial review, often engaging George E. Doty of Lybrand, Ross Brothers & Montgomery (later Coopers & Lybrand) to do the study. Recalls Doty, "Gus Levy had a small group of loyal and very closed-mouthed clerks working directly for him. They kept all the very complicated and long-lasting records that were needed in railroad arbitrage. Their rules of conduct were simple and clear: 'Don't *know* anything and don't *say* anything.' "

To build business volume and create demand, Levy was always going out on the telephone, offering the new securities to different institutions. In the course of talking up these offerings, Levy would say, "If you want to *sell* something to raise the money for this, I will take it off your hands," or, "If you don't want to buy MoPac [Missouri Pacific Railroad], is there something *else* you'd like to buy?" And that was the beginning of Goldman Sachs talking to institutional investors about *transaction* ideas rather than *investment* ideas. It was of course, a small beginning. The equity-trading desk consisted of only three people. Levy later said, "We didn't have any electronic quote machines, so it was essential to watch the tape and to know where the last sales were and what the markets were doing."

The increasing size of transactions, the need for capital commitments to make trades happen, the speed of decision required to seize fleeting market opportunities, and discretion bordering on secrecy were all required in arbitrage—and they were splendid preparation for the changes in the nature of the stockbrokerage business caused by the surging increase in institutional activity. These changes created a rapidly expanding opportunity for those who, like Gus Levy, were prepared and determined to exploit any opening.

In the mid-1950s the climate on Wall Street began to change. Men who had known firsthand the difficulties faced during the Depression were completing their careers and leaving the Street, taking their fears and worries of another Depression away with them. Younger people with new ideas and high ambitions were beginning to come into the business. Still, the early indications of change were small and easily overlooked. In 1956 the total revenues of Goldman Sachs's "institutional business" were only three hundred thousand dollars—a business small enough to go unnoticed by senior partners at well-established firms who were members of wealthy families with well-established patterns of life. Such personages, preferring to consider themselves *investment bankers*, saw the stockbrokerage sales and trading operations as somewhat demeaning activities pursued only as necessary for securities distribution sufficient to maintain their position in underwriting syndicates. Yet for those who were hungry to get ahead, even small changes could be seen as harbingers of interesting possibilities for advancement.

Since most of the people working at Goldman Sachs had no family wealth, they knew they'd have to work hard to make it, and as outsiders they had little to lose by taking risks or being "different." Bob Menschel, a young NYSE floor specialist, played a key role in getting Goldman Sachs into institutional block trading by convincing Levy to dedicate some of his extraordinary energies toward this nascent business right from its beginning.[7] "In those days," recalls Menschel, "the floor was very quiet, so we were always looking for new ways to do more business, particularly in companies where we were the specialist." Increased market activity linked to a possible merger involving a company where Sidney Weinberg was a director gave Menschel a pretext to call on Mr. Weinberg. A year later, Menschel wrote to Weinberg recalling their earlier appointment and explaining that he'd noticed a change of some interest: Trades of one thousand and five thousand—sometimes even ten thousand—shares were being done by institutional investors. "I noted that this was something new and might develop into an important opportunity to do business with insurance companies and other institutions. Trades of five thousand or ten thousand shares were too large for the specialists, who were used to working on trades of one hundred or two hundred shares and did not have the capital to handle these larger trades."

Weinberg sent the letter along to Levy with a note saying, "Not sure I recall, but please see him." Levy, who was interested in any new market development, had coincidentally been courting the specialists, saying, "I'll participate with you in trades of five thousand and ten thousand shares." When they met, Levy was taken with Menschel, agreed something important might be developing, and arranged for all eight Goldman Sachs partners to interview him. Six months later, Menschel joined the firm. "My uncle was furious. He couldn't believe I'd give up the floor. Most of the partners at Goldman Sachs found it hard to believe themselves: Like most people on Wall Street, they generally aspired to own a [stock exchange] seat someday at the peak of their careers. But I was bored on the floor. You need to be a real poker player to thrive on the floor, and I'm not a poker player."

Levy's and Goldman Sachs's experience in arbitrage gave the firm a different way of thinking about the time and risk aspects of market making. At other firms, the profit and loss on trading "principal" positions was calculated daily. Daily measuring made sense for the over-the-counter market-making business, which was all about separate, stand-alone transactions where there were no "relationships" that might link one trade with another. But what worked well in the retail trading business inevitably led to wrong decisions for the institutional trading business, which was all about relationships and the recurring transactions of regularly repeating customers. Additionally, the OTC dealer's focus was on protecting the firm's *owners'* capital from trading mistakes or losses by *employees*. At Goldman Sachs, the capital at risk was the partners' capital and partners were making the trades—the employees *were* the owners. They knew the accounts' traders well because they did business with them almost every day. To make profits for Goldman Sachs, their focus was not on protecting against taking a loss on each transaction, but on developing profitable relationships that would over time make money for the firm. They took a long-term, principal's view of trading as an ongoing business. By combining risk capital with superb service, trading could be made a continuing business. Rough and tumble, often painful, always competitive, and requiring special skills plus a willingness to take significant risks, block trading was transformed by Levy's Goldman Sachs and a few competitors into a relationship business that was like riding a bucking bronco but could be successfully managed at substantial profit with longer-term orientation.

The block-trading business grew in several ways. The number of block trades increased. The size of block trades increased, and the number of institutions active in buying and selling blocks of stock increased. As the volume multiplied, so did the profits and the competition. Levy was determined to dominate this remarkable, fast-growing new business because he understood that the best profits went to the market-leading firm, and he was determined that that leading firm just had to be Goldman Sachs. "Gus was always one hundred percent committed, and that commitment could unnerve people *or* it could bring out the best in each person," says Menschel. "He was so intent on doing *every* trade that he could get catatonic if he felt we'd missed one. Gus would be storming around, bemoaning our failures: 'We're losing out! We're not in the market anymore! We've lost it! We're not *competitive* anymore!' To build the business, we had to find ways to keep Gus calm—or at least at bay."

Menschel believed that "originating a trade is a lot like fly-fishing: Both take patience and quiet persistence to land the really big ones." He created a quantitative index of the total block-trading business and of the firm's percentage—in number of trades, in number of shares traded, and in different sizes of blocks—to prove to Levy each day that the firm was actually doing very well. (About this time, Levy began using a string of worry beads given to him by a friend in Greece.) Eventually, Bob Menschel and L. Jay Tenenbaum would both decide they had to quit the business because Levy's unrelenting driving was too much for them—it threatened to kill them both. But in the meantime, Levy's drive and leadership paid off handsomely: By the late sixties Levy's trading produced half of the firm's profits. And Levy, who at his peak owned ten percent of the firm, was becoming the recognized leader of Goldman Sachs.

Levy said he would never forget the day he first knew he was important: Sidney Weinberg had quietly asked if he would like to sit next to him at the partners' annual dinner. When it became time in 1969 for Weinberg to turn over operations to a successor, Levy *had* to be made managing partner of Goldman Sachs. As the major rainmaker who commanded great personal loyalty within the firm, he was the obvious choice* as the firm's leader for a simple, compelling reason: He was already leading. As John Weinberg put it, "If Gus asked me to do *anything*, I'd do it—anytime!"

However, while Sidney Weinberg accepted the investment banking business Levy brought in and respected Levy's profitability and his internal leadership, he took no pride in Levy's block-trading business nor in the "ragtag" conglomerate companies Levy and his trading prowess attracted to the firm as investment banking clients. Levy always wanted to find a way to do the deal, which was a concern for Sidney Weinberg, who worried about the companies and people Levy did business with—conglomerate wheeler-dealers like Jimmy Ling, Norton Simon, the Murchisons. But that's where the business was to be done, and Levy went for the business. As John Whitehead observed of Levy,

---

* Not to everyone. Stanley Miller was a long-term partner in investment banking who had been brought in by Sidney Weinberg to develop an international business and as a possible successor. In 1974, when stockbrokerage was losing money, Miller made his move to be the leader. It came to a head one day with Gus Levy in Miller's office. Voices got louder and louder until Levy, a former Golden Gloves boxer, grabbed Miller by the top of his tie, commented on his Episcopalianism, observed how self-centered his activities had been, and delivered in disgust the conclusion that Miller was being disloyal to Goldman Sachs. Levy had the solid support of most of his partners, so the conflict was soon over—as was Miller's career at the firm.

"He had only one central idea: More! Gus would take almost anybody as a client. Just as he avoided the paneled offices on the seventeenth floor in order to be in the trading room on the thirteenth floor, he reached for the *doers* rather than for *class*." While respecting Levy's prodigious business-building capabilities and extraordinary capacity for work, Weinberg could never fully trust someone with the instincts of a trader to be solely in command of the firm. Weinberg was hard on Levy, and Levy went to Weinberg's son John to complain, "I've gotta leave this firm!"

Just before Levy was made managing partner, Weinberg, anticipating his own retirement, organized a management committee and filled it with partners he knew were loyal to him to control and restrain Levy—to prevent him from converting Goldman Sachs from a banking firm into a trading firm, as Bear Stearns had become under a strong trader, Levy's close friend Sy Lewis.[8] As managing partner, Levy would have forty-nine percent of the votes, so, as George Doty explains, "To block Gus, you'd need one hundred percent opposition, but to get anything done, Gus would always need to win at least one supporting vote." During Levy's initial years as managing partner, Weinberg knew that members of the management committee would, as his personal surrogates, always seek his opinion on key decisions and then vote as he told them to vote. Even with this governor established, Weinberg still had reservations, so he continued on as senior partner and sole decision maker on partnership percentages.

Levy—always calling him Mr. Weinberg—accepted the form but not the function of the management committee. Meetings were held every week, but they were kept short, usually only fifteen minutes, and there was minimal discussion, no agenda, no minutes—and no chairs. The group met in Levy's office, standing, and Levy often took phone calls during meetings to show how little importance he really gave to the committee. As John Weinberg acknowledges, "Gus always resented Sidney's having created the need for him to get committee approval." And as John Whitehead observed, "Gus was always afraid he would fail to fill Sidney Weinberg's shoes."

"Sidney and Gus were different in many, many ways," recalls Doty. "For example, Sidney would listen quite solemnly and intently to all you might want to say, and then simply ignore you. Gus would not listen—interrupting all the time and arguing—but he'd take your advice and information to heart and would *use* it."

On decisions that came to him, Levy required very short memoranda stating the situation and the specific recommended action; known across the firm as Gus-O-Grams, they had to be so carefully thought out that they were usually only four or five lines long. Otherwise he believed you weren't ready to act. Extensive examination of the facts of the matter and wide consultation within the firm were certainly expected, but having been done, the complete homework did not need to be paraded in the action recommendation. And Levy always came back within twenty-four hours. "Getting time with Gus was always hard," recalls partner Peter Sacerdote, "but he always read your memo and he always got back to you in time." Levy returned internal phone calls the same day—and usually the same hour. And his calls were always *very* short.

Levy routinely cut off discussion as soon as he was ready to decide a matter, and he was nothing if not decisive. As John Whitehead puts it, "Gus was indefatigable and never wasted a minute. There was no idle chatter with Gus, ever." When he asked questions, Levy wanted answers that were short, direct, and specific. He abhorred ambivalence and uncertainty. When one of his colleagues offered tentatively, "We may be able to do something that may help," Levy cut him off: "*May* is just a month between April and June. It has no place here at Goldman Sachs."

"Sometimes, you could get your way with Gus just by taking longer to talk about something and taking up more time than he was willing to give to the decision you were discussing," recalls Doty. "[Partner] Walter Blaine, a very upright sort of guy, would take *forever* discussing something. Sometimes, Gus accepted Blaine's decision not because he agreed with his views, but because he felt he couldn't afford the time Blaine would take discussing details and ramifications all too fully before a better decision could be hammered out. Gus's conclusions were often far better than the reasons he would give you. He was very intuitive and fast in his thinking." As partner Ray Young recalled, "Gus had a very quick mind, particularly with numbers. His one wart was this: He rarely if ever would compliment people for what they had done." Nor did he waste time on pleasantries with spouses when, as he often did, he called at home—early or late.

Decisions that did not require Levy's authority were expected to be made by others. "Gus was a great delegator *if* he trusted you," observes a banking partner. "He could also get *totally* involved." Levy was both decisive and remarkable in his good judgment. "He was not the most brilliant guy in the world," a contemporary once observed of him, "but then the average genius on Wall Street, when you meet him, usually turns out to be just a clever guy. People aren't stunned by his brilliance, but they feel sure that Gus will get things done."[9] Levy had an intuitive sense of what might be doable, an instinct for action, an understanding of the risks that would have to be taken, and the fortitude to take the risks required to get things accomplished. In a persistent search and striving for advantage, he was always negotiating.

"Gus was very resourceful in the way he engaged in person-to-person negotiations inside the firm as well as with those outside the firm," says Doty. "He'd be very careful to give me the impression that such-and-such had already been agreed upon by so-and-so and therefore his hands were tied, so he and the firm would just have to live with it. Several times, he really had me 'solved' that way. But if you refused to accept it, you'd find out that, amazingly enough, he would still be able to renegotiate the supposedly final settlement."

Levy "negotiated" others, but he certainly expected no one to negotiate him. That's why "Two in the red!" may have been the riskiest outcry in the history of Goldman Sachs. A not particularly competent salesman (who later sued the firm for age discrimination when he was finally let go) had two box seats for a 1972 NBA playoff game between the Knicks and the Celtics—one of the most in-demand games in the history of basketball. Henry Ford wanted to go. He called Gus Levy and said so. The salesman had the only pair of tickets around, so Levy asked him to do this favor for a great friend of the firm. The salesman refused, saying, "Gus, my word is my bond. I promised a *client*. Even for Henry Ford and you, Gus, I can't renege on a client commitment." However reluctantly, Levy accepted. A promise is a promise and a client is a client. But as the crowd poured into Madison Square Garden that night, the salesman could be seen waving two tickets high over his head—both in the coveted "red" section—from the top of the steps. "Hey! Two in the red! Buy these tickets! Buy 'em now! I've got what you want: two in the red!" It was lucky for the salesman that word never got back to Levy.

Levy missed very little and was able to do so many things because he had extraordinary self-discipline, planning each day's many activities and closely monitoring actions taken. He kept a long yellow legal pad with a list of items he wanted to get done, usually one line for each item. He'd get up at five thirty, run on his treadmill, say his prayers, and be at work by seven each morning. Then he'd take up his long yellow pad and start calling. Levy was an extraordinarily *operational* presence. As the CEO of Monsanto recalled with wonder, "Gus would call in the morning and give me price quotes on various stocks—for no particular reason—and then say, 'Well, I thought you'd be interested,' and hang up." He made those calls by the dozen day after day. Always pleasant, his calls seldom went over thirty seconds. And when return calls came in, Levy picked up his own phone. So did everyone else. Levy wanted no secretaries in between customers and sales traders. That "separated" customers from sales traders and wasted valuable time. Intensity and speed were crucial to Levy.

"If he called me on a Monday about something," recalls Doty, "and I explained that it would take, say, three full weeks to get that thing done, he wouldn't wait the three weeks. He'd call again the next Monday, wanting to know if I'd gotten it done yet. So I'd explain again all the reasons it would take the three weeks we'd already agreed upon. But the heat was clearly on, and he just might needle me into getting it done faster—and *surely* not any later." One evening, Levy gave a competitor a ride uptown in his limo. He had more than a page of foolscap listing, one per line, the calls he had received that day but had not yet been able to return. Given the late hour, his passenger noted that it was too late to make the return calls. Levy's tense reply: "They'll *all* be called by midnight."

A salesman who worked out of the London office had a typical experience. "Having flown into New York from Europe the night before, I woke up early and couldn't get back to sleep because of the different time zones, so I decided to go on down to the office instead of just sitting around my hotel room killing time. It was ten before seven in the morning when I got on the elevator to go up to the office. Another man got on just behind me: Gus Levy. Two weeks later, I was back in New York again; couldn't sleep again; and decided again to go on down to the firm early. It was a quarter to seven. And there was Gus again. Let me tell you, that sort of thing sets real standards in a firm and builds wonderful loyalty." Levy kept two very productive secretaries—Inez Sollami and Betty Sanford—very busy, and they too came in by seven. As partner Jim Gorter recalls, "Gus Levy was a shirtsleeves, no-frills guy. In the office before seven every morning. Worked like a dog! Gus set an example by his own dedication—and he expected *everyone* to do the same." Retired partners agree that the dual emphasis on individual performance and on teamwork at Goldman Sachs came from Gus Levy.

"The firmwide work ethic really set them apart," says a block-trading competitor.[10] "At most firms in the 1970s everybody was in by nine a.m. At many firms, people were in by eight thirty; and at some, by eight. At Goldman Sachs, *everyone* was in by seven in the morning—because they truly *wanted* to be in. It made them feel different; they believed they *were* different. Gus set the standard by being among the very first ones in every day."

As Levy himself put it, "We have real spirit. We love to do the business. We get a kick out of it, and it's fun. While none of us wants to deprive a guy of a family life and a home, we do demand a full day. We want to make Goldman Sachs a close second to his wife and family. A *very* close second." Recalls Fred Weintz, "Gus had awesome standing in the firm. He once joked about how committed he was, saying, 'Just stick a broom up my ass, and I'll sweep up, too!'"

Levy was notorious for being "everywhere at once"—often having two different dinner engagements scheduled on the same night, with at least one at "21." Citibank's Walter Wriston once explained: "About six o'clock each evening, there really are *two* Gus Levys, both in tuxedos and both going to dinners in Manhattan—and both in a hurry." Levy, like many Wall Streeters before and after him, was busy in other ways; as his lifelong friend Tubby Burnham of Burnham & Company summarized, "Gus liked girls." Levy was also active in both politics and charities and was a director of twenty-one corporations, including Braniff, Studebaker, May Department Stores, Worthington, Witco Chemicals, and Lanvin-Charles of the Ritz. As John Whitehead admiringly explained, "Every CEO [of a company Gus served as a director] used to say that Gus Levy was his best outside director. Well, it's easy to be the best outside director of one company, but to be regarded so highly by *all* the companies whose boards you're on is really quite remarkable. And yet that's what people said he was." Then he had a whole further life in the world of nonprofit organizations, particularly Mount Sinai Hospital, where he was the active president and chief executive officer for years—in addition to all his fund-raising and political activities. He was treasurer of Lincoln Center, trustee of the Museum of Modern Art and the

Kennedy Center, and commissioner of the Port Authority of New York and New Jersey, and three times was treasurer of the United Jewish Appeal.[11]

On the board of directors of Lanvin-Charles of the Ritz, Levy was not like the other directors and not at all like the urbane, sophisticated CEO, Richard Salomon. He cared not at all for decorum. For example, while the other directors sat around a table in the boardroom, Levy sat separately in a corner, following closely the directors' discussions while talking to one person after another on the phone. His language was notoriously coarse as he talked from the boardroom to people at the firm: "That bastard is always trying to screw us. Fuck the fucker! He can't fuckin' fuck us. Tell him to go fuck himself."

"Gus was a leader, but not a manager," says L. Jay Tenenbaum. "Gus never had plans. Everything was daily—or even shorter—and very transactional. He only dealt with the crises. And if Gus found a part of the business we weren't covering, that was a crisis. Gus hated not covering *everything*. I can hear him now, nearly screaming, he was so upset: 'L. Jay! We are falling short in *options*! We're behind in *options*!' And he would want me to jump right to it and build up an options business, saying, 'What am I *paying* you for?' If Gus wasn't complaining or disgusted or shouting at you, you could figure he thought you were okay. He was a very bad teacher. Never explained anything or how to do anything. Gus always *knew* he could have made the call, done the trade, or whatever better—a lot better—if he'd only done it himself."

"In trading, 'being there' really matters," explains an admiring competitor, "and Goldman Sachs was always 'there' for their accounts. They knew how to take their little losses—and did—so they were very much in the flow when the big payoff opportunities came along, so they could—and would—win big by doing the major trades. And they were not above finding their full share of those numerous opportunities to pick up a little extra profit by anticipating a trade, going short a few thousand shares before a big block came onto the market—all of which was part of being in the block-trading business in those days."

Levy's constant pressure on others—always matched by the pressures he put on himself—produced an efficient, internally cooperative organization of people who were intensely competitive externally, people who again and again earned extra business and extra profits. At TIAA-CREF, a major institutional investor, Rodger Murray was managing the stock portfolio. After careful study, he decided in late December one year to restructure the portfolio and decided the best way to do that was to complete the restructuring before year-end. Goldman partner Gene Mercy recalls with a smile, "Rodger called me from his home where he was working on Christmas Eve to say, 'We have a major market operation that we need to get done—now. Other firms are already closed for Christmas, so we're turning to you to do a series of large trades in utilities.' We reviewed the stocks in their portfolio and agreed to trade them at the close. With the music of the Salvation Army Christmas players outside, Rodger gave the go-ahead, and we did fifteen percent of the total NYSE volume that day in one minute at the close of trading—at the old fixed rates, for $425,000 in commissions—just for always being there, even on Christmas Eve, to pick up the phone."

In another case, when the Navajo Indians won an enormous cash settlement with the federal government, it was reported on a Thursday. By Tuesday, Citibank executives were in Arizona, determined to be the first to speak to the tribal elders. They were understandably stunned to hear, "But we already have a financial adviser. Gus Levy came to see us on Saturday. Gus Levy is our investment banker."

In Memphis, to help partner Roy Zuckerberg build up the firm's individual-investor business, Levy was all Southern charm. Speaking to a group of local business leaders, he began, "Ah'm from aways down rivah," gently and colloquially separating himself from New York and up-North and Yankee while genially and modestly making the connection between Memphis and his own hometown, New Orleans. As they reviewed that session afterward, Zuckerberg gently, but somewhat critically, pointed out that Levy had not actually asked for the business. Levy appeared preoccupied and not really listening, but at a subsequent meeting a few months later, with two dozen business leaders and wealthy prospects in Los Angeles, Levy's first cards off the deck were blunt: "We've come all the way from New York City to Los Angeles because we want your business!" After dinner, Gus asked, "How'd I do?" and Zuckerberg suggested he might have been perhaps a bit too direct. Levy retorted, "But Roy, that's what you *told* me to do!"

An important part of Levy's remarkable ability to produce business was his extraordinary range of personal connections. A devout Catholic, George Doty went to Mass every morning before coming to work by 7:30, gave generously to the Church, and made Fordham University *his* charity organization. Levy saw Doty and asked: "George, do you know the cardinal?"

"Of course, Gus. Cardinal Spellman."

"But, do you *know* him. You ever met?"

"No, Gus. Never."

"Come with me Wednesday. I'm having lunch with the cardinal. I'll introduce you. He'll be glad to meet you."

Similarly, George Bennett was the Man in Boston: treasurer of Harvard, the country's biggest endowment; a dominating managing partner of State Street Research & Management, then one of Boston's largest and most prestigious institutional accounts; and a director of Ford, Hewlett-Packard, and other major corporations. Once or twice a year, Levy visited accounts in Boston, where State Street was a key client, and Bennett was the strong man, so Levy went there. They would hug each other—neither man was ever considered a hugger or huggable by his own associates—and go into Bennett's office, close the door, and talk "serious talk" about politics, Ford, Harvard, Florida Power, and people.

For Steve Kay, a thirtysomething salesman who focused on traders, nothing could be more helpful to his ability to do business than having—and everyone at State Street knowing that he had—a special relationship with managing partner Bennett. "Steve, come in here so George can get to know one of our very best, fast-rising young professionals." And, never pausing, Levy moved right into sharing the inside scuttlebutt that everyone treasured from their time with him because he always seemed to know *all* the important people.

Later Levy called Kay. As usual, he was direct and brief: "I'll cover Bennett. You get to know Smith." And that was all Steve Kay needed to hear to know what nobody at State Street would know for a year: Charlie Smith was going to be George Bennett's chosen successor as managing partner. This gave Kay plenty of time to get close with the affable Smith, who privately resented being ignored by most Wall Streeters. Kay would soon have their relationship firmly established— long before anyone else in Wall Street had the first clue about the power shift— and Goldman Sachs would continue being State Street's most important and most profitable stockbroker, getting nearly fifteen percent of its business while the runner-up broker would get less than ten percent, and much less profit, for working equally hard. The difference was close to one million dollars in revenue.

As more and more Wall Street firms organized "asset management" divisions to get into the fast-growing business of managing pension funds, Kay, as head of the Boston office, came under heavy pressure from institutional accounts to stay out of the lucrative investment management business. "Don't compete with us; we're your *clients*—and investment management is *our* business!" Loomis, Sayles & Company was particularly concerned about competition from brokers and had a strict rule: If a broker stole one of its accounts or even one of its people, Loomis Sayles would do no business with that firm. But as an old-line, conservative Boston firm, Loomis Sayles didn't pay competitively, so its best young people kept getting bid away. After Goldman Sachs had taken a *second* person, Dick Holloway of Loomis Sayles called to remind Steve Kay about the Rule, and Kay called Levy, telling him of the loss of a large account. "I wanna see 'em," was all Levy said, and he hung up. This put Kay in a box: He couldn't say no to Levy, and why would Loomis Sayles agree to see anyone from Goldman Sachs after it had broken the Rule a *second* time?

Dutifully, Kay called Holloway to plead for a short visit.

"Gus Levy wants to see *us?*" Holloway exclaimed, adding that he would call back after checking with his CEO. In less than an hour Holloway was back on the phone: "We'd be *glad* to meet with Gus Levy. No, don't come to Boston. We'll come to New York. When would be most convenient?"

A luncheon at Goldman Sachs's office was arranged for the men from Loomis Sayles with Kay, Levy, and research director Bob Danforth. Levy was obviously preoccupied and didn't participate in the conversation. Then one of his secretaries, Inez Sollami, came in to say, "Governor Rockefeller wants to reschedule your meeting for two o'clock and wants to move it to the Roosevelt Hotel instead of Pocantico Hills. He asks that you come in by the freight elevator so you won't be spotted." (The New York City hospitals were going on strike, and Rockefeller was personally involved in the negotiations because he feared racial problems if the hospitals were closed.) Levy took two other calls—both from prominent corporate executives—and then briefly focused entirely on his two guests. "I know we hurt you, and I apologize for that. Now we'd like to *help* you. Steve, let's see what we can do here to get these good clients of ours some nice new business. I'll call Bob White at Ford and recommend their services as pension fund investment managers—and Jimmy Ling needs someone too." Then, apologizing for having to go so soon to meet Governor Rockefeller, Levy left. He probably never knew the names of his guests. But he knew his business. When they got back to Boston, the men from Loomis Sayles made Goldman Sachs one of their most important brokers.

S ince every mutual fund had to report its shareholdings quarterly, it was easy to figure out who was selling after two or three blocks had been executed. On one big series of trades, Steve Kay in Boston knew that MFS, a big mutual fund organization, was the seller and that it had an exclusive with Salomon Brothers. Inez called: "Mr. Kay, Mr. Levy would like to speak with you." Gus Levy never called to say, "Well done"—so Kay knew as he waited on the line that there could only be one reason for Levy's call: to chew him out. "You've missed three big trades so far today. Don't you Boston guys know your accounts any better?"

"Gus loved doing business," observes Lew Eisenberg, who headed institutional sales in the 1980s. Long before Levy called him by his real name, Eisenberg was known as "the kid from Hartford," not because he was born or raised there—he was from Chicago—but because that's where his initial group of institutional accounts were located. After a few years of covering the Hartford accounts, Eisenberg got up the courage to propose to Levy that they make a joint trip to Hartford to visit the financial vice president and the treasurer of the Travelers Insurance Company.

During the plane ride to Hartford, Levy hardly spoke two words to Eisenberg. Same on the return flight. Nearly a week later, Levy received a call from Travelers saying the client felt their meeting had gone well and Levy could tell Eisenberg that he would soon be the selling broker for the first block trade in history to be done at negotiated rates. The size of the block would be 250,000 shares, with a commission of seventy-five thousand dollars—unless, with the firm's usual hustle, that commission could be doubled by finding buyers for that block and doing a cross (handling both sides of the transaction) generating total commissions of $150,000. Levy clearly expected the trade to be a cross at $150,000.

Once inside Goldman Sachs's trading room, Levy focused entirely on doing business. He had tinted-glass partitions around his desk, which was in the center of the trading room. Through the glass he could see all and hear all, checking the status of every big position or every possible trade while seeing visitors—mostly insiders, and as many as ten an hour—and taking and making calls all the time, often two or three calls at the same time. He had sliding windows in the glass partitions so he could open them quickly to bark instructions, as he frequently did. "Why do I do it? It drives me. I don't know why, frankly. It's responsibility—trying to do the best you can. It's not a question of getting ahead, because I can't get ahead much farther. Now I just try to be afloat."

Challenged to explain why he had a general reputation for toughness, Levy said he recognized that he got "such a kick out of making a transaction that I guess I get excited and I say things I don't really mean. Then my conscience gets the best of me and I apologize—despite the fact that that's the one thing I hate to do." Levy's self-appraisal was that he was too open and not tough enough: "I think people at Goldman Sachs know that my door is always open. I have certain opinions, but they are not built in concrete. I'm willing to listen to reason."

"Gus was remarkable," says John Weinberg. "He had a tremendous capacity to do a huge number of things and do them all very well." Levy left Goldman Sachs every day at three thirty so he could be at Mount Sinai to run the executive committee from four to six—and then would take a Goldman Sachs client to dinner, usually to "21." And Levy was always networking with powerful people—in philanthropy, finance, or politics. "Gus Levy and Nelson Rockefeller, as powers in the New York Republican Party, would go to a small room with [NYSE floor specialist] Bunny Lasker and others to swap stories—crude dirty jokes, political gossip, and personal insights into powerful people."

Levy lamented: "I guess I'd have to admit that it's very hard for me to say no. I'm a bad naysayer—except where a principle is involved. It's very hard for me to turn a guy down. I wish I was harder. Mr. Weinberg used to say that if I were a woman, I'd always be pregnant because I just can't say no." Levy repeatedly promised one or another of his friends to give the friend's son a job at Goldman Sachs, usually in sales, and sales manager Ray Young would call to protest, "Gus, this is *my* job and *my* department. If you don't stop stuffing dopes on me, I'll quit."

Levy affected a gruff exterior, but he was there to help anyone in the firm who had a real crisis. On any serious personal problem, he would never say no. When a plane was hijacked in Israel with the daughter of one of the firm's older messengers aboard, Levy called the messenger to come right up to Levy's cubicle on the trading floor. The poor guy was scared to death to go. When he arrived,

Levy said how concerned he was about the man's daughter and that he wanted to help in any way he could. This was, of course, very nice to say. But then Levy picked up the phone and said, "Get me Bill Rogers"—when William Rogers was secretary of state—and in minutes, he was put through to the secretary himself. Levy knew Rogers from his days as a New York lawyer and their shared interest in Republican politics, so he spoke directly, explained his reason for calling, said, "Keep me posted," and hung up. The lasting impact Levy's call made on the old runner—and others in the firm—is easy to imagine.

Levy was a voracious and persistent learner, always striving to do better and to be better in every way. "Don't tell me where we're good. We can't do much about that. Tell us where we're weak, where we can improve, because that's what we are determined to do." Goldman Sachs got better and better under his leadership, and Levy's personal stature rose steadily higher.

As Doty recalls, "With his amazing memory for people and numbers and situations, he had a phenomenal list of people he could call and say, 'I need you to help me, and it won't hurt you.' Then he'd explain what he wanted—and he'd get their help. He was out of the Wild West as a young man, a loose cannon calculating what he could do, what he could get away with. And he was 'too Jewish' for Sidney. But when he became chairman of the New York Stock Exchange and a prominent figure on the national scene, although we had many arguments within the firm, Gus became much more conscious of the importance of process and order."

"Gus was very proud of being the first Jew to be chairman of the Board of Governors of the New York Stock Exchange," said his friend Tubby Burnham. "He considered that position very important in his life. However, Gus was really not a great chairman because he couldn't separate his thinking from what was in his own firm's interests. He was always favoring Goldman Sachs. More important than his two years as chairman of the Big Board, Levy was truly the father of NASDAQ's national market system. I know because I was there. In 1976, when Rod Hills was chairman of the SEC, he called me as head of the Securities Industry Association and said, 'Tubby, we've gotta have a *national* system for the over-the-counter business. And you've gotta come up with a system—and quickly—or we at the SEC will have to impose a system on you.'

" 'How much time will we have to get this done?' "

" 'Six months. It's not much for a major thing like this, but that's all you can have.'

" 'Thanks, pal. Thanks a *lot*.'

"And as soon as I hung up, I called Gus because he knew the OTC markets so well. He was in Bermuda. 'Gus, you've gotta chair this committee and work out a solution.' And I promised him he could have any people he wanted. Gus's committee came up with the system where every OTC dealer and every market—Pacific, Chicago Board, and all the rest—had to show their bids and asks through a central computer screen and had to be good for one thousand shares on either side. And that was the whole secret to our country's having the national over-the-counter system, or NASDAQ, that now handles more daily volume than the NYSE."

Levy respected toughness, particularly in competitors, and had remarkable inner capacities to rise to any occasion. One illustration is the way he handled a dramatic change that confronted the New York Stock Exchange, where he was an increasingly prominent power. As head of Donaldson Lufkin & Jenrette, Dan Lufkin arrived in 1970 at his first-ever meeting as a new member of the NYSE Board of Governors. The meeting was in the ornate amphitheater appropriate to the knights of capitalism who were gathering together. Lufkin carried two large, heavy boxes tied with sisal cord with wooden handles—just in from the printers.

Lufkin had met the night before to brief his friend and incoming NYSE chairman, Bunny Lasker, about DLJ's decision to break all tradition and go public—and to tell him that the preliminary prospectus or "red herring" would be filed with the SEC at noon the next day. As the Board of Governors meeting came to order at three thirty on the day of filing, Robert Haack, NYSE president, was handed a news item that had just come on the broad tape announcing that DLJ had filed for its initial public offering.

Lasker announced: "We have an important news report that concerns us all—DLJ has filed an IPO with the SEC. Fortunately, we have Mr. Lufkin here to explain." Lufkin then opened the boxes and asked that copies of the preliminary prospectus be passed out. Taking a deep breath to maintain composure, he began explaining the revolution that an "upstart" firm, not even fifteen years old, was provoking. Angry feelings were widespread. "You are Judas!" exclaimed Lazard Freres's Felix Rohatyn, saying the NYSE's only option was to expel DLJ immediately from membership.

That evening at the traditional transitional dinner for incoming and outgoing exchange governors held uptown at the Brook club, Lufkin—clearly and obviously being avoided by everyone—was standing alone at the bar nursing a beer when Levy, as outgoing chairman, arrived and went over to say: "I don't agree with you, and I don't like what you did today."

Lufkin started to counter with "I hope you will see things differently soon and..."

Levy cut in: "I haven't finished"—and continued admiringly, "But you have guts coming to this dinner after all that."

While deeply Jewish, Gus was an exemplar of Christian virtues," says George Doty. "He was always giving. And he taught me the joy of giving. He gave both in dollars and of himself and his time. If you asked his help with, say, a dinner, he would never pause or beg off. He'd open his appointment book right away, and if it was possible, he'd sign up then and there. Gus would work for *any* charity. That's how he got to know Cardinal Spellman: as a Jew working for Catholic charities."

"Gus Levy was the first one to ask 'How much?' *publicly* at appeals," recalled Tubby Burnham, who explained the way it happened. A meeting was held at Lehman Brothers where the senior leaders of the Jewish community on Wall Street—André Meyer, Joe Klingenstein, Bobby Lehman, and the others who had been the young Turks back in the twenties and thirties put the challenge on the table: How could the younger Jewish leaders organize *their* generation to give in significant size? "We didn't have their kind of money, so Gus, who was our natural leader, said it would be necessary to solicit many more people in order to match the personal giving of the older, wealthier leadership."

At the next annual dinner of the Federation of Jewish Philanthropies, Levy took the microphone and launched right into a new kind of public solicitation. Without ever pushing or demanding, but by publicly asking in a nice way that included calling out the donor's name, telling something about him and his family and his business and the good things he'd been doing at work and in philanthropy—really the person's life history—Levy would end with, "And last year, you gave fifteen hundred dollars to the Federation, and we're all wondering what your gift will be *this* year?" And then in that moment of silence, the recipient of Levy's nice words would say, "I'll give...two thousand dollars." And Levy would reply warmly, "That's a very nice gift. Nice increase too. Thank you very much."

Levy would then turn his charm and the audience's attention to the next donor. Of course, he already knew each of his prospects and what they could give; he'd done his homework. He knew whom to ask first and who, like Charles Revson, needed to be a big shot and get featured with a lot of attention, and he knew exactly when to call on each of them. In that one evening, Gus Levy raised three times more money than had ever been raised before. And of course the calling out of names and stating specific amounts has gone on and on because it works so well. Now, it's a tradition—but it all began with Gus Levy.

"Gus was very extroverted, gregarious—and generous," recalls Peter Sacerdote. "One year, he gave one million dollars to the Federation and, in his speech, he said it was really not a big deal—that it had been more of a stretch when he gave one dollar that first year he was at the YMHA." More than money, Levy gave his time. He worked for hours every weekday for years as chairman of the executive committee to build Mount Sinai Hospital almost single-handedly.[12] Honored with an award for lifetime service, Levy took the mike to say simply and memorably: "I never expected this. I certainly don't deserve it—and I'll never forget it."

Levy was as notoriously intense in his private life as he was at Goldman Sachs and in philanthropy. His friend Burnham recalls: "Gus and I went all the way back to when he first got to New York. We talked at least once every day and played golf on weekends. Gus called me on Friday night from California: 'The grim reaper's got me, Tubs. My heart.'

" 'Did you see a doctor, Gus?'

" 'Naw. I'm not going to a doctor. I'll meet you on the first tee at eight tomorrow morning. I'm taking the red-eye in.'

"Next morning, just before eight, Gus comes up to the tee. 'Do you guys mind if I jog?' We all know Gus and what he has in mind. He'll hit his ball, run to it, wait for us to catch up, hit again—and jog off. We agree he can jog and we double the stakes. By the end of the ninth hole, Gus is down eight—and finally decides to play like the rest of us."

. . .

A strong record of past achievements and profit making had led to Gus Levy's being selected managing partner, but leadership authority and power in Goldman Sachs, as in all Wall Street firms, has to be earned over and over again every time the leader gets challenged—just as a male lion has to keep defending his pride of lionesses. Gus Levy knew and understood all this. What he did not know or anticipate was that his greatest threat would suddenly bolt out of the firm's oldest business—commercial paper—where Goldman Sachs, over the past hundred years, had made itself the leading dealer.

THE WRECK OF THE
PENN CENTRAL

Without commercial paper, Goldman Sachs would have been unable to expand beyond the core of Sidney Weinberg's corporate clients—and even they would be at risk as competitors kept forcing the question: "Without Weinberg, why work with a second-tier firm that's only able to provide one specialized short-term financing service?"

In the early 1970s—before the boom in corporate bonds, before international bonds were anything more than rare oddities, before the invention of mortgage-backed and asset-backed bonds such as GNMAs, before high-yield bonds, before medium-term notes, floating-rate notes, and the myriad other aspects of today's enormous bond markets, and long before the derivatives and computer models that tie all these disparate instruments into one massive, complex debt capital market—commercial paper was far more important than a current observer might first imagine. And it was the strong basis, over the years, for the firm's expansion into money-market instruments and then on into bond dealing. Commercial paper was not only Goldman Sachs's oldest business, it was the only corporate product where the firm was the acknowledged market leader, and it became the single, vital point of entry on which John Whitehead was striving to build an important and eventually highly profitable investment banking business.

During the fifties and sixties, use of commercial paper increased significantly. As interest rates rose and rose again, issuing commercial paper became increasingly attractive as an alternative to bank loans for more and more companies. And even if the commercial-paper alternative seemed not really the right way for a particular company to borrow right now, it was surely worth considering for the future, so discussing its advantages with the man from Goldman Sachs was easy to justify. Commercial paper also made considerable progress as a way for many corporations to temporarily invest surplus cash. Interest in buying commercial paper as a short-term, money-good investment increased substantially because the Federal Reserve's Regulation Q limited the interest rate that banks could pay to attract time deposits; commercial paper offered higher rates. The "unique selling proposition" of commercial paper—unsecured short-term borrowings that were cheaper and more flexible than bank loans—was attractive, very attractive. So doors opened and conversations began at more and more companies. Without commercial paper, Whitehead's ambitious strategy in investment banking would never have succeeded, but with commercial paper, it was almost certain to succeed—or so it seemed.

For Gus Levy, early 1970 promised a great year. His institutional block-trading business was so successful that even without a retail-customer business, Goldman Sachs ranked third in NYSE commissions and was much more profitable than any other stockbrokerage firm, earning at a record rate of 40 percent on the forty-five partners' fifty million dollars in capital. Confidence was spreading throughout the firm, including confidence in the leadership of Gus Levy and in the direction he was taking the firm.

The securities business was changing, and change creates opportunity, particularly for aggressive innovators. The era was replete with business opportunities and challenges, and Levy was flat-out committed to capturing every profitable business opportunity for his firm. Maintaining intensity of commitment was essential to the firm's continued progress and would have been a great challenge for any leader, particularly anyone coming after someone as dominating and effective as Sidney Weinberg. Levy believed he was up to the challenge but knew that leaders are only as effective as their followers' confidence and commitment make them. Committed to attack and expansion, he had no spare capacities or resources for defense or to deal with new troubles. Levy certainly wasn't looking for any new trouble, but new trouble found Levy.

He got hit by the largest railroad company in America: Penn Central.

On June 21, 1970, Penn Central Transportation Company—the eighth-largest corporation in the nation and the largest owner of real estate—petitioned for reorganization under Section 77 of the Federal Bankruptcy Act, and at 5:45 p.m. U.S. District Court Judge C. William Kraft signed the petition. It was the largest bankruptcy in history.

Although its assets and book value were immense, Penn Central's stock price had plunged to ten dollars—down 88 percent from a high of $86.50 two years before. Between April 21, the day before it announced a $62.7 million loss for the first quarter (versus a much smaller $12.8 million loss in the same quarter a year earlier), and May 8, maturities and payments on its commercial paper exceeded sales by $41.3 million, leaving a balance outstanding of $77.1 million. Six weeks later, with Penn Central in bankruptcy, the market value of its commercial paper plunged, imposing large losses on clients of the issuing dealer for Penn Central's commercial paper, Goldman Sachs.*

Penn Central was Gus Levy's personal client, and the loss it threatened to impose on Goldman Sachs was not only larger than any prior loss, it was larger than Goldman Sachs.

The trouble was quickly contagious. Nearly three hundred other Goldman Sachs commercial-paper issuers faced a rush by investors to redeem their paper. That meant the clients suddenly had to borrow from their banks to buy back their own commercial paper.[1] The Federal Reserve had to take swift and substantial action to ensure liquidity in the U.S. banking system. Standard & Poor's cut Penn Central's bond rating from BBB to Bb. According to Standard & Poor's Guide, a BBB security is "borderline between definitely sound obligations and those where the speculative element begins to predominate." The Bb securities have "only minor investment characteristics."

---

* Penn Central was not the first commercial-paper issuer to default. In late 1968, Mill Factors, another Goldman Sachs client, had defaulted on $6.7 million of commercial paper, and two holders—Alexander & Baldwin and Worcester County National Bank—sued Goldman Sachs. The firm paid out fifty thousand dollars.

Clients who had bought Penn Central commercial paper through Goldman Sachs could be expected to sue. Eventually over forty investors did sue, seeking recovery: Their claims totaled over eighty-seven million dollars. With partners' capital of just fifty-three million dollars, Goldman Sachs didn't *have* eighty-seven million dollars.[2] Penn Central–related lawsuits could wipe out all the firm's capital and more.

Losing the partners' money—or even a significant fraction of it—was devastating to contemplate. Beyond the money, it could cost Levy in loss of authority and strength of leadership. Partners close to Sidney Weinberg, who had worried about Levy's being too much of a trader with "ragtag" friends, could have withdrawn or reduced their crucial support.

Levy and others had assumed that gigantic Penn Central could always raise capital—if necessary, by selling off some of its enormous real estate assets—and had trusted Penn Central's chief financial officer, David Bevan. But Bevan had lied to Levy and to his fellow employees at Penn Central and to all his friends. In the exhausting series of misadventures since the merger that had produced Penn Central, Bevan had been scrambling to create liquidity for the asset-rich money-loser and had come to believe he had a "higher responsibility" to do anything and everything to save his company—at least until some of its real estate could be converted into liquid assets. Bevan was in over his head, struggling to keep up. As John Whitehead later recounted: "David Bevan was a nice enough guy, but as Penn Central's problems got worse, he was way out of his depth. He didn't know what to do and decided his responsibilities were to his company and the people he knew personally, so he deliberately lied to Penn Central employees and to his friends—including Gus Levy. He was entirely wrong, of course, but that's what he was thinking."

Bevan's struggles and poor judgment led to serious mistakes. Just ten days before the bankruptcy announcement, Penn Central appointed a new CFO[3] because Bevan faced criminal charges. Bevan had tried to force a bond underwriter's law firm to remove a lawyer who was working on a Penn Central bond issue and who "was particularly diligent in demanding full and unvarnished disclosure." This led to investigations that revealed various misfeasances: self-dealing by Penn Central executives, lavish expenses charged to subsidiaries, and insider trading. The offenses were not limited to Bevan. The SEC report charged that "the board repeatedly failed to act despite direct and clear warnings."[4]

Bevan's personal failings were a particularly explicit symptom of the malaise within Penn Central, which was a merger only in legal terms. In the largest railroad combination in history, the New York Central and the Pennsylvania Railroad had combined into one massive transportation and property complex with 20,530 miles of track. But after a century of archrivalry, the intensive competition between "Central" and "Pennsy" never stopped. Disputes, often quite serious disputes, continued between the "green hats" and the "red hats"—the premerger colors on the two lines' boxcars. Worse, the president (Stuart Saunders from Pennsylvania) and the chairman (Alfred Perlman from New York Central) bickered even at board meetings and fought over key appointments until, two years after the merger, Perlman finally gave up and agreed to step aside as chairman so a new president[5] could be brought in from AT&T's Western Electric unit. Instead of increasing operating efficiency, the merger increased chaos: Freight cars got lost; switchyards got jammed up; every day twenty to eighty trains got delayed because there were no engines to pull them; the computer systems were as incompatible as the people; and freight customers and passengers complained bitterly. As operating losses mounted, the dividend was cut and the stock price crumbled.

Amid these crises, Penn Central management cited numerous optimistic numbers: a 6 percent freight-rate increase authorized by the Interstate Commerce Commission would add eighty million dollars; a change in interline freight-car rentals would add sixteen million dollars; merger savings were running at thirty-four million dollars, twice what had been expected; thirty million dollars in extra costs of integrating the two lines were nearly over, and the Connecticut commuter lines that had lost over twenty-two million dollars annually would soon be taken over by the state, which would pay eleven million dollars for rolling stock and four million dollars in annual rents. In addition, executives observed, if it ever needed to raise money Penn Central could sell off pieces of its three billion dollars of nonrail assets—largely New York City properties like Madison Square Garden and Midtown apartment buildings.

Penn Central had ample assets but too little cash. And as its troubles got worse, its lack of financial flexibility got worse even faster. As recently as the summer of 1968, Penn Central had made public a plan for a new mortgage-bond issue that would consolidate more than fifty different debt issues of the Pennsylvania and New York Central railroads. This umbrella issue was sure to exceed one billion dollars and was to be backed with the combined railroads' real estate holdings, including prize parcels of land in Manhattan. Penn Central also planned to raise one hundred million dollars of commercial paper as part of this massive restructuring and began using Goldman Sachs as its commercial-paper issuing dealer.

However, there were ominous signs. One ICC commissioner even spoke of a possible bankruptcy, saying, "The most discouraging thing is that the company is way ahead of its savings goals, yet the deficit is getting worse. If the Penn Central goes into receivership, anything can happen."[6] Others scoffed at the notion of bankruptcy for the nation's largest railroad. "They have assets up to their ears," said a federal official at the time. "The question is how fast they can liquidate assets into quick cash. Hell, they are the largest real estate holding company in the country."

Among a long series of negative events, these were major: In a crucial change following objections from Congressman Wright Patman, the Defense Department decided not to guarantee a two-hundred-million-dollar borrowing. (Goldman Sachs had been told of this confidentially in February.) After this setback, the company[7] was unable to float a bond issue of one hundred million dollars even at a high interest rate of 11.5 percent. In the preliminary prospectus for that aborted issue, the company revealed that it was having difficulty rolling over its outstanding commercial paper as it came due in the twenty days from April 21 (the day before the railroad announced the big first-quarter operating loss) through the day the prospectus went to press on May 8. In what might have been seen as a desperate tactic, the company borrowed fifty-nine million dollars in Swiss francs—with just a one-year maturity—at a high average interest rate of 10.1 percent before reporting a loss of $56.3 million for 1969 and another loss of $62.7 million for the first quarter of 1970.[8]

After the merger, both real estate and railroading had needed cash: In early 1968, the Penn Central was using up cash at the rate of seven hundred thousand dollars a day.[9] Less than two years later, in June 1970, Penn Central was bankrupt.

With so many variables—some positive and some negative—securities underwriters and rating services would have been expected to insist on rigorous due diligence. But instead of conducting an up-to-date and independent evaluation of Penn Central and its finances, Allan Rogers of National Credit Office, a subsidiary of Dun & Bradstreet, that acted as a rating agency for commercial paper, simply called Goldman Sachs and spoke with partner Jack Vogel on February 5, 1970, to get the firm's current opinion. Vogel gave assurance that, despite the disappointing earnings, with the railroad's massive real estate assets Goldman Sachs was definitely continuing to offer Penn Central's commercial paper. This kept NCO from lowering its "prime" rating. But Vogel had not given NCO the full story, particularly the actions taken to protect Goldman Sachs.[10]

On the day it heard of the big first-quarter loss, Goldman Sachs had insisted Penn Central buy back from the firm's inventory ten million dollars of its commercial paper.[11] And to avoid the risk of carrying Penn Central paper in inventory as issuing dealer, Goldman Sachs converted the offering to a "tap issue." (Taking no market risk whatever, Goldman Sachs would no longer buy commercial paper from Penn Central nor hold twenty million dollars of Penn Central paper in inventory for resale, but would instead have Penn Central issue commercial paper only when a specific buyer of the paper had identified itself to the firm.) These self-protective actions were not reported or explained to NCO nor to any customer of Goldman Sachs.

Bankruptcy for giant Penn Central had been truly inconceivable. Startled by the crisis of a major issuer's bankruptcy, the commercial-paper market panicked and demand plunged. Dealers were forced to buy back recently issued paper; nearly three billion dollars of commercial paper was cashed in and $1.7 billion in Fed funds was borrowed from the Federal Reserve banks in a single week in July. Interest rates spiked higher, and liquidity dried up as corporations all across America scrambled to borrow from their commercial banks to pay off commercial paper. The Federal Reserve had to take direct action to ensure the liquidity of the nation's banking system.

After Penn Central went bankrupt, information on the corporation's finances may have been interesting but wasn't important to commercial-paper investors: They had large losses on what was supposed to have been a safe investment. What they wanted to know was obvious: What was Goldman Sachs going to do now? Would Goldman Sachs make good the customer losses? Were any of the firm's three hundred other issuers also at risk of bankruptcy?

With eighty-seven million dollars in Penn Central's paper issued and outstanding—and now defaulted—the firm itself was clearly threatened. How large would its losses be? Since all the capital in the firm was the personal wealth of individual partners, losses were not "corporate," they were *personal*, and the pain of loss could be sharp and feelings bitter and divisive. Could Goldman Sachs absorb the pain?

Knowing from his experience in block trading how important it was to move quickly to make some kind of an offer—no matter how low or how unlikely to be accepted—to keep the market alive, Levy sent John Weinberg to meet with clients in the Southeast and make them an offer: fifty cents on the dollar. Weinberg had been a partner for fifteen years, was Sidney Weinberg's son, was great with people and a member of the management committee—but none of that mattered. No one was willing to negotiate, and everyone was angry. The mission was a failure. The issues and the recovery of losses would be resolved in the courts of law.

On November 17, 1970, four investors—led by Anchor Corporation and its mutual fund Fundamental Investors, which had bought twenty million dollars of the paper in four five-million-dollar pieces between November 28 and December 8, 1969—sued Goldman Sachs for a total of twenty-three million dollars in a joint action with Younker Brothers of Des Moines, Iowa, C.R. Anthony Company of Oklahoma City, and Welch's Foods, the grape juice producer, which had lost, respectively, five hundred thousand dollars, $1.5 million, and one million dollars.

The plaintiffs asserted that the firm had made "promises and representations as to the future [of Penn Central] which were beyond reasonable expectation and unwarranted by existing circumstances" and "representations or statements which were false."[12] The companies were at least somewhat pressured into suing by fears that if they didn't sue, they would get sued themselves for not protecting their own shareholders' interests. The plaintiffs alleged, among other things, that Goldman Sachs didn't give them numerous material facts it should have known about the quality of Penn Central commercial paper; the paper was and is "worthless or worth substantially less" than they had paid for it; Goldman Sachs didn't adequately investigate or regularly review the financial condition of Penn Central to evaluate the investment quality of its paper; when Goldman Sachs participated in the fall of 1969 in a Penn Central application to the Interstate Commerce

Commission for approval of the company's issuance of commercial paper, the ICC had "expressed serious concern over the heavy dependence of Penn Central upon short-term financing"; Goldman Sachs was the "confidential financial adviser" to Penn Central and "otherwise had obligations and loyalties to Penn Central which conflicted with its obligations, loyalties and duties to plaintiffs"; and Goldman Sachs was guilty of stating a long list of material untruths in its sales of Penn Central paper. Among these were alleged statements that Penn Central paper was "prime quality"; that Goldman Sachs had made an "adequate investigation of, and kept under continuous current review, the financial condition of Penn Central"; and that Goldman Sachs would, "at the request of plaintiffs, repurchase said commercial paper."

In rebuttal, Robert G. Wilson, the partner in charge of commercial paper, said in a prepared statement, "There is absolutely no merit to the claims which have been made against Goldman Sachs." Wilson stated that "during the entire period in which we were selling Penn Central Transportation Company commercial paper (which ended in mid-May), we were confident that the transportation company was creditworthy. The financial statements of the company showed a net worth in excess of $1.8 billion at December 31, 1969.... There also was ample evidence to justify our belief that the transportation company had access to credit at least sufficient to cover its current obligations and repay commercial paper as it became due."

John Haire of Fundamental Investors, as by far the largest claimant, took the lead in private settlement negotiations with Goldman Sachs. A major mutual fund organization and a major securities dealer would have many ways to do creative business together and would have ample reason to put a confrontation behind them, and Haire and Levy worked out a settlement in April 1972 for $5.25 million in cash and the balance in certificates of participation in any future settlement. But the farmers in the Welch's cooperative had had a bad harvest in 1970 and felt they needed 100 percent restitution, while the two Midwestern organizations saw the case as a matter of dishonest dealing and felt morally right in insisting on full recovery.

If all losses were settled at 20 percent to 25 percent of the face amount, Levy's firm would lose nearly twenty million dollars—a massive blow, but one Goldman Sachs could survive. In all, forty-six lawsuits were filed. In May 1972, eight suits[13] involving $13.3 million in Penn Central commercial paper were resolved for 20 percent of the face amount with the plaintiffs executing stipulations of dismissal. This left holders of fifty million dollars face amount yet to reach resolution. Meanwhile, the federal government continued its investigations. Once the federal findings of fact were completed, private civil suits for financial recoveries would follow. All these recoveries would have to be paid by Goldman Sachs.

The SEC staff investigation of the Penn Central collapse concluded in August 1972, with a public report of eight hundred pages based on testimony of two hundred witnesses representing 150 financial institutions. The SEC staff report said that up to May 15, 1970, Goldman Sachs had continued to offer the railroad's commercial paper to its customers even when the firm had received warnings that the Penn Central's problems were "critical" and that Penn Central, when unable to obtain further financing in this country, had turned to foreign creditors as a last resort. "During this time, Goldman Sachs became aware of information which cast doubt on the safety of this commercial paper. Most of the nonpublic information...wasn't disclosed to customers. The information they did disseminate was out of date." The report went on to say that Goldman Sachs had reduced and was eliminating the Penn Central commercial paper held in inventory and that Penn Central paper was meeting strong resistance from buyers.

Levy testified he had been assured by his own partners that Penn Central's three billion dollars in assets was more than sufficient to raise the capital needed to meet all its obligations. Levy also testified that he was so certain of the Penn Central's future that he held on to stock worth nine million dollars in a trust he managed for Walter Annenberg, America's ambassador to the Court of St. James's.

Sale of Penn Central commercial paper was aided greatly, the SEC staff said, by the receipt of a "prime" rating from the National Credit Office. NCO rated Penn Central commercial paper prime—its highest commercial-paper rating—until June 1, just three weeks before the bankruptcy announcement. On June 1, NCO "reserved" Penn Central's rating—meaning the company's situation was too ambiguous to give a rating—and told subscribers it had learned Penn Central was "rearranging its financing." The SEC staff said that the prime rating was given without adequate inquiry into Penn Central's financial condition and at a time when the facts didn't support such a rating.

According to the SEC staff, Penn Central sought to inflate earnings artificially and to cover up losses of the merged railroad to disguise its critical financial condition in 1968 and 1969. Among the SEC's other charges: Penn Central directors approved the payment of one hundred million dollars in dividends to convey a rosy picture of railroad operations at a time when the carrier actually was losing more than $150 million a year and borrowing millions of dollars just to remain liquid. In furtherance of a scheme to "improperly increase the reported earnings" of Penn Central and its parent company, the commission report said, Saunders and Bevan failed to include charges to the corporation arising out of its ownership of the Lehigh Valley Railroad Company, the New York, New Haven & Hartford Railroad Company, and the Executive Aviation Corporation. The Penn Central complex was facing continuing cash drains, the SEC report said, that created "an increasing need to conceal the true conditions" of the operation, intensifying the search for accounting methods that would inflate Penn Central's reported earnings.

The SEC report continued: "Goldman Sachs gained possession of material adverse information, some from public sources and some from nonpublic sources, indicating a continuing deterioration of the financial condition of the transportation company. Goldman Sachs did not communicate this information to its commercial-paper customers, nor did it undertake a thorough investigation. If Goldman Sachs had heeded these warnings and undertaken a re-evaluation of the company, it would have learned that its condition was substantially worse than had been publicly reported."

In his cover letter for the staff report, SEC chairman William Casey described the company's actions as "an elaborate and ingenious series of steps...concocted to create or accelerate income, frequently by rearranging holdings and disposing of assets and to avoid or defer transactions which would require reporting of loss." The SEC staff said, "Saunders established the policy and looked to other members of top management team to implement it."

In May 1974 the SEC filed civil suits in both Philadelphia and New York, charging that Stuart Saunders lied about profits in 1968 and 1969 and covered up losses; that David Bevan not only misrepresented operations, but also personally profited from illegal insider trading in selling fifteen thousand shares at prices between fifty and sixty-eight dollars to pay off a $650,000 loan that had allowed him to exercise his options; that Bevan had misappropriated four million dollars in corporate funds; and that Peat, Marwick, Mitchell & Company had filed false financial statements for the railroad.[14]

The Securities and Exchange Commission censured Goldman Sachs, saying the firm had violated the law by not informing customers about the continuing financial deterioration of the railroad. The SEC enjoined the firm from further violations, and Goldman Sachs, while denying any wrongdoing, agreed to a consent order[15] barring it from making any misleading or fraudulent statements while selling commercial paper in the future and agreed to set up additional procedures to protect buyers of commercial paper.[16]

Within hours of the entry of the SEC consent decree, a long-distance controversy erupted between counsel for Goldman Sachs and the SEC as to the exact nature of the charges to which Goldman Sachs had agreed. Michael M. Maney, who handled the consent agreement as outside counsel for Goldman Sachs, said that while the action was brought under the antifraud provisions of the Securities Act, the firm was charged only with negligence in failing to inform itself and its customers of the actual state of financial affairs of Penn Central. Counsel for the commission insisted, on the other hand, that the intent of the complaint was, indeed, to charge fraud under a section of the Securities Act entitled Fraudulent Interstate Transactions.

In a statement for Goldman Sachs, Robert G. Kleckner Jr., the firm's in-house counsel, said, "The decision to consent to the SEC injunction was made as a matter of business judgment. We did not violate any law or regulations, and we believe we acted honorably and responsibly in selling the commercial paper of Penn Central Transportation Company." Then, apparently to deflect accusations that accepting the consent agreement implied that Goldman Sachs had done anything that was not normal industry practice, Kleckner continued: "We support the policies and procedures for commercial-paper transactions embodied in the injunction. It is our understanding that the commercial-paper industry generally is expected to apply them."

Then things got a lot worse. The suit filed by the three investors—Welch's Foods, C.R. Anthony Company, and Younker Brothers, which had originally joined with Fundamental Investors but had not agreed to settle—had been winding its way through the courts for four years. Now it came to trial.

Marvin Schwartz, Sullivan & Cromwell's senior securities litigator, had sought to bring all the cases against Goldman Sachs together into a unified case and to have the case assigned for trial in Philadelphia as part of the Penn Central bankruptcy case. Lawyers for the plaintiffs, led by Daniel A. Pollack, kept the commercial-paper case separated, so it was tried in New York City. David Bevan, Stuart Saunders, and thirty-three other witnesses, including Gus Levy, were deposed.

As the trial proceeded, Goldman Sachs decided it needed to change litigators; Marvin Schwartz was relieved, and another Sullivan & Cromwell partner, William Piel Jr., fresh from defending Ford in a major antitrust suit, took over the defense on September 23, 1974, in the third week of the trial. He argued that Goldman Sachs's customers were sophisticated investors capable of making their own investment decisions; that the firm's obligation was to act merely as a conduit for such paper without making recommendations on the paper's quality; that customers could have gotten their own information because Penn Central was a publicly held concern; and that Goldman Sachs did disseminate information to customers on certain occasions. Gus Levy told a reporter: "The whole thing is unwarranted and the facts don't support a single complaint against us. These are professional investors who knew as much as we did about Penn Central or probably more."[17]

Pollack's strategy for the plaintiffs was to simplify and clarify the issues so the six jurors and two alternates—all blue-collar workers—would be confident they understood the issue and their decision. It helped that the litigators from Sullivan & Cromwell underestimated Pollack, seeing him as young and inexperienced and not from a major law firm, instead of as a tough, talented litigator, keen to propel his career and aware that with daily press coverage this was a high-profile case. The first phase of Pollack's strategy was to rehearse the extensive record of depositions so the jurors would become familiar with the arcane terminology of the commercial-paper business and would have plenty of time to become comfortable with all the ins and outs of the business and not be intimidated. Testimony took thirty full days.

Pollack often read to the jury long passages in the transcripts from the depositions—particularly Gus Levy's:

QUESTION: "Were you aware that Goldman Sachs was selling commercial paper of Penn Central while it possessed nonpublic information on Penn Central?"

LEVY: "I was aware that Goldman Sachs was selling commercial paper, but I didn't know whether—yes, yes, the answer is yes."

QUESTION: "Did you do anything about this situation?"

LEVY: "Did I do anything about it?"

QUESTION: "Yes."

LEVY: "I didn't do anything about it because I didn't know what Wilson told the people."

QUESTION: "Were you aware that on February 5, 1970, O'Herron told Wilson [both were partners in the commercial-paper division of Goldman Sachs] that he did not think Penn Central could get $100 million in standby lines?"

LEVY: "The answer is yes."

QUESTION: "Was that nonpublic information?"

LEVY: "I presume it was."

QUESTION: "Did you instruct disclosure of that fact?"

LEVY: "I did not."

QUESTION: "Were you aware that on February 5, 1970, Wilson told O'Herron that in the future, Goldman Sachs probably would handle their paper only on a tap-issue basis where Goldman Sachs did not inventory their notes?"

LEVY: "It was in the memorandum, so I knew about it."

QUESTION: "Was that nonpublic information?"

LEVY: "I guess it was."

QUESTION: "Did you instruct disclosure of that fact?"

LEVY: "I did not."

QUESTION: "Were you aware that on February 5, 1970, Wilson asked Penn Central to buy back $10 million of its commercial paper from the inventory position of Goldman Sachs?"

LEVY: "That was in the memorandum, and I presume I was aware of it."

QUESTION: "Was that nonpublic information?"

LEVY: "That was definitely nonpublic information."

QUESTION: "Did you instruct disclosure of that fact?"

LEVY: "I did not."

QUESTION: "Were you aware that on February 5, 1970, Penn Central agreed to buy back $10 million of their notes from the inventory position of Goldman Sachs?"

LEVY: "I believe I was. It was in the memorandum."

QUESTION: "Was that nonpublic information?"

LEVY: "I believe it was."

QUESTION: "Did you instruct disclosure of that fact?"

LEVY: "I did not."[18]

At trial, it was revealed that Goldman Sachs produced research on commercial-paper issuers on two very different levels: Green Sheets (duplicated on green paper) went out to customers, while Blue Sheets were strictly for internal use. Worse, in the confidential Blue Sheets Wilson wrote a clear "smoking gun" statement: "We don't want Penn Central paper in our inventory." As Pollack explained to the jury, the firm could have said to its customers, "We're going to re-put [sell back to Penn Central] the paper we hold in inventory, so if you'd like to re-put your paper, let us know." He made it clear to the jurors how easy it could have been.

In cross-examination, Pollack got Levy to say that the firm did not disclose to investors important information in its possession:

QUESTION: "Mr. Levy, I take it from your direct testimony this morning that you admit that Goldman Sachs possessed nonpublic information on Penn Central. Is this correct?"

LEVY: "Yes, sir."

QUESTION: "You knew at the time, in 1969 and 1970, that Goldman Sachs possessed nonpublic information on Penn Central, is this correct?"

LEVY: "Yes, sir."

QUESTION: "You did not instruct disclosure of that information to the commercial-paper customers of Goldman Sachs, did you?"

LEVY: "It was our policy, Mr. Pollack, not to disclose confidential information on any of our issuers or any of our corporate clients."

MR. POLLACK: "Your Honor, I expressly ask that the witness be directed to answer the question."

THE COURT: "I think the question should be framed with respect to these three plaintiffs, Welch Foods, Younker, and C.R. Anthony."

QUESTION: "Mr. Levy, you did not instruct disclosure of this information to Welch Foods, Younker Brothers, or C.R. Anthony Company, did you?"

LEVY: "I did not. It was against our policy."

MR. POLLACK: "I move that everything after 'I did not' be stricken as not responsive, your Honor."

THE COURT: "Yes, I will strike it."

QUESTION: "Penn Central financial officers did not ask you to withhold this information from Welch, Younker, and Anthony, did they?"

LEVY: "Not to my recollection."

QUESTION: "On another subject, Mr. Levy, is it a fact that you had no opinion yourself of your own as to the creditworthiness of Penn Central in 1968, 1969, or 1970?"

LEVY: "Well, it is true I relied primarily on the credit judgment of Mr. Wilson and his credit man, Mr. Vogel, but obviously I was involved February 5th and 6th—rather, February 6th—and I followed the credit memorandums, so I had some idea what was going on and I knew a lot."[19]

In another cross-examination, John Weinberg, the partner to whom the commercial-paper division reported, explained that he got many pages of Green and Blue Sheets, seldom more than skimmed them, and promptly tossed them into his office wastepaper basket, saying in the straightforward way that usually established his credibility with all sorts of people but this time would backfire with the jury: "I throw them away. I'm a big wastebasket man." Pollack would return to this phrase. It had a real impact on the jurors in his summation to the jury.

Pollack began his summation by asserting that the "test of basic honesty is clear: treat your clients as well as you treat yourself." Then he took advantage of Weinberg's candor about top-level supervision not being careful or close: "In supervising and controlling the profitable commercial-paper business, where was Mr. Weinberg, who was responsible for management and oversight? Where was—and I quote—the 'big wastebasket man'?"

Then he summarized the way the jury should proceed in its deliberations: "The North Star in this case is clear and simple: did Goldman Sachs know—and not tell? If you find that they knew and you find they did not tell their clients, then those clients are entitled to full recovery."

In a lengthy opinion, the court ruled that there was ample "objective data to lead a reasonable observer" to conclude that Penn Central's commercial paper "was not prime." The judge brushed aside Goldman Sachs's argument that it was so rated by Dun & Bradstreet's National Credit Office: "The private determination of that branch of Dun & Bradstreet cannot bind investors or the courts."[20] He then pointed out that there was at least some evidence of circular reasoning: that National Credit Office had based its prime rating on Goldman Sachs's continuing to offer the paper, plus Goldman Sachs's assurances of Penn Central's wealth in real estate.[21]

In late October 1974, the jury of three men and three women, after the month-long trial, found unanimously that Goldman Sachs knew or should have known that the railroad was in financial difficulties that would put it in bankruptcy, and ordered the firm to pay back the three million dollars the plaintiffs had paid for Penn Central commercial paper between January and April 1970, plus nearly one million dollars in interest.

In defense of the firm's failed trial strategy, a partner contended, "We drew an anti–Wall Street judge, so we went for a jury trial, with Sullivan & Cromwell advising that the firm would be okay because commercial paper is specifically exempted from the Securities Act, so it is not a security. However, the issues were too complex and too subtle for the jury to parse, so Goldman Sachs lost."

In March 1975, Goldman Sachs settled out of court, for $1.4 million, a suit by Getty Oil that had sought two million dollars plus five hundred thousand dollars accrued interest for losses on Penn Central commercial paper purchased five months before the bankruptcy.[22] The settlement at fifty-eight cents per dollar of face amount plus accrued interest—more than double any previous negotiated settlement in the Penn Central bankruptcy—was apparently made because of the federal court's jury award at 100 percent plus accrued interest five months earlier. This left nearly twenty lawsuits worth twenty million dollars still pending.[23]

In October 1976, Goldman Sachs lost another suit as Judge Morris Lalter of the federal district court in New York decided against the firm and awarded six hundred thousand dollars plus interest to the University Hill Foundation, a fund-raising unit for Loyola University of Los Angeles.

In December 1975, after a nine-day trial, Goldman Sachs was ordered by Federal District Judge Charles M. Metzner to pay five hundred thousand dollars—100 percent of the claim made by Franklin Savings Bank. The president of Franklin had called Goldman Sachs on March 16, 1970, expressing interest in buying $1.5 million of commercial paper, and was offered five hundred thousand dollars of Penn Central paper due to mature June 26, 1970, and one million dollars from a different issuer.[24] The judge said Goldman Sachs didn't disclose its self-protective actions to Franklin Savings before the bank bought the Penn Central paper, and added that while such disclosure might have done great harm to Penn Central, Goldman Sachs had an obligation to either make the disclosure or abstain from trading in or recommending the securities concerned.

"I understand the reluctance of Goldman Sachs possibly to be the cause of such calamity to our economic structure," Judge Metzner wrote. "In addition, it had close business if not personal ties to the Penn Central management which would be jeopardized in the event of collapse. However, it is disclosure of just such information...to which the antifraud sections of the securities laws are directed." The judge added that he believed this to be "the perfect example of an omission to state a material fact necessary to make the statement not misleading. When Goldman Sachs sold the commercial paper, it was understood that it was holding out the paper as creditworthy and high quality. The information that it failed to disclose was clearly material."

In August 1977, another decision—a decision in favor of Goldman Sachs—was reversed. Back in June 1976, the firm had won its first victory as Federal District Judge H. Kenneth Wangelin had said that Alton Box Board Company was not "a widow defrauded in a blue sky scheme," but rather a "sophisticated investor," and had dismissed Alton's $625,000 claim.[25] However, the Circuit Court of Appeals overturned that ruling and ordered Goldman Sachs to pay Alton $599,186 plus 6 percent interest, noting that the firm had confidential and undisclosed information about the railroad it did not disclose to Alton and that eight days before the sale, the firm had been told by Penn Central of an impending heavy loss in the first quarter.[26]

Gus Levy's friend I. W. Burnham summarized the end result: "Penn Central

really hurt Gus—and came awfully close to seriously hurting Goldman Sachs."
If all the investors in Penn Central's commercial paper had gone to trial as effectively as Welch's, C.R. Anthony, and Younker Brothers, the firm could have
been liable for financial settlements far beyond its capital. The adverse publicity
that would have come with large losses at trial would have badly hurt the firm's
long-term efforts at reputation rebuilding after Goldman Sachs Trading Corporation. Moreover, with the sharp downturn in the 1973–74 stock market, the firm
was running at only breakeven. For a partnership, the combination of break-even
operations and a large cash settlement could have been severely destabilizing, and
the history of Goldman Sachs could have been, in a word, derailed.

But that full nightmare did not develop. The firm lost less than thirty million
dollars spread over several years.

George Doty found a silver lining: "Some real good came out of it. All the
partners pulled together to work through a life-threatening situation. There were
no recriminations and no fault-finding. The firm was seriously challenged, and it
rose to the challenge. Another benefit was less obvious: Humbled and chastened
by Penn Central, Goldman Sachs avoided the disease of arrogance that did long-
term harm to other firms on Wall Street."

John Whitehead later acknowledged, "Penn Central really hurt and did real
harm to the reputation of Goldman Sachs. Naturally, we increased our controls
to prevent such events, and in particular made a clear division of responsibility
between credit approvals and client service." The firm operated for ten years
under the terms of the SEC consent decree.

Senior debt held by the firm was converted into Penn Central stock at zero
cost basis. With the firm's partners all in the 70 percent tax bracket, the loss was
partly covered by insurance and partly written off. Years later, at a much lower 25
percent capital gains tax rate, the shares regained some value and were sold, and
Goldman Sachs came out ahead. As Gus Levy laconically commented, "We may
have made some money on all this, but I can assure you, it was not the approved
method."

Daniel Pollack, attorney for the plaintiffs in the decisive New York trial,
served Foster Grant Corporation as a director. So did Gus Levy. After the trial,
Pollack was quietly advised that when his term ended at the next annual meeting
he would not be renominated.

Less than a decade later, an entrepreneurial initiative would have Goldman Sachs establishing an important relationship with the federal organization that had taken over Penn Central's railroad operations. In 1981, Mike Armellino of Goldman Sachs, Wall Street's leading railroad analyst, read an official notice in the Federal Register that Conrail would at least consider going public. This large-scale transition would involve a complex series of transactions and would provide a splendidly lucrative opportunity—if all went well—for a major Wall Street firm to act as lead underwriter. While Goldman Sachs had virtually no business record in railroad finance, other than its notorious experience as Penn Central's commercial-paper dealer, Armellino reckoned that, if the firm could get involved in an advisory capacity well in advance of any public securities offerings, it would be poised to compete for a lucrative position in any future underwriting. He wrote an internal memo recommending his idea and asking if anyone could lend a helping hand. Within days, a copy was back on his desk with a longhand comment from John Whitehead saying he knew secretary of transportation Drew Lewis quite well and would be glad to arrange an introduction.

Goldman Sachs became investment adviser to the Department of Transportation in 1982 with a team composed of Armellino, Don Gant, and Eric Dobkin, who recalls: "Winning the business? Absolutely. That was my mission in life. I *had* to win!"

In late 1986, Morgan Stanley attempted to force its way in as co-lead manager by going through Congress to get legislation requiring a reconsideration, but Transportation simply went through the motions and then chose Goldman Sachs again to lead six investment banking firms that all participated equally in the sale for $1.6 billion of 85% of Consolidated Rail Corporation—one of the largest public offerings of that era, with commissions estimated at $80 million.[27]

Though wounded by the Penn Central trials, Gus Levy soon seemed back in form. "Gus never reached his limit, never topped out, was always increasing his capacity," observes Whitehead. Doty agrees: "Gus was always changing and growing. He was still growing; his judgment was still improving—and so was his effectiveness."

8

GETTING GREAT
AT SELLING

B y the 1960s Goldman Sachs was already well along in developing one of its decisive competitive strengths—selling securities more effectively than the rest. But that strength began as a real weakness.

Although a member of the New York Stock Exchange, the firm hardly had a sales force in the thirties and forties. Half a dozen old and tired men—too old and too tired to switch to better jobs during the Depression and the war—were really just order takers, serving out time. As Bob Menschel remembers, "Institutional investors were not active in the market and were being very lightly covered by a group of older guys who sold anything and everything—stocks, bonds, convertibles, and municipals—but their approach to sales was not at all effective." In the department then called retail sales (later securities sales and later still the equities division), Goldman Sachs's weaknesses were so obvious that they presented an opportunity. As partner Ernest Loveman sardonically observed, "We're so far down, if we change at all, we *have* to rise."

At most Wall Street firms, the majority of front-office people were "family" or "money" or children of clients, and each group brought its own form of office politics and resistance to change. But for those who had little and were hungry to get ahead, even small changes could be seen as interesting possibilities. As outsiders, the people of Goldman Sachs had little to lose by taking the risks of being different.

So in the fifties, when Ray Young, widely recognized within Goldman Sachs as a great team captain, began looking for ways to develop a sales force that would concentrate on building the firm's business with the still small but rapidly growing "institutional" investors, his plans encountered little resistance.[1] By contrast, entrenched retail salesmen at many other brokerage firms greeted similar efforts with turf-protecting fights and internal squabbles that often seemed interminable.

Traditionally, the business to be had from retail brokerage customers was most definitely not controlled or "owned" by the brokerage firm. Accounts with individual investors were jealously guarded by the individual brokers who had found them, prospected them, and brought them to the firm where they happened to be working. Each broker would split the brokerage commissions generated from each of *his* accounts with whichever firm provided him the best support services, such as space, statistics, custody, executions, and record keeping—and the best deal on the commission split. The firm did not choose the broker; the broker chose the firm. If the broker could not get the deal he wanted with the firm he was at, he simply moved to another firm—and took his accounts with him.

At firms with well-established retail sales forces, a "good producer" would concentrate on his core business with traditional retail accounts—doctors, lawyers, entrepreneurs, and those who had inherited wealth. He might have a few institutional accounts—banks, insurance companies, or investment companies—where he had an in with one of the decision makers, but most institutions were house accounts that the broker could not take with him, and for these, the broker was expected to meet the institution's modest expectations for routine service and little more. He understood reality: He had no good way to increase institutions' volume of business. The typical retail broker didn't compete for a large share of the business done by the institutions he covered for his firm—he didn't have the abilities or the social acceptability to do much more than not screw up. But times were changing.

Institutional investors were getting larger and more active, and the commissions they generated were also getting larger—and larger. For their ballooning commissions, institutions wanted more service and better service, particularly thorough research on the economy, major industries, and specific companies. The traditional retail stockbroker's abilities were not competitive with the research- and service-intensive approach being taken by a new group of specialized institutional brokers.

The need for conventional brokerage firms to reorganize to compete better was real. Still, the retail broker would fight to hang on to his institutional accounts, even if he was seriously underproducing with these accounts, because their scraps of business were lucrative: The broker got 30 percent to 40 percent of the gross commissions collected by the firm. Some of the major retail firms were still fighting account by account over these turf issues twenty years later. Resolutions of these disputes were typically grudging compromises—determined by short-term political considerations but clearly not optimal for building a vibrant long-term business.

Goldman Sachs had few conflicts over who "owned" each institution because it had few retail salesmen with assigned accounts. The firm was free to organize its institutional business in the way Ray Young wanted, and Young took full advantage of this opportunity to innovate. He had all of the institutional units reporting to him—research, research sales (salesmen who merchandised the firm's research to institutions), and sales trading (salesmen who developed important relationships with institutional traders and managed their market orders).[2] "Ray really got us started," said John Weinberg appreciatively. "He was a great recruiter and trainer." While Gus Levy—with his penchant for foisting the sons of his friends onto sales—could be a problem for Young, nobody else would dare. Young was recognized as tough and absolutely straight-arrow, particularly in the management committee, where it mattered most. No matter who was in an argument, everyone in sales accepted Young's judgments. They had to. "I've heard you," Young would say. "Now, I'll tell you what we're going to do." And if facial expressions suggested Young's conclusion was not fully accepted, he would add: "You should consider immediate and total acceptance of my decision an absolute condition of employment. Period."

"Ray Young knew that in a service business, the client *always* comes first," recalls Bob Menschel's brother Dick, also a partner. "He was always explaining to us that putting the client first was always—over the long term—best for the firm and for each individual. Ray was beloved. He was scrupulously fair and non-political within the equities division and was known and trusted to be a strong advocate-representative for the division on the management committee because Gus and L. Jay both respected Ray, and everyone knew it."

R ay was all about integrity and clients," partner Lew Eisenberg recalls. "He came to my desk one day, collaring a young sales trainee, and asked: 'Is this kid with you?' I said yes, and Ray laid it on the line: 'You have one hour to decide whether he's out or he stays,' and strode away. The trainee had gotten a really good order in Allied Chemical—and then was heard taking about it in the elevator to another trainee. Ray was very clear about the rules, and rule one was that nobody *ever* talks about clients or clients' business. Half an hour later, after a very serious talk with the trainee, I told Ray my judgment was we should keep the kid. Ray called us both down to his office and asked the trainee gruffly: 'What have you learned?' The answer showed he had gotten the message: 'To keep my big mouth shut—sir.' That was acceptable to Ray—this one time." Here's how David Feinburg, who was with Goldman Sachs for the next seventeen years, recalls the same event:

"I had just graduated the training program in early 1980. Tom Tuft and I were heading to a lunch for our pharmaceutical analyst Fred Greenberg and clients in midtown (our offices were at 85 Broad Street with equities on the fourth floor at the time). Tom and I entered the elevator and ran into Fred. I said to Fred, 'Thank you for your help with New Jersey; they bought Merck through us because of your help.'

"As I was saying this I noticed Mr. Young at the back of the elevator and immediately realized I had screwed up. When the elevator reached the ground Ray pulled me aside, placed his now bright red face about two inches from mine, and started screaming at me that if he ever heard me use a client name in public again that I would be gone from the firm. The F word was used about ten times.

"I attended the lunch (in a very quiet fashion) and was called in by my boss Lew Eisenberg upon my return. He said that Ray had told him he had gone a bit hard on me, but asked if I had learned a lesson. I told him yes—and added that I would take the stairs from now on. I was quite shaken."

Young called one of his salesmen, Eric Dobkin, late one morning. "Are you going out to lunch with a client?"

"No, I'm eating at my desk."

"Come on up. I'm in town." And that's how Dobkin was told he was going to Chicago—for six years. At the end of those years Young phoned Dobkin again, again asking if he was free for lunch. "But since I'm in Chicago, he can't mean today," Dobkin recalls, "so I ask, 'What about tomorrow?' So I flew to New York City for a meeting with Ray, Richard Menschel, and Jim Timmons, who had been running the [SEC Rule] 144 restricted-stock business and was leaving the firm. They wanted me to take Jim's place. All I wanted to know was if I'd be able to make partner. 'That seat has a partner now' was all they said—and all I needed to hear."

Young was decisive, a characteristic that salespeople appreciated. He built a strong sales team partly because he really knew the business and partly because everyone knew he believed entirely in the code of loyalty up, loyalty down. "Once when I was thinking about firing a salesman," recalls partner Jim Kautz, "Ray asked me, 'Have you ever been fired?' I said no, and Ray said, 'I thought not. Always remember, when a guy gets fired, he *never* forgets it—for the rest of his life.' Ray understood salesmen and sales management and was instrumental in the firm's hiring MBAs into sales."

The strategy to build strength into sales was to get really close to the customers, looking for ways to be helpful and asking for a chance to show what Goldman Sachs could do. "If we could get a start, a foot in the door, we knew we could prove we were decent, likable guys doing business in a truly professional way," remembers Bob Menschel. "We really lived with our customers—at IDS, Fidelity, Capital Research, Dreyfus, Morgan, and the insurance companies in Hartford. Over and over again we suggested, 'Give us a try. When none of the other firms can do your trade, we believe we can. If you ever have a difficult block, we'd like a chance to show what we can do.' Many, many threads had to be found and pulled together to make the whole really work well. Goldman Sachs had very little franchise in those days, and we were always looking for an entry point. We put together a group of enthusiastic younger guys who liked the securities business, enjoyed sales, and wanted to do a professional business. Our group wanted to do everything *differently*—and started by buying out the older guys with one- and two-year guarantees of their past level of business. Then we turned our attention to building a real business, knowing we would have to do things very differently."

Harold Newman, a particularly effective salesman, adds that the people recruited into securities sales, as the department was known in the sixties, were a breed apart from the conventional stereotype of a stockbroker: "We were identified as people with standards and focus who were creative and spoke straight."

A trip to Las Vegas in 1963 was the beginning of a practice that contributed mightily to Goldman Sachs's later success: teamwork in sales. For years, a group of friends within the fledgling securities sales group had gone to Las Vegas twice every year—in March with their wives and on their own in October. Included in the group were Young and two retail salesmen, Harold Newman and David Workman. Speaking for the pair, Newman proposed to Young that they would be more productive if they could combine their efforts—with one man always in the office to take customers' orders, while the other was always out prospecting for new business—and then pool all their commissions as partners with a fifty-fifty split. "David did not like cold-calling, but I didn't mind it," recalls Newman. "But when I was out I needed someone to cover for me if one of my customers called. So our proposition was that we'd work as a team and one of us would always be in the office to take the calls while the other was always out drumming up new business."

Richard Menschel, knowing the usual problems of such an arrangement, was strongly opposed. "Conflicts will abound. You'll never work it out. The details will lead to arguments that will ruin you." But Young was game to try it. The proposition fit well with Gus Levy's dual emphasis on individual performance and teamwork—and it worked so well that more pairs of salesmen, and then larger and larger groups, were soon going "joint."

Before, each salesman had typically been on his own with a "you eat what you kill" approach to work and compensation. Bob Menschel worked out a teamwork-motivating system of compensation for institutional sales. First, Menschel got agreement from the firm that sales would get payouts of 15 percent of gross commissions. Then the group agreed that all institutional commissions would be put into one pot and each salesman on the team would get a certain percentage of the total for the year—with annual percentages reset by Menschel. Recognizing that it would be difficult to predict who the winners would be for the coming year, Menschel reserved a third of the total so he would have managerial discretion over a significant part of the pool and could reward those who did the most for the sales partnership, which grew to over forty participants. With this innovative compensation structure, "everybody focused on one thing: total gross credits," recalls Bob Menschel. "We all saw all the tickets because sales and trading sat next to each other. For the true team player, with this setup the opportunities were virtually unlimited."

While Bob Menschel developed institutional-sales teamwork through commission pooling, his brother Richard organized the high-net-worth sales force for focus. "Dick Menschel conceived of specializing in sales," recalls partner Lee Cooperman. Menschel believed in covering a specialist buyer with specialist salespeople for research or trading or convertibles or preferreds, particularly if any competitor firm had a specialist salesman covering a specialist buyer. Research sales was separate from sales traders, and listed sales traders were separate from OTC sales traders. But if five or six salespeople covered a major account, they pooled all their business and shared the total in previously agreed percentages.

Pooling commissions in partnerships became an increasingly important part of the Goldman Sachs way. Another important part of the firm's compensation was simply that Goldman Sachs salesmen were paid more. They believed they were special, took pride in their work, and knew they worked harder and for much longer hours than most competitors.

"We had very low turnover," recalls Eisenberg—usually only 5 percent a year when at other firms it was 20 percent or higher. "Some might even say our turnover was too low." But the customers did not complain. They liked continuity with highly motivated, entrepreneurial salesmen always looking for new and better ways to be helpful. The firm's typical salesman-customer relationship was well developed, comfortable, and important to both sides, while competitors' relationships were often new and still "in development." The difference was huge. Goldman Sachs was the number one stockbroker for a large majority of all institutional investors, including nearly all the largest and most active institutions.

"We were particularly focused on recruiting very smart people who really cared about and wanted to be part of a real team," says Dick Menschel. "We were thorough in our interviews, and lots of interviews were required before you could gain admittance to our team. Knowing how hard it was to get accepted, we all respected anyone who had passed the intensive screening of all those interviews. If they had passed that process successfully, we knew they belonged. And we all had staying power. Teamwork was crucial. We were always backstopping each other—and we *liked* each other. We had a passion for the business and lots of fun."

Menschel hired salesmen carefully. His screening criteria were always the same: Candidates had to be very presentable and very bright. If a candidate made it past the first round, judgments centered on one key driver: How hungry was he, how much did he need to succeed? Having some family money—in the sixties, still the first screening criterion at most firms—was not a positive at all: It was a real negative. Menschel wanted driven people, because he wanted a driven sales organization that would accept his strict discipline.

In 1968, when ten million shares of trading volume was a good day on the NYSE and a block cross of ten or twenty thousand shares would certainly be the event of the day, Eisenberg got a call from an excited trader at a major institution in Hartford with an outsize order: Sell fifty thousand shares of American Cyanamid!

Quickly, Eisenberg, Bob Mnuchin, Ray Young, and Gus Levy huddled and decided to position the block at a price half a point below the market. They made their bid, and the institutional trader, clearly pleased, said, "Print it." As the trade showed on the tape, Eisenberg felt a wave of private pleasure. A few minutes later, Gus Levy came by and silently patted Eisenberg's back. Ray Young took the new hero out to lunch, a rare and therefore significant sign of celebration.

All very satisfying. But not to last.

Returning to his station after lunch, Eisenberg found twenty pink message slips—all from the same institution's trader. Eisenberg called. The trader blurted out: "You're not gonna believe this. I'm virtually certain to get fired. I messed up on that order. It was not an order to sell. The order was to *buy*. And if you think that's bad, here's what's really bad: I added a zero. It was for five thousand shares, not fifty thousand!"

Eisenberg slumped in his seat, astounded. He had to tell Levy right away. But tell him what? As he moved to Levy's dark-glass cubicle, he knew he'd have to tell it straight. "Gus, there's a terrible problem. There was an error on that big trade."

"Whose error?"

"The account's. The order was totally incorrect."

By this time, the market price of the stock had moved up one and a half points, or more than seventy-five thousand dollars.

"How well do you know him? Is he stupid or a crook?"

"Gus, I believe the guy simply made a dreadful blunder—a straight-out, *very big* mistake."

"Okay. Then we're gonna make him into a very good client of ours. We'll take the error. The loss is ours."

Eisenberg assumed his career was virtually over and was thinking how to tell his wife that night. But he was wonderfully wrong. Within a week, the institutional trader and his boss were taking Eisenberg to lunch to thank him: "You and Goldman Sachs have shown us the utmost professionalism. And we will demonstrate our appreciation to you by being a very major client of Goldman Sachs for a long, long time." The institution proved true to their word.

Speaking of Levy, Young, and their sales teams, Al Feld says, "They weren't gods; they were only human. But when push came to shove, they would always do what was *really* right." Leaders are known by two things: the people they hire and bring together and the beliefs they hold to when they really have to choose. You only know what a person *really* believes in when he chooses to do something even though it costs him—because he really believes it's the right thing to do.

When Ray Young retired in the seventies, Dick Menschel took over sales management.[3] There were no middle managers: Everybody in sales reported directly to Menschel, who had exact knowledge of each salesman, his accounts, and his standing at each account. "Menschel was a motivating mentor," recalls partner Bill Landreth, "precise in his memory of specific details. He insisted that every memo have the correct middle initial of both the writer and the addressee. It might have just been another dimension of his controlling style, but we all believe *he* believed it showed greater respect."

While every other firm worked to maximize cooperation between sales and trading, at Goldman Sachs securities sales was separate from trading because Dick

Menschel and Bob Mnuchin couldn't get along. Their personalities and their ways of working were just too different. Menschel was all about process and the value of details, facts, and accuracy, while Mnuchin was disruptive and often deceptive. As one partner explained, "Dick never allowed any swearing or funny business, while Bob ran a locker room, where guys played games, and cursed the stars." For management committee meetings, Menschel would prepare meticulously for six to eight hours and arrive with a series of rigorous questions about details; Mnuchin would come to the meetings with his copy of the preparation papers still unopened and, perhaps just to twit Menschel, would deliberately make a show of opening them for the first time at the meeting table. Menschel kept careful records of his personal expenses, while the firm's bookkeepers couldn't close their accounts because Mnuchin had several paychecks shoved inside his desk drawer uncashed.[4]

By the 1970s Dick Menschel had further differentiated Goldman Sachs's sales operation from the pack by developing a comprehensive training program. New salespeople rotated through all the firm's business units for on-the-job training, with formal sales training sessions twice every week. Cases and role-playing were used, and the sessions were taped. The whole group would critique each trainee's performance. It was fun and professional. Training ran for six or seven months, with retraining required every five years. Starting with a dozen trainees in the early seventies, the program peaked with nearly forty in the late eighties, then dialed back to two dozen in the early years of the new century, when changes in the markets reduced the need. Scheduled from 5:30 to 7:30 p.m., always on Friday night, New York's major social evening, the sessions invariably started late, usually around six or six thirty, and then ran until eight or eight thirty. Menschel was then single, so he was okay with running late, but others had waiting families and dinner commitments. Most students thought running late was deliberate—another way to test each person's determination to master the business and show deep commitment to the firm.

Addressing a large group of trainees, partner Roy Zuckerberg once asked: "Are you bullish on the market—or bearish?" As he went around the room, calling on one after another of the trainees, each gave his answer to the question. Some were bullish, some were bearish—all with good, sometimes complex reasons. Finally, he called on a Japanese trainee who was so exhausted from his flight in from Tokyo that he was unable to keep from dozing off in class. Zuckerberg's questioning gaze focused on the trainee as his neighbors poked him awake. Still groggy, he blurted out: "I'm bullish. I'm always bullish."

"Right!" exclaimed Zuckerberg. "In the securities business there's only *one* way to be—and that's bullish! *Always* bullish."

The main feature of each week's Friday session was role-playing with intensively critiqued mock presentations to prospects or customers—with Menschel or Zuckerberg pretending to be the hypothetical customer and asking all sorts of difficult questions. Some questions were information difficult; some were personality difficult; some were policy difficult—and some were difficult in multiple ways. As Bill Landreth recalls, "If Menschel and Zuckerberg were taking sadistic delight in torturing their students, they couldn't have made the experience more challenging—or more educational."

Menschel, pretending to be a big fund manager, would give a role-playing final exam. The sales trainee would come into his office, tell him what stock he was going to recommend, and launch into a sales pitch. After five minutes—when the salesman might be just one-third of his way through his presentation—Menschel might cut in and say, "That's wonderful. Really interesting. You've done a great job of research. I'm really interested. Why don't you buy me ten thousand shares?"

If the trainee wrote that order down on his order pad and returned to giving his presentation—no matter how brilliant and articulate—he would get a failing grade. Why? Because he had already gotten the order and was now, by continuing to talk on *after* getting the order, running the risk of perhaps saying something that might unravel the buyer's conviction. If that happened, there would be no sale: The salesman would have "bought it back."

In a typical role-playing session, Zuckerberg would be on the phone, with everyone in the training program listening in. One night, the student salesman whose assignment was to convert this prospect into a new customer for the firm had been kept in the training program for more than the usual six months, so he felt strong pressure to finally "make it" by showing he had developed the skills and competence to pass the test and get going on his career.

Zuckerberg's hypothetical prospect was typical: a man in his early sixties who owned a small but profitable business—in this case, a nursery for residential landscaping. The pitch was also typical: Goldman Sachs is an unusually capable organization with many capabilities, enjoys considerable stature within the industry and an outstanding reputation, and is interested in helping this particular prospect build his net worth through investments. The firm wants to build an important relationship with this man, so the salesman wants to know how best to be helpful now so they can get started working together.

The trainee was determined to achieve a win-win with this prospect and had been doing well in the early minutes of the call, so Zuckerberg picked up the pace and the challenge.

"Young man, you say you really want to help me do well, is that right?"

"Yes sir! We at Goldman Sachs want to work *for* you and *with* you. We want to help you do well—*very* well, sir!"

"You know my business is growing fine shrubs and trees for residential landscaping?"

"Yes, sir."

"And you'd like—your firm would like—to help me. Right?"

"Yes, sir. We want to help *you*."

"Well, I know one way you can help me—even while I'm helping you. Are you interested in helping me help you?"

"Yes, sir!"

"Good. Here's our plan. You send me a list of your senior people with their home addresses and phone numbers and then I'll call and tell them what we can do to help them make their homes truly beautiful. This will be good for them—and, as you say, will help us too. Okay?"

"Yes, sir!"

Buzz! Buzz! Buzz! "You failed! You got it *all* wrong! You're on the phone for *one* reason—and *only* one reason! Sell securities! You dumb schmuck, you're not supposed to *buy* anything—and certainly not supposed to set up the partners of the firm as prospects for some goddamn *plant* salesman by giving away their home phone numbers and addresses! How dumb *are* you? Class dismissed!"

Delaware Management was one of the largest and most active institutional accounts in Philadelphia when Eric Dobkin was assigned in the late sixties to see what could be done to increase Goldman Sachs's share of its business. Knowing that the people at Delaware already thought well of Goldman Sachs, Dobkin needed to find a specific lever to increase the firm's business significantly, so he made an appointment to see John Durham, Delaware's top portfolio manager, after the NYSE's close and asked him what should be done to earn more business. Durham answered, "Tell me your best research ideas."

"I'll do that—and I'll do even better," replied Dobkin. "After the close each day, I'll call you with a complete—and unique—rundown on which stocks are being bought and sold by the really smart institutional fund managers."

"Call and Stephanie will put you through."

"For the next ten days," recalls Dobkin, "I called and Stephanie put me through. I gave Durham the rundown on what the major institutions were doing, but there were no direct responses to anything I'd been saying. So, to move forward, I asked very respectfully, 'How am I doing?'"

'Fine.'

'So John, what are *you* doing?'

Click. Durham hung up.

"I was obviously wasting time and getting nowhere," recalls Dobkin. "I needed a different approach. So I studied the Delaware Fund prospectus and its list of stockholdings and put myself in Durham's position, trying to guess what he might be buying or selling."

Dobkin calculated that if he could give Mnuchin a good indication of what Durham might be buying or selling, Mnuchin would give him five thousand or ten thousand shares to work with. If Durham took the bait, Goldman Sachs would know which way Durham was moving, so the firm could go out to find the other side and create some sizable block-trading business. "I gave Mnuchin my best sense of what Durham was doing. Bob enjoyed playing cat and mouse, and pretty quickly we created better and better trading volume with Durham, and the classic more-the-more phenomenon [the more business you do, the more business you get] took hold and our commission volume really took off. We did increasing business in blocks, options, converts, and we were soon number one across the board for Durham and Delaware."

On another occasion, Goldman Sachs had "positioned" a two-hundred-thousand-share block—over eight million dollars' worth—of a Midwest utility's thinly traded stock and had found only one institution that might be a buyer of that much: Delaware. But Delaware's trader was not ready to pay the price. Gus Levy was convinced it was the right price. They were only an eighth of a point away from a cross, but each side was waiting for the other to move. Gene Mercy was on the call and was feeling the pressure coming from Levy. Mercy decided to take a risk and go over the trader's head and speak with John Durham.

"John, we've done a lot of trades together over the years. In putting them together, I've come your way when you needed some help. Do I have any chits that I might call in?"

"Probably."

"Okay. I need you to come up an eighth on this utility block, John."

Pause.

"Okay."

Gus Levy *almost* smiled and *almost* said something.

I n 1979 Mnuchin and Dobkin developed a new niche product—debt-equity swaps—and did a lot of business. "Then we invented installment sales, which became a very big business for the firm. With a forty-nine-percent tax rate on short-term capital gains, when a takeover involved a cash tender offer the install-ment sale enabled the selling shareholder to defer the date on which the IRS recognized his gain, so he got a lower tax rate. This arrangement was a very easy service to sell, and we usually knew which investors to go after. We went around to all the best law firms, explaining exactly how it worked, so they would bring us any potential customers we'd missed. We met many interesting people and inter-esting families—when [former deputy secretary of defense] Paul Nitze's family sold the Aspen ski resort we 'installed' their sale. In our best year, installment sales accounted for a full three percent of the firm's total earnings and was a very good feeder of extra business for PCS [Private Client Services]."

Being *a* broker, even a major broker, is not comparable to being the number one broker for a major institutional account. Over and over again, the typical large institutional investor does about 12 percent or 13 percent of its total com-mission business with its number one broker, 10 percent with number two, and 8 percent with number three. If Goldman Sachs focused all its skills and energy on being number one while other major competitors averaged third or fourth rank, the firm would generate a full 50 percent more business—at a much higher profit margin because its costs were nearly the same as the competitors'. And in trading, "them as gots, gits," so even in one of the most open and competitive free markets in the world, it would be possible to build up a defensible and sustainable competitive advantage. Goldman Sachs's continuity of sales coverage and superior sales skills enabled it to be number one broker for many, many institutions that grew larger and larger in terms of assets under management and commissions generated. As in every service business, continuity and strong relationships matter.

That's not all. Goldman Sachs decided in the eighties to focus on the giant accounts—the one hundred largest accounts in the world. This was not as narrow a focus as it might seem at first. In the United States the fifty largest institutions now execute 50 percent of all the trades on the New York Stock Exchange and an even larger proportion of the equally large volume, in underlying dollar value, traded each day on the Chicago Board Options Exchange. And these same giant accounts are even more important in the distribution of new-issue underwritings.

Not all the largest accounts were in America. One was in the Middle East. In London, Bill Landreth was in an important telephone conversation with David Buchan of the Kuwait Investment Office, and Buchman could hear Mnuchin on Landreth's SS1 squawk box in the background.

"Bill, what was Bob talking about?"

"We have a big sell order in GE. It's for 750,000 shares."

"Bill, is it for sale at the market?"

"Yes."

"Bill, we'll take it."

That meant a perfect cross—with Goldman Sachs dealing for both buyer and seller and earning commissions on both the buy order and the sell order. That meant commissions on 1.5 *million* shares of stock. In market value, it was the biggest trade ever done—with no capital and no risk. Right people, right place, right time. Stars and moon in alignment. All within minutes. For Mnuchin, it was just too much. The iron man was blown away. He had to get an explicit confirmation: "Bill, I'm calling you right away on a secure line. Be ready for my call."

Kuwait Investment Office soon became a major account. "They were good traders—and good buyers," remembers Landreth. They were great clients, too. Kuwait helped save Goldman Sachs from what could have been one of its worst embarrassments. When Landreth offered to introduce the bizarre British publisher Robert Maxwell—who was doing a lot of trading—Kuwait Investment Office executives had no doubts. No doubts at all. "No deal, Bill. We won't work with that man or his company. Period. Ever." Later Kuwait Investment more directly helped Goldman Sachs by buying a major position the firm had gotten stuck with in underwriting British Petroleum.

B ill Landreth got a call late one night in 1979—just before midnight. "Bill, this is important. Very important. You'll have to trust me because I'm absolutely sworn to secrecy—so trust me and get dressed and come *now* to Heathrow Airport. I'll give you the exact address. It's the strictly confidential location of a safe house. And, Bill, come alone."

Landreth dressed, got in his car, and drove through the nearly empty streets of London to the area near Heathrow and the safe-house address he'd been given. Bodyguards were obviously everywhere. Landreth was patted down and taken inside and into what was clearly a very private room. Through another door, a slim man of average stature in a well-tailored suit entered: a representative of the shah of Iran. "The shah is going to sell his entire portfolio of U.S. stocks—for immediate cash payment. The certificates are held in custody at a major Swiss bank. Knowing this is an unusual transaction, I am prepared to accept a thirty-percent discount from the market. Will Goldman Sachs bid for this 'cash now' portfolio transaction?"

"I understand the question," Landreth replied, "but before I can give you an answer for my firm, I'll need to speak with my partners in New York. May I use a phone?" It was already past 7 p.m. in New York, but people were still in the Goldman Sachs trading room, attending to details of the day's trading and preparing for the coming day's activity. Fortunately, Bob Mnuchin was still there.

Landreth spoke with Mnuchin. The appeal was obvious: At a 30 percent discount, Goldman Sachs could buy a hundred-million-dollar portfolio of diversified blue chip stocks and sell them as blocks at prices sure to be more than 40 percent above the early morning bid. The firm could make over twenty-five million dollars!

The reward was clear—but so was the risk. In a few days, the shah would not be the shah anymore. Ayatollah Khomeini would be in authority, with ample power to present extraordinary nonfinancial risks—like explosives in Goldman Sachs offices or cars or homes. Too much "specific" risk. So the decision became obvious: pass. It was the first and only time Goldman Sachs refused to bid on a record-breaking trade. If any other firm took on the trade, the news stayed secret.

During the late 1980s and early 1990s, the equities division was a major contributor to the firm's profits, but with competition continuously pressuring commission rates down to lower and lower levels and costs rising and electronic trading networks taking larger and larger shares of the available business, division profitability would fade away. During the golden years of institutional stockbrokerage, however, the firm had made the most of its opportunities.

9

BLOCK TRADING

THE RISKY BUSINESS

THAT ROARED

Bob Mnuchin took the call one morning in January 1976—the most important call any block trader had ever taken: a one-billion-dollar order that confirmed Goldman Sachs's leadership in block trading. The firm was being asked to execute the largest block-trading operation in history.

The head of New York City's pension fund[1] had decided to convert a five-hundred-million-dollar portfolio of common stocks into a specific portfolio of stocks that would replicate the stock market—an index fund. This massive change required five hundred million dollars of stock sales and another five hundred million dollars of stock purchases. Goldman Sachs would have to bid a single price to buy the whole portfolio and create the exact new portfolio the city's pension fund manager specified—and to do so not as an agent, but as an "at risk" principal.

The firm would commit to a total exposure of half a billion dollars. A principal trade this big obviously had to have the approval of the management committee, so Mnuchin and his team went, prepared for a thousand questions. "They asked only five questions," remembers Mnuchin. "And each question was laser-like in its focus on a key trading factor. We answered the five questions and there was a moment of silence and then everyone agreed. It was a go!"

With large yellow pads, Mnuchin and his team worked the whole weekend with price charts, recent research reports, and all their years of market trading experience, plus all the bits and pieces of information they could pull together about what each of dozens of major investing institutions might be willing to buy or sell. "Then we had a plan."

Starting with closing prices on February 4, Goldman Sachs guaranteed the pension fund that the maximum total cost of executing trades of nearly twenty-five million shares would not exceed $5.8 million—including the risk of paying more for purchases or getting less on sales than the closing prices on February 4.

"Wall Street is a very small community," says Mnuchin. "[Normally] you can't make a major move without everyone knowing it. It was so very big, it was like everyone at a World Series game getting up and leaving Yankee Stadium in the second inning—and nobody noticing anything." To avoid being noticed—particularly by competitor firms—Mnuchin and his team worked out a careful strategy. As Mnuchin recalls: "We agreed we would be active every day—no matter what—and that we'd never let the total buying and total selling get separated by more than $5 million. Security was obviously essential—any leaks and the other brokers would trade ahead of us—so a code name was used: Operation Eagle. Small blocks of at least some holdings were sold every day, but for each particular stock, the firm was active one day and then quiet for two or three days. One block of 330,000 shares was sold in seventy-eight separate lots, of one hundred to thirteen thousand shares. Over five weeks, twelve million shares in fifty-two positions were sold and 231 positions purchased in Operation Eagle."

When the last trade was finally executed, Mnuchin picked up the hotline phone to announce, "Eagle has landed." In mid-March, New York City's pension fund announced that Goldman Sachs had secretly finished executing the largest-ever purchase and sale of stocks. The final cost to the New York City pension system for transactions totaling one billion dollars was only $2.9 million—less than one-third of 1 percent—for the largest and one of the most complicated trades in history and an apt demonstration of Goldman Sachs's prowess in block trading.[2]

Most major securities firms shunned block trading. Indeed, they didn't understand and didn't like the whole institutional business, for several reasons. The leading and most active institutional investors were young, irreverent, well dressed, and well educated—admiringly dubbed a new breed on Wall Street—with limited respect for people they considered old fogies or for the traditional hierar-chy of Wall Street. These newcomers wanted new and different services that were expensive to produce, such as in-depth investment research on all sorts of com-panies and industries, and they wanted much more sophisticated sales attention than most firms were willing to provide, especially to MBAs they considered too young, too irreverent, too well dressed, and too overpaid.

Among the many services these young new-breed fund managers wanted, block trading seemed surely a sucker's game. The "money" partners at most firms saw no reason whatsoever to get involved in such a certain money loser. They were *agency* brokers and underwriters, not risk-taking *principal* market makers and dealers. Buying what smart institutional investors wanted to sell was danger-ous: The sellers might know something important. Why take a big risk that the stock really should be sold? And why tie up the firm's limited capital buying and holding, for *days* or *weeks*, big blocks of stock that nobody wanted? Most firms had no interest in the trading business, and buying big, dangerous blocks from aggressive young hotshot institutional investors looked like the worst bet of all. The august partners didn't do trading themselves and looked down on their firms' traders as mere employees. Why should they entrust their family wealth to a mere trader—someone they would never take home for dinner?

As Bob Menschel explained, "Bobby Lehman had the capital at Lehman Brothers, but he could not live comfortably with having his personal fortune put at risk by somebody else, particularly by one of his *employees*—and all the traders were just employees. In block trading, the money must not know who owns it. You can't afford to be too personally involved, particularly in an emotional way, any more than a surgeon should ever operate on his own children. Block trading is a business: It requires lots of rational business decisions being made in a very nonemotional, businesslike way."

At the New York Stock Exchange, commission rates had always been set in terms of one-hundred-share "round lot" transactions with fixed rates per one hundred shares that varied only with the share price.[3] Commission rates were set, naturally enough, at levels considered appropriate for a *retail* stockbrokerage busi-ness, because retail activity had always dominated the stock market. Daily volume averaged less than one million shares through the 1930s and 1940s and just over one million shares a day in the 1950s. Overall, commissions covered a securities firm's costs. All the profits came from underwriting new issues. During the Depression and World War II there was little underwriting, so firms had learned how to avoid all unnecessary costs. The demands of serving institutional investors—particularly block trading—appeared to bring *very* unnecessary costs.

Then, in the 1950s, the stockbrokers' world began to change. The profile of the "typical" investor was changing, from the moderately affluent individual investor occasionally buying or selling a few shares through his retail stockbroker to the continuously active, professional institutional investor who was active in the market all the time, buying and selling positions in dozens of different stocks every day. Because the institutional investors were growing and managing portfolios more intensively, the volume and price of trading increased again and again. In 1960, NYSE daily volume averaged nearly two million shares. By the end of the decade, average daily volume doubled to four million shares as institutional investors, competing for "performance," increased their buying and selling. Daily volume growth continued to expand, reaching 1.5 billion shares a day in 2007—one thousand times the volume fifty years earlier.

Institutional investors were and are very different from individual investors. Their decisions are much larger. Orders are not for one hundred shares, but for one hundred *thousand* shares—and they want to execute their large transactions quickly and at a definite price. Their new demand produced an opportunity for Goldman Sachs and a few other firms that were led by aggressive, experienced traders to create a whole new kind of business: block trading.

When a portfolio manager wanted to sell fifty thousand or a hundred thousand shares of a particular stock to raise cash to pay for another, more promising stock, he contacted one of his major stockbrokers (who were getting well paid—often more than a million dollars in commissions every year—for executing the institution's high-commission, risk-free agency orders). If the block-trading stockbroker could not find the other side for an agency trade, he would be expected to buy or "position" the block with the firm's own money and take the risk of a sudden trading loss.[4]

Block trading was clearly risky business, because the institutions had reasons to sell—often compelling factual reasons such as a company's serious earnings shortfall. If the selling institution had just found out about a real problem and got out slightly ahead of the crowd by selling a block to a Wall Street firm, everyone knew that other institutions would soon learn the same bad news and become sellers too. The price of that block might suddenly drop, so the pain of loss on a "positioned" block of stock could be sudden and awful. As long as no buyers were found, the firm's capital would be tied up, which could put the firm, at least temporarily, out of the trading business. As Dick Menschel explained, "The merchandise has to be moved swiftly. Otherwise, it ties up your capital, which means you're out of the business flow until you get liquid again. But also, tired merchandise can go rotten awfully fast and cause big losses."

Time clearly is money in block trading. If firm A doesn't "create" a trade very quickly, firm B or firm C or D will try to steal the trade away. With high fixed-rate commissions, the incentives were powerful. A broker with an order to sell ten thousand shares of a typical stock would earn a commission of forty cents a share, or four thousand dollars for the block. For one hundred thousand shares, the commissions were forty thousand dollars. If the broker was able to find a willing buyer and execute the trade as a cross—acting for both buyer and seller, he'd earn the commission on both the buy side and the sell side—they were a total of eighty thousand dollars. If a firm could execute a single hundred-thousand-share cross every trading day for a year, the extra annual revenues would be twenty million dollars, with little or no incremental costs. Adding two such crosses would add forty million dollars. Adding one 250,000-share cross each day would add fifty million dollars. As Senator Everett Dirksen might have said, "Pretty soon you're talking real money."

"Gus stands out as a real innovator in block trading," says Dick Menschel. "Gus was well positioned to do this for two important reasons: He knew the arts of successfully 'positioning' blocks through his experiences with block trades and taking on positions when running arbitrage, and he knew the skills needed for what we now call the capital markets business—who owned and might sell; who might buy and why; how the market did work and could work; and how to develop others' trust so he could 'make it happen' on specific trades." From 1955 to 1965, Goldman Sachs had had almost no competition in block trading. Levy worried about other firms getting into the business. As one way to keep competition away, Goldman Sachs partners would often bemoan publicly how tough and costly the block-trading business could be—and never acknowledged how profitable it really was. Meanwhile, Levy was bolder and more aggressive than any other block trader. As his friend I. W. "Tubby" Burnham would recall, "Gus was making markets for far bigger blocks than any other firm. Gus liked and understood risk."

The "secret sauce" of the block trading business was to attract the business by developing a reputation for having capital and being ready to commit it to position blocks of stock whenever an institution wanted to sell, while at the same time not using the firm's own capital. It was often possible to find the other side of a pure agency trade, usually within hours and often within minutes, by being constantly in touch with all the potential buyers. The risk-control imperatives for success in the business of block trading were clear. First, buy blocks only from institutional traders whom the broker could trust to treat his firm fairly and who, if the position nose-dived, would make up a firm's losses by doing extra business later. Second, be able to resell blocks *very* quickly so the inventory kept turning over. Ideally, business would be attracted by the availability of capital and would be priced as a risk-taking *principal* trade but then executed quickly as a no-risk *agency* trade.

The keys to swift reselling were market information and close client contacts at all the major institutions. In addition to a sales team that could quickly man the phones, searching among dozens of institutions across the country for potential buyers, Goldman Sachs also needed a systematic way of knowing who was about to become a buyer and how to encourage potential buyers to "get real" and take action. A firm that is known to have the *sellers* will attract the buyers, and a firm known to have the *buyers* will attract the sellers. In market making, business begets business. And perception matters greatly: If the important buyers and sellers perceive that a particular firm is the place to go, that firm will have the decisive competitive advantage of getting the first calls. If a firm gets the first calls, particularly the first calls on important blocks, that firm's reputation as the go-to firm goes up and up.

Block traders worked to develop "the other side" with the NYSE floor specialists by inviting specialists, who regularly made markets of a few hundred shares for the traditional retail investor, to participate in larger institutional blocks for, say, one thousand or five thousand shares. Block traders also worked with floor traders (exchange members who roamed the NYSE trading floor, "taking the other side" when an excess volume of either buying or selling temporarily distorted the market) by welcoming them to make a market in that stock for that trader.

To become that go-to central clearing firm for buying and selling, a wide-ranging communications network of good, active contacts is essential. The quality of contacts is measured by the institutions' speed in taking a particular firm's calls and their willingness to show trust by opening up and talking about what they are doing or might be doing. The other key factor is the ability to influence *potential* buyers (or sellers) to commit to action now. The best way to reduce the risk of getting caught with a block that can't be moved is to increase the order flow—the volume of buying and selling that the firm sees and can participate in. The best way to increase Goldman Sachs's order flow was to develop superior service relationships with the traders and portfolio managers at the major institutions and convince them that Goldman Sachs was the go-to firm for block trading—that Goldman Sachs would provide the most help when an institutional trader needed to sell a particularly difficult block of stock. "Somehow, it all came together," says Mnuchin. "A group of really quite extraordinary people of great talent at a time when the basic nature of the business was changing very rapidly. Teamwork. Working together. Focusing on customer needs and how to solve *their* problems. That's what we were all about in Trading." Teamwork at Goldman Sachs was becoming a whole-firm phenomenon. As partner Gene Mercy explains, "We did trades the desk didn't want to do because a salesman had been working on a particular customer for weeks, and this was our first chance to show what the *firm* could really do."

Levy drove Goldman Sachs to be the dominant firm in institutional block trading, creating supply or demand or both to trade ever larger blocks of stock—ten thousand shares, fifty thousand, and more. Levy organized, inspired, and drove the firm's sales traders to develop the closest working relationships with every major institution's senior traders and to make more calls more quickly to more customers than any other firm. Goldman Sachs matched this effective service organization by committing its own capital to buy or sell millions of dollars of almost any stock to match supply and demand and "do the trade, get the business."

Levy rose to prominence on Wall Street as block trading emerged from being just an offbeat occasional specialty into being the most important part of the institutional stockbrokerage business. During the 1960s and 1970s, block trading gathered momentum as mutual funds and pension funds grew rapidly in assets, shifted the mix of their ballooning portfolios toward equities, and increased the speed of portfolio turnover in their accelerating competition to achieve superior investment performance. The rapidly expanding business of block trading was concentrated with the few stockbrokers who were willing to take risks by using their firm's own capital to "take the other side," buying what institutions most wanted to sell or selling what institutions most wanted to buy.

Still, block-trading risk takers were unusual on Wall Street. Most Wall Streeters kept thinking of the trading business in one historically valid but increasingly obsolete way: Every trade was separate from every other trade; nobody owed anybody any favors; *caveat emptor* and *caveat vendor*. If an institutional seller came to a dealer looking for a bid, the dealer and the account both knew they were adversaries in a zero-sum game—just as they are today in commodities, fixed-income securities, currencies, and derivatives. Most Wall Street firms were so used to thinking of their business in this day-by-day and trade-by-trade way that they were unable to see the business that could be developed by combining intensive service with risking capital and accepting occasional losses as a necessary cost of developing profitable long-term relationships with the major institutions' senior traders. Nor did they understand that executing a large, repetitive share of each institution's continuous and increasing flow of commission business would, over weeks and months, earn large profits. The institutions' senior traders needed the block-trading firms to satisfy their portfolio managers' liquidity requirements, and only a few firms could and would provide that liquidity consistently.

Levy's unrelenting drive to do the business—*all* the business—was so intense that customers would actually commiserate with the Goldman Sachs traders and salesmen covering them, crying and laughing together at the intense pressure Levy put them under. One example of the fun to be had was a cross-stitched "sampler" that Bob Menschel had made up, framed, and placed prominently in the institutional sales department adjacent to the trading room:

A 250,000 SHARE
BLOCK A DAY
WILL KEEP GUS LEVY
AWAY

A thousand copies were made up and sent out to clients. Hundreds of clients proudly put them on the walls of their trading rooms all across the country.

With such incentives, as more and more shares were traded in blocks, all the block traders made special efforts to develop close relationships with the institutions' senior traders, flying to Boston for dinner at Locke-Ober's or to Chicago for hockey or basketball games or going fishing, golfing, or skiing—and always by calling and calling and calling, sometimes calling the same buy-side trader at an institution fifty or more times in a single day. Soon hotline direct wires were installed at the institutions' trading desks, connected directly to the trading desk at Goldman Sachs. Having hotlines became so important that one institutional portfolio manager managed trading relationships with masking tape—taping over the lines of block-trading firms he thought were underperforming.

Gus Levy made markets for bigger blocks than any other trader because he understood risk and liked taking risks. Goldman Sachs's main rival as king of the hill in block trading was Bear Stearns. Sy Lewis, managing partner of Bear Stearns and a fierce competitor in block trading, was Gus Levy's personal rival and personal friend. Both men were determined to win the competition—and winning was not just a matter of pride. They were competing for control of a big, profitable business. Just as Olympic gold medals are often won by differences of less than a tenth of a second, small differences between block-trading firms were often decisive. That's why Levy was unrelenting in his pursuit of every possible piece of business. "God forbid you missed a trade and Bear Stearns got it," remembers partner David Silfen, "because Gus knew he'd be playing golf on Saturday with Sy Lewis, and Gus didn't want any razzing from Sy or from the others in their group." Nor did he want any razzing from his partners about taking losses in block trading.

When the firm incurred trading losses early one year, Levy told *Institutional Investor*, "The only reason we ran in the red any month was not because of normal business, but because of inventory losses. And that's the nature of this business. If you're in the dealing business, you know you have to lose some money sometimes. It's not major; in fact, it's very *un*major. I think we've learned a lesson. We're not going to be so high, wide, and handsome next time. This means we will turn our inventory, or try to turn it, quicker. We aren't going to play wishful thinking. There is an adage, and it still holds true on Wall Street: something well bought is half sold. That's the trick of the trade." Within the firm Levy made it even clearer: "A good trader eats like a canary and shits like an elephant."

Competition between stockbrokers developed in two ways of particular importance to the largest and most active institutions: research and trading. Research was increasingly important to the institutions. While most individual investors' buying and selling were primarily "informationless" trades occasioned by nonmarket events such as receiving a bonus or an inheritance or needing money to buy a house or pay college tuition, the institutional investors were in the market every day buying and selling shares. They based their trades on the relative attractiveness of the stocks they owned versus stocks they were considering, so they wanted to be well informed about what they might buy or sell and why. They demanded accurate, detailed, up-to-the-minute information and shrewd analysis of important trends that could affect a company's future earnings.

In addition to courting the institutions' senior traders, Goldman Sachs and the other block-trading firms made direct contact with the portfolio managers, who told the senior traders what they wanted to buy or sell. At the same time, to serve the institutional investors' needs for information and knowledge, a new group of "research" brokerage firms built their business with a heavy emphasis on in-depth investment research communicated through long, detailed reports, conferences, telephone calls, and personal visits by their expert analysts. Their research enabled the best of these brokers to gain market share in the rising tide of institutional transactions. Still, the best competitive position was to have strength in both research and trading. And that's what Levy insisted on at Goldman Sachs, so it became the leading institutional stockbroker.

Levy worried that other firms, particularly Salomon Brothers, with its bold, risk-taking trading reputation in bonds, would muscle in on his lucrative block-trading business in stocks. His fears were realized in the seventies. "When Billy Salomon decided to learn the equity block-trading business," recalls Bob Menschel, "he offered to put up the capital to take on half of all our positions. We all knew that meant Solly was going to get into the stock business with the same competitive intensity they were showing in the bond business. But, as I told Gus, 'He will do this with somebody, so why not with us for now?' So we were soon in business together."

Levy wanted "all our share" (and he really saw no need for the second and third words in that short phrase) of the ballooning institutional business, so he took three bold initiatives. First, Goldman Sachs would allow any institution to allocate all or part of the total commissions on a trade executed by Goldman Sachs as a "give-up"—paid by the firm's check to another broker for its research.[5] This shielded institutions from pressure to trade blocks through research brokers to pay for their research services, or to compensate retail brokers for selling mutual funds, or to compensate the brokerage firms for maintaining large bank balances with them. It also discouraged research firms from developing block-trading skills and becoming direct competitors.

"When give-ups came along, other firms fought it," recalls Menschel. "We accepted reality, saying 'So be it,' and sought to make the best of it, welcoming the chance to do the trades and then sending out the give-up checks to other brokers. We were confident that if we executed the trades, we would maximize our breadth of inquiry [the future trades that would come to Goldman Sachs first]." While the rates at which brokerage commissions were charged were fixed by the stock exchange, the proportion that would be given up was fully negotiable. Years later, the commissions themselves would be made negotiable.

Second, Goldman Sachs would commit large amounts of its own capital to position blocks of stock that the institutions wanted to sell, accepting the inventory risk of buying the unwanted block before other institutional buyers could be found or rounded up, and before competing brokers could jump in and "steal the bacon." Levy's team would work the phones, urgently striving to find potential buyers and bringing them to the point of decision so the positioned block could be resold. With Levy's driving leadership, with thirty million to forty million dollars of firm capital made available for positioning blocks, and with an extraordinarily effective sales organization covering all the active institutions, Goldman Sachs set record after record for giant trades. In October 1967, Levy traded at the close of trading a block of 1,153,700 shares of Alcan Aluminum at twenty-three dollars, off 1⅛ from the previous trade. Valued at $26.5 million, it was the largest trade that had ever been done. On one day in 1971, Goldman Sachs did ten blocks of seventy-five thousand shares or more, including four over two hundred thousand shares; that year, largely on the strength of block trading, the firm earned record net income. In 1976 it traded over one hundred million shares in blocks on the NYSE.

"In evaluating leaders," says Dick Menschel, "the central question has to be 'Who made a difference?' and on this criterion, Gus Levy stands out as a real innovator in developing the business of block trading." Levy and his key lieutenants had that unstoppable drive to build a major, very profitable business, and they built the organization that would do it. One part of that firmwide focus was the buildup of research, but research was always a means to better trading, not an end in itself.

Levy insisted his salespeople make frequent direct contact with the portfolio managers and analysts who originated investment decisions that the traders executed. The question was how? The answer was investment research, but not the research on "interesting small companies" in which Goldman's research department had specialized under partner Bob Danforth, looking for investment ideas for the partners' personal accounts. Research had to focus on the major public companies, the ones most of the major institutions owned most and traded most.

Already, portfolio managers at Levy's largest trading accounts—Dreyfus, Fidelity, J.P. Morgan, and State Street—were pointing out that Goldman Sachs was their largest broker, often doing as much as 15 percent of their total brokerage business, but was not providing anything like an equal portion of the investment research they needed on large corporations. If Goldman Sachs didn't change and become far more helpful in research on major companies, Levy's largest accounts bluntly told him, Goldman Sachs would not continue doing nearly so much of their trading business. They would cut him back—way back.

Levy knew that any reduction in order flow would harm Goldman Sachs's ability to create the other side of block trades and to generate the liquidity to get out of unsold block positions by selling smaller lots on the market. Any unwinding of the "more, the more" compounding of Goldman Sachs's block-trading business would be costly: Block trading was the real money spinner at Goldman Sachs, and because block trading was *his* business, it was an important part of Levy's strength as the firm's leader. So his third initiative was to transform research. As usual, Levy got the message quickly and was soon saying, "One mistake we made in research is that we really didn't—with the exception of IBM and a few others—concentrate on the big stocks. That has been a very big mistake." Goldman Sachs had to become a leader in research on large corporations now, not because anyone really wanted to, but because Gus Levy said they had to.

Having research that really mattered to the institutions would give Goldman Sachs the powerful advantages of *time* and *access*. If the firm's analysts and salespeople were recommending Merck or Sears or IBM through in-depth written reports and one-on-one visits to the analysts and portfolio managers at all the major institutions, they would know more and sooner which institutions were most likely to become buyers if Goldman Sachs had a large order from a seller— or sellers, if the firm had a big buyer. Combining valued research with intensive service at all levels of the decision process, the firm was often able to anticipate what the traders at these institutions would otherwise find out about only several days later. Having insight into potential buying or selling decisions well in advance of their actually being made was a wonderful advantage in getting more and more of those big orders.

Simultaneously, Levy decided that Goldman Sachs was capable of serving as investment banker to large corporations—particularly the new conglomerate companies. The conglomerates were doing most of the acquisitions and thus were most often in the capital markets for financing and most eager to know what the arbitrageurs and key people at the major institutions were thinking and doing, and likely to do.

In 1969 Levy announced, in his "no questions expected" way, that from then on, Goldman Sachs would concentrate on major companies in *all* its work—and obliged each of his key lieutenants to lead in making this new strategic commitment work in research, trading, and investment banking. Not only did the change mean deliberately abandoning the firm's traditional focus on smaller companies in investment banking and in research, it meant committing the firm to a business strategy in which other larger and more prestigious investment banks were already well established.

Fortunately for Levy and Goldman Sachs, America's major corporations were entering a strong growth phase and not only needed more capital, but also were adding investment bankers to their traditional syndicates. As the tide of institutional investors' interest turned from "small caps" to "large caps," Goldman Sachs was ready and caught the wave. The firm's underwriting business expanded rapidly, capitalizing on the powers of institutional distribution developed through equity block trading. As he did so often, Levy visibly led the charge, convincing one major company after another to make more and more use of Goldman Sachs

Investment Banking Services, the business development organization that had become increasingly effective under John Whitehead's leadership, was now prepared for the challenges of competing with the major establishment firms that made up the formidable "bulge" bracket—the recognized leaders in investment banking. In addition, advice on mergers and acquisitions was beginning to develop as a separate product line under the leadership of Steve Friedman. The profitability of this business could and would be stunning. Still, even as other divisions blossomed, the core of Goldman Sachs's business was block trading.

I want you in Gus Levy's office—*now!*" Bruce McCowan, who had replaced Danforth as partner in charge of research, was about to get direct, absolute, imperative instruction on where research stood in the hierarchy from the dean, Bob Mnuchin. Less than an hour earlier, McCowan had been asked for a research perspective on a stock that Trading was working on as a block trade. McCowan had been distracted by a customer's call. When asked just a few moments ago for an update, he had said he would now be returning to the matter and would call when he had an answer. That would *not* do. Not at all. That's why he got the command call to be in Levy's office—*now*.

Once inside Levy's small glass office on the trading floor—as Levy watched, solemnly puffing his cigar—Mnuchin poked McCowan's chest to command attention and laid it on the line: "When I say jump, you say 'How high?' *This* is where the firm makes its money. This is where *everything* and *everyone* must focus." No ifs, ands, or buts. None at all. Research was only important when it served trading.

Mnuchin's waiting periods rarely extended beyond "right now." The morning call every day was at eight thirty in New York. But that was 5:30 a.m. in California, so one of the sales traders in Los Angeles would listen in from his home and then drive in to work. One day, Mnuchin had a series of major positions he wanted to sell and called each office to hear what help they could give him. When he called L.A., the trader's wife answered and said he was taking a shower. Mnuchin went nuts.

I n building up the block-trading business, which in the early 1970s produced over two-thirds of the firm's annual profits, Gus Levy had plenty of help. Among the people who performed strong roles as members of the "phalanx" were two standouts: Mnuchin, who ran the institutional block-trading desk, and L. Jay Tenenbaum, who managed the overall trading department, which included over-the-counter brokerage, convertible bonds, and risk arbitrage.

"L. Jay Tenenbaum worked *under* Gus," explains John Whitehead. "Gus was never abusive, but you wouldn't work *with* Gus, but *for* Gus. L. Jay stayed as long as he could stand working under Gus. They were very close in many ways, but the cumulative pressure of the moment-to-moment intensity of working for Gus was very hard to sustain indefinitely." Levy would frequently call members of his team at home—before seven in the morning and after eleven at night, or even two in the morning—usually saying only, "Gus—is he there?"

Mnuchin was ambitious and cheerfully admits that "partly by assignment and partly by initiative, I began to back Gus up." From the first, Mnuchin had hustle. Recalls a colleague, "Whenever a trader went to the bathroom, Bob was in his chair."

One day, Levy was out of the office for a few hours when a call came in from an institution that wanted to sell seventy thousand shares of RCA, a tremendous block in those days. "I wasn't second or third in command," Mnuchin recalls, with a grin like the old-time comedian Joe E. Brown's that comes easily to him, "I was just there. I called some accounts, but I couldn't get a firm bid. So I made a bid—forty-nine and a half, I think it was, three-quarters of a point down from the last sale. Then I called back the one institution that had showed a real interest and asked if they would now buy at that price. I held the phone for at least five minutes. You don't know how long those five minutes lasted. But they bought it. When Gus came back, he was very complimentary." And Mnuchin was in.

While never close personally, Mnuchin and Tenenbaum had great professional respect for each other. Tenenbaum, whose mother, like Mnuchin, had been a champion bridge player, observed, "[Trading] involves the same skills—the ability to determine where all the cards are sitting and the way the bidding is going and the ability, too, to keep all the separate situations clear."[6] Mnuchin himself observes that a big factor in block trading is memory—"training yourself to retain facts, the almost unconscious ability to have a mental filing cabinet."

It was a long time before institutions found it as natural to ask for a block *offering* when they wanted to buy stock as they found it to ask for a *bid* when they wanted to sell. In the early days, they tended to use block trading only when they were selling—and their selling tended to be in down markets. As Mnuchin explains, "The entire habit or process of active institutional transactions—of their revisiting their portfolios and making changes—was in its earlier stages. So, if you had, for example, a block of twenty-five thousand shares you wanted to sell at forty-nine dollars, it was very unlikely that you would find another institution that wanted to buy that size block at that specific price at that specific time. The frequency of finding the other side of a trade was small, very small, but this created opportunity. Once block trading became a product with a relatively broad base, as opposed to an occasional pick-your-spot situation, the positions we wound up holding were not a profit center in themselves, but the volume we created and the aggregate commissions we generated—minus the loss on positions—for the most part became, overall, a profitable business."

The real risk in block trading comes when things suddenly go wrong and the block trader has bought or sold a block and cannot find the other side. "The hardest aspect of this business is the problem position," says Mnuchin. "When you can get out of a stock that you're long at a small loss and buy back a stock you're short at a small loss, that's an easy decision. It is painful when there isn't an apparent opportunity to unwind a position or the price moves farther and faster away. Then you hesitate. Then you pray. You hope that it will get better—or you use the wrong judgment and believe that it *will* get better. Those were situations when it was absolutely fantastic to work with Gus Levy."

Mnuchin recalls Levy's support "during the hardest single time I had before becoming a partner in 1965." An institution wanted an offer on Motorola for what was then a very large block, about 100,000 shares. He offered to provide the stock at nearly a point above the price of the last sale, and they said they'd buy it. "Well," he says, "you never know which trade is the one that will not create supply and demand. On this particular transaction, no supply of Motorola filled in. We were short *all* of it. I handled the position very badly, and the stock was just a steamroller. It wouldn't stop. We did this transaction at a price in the mid-sixty-dollar range, and, if I recall properly, we covered the last shares of the short at $109 or $110. It was a monumental loss—significant seven figures. I wasn't thinking about my partnership prospects—I was worried about my *employment* prospects. I had some genuine concern that I'd be fired as a result of this Motorola deal. Well, Gus was absolutely terrific about this one. Instead of getting fired, I was shortly thereafter made a partner."

Known as the Coach for his hands-on, "get the customer on the phone and start talking—and stay with it" management style, Mnuchin would do much the same sort of thing for others on the team that Levy had done for him. "It may sound corny," he says, "but this business is really like a football team. I'm the playing manager. Or maybe the quarterback. Good quarterbacks are only made by good teams, and I like to think I'm a good quarterback. And a good quarterback can sense when his linemen are blocking hard and when they're just blocking. You have to get yourself up for this business every day. You have to be up emotionally, and keep everybody else emotionally keyed up, all the time. You've got to drive and motivate people. If you're placid or a little bit tired or depressed, you won't turn the routine calls into something. You won't create the big business."[7]

Mnuchin, as everyone in that part of the business did, used smoke and mirrors and said slightly different things to different people, but he could keep all those differences clear in his head and always knew exactly what he'd said to each account—so he never got caught. Bob Rubin once observed, "Bob had tremendous charisma within the firm. When, every once in a while, you'd have a time when markets would fall apart on you, Bob would go on the trading desk, be supportive and keep everything going." Adds partner Bill Landreth, "On the SS1 open-line communications system, Bob Mnuchin's commitment and the motivation he inspired in his global sales organization were truly electric." It would have been an exasperating and frustrating existence if he hadn't loved it so. "And I do love it," avows Mnuchin. "I think to be good at it, you have to. It's not a science. There's no one right way to do things, no contract with specifications. Every piece of business is different, and you never know what's coming down the pike. And aside from the money you make, it's tremendously exhilarating when you do a big trade—when everything works." Mnuchin enjoyed playing the block trader's equivalent of "chicken," calling institutional traders and offering to buy blocks—*any* blocks—at either the last sale or on an uptick.

Mnuchin laughs knowingly: "Some of our worst trades have resulted from pride. When it goes wrong, it is a lonely, desperate feeling, even though the partners are terrific and supportive. There's a tendency to be either very high or very low. So when I'm high, I temper it, knowing another day will come. And when I'm low, I temper that, too, so I don't make it worse emotionally. Then afterward, I try to learn from the defeats and repeat the victories."[8]

In a rare compliment, Levy observed, "Bob is the best trade-putter-together I know of in the business." The senior trader at a major institution, reflecting the intensity experienced by those on the receiving end of the Mnuchin treatment, said, "Mnuchin is the most aggressive guy on the Street. He'll move heaven and earth to get a trade."[9]

Levy's focus on what was best for Goldman Sachs could, on rare occasions, cause him to be badly out-traded—most obviously during the SEC's drive for negotiated commissions. The Antitrust Division of the Department of Justice fired the first warning shot when it concluded in the late sixties that fixed rates were a monopolistic practice; it wrote a letter to the SEC asking why fixed rates should not be disallowed, particularly since firms were clearly discounting them regularly to favored institutional customers. Caught off guard, the SEC rushed to get organized and initiated a major study of institutional investing and related brokerage practices. Levy was not only the head of Goldman Sachs, he was also the chairman of the New York Stock Exchange, so he might have felt he was conflicted in serving two masters. Most exchange members wanted to keep fixed commissions as long as possible—preferably forever. Knowing the other major block-trading firms had a special-interest reason to be against give-ups, Gene Rothberg, a smart, tough senior SEC staffer,[10] saw an opening and gave Levy a choice: The give-ups were really a form of price negotiation, so Levy should either agree to negotiated commission rates or give up give-ups.

Since "where you stand is where you sit," and Goldman Sachs was distributing many millions of dollars of give-up checks to other brokers, Levy immediately saw that Goldman Sachs would be far better off by giving up give-ups—so he went for it. What he didn't recognize was that this would be the fulcrum on which the government would eventually oblige "voluntary" acceptance of negotiated commission rates. Nor did he recognize that he had just been strategically out-negotiated.

In Levy's second round with the government, he took another loss: He spoke in favor of negotiated rates because he really thought commissions—particularly for the large, difficult trades in which Goldman Sachs was the undisputed leader—would go *up* if they were no longer fixed. He just *knew* that the other firms could not keep up with Goldman Sachs, so for Levy, it stood to reason that his firm would gain market share and would be able to insist on higher rates for doing the tougher trades if rates were negotiable. Later on, Levy could see that rates would probably decline some, but he still believed Goldman Sachs would gain revenue and profits overall, because he was sure he would gain market share. In the days before May Day in 1975, Levy toured the major institutions, confidently saying, "If commissions drop more than twenty percent, we'll get *all* the business." He was very wrong. During the first day of negotiated rates on very large trades, senior trader Bill Devin called from Fidelity: "We're seeing a lot more than 'down twenty'—and from good firms." It was the start of a thirty-year collapse in commission rates from forty cents a share to well under four cents.

The persistent search for opportunities to do business—to dominate and control the market, partly to maximize volume and partly to preempt any business going to any competitor—can be illustrated many, many times in the ambitious development of Goldman Sachs. One example was in the sale of stock by corporate "insiders," which was strictly limited by the SEC's Rule 144 to 1 percent of NYSE trading volume in any six-month period—unless the seller was responding to an unsolicited bid. On Dick Menschel's initiative, Goldman Sachs developed a specialty business of showcasing its institutional block-trading activities to large individual holders of "Rule 144" stock. Far from feeling pestered or annoyed by calls from Goldman Sachs salesmen, corporate executives with Rule 144 stock saw these calls as an invitation to be included in the action—and as a potential source of those valuable unsolicited bids.

As the leader of the firm's Rule 144 business unit, partner Jim Timmons limited his calls to people with at least twenty million dollars in stockholdings to stay focused on his prime prospects. To gain maximum coverage of the whole market, Timmons got weekly reports from a Washingtonian who rode his motorbike to SEC headquarters each week to be the first to receive the regularly released insider stock activity reports, which were available only there. And in New York City, he organized an innovative information network on which the firmwide business development operation was based. He made Goldman Sachs the clear leader in Rule 144 business and fed good new-business leads to the Private Client Services brokers. An executive who sold a block of Rule 144 stock suddenly had five million dollars—or ten million dollars, or more—of cash to reinvest.

Another niche market tapped by Goldman Sachs was the business of corporations' repurchasing their own common stock. Goldman Sachs built up a business specialty that required no investment in research, put no capital at risk, and was a productive feeder for other businesses of the firm. While most stockbrokers considered share repurchase just a minor sideline, at Goldman Sachs the minor sideline grew to generate high-margin, risk-free business with annual revenues of one hundred million dollars.

The firm had regular access to corporate treasurers through its large commercial-paper business, and treasurers whose companies had large-scale programs to repurchase their own shares found accepting Goldman Sachs's calls offering a block of stocks doubly attractive. The treasurers saw buying blocks as far more convenient and cost-effective than a long string of hundred-share purchases could ever be. In addition, they could avoid intraday price disruptions. If Goldman Sachs could get a corporation's buy order for a large-block share repurchase, it could then scour the institutional market, looking for a willing seller—and another block-trading "crossing" opportunity.

When "NSI 100,000" appeared one day in the early seventies on the illuminated, outsize ticker tape that dominated the far wall of the trading room, Timmons was stunned. This was supposed to be *his* block of one hundred thousand shares of Norton Simon common stock. He had been promised the trade by the company as part of its share-repurchase program, and he had been able to find a willing seller for a perfect cross and a full commission of seventy-five thousand dollars. Even more important, Timmons had confidently assured the others in the trading room nearly a week ago that he had it all set up—and far more important, he had given that same confident assurance to Gus Levy.

Now, having lost the trade completely, he'd have to face Levy. But first Timmons reached for the phone to call Norton Simon Inc. When the treasurer came on the line, Timmons spoke quietly and directly: "One hundred thousand shares of NSI just printed on the tape. You promised that trade to me five days ago. I'm calling to ask your help. You've got to explain it to me, because I have to go explain it to Gus." Timmons was no clerk; he was a Goldman Sachs partner.

"Jim, I owed business to Bear Stearns. This trade was my best way to give them some business. I knew one of us would have to face getting chewed out by Gus. Better you than me, Jim. So yes, I lied to you."

Timmons put down the phone, pulled himself up out of his chair, and began the long, long walk across the trading room to the darkened-glass cubicle. Levy didn't look up when Timmons got to the door. Timmons stood waiting for the usual slight indication of recognition, but there was none. As more and more seconds passed, Timmons knew he wasn't going to be acknowledged.

Levy rose from his desk as though he were alone, moved past Timmons, and walked deliberately to the center of the trading room where he silently took up a position next to Bob Mnuchin. Not dismissed, Timmons stood frozen as he realized the obvious: Levy was not going to speak to him.

Feeling the full burden of failure, Timmons began the long walk back across the cavernous trading room toward his seat. As he passed the desk of Bob Rubin, known to be one of Levy's few favorites, Rubin's barely audible voice gave this saving counsel: "He only does that with guys he knows he can trust." Levy's lesson was clear and indelible. Never, ever ease up on the unrelenting execution of *any* transaction until *after* it has been absolutely completed.

A quarter-century later, Timmons's memory of that experience, and the lesson learned about how to get business done, was still vivid.

10

REVOLUTION IN
INVESTMENT BANKING

The Ford stock offering, a triumph for Goldman Sachs and Sidney Weinberg, also helped launch the career of John Whitehead. With his friend and partner, John L. Weinberg, Whitehead would lead the firm in decisively changing the basic structure of Wall Street and advance Goldman Sachs from the cluster of firms in the lower middle ranks of investment banking all the way up to global leadership. Unusually talented, shrewd, and classically upwardly mobile, the good-looking, soft-spoken Whitehead was typecast for Wall Street leadership and ambitious for his firm and for himself. As a competitor later summarized, "John was the consummate investment banker of his era."

Successful people and successful organizations seldom favor change, particularly change in their own sources of success in accumulating great wealth. They oppose disruption and strongly favor stability, consistency, and reliability in the business norms and personal behavior that they know best and that have worked so wonderfully well for them as individuals. Investment banking was steeped in traditions that had brought great wealth to many. Over fifty years, the ways of Wall Street had been more and more carefully developed in greater and greater detail and had become increasingly stable. Nothing was more codified on Wall Street than respect for other firms' client relationships.

Through the 1970s, proudly traditional Wall Street firms would not deign to solicit business. "Nobody called on corporations," explains partner Jim Gorter. "It just wasn't done. The old school ties governed, and changes, if any, came very slowly. For example, Motorola [founded by Paul Galvin] used Halsey Stuart because Mr. Galvin had a personal friendship with Mr. Stuart. That's the way it was and the way it had always been. Investment banking firms expected clients to come to them." Even into the late 1970s, elite firms like Morgan Stanley and First Boston would send engraved invitations to specific corporations—and even the government of Mexico—informing them that they would now be welcome to make an appointment to visit the firm at its office to discuss the possibility of becoming clients.

Within all the leading investment banking firms, individual partners had *their* client corporations, on whose boards of directors they usually served. Thus they would always know well in advance if any financing were to be done; they would be involved from the beginning in shaping the nature and timing of that financing and be alert to repel any competitors that might presume to offer their services. And while syndicates were organized firm by firm, the economics of every firm depended on the productivity of the individual partners. They jealously guarded their particular clients because in an "eat what you kill" world, their incomes depended on the business they personally brought in.

As Whitehead recalls, "Back in the old days of the forties and fifties, the 'historical' syndicates of underwriters were taken terribly seriously and were considered absolutely sacrosanct. Once a firm was in a particular underwriting syndicate as a major, it was a major for life. Changes came very rarely. I can remember resenting quite bitterly the fact that Kuhn Loeb and Dillon Read— which I considered at the time to be old-fashioned and not up to Goldman Sachs in their talents—were included in the 'bulge bracket' as leaders in all the underwriting groups that Goldman Sachs was not in. Nobody was willing to face the reality and change those historical structures."

Attentive service to each firm's own clients was extremely important. There was little or no shopping around for different investment bankers and very little price competition. Moreover, few companies, other than utilities, turned regularly to the capital markets to raise either debt or equity capital, and if they ever did, they certainly wouldn't abandon their long-standing traditional banker and risk such an important transaction with a different firm—particularly a small, stigmatized, second-tier firm like Goldman Sachs.

During their time together working on the Ford offering, Whitehead had earned Sidney Weinberg's confidence. Even though he was not yet a partner, he was able to get Weinberg's okay that a study of Goldman Sachs's new-business activities might be worth undertaking. The study was authorized on January 20, 1956, and completed several months later. But on the advice of his friend John Weinberg, Whitehead cautiously kept in his desk drawer the crucial report—which explained the risk of depending on one single person, even one as remarkably effective as Sidney Weinberg—until *after* his formal admission to the partnership.[1] Whitehead says knowingly, "Rocking the boat did not pay off with Sidney Weinberg."

Whitehead's memorandum advocated a complete change in the firm's organizational structure—a change that would, in time, decisively accelerate Goldman Sachs's becoming the nation's and then the world's preeminent investment bank, and in time would cause every major competitor in the investment banking industry to restructure too.

Redefining a business and reinventing the firm—often very substantially changing itself and its way of doing business—are themes in the extraordinary growth and expansion of Goldman Sachs. Yet almost always the firm projected smooth consistency that masked its unrelenting determination to advance in competitive position and increase profits.

The most sincere business compliment is when competitors change their strategies and organizational structures to imitate another firm's business strategy and the structure through which that strategy is being realized. The compliment of replication is all the more substantial when competitors believe the particular business they are adjusting is the crucial core of their own strategies and when their previous organizational structure has been the pathway by which their senior executives have achieved their prominence, power, and affluence. At Goldman Sachs, Sidney Weinberg had been succeeding greatly within the old, established structure. In his irreverently unique way, he had become a master of that traditional structure, and it had enabled him to become accepted as an effective, powerful leader. So why would he be open to making *any* change, let alone endorsing major change?

Into this unpromising environment, Whitehead proposed to separate executions from solicitations and to have everyone in investment banking at Goldman Sachs work either on soliciting business and managing relationships *or* on executing specific transactions. Nobody would do both, even though that was the way it had always been done on Wall Street. The idea of soliciting business with a team of people who did nothing else was entirely new and different for investment bankers. It was distasteful to many—including Sidney Weinberg, who knew how important *he* was—and to many it seemed a sure waste of money because it could not possibly be effective. Who, after all, could compete with Sidney Weinberg or with any of the other leading bankers at Wall Street's leading firms, who as professionals all took pride in delivering the services they sold and sold only the services they themselves delivered? Everyone knew that all investment banking business had always been done at the highest executive levels and could only be handled by skilled and experienced partners. Weinberg naturally believed he had unique skills and abilities to develop relationships—skills and capabilities that were not about to be matched by a mere commercial-paper salesman. Like other traditional investment bankers, Weinberg believed that only the banker who would actually execute the transaction could possibly fully understand what to promise or propose, and he saw soliciting other firms' clients as unprofessional. Sidney Weinberg would see no merit in making any change.

He certainly made no response to the copy of Whitehead's memorandum he eventually received, and Weinberg was none too pleased when he learned that copies had also been distributed in blue covers with a spiral binding to each of the firm's partners. However, since Whitehead's proposal had been developed in response to Weinberg's own written directive, it was automatically on the agenda for the next partners' meeting. After Weinberg's dismissive introductory observation that "Whitehead has some crazy project on his mind," Whitehead explained his plan.

As he presented the proposition, it was simple: Pointing with deference to Mr. Weinberg's formidable success in bringing business to the firm—and making no mention of the obvious risks in Weinberg's clearly getting older—Whitehead explained that if *ten* men were out selling and each of them could produce just 20 percent of what Mr. Weinberg produced, they could, as a group, produce *twice* the business the firm was then getting through Mr. Weinberg.

In suggesting the separation of the sales and service function from the production function, Whitehead used the example of manufacturing companies like Ford. The successful automobile salesman doesn't go out on the factory floor to make the product; he goes back to sell more and serve his customers because that's what he is best at—while others do what *they* do best: make cars. "Production and distribution are quite different," Whitehead said. "Building relationships to bring in the business is one function; executing the specific transactions is a very different function. The different functions need different skills, drives, and personalities. Demand versus supply. Most people—by skills, interests, and temperament—are better at one or the other, and the opportunity for management is to match each person to the role where he has the best fit, will have the most interest, and will do the best work."

For Whitehead, there were two important dimensions to the problem with Wall Street's traditional practice of just one investment banker doing it all for his client. First, sales and selling were not demeaning; they were the vital strengths of a great organization and should be so recognized. It takes time and thoughtful attention to each client organization to become an expert on the opportunities and problems that particular client must deal with successfully; to understand how those problems and opportunities are changing and might change as time passes and circumstances develop; to keep all the relevant people at each client fully informed about and confident in the firm's special ability to serve effectively; and to make them confident and comfortable that the firm to use for each major transaction is, naturally, Goldman Sachs.

Second, selling should be separated from manufacturing to be sure the best manufacturing skills are dedicated to making the best product. Producing the best-manufactured product is key to delivering the best service, and there are just too many specialized products in investment banking for anyone to be a true master of each and all of them.

Weinberg briefly expressed offhand skepticism in the meeting and was clearly not supportive. "He rather obviously ignored the whole idea," recalls Whitehead, "but it was important that he did not explicitly reject the idea either."

No formal vote was taken. With no direct opposition, Whitehead boldly and quietly decided to act. "Since there was no vote," he explains, "we had not voted no. So I just went ahead."

Weinberg never did endorse Whitehead's concept.

Jim Gorter, who built the core of Goldman Sachs's national power in the Midwest and ran the firm's important Chicago regional headquarters for many years, explains: "While the actual implementation was somewhat different from the proposition as written, this was the decisive event in the development of Goldman Sachs and of investment banking as an industry." "Of course," acknowledges Whitehead, "it would take ten years and several false starts to get the proposition all worked out in operation, but it was clearly different. And we knew that Goldman Sachs had to be different to make a real change in our competitive position in the business." Observes Jim Weinberg, "Most great ideas develop rather slowly with a few lucky breaks and then gather momentum. Only later do they appear to be the stroke of genius."

So that there would be no incremental cost for the firm—which could provoke objection—Whitehead's first step in the early days was to invite two commercial-paper salesmen to add some of the firm's other products to what they were already offering in their regular marketing territories. "As salesmen, they were naturally interested in this enlarged opportunity," says Whitehead. (Years later, he acknowledged that it was "a rather sleazy gambit" to start with the firm's commercial-paper salesmen, but it was a start and there were no alternatives.) Whitehead soon added men from the buying department, such as Alan Stein in California and Fred Weintz in the Midwest, and called his unit the new business department—later renamed Investment Banking Services and called IBS. IBS men became more and more effective in developing relationships and winning business, and success in executing transactions deepened their confidence that the product professionals they represented were so intensively specialized and experienced in their particular product that they must be among the best in the entire industry. The central question became, where should the firm's relationship managers concentrate so they could be most productive?

"As we looked at the overall market, the hundred largest corporations were all pretty much locked up by the leading Wall Street firms," says Whitehead. "Most had just one major investment banker, and often a partner of that firm was already sitting on their board of directors, determined to protect his firm's relationship and keep all the available business—so there wasn't much chance in those early days to get them to change to Goldman Sachs. But there were many, many *other* corporations, so we focused on them." Into the mid-1970s, Goldman Sachs concentrated on smaller and midsize corporations, the so-called Fortune Second 500—and many even smaller companies. Whitehead's group initially worked with a list of five hundred companies. This list was soon expanded to one thousand and then to two thousand. As more people were added to IBS, the list each covered was cut from two hundred down to one hundred companies, so more and more companies were covered more and more intensively. By 1971 every one of the four thousand U.S. corporations earning one million dollars or more had an investment banker at Goldman Sachs responsible for trying to do business with it. In the five years between 1979 and 1984, the firm added five hundred new clients, literally doubling its clientele. Within a generation, every major firm on Wall Street was obliged by competitive realities to adopt Whitehead's organizational concept.

Having gotten their selling experience in the commercial-paper business, the commercial-paper salesmen knew the disciplines of patience, persistence, and procedure. They had to build comprehensive credit files on prospective issuers long before they did any business so the firm could respond swiftly if and when a company might call to say it had decided to issue commercial paper. As Fred Weintz recalls those early days, "An IBS man would write a report to the buying committee explaining the company and what it wanted to do with the capital. Then there would be extensive checks with competitors, suppliers, and customers to find out what the company and its management were really like. I was always making new calls, but we wanted to develop *relationships* and would try like hell to do a good job for each client. We knew that if we did our work really well for each client, more business would follow and we'd get recommended to others. Our competition for underwriting consisted of Blyth, Merrill Lynch, First Boston, and McDonald."[2]

But Whitehead wasn't looking for mandates to sell just commercial paper: "I was always looking for some other things we could sell. So I might see a possibility at one of the companies for, say, a debt private placement and say, 'Ted, why don't we also sell these folks a private placement?' And Ted would try it out on his next visit and write it up in his call report. And then I'd say to Bob and others, 'Did you notice that Ted's already talking to company X about a private placement? Looks like a good idea.' And pretty soon, Bob would report on *his* call reports that he was recommending a private placement to company Y"—with Whitehead deliberately and repeatedly taking note of Bob's good initiative when talking to the others in IBS and to Bob himself.

Acknowledging how closely he monitored the sales effort, Whitehead recalls, "I read all of the call reports, often sending them back with notations like, 'Did you try to offer them service A?' or 'Did you ask about service B?' Soon enough, one of the men somehow got a mandate to study a company's dividend policy for a fee of twenty-five thousand dollars. Not much of a fee, even in those days, but recognized as business we'd never have had except for his efforts. A memorandum celebrating this wonderful accomplishment went to all the partners. The triumph for a whole year would be that Goldman Sachs had persuaded some company not to use Lehman Brothers for some issue and instead to use Goldman Sachs, or to add Goldman Sachs as a joint manager in addition to their historical banker, Morgan Stanley. Those small gains were celebrated as great achievements."

Whitehead was optimistic—and determined. As he recalls those years, "Pretty soon we'd get another mandate and do another transaction, and would celebrate that fine achievement rather widely and visibly. We kept doing this until the whole team was engaged in selling our broader and broader product line." With Whitehead's persistent and cautious "prune losers, feed winners" style of management, the whole IBS organization became constructively infected with commitment: first to specific actions and transactions and later to an overall strategy—and eventually to a firmwide culture and a commitment to a new, organized way of doing business.

By making relationship management conceptually equal in stature to executing transactions, Whitehead was able to recruit skillful people into an organization that became notoriously effective at finding business and distributing new product ideas. It gave Goldman Sachs a decisive competitive advantage over other Wall Street firms, plus a growing reputation for competence and commitment among corporate prospects and clients. No other firm could match it. Even competitors called it "the machine."

Whitehead recalls with a smile how the business was built: "We would, of course, defend and protect our own clients, taking full advantage of our being their traditional investment bank, and saying to a CEO who had just come into office at a firm client, 'Oh sir, you wouldn't even *think* of changing your company's long-established investment banking relationship, because this is something that has gone on for generations before you came on the scene. You'll be CEO for only a few years, but the relationship between Goldman Sachs and this company will certainly continue on forever.' But then with other firms' clients, of course, we talked a very different line, saying 'Who does Morgan Stanley think they are, to claim that they *own* you? You are an *independent* company. You have every right to pick your own investment banker based on whoever you think is the very ablest, and not be bound by past history.' "

Whitehead's first task was to build IBS into an organization that could successfully initiate, develop, and build business relationships with many, many corporations. The second and simultaneous task was to elevate the stature of IBS within the firm to equal the traditionally dominant buying department where skeptics and resisters were numerous. This equality in stature would depend on the ability to recruit and keep exceptionally talented and ambitious professionals working in IBS for their full careers. For several years, Whitehead led the recruiting each year at Harvard Business School. He was also always looking for unusually capable commercial bankers who might transfer for more opportunity, and he recruited people from other firms, concentrating on ambitious younger people who had good training and experience but might feel stymied in their careers. Whitehead would offer them the opportunity to have their own accounts and a promotion to vice president.

Fred Weintz recalls how things were: "Not long after John Whitehead put forward his plan to establish a new business department, Jim Weinberg persuaded me to apply for a transfer from commercial-paper sales. Commercial paper was not very profitable, but it was a good way to get started with a company while looking for a chance to do a future public offering if the company earned at least one million dollars. And obviously, it had to be a *quality* company to pass with Sidney Weinberg. The firm was also trying to recruit commercial bankers on the theory they knew how to call on companies for financial business, and was offering them twelve thousand dollars a year. But when I was taken on as an internal transfer, it was for only $7,500 because the firm's cost controls were so very strict.

Following the pattern used for commercial-paper sales, we were organized by geographic areas, with five men in New York, two in Boston, one in Philadelphia, and one in St. Louis. I had Ohio and Indiana—except, of course, for any companies in the territory that were Mr. Weinberg's. We were always striving to rationalize our business and the operation of the new business department. We knew we were nowhere in oil, and Morgan Stanley and First Boston had most of the top one hundred corporations. Goldman Sachs had a few in the top one hundred list, but most of our clients were spread across the next thousand. We had group meetings all the time trying to figure out ways to improve our business."

Whitehead recalls, "Since there were hardly ever *any* changes in investment banking relationships in those early days, our task of breaking in was daunting. We would evaluate our performance by how many new clients we added in a year versus how many we lost. After a long year's work, we might be up three or up six or something like that." It didn't seem to work at first. New Business took the credit for things, and the overheads went up, and small gains were celebrated as great achievements, but the flow of business did not really increase. The idea that commercial-paper profits would "finance" the expanded new business organization looked to some like wishful thinking. As George Doty observed: "Goldman Sachs's new business development organization was by no means an overnight success. For several years, it was a money loser. That's one of the main reasons other firms did not duplicate it. Who wants to duplicate an experiment that is a radical departure from the tried and proven, and doesn't seem to be working all that well?" It would take ten years and several false starts before Whitehead's innovation worked out. Sidney Weinberg never did like it or support it and was, according to Whitehead, "number one in new business until the day he died."

Whitehead gave more and more of his attention to things managerial, particularly business planning. One day in late 1963, Gus Levy, the intuitive, forceful, deeply engaged frontline leader, had cornered Whitehead in the hallway to bemoan the dreadful news that with all its hiring of people, the firm was now saddled with a huge annual overhead of twelve million dollars. Levy worried aloud, "We'll have to take in a million dollars every *month* just to break even!"

Whitehead offered reassurance that, with some planning, this apparently awesome cost burden could actually be covered by normal and expected operations. For starters, Whitehead said he would estimate that the investment banking part of the firm would do at least one private placement a month—and, taking a pad of paper, wrote down "12 x $50,000" to record the fees that might be expected from this line of business, which, at the time, was a major product line for the firm. Then he added a line for commercial paper and then another line for a third service and so on until he had accumulated six million dollars in expected revenues, all from investment banking.

Then he asked Levy, who ran both arbitrage and stockbrokerage, "And what would you guess you can expect to do?" Responding to an implicit competitive challenge and quickly catching onto the play of the game, Levy ventured an estimate of the commissions to be generated by each of his twenty-five largest stockbrokerage clients—and then those likely to come from the next fifty—and then added something for arbitrage. As each new item was put forward, Whitehead wrote it on his pad. Then, noting that the total came to more than the previously daunting twelve million dollars, Whitehead had a rough business forecast for the coming year and wrote across the top, "1964 Budget." With this simple start, the discipline of planning was on its way to becoming a hallmark of the firm. Revenues were soon twenty million dollars, with expenses at fourteen million dollars—and pretax profits were six million dollars.

The investment banking business began to change in the 1960s as the volume of underwritings and the mergers-and-acquisitions business both picked up and institutional investors rose to dominance in the debt and equity markets. Even more important, major companies wanted more than one banker, and they began to use joint managers for their underwritings. More and more, investment bankers lost their "captive" clients.

Investment bankers traditionally prided themselves on being generalists who could execute any transaction or perform any banking service that client companies might want or need. Whitehead's organizational innovation was to divide and conquer. By focusing each banker on one specialty, Goldman Sachs would be able to deliver the best of both and do so over and over again, eventually anywhere and everywhere. Pairs of specialists—one expert on the product or service and one really knowing the company and all its key people and how they made decisions—could beat the generalist investment bankers from traditional firms, occasionally at first and then, increasingly, time after time.

"Pretty soon the system began to work pretty well," recalls Whitehead with characteristic understatement. "Prestige for this group would necessarily come later—with the results." If the rest of the firm had doubts about the stature of the group, that was resolved decisively by Whitehead's persuading Sidney Weinberg's highly regarded elder son, Jim, to leave Owens-Corning Fiberglas and join IBS, where he was very successful *and* a Weinberg. In addition, as the years went by, others within the IBS group were promoted to partnership.

After an IBS new-business relationship manager won a mandate, he would turn over full responsibility for the execution to a specialist in that particular type of transaction. The relationship manager who developed the business would continue to be responsible for seeing to it that the client was pleased with the transaction and for seeking additional business. Meanwhile, the execution specialists, as they accumulated more and more experience, became leaders in their specialties. They could focus all of their time, skill, and energy on what they did best, knowing that the relationship professionals would bring in more—and more interesting—work for them to do on behalf of major clients who would already be committed to the undertaking. As Whitehead summed it up, "When our selling people knew they were representing the very best, most experienced, and most skillful *product* specialists, they could speak with pride and conviction when advocating a specific transaction to one of their clients. And they also knew they could turn the execution entirely over to the firm's product specialists, while they continued to devote all their time and energies to doing very well what they did best: working closely with each of their clients to be sure they kept bringing in the most business. They knew their prospects and their clients would get 'best execution'—and it was always easier to brag about a colleague than about yourself."

The combined strength of pure relationship managers doing what they did best, matched by pure product experts doing what they did best, would, in time, give Goldman Sachs a decisive—"unfair"—competitive advantage and a steadily growing reputation for competence and commitment among corporate prospects and clients. Gradually but steadily, the transaction specialists became confident that the relationship specialists really knew their companies and were good at finding and developing business opportunities and would call them in only when a company was genuinely interested in their transaction specialty, so their time would always be well used. And the relationship specialists steadily gained confidence that the transaction specialists had more experience than their counterparts at other firms in their particular product specialties and knew the inside stories on all the most recent transactions—which gave them special credibility in competing for new business. As both groups eventually learned they could depend on each other, this was good for esprit de corps. And this interdependence fit well with the Goldman Sachs culture of teamwork and the subordination of "I" to "we" that had originated with the Sachs family, was consistently advocated by Gus Levy, and was always insisted upon by John Whitehead and John Weinberg.

S pecialization by industry—in addition to specialization by geography— began institutionally in the early 1960s with partner Dick Fay focusing on finance companies. Then Burt Sorenson, also a partner, started to focus on utilities. When Barrie Wigmore, a Canadian, joined the firm in 1971, Whitehead's strategic objective was to accelerate the pace at Goldman Sachs by recruiting people like Wigmore, who wanted to achieve something special in their careers, were more than willing to work long hours and weekends to make it happen, and saw change as exciting and fun.* The original plan was to pair Wigmore with Charlie Saltzman, a retired general who had served at a senior level in the State Department before he was hired into the firm by Sidney Weinberg. Already in his sixties, Saltzman was near retirement, so Wigmore was in line to take over coverage of his companies in a year or two. But before that change ever took place, Whitehead decided it would be better to put Wigmore in charge of trying to develop business for Goldman Sachs in the huge public-utilities business.

Corporate-bond issuance was dominated by public utilities, but Goldman Sachs had no fixed-income research and no strength in bond sales. Moreover, most utility issues were competitively bid; Goldman Sachs historically had little interest in that low-margin business. But Whitehead still saw possibilities.

* Wigmore was surprised by the pace he found. Used to working on weekends, he came in on Saturday to find the doors to Goldman Sachs closed and locked. Nobody came in back then on Saturdays. Similarly, late-afternoon meetings would be brought to an abrupt end in those days by statements like, "Uh oh, time for my train!" Wigmore's readiness to extend the workweek was seen as an inconvenient nuisance by others at the firm.

To Whitehead, utilities represented a major opportunity—not because they did over half of the total public securities offerings by corporations; not because they were sure to continue to be major users of Wall Street underwritings in good economies and bad; not because there were so many of them; not because they were located all over the country; and not because utilities were important to such prestigious investment banking firms as Morgan Stanley, First Boston, Merrill Lynch, White Weld, and Salomon Brothers. In Whitehead's view, utilities represented a major opportunity because Goldman Sachs had almost no business with utilities—so "the opportunities were unlimited." Whitehead explained the opportunity: Wigmore could develop his own strategy, wasn't expected to spend time protecting existing business with old clients, and could go anywhere and do anything.

The one utility that the firm did any business with in the early seventies was the right one: Telephone. In truth, AT&T was not a firm client; it was a Gus Levy client. AT&T habitually sold common stock on rights offerings through warrants, and this automatically created an arbitrage situation involving the "when issued" shares. Since Levy headed the firm's arbitrage desk, he automatically became an important participant in the underwriting process and soon established a reputation with AT&T as an expert on share pricing—an expert whom AT&T wanted to consult before setting the terms of each new offering. Levy, who was chairman of Nelson Rockefeller's campaign finance committee, had become a member of New York Telephone's board of directors, so his firm frequently was listed as a comanager of AT&T's new issues—but never as the lead manager. Levy had developed such a strong relationship with AT&T's treasurer that even though Goldman Sachs lacked retail distribution and was weak in bonds, it would get a call announcing how much business it would be getting in each new underwriting—prestigious business the firm was glad to have.

So AT&T was a start. But would there be any followers? Wigmore took an inventory of his weak strategic position: Utility stocks were of no interest to most of the firm's institutional clients—and all of its important accounts. The firm had none of the small retail customers who traditionally bought utility stocks. The firm itself had little interest. Ray Young, head of sales, was clearly opposed: "We have no business in selling utility stocks." The firm's total revenue from utility business in 1970 was only twenty-five thousand dollars. Every utility already had long-established, stable investment banking relationships, and utilities were notoriously cautious about changing their sources of finance. Changing these settled relationships would be difficult. The firm didn't know the complex ins and outs of the many and arcane utility regulations—regulations that were important and differed from state to state and from one type of utility to another. Wigmore didn't know anything about the rating agencies and how they did their work—except that they were important. And Wigmore didn't know the lawyers of the utility bar, but he did know he had to get to know them. Wigmore didn't know any utility executives, and they didn't know him.

Barrie Wigmore was a long, long way from his family home in Saskatchewan. But things were changing at Goldman Sachs. Under Whitehead's leadership, the investment banking department was developing a new aggressiveness. New-business developers were calling on clients and nonclients alike in search of business, and the specialty departments around the firm were encouraged to provide a constant stream of new ideas. Thanks to an unparalleled recruiting process, a lot of smart young people were generating ideas.

Structural changes are always resisted and always difficult to implement successfully, and the firm had a long-established tradition of all relationship bankers being generalists. This was important from a management perspective because as different opportunities waxed or waned, people could easily be moved around and redeployed. This tradition added two key elements to Goldman Sachs's strategy: low fixed costs and ample resources with which to pursue and maximize gains from any unfolding opportunities. People at other firms would say, "We should do this for the prestige" or "for our rank in the league tables" or "to protect our relationship" or "to show our commitment." Not at Goldman Sachs. Goldman Sachs has always been more clearly and more consistently focused on *profits* than the other firms.

Goldman Sachs was also more consistently aggressive, as illustrated by Wigmore's pursuit of an appointment with an important prospect in the early 1980s:

"Sorry, Mr. Wigmore, my whole day is fully booked."

"When do you start your day?"

"Six o'clock."

"If I came in at five forty-five a.m., could you see me?"

To develop business with utilities, Wigmore knew he would have to outflank the established firms and be innovative, so he searched for ways to differentiate his business-development initiatives and capitalize on firm strengths that had not yet been applied to utilities. As an outsider, he had to be ready for possible breaks when and where innovation might be welcome. Wigmore's team eventually included over thirty professionals—analysts, IBS relationship managers, and product execution experts. Every Monday morning, they all gathered at 8 a.m. for breakfast and open discussion, reporting on every aspect of the unit's business and probing guests from other departments for new ideas. While the specifics would differ each week, the agenda was always the same: What's new and changing? What smart, new things are competitors doing that we can learn from? What opportunities might be developing?

Everyone was encouraged to come up with new ideas, no matter how far out, and to test them. "It was good for business and great for morale. We tried out all sorts of ideas," recalls Wigmore. "Some were nonstarters. Some were crazy. But some of them really worked. It was exciting to be in the hunt, and it was really exciting when we developed a winner. Pretty soon, we were earning a reputation in the industry for being well informed and imaginative, so more and more people wanted to talk with us and hear what we had to say and work with us on developing new ideas."

Most of the new ideas applied to the capital-hungry electric utilities industry. Some of the new ideas that worked:

- The firm arranged the first nuclear-fuel lease with commercial-paper backup. In these transactions, the firm bought nuclear fuel in a special subsidiary, Broad Street Services Corporation, financed it with commercial paper guaranteed by bank letters of credit, and then leased it back to the utilities. This used the firm's strengths in commercial paper and in leasing, an unusual specialty few competitors knew much about. A similar opportunity was found in equipment leasing.

- Pollution-control revenue bonds capitalized on the firm's strength in tax-exempt finance.

- The aggressiveness of the private placements department opened up new opportunities. When an institutional investor told one of the Goldman Sachs private placement experts that he wanted a specific type of bond, Wigmore's team would quickly scour the utilities side of the market, asking, "How would you like to borrow ten million dollars now at such and such a rate?"

This unorthodox approach—the exact opposite of the traditional approach, where a borrower prepared an elaborate offering statement and initiated the process—worked well and soon made Goldman Sachs a go-to intermediary in this new and fast-growing segment of the capital market.

- Eurobonds, sold through the Netherlands Antilles, opened another niche market and provided a way for American utilities to get their names and creditworthiness known in Europe's expanding capital markets.

- SAMA—the Saudi Arabian Monetary Authority—had huge cash flows to invest in the late 1970s, and interest rates were not as important to SAMA as credit quality. Through the contacts of partner Thomas "Dusty" Rhodes, the utility group arranged two- to five-year private placements with SAMA for many of the highest-grade U.S. utilities.

- Utilities that wanted coal-fired power plants could negotiate long-term supply contracts with coal-mining companies. But the coal companies could not afford the investment—as much as one hundred million dollars—in the outsize dragline equipment sometimes needed to mine the coal. Nor did the coal companies have enough taxable income to use the huge depreciation charges from such an investment. Solving this problem was easy: The utilities would arrange the financing for their coal suppliers through Goldman Sachs—and another financing specialty with good profit margins was developed and systematically offered to every utility that was a potential user.

These innovations were successful and profitable for the utility group, but they were all concentrated in the debt markets. Innovations there might gain Goldman Sachs respect and business within the utility industry, but common-stock equity financing was the utilities' lifeblood and ultimately determined whom they considered to be their investment bankers. Goldman Sachs needed to penetrate the equity market. But the effort faced big obstacles both outside the firm—competitors were entrenched and determined to defend the business—and inside. Things began to change, however, when Ray Young, the leading resister inside Goldman Sachs, retired, and Dick Menschel became head of sales. Open to new ideas, Menschel listened to Wigmore's proposition: "The sales force doesn't know much about utilities. If you'll give me *one* guy—part time—so we can teach him all about utilities so other sales people can feed off his knowledge, I'm sure we can really do some business in utility stocks." Fortunately, Menschel assigned Tom Tuft to work with the utilities group. Tuft would become the leading institutional seller in the country of electric-utility stocks and go on to become the chairman of the firm's equity capital markets group.

Working with the research department, Tuft and Wigmore developed an easy-to-use sales tool that could be run off the computer every day. It showed, in rank order, the deviation in every utility stock's yield from its historical relation to the industry's average yield. Taking the simple assumptions that the market was usually right on its pricing of *each* utility relative to *all* utilities and that reversion to the mean would tend to bring any "wanderer" back toward the norm, money could be made by selling the "highs" and buying the "lows." Casualty-insurance companies—able to exclude from taxes 85 percent of dividends received as income—learned to use the information. Trading off the model, they became increasingly active trading customers with, of course, Goldman Sachs.

For Goldman Sachs, with its leadership in block trading, the next steps were easy, at least in retrospect: Offer blocks of new-issue utility stocks to institutions it knew were buyers, without the cumbersome, expensive, and time-consuming process of organizing a retail-oriented, multifirm underwriting syndicate and conducting a road show all around the country. Now, through just one firm— Goldman Sachs—utilities could raise fifty million to one hundred million dollars of low-cost equity capital in just one day. There was none of the usual "market uncertainty." And the execution cost to the issuing utility was compellingly low: only 1 percent to 2 percent instead of the customary 3.5 percent underwriting spread.

The next step would be continuous offerings. The firm persuaded the utilities that doing one big offering every year or so was not as likely to achieve their objective of low-rate financing as using a shelf registration (one registration statement covering several future issues of the same security) and taking advantage of market opportunities as they developed. Recalls Wigmore, "We began this sort of offering with medium-term notes, which were just one step along the maturity curve from the firm's great strength in commercial paper."

Advancing to longer-term debt and then to equity offerings was, at least in retrospect, a natural progression. If an institutional investor was interested in buying one hundred thousand shares of common stock, that buyer interest would be taken directly to the utility as an offer. With its stock facing none of the market pressure so often caused by a major syndicated equity offering, the issuing utility typically got a better price for its shares. Goldman Sachs became known as unequaled in efficient execution of institutional stock purchases, and this added to the firm's overall credibility.

With these new underwriting tools and Tom Tuft's leadership, the firm gained new respect in the equity arena. It could increase its business by getting a bigger share of each underwriting—which it pursued vigorously. The turning point came on a deal for Florida Power & Light, traditionally one of the smartest companies in the industry, when it agreed to do a major nonsyndicate offering through a three-firm team: Goldman Sachs, Merrill Lynch, and Salomon Brothers. "Goldman Sachs was absolutely focused on placing those shares. The two other firms were not so focused on making it happen. This gave us a real opportunity," recalls Wigmore. "First, we sold all of our own allotment. Then we took back *all* of Merrill Lynch's allotment—and sold one hundred percent. And then we went to Salomon, who told us they still had eighty percent of their allotment. So we took that back and sold all of it, too."

Of course, this aggressiveness upset established underwriters like Merrill Lynch and Morgan Stanley as Goldman Sachs began picking off more and more business from 'their' clients, but it was great business for Goldman Sachs. No underwriting risk. No capital tied up. And no disruption to an established business relationship. "The utilities loved it too," recalls Wigmore, "so they began giving us other business as well. It was great, really great."

The firm's experience and effectiveness in distributing utility securities in the United States spliced nicely with its drive to build up business in the United Kingdom, where, starting in 1979, Margaret Thatcher's new government was strongly committed to privatizations. If Goldman Sachs could win those enormous, highly prestigious assignments from the British government, it would be taking a giant step forward in establishing itself in London and on the Continent. The firm had several things going for it. First, it was no stranger to UK institutional investors that were experienced, major investors in utilities. Scottish institutions in Edinburgh, Dundee, and Glasgow had been especially regular customers for utility underwritings, so they had gotten to know the firm and the firm knew them.

More important, Goldman Sachs had been developing expertise in underwriting offerings for investor-owned utilities. As Wigmore says, "We really understood the investors; we knew the market." Wigmore demonstrated Goldman Sachs's usual competitive intensity—flying over on the red-eye, meeting for luncheon in London with senior UK Treasury officials, and then coming right back to New York on the late afternoon flight. Her Majesty's Treasury got the message: Goldman Sachs was committed.

Almost simultaneously, Tom Tuft, frequently working with Bob Rubin, had success in utility privatizations in Mexico and Spain. The utility group had a parallel success with the gas-pipeline industry. Because the firm still had a weak hand with electric utilities, Wigmore concentrated at first on the pipeline industry, which had a more industrial mind-set that suited Goldman Sachs's traditional skills. Fortunately, White Weld, one of the traditional pipeline investment bankers, was in decline at the time, and other firms were slow to specialize in pipeline business. In new issues by pipeline companies, the firm went from zero to ranking number one. "But at first," says Wigmore, "we started, as always, beating our heads against the wall with the intensity of our calling and calling." Fortunately the pipeline companies saw themselves as industrials, not utilities, so they liked that Goldman Sachs was an industrial underwriter.

As pipeline companies tried to diversify, Wigmore saw the opportunity to apply the firm's mergers-and-acquisitions skills in the gas industry. Then, in the mid-1980s, when unfriendly tender offers became popular, Wigmore had a revelation: "The pipelines were sitting ducks—targets for hostile takeovers. The numbers were staring me, and anyone else who would look, right in the face." So he made the rounds of the pipeline companies to warn them: "You'll get raided—or LBOed!" This warning was more correct and timely than even he realized. When Cities Service was forced to sell off its gas pipeline in 1984, it attracted an astonishing twenty different bidders. "It was so obvious what that meant: The whole pipeline industry was now in play. All I could say was the obvious: 'Watch out! Here it comes!'"

As one of the first units organized to serve investment banking clients in a single industry, the utilities group broke the firm's traditional geographic mold—because, by intense specialization, it made more profits. In 1985 the merger of American Natural Resources and Coastal States Power produced the largest fee the firm had ever earned. Then Northern Natural Gas merged with Houston Natural Gas. The utility merger business exploded. M&A bankers like Mac Heller, Mike Overlock, and Peter Sachs joined in, and the transformation was under way. As volume continued to expand, the firm could justify forming more and more industry-focused groups. David Leuschen started the highly successful oil and gas unit. Joe Wender started the banking group, which soon expanded into all finance industries. Other specialties included telecom, retail, health care, and forest products—each of enough size that it could flexibly adapt to opportunities developing within its industry.

Whitehead's "phalanx" organization—ad hoc combinations into effective teams of interchangeable specialists—was virtually unstoppable against any competitor organized in the old-fashioned "one banker does it all" star system that divided each banker's time and experience between executing a variety of different kinds of transactions and developing numerous client relationships.

Fortunately for Goldman Sachs, the effectiveness of Investment Banking Services was well established before the proliferation during the 1970s of investment banking products. The investment banking business changed then as the volume of underwritings and the mergers-and-acquisitions business both picked up. Investment bankers lost their captive clients as companies wanted more than one banker and increasingly chose to use joint managers for their underwritings and other firms for specific specialties. With the professionalization of the debt and equity markets through the increasing dominance by large, sophisticated institutional investors, the traditional power of the investment banker was no longer determinant. The markets themselves were increasingly dominant because the rise of active institutional investors made them faster, cheaper, more price-certain, and responsive to innovation. Companies could choose different investment bankers for different services, shopping for the best firm for each transaction.

This opening-up played directly into the expanding array of capabilities at Whitehead's Goldman Sachs. While another firm might have better individual bankers, they could not be masters of every product specialty, and while a traditional banker concentrated on executing a transaction, he could not be out soliciting more business or defending a client relationship with extra services. Goldman

Sachs was designed for competitive advantage, and with each passing year, that advantage got stronger and stronger. No matter how brilliant a competitor's banker might be, he found it harder and harder to keep up with the IBS machine.

Whitehead's IBS organizational structure also made it possible for Goldman Sachs to follow a low-risk and high-impact "fast follower" strategy on new products and services. Let other firms be first with new ideas, absorbing the costs and pains of being on the "bleeding edge" of innovation. Study what worked and improve it if possible; sort quickly through more than a thousand client relationships to select the most likely prospects for the new service; then, using IBS as the delivery system, take the transaction specialist to all the most promising prospects; and finally, by outselling the innovating competitor, come from behind quickly to do the most business and become the recognized experts in the new service.

Sidney Weinberg's very individual way of building relationships and executing transactions made him the best banker of his era, but his way never would have worked in the greatly changed business of the sixties, seventies, and eighties. Ironically, Sidney Weinberg had mastered the investment banking business that his protégé, John Whitehead, made obsolete. Each man, in his own way, was crucial to the success of Goldman Sachs in his own era. Intermediaries, particularly in a dynamic, fast-changing business like wholesale financial services, must always be changing and reinventing themselves and their ways of doing business to advance against the strongest, most skillful and aggressive competition in what economist Joseph Schumpeter accurately described as creative destruction—even when what's being destroyed is a firm's own business.

While understandably proud of the deals and transactions he brought in for execution and of the client relationships he developed, Whitehead acknowledges that his principal and most enduring contributions came from his organizational initiatives, particularly reorganizing investment banking. Still, he was very effective as an aggressive, frontline competitor for business.

Surprised once to learn that another firm had proposed a financing and that one of his best clients had decided, since it fit their needs, to go forward with the competitor's proposal, Whitehead immediately called the company's CFO. After the personal pleasantries typical of close relationships, Whitehead turned to the real purpose of his call: "Having just learned of your decision to do this specific financing, would you be okay—if, of course, this other firm would agree—since we are so well recognized by investors as your principal banker, to comanage this particular offering? I'm confident that, with both of us working together, you would get a better market reception and, most probably, a better price." Naturally, with nothing to lose and potentially a real benefit, the company agreed, if the other firm would go along.

Whitehead than called the banker at the competitor firm. "We've been bankers for a very long time for this company and it would be awkward for us to have your firm acting as the sole senior manager on a public offering by the company. I've spoken with my friends at the company and, while they like your initiative on this particular financing, they would have no trouble at all with our jointly managing this offering. Of course, as we both know, there are always many, many ways for friendly firms in Wall Street to help one another as the years go by. And, candidly, it would mean a lot to us at Goldman Sachs if you could see the merit in not excluding us, since we are their traditional investment banker." Whitehead went on a bit more, but the other banker had already gotten the message, and knew he would be wise to accept reality and to do so promptly: "John, why don't we agree right here and now to comanage?"

At the company's headquarters, Whitehead and the competitor banker met with the CFO to determine the terms of the transaction. Graciously, Whitehead—apparently recognizing the competitor's having initiated the transaction—said, "Why don't you begin with your thoughts on pricing?" The bait was out and the other banker went for it. "We think the interest rate we can go to market with is fifteen and a half percent, and that at this rate we can raise twenty million dollars."

"Why not develop how you arrived at your pricing conclusion," prompted Whitehead. So the other banker explained his reasoning, making it clear that, in his firm's carefully considered opinion, this was the very best possible price—and maybe even a bit of a stretch. This locked him into his position and made it easy for Whitehead to go right around him. "At Goldman Sachs, we look at this issue and the market somewhat differently. If that's the best our fine competitor can do, then I'm pleased to say that we at Goldman Sachs are prepared to offer a full twenty-five basis points *lower* cost to our good client." Two weeks later, Goldman Sachs was sole manager of the offering.

When they saw each other again a year later, the competitor said, "John, you taught me a lesson—a very expensive lesson." Whitehead replied: "Maybe it seems expensive to you in the short run. But in the long run, you'll never leave yourself so open to a competitor. You're young. Over the years ahead, I'm sure you'll profit from the experience."

Shortly thereafter, Whitehead invited the banker to luncheon in one of the firm's private dining rooms. This time, his interest was more personal: Whitehead wanted to know if he might be interested in joining Goldman Sachs. This inquiry was not unusual. Over the years, Whitehead developed the practice— and strongly encouraged all others in IBS to join him—of recruiting the best people at competitors. This concept soon became codified: It was almost okay to lose an important transaction if you recruited to IBS the competitor who won.

Whitehead recognized early on that dividing the spoils, or allocating credit for transactions among Goldman Sachs people, could easily become divisive. After all, how and why would relationship specialists fully appreciate all the contributions that had been made by transaction experts—and how and why would transaction experts fully appreciate all the important contributions made by the relationship specialists to the firm's overall success? So Whitehead installed a win-win approach to compensation that would help avoid confrontations and help build strong teamwork and encourage everyone to concentrate on making the phalanx system work: 100 percent credit for each transaction would go to *both* sides. If a client assigned to Murphy did a transaction with the firm, Murphy got full credit, whether Murphy actually did anything or not. So there was zero reason to try going around Murphy or to ask potentially ugly questions about whether Murphy was 60 percent responsible or only 50 percent, or merely 30 percent, responsible for the completed transaction—"delineation perfection" that could easily hurt feelings and distract people from focusing 100 percent on working for the client.

After each transaction, an internal memorandum would detail the specific contributions of each banker. So all got recognition for what they had done, and all saw the importance to the firm's success of all the other contributions, clearly emphasizing the importance of the firm's commitment to teamwork. As Whitehead explains, "Talented people want recognition and respect for their skills and their achievements even more than they want money. They need and appreciate acceptance and respect."

When approaching the annual compensation review period, Whitehead would send a memo to all members of IBS asking for input, "so we'll be sure to know all you've done this year." Each person would write up his own report card, which Whitehead and others would carefully study. While other firms concentrated on "production"—the volume and profitability of transactions—Whitehead established at Goldman Sachs that half of a banker's bonus depended upon evaluations from others of how helpful he was to them, a compensation process that strongly encouraged everyone to focus on making the firm's phalanx system work well. These evaluations were written and collected into what became known ironically as the "slam book." To encourage reaching out across organizational lines, compensation for teamwork across organizational boundaries was celebrated and rewarded. So were individual achievements: "Of course we all care greatly about real teamwork," Whitehead would say, "so we're very glad you gave a lot of credit to so many other people. We just want to be sure you know how very much we really appreciate all the good work we know *you* have done!"

If there was a fault in Gus Levy's management style, it was that he was not a very good delegator," says Whitehead. "Gus was not a planner; he was a day-to-day operator. To Gus, short range was what's happening this morning—and long range was what's going to happen this afternoon. He felt that Wall Street was a constantly changing field in which it was hard to plan, maybe almost impossible to plan. You just sort of took advantage of the opportunities when they appeared. It was a trader's instinct that created his success. And so others of us, rather than Gus, were the ones who thought in terms of looking ahead and what activities we should go into."[3]

Planning concentrated the partners' energies on generating the firm's growth. To get closer than competitors to the market, planning meetings were held not in October and November as at other firms, but in January and February. To avoid taking productive people away from their line responsibilities, these planning meetings were held on weekends—actually, three consecutive weekends—when plans were presented, challenged, and revised until approved for immediate action. This was a two-sided coin. On one side was the intense, hands-on engagement of the partners in every aspect of the firm's operations that had made Levy such an effective player-leader. But on the other side was the risk of simply projecting incremental improvements in the same old businesses, not reaching for significant discontinuous change and innovation. Some plans were too cautious, some were too ambitious—depending on the personality of each department head. To overcome this, financial reporting during the year matched plans to actual revenue and actual costs. "Soon both the cautious and the dreamers learned to do better and better annual planning *and* execution," says Whitehead. While remarkably sophisticated in later years, the planning process was ponderous in the beginning. After sitting through branch-by-branch reviews of each and every line of business, Whitehead decided, "By God, that's the last time I'll sit through plans for both Albany *and* Detroit." He decentralized the firm's planning process to the divisions and departments.

In sustained pursuit of his strategic goals, Whitehead combined disciplined planning with reserved affability. He was quite unconcerned about being demanding of others. Smoothly rational rather than emotional, he never fraternized with the troops or had pals within the firm. Respected, but not loved or even particularly well liked, and often considered aloof from the others, who regularly socialized together, Whitehead was called, behind his back, the great white shark. He never cajoled or coddled and could be hard on investment bankers who sought praise or had a high need for ego celebration. Whitehead calmly obliged conformance in large matters and small. To ensure completion of call reports and expense reports, Whitehead once simply instructed the financial manager to hold onto everyone's monthly paycheck—partners included—until each person's call reports and expense reports had been correctly filed.

"Investment bankers are quite sensitive to public versus private critique," says partner Roy Smith, who played a key role in the early years of building Goldman Sachs's international business. "They'll accept private criticism, but never public ridicule. John could twit bankers in public, and they didn't like it one little bit. They resented it."

Whitehead not only designed and staffed his productive organization, he *made* it work, saying to one banker after another, "You *can* do it," and always clearly implying, "and if I hold you to it, you *will* do it." "John was almost regal in the way he acted," says Smith. "I never met anyone else like that in my life.

It's really quite amazing. He tells you exactly what he wants you to do; gives you the clear understanding you have no alternative and *must* do it; then proceeds to encourage you to believe you might very well be *able* to do it; and then continues on to give you the feeling you might even *enjoy* doing it, particularly if you commit your every effort to be *sure* you'll succeed."

"We had no big *and* bad ideas," explains Whitehead with evident satisfaction as he reflects on the firm's development. "We knew it would take a generation to complete the change of our position in the marketplace. Doing thousands of little things, day after day, inching along as consistently as you can, in the right direction as best you can tell, is *management*—and motivating or inspiring everyone to work together for long-term purpose is *leadership*." Whitehead didn't waste any energy, gaining force and effect through the "no waves" consistency of his commitment to a few long-range objectives and his steady, rational approach. The firm's development was not organized around grand strategies, but grew out of a continuously aggressive drive to move ahead. "As we made changes almost continuously, we had many, many failures," concedes Whitehead. "But they were almost always *little* failures that could be stopped without harm to the firm. We never felt the way to go forward was with a handful of superstars or some big acquisition."

If Goldman Sachs wanted to get into a business, it preferred to give the challenge to some of its own most promising young people. "When, as we rarely did, we decided to go outside the firm for talent, we avoided hiring whole groups or teams. Instead, we would identify the very best people, get to know them well, and bring them over individually. These new individuals would learn the Goldman Sachs culture and either blend into the firm or they would not make it at Goldman Sachs. We always tried to be creative with the new techniques and new financial products, but I never thought we had to be first with everything. I was perfectly happy to have another firm be first with a new idea because I was confident that with our superior marketing organization, we would improve the product and then achieve dominance through distribution, while those other firms put their reputation at risk if it didn't work. We control our growth rather tightly so things don't get away from us."

Whitehead remembers Gus Levy saying, "We're greedy, but long-term greedy, not short-term greedy." "Gus," he says, "wanted to do what was right for Goldman Sachs in the long run and didn't deny that he was greedy for that, but he didn't want to be greedy in the short run if it . . . well, you can see what the phrase implied."

As George Doty noted, "Gus would *never* have retired." On October 26, 1976, as always working himself much too hard, Levy flew on the red-eye from the May Department Stores board of directors meeting in Los Angeles to New York City for a full day at Goldman Sachs plus a meeting of the New York Port Authority. During that meeting, he had a stroke. Nobody noticed at first, assuming his blank stare was partly fatigue and partly his ability to tune out for a while to focus on some problem—but then he collapsed. He was in a coma at Mount Sinai Hospital for several days and then died on November 3. He was sixty-six. "Gus killed himself by working so very hard," said John Weinberg, "knowing he had a bad heart. But he wouldn't have been willing or able to live his life any other way."

While Levy lay in a coma, Weinberg went to visit and was there when an elderly American Indian quietly entered the room. Weinberg spoke first: "Hello, I'm John Weinberg, a longtime friend of Mr. Levy's. Can I help you, sir?"

"No, thank you. I'm here to help Mr. Levy find his way to the happy hunting ground. No help will be necessary, thank you." The Indian, perhaps a Navajo remembering Levy's long-ago service to the tribe, spread out the prayer rug he carried, knelt on it, and softly began praying. Two days later, after Levy had died, he rolled up his rug and left as quietly as he had come.

Bob Mnuchin had worked under Gus Levy for nineteen years. Their relationship was marvelously productive in business results, but through all the daily pressures of doing the business as they did it, their personal relationship had absorbed the many stresses of the block-trading business. Levy had traditionally begun the morning call that engaged all nine regional offices in a concerted campaign to do *all* the business that might be doable that day. Mnuchin traditionally came on the speaker system second. Now he was alone.

Mnuchin was direct: "As you've all heard, Gus Levy died yesterday of a stroke. There'll be time to discuss his contributions at a later time. Right now, as he taught us so well, it's important that we all get on with our work and the job to be done today. That's what Gus would have wanted." Mnuchin then turned to the work of the day.

At Levy's funeral, over two thousand people came to the imposing Temple Emanu-El on Manhattan's Fifth Avenue. The prayer was given by Cardinal Cooke, and one eulogy was given by I. W. Burnham, Levy's old friend and a Wall Street leader. The other eulogy was given by one of the richest men in America and one of the great powers in the Republican Party, particularly in New York, Governor Nelson Aldrich Rockefeller. His repeated theme in his eulogy for Gus Levy caught the sense of the congregation: "Oh, what a man he was!"*

"Gus was always gruff—and always very fair," recalled a former partner. "He could put the fear of God into you if you missed a trade. But you knew he wanted you to do well and you knew if you ever needed him that he'd be there for you. One Friday after Thanksgiving, I took my young son in to see the firm and showed him around. I called Inez to see if it would be okay to go down to the trading floor, and she called back to say it'd be okay at lunchtime. While we were there, I noticed Gus's cubicle was empty, so we went over. Just then, Gus came along and naturally wanted to know what was going on, so I introduced my son. Gus shook his hand and we left. Back home, my son drew a picture of a stick figure with a big cigar and wrote "Big Gus Levy" under it. A few days later, I asked Inez what she thought of my giving it to Gus, and she thought it was a great idea. Years later, after Gus died, she was cleaning out his desk—and there it was. He'd saved it all those years."

After he and John Weinberg jointly succeeded Levy as head of the firm, Whitehead's effectiveness on high-level strategies and policies was matched by a focus on clients' operations. "John was consistently very clear-minded and insightful," said partner Jun Makihara. "When we brought TGIF, a fast-growing restaurant chain, to the executive committee and presented all the great numbers for this fast grower, John said, 'I've never been in one of these restaurants, but this is clearly a fad. It can go as fast as it has come. We need to watch closely— and report to this committee—same-store sales every month.' He was certainly focused on the right thing. Within months, problems were starting to show, but

---

* The eulogy was written by Goldman Sachs's public relations manager, Ed Novotny, who met briefly with Governor Rockefeller just before the service began to give him the text, as requested. "I can't read this!" exclaimed Rockefeller. "I'm dyslexic!" The text was quickly retyped on a special typewriter so the governor could read it at the appointed time during the service.

they were only visible on the one measure John had made us focus in on. You learn a lot when people like John Whitehead are reviewing your work."

Looking ahead, Whitehead had no great plans to change—just to improve. "We will continue to expand internationally. However, we must be careful not to let the firm grow too big and lose the intimacy that we and our people treasure."

Later others would argue that Whitehead's deliberate, careful approach was not as aggressive as the firm should have been, partly because the increasingly competitive markets were changing and partly because Goldman Sachs had been changed by Whitehead and Weinberg so it *could* be more aggressive and more innovative. "John Whitehead believed in the IBM approach," says Steve Friedman. "Develop superior, strong relationships with the maximum number of clients and be conservative with new product and service introductions because they don't all work and you don't want to harm those relationships that took years to develop and that you'll want to come back to again and again. This leads to cautious incrementalism on the product side and no big, breakthrough innovations, because if you're not looking hard for innovations you certainly won't find them. And the general feeling was: Don't innovate. It's not wanted and in fact was clearly *un*wanted. So innovators were taking career risk, and risk was the major no-no."

In 1985, after thirty-eight years at Goldman Sachs, Whitehead was asked to become deputy secretary of state to George Shultz and served until early 1989. He has since served in a broad range of powerful public positions—chairman of the New York Federal Reserve Bank; chairman of Lower Manhattan Development Corporation, the organization responsible for rebuilding and revitalization after 9/11; and trustee of an impressive set of educational, artistic, international, and social institutions. His corporate activities have been confined to AEA Investors, a private-equity investment company, where he "can see lots of old business friends roughly my own age."

EXCELLENCE, reads the small sign on Whitehead's desk. He had it with him throughout his years at Goldman Sachs. He also had it on his desk at the State Department, where many spoke French and some asked: "Is it a noun—or a title?"

11

PRINCIPLES

The longest-lasting, most visible, and perhaps most important of John Whitehead's contributions to Goldman Sachs materialized in just one Sunday afternoon in the late 1970s when he was alone at his home in New Jersey writing longhand on a legal pad. In writing, recalls Whitehead, "I tried to be direct, even pithy—and tried very hard to avoid anything that might read like motherhood." Contemplating the growth of Goldman Sachs, he had realized with concern several weeks before that even with the firm's remarkably low staff turnover of just 5 percent, steady increases in business were producing a 15 percent annual increase in staff. In just three years, over half of all the firm's people would be *new*. Thinking through the implications, Whitehead became uneasy. With the firm steadily getting larger and more diverse and adding so many new people, the traditional but inherently slow one-on-one "apprentice" approach of passing along the core values of Goldman Sachs would surely be overwhelmed by the number of new people. Without appropriate action, the core values could not be successfully passed on to the increasingly large and diverse staff. The firm's unique culture, which Whitehead believed was crucial to its growth and success, would be put at risk by the firm's own success and growth.

Whitehead kept coming back to a gnawing question: "How could we get the message to all those individuals who were new to Goldman Sachs in such a way that they would understand our core values, come to believe in them, and make the firm's values *their* values in everything they did every day?"

Whitehead collected what he thought were the existing but unwritten principles of Goldman Sachs, thought about them for weeks, and then spent that Sunday afternoon writing them out longhand. The list began with ten major statements, but Whitehead soon heard from George Doty, a devout Catholic, that that seemed sacrilegious. A list of ten principles was too close to the Ten Commandments—so the list was expanded.

With a few changes by other partners, "Our Business Principles" was set in type and copies sent to all employees and their families at their home addresses. As Whitehead explains, "Our annual review was being issued at just this time, so I made sure we clipped 'Our Business Principles' on the front and had copies sent to all Goldman Sachs employees' homes. And, just to be sure, envelopes were carefully addressed to John Smith *& Family*, so they and the members of their families could read them and enjoy reflecting with some pride on the nature of the firm with which they were associated. We thought the wives and children of our employees would enjoy seeing what kind of firm their men were working for and what values they lived by at work, recognizing that many were absentee fathers. We got great feedback on this, particularly in quite moving letters from spouses."

The Principles have been featured in every subsequent annual review published by Goldman Sachs. For example, the firm's 1990 annual review stated: "Our Business Principles are inviolate. They are the core around which everything else has been built. One of the major tasks in the 1990s will be to ensure that these values are clearly understood in our increasingly complex, international firm. Teamwork, integrity, placing our clients' interests first, and the other core values expressed in these Principles are the center of our competitive strategy and represent the only kind of firm at which any of us wants to work."

Despite major changes in the firm's size, organizational structure, and business, the Principles, with minor changes for political correctness over the years, have endured. Featured somewhat self-consciously in each year's annual report and referred to frequently, they have taken on totemic significance within the firm. The Principles now are:

1. Our clients' interests always come first. Our experience shows that if we serve our clients well, our own success will follow.

2. Our assets are people, capital, and reputation. If any of these are ever lost, the last is the most difficult to regain.

3. We take great pride in the professional quality of our work. We have an uncompromising determination to achieve excellence in everything we undertake. Though we may be involved in a wide variety and heavy volume of activity, we would, if it came to a choice, rather be best than biggest.

4. We stress creativity and imagination in everything we do. While recognizing that the old way may still be the best way, we constantly strive to find a better solution to clients' problems. We pride ourselves on having pioneered many of the practices and techniques that have become standard in the industry.

5. We make an unusual effort to identify and recruit the very best person for every job. Although our activities are measured in billions of dollars, we select our people one by one. In a service business, we know that without the best people, we cannot be the best firm.

6. We offer our people the opportunity to move ahead more rapidly than is possible at most other places. We have yet to find the limits to the responsibility that our best people are able to assume. Advancement depends solely on ability, performance, and contribution to the firm's success, without regard to race, color, age, creed, sex, or national origin.

7. We stress teamwork in everything we do. While individual creativity is always encouraged, we have found that team effort often produces the best results. We have no room for those who put their personal interests ahead of the interests of the firm and its clients.

8. The dedication of our people to the firm and the intense effort they give their jobs are greater than one finds in most other organizations. We think that this is an important part of our success.

9. Our profits are a key to our success. They replenish our capital and attract and keep our best people. It is our practice to share our profits generously with all who helped create them. Profitability is crucial to our future.

10. We consider our size an asset that we try hard to preserve. We want to be big enough to undertake the largest project that any of our clients could

contemplate, yet small enough to maintain the loyalty, the intimacy, and the esprit de corps that we all treasure and that contribute greatly to our success.

11. We constantly strive to anticipate the rapidly changing needs of our clients and to develop new services to meet those needs. We know that the world of finance will not stand still and that complacency can lead to extinction.

12. We regularly receive confidential information as part of our normal client relationships. To breach a confidence or to use confidential information improperly or carelessly would be unthinkable.

13. Our business is highly competitive, and we aggressively seek to expand our client relationships. However, we must always be fair competitors and must never denigrate other firms.

14. Integrity and honesty are at the heart of our business. We expect our people to maintain high ethical standards in everything they do, both in their work for the firm and in their personal lives.

"I was simply putting down on paper the things that we really lived for there as long as I could remember, and tried to foster," Whitehead said. In a follow-through typical of his persistence, each department head was told to assemble all his department's employees for a public reading of the Principles—"Our clients' interests always come first." . . . "If we serve clients well, our own success will follow." . . . "We stress creativity." An open discussion in small groups of what the Principles really meant in that particular department's day-to-day working experiences was to follow, so everyone would see how those abstractions could be made operational in their own particular work. The discussion might run: "On bidding for blocks of stock, for example, if the price is really good for our client, the institution, is it really the right price for Goldman Sachs to buy at? And what if the price drops after we've bought it?" Formal minutes of these discussions were to be prepared in some detail and submitted by the department head to the management committee for review. Even Whitehead's admirers are skeptical that such obedience was ever fully achieved, but it would be hard to find any other organization where so much prominence and serious attention is given to a corporate belief statement for so many consecutive years.

"The Business Principles were not just about the style of the firm or its culture," explains Roy Smith. "They lay out a series of dicta about how to conduct business and how to be truly professional. Considering that John was then an important but not a leading partner, it was all the more audacious to compose and promulgate this set of rules for success." Whitehead, mentioning that he's still somewhat surprised by the organizational significance the Principles have acquired, says: "Since investment banking *skills* are pretty much comparable among the major Wall Street firms, it helps to be recognized as a firm that is unusual in its focus on being ethical."

The Principles are an easy target for those who think they are too many. Some argue that nobody can implement so many beliefs with sufficient rigor and vigor to make all of them equally important. As Steve Friedman put it years later: "When you are waked up in the middle of the night, how many principles can you rattle off while you're just coming awake—three? Maybe four? That's where we should all focus so they are always on our minds and in our thoughts." Others appreciate the comprehensive construction. As Roy Smith puts it, "Those principles are a complete prescription of the firm's business strategy. No other firm in the securities business—and almost certainly, no other firm in *any* business—can say and mean those statements because they cannot commit to and live by *all* of them. But those simple declarative sentences describe the essential nature of Goldman Sachs. And they explain how and why the firm really works."

The Principles not only imply an overarching business strategy for Goldman Sachs, they provide clear guidance on operational tactics. "My commitment to the corporate culture at Goldman Sachs is certainly not religious," says Gene Fife. "It's because it's a very smart way to do very good business." While some other banking firms tried to manage and control with top-down rules, a rules-based management couldn't possibly keep up with the speed of change in the securities business and couldn't penetrate the complexities of many different lines of business in many different markets to address specific situations where values-based decisions might be needed. With a principles-based management, responsibility for decisions is pushed down to the men and women on the firing line. Since they know the concepts of the Principles *and* they know the detailed realities of their specific business, they can be held accountable for knowing and doing the right things in the right way. Hard decisions about doing the right thing are always in the gray zone and usually somewhere in the middle of that gray zone—and they come up for action much too quickly for leisurely deliberation. Action must be swift. The tight-loose management that is so clearly expected and expressed by the Principles distributes decision-making responsibility very widely throughout the firm without senior management ever delegating its final authority. Trying to formulate all the rules that might be needed would produce such inconvenient bulk—like the IRS Manual—that only a few could ever figure things out even if they had all the time in the world. The Principles have become totemic because they work.

Never content to be a one-trick pony, Whitehead put out another set of guidelines or tactics for IBS business development in 1970—and these *were* ten commandments:

1. Don't waste your time going after business we don't really want.
2. The boss usually decides—not the assistant treasurer. Do you know the boss?
3. It's just as easy to get a first-rate piece of business as a second-rate one.
4. You never learn anything when you're talking.
5. The client's objective is more important than yours.
6. The respect of one person is worth more than acquaintance with 100.
7. When there's business to be done, get it!
8. Important people like to deal with other important people. Are you one?
9. There's nothing worse than an unhappy client.
10. If you get the business, it's up to you to see that it's well handled.

The real culture of Goldman Sachs was a unique blend of a drive for making money and the characteristics of "family" in ways that the Chinese, Arabs, and old Europeans would well understand. More than any other Wall Street firm, Goldman Sachs became tribal: To be successful, it was important to have a "rabbi" who would coach you, sponsor you, and protect you. Teamwork and team play were celebrated—and required. Individuals—Jim Gorter and Terry Mulvihill in Chicago, Steve Kay in Boston, Ray Young, Fred Krimendahl, and L. Jay Tenenbaum in New York, George Ross in Philadelphia—were especially admired as culture carriers and exemplars. Some expressions of "our crowd" were simple. As Terry Mulvihill admonished young partners: "Go to *every* employee's major life events—every wedding, every funeral, every bar mitzvah. Always get there early and make sure you're visibly social." More than at any other firm, the partners of Goldman Sachs turned out, over and over again, for weddings, funerals, and other family events.

Absolute loyalty to the firm and to the partnership was expected. While strong feelings—including personal dislikes and flashes of anger—were evident to the partners *within* the partnership, an impenetrable wall of silence kept almost all internal tensions invisible to outsiders. No other major firm came even close. One remarkable demonstration of the we-they separation between insiders and outsiders was the speed and clarity with which long-serving partners who left went from being insiders to being outsiders and were soon forgotten. While this may have strengthened the internal bonding, it was an obvious missed opportunity for the organization—and a personal loss for those who, after devoting the most important years of their careers to the firm, were now almost ignored.

The answer to one key question again and again dominated both tactical and strategic decisions: "What is best for the firm?" Even though divisional profit was clearly of great importance—divisional profits eventually drove partnership percentages and the stature of individual partners—partners would time and again defer to other partners if that would make money for the firm.

Personal anonymity is *almost* a core value of the firm. Most things that other firms might celebrate or dramatize are deliberately understated. Morgan Stanley, for example, has elaborate, large, neon-lighted signage with stock quotes visible from several blocks away. In New York, London, or Tokyo, there is no indication whatsoever of Goldman Sachs's presence—other than well-dressed young men and women coming briskly into the building early and going out late.

The Sachs family believed public relations was a bad thing and would have none of it. This was the background within which John Whitehead proposed to compile and produce an annual report on Goldman Sachs. As he explains, "The limits necessary to achieve a compromise seemed pretty strict: no financials; plain, no frills; and a list of our services. And, on advice of Sullivan & Cromwell, we were prohibited from using the terms 'bank' or 'investment bank.' The text began with this sentence: 'Goldman Sachs is today a leading firm in the investment business.' The back page said only, 'Established in 1869.'"

Walter Sachs's reaction to Whitehead's plan for distribution was not positive;

it was "No!" The slim reports would not be mailed out. Copies would only be given out by hand, if and when appropriate. Modesty and understatement were matters of principle at Goldman Sachs.

With actual capital of thirty million dollars, the firm's claim—the only even tangentially financial detail in the report—was restrained: "over $20 million in capital." Goldman Sachs continued to use this figure even when actual capital had accumulated to over one hundred million dollars.

The firm does produce annual reports, but except for the top one or two executives, all employees are clearly shown not as individuals, but grouped as members of the team. The principal responsibility of those who labor in public relations is to minimize the number of articles about the firm, to discourage pieces about individuals, and to project a tone of modesty and moderation. The head of public relations over many years, Ed Novotny, was not even an employee. Even though fully dedicated to the firm, he had a separate office and phone and styled himself as just a consultant.

The firm's precepts didn't stop with the written ones. Making money—always and *no* exceptions—was a principle of Goldman Sachs. Nothing was ever done for prestige. In fact, the prestigious clients were often charged the most. Every banker was expected to succeed on *two* standards: Serve the client and make money. Both were top priority—always. No exceptions. Be strong. If you must cut fees to win or keep business, do *not* cut fees.

Cost discipline was another principle. Fly coach. Staff leanly, because with the very best people, you can be lean *and* cost-effective—and therefore more profitable.

Open dialogue was another principle. Part of this was posting: keeping *everyone* informed. Part was the deliberately flat organizational structure. During the seventies, the firm initiated monthly meetings of partners. Any partner whose area was doing better or worse than anticipated would be expected to stand and explain the difference. If the difference reflected a problem, then the solution was also expected.

Aggressive salesmanship was obviously a principle. So was working harder for much longer hours than the people at any other firm.

Deliberately taking risk—and being first to learn how to take and manage risk in any emerging new market—was also a matter of principle. In investment banking, the firm continued to avoid risk as a cautious "fast follower," but in trading, while most competitors tried to avoid or minimize risk, Goldman Sachs was almost always alone in the early days of new markets. Therefore it was able to earn high risk-adjusted profits and learn how to succeed in each market over the long term.

Goldman Sachs's capital kept growing, but the firm always needed more capital than it had because its people were so entrepreneurial. The tension between supply and demand provided a constructive discipline.

Independence or freedom to decide was balanced with authority and responsibility as a matter of principle at Goldman Sachs. When a tough negotiator was trying to bully young partner Barrie Wigmore on the terms of an offering, one of his colleagues left the room where they were meeting and called the office. The management committee was meeting, and he was put though on a speaker phone. After hearing his description of the negotiations, the committee decided not to accommodate the prospective client—while Wigmore was continuing to negotiate. When his colleague returned with the decision of the firm's senior management, Wigmore—who was all of thirty-one—said, "No! What business is it of theirs? Pricing a service is *my* responsibility," and that was that.

Independence *and* responsibility were pushed out to those on the firing line because they knew the most. But independence did not mean everyone for himself. Responsibility included responsibility for any negative side effects on other divisions of the firm.

12

THE TWO JOHNS

Gus Levy's unexpected death, at the peak of his powers inside and outside the firm, left Goldman Sachs with no clear answer to the urgently obvious question of who would now be the senior partner. More precisely, which of the Two Johns would take over leading Goldman Sachs? John Weinberg, popular and decisive, managed most of the firm's major corporate client relationships, most of which had been his father's, and to many it would be fitting for him to lead what was still widely considered Sidney Weinberg's firm. John Whitehead was older and had been at the firm longer, but while he had strong advocates, he also had silent skeptics. The Two Johns worked well together and had great respect and affection for each other, but both were alpha males. A contested choice between the two natural leaders could have hurt the firm.

John Whitehead's long-standing interest and leadership in strategic planning; the increasing success of his innovations in investment banking; his considerable visibility in Washington and in the Investment Banking Association; and his initiatives within the firm in promulgating the Principles and in recruiting, public relations, and organizing and upgrading internal operations—all these made him, in his own mind and the minds of others, the natural first choice. But

Whitehead had to know he could only succeed in the senior partner role if he had the explicit support of his friend. He knew that many partners had strong positive feelings about Weinberg—warm, affectionate feelings that differed from their cool, respectful feelings about him.

Outside the firm, Whitehead was generally recognized as the strategic and conceptual leader. Insiders liked Weinberg better. "John Whitehead was clearly a brilliant strategist," said one partner. "But he didn't have that 'connectedness' that's so often vital to great leadership."

"John Weinberg understood people better than anyone else in the firm," said Ray Young. "Like his father before him, John would get it right with people. They *knew* they could trust him and his decisions. John Whitehead was very ambitious and always had his own agenda. We were all ambitious, but our ambition was for the firm. John Whitehead cared about recognition for his personal achievements and his charitable contributions. Later in life, John Weinberg probably gave just as much—but always anonymously."

The consistently cool and articulate Whitehead, aptly described as a "gentleman's-C's type who gets straight A's,"[1] was calmly guarded and one step removed from others as he concentrated on policy and strategy, in contrast to Weinberg's spontaneous emotional directness and earthy candor as he concentrated on transactions. Whitehead inspired respect; Weinberg inspired trust and affection. Everyone at Goldman Sachs knew where and why Weinberg stood on every decision, but many wondered about the core hidden many layers behind Whitehead's smooth exterior. It was amusingly ironic that Whitehead, the patrician, had to work his way through school while Weinberg, the Common Man, had been raised in affluence and gone to all the "right" schools: Deerfield, Princeton, and Harvard Business School.

With Levy gone, everyone expected the Two Johns to resolve the leadership succession. Whitehead had a sensible solution: The Two Johns would take turns. He proposed a "first me, then you" sequence in firm leadership. As the senior of the Two Johns, he would succeed Levy now and would then, after some years, pass the baton to Weinberg and move on to a career in Washington or at a major corporation.

But Weinberg didn't buy it.

What could easily have become a personal "him or me" confrontation became instead one of the great personal combinations in management as White-head deftly offered a different proposal: The Two Johns could lead their firm together as co–senior partners. Forcing a "him or me" choice would have caused division within the firm when it was most vulnerable. It wasn't clear who would have won, and in any case there was too much important work for any one leader, particularly if there were any hurt feelings—and there surely would have been some. Weinberg, who was so often almost instinctive in his good judgment, agreed immediately to what must have seemed a most improbable and unwork-able managerial proposition to those who first heard about their unusual plan.

In fact, the first thread leading to this unique proposition was in Gus Levy's will. Levy had identified the Two Johns as coexecutors of his estate. Later Levy took this thought further, as L. Jay Tenenbaum recalls: "When I asked Gus who he had identified as his successor, he told me of his plan to have the Two Johns take over, and I told him: 'Gus, that won't work at all well. You have to have one guy who has the final say.'" Then in 1976, recognizing that the Goldman Sachs part-nership could become divided—with some partners wanting Weinberg and some wanting Whitehead—Levy announced that he didn't want to choose between them and had decided to endorse "our usual formula for success in virtually all endeav-ors: teamwork." The legend within the firm has it that on the day he had his stroke, Levy had a memo on his desk about the advantages of the Two Johns succeeding him—together.

The official announcement of Levy's stroke explained that Weinberg and Whitehead would serve together as acting cochairmen.[2] A week later, they announced they would serve together as senior partners and cochairmen—not with each taking responsibility for half the firm, as others might have done, but with both taking undivided responsibility for the firm as a whole. In establishing their dual leadership, the Two Johns took advantage of their friendship, formed over many years of discussing what they were going to do when they eventually headed Goldman Sachs, as they believed they would, while eating chicken salad sandwiches at Scottie's Sandwich Shop on Pine Street. If either had a strong view, the other deferred, so they maintained broad agreement on strategy and policies. The eventual decision to co-lead Goldman Sachs soon seemed as natural to the Two Johns as it was unusual on Wall Street.

Weinberg reminisced, "During one summer before going to [Harvard

Business] school, I had worked at McKinsey. It was my father's idea, and a good one. I got to know Marvin Bower, the senior partner of McKinsey, who knew a lot about the workings of organizations. When he heard that John and I had it in mind to serve as cochairmen and senior partners, he said it would never work, and that when we had the whole firm really screwed up he'd come down and help us unscrew it. He was great. But somehow we made it work."

The Two Johns sustained a "we two" relationship, as successful parents so often do, based on mutual respect and different priorities—one largely internal and managerial and one largely external with clients—and avoided competition by coordinating frequently. "Though we are very different kinds of people, we happen to be very simpatico," Weinberg once explained. "Our offices are close together. We communicate a lot. We really wear out the carpet between our offices. We have a very collegial approach to management of the firm. John Whitehead and I think very much alike on all sorts of things. We speak on the phone almost every day, and every Sunday evening we talk about the agenda for the next day's management committee meeting and agree on what we need to do."[3]

Whitehead and Weinberg—"the Two Johns" to all at Goldman Sachs—never competed with each other but were intense competitors with the rest of Wall Street, determined to drive Goldman Sachs just as far as possible up into leadership among investment banking firms. Their agreed priorities were clear: recruit the best people, develop more and better long-term corporate relationships, build up capital, tighten managerial discipline, require teamwork, avoid big mistakes, expand the business, persistently increase market share, upgrade the staff and upgrade the clients, increase profitability substantially, grow from within, minimize personal publicity while building the firm's reputation, and keep accelerating. A few years after the Two Johns took over, a senior competitor would say, "Goldman Sachs, as an entire firm, is *driven*—on this it is consistent and unrelenting."

Always determined but cautious, the Two Johns favored a fast-follower strategy in business development and had no room for heroes or stars. "To be a star," advised Weinberg, "getting your name in the paper and all that, is not popular in Goldman Sachs because it's against the culture. If you did that, everybody would call you a showboat. If people want a career here, then go with the system."[4] Office politics were verboten. "With John and John everybody knew: Don't ever screw around," recalls partner Bob Steel. "They allowed *zero* politics. With strong, respected leaders like John and John, everybody knew not to play politics, particularly politics that were negative about other people. And they had *no* favorites within the firm. With John and John, you knew not to push the boundaries, or to squeeze. They had no fear of anyone or anything. And both men were always ready to make the very tough calls."

Both Johns were clear on what was wrong and what was right. They had deep experience with moral standards from their service in World War II. Changing the norms of personal behavior from the "don't ask" laxity of the past called for swift, decisive, and visible decisions on people, including terminating partners. "Some days, I really hate my job," observed John Whitehead to another firm's CEO, explaining that he had just fired a superbly talented young partner who, under extreme pressure to produce a document for a client, had gotten unacceptable work from a typist and had lashed out at her, calling her a "stupid cunt." A few years later, John Weinberg fired a divisional head for having an affair with his secretary and not coming entirely clean with Weinberg when the story, which mushroomed into a high-visibility embarrassment for the firm, first got reported in the press. Sexual exploits were tolerated if kept private, but the boundaries of privacy were tested in various ways. One man was so extensive in his multiple "private" adventures—usually going by radio-connected Dial Car, the firm's exclusive provider, to his numerous and varied assignations—that drivers could be overheard bantering in amazement on their radios about his heroic exploits, and one day the trading room was a sea of smirks when an attractive young woman came onto the floor looking for more.

"Assuring professional ethics are really lived by is a bit like being a zoo-keeper," says partner Roy Smith. "You need lions and tigers to have a really good zoo, but you must also keep them under control—or reasonably so." Everyone in Goldman Sachs was supposed to be interchangeable, a member of the phalanx. "We were like horses competing to pull the wagon. You might stop to complain, eat some oats, and go right back to pulling the wagon." At that time Goldman Sachs was strategically a lot like Procter & Gamble: few real innovations, but skillful and unrelenting in execution. When a competitor introduced an interesting new product, the firm would immediately study it and learn all about how to do it really well—always driving to improve the product as much as possible—and then present the improved product extensively through Investment Banking Services and execute effectively and consistently. With IBS's corporate relationships well established, any new, improved product could be taken rapidly and effectively to large numbers of potential users—in the order of their probability of signing up—often quickly producing substantial market leadership.

The Goldman Sachs that the Two Johns had found in the 1950s had been a "not" firm: *not* intensely competitive, *not* exciting, and *not* important. But competitive intensity came naturally to them. Both men had seen combat. Both understood how successful organizations could be if they always moved faster and more aggressively than their competitors. Both were ambitious as individuals and for their firm. Both believed in understated but unrelenting aggression versus competitors, and both believed that in any competition, the organization that had the best people, made the fewest mistakes, and showed the most commitment to *working* to win would win out. They always played to beat the other firms, to win on every dimension, believing that that was what their toughest competitors would always do, too.

Their remarkable partnership and friendship had its origins when, three years into his rapidly rising career at Goldman Sachs, Whitehead was told by Sidney Weinberg that his son John would be coming to the firm for the summer months between his first and second years at Harvard Business School and that Whitehead should show him the ropes. A year later, John Weinberg joined the firm full time and the Two Johns began the person-to-person partnership that lasted over thirty-five years. The two men became partners on the same day and held the same percentage ownership in the firm throughout their careers.

In the beginning, the two young men set their desks back to back in the squash court. As they ate chicken salad sandwiches at Scottie's each day, they talked freely and exchanged thoughts and ideas on virtually everything—including their frustrations with the way the firm was *not* run. Whitehead explains, "We were only serving time, not learning much and certainly not working at our capacity. John and I were resolved to put much more responsibility to the young people in the firm." As they talked, both Johns became more and more convinced that they knew many ways to make the firm stronger and better. "We found we thought alike on many, many things. We had the same hopes for Goldman Sachs, and while we shared enormous respect and affection for Sidney Weinberg, we shared major frustrations with him too."

The firm's carefully monitored team atmosphere meant there were fewer of the petty turf battles that plagued the rest of the Street. Goldman Sachs became recognized as "a company—rather than a collection of individuals—that acts more like an organism."[5] Still, the competition for advancement, particularly to partnerships that would go to only a few, was intense. All the people who joined Goldman Sachs were capable and hardworking. Those who made partner had to make a larger commitment to the firm—strive more, devote more time, and take more pressure on themselves and on their families.

"Goldman Sachs was an investment banking firm that added on trading," says Jim Gorter. "So did Morgan Stanley. Salomon Brothers was a trading firm that added on investment banking. At Goldman Sachs, the bankers generally ran the firm, and more partners came from banking than any other division. But the point is that everyone worked *together* all the time. Or certainly almost all the time, because as in any situation there were tensions to work out. The concept or commitment to real teamwork—and no stars because stars denigrate all the others—traces right back to Gus Levy, but was brought home and institutionalized by John and John."

"We were sort of shabby in our offices and low key, low visibility in terms of personal heroes," says partner Roy Smith. "We tended to resent heroes if any were to emerge because we all knew that it was the team approach—the phalanx—that made the difference . . . plus not letting our egos get out of line. We produced a somewhat hard-to-classify mystique of efficiency without too much identity. That sometimes frustrated us when we felt we had a lesser public image than some of us from time to time would like to have seen."

Teamwork was mandatory and celebrated. "I," as in "I did this" or "I won that," was clearly to be avoided. Everything was "we"—"We did this" or "We won that." As one partner quipped, "The I word is so strongly avoided that some people won't even go to see an eye doctor!" Teamwork mattered to clients as much as to those within the firm. Ford Motor Company's president, Philip Caldwell, explained what made Goldman Sachs outstanding: "First, they know their business. Second, they don't seem to have any internal struggles or strife."[6] The Two Johns worked consistently to develop the leadership and management capabilities of strong performers. Pairs of young "future leaders" were assigned to various managerial slots to see how they would perform together and handle shared power and responsibility.

Another way of building teamwork was to share the profits in good years—and protect people in bad years. To spread participation in the success of the whole firm, the partners contributed 15 percent of profits to a pool divided into "profit shares" in a program administered by each division. In combination with salary and bonus (and the future possibility of partnership), the profit shares were an important part of the firm's ability to make an attractive economic offer to prospective associates. During the stock-market doldrums of the mid-seventies, when the firm scrambled to barely break even, layoffs were avoided, and not only were decent bonuses paid out widely through the organization, but young partners were subsidized so they could make it through the adversity. Really being there for people when it mattered counted a lot in the organization the Two Johns were building.

"Balance was key," says partner Lee Cooperman. "More than any other firm, Goldman Sachs had strategic and organizational balance across all areas of the business. It was a conglomerate that worked. Key to Goldman Sachs's success was that the firm not only had great balance and strength, it also shared the benefits of that balance widely within the firm. Everybody pulled on his own oar and all pulled together. Everybody was part of—and all believed in—the Team. Sure, there were some politics—and as the firm grows, it's probably increasing—but compared to any other firm, the problem of politics at Goldman Sachs was small. The real indicators of teamwork and cooperation—not just within divisions, but also across divisions—are the *certainty* of cooperation and the *speed* of cooperation," says Cooperman, who gives this simple example: "A lawyer at a major Wall Street firm wanted an introduction to the key people in project finance [at Goldman Sachs] and asked a securities salesman how to go about it. 'I'll find out for you.' The lawyer expected to hear in a week or two. That same day, the lawyer was called with a confirmed appointment already set up. The lawyer was startled, but that's typical of the way it works."

Goldman Sachs had a relatively flat organizational structure with virtually no hierarchy. Teamwork, interaction, and swift, extensive interdepartmental communication were stressed. One of the first lessons taught new associates was "posting." Is there *anyone* else in the firm who can use this information? The firm developed its own culture, based on management by owner-producers and a highly charged, intensely meritocratic environment. "We believed we were the financial world's equivalent of a team of professional athletes," says Roy Smith. "We were very competitive and worked and trained hard. We were good at what we did and wanted to be the best—the world champions."[7] The sustained striving that was so essential to becoming champions needed to be balanced by a perspective that protected the firm and its individuals from going too far. Asked what could derail the firm's strategy, Bob Rubin was candid: "Ego, arrogance, a sense of self-importance. If you allow them to develop, that's when you fall off the track."[8]

"When the firm was small in the sixties and seventies, it was easy to recognize the really bright guys," says George Doty—to see "who were real players and who were just spectators." But as the firm grew, more structured communications were needed. To encourage teamwork and to be sure everyone involved in the important transactions was fully recognized and also knew how important the contributions of others had been, Whitehead and Weinberg insisted on "credit memos" being written to specify each contributor's contributions, and that those credit memos be circulated to all concerned. Still, Doty could feel frustrated: "There are two types of those memos that really get to me. First, is the 'Gee, I'm great' type. Second, and almost as bad, is the 'My people are so great' type with the all-too-obvious implication that the writer must be a superb leader to have so inspired his team." Still, the determination to identify and visibly recognize everyone's contribution minimized misunderstandings, showed everyone how important all the other members of the team were to achieving success, and, while celebrating each person's particular contributions, encouraged realistic modesty. Teamwork and subordinating individuals to the organization helped build Goldman Sachs as a unity both inside and outside.

"Fear and accountability were important, too," recalls Cooperman. "You wouldn't ever want to leave anything not yet done that might or could be done. You were responsible for being the best at each client and for doing the most with each of your accounts. The pressure was always on to do more and to do better.

The firm didn't give any medals or bouquets for doing a good job, but it was very quick to focus on negatives that needed to be corrected. John Whitehead could be very cutting. I'll never forget his memorandum that said: 'We appreciate the business you've brought in. We are also conscious of the other business you have not yet brought to Goldman Sachs.'"

"The Two Johns saw nothing at all wrong with people working very hard and carrying a heavy load," recalls partner Roy Smith. "They were convinced it was better for you to carry more work responsibility—perhaps half again more than your normal capacity—because that meant you accumulated more experience and you would learn more and know more. You'd advance up the learning curve more swiftly and get to a higher level of performance. And sooner or later, if as a result of your hard work you were the best trained or had the most developed skills, you'd be doing transactions for clients that other firms couldn't do as well." Whitehead confirms that view: "Goldman Sachs believes in working very hard because the more work you do, the more practice you'll have and the more you'll learn. In an inherently fast-changing business, you'll develop better skills and greater understanding than your cohorts inside the firm or your competitors outside the firm."

Under the leadership of the Two Johns, Goldman Sachs was sometimes criticized for being slow to innovate or too cautious. Weinberg objected: "We don't perceive ourselves as being slow. We think we're like the tortoise in the race with the hare: we get there, but we don't get carried away with unproven ideas. When it's all your own money in a partnership and you have unlimited liability, you try to take only sensible business risks. Despite our reputation for planning, most of what we did was to see an opportunity and take an action—advancing one step at a time, usually with no clear sense of direction, let alone destination. John concentrated on planning and management, while I concentrated on clients. John had vision. He was tough, too. He would tell people what to do, without messing around."[9]

While Goldman Sachs became capable of making major tactical changes in the way it does business, continuity of strategic vision was long a consistent hallmark. In 1983 Whitehead described the firm's objectives: "Our long-range goal is to become a truly international investment banking and brokerage firm. We want to have as many clients around the world as we have here in America and to be as highly respected in London, Paris, Zurich, and Tokyo as we are in New York, Chicago, and Los Angeles."[10]

Developing 'franchise' earning power is what every investment banking firm looks for," explains Roy Smith. "The trick is to maximize risk-adjusted earning power as a firm. But of course each individual is looking for maximum earning power too. With thousands of employees—each making his own trade-off of risk versus return and short term versus long term and individual relative to firm and client relationship versus specific transactions—the challenge for management is very great. With all the many conflicts and challenges, and they are *always* changing, it's hard to find and sustain harmony and balance." The ultimate risk is that the truly great individuals like Gus Levy and the Two Johns, as well as everybody in leadership positions in each of the business units, will feel constrained or frustrated by the organization. The creative genius needs to be disruptive and different to be truly innovative. But the larger the organization gets, the more it will seek—and will insist on getting—order and stability. Both are needed, but each is in conflict with the other. Managing these conflicts is what real management is all about in the securities business.

The challenge compounds. With opportunities seized, the firm grows. As the firm gets bigger, it's harder and harder to recruit or fully use or even keep the remarkably gifted, creative, and driven individual performer. Almost inevitably, there is an institutional hardening and the organization ejects the great individual performers, even though it was the great individual performers of the past who enabled the organization to create growth. So management's dilemma is that the organization's franchise—vital to maximize long-term risk-adjusted earnings—must always be protected from the short-term urgency of specific transactions or deals. "Protecting against short-term expediency must be balanced against the opposite problem," says Smith. "If you're too conservative, you'll force out or lose the great individual contributor. Or they won't even join you. If you're not conservative enough, individuals will get out of control and do self-aggrandizing transactions that will harm the whole organization. The more complex the organization and its business, the more difficult this vital role of management will be."

In building the organization they wanted Goldman Sachs to be, the Two

Johns had long been recruiting key people at senior levels. Two of their most successful imports were Jim Weinberg and George Doty. An original and sometimes contrarian thinker, Jim Weinberg was consistently unpretentious, congenial, and insightful. He was his younger brother's closest and most objective confidant and adviser on policy and strategy. In a crowd of intense, controlled egos, Jim Weinberg was cheerfully modest, pragmatic, and gracefully at ease within himself—and found keeping faith with his brother's privacy entirely natural. He wisely identified numerous people for advancement to important positions of leadership, and he was completely unpretentious. He took subways and once, at a fabulous Los Angeles restaurant, asked the captain, "Don't you have anything less expensive?"

Doty, who had been recruited in the sixties, was tough and shrewd as he concentrated on operations and fiscal discipline. As a senior partner in Lybrand, Ross Brothers & Montgomery, later Coopers & Lybrand, Doty had been a major presence, with Chase Manhattan Bank and Dillon Read, among others, as his clients. "I was in some danger of becoming the senior partner of our accounting firm, was forty-six years old, and felt I had the world by the throat. The only man who might have gotten the job instead of me said he would be glad to step back if I'd take it. Still, I had some reservations about Coopers. I'd been disappointed to see how that firm seemed to prefer 'cue balls' as partners—you know, guys who had nothing wrong with them and who were smooth operators—and would steer away from making partners of guys who might be awkward or had faults, but also had some really strong *talents*. Goldman Sachs was different—as I'd been learning at my Naval Reserve unit where John Whitehead and I both served as officers. We had been having long talks about how to build up a truly great professional firm. We got along well and I felt he really had something going at Goldman Sachs."[11]

Whitehead was impressed with Doty's detailed knowledge and managerial understanding of the operations of various little-known units in what most investment bankers rather contemptuously referred to as "the cage"—the place where millions of dollars of cash and negotiable securities were handled daily, which is why it had heavy wire screening for security. Knowing that the best way to get a decision made *and* implemented was to set it up carefully and then hand it off to Sidney Weinberg, Whitehead introduced Doty to Weinberg. "When

Sidney invited me to lunch," recalls Doty, "his timing was perfect. Still, I told him I had real doubts. 'It's not religion, is it?' he asked me. I'm Irish Catholic. I assured him that religion wasn't it. My family was leaving for a long-planned vacation and I promised to give him my answer when we returned. 'Sounds like a furniture store!' was my wife's first reaction. She was thinking of Saks Fifth Avenue, but the plain truth is the firm was not very well known back then. Goldman Sachs was not as profitable as the other firms I knew, but the firm was always more professional, always striving to do what was best for the client, convinced that if the firm really solved the clients' problems for them, in the long run everything would work out well for the firm. This may be a somewhat archaic concept, but it has put the firm in a truly respected role. Other firms were then—and are now—more cash-register oriented."

From the day of his arrival, Doty was powerful: He began as a member of the commanding management committee and had the fourth largest partnership percentage, after Gus Levy and the Two Johns.[12] He was powerful partly because he built an encyclopedic knowledge of how the increasingly complex organization of Goldman Sachs worked and could be made to work; partly because others did not have that knowledge; partly because operational efficiency and effectiveness were becoming decisive in determining the firm's ability to make strategic choices and fulfill objectives while competing with other organizations in a faster-paced and increasingly complex business; and partly because Doty was tough, tenacious, and unflappable.

Even in developing an internal financial management organization, the Two Johns were competitively aggressive, once hiring some financial managers from Merrill Lynch because they thought Goldman Sachs would learn a lot about the competitor's presumably advanced financial management system—only to be surprised to learn how little sophistication that competitor had. Developing talent from within, the Two Johns made Jonathan Cohen their chief of staff and a partner because they had learned they could trust him with anything. John Weinberg once joked, "Jon, when we leave, you'll know so much we'll just have to kill you."

While Whitehead and Weinberg were considered conservative as firm leaders, Doty was *very* conservative in managing internal operations. "Much as I admired and liked George, he could be awfully negative about new things," recalls Whitehead. "More than a few times, I had to take him aside and say, 'Now George, new ideas are quite fragile in their newness. You really must be careful because there are always more people who can kill a new idea than there are people who can help it grow up from something hopeful, but still quite young and weak, into something truly useful.' He would lobby other partners to organize resistance to things we wanted to get accomplished." Whitehead adds with a smile: "And he could get me pretty irritated, too."

Doty was all about control, and for him financial control came first. Expenses were watched closely. All partners' tax returns were either done through the firm or turned in promptly for careful review by the firm. "We didn't want anyone not paying any taxes. I'd been infuriated to see Bobby Lehman making millions one year and paying a tax of only twenty-five thousand dollars. I didn't want that sort of thing to hurt Goldman Sachs. We had a policy that partners could not borrow unsecured without the firm's permission. We wanted everyone to focus on the firm's work *all* the time. We didn't want anyone to be worried about paying off debts. Our policy and our practice were simple: 'Mother's lookin'!' "

Doty knew that in all large securities firms there is always the risk of corner-cutting, cheating, misfeasance, and malfeasance. As an experienced auditor, he knew that the best way to prevent big trouble is to be persistently diligent on small troubles and that access to early information depended on employees' volunteering that information. Doty explains, "People who know about something that's not quite right won't say anything to you unless they know you want to hear and know you will be listening. In the most casual conversation, they'll leave a verbal thread out for you to see—if you're looking—and hope you'll pull on that thread. Some of the finest people on integrity have the least education. If they know something's wrong and know you're breathing on it, they'll steer you right. When we set up an enormous trading room, we deliberately built it on one floor and had only one men's room. Standing side by side at urinals, everyone's an equal. You can mention anything that looks funny. I went to the bathroom as often as I could in those days—and always with an announcement, 'I'm taking a break, guys,' and then I'd get up a little slowly, so it was easy to follow me. I pay close attention in deciding which people I'm going to give full access to my back."

Doty was responsible for the sensitive discussions held with each new partner to determine his appropriate capital contribution. New partners came in as a "class" with equal participations in the earnings of the firm, but each one had a different personal balance sheet and a different ability to contribute capital. Some had family money; others had none. Investment bankers, to keep up appearances, usually had themselves pretty loaded up with nice homes on Park Avenue, while traders would be quite liquid. Ironically, the bankers all wanted to put up the *maximum* affordable to make a "statement" while the traders would try to get by with the *minimum*. George Doty decided how much each new partner would be told to put into the firm after examining a new partner's complete financial statement. Doty would ask skeptically, "Is this *all* you've got?"

"Yes, sir."

"Are you *sure?*"

Doty's job was to find the right number, the amount that meant each new partner would feel really at risk and each would have enough of a stake to be credible on any major decision on which he might be speaking before the partnership. As Doty explained, "Your participation in profits would be a function of your business contribution, while your capital commitment was a function of your personal wealth."

Doty's disciplines were not limited to capital contributions. When Gene Fife became a partner, two workmen arrived in his office in San Francisco and started measuring the furniture. "Hey, fellows, why are you doing that?"

"Mr. Doty told us to."

So Fife called Doty in New York: "What's this all about?"

"As a partner, you can have certain kinds and amounts of furniture. You have more than that in your office. That's okay; it's your choice—but you'll have to pay for it. The firm does *not* provide it."

"But it was there when I moved in."

It didn't matter, Doty wasn't listening. Welcome to the discipline of the Goldman Sachs partnership.

With newly elected partners, the Two Johns would execute a classic "good cop–tough cop" sequence, with Weinberg all smiles and virtually hugging the new partner in a warm, man-to-man way: "You're so great. We always knew you'd make it. We're so happy to be your partners. Welcome aboard. You'll do great things and be really great for the firm. Well done!"[13]

Then Whitehead would take the same new partner aside and quietly perform the tough side: "You must know as well as we all do that you're joining a very capable, very hardworking group of the very best in Wall Street, so to keep up with the pace of accomplishment here, you're going to have to work very, very hard and really pour it on. Today's announcement is really just the beginning, because Goldman Sachs partners take on more responsibility and are expected to accomplish much, much more when they are partners. The standards set by those ahead of you are very high—and lots of young lions and tigers are coming right behind you. The firm wants to be the very best. So that means you will be expected always to be your very best and that really means from now on you are challenged to *increase* your productivity and set a very high standard. We'll be watching you very closely in everything you do—particularly now that you're a partner—so be sure you focus on real achievement and real results. Show us what you can do at your very best . . . or recognize we'll know you're not. We're not playing to play here at Goldman Sachs. We expect you and everyone else, every single day, to play to *win*."

The words were strong, and actions spoke louder than words. There was no tenure. Partners who did not perform strongly were cut back in partnership percentage or taken right out of the line—with no regrets.* "To function around here," said Weinberg, "you really have to work hard and give up a lot of your outside activities—even, frankly, your family life to some extent. To do that, you really have to be ambitious and hard driving. Everybody works hard around here. If they don't, they have to leave."[14] As a partner explained, "There's no let-up for the seniors. If they can be pushed out, out they go—so their partnership shares can be divided up among the best and most aggressive people right behind them. In this constantly unfolding, Darwinian process of evolution, the finer, nicer people don't always win out." Still, as a competitor put it, "What's also amazing is that nearly everyone there is nice to each other, at least insofar as outsiders would see."[15]

Weinberg and Whitehead were not only playing to win—to win clients, mandates, and deals—they were also playing to increase market share and "share of wallet" with each client, and then go right on to win still more. Given the drive they inculcated, some competitors would see the firm as a predator: "It's the

---

* A partner leaving would "go limited" and be paid 50 percent of his accumulated capital immediately and the other half over six years, during which time he would get an above-market-rate fixed rate of return.

Goldman Sachs syndrome: what's mine is mine, and what's yours is half mine," claimed a rival banker.[16] Competition was not limited to other Wall Street firms or even to international competitors. The Two Johns worried about commercial banks, and one of Whitehead's major contributions was his successful lobbying to extend the life of Glass-Steagall, the federal law that kept the commercial banks out of the securities business for decades.

The differences in the ways the Two Johns expressed themselves went on display at the firm's annual investment banking conference when someone asked, "Why is the firm so worried about the commercial banks getting into our investment banking business?" Weinberg, direct and blunt as ever, simply said, "Because they'll screw it up!" Whitehead then rose to give a typically erudite and articulate, and in this case lengthy, explanation of the significant differences in cultures, capital, people, management, and strategic priorities—until he paused, looked over at Weinberg, smiled broadly, and said, "Just as John said, they'll screw it up!"

"John and John *never* had a conflict," says Bob Steel. "At least nobody ever saw any conflict whatsoever. They were each very comfortable being who they were, different as they really were, with Weinberg instinctive and spontaneous and Whitehead the very model of self-control and circumspection—and without any jealousy of each other's successes."

The Two Johns could have made all the decisions, but they chose to respect the strong group they had assembled on the management committee, including Jim Gorter, Fred Krimendahl, George Doty, Dick Menschel, Steve Friedman, Bob Rubin, and Bob Mnuchin. And the committee members appreciated the respectful way they were treated by the Two Johns, so they took their responsibilities seriously and were certainly not yes-men. Still, it was understood that department heads were generally free to run their different businesses their own way. There was an almost senatorial courtesy of assuming that if there were a problem in a man's area, he would work it out. There was none of the "digging right in" insistence on detailed accountability that came later with Bob Rubin and Steve Friedman.

Asked years later to explain the "secrets" that enabled Goldman Sachs to become what was widely considered Wall Street's best-managed firm, Whitehead explained: "We stick to our knitting. This permits us to spend our time trying to be better at what we do without the diversion of being in businesses that we are not comfortable with. I've always felt it's easier to increase your market share from thirty percent to thirty-five percent in something you are already good at than it is to carve out a five-percent market share in some other business that you don't know anything about. We control our growth rather tightly, so things don't get away from us."

The Two Johns accelerated the pace at Goldman Sachs, expanded the investment banking business enormously, recruited and developed numerous business leaders, and built up the firm's profitability and capital. They led the partners to a series of important commitments to "investment spending" that transformed the firm from domestic to international in scope, lifted it from midrankings to first place, filled out the product line of services and capabilities, and laid the foundation for major long-term growth.

"We never made big strategic bets," says Whitehead. "We fed our successes and gave the winners more and more leeway to do better and better with what they had." New ideas got limited pilot-plant support until they proved their worth—and then the Two Johns fed the winners. Patience, prudence, and unrelenting persistence characterized the Two Johns' leadership—making many modest "three yards and a cloud of dust" incremental advances in market share and in stature. Weinberg and Whitehead were particularly careful not to build up costs and overheads in anticipation of hoped-for business and avoided "swing for the fences" risks. As Bob Rubin observed at the time, "Our approach *is* dull. But it's not a bad way to run a business."[17]

The Two Johns were always "in there" doing the business with the others, never insulated from either the business or the other partners. "You can't overvalue those two guys," says Steel. "They had their offices at the center of the action—classic John and John. Other firms had executive offices on a separate floor, so as the pace of the business picked up, the senior management got more and more out of touch."

The firm's reputation for preferring to follow and be prudent rather than innovate was a strategic style that fit with its determinedly low profile. Two examples of its success compare it with Morgan Stanley. In 1989 Morgan Stanley took a lot of heat from angry institutional clients and negative press when it bluntly announced a move to rationalize its institutional stockbrokerage business by concentrating attention on the 150 largest accounts, which represented 80 percent of its institutional business, while shunting all other institutional accounts off to its retail brokers. Goldman Sachs effected much the same change at almost the same time, but did so over several months of quiet explanatory meetings with each individual institutional client, carefully explaining that service levels would actually increase when the account went from being an institutional salesman's smallest account to being an individual-account salesman's largest account. And in 1993 Morgan Stanley was prominent in the press for wresting an enormous tax deal from New York City and State after publicly threatening to move its headquarters and operations to Stamford, Connecticut. Goldman Sachs got a similar tax break, but very privately and quietly. Both firms remained in Manhattan.

I think that labels, good and bad, peel off slowly," said Bob Mnuchin. "I think that we clearly had a label of being somewhere between cautious and maybe overly cautious. And I think that started changing in the late eighties." Steve Friedman confirmed that view of the era of the Two Johns era a few years later when he and Bob Rubin had taken over: "I think historically that was a valid criticism, but certainly not in recent years since we have been at the forefront on innovation. We're a dramatically different firm than we were then."[18]

In one of their annual reviews of the firm's progress, Whitehead and Weinberg noted the increasing speed and complexity of finance and the sort of organization they felt would prevail in such an environment: "Financing activity today is increasingly spontaneous as well as international in scope. In this environment, traditional investment banking relationships—once characterized by long-pondered advice followed by measured preparation for entry into market—have been put under tremendous strain. Investment bankers best able to serve their clients today are those who are knowledgeable about and sensitive to markets, domestic and international; are able to muster resources and act quickly; possess and willingly commit capital to facilitate transactions; and provide considerable ingenuity in designing and marketing securities. It is an environment that tests the mettle of investment banking firms. Those with resources—professionals of top caliber, capital, presence in all markets, a well-honed organization, and a high level of concentrated energy—will assume leadership. Inevitably, investors and issuers alike will turn to the firms that demonstrate these capabilities." They went on to observe proudly that the firm was "at the top or near it in every one of the more than forty services we provide to our investing and financing clients."

Great and enduring organizational change at a firm like Goldman Sachs does not always come in the form of dramatic events, but rather in the steady no-waves and no-nonsense pursuit of central beliefs. Core beliefs may appear almost intuitive but are actually based on the sort of deep understanding that enables great leaders with the will to excel to inspire many to follow—and oblige others to come along too. If Goldman Sachs was not particularly creative or innovative during the Weinberg-Whitehead transformation, it was responsive to market opportunities, to competitors' moves, and to changes in the environment in the 1970s and the 1980s, so that by the 1990s the firm was well prepared for an enormous surge in business. Profits of only fifty million dollars when John Whitehead and John Weinberg became co–senior partners mushroomed to eight hundred million dollars by the time Weinberg retired in 1990.

As readers will see dramatized over and over again, Goldman Sachs was entering into a period of accelerating transformation. Part of the transformation came externally, with explosive growth in institutional investing, increasing volume in block trading, expanding and accelerating merger and acquisition activity driven by the emergence of conglomerates and a deliberate reduction in antitrust activity—plus increasingly active competitors like Morgan Stanley, First Boston, Merrill Lynch, and a host of domestic and international banks. Part of the transformation came from within the firm, as recruiting brought increasing numbers of talented and highly motivated individuals to Goldman Sachs who were too skilled, well trained, and ambitious to wait for things to happen. Part of the transformation came with the increasing magnitude of compensation that could be earned by creativity, risk taking, and entrepreneurial determination. Part came with serial successes leading to increasing self-confidence, which led to more successes, which fostered greater confidence that hard work, superb client service, and discipline really would pay off. And part came from the Two Johns' determination to make Goldman Sachs preeminent; while driving individuals to work longer and harder to serve clients unusually well—and to copy and improve on other firms' best ideas—they insisted that everyone always work as part of the team. Part came from the strategic power of the IBS system. Part came with Bob Rubin and Steve Friedman showing that success and rewards would go to those who achieve major results, causing the whole firm to accelerate its pace with increasing self-confidence and greater use of its strategic resources: knowledge, relationships, and capital.

All financial intermediaries must adapt to changes in supply or demand, or both. Most adapt defensively by gradual acceptance and accommodation to the imperatives of change. Those that fail typically accept and adapt too slowly. Those that succeed adapt actively and even aggressively. They hold high standards of performance, have a long-term focus, think and act strategically, gladly drop fading lines of business and search diligently for opportunities for profitable business creativity. Those that succeed adhere to consistent long-term beliefs and policies; they greatly demonstrate a will to excel in strategic initiatives and innovations, and in daily routines of such superb execution that they become anything but routine. As though it had always been its natural destiny, the firm continued its metamorphosis toward the global juggernaut it would become as today's Goldman Sachs.

The great changes brought to Goldman Sachs by the Two Johns eventually had an obvious consequence. Sidney Weinberg's dream was realized: Goldman Sachs became America's leading investment bank, creating the base from which the firm would go on to worldwide market leadership.

Of all the changes brought about by the Two Johns, perhaps the greatest was a profound shift of attitude and self-perception in the minds of their partners. At the start of their era of coleadership, Goldman Sachs was a second-tier contender with many visible weaknesses and only three distinctive but quite separated strengths—block trading, commercial paper, and risk arbitrage—with its investment banking business, except for that flowing from Sidney Weinberg's directorships, largely confined to smaller "middle market" companies, particularly those that might decide to sell out. By the time the Two Johns stepped down, the firm was on its way to being an integrated market leader in every major line of the securities business. Holding the leading position in investment banking with the leading American corporations, it was poised for expansion to global leadership.

Ironically, it would be the remarkable combined successes of the new lines of business spearheaded by the Two Johns and of the firm as a whole that would

214 · THE PARTNERSHIP

convince their successors that Goldman Sachs should go public—a decision the
Two Johns would vigorously and unsuccessfully oppose after their time of leadership had passed.

W hitehead and Weinberg made one of their greatest contributions to Goldman Sachs by agreeing, out of their great mutual respect and personal
affection, *not* to take one particular action. That example of deference to partnership literally saved Goldman Sachs from disaster.

Through his work with the New York Port Authority, John Whitehead
learned of an unusually attractive opportunity to lease a large block of open-
architecture floor space, ideal for a large trading operation, near the top of one of
the major buildings in the Wall Street area. This one lease would allow everyone
in the firm to work together on connecting floors in one major building—with
a spectacular view. The lease would run for twenty-five years—well into the
twenty-first century. The financial terms were attractive; the firm clearly needed
substantial new space in the Wall Street area; and the time had come for Goldman
Sachs to set aside its past penchant for low-key, shabby offices. The physical space
was perfect, and being headquartered in that iconic space would be a perfect symbolic declaration: Goldman Sachs had become a dominant global leader in investment banking.

Whitehead sketched out the splendid opportunity, but he could see that
Weinberg was, for some reason, not buying in. So, out of respect for his partner, he decided to let the subject drop for a week or so because it was not all that
time-urgent. He would give his friend time to get on board. Given time, the idea
itself was sure to win Weinberg's enthusiastic support.

A week later, Whitehead brought it up again, but got even *less* interest. So
he deferred for another week. When he brought it up a third time, Weinberg surprised Whitehead by saying he knew Whitehead had brought the matter up twice
before and seemed quite excited about his deal, but even without getting into the
details, he would never support such a move.

Whitehead wanted to know why, so Weinberg explained: "I get claustro-
phobic when I'm in a building where the windows are sealed and can't be opened.

The windows in that building are all sealed—and the space you've been looking at is ninety floors high. John, I could never work in that building, I can't possibly work way up there with windows you can't open."

With that very human explanation, Whitehead deferred to his friend, and they never spoke again about leasing floors for the whole firm near the top of One World Trade Center.

13

BONDS

THE EARLY YEARS

Bond dealing was not important to Goldman Sachs in the fifties and sixties, and Goldman Sachs was certainly not important to bond dealing—until Gus Levy read Salomon Brothers' first-ever annual report. It showed him that a competitor firm was making large profits in bonds, a line of business he and Goldman Sachs had been ignoring. Focused as always on making larger profits, Levy declared, "We gotta get major in bonds. There's big money being made, and Goldman Sachs should be there."

The firm's bond business had been small—very small—because everybody "knew" the bond business was just a prosaic "accommodation service" to investors that tied up capital, made little money—and depended on a firm's being a major new-issue underwriter of bonds, which Goldman Sachs most certainly was not. That had to change.

In fact, Levy was misled. What he didn't know was that a large part of Salomon Brothers' reported profits actually came not from bond dealing, but from its equity position in a Texas energy company, Haas Oil. Salomon Brothers' CEO, William Salomon, had insisted on putting out the confusing report as "advertising" for the strategic thrust he was determined to make into investment banking.

He had decided that the best way Salomon Brothers could become a major underwriter was to show the world how powerfully profitable it had become. He also authorized a major newspaper advertising campaign organized by Ogilvy & Mather around large pictures of his firm's cavernous bond trading room—heralded boldly in full-page ads as "The Room"—to celebrate the market power of Salomon Brothers' trading. But his understandable bragging—which Sidney Weinberg would never have allowed for this very reason—was soon attracting competition from a suddenly awakened competitor: Goldman Sachs.*

Building on its leadership in commercial paper, Goldman Sachs first expanded into a full range of the proliferating variety of money-market instruments. Henry Fowler, the former secretary of the Treasury,[1] was recruited to Goldman Sachs in 1968 by Sidney Weinberg, who had known him from their days with the War Production Board. "With his experience as secretary of the Treasury, Henry Fowler really knew quite a lot about the Treasury bond business and felt strongly that we should be in it in a serious way," recalled John Weinberg. Cheerfully, Fowler began to open doors to the offices of his former counterparts and acquaintances at other countries' central and commercial banks. But his low-key diplomatic approach was not sufficiently aggressive to match Levy's strategic aspirations.

With increasing strength in other money-market instruments and steady expansion in investment banking adding to the firm's well-established leadership in commercial paper, Levy thought it was obvious that Goldman Sachs should complete the strategic triangle and build a major business as a dealer in taxable bonds. He proposed to do so by adding corporate bonds to the firm's commercial-paper business relationships—relationships developed over the years with hundreds of corporate issuers and thousands of institutional investors. As usual, he was unrelenting in his drive to make it all come together. He saw Goldman Sachs as the "sleeping giant" in bonds: All it needed, he thought, was to be roused from slumber and taught how to *change*. "We've expanded our bond business recently,"

* Salomon Brothers's focus on profitability and on wholesale business—disparaging any business done with less than the largest institutions, corporations, and governments—was actually taking it in a radically different strategic direction. It soon dropped out of municipal bonds, where it had been a leading competitor, and out of commercial paper, where it had been only a small player. Salomon Brothers made a major, strategic thrust into block trading, Goldman Sachs's home territory, and into investment banking, mortgage-backed-bond dealing, and, through merger with Phibro, into commodities. That merger would soon be a significant factor in Goldman Sachs's decision to combine with J. Aron.

said Levy in 1969. "We plan to be number one in the bond business. We never plan to be number two in anything."

At Levy's direction, George Ross led a partners' committee[2] in a major study of the business possibilities in corporate bonds. It showed that opportunities for large profits were significant in both underwriting and dealing in the secondary markets. So Levy summoned Ross from Philadelphia to take over from Fowler and run the bond business out of New York. Levy's charge: "It's a big business and a big opportunity for Goldman Sachs." But senior bond traders refused to cooperate. They believed Ross was too interested in friendly client relationships to succeed in the confrontational arena of the bond business, so he went back to Philadelphia after two years and John Weinberg was put in his place, reporting to Ray Young.

"Gus put me in charge of the bond department," recalled Weinberg. "I objected: 'Gus, I don't know bonds.' But Gus said, 'You know how to control the traders, so you're it.' And that was that." Weinberg's main job was to find the right leader to build a major bond business. "So I start looking around at our guys and quickly realized that we didn't have anyone who could be a real leader. Then I find a guy at Salomon—Bill Simon, who was later secretary of the Treasury—and was going to hire him when our traders threatened to quit if I hired anyone in over them.[3] I'm not about to be threatened by those clowns, so I laid it out clear and easy: 'You guys have fifteen minutes to come to me and say we'll go along with you and really support this new guy as our head, or *out you go!*' So most of them left that very same day. Fine with me. Then Simon got a big counteroffer from Salomon Brothers and decided not to move to Goldman Sachs. The next day, I'm desperate to find somebody who can take the responsibility for managing our bond positions when I remember Eric Sheinberg is running our convertibles operation. Convertibles are bonds, so I go tell Sheinberg he's got a new job. He argues that converts are almost completely different from straight bonds; they're much closer to common stocks. But I say, 'Cut that: you've been *drafted!*' So he accepts the inevitable and agrees to run the bond positions for a while, while we go looking for someone else—someone who can really do the job and put us into taxable bonds in a major way."

But taxable bonds were only one area of the bond business. While Weinberg was looking for a new head of taxable bonds, a separate effort was being made in tax-exempt municipals. John Whitehead had recruited Bob Downey, whom he had met through Don Gant, to leave R.W. Pressprich, where he was working in municipals, to lead a major buildup in municipal bonds at Goldman Sachs.[4] As a lifelong Republican, Whitehead's proposition was that municipal finance was sure to grow because the states and municipalities would need the money, particularly with the Democrats in power.[5] Downey was so persuaded to focus on the exciting future opportunity Whitehead projected that he took a significant pay cut.

"Do it right" was Whitehead's charge to Downey. "You don't have to do it all at once or achieve everything this year. Don't stretch. Be the *best*." But despite those words, Downey understood Goldman Sachs's drive: "Of course, we worked our asses off because we knew, in the final analysis, that John really expected the business to grow rapidly and put Goldman Sachs at the top of the league tables *very* quickly, and that he required we do it in a first-class way." At the time, it was not at all obvious that Goldman Sachs would be a significant beneficiary of the expected increase in municipal-bond volume. In 1969, the year Downey took over, the firm was not even in the top fifty among new-issue municipal underwriters. As usual, breaking into the municipal-bond business would require an imaginative new product, an innovative marketing focus—and a sustained, driving commitment.

The first major advance came in 1970 when Goldman Sachs invented the Vermont State Municipal Bond Bank, which enabled small municipalities across the Green Mountain State to gain access to the municipal-bond market on much more favorable terms than they ever could get for their individual financings. As Downey explained, "Small issues got no attention from Wall Street or from investors. For example, one bond was issued for Peach, Vermont, with a population of only 19,000. The Vermont banks—the traditional buyers for small, local issues—were out of money to buy local bonds, so there was no market for Peach's bonds without the bond bank."

The Vermont Bond Bank offered bond issues of at least medium size—which made them liquid, or tradable in the secondary bond market—by pooling numerous municipalities' small bond offerings and adding the imprimatur of the state of Vermont, which had a triple-A credit rating. While the state wasn't legally responsible for the bond bank's debt, the bank's credit was based on the state's moral obligation and was rated double-A. The key to success with this innovation was coordination: putting it all together and making it work politically and then financially by aligning payment dates and handling defaults, among other things.

"We went to lots and lots of town meetings and met with lots of town selectmen," recalls Downey. "That December, we raised a total of forty-six million dollars for fifty different municipalities, and we were off and running with our better idea. We brought Maine in two years later with the Maine Bond Bank."

In building the firm's municipal-bond business, not doing the wrong things was almost as important as doing innovative things. For instance, credit analysis was an important part of the firm's strategy in municipals. "But we didn't publish [our reports]," says Downey, "because we didn't want to miff our issuing clients. Merrill Lynch and others did publish—and they got into real troubles with their published research on clients." Instead, he explains, "We would [privately] show a list of the duds we had avoided—like West Virginia Turnpike. While it's not good to get a reputation for being *too* cautious or even chicken, it's always important to know when to say no. And saying no is not the *last* thing you can ever say because you can always come back to the table. You don't want to be just some idiot who is only avoiding bullets. You do want to compete, so just like in the Marines, you have to know when to duck and when to move up and engage. Sometimes you duck first and then engage on the very same issue."

Downey liked to take astute market risks. When Executive Life—which CEO Fred Carr would later drive into a spectacular bankruptcy—issued insured, guaranteed investment contracts, or GICs, they got a triple-A credit rating. The money invested in those GICs came mostly from municipalities that raised money through tax-exempt bonds sold through Drexel Burnham. The municipalities were profiting, at least temporarily, from arbitraging the interest-rate spread between the tax-exempt and taxable bond markets. "But," recalls Downey, "even in a large, diversified portfolio, junk bonds are *not* triple-A. So we stayed far away from the Executive Life issues when originally offered at par. But later"—after Executive Life hit the skids—"at a market price of just forty dollars for every hundred dollars of face value, those same bonds were selling at a sixty-percent discount, and we went in at that market price and did beautifully as the price later rose to eighty. Still . . . there were moments." The price of those bonds once dropped briefly to twenty-five dollars on a rumor that the courts might rule that secondary-market investors were just speculators and would not be treated equally with the somehow more legitimate investors who had bought at the offering. Fortunately for those who bought in between forty and fifty dollars, that rumor soon evaporated. "By saying no back at the original underwriting, we had a leg up when it was time to organize the bailout financing," Downey says. "It was hard work, but we really did our homework and earned a reputation for professionalism. With our reputation established, business was really coming in and the municipal finance department was making real money."

Confident that the firm would recognize the unit's success in municipals, Downey and others expected Municipal Finance to win its first partnerships. But it didn't quite happen. The division got *one* partnership, for a banker named Charlie Harmon. "We were very disappointed because we believed very strongly that our Frank Coleman was too good to pass over. So we wrote a letter to Gus, saying, 'We truly believe Goldman Sachs is the best firm, but we want you to see our department as being important to the firm.' We got no reaction from Gus—and certainly no promises." Disappointment spread quickly across the municipal group.

Downey and his three-man team decided that if partnerships were not going to open up at Goldman Sachs, they had better talk with other firms. After three months of carefully confidential discussions, they agreed to leave Goldman Sachs and go over to Donaldson, Lufkin & Jenrette. Because the formal announcement would be made the next day, their wives had just received big bouquets of "welcome aboard" flowers. It looked all settled when Dan Lufkin, chairman of DLJ, asked his partners: "Have you spoken with Gus?"

"No. Why?"

"As a courtesy—because that's the way it's traditionally done on Wall Street. If you haven't called Gus, I will." And off he went to make the call.

When Levy got the courtesy call on the "done deal," his sixth sense gave him the intuition that the deal for his municipal-finance team to leave Goldman Sachs and join DLJ was not absolutely airtight. During that simple courtesy call, Levy kept the conversation going, personalized it some, and then, moving on to other related topics, got Lufkin—who had known Levy through their work with the Republican Party—to concede that the deal, while agreed verbally and with handshakes, did not include a written contract, so it was not *absolutely* locked up as a 100 percent done deal. No, Lufkin indicated, it was not quite *absolutely* locked up as a 100 percent done deal.

That small opening was all Gus Levy needed. He called Downey down to his office and went to work on him, getting Downey first to wonder and then to worry about how much he could really trust the other firm if they would talk to Levy without first clearing such a sensitive call with him. "What can we do for you that'll cause you to stay?" and "Make Frank Coleman a partner of Goldman Sachs" and "This is not a partnership year, so that'll be really difficult . . . but . . . it will be done at year-end."

Less than half an hour after Lufkin's call to Levy, Downey was on the phone to DLJ, saying, "Your chairman told Gus Levy that our deal is not closed," and within hours the deal completely unraveled. Downey and his municipal-finance team stayed with Goldman Sachs and soon got that second partnership for Coleman. By the end of the twentieth century, negotiated municipal-bond deals had grown to represent over three-quarters of the overall tax-exempt market and Goldman Sachs dominated in lead-managed, negotiated bond underwritings during the century's last thirty years.

S till needing strong sales leadership in taxable bonds, Weinberg reached for a young star who, if he was successful where others had failed, would be declared a hero. Months before, one of the bond traders had asked David Ford, "You cover Atlanta, David, so why don't you come with me to visit some accounts in Atlanta?" The trader continued to explain, "That way, I won't have to pay for my vacation trip to Augusta this year." So Ford went on a three-day series of account visits and the trader got his transportation paid by the firm. While they were away, telephone calls came in. First, Dick Menschel called. Then John Weinberg called—both looking for Ford.

"Where in hell have you been?" Weinberg demanded when Ford phoned back.

"Calling on accounts."

"Well, then you must be ready to get to work!" and Ford was switched to fixed-income sales in Philadelphia on the curiously convoluted assumption that since he was effective when working with high-net-worth clients, he must have good quantitative skills—and this in turn meant he could be transferred to fixed-income sales, where numeracy was essential.

A few months later, Weinberg invited Ford to have dinner with him in New York City because he was ready to make Ford, at thirty, national sales manager for corporate bonds. Ford: "I know you're also looking for a head of the whole division, and he'll want to hire his own sales managers. But my dad was in the military, so if you say that's what you want me to do, I will. If you still want me to take the job, I'll need at least six months to get the key hires in place and get myself established."

"Done."

Ford was brushing his teeth at home in Philadelphia when his wife asked: "How did your dinner with John Weinberg go?"

"Well! He offered me a major new job: national sales manager."

"What did you say?"

"Yes!"

"But you didn't talk to *me*."

The Fords moved to New York, but they never felt comfortable in the city. He soon gave up the sales manager job, and they moved back to Philadelphia.

By the early seventies, Whitehead and Weinberg, as coheads of Goldman Sachs, were determined to move ahead in the secondary markets, for previously issued bonds—first in municipals, where the firm could capitalize on the strengths Downey had established in the new-issue or primary market, and then by expanding in corporates and governments. In 1972 all bond operations were taken away from the regional offices and consolidated in New York City as a first step. Don Shochan, recruited from Discount Corporation, was put in charge at first. But Shochan was eventually recognized as a "crapshooter"—he managed positions by changing portfolio maturities in anticipation of changes in interest rates—and was let go in 1977. Goldman Sachs was again looking for a leader and a strategy to break into bonds.

"Frank Smeal was our man," recalls Weinberg. Smeal had been approached a year earlier by Levy, Whitehead, and Weinberg when they correctly sensed that Smeal was no longer a leading candidate to be chosen CEO of Morgan Guaranty and might be receptive to their offer. But Smeal refused. As he later explained: "I wouldn't work for Gus Levy. But after Gus was gone, it was different." The change in leadership at Goldman Sachs was one major factor in Smeal's decision. Another difference was that Smeal had just been badly disappointed when finally passed over as CEO at Morgan Guaranty. In negotiating the terms for his join-ing Goldman Sachs, Smeal proved he was a good trader: He came over in April 1977 with an annual guarantee of five hundred thousand dollars and a significant partnership percentage—nearly equal to Weinberg and Whitehead—with a slot on the management committee.

Smeal moved quickly to develop a strong, customer-oriented sales organi-zation, started producing value-added research, and expanded the firm's market making. He was soon making real progress. However, the whole world of bond dealing was about to go through a once-in-a-lifetime transformation and, as oth-ers would soon see, the service-intensive strategy Smeal understood best would be pushed aside by capital-based, quantitative, risk-taking strategies that focused on principal trading—buying and selling for the firm's own account rather than just executing customers' orders. But the transformation was not yet visible. Smeal was moving to establish a traditional organization for the traditional bond business.

Jim Kautz had been in bond sales in the St. Louis office when he declined a 1975 "invitation" from Gus Levy to go to New York to head municipal sales. "That was the longest plane ride in my life—an hour and a half with Gus Levy, who was returning to New York from a May Department Stores directors' meet-ing in St. Louis. Gus spent the whole flight telling me why I should change my mind and take the job." A few years later, when Smeal gave Kautz another offer to be overall sales manager for the fixed-income department, he quickly took it.*

In a thirty-year career at the Morgan Bank, Smeal not only had been exec-utive vice president and treasurer, but also was important in the Bond Dealers Association. His name and reputation were far bigger than many at Goldman Sachs realized, but his style hardly matched the firm's. A connoisseur of fine wines and great restaurants, he went out almost every evening with customers and com-petitors, networking extensively in the old-school way he knew so well from his years at Morgan. He wore tailored suits, expected younger people to defer to him as "Mr. Smeal," and believed serious meetings were held in conference rooms and scheduled for specific times at least a few days in advance so everyone could prepare properly. But at Goldman Sachs, everybody used first names, nobody

* Kautz's predecessor as head of bond sales was John Gilliam, who had joined the firm in the 1950s, fresh out of Prince-eton, and sold stocks in the Midwest. He and Smeal never bonded. Gilliam says, "Frank Smeal was a fake."

wore suit jackets, and the most significant meetings were "on the fly," impromptu trading-room gatherings to make urgent decisions.

Smeal's style conflict was first seen in recruiting: He assumed that as department head, he would do his own recruiting. An early casualty of this misunderstanding was Victor Chiang, who had been recruited in 1977 to Chase Manhattan Bank from Chicago's Harris Bank to run Chase's government and municipal bond operations. At the Greenbrier Hotel for a major dealer's conference in 1979, recalls Chiang, "as I came off the tennis court, Frank asked me to sit with him under a tree." Chiang knew a lot about Goldman Sachs and was impressed with the firm's commitment to recruiting college graduates and MBAs while Salomon Brothers was still looking to upgrade back-office clerks with few or no credentials beyond street smarts and a lot of hunger. Chiang also recognized the significance of the powerful changes that were coming rapidly to Wall Street with derivatives like T-bill futures, which were just being introduced on the Mercantile Exchange in Chicago. Derivatives would soon change the scale and the basic nature of the bond markets. These sophisticated new instruments would bring important opportunities for bond dealers to manage their business in an entirely new way without taking major market or interest-rate risks.

"Frank asked me to join Goldman Sachs as head of trading and research in governments and mortgages," recalls Chiang. "After three days of intense consideration—because I knew there was a real need at Goldman Sachs for my skills and experience with derivatives—I accepted. Then, suddenly, surprise! One day later, Frank told me he had not made an actual *offer*." Backpedaling, Smeal— who had just been told that in a partnership, recruiting decisions were always made collectively by at least a dozen people—said his offer was not definite, but rather "a proposition to consider as an adventure"! But since Chiang had already made his commitment, meetings with several partners were hurriedly arranged, and after a few days of intensive interviews, the "proposition to consider" was made a real offer and Chiang joined the firm. "But there was no office space for me," he recalls, "except a small interior room with no windows—and two doors."

Chiang's most important changes were initiating the use of derivatives and hiring two future leaders, Jon Corzine from Continental Illinois National Bank and Mark Winkelman from the World Bank. Chiang never fit into the firm personally. Some said he was "too ivory tower"; others said he was felled by internal competition. "In the end," recalls Chiang philosophically, "Frank fired me solo—the same way he had tried to hire me."

That wasn't the last of Smeal's difficulties. His experience at the Morgan Bank had been in municipals and Treasuries, but the major business challenge at Goldman Sachs was in taxable corporates, a very different business. Smeal was an experienced administrator who knew lots of senior people and greatly enjoyed the old-school relationship diplomacy. But that was no longer the way the bond business was being done and not the way to build up a major business rapidly in the face of huge, rough, risk-taking, richly capitalized, and determined competitors like Salomon and First Boston. They understood how vital it was to *their* future to keep and defend their market leadership, which was key to their profits and to their status in corporate underwriting. "Not only did he not know the Goldman Sachs culture or the firm's ways of doing business—informal, fast, open, etc.," recalls a partner, "he wasn't up to speed on the mathematics that were coming into dominance in the bond-trading business. He never really understood how modern bond traders make money for the firm. Frank should have been a senior adviser, not responsible for hands-on leadership charged with driving the unit to build a major business. Looking back on those days, Frank's real role was as a high-grade placeholder until the firm could put some business builders in charge that understood the Goldman Sachs culture and could hire the strong hitters we needed to build the business. Frank's true role, whether he or anyone else realized it at the time, was to give us some external credibility when we were so very far behind Salomon Brothers and First Boston, and we could see that Lehman Brothers, Morgan Stanley, and Merrill Lynch were all moving up strongly."

For a few years Smeal seemed to achieve a major success. Fixed Income went from barely break-even to what appeared to be a highly profitable division of Goldman Sachs. But profit reporting can be very misleading. The division was reporting robust profits only because it was liquidating the firm's base of business in corporate bonds.

Steve Friedman laid out the problem to John Weinberg. Sure, there were signs of success that hid the core problem. Reported profits were up a lot. The firm's increasing strength as a municipal-bond underwriter in the new-issue market was being matched by sales and service operations in the secondary market. With the help of former treasury secretary and now partner Henry Fowler, the firm was establishing itself as a government-bond dealer. Fixed-income research had been introduced and was becoming a competitive strength. Trading risks were carefully minimized.

But in corporate bonds—the business that was new to Smeal because commercial banks like J.P. Morgan had not yet been allowed to underwrite or make markets in corporate issues—Goldman Sachs was losing lucrative corporate-bond underwritings from such traditionally important clients as Sears Roebuck and Texaco. Both had sold one billion dollars of bonds through other underwriters. In three years in the early eighties, Goldman Sachs's rank in managed corporate-bond underwriting had dropped from first to third to fifth. Its market share had shrunk over those years from 11 percent to 9.6 percent, while Salomon Brothers's share had risen from 16.2 percent to 25.8 percent. The changes were a serious threat to Goldman Sachs's position as an underwriter. Competitors were using their rich profits in surging new markets like mortgages to cover their losses in corporates, where they were cutting prices to gain market share.

Friedman and Rubin were convinced that the firm could make major money in bonds only by committing in a big way to proprietary trading for the firm's own account, because the bond markets were radically changing. Mortgage-backed securities and an increasing variety of asset-backed and lower-grade, high-yield bonds were exploding in volume and in dealer profits. Smeal continued to favor the traditional, customer-oriented agency business. Friedman feared that if Goldman Sachs stuck with Smeal's suddenly obsolete business strategy for another three years—while Salomon Brothers, Morgan Stanley, Merrill Lynch, and First Boston kept building their risk-embracing business, making big profits as principals, not small profits as service-intensive agents—the firm risked being shoved aside as a major corporate underwriter. Friedman and Rubin recognized the strategic problem; knew Smeal could not discard all he knew from long experience; and decided that the better option was for them to take over leadership of the fixed-income group. Weinberg endorsed the change, partly because it gave his two protégés a challenging opportunity to develop and demonstrate their abilities as coleaders away from their "home bases" of M&A and arbitrage, and partly because the firm's earnings in bonds paled in comparison to the enormous profits Salomon Brothers, First Boston, and a few other bond dealers were making. Weinberg wanted to test the pair with greater managerial responsibilities as he groomed them to be his successors. He expected them to figure out how Goldman Sachs could join in making big profits in the bond business.

A strong dealer position in the secondary bond markets had become essential when competing as a new-issue underwriter, and new-issue bond underwriting was booming. Not being a leading dealer in bonds was already hurting the firm competitively and, without major change, would become a dominating strategic liability in corporate underwriting. All the other majors were strong in both debt and equity, and no corporation would want to depend on a one-trick underwriter. Moreover, if competitors were making big profits in *any* line of business—like proprietary trading in new kinds of bonds—those profits would surely be used to move in on other lines of business or to pay up in recruiting talented people, including those at Goldman Sachs.

In 1985, at age sixty-seven, Frank Smeal retired. This opened up an opportunity for major change. Steve Friedman recalls, "I couldn't sit on the management committee with Smeal and not know that something was missing—something really important—when he talked about London having lost twelve million dollars on a trade and didn't even know why. They *had* to know why they'd taken such a loss so they could learn from the mistake so it could be prevented the next time. I knew that Tom Saunders at Morgan Stanley had everyone and everything reporting into him on the trading floor, so they had close communication and good coordination. By contrast, we had guys spread across three different floors. Talk about frustration!"

A year later, Bob Rubin called David Ford again: He wanted Ford to relocate to New York and take on sales management again. "You're really asking two different things," Ford responded. "First, will I take the job? Second, will I move to New York? If you can judge my work by the results accomplished and not by how much face time I put in in New York, I'll take it—but only on that basis."

"I'll want to discuss this with Steve. Can I put you on hold?"

"Sure."

Ford was on hold for less than one minute and would never know whether Rubin actually asked Friedman anything before coming back on the line to say, "Done."

To make fixed-income sales effective, Ford knew he would need to offer a service that would enable his salesmen to "sit on the client's side of the desk"—offering solutions to pressing problems—by delivering research that would help clients make better investment decisions. Gary Wenglowski's extensive macroeconomic research—although originally organized to support equity research—was adaptable to fixed-income research and proved helpful. So was the work of Stanley Diller, who joined Goldman Sachs to build a bond-research department in the late 1970s and was the firm's first "rocket scientist" quantitative analyst. Diller, a professor at Columbia, came to do research on portfolio strategies as a way to differentiate Goldman Sachs and to generate research-based transaction ideas for customers instead of simply risking firm capital buying any bonds that customers wanted to sell. Unfortunately, Diller needed enormous amounts of computer time to run his complex models, and this caused conflicts with others in research. When Diller lost his temper one day and called Lee Cooperman a "Hitler," his career at the firm was suddenly kaput.

Also in the late seventies, Joel Kirschbaum, who had ranked at the top of his class at both Harvard Business School and Harvard Law School before coming to Goldman Sachs, switched from banking to build a mortgage-backed-securities business and catch up with Salomon Brothers, which was making a fortune in mortgages. To trade mortgages, Kirschbaum recruited Robert From, a trader from Blyth, who recognized that when portfolio managers wanted to hedge their portfolios of mortgage-backed bonds against market risk, they were short-selling the bonds' initial maturity strips. (In another of many "product" innovations from Wall Street, mortgage-backed bond issues were sold in strips, divided by maturity like slices in a loaf of bread.) With this simple insight, he would accumulate a big position in those initial maturity strips, buying in the floating supply, and then squeeze the short sellers—hard. As the shorts scrambled to get securities to deliver, they had to pay higher and higher prices. Panicked as prices went up and up, they would bid the price up even faster and even higher. This caused major spikes in market prices that only the former Blyth trader could anticipate because he was the one forcing the shorts to cover. He made huge profits for Goldman Sachs.

Soon Kirschbaum was asking the brightest people he could find one key question: "Who is the one person I most want to have to build a truly great research unit in mortgages?" Some of Professor Richard Roll's UCLA students were at the firm, and they all pointed to Roll. "Joel flew out to Los Angeles, grabbed me by the throat, and just would not let go," recalls Roll. He joined the firm in 1985 and over the next two years built a fifty-five-person research unit specializing in mortgages. "The firm had some of the smartest people I've ever met," says Roll, and "while the firm, more than any competitor, has used more people with advanced academic training, their regular employees are every bit as talented. Goldman Sachs used academics like me as catalysts to get their own people thinking in more rational and sophisticated ways."

John Weinberg was set appoint Steve Friedman to head fixed income, but Bob Rubin heard about it and quickly convinced Weinberg to appoint him as co-head to be sure trading skills would be at the top of the division. Looking back on Frank Smeal's departure, Friedman recalls: "Our bond business was *really* disturbing. It had the wrong strategy. Frank was going backward, not forward, when recommending a relationship salesman to succeed him as head of the division. We said, 'Over our dead bodies!'" Smeal's candidate was not up on the sophisticated analytics that were becoming central to proprietary trading and were sure to be the main source of profits. "One month after Bob and I got involved, a major crisis hit the markets. The fixed-income division was all stovepipes and fiefdoms, so traders were looking only at one part of the market and paying no attention to how other parts of the market were affecting their own. They had no understanding of the basic mathematics of embedded option values [such as call protection or mortgage-refinancing rights], which were absolutely essential. The top of that division was an intellectual vacuum."

Rubin and Friedman changed the compensation arrangement from straight commission on volume to "managed comp" that could at least include whether the firm *wanted* the business a salesman was doing. "We had guys getting paid on volume when the key to *their* volume was *our* losses in market-making," laments Friedman.

In 1985, convinced that new leadership and new strategy were needed in fixed income, Rubin and Friedman recruited a group of experienced risk-taking bond dealers from Salomon Brothers into Goldman Sachs to force change in the fixed-income division's culture and alter its concept of the business from service-oriented and risk-avoiding over to a bold, risk-embracing, capital-intensive, proprietary business model. Most left Salomon Brothers because they had felt shortchanged, and most subsequently left Goldman Sachs after a few years because they couldn't adapt to the teamwork culture, but by then they had already helped change the firm's way of doing bond business.[6] By 1986 over one thousand people worked in Fixed Income.

Thinking more rationally and in more sophisticated ways was not limited to tactical changes. The changes that Rubin and Friedman put through were massive—and would help change the character of Goldman Sachs forever. But favorable change did not come swiftly or easily.

As interest rates fell in 1986, dealers with long positions in corporate bonds and mortgage-backed securities were not getting the rising prices they had expected, but their short positions in U.S. Treasuries *were* rising right on schedule—so Goldman Sachs dealers were taking huge, repetitive losses. Arbitrage losses in Fixed Income surged to one hundred million dollars—not a good start for Rubin and Friedman as new coheads of the division.

"What in hell is going *on?*" exclaimed Friedman.

Nobody knew—and nobody knew for days on end—until somebody realized the obvious: As interest rates fell, homeowners were refinancing their mortgages and corporations were refinancing their bonds by exercising call provisions. That explained why the Wall Street dealers' long positions in corporates and mortgages were not rising as rapidly as their short positions in Treasuries, squeezing the spreads that dealers were counting on.

Goldman Sachs needed better models that more accurately reflected the impact of changing interest rates on the different bonds' embedded options. This need surfaced during one of the postmortem review sessions Rubin held each Saturday. He always made sure that each person present had his chance to speak—including in-house guru Fischer Black, the codeveloper of the Black-Scholes formula for valuing stock options, who sat in a corner and was silently listening. Rubin, who respected people who, like himself, knew how to listen, said, "Fischer, you've been pretty quiet. Is there anything you'd like to add?"

Noting that the embedded bond options to refinance were not being valued correctly, Black said that correct valuation of those embedded options could probably be obtained if the quantitative-model builders at the firm went to work on the problem. While the Black-Scholes formula for valuing stock options couldn't work well on bond options, over the next several weeks, working with Emanuel

Derman and Bill Toy, Black developed a practical computer model that incorporated the decisive difference between stocks and bonds.[7] All bonds have an exact value on the exact date when they mature, and this enables analysts to translate each bond's yield curve and price volatility into a consistent pattern of future short-term interest rates and volatilities. And that pattern can be used to price *any* other fixed-income security, including derivatives, in ways that are all internally consistent.[8] This insight revolutionized the bond business at Goldman Sachs and the bond markets all around the world because it integrated futures and cash trading in every market, everywhere. What began with Rubin's habitual question-invitation soon became another transformational revolution.

14

FIGURING OUT
PRIVATE CLIENT SERVICES

Ray Young and Richard Menschel saw an opportunity in the early seventies to develop a substantial new business by harnessing two established strengths of Goldman Sachs. If executed well, this new business would have high margins, require little or no capital, and be a steady long-term moneymaker. Good execution would depend on an entrepreneur who was ambitious, unusually presentable, and tough—tough enough to cold-call persistently in many different cities over many years.

Except for one crucial distinction, the business opportunity Menschel and Young had in mind was the basic business of Wall Street: retail stockbrokerage. The crucial distinction was focus—focus on wealthy individuals, particularly on individuals who had became wealthy by building businesses and whose wealth had suddenly become liquid because Goldman Sachs or another firm had helped sell their companies. The focus would give Goldman Sachs an important "unfair" competitive advantage. Since the firm already had strong research and trading capabilities in place to serve its institutional accounts, any business with wealthy individuals would be almost entirely incremental, so the profit margins would be high as volume built up.[1]

Through its "seller rep" specialty, Goldman Sachs was the Wall Street leader in helping the owners of small and medium-size companies sell out on favorable terms. After a sale, each of the major shareholders suddenly had money—usually lots of money—and Goldman Sachs knew exactly who they were and how much they each now had to invest, weeks before any other firm. In addition, each of these newly wealthy people would have a quite favorable predisposition toward the firm that had managed the sale of the company. Said Menschel: "You couldn't ask for a better opening opportunity for a securities salesman." If Goldman Sachs managed an IPO and the company's CEO came into millions, a young salesman—also from Goldman Sachs, but often not with the same maturity as the attending investment banker—would call about managing his personal investments.

During the conglomerate era of the sixties and seventies, acquisitions were at an all-time high. For example, U.S. Industries Inc. alone made one hundred acquisitions in half as many months—creating at least one or two, and often as many as a dozen, freshly minted millionaires in each of one hundred selling companies. As Menschel noted, "That's hundreds of prospects from just that one acquisition-active company. And there are bigger deal makers, like Jimmy Ling, the Murchisons, and Derald Ruttenberg, all doing deals and creating big, liquid personal portfolios."

Once a few successful entrepreneurs in a city had become clients and experienced the firm's first-rate service and solid investment results, they would be more than happy to introduce their wealthy friends to Goldman Sachs. This would give the firm an expanding perimeter of competitive advantage in building its individual-investor business. Some of these new customers could also become clients for the firm's seller-rep business—a perpetual virtuous cycle.

Menschel thought he knew the right man for the job of building a significant business on his ideas. Menschel had been assembling the firm's institutional sales force, one person at a time, with great care and high standards, because he recognized that year after year, the firms with the best relationships with institutional investors got paid significantly more than the second- or third-ranking firms serving those same institutions. The key factor in having the best relationships was having the best salesmen. That's why Menschel was exacting in recruiting and training salespeople and supervising their assignments and their advancement. He concentrated recruiting at Harvard, Stanford, Wharton, and Columbia, and was alert to unconventional candidates who were exceptions that proved the rule—like Roy Zuckerberg, whom he had hired a few years before.

Looking over Zuckerberg's one-page résumé, Menschel, who liked to test candidates to see how they reacted, had said, "I see you didn't go to business school, Roy. We're hiring most of our new salesmen from the very best business schools. Can you tell me why I should hire you when you didn't even go to any business school?"

"No, I didn't go to business school," replied Zuckerberg smoothly. "I studied business in the real world—where you actually do things, not just talk about doing. While the others studied business, I did business."

"So what did you accomplish in your school of hard knocks?"

"I reorganized sales, cut costs, and increased revenues threefold in eight years, and changed the way the business was done. I managed people. I built relationships. I built a business and made it far more profitable. You learn a lot when you do real business."

"And what did you study at . . . was it . . . Lowell Tech?"

"Textile engineering. My father was in the industrial textile business."

Menschel was impressed but still skeptical. Virtually all his hiring was at business schools, particularly Harvard Business School—partly because he'd gone there himself, partly because John Whitehead and John Weinberg both favored HBS graduates strongly, and partly because the training there made his salesmen highly presentable to clients—particularly after an offhand comment like: "Your salesman will be Sam Jones. He went to Harvard Business School, you know." But Lowell Tech, followed by no business school at all—that would never impress anyone. Yet Menschel was intrigued. This guy Zuckerberg had charm, was clearly driven to get ahead, and showed considerable selling skills. He was certainly good at selling himself. More important, L. Jay Tenenbaum, a good judge of people, had recommended him to Menschel. Tenenbaum had been instrumental in bringing into the firm a series of future leaders: Bob Mnuchin, David Silfen, Bob Rubin, Steve Friedman, and Bob Freeman. Tenenbaum had agreed to see Zuckerberg for fifteen minutes because his friend Bruce Mayer had asked Tenenbaum to interview him as a favor. On learning that Zuckerberg was about to take a job in operations at Bear Stearns, Mayer had said, "Oh no, Roy, you belong in sales," and called Tenenbaum. Busy as he was on the arbitrage desk, Tenenbaum continued the interview for nearly three hours and concluded by saying, "I don't know how, but I'm going to help you get you a job here at Goldman Sachs. I'll introduce you to our heads of sales, Richard Menschel and Roy Young."

Menschel might have been even more intrigued—and more skeptical—if he had known more of the details of young Zuckerberg's education. In high school, Zuckerberg realized that he was very smart because he got high grades without doing any homework. When other kids told him he would be in trouble if he kept skipping homework, he elected the toughest course he could find—math—and bet ten dollars he would get a grade of seventy-five or better without any study. He won the bet with a seventy-eight. He then went to Lowell Tech and then to work at his father's "textile" company. In dry-cleaning women's dresses, the mannequins that take the abuse of heat, pressure, and chemicals have textile covers that must be replaced regularly. Roy's father's textile business was providing those covers—a tough business, but not as tough as Sam Zuckerberg, who announced how his son's first day on the job would begin: "You'll start working tomorrow at five a.m. Be there!"

"Gimme a break, Dad. I've had no vacation since leaving school."

"You've had twenty-two years of vacation! Five a.m.!"

When, after a few years, Roy decided he would have to quit, he went to his father to explain his decision. As soon as Sam Zuckerberg realized what was coming, his eyes narrowed and his voice hardened: "Turn in the keys—now! That's a company car!" The son protested that he needed the car to get home, twelve miles away. The father had no problem with that: "Turn . . . in . . . the . . . keys!"

Zuckerberg started in securities sales at Goldman Sachs in 1967 and in 1972 was also running the sales training program when Menschel said, "Roy, why don't you give up your institutional accounts? We both know that because you came into sales late, you don't have the best list of accounts. You should drop your institutional accounts and go full time into selling securities to wealthy individuals. You do well with the individuals you work with now. You have a good understanding of how to do significant business with individuals, and there are good individual-investor accounts all over the country, so the opportunity is unlimited—and it's a fast-growing business, particularly if you concentrate on the wealthiest of the newly rich." Menschel had developed a decisively differentiated model of how the individual-investor brokerage business could and should be developed, and now he wanted someone to run it, someone who could develop it into an important business for Goldman Sachs.

"All the newly rich selling shareholders need somebody," Menschel told Zuckerberg. "All you have to do is to make sure that that somebody is Goldman Sachs. You'll have more good business than you can handle, and you can build a significant organization to serve this large and growing market. And Roy, all the business will be incremental, so the profit margin will be very high. This is your great opportunity!"

Zuckerberg started building the individual-investor business in 1972 and ran it for sixteen years. "I traveled extensively to work with our regional people to meet with their clients and prospects," he remembers. When any corporation sold out, with the help of Goldman Sachs or any other firm, Zuckerberg and his team would call on every important stockholder within twenty-four hours of the deal—usually first thing the very next morning. Zuckerberg recalls, "Dick told me the secret—in fact, he insisted on it: 'Go after the very rich. They're only different from everyone else in one single way: They have much more money. It's just as easy to sell to the very rich man as it is to sell to an ordinary account.'"

Soon Menschel had another idea: "You need a name! This business is becoming important, and every important business has a name." The business had simply been called Securities Sales–Individual, to separate it from the dominant business, Securities Sales–Institutional. Even the order tickets were "institutional"; designed for a cash-on-delivery institutional business, they were so complex that most individual customers found them frustrating. The business's comforting new name became Private Client Services.

In addition to going after more and more new accounts, Menschel and Zuckerberg thought strategically about how to organize and build a strong, scalable business for the firm. Adding clients often required a major educational job because the prospects knew so little about securities or the markets. They were not investors. They were and had always been business managers, and investing in securities was very different both objectively and subjectively. "Night after night, I'd sit with a legal-size yellow pad and make long lists for myself of what we should do," Zuckerberg recalls.

By the early 1980s, Goldman Sachs was consistently one of the top three underwriters of negotiated municipal-bond issues. This meant PCS clients had plenty to choose from and could buy new bonds at wholesale prices (with sales compensation paid by the issuer). At the same time, strong individual-investor demand from PCS clients was great for the firm's reputation as an underwriter: PCS got broad distribution, and the bonds would often be held to maturity—not get sold back into the market.

In addition, the firm's solid equity research was well suited to the high end of the individual-investor market. Definitive reports on industries and leading companies could intrigue entrepreneurs leading smaller companies in the same business and showed how broad and deep the analysts' knowledge was. PCS salesmen would send research reports to people likely to be interested with a note such as, "Thought you'd be interested in George Owens's research. If you'd like to hear from George directly, we can set up a conference call." Finally, as Zuckerberg and his salesmen would explain to prospective clients, Goldman Sachs did not accept "retail" accounts; it took on personal business only if the account was very large and the individual was "qualified" for admission to what appeared to be a special insiders' club.

Later on, PCS got into real estate, tax-advantaged investments, and then private equity, international, and hedge funds. In private equity, the sales pitch was different: "How would you like to invest side-by-side with the partners of Goldman Sachs? They're the lead investors in this fund and are contributing twenty percent of the total." Adding another 10 percent to 20 percent from individuals was important in the sales process—it helped the firm preempt efforts by large institutions such as state pension funds to get a fee break in exchange for an early commitment. Year after year, the business grew larger and larger. As Zuckerberg recognized, "We had everything going for us."

Building on the process that had brought Zuckerberg in years before, Richard Menschel developed the core strategy that so differentiated PCS from the ordinary retail sales organization. Most stockbrokers were hiring college graduates, training them only to pass the basic New York Stock Exchange Series Seven exam, and then sending them out to sink or swim—with most sinking in a year or so. Goldman Sachs recruited MBAs from top schools, people who were academically and motivationally equal to those who covered the major institutions as sales people. To achieve consistency in training and instill its culture, the firm took almost no laterals—while most competitors were poaching each other like crazy to bring over books of business. Goldman Sachs generally hired only those for whom PCS was their first serious job.

Hiring involved several rounds of interviews, always including some with partners, and all final interviews were in New York City. By the time a candidate was hired, she or he knew quite a few people and knew what to expect. PCS people received a salary and were given time, training, and a full array of support services.

At Goldman Sachs, training took six to nine months, compared to about ten weeks at other firms, and went from 7:30 a.m. to 7:30 p.m. every day. None of that time was spent on prepping for the Series Seven exam. That was to be done on your own time—on nights and weekends. Research got special emphasis, and each tyro would be given a month to master every aspect of two or three recommendations for presentation at group meetings. Friday night sessions often ran as late as nine thirty. Are you sufficiently dedicated? If you feel the firm is demanding, fine. Get used to it! The moment of truth for a trainee came in a role-playing test: Can you demonstrate that you know more than any other salesperson? This required mastering annual reports and 10-K reports and knowing the directors—all at least as well as an institutional salesperson.

The test of a relationship, the trainees learned, was this: Will the person take your call even when it's really inconvenient? During training, salespeople were advised to develop good relationships with as many internal Goldman Sachs people as possible so they could always call for help and gang-tackle situations.

So there would be no temptation to churn accounts, newly trained salespeople were not put on commission for a year or more—until they had built a large enough book of business to support their draw. Teaming was standard operating procedure—originally in pairs, but with more and more specialties like private equity, municipals, and options and other derivatives, teams of three or four were not unusual. Even for new-business solicitations, teams were used. A group of four specialists who worked well together would make a powerful and differentiating impression on a prospect.

The firm invested in continuing education, including regular two-day research seminars. It was expensive to take people out of sales production, fly them to New York, and put them up at a hotel, but it brought everyone together and generated bonding. (Anyone who missed a session would get a call.) Also, when firm analysts would visit the regional offices to meet with institutional investors over breakfast and lunch, a few PCS salespeople were invited to listen in.

Zuckerberg recruited people carefully and worked with them closely and individually to train them to be effective business producers. "We trained and trained so everyone knew and understood every product and how to use it. And we built pride and esprit de corps, so we had very low turnover, which meant a lot to the clients. We had great client loyalty to the firm and to the individuals in PCS. And that really helped us build a very solid, steady business on a very large scale."

Managers of regional offices—successful salespeople who showed an interest in management and were potential partners—were taken out of production and relied on Menschel's judgment for their compensation. Their job included recruiting stellar salespeople and helping new joiners develop their skills and their books of business. Managers were also expected to know as many clients as possible, particularly the more active and important clients in their region.

Only "significant" accounts were accepted. As Menschel and Zuckerberg said over and over, the only real difference between the affluent and the very rich is the size of their orders. In the seventies, an account had to have one million dollars in the market. Then it was five million dollars. Then ten million dollars.

Most retail stockbrokers try to cover two hundred or more accounts and assume they'll lose and replace 20 percent of them a year, so they go for major commission-generating turnover in the accounts while they have them. But at PCS, losing an account was like an earthquake, because the strategy was to have only a small number of major accounts—as few as twenty—but to keep all of them forever. The typical brokerage customer who stays with one firm will go through six different representatives in a decade. At PCS, the strategy was to have such capable salespeople that they kept clients so long that they really got to know their hopes, fears, worries, and predilections—and attended their family weddings and bar mitzvahs—with a clear focus on understanding their needs and expectations.

Selling is all about listening, and listening is partly about being quiet and paying close attention and partly about asking good questions to learn the real meaning and feelings behind the words. Good listeners give people the feeling that they are "in it together" and "on the same side of the table" and comfortable with each other. In the seventies partner Gene Fife noted that the developer of Pringles potato chips had just sold his company for eighty million dollars. It was too late for Goldman Sachs to be his seller representative, but the firm could become his investment adviser. So, with one of Zuckerberg's PCS salesmen, he went to Idaho Falls and from there to a remote fishing camp for an afternoon and dinner, an overnight stay, and a hearty breakfast. Conversation ranged over many, many topics, but no business was discussed. Two other New York firms' representatives who were soliciting the business made similar visits. A month later, Fife's telephone rang. "Well, Gene, you've got the business."

"Well, that's just great! Thank you so very much! I'll arrange to have one of our best people come out and take care of the necessary arrangements."

"Don't you want to know why you won?"

"Oh, sure. Why?"

"The missus and I talked it all over. You and the other two groups all talked the same, looked the same, and dressed the same," . . . pause . . . "but after dinner, you pitched in to clean up and wash the dishes. That was different. We felt you were really listening and understanding us as people—so we felt comfortable with you. And that's why you won the business."

Zuckerberg recognized early that the key to success in PCS was being effective not so much in investing assets as in gathering assets—attracting clients. "The secret is that there is no secret," he says. "Show people that you really care. Be sensitive to people's needs and their tolerance for risk. The clients we want are all smart, way too smart for any baloney. And they get lots of calls from all the other firms, so they have lots of choices. They know they'll get pretty smart people at any firm, so they look for something meaningfully special. And that special something is understanding what they really want—and that we care."

He adds: "I made it clear that I would go at any time to any city for a luncheon or a dinner with a prospective client and often would bring along a guest speaker such as Lee Cooperman, our investment strategist, or a top research analyst. And when I say go anywhere, that includes Boise, Topeka, Little Rock, and Shreveport. For years, I traveled a lot to smaller cities most people have only heard about, and I ate a lot of meals with PCS prospects and clients, building relationships and building our reputation in each of these communities. We built the business the old-fashioned way—one relationship at a time."

The years 1972–73 were a growth period for PCS, but in the severe bear market that followed, Zuckerberg—who took it all very personally—was discouraged. Bob Rubin chose that time to ask how much business volume was being done, and Zuckerberg said, "Six million dollars." Rubin's response was just what Zuckerberg needed to hear: "That's pretty good these days, particularly in a new business." Zuckerberg looks back on that simple exchange and smiles: "Bob's reaction was very important to my staying focused on PCS." With Zuckerberg's focus, PCS grew steadily—up nearly 20 percent a year for more than fifteen years. With over 375 PCS account reps—three hundred in the United States and nearly one hundred overseas—managing seventy-five billion dollars in assets, revenues grew from six million dollars in 1974 to $220 million by 1990. That carried Zuckerberg to the management committee. By 1998, PCS revenues exceeded one billion dollars.

Along with the surging revenues, PCS reported strong profits all the time. With larger and larger balances in clients' margin accounts, PCS earned important profits on the spread between the rate charged to customers and the firm's cost of funding. Another layer of profits came from the stock-loan business. The firm found more and more ways to earn profits from Private Client Services—brokerage commissions, dealer spreads, underwriting fees, private-equity management fees, interest-rate spreads, stock lending, foreign-exchange spreads. And PCS helped the firm's investment bankers by having large amounts of controlled business that could be delivered to "make it happen" on important underwritings. Zuckerberg and his legions kept adding more and more accounts. "I always believed everyone would eventually want to do business with Goldman Sachs," says Zuckerberg.

His efforts to build up the margin-account business had drawn early resistance within the group: Oh no, Roy, if one of our customers can't afford to pay cash for his purchase of shares, then that's not the kind of customer business we really want to have. Exasperated, Zuckerberg explained that if a customer used margin to double the number of shares purchased, PCS would get double the commissions—with no increase in costs or sales effort—and would also earn extra income through the fees on the margin balance. Later the services developed for PCS would be adapted to service hedge funds and create another stream of profits.

PCS's well-organized, well-managed, almost automated process of business development depended heavily on personal contact through carefully orchestrated dinners. Often the speaker was Cooperman, who was a great "switch hitter": He could give an erudite, statistics-laden disquisition on the economy and portfolio strategy, or he could switch over to hilarious Jewish jokes or do both, as suited the particular audience. Another part of the process was the systematic collection of information so every call built on all prior calls. For every guest, a briefing memo—telling everything anyone could find out—was required. "By reviewing those files before the dinner, we knew what we didn't know and what we should be finding out. After every client and prospect dinner or luncheon meeting, we met to decide how we would follow up on our conversations with each guest and to add any significant new information to our understanding of their situation and interests. If you know what you're looking for, your chances of finding it are pretty good."

After one of those many dinners—this one in Tulsa—Zuckerberg had his team sit down right after the guests had gone home to review each guest so they could add to their notes anything they had learned about that guest's financial situation and interests or concerns and how best to improve PCS's business prospects. When they got to a Mr. Livingstone, Zuckerberg called out his name.

"He didn't come, Roy."

"Any idea why not?"

"This club is restricted."

"How could you possibly have decided to host a Goldman Sachs dinner at a club that's restricted? That's embarrassing! And dumb! Call Mr. Livingstone right now and apologize."

"It's after nine, Roy."

"I don't care. Call him, I want to speak with him and apologize for putting him in such an awful, embarrassing position."

The call was made; Mr. Livingstone came on the line, and Zuckerberg apologized profusely. Mr. Livingstone said not to worry. Zuckerberg said he'd like to meet Mr. Livingstone and apologize in person. Mr. Livingstone said that was not at all necessary—but if Zuckerberg really wanted to come out, he'd be welcome for breakfast. Before accepting, he should know that the Livingstones were early risers and breakfast would be at 7 a.m.

The next morning, Zuckerberg was up very early and made the 7 a.m. breakfast. On the walls were pictures of Mr. Livingstone with Golda Meir, with David Ben-Gurion, and with others—always clearly in Tulsa, the headquarters for LVO Corporation, Mr. Livingstone's company. The breakfast was cordial, and Livingstone eventually became a good client. Zuckerberg's takeaway: "Fix it! Everybody makes mistakes. Whenever you make one, fix it right away."

PCS became a key part of Goldman Sachs's international expansion strategy. Since there are rich and well-connected people in almost every part of the world, each PCS salesperson could make himself profitable on his own initiative. And wealthy people could often provide entrée to promising leads to investment banking opportunities, particularly with the midsize, privately owned companies that are important everywhere. PCS added strength in Europe and was Goldman Sachs's "first mover" in Asia. Joe Sassoon, hired by Zuckerberg in 1979 as he was completing his PhD at Oxford, recruited other good people to PCS in each of Europe's major countries and built a large European private-client business. Sassoon took a philosophical approach: "Wealthy people are difficult to deal with. Most are, of course, older and understandably tend to be defensive, particularly about their personal wealth. They know they cannot live forever and this reality is always on their minds, so they often come across as complainers. And, of course, as wealthy people, they have gotten used to being given lots of attention and rather expect it, particularly in regard to their wealth, which has often become their last focus of attention."

PCS opened in Hong Kong, Tokyo, and Singapore—and in Miami, which linked the firm to accounts in Brazil, Venezuela, and the rest of Latin America. In the early 1990s, it became clear that non-U.S. clients would like having a Swiss bank and numbered accounts, so the firm acquired a bank and two years later got a license to run it as Goldman Sachs Bank.

As a result of Menschel's careful recruiting and the economic advantages of his business model, PCS continued to have low turnover and high morale. Like all retail brokers, the people in PCS were paid entirely on commission, and they were making real money: On a payout of 30 percent of gross commissions—one of the lowest percentage payouts on Wall Street—personal incomes of two million dollars were not unusual for brokers with no managerial responsibilities, and some earned even more. This did not go unnoticed by the partners, who typically earned two million dollars to five million dollars a year and had to spend time in management and recruiting, activities that were recognized as important for firm building but took them away from making more money.

Complaints began to arise around the firm that the highly paid PCS salesmen were trading off the reputation of Goldman Sachs while their investment results were not always "firm standard" in quality or consistency. So the firm began to monitor account-by-account performance, with particular focus on potential risks and portfolio turnover. The source of the worst investment ideas was soon discovered: Most came directly from the customers.

Goldman Sachs was understandably happy, even a little complacent, about the progress of PCS. In 1989 Bob Rubin asked for an analysis of PCS's profitability. The results were clear: PCS was a money spinner. Profit margins were consistently 22 percent to 23 percent. But in any multidivisional business like Goldman Sachs, with large core costs allocated to revenue-producing units, the profitability of individual operations can be changed a lot by changes in the allocations of those core costs—costs like the multimillions spent on research, which were then allocated to the operating units. Before Zuckerberg left the firm in 1998, John McNulty arranged to merge PCS into the still-not-profitable business of Goldman Sachs Asset Management, and allocations of support costs were "revisited." When the allocations to PCS were recalculated, PCS was declared "not really profitable." In another reallocation, profits on bond purchases by PCS clients were shunted away from PCS and over to the dealers making each bond's market. "I don't believe I ever witnessed a larger reduction in business value," was Lloyd Blankfein's summary of the impact of reevaluating PCS.

In 1999–2000, Phil Murphy, the new head of PCS, reorganized compensation to align individual incentives with the firm's objectives. This typically cut pay-out ratios to brokers from 30 percent to 20 percent. This reduction and realignment caused dozens of PCS salesmen to look at moving to other firms that were trying to break into the wealthy individual investor business. Other firms offered gross commissions as high as 40 percent—in some cases well above the firm's new payout—to attract major producers to leave PCS. While most chose to stay, some of the most productive PCS brokers checked the market for their capabilities and traded themselves to Merrill Lynch, Morgan Stanley, UBS, or Bear Stearns after commanding rich signing bonuses as well as higher commissions. The leaving was often unhappy, even bitter.

With a substantial reduction in its profitability and with both Zuckerberg and his successor Bill Buckley leaving the partnership, it was almost inevitable that the whole concept of PCS would be challenged—and reinvented. McNulty and Murphy led the transformation. "The PCS business model was flawed," said McNulty. "At the end of the year you had to start all over again. We were paid by the number of transaction tickets written—and paid very well for placing IPOs. But that was not an investment-advisory business." The PCS salespeople thought they were asset managers, but they were actually confusing two very different businesses. The first business was based on developing personal trust and personal relationships, which they were good at, but from the firm's perspective, PCS was too dependent on those individuals. The second business was the investment business. PCS was a series of personal proprietorships, but it was not a scalable, manageable business, and the real "owners" of the business were the individual PCS people, not the firm.

As McNulty explained, "The PCS people were not all great portfolio architects or great stock pickers or great investment strategists—and the world of investing was developing skills and expectations of capability and professionalism that were rapidly outpacing them." McNulty and Murphy converted PCS from the entrepreneurial business model developed by Zuckerberg and Menschel into a corporate design in which PCS people were "asset gatherers" and the investing was increasingly done by the firm through GSAM and firm-sponsored funds.

Some very large accounts—particularly those with assets over one hundred million dollars and poor results—were taken away from individual salesmen and made firm accounts. Investment management was shifted away from the individual PCS salesman in two ways: The investment "product" was broadened to include more asset classes and made more consistent—less dependent on the individual PCS salesman. An "open architecture" approach to product sourcing brought investing capabilities from outside GSAM.[2]

After he retired, Zuckerberg went to the firm's office at 7:45 one morning in 2004 and was surprised to see what was now called the Private Wealth Management area almost empty. "Where is everybody? Where are all the people?" Someone heard him, knew who he was, and understood what he meant: "Roy, it's different now."

And so it is. Now everyone is part of a large organizational effort, and the role of the PCS people is concentrated on bringing in the accounts and servicing them. Other people, chosen because they were professional investment managers, would run the money. Goldman Sachs has a highly profitable, scalable business, PCS people get paid well, and the profits are more predictable. Within the firm, some miss the old PCS hustle, but most believe it's all just as well.

Goldman Sachs has produced two important businesses out of PCS. Private Wealth Management, serving wealthy families and individuals with a wide array of investment products produced both by Goldman Sachs and by an array of outside investment managers, became one of the best among the firm's many businesses when it was expanded globally. And an even better business—if not the best of all businesses that came out of PCS—is prime brokerage.

In the spring of 1983, based on the work being done for one client—Steinhardt, a hedge fund assigned to PCS because it used margin-account borrowing and required special handling—Roy Zuckerberg had an idea. It got him so excited that he felt he had to discuss it with someone—someone who could take it from a mere thought into a really good business. Zuckerberg called Dan Stanton, who was managing the Boston regional office, a proven business builder and good with people.[3] "Dan, if you were presented with the right opportunity, would you be willing to make a change?" Stanton said he liked what he was doing, but yes, he would move for the right opportunity. Zuckerberg said, "I'm coming up to Boston to see you. Let's meet in the Café at the Ritz-Carlton tomorrow morning." That next morning, the two men were in deep conversation, with Zuckerberg drawing squares and lines on a paper napkin to make his points.

"We do a lot with Mike Steinhardt. We could do the same, and more, for other hedge funds if we package it properly, deliver the service properly, and price it properly." Morgan Stanley was already doing what Zuckerberg had in mind—coordinating the many specialized financial services that hedge funds require—for Julian Robertson at Tiger Fund and for George Soros. Bear Stearns was doing part of it, but its business model was based on its clearing brokerage business for the smaller regional firms and wasn't really right for the hedge funds. Zuckerberg was enthusiastic: "This is going to be big because hedge funds are going to be big. More hedge funds are being organized all the time, and they are going to keep growing because the compensation economics are so compelling." Stanton was at least as interested as Zuckerberg.

Hedge funds manage their assets very intensively, so they need accurate reports on their positions every day and accurate, swift clearance of all their trades, many of which are complex. Margin lending is important for all hedge funds because they use leverage boldly, and margin-lending brokers need to know exactly how much good collateral each hedge fund has to support its borrowing. It makes no sense for a hedge fund to work with twenty or thirty different brokers and try to consolidate all their reports into one database when all that work can be done by one "prime" broker who can keep accurate daily records for the hedge fund of what it is doing with all its separate brokers. Because hedge funds trade so actively in all sorts of securities, serving as a prime broker is operationally exacting and depends on sophisticated computer capabilities—capabilities that can easily cost one hundred million dollars every year. Developing the capacity to find and deliver securities that the hedge fund is selling short is essential. Easy in concept, this can be hard in day-to-day practice. "We travel the world to develop supply and make an unrelenting drive for superb relationships with the master trustee custodians who supervise most securities assets," explains Stanton. Short-term cash balances—both credit and debit—stay with the custodian broker, who earns some interest income on the funds every day, including Saturdays and Sundays. The funds' record-keeping computers are integrated with the firm's computers so the work can be done machine to machine. The prime-brokerage business has grown almost as rapidly as the hedge-fund business. In the seven years from 1993 to 2001, total hedge-fund assets multiplied six times from one hundred billion dollars to six hundred billion dollars; they will probably triple again by 2010. Securities lending is the key product in the prime-brokerage business. Since borrowing hard-to-find securities could also be critical to the firm's proprietary-trading desks, their heads didn't want the prime-brokerage operation to lend securities to the hedge funds. Others argued that preventing this would be a subsidy to the "prop" desks. As one proprietary trader said, "If we really need a subsidy, we shouldn't be in this business." Prime Brokerage kept the right to lend securities.

"Every real business has a name," said partner David Silfen, like Dick Menschel before him. "So you should come up with a good name for your business, Dan." Stanton thought for a while and proposed "Global Securities Services," or "GSS." Since "GS" often stood for "Goldman Sachs," many people thought the name must be Goldman Sachs Services. "There was a lot of confusion about the name, but no confusion about the business of making money for Goldman Sachs."

Stanton and his group were making bigger and bigger profits, but nobody in senior management seemed to know or care. Ed Spiegel, a leader in equity sales, proudly introduced his partner: "This is Dan Stanton. He runs our back office." Almost nobody came down from the executive offices on the twenty-eighth or twenty-ninth floor to visit GSS on the seventh floor. Among the partners, John Thain got it. Hank Paulson knew he should have had more of an understanding but felt he never had the time. Yet even as the profitability and the compensation in Equities kept getting squeezed, the profitability of GSS kept rising over the years. By the millennium, the status of being in GSS was equal to that of being in Equities, if not higher. For a while, it was disconcerting for many at the firm to know that GSS people without MBAs were making more money than Harvard MBAs in other divisions, but profits always drive power and status in the firm. Today being in GSS is clearly high status, so talented, ambitious people are migrating there.

"Being underappreciated and ignored by the top brass, who really didn't understand our business, was a real benefit—because they left us alone," says Stanton. "Even during the '94 cost cutting—or should I say, cost slashing—we refused to ease off on our commitment to recruit the very best people and deliver the very best service. And we never backed off on our absolute commitment to information technology—never, even when everyone else was taking a blowtorch to IT." That commitment has really paid off in building Goldman Sachs a great business. When Thain and John Thornton, serving as co-COOs, conducted a "Q&Q" study in 2000, to measure the quantity and quality of earnings in every business of the firm, two lines of business stood out: M&A and GSS.

GSS is a Warren Buffett dream come true—a simple, great business with a wide, impenetrable protective moat around it. GSS has it all: rapid, steady annual growth of nearly 40 percent, compounded; high—very high—profit margins; and few competitors and tall barriers to competitive entry because the huge computer costs make a large scale of operations essential to be cost-competitive. Even more important, the service is absolutely necessary to the customer, the cost to the customer is tiny compared to the value delivered, and the service and how it's delivered are opaque, so there's almost no pressure to reduce fees. That's why it would make no sense for the market leaders—Goldman Sachs and Morgan Stanley—to compete with each other aggressively on price. Even as volume has multiplied many, many times, prices have eased down only 20 percent since the late nineties. Finally, the extensive network of working relationships is crucial in the all-important core of the business, securities lending. As Stanton says, "It can't get any better than this."

15

J. ARON

UGLY DUCKLING

B ob Rubin looked up slowly from the business plan he held in his hand and, as usual, spoke softly: "Mark, you'll have to set your sights higher—a *lot* higher."

Two years before, Rubin had put Mark Winkelman in charge of the commodities firm J. Aron, Goldman Sachs's first important acquisition in half a century. After years of increasingly lush profits before the acquisition, J. Aron had faltered badly. It lost money in its first year as part of Goldman Sachs, and with lots of work and many changes had just barely climbed back into the black with a five-million-dollar profit. In his business plan for the coming year, Winkelman had been aiming to stay in the black—and *double* profits to ten million dollars.

Smiling sympathetically, Rubin handed Winkelman's business plan back to him. "Mark, ten million dollars is *not* why we bought J. Aron. Tell us what we need to do to make profits of a hundred million *this* year!"

"What?"

Mark Winkelman was brilliant, but he had no idea what Rubin might be thinking. He was dumbfounded. Even with his extraordinary respect for Rubin's judgment, he couldn't believe Rubin was really serious. But the look in Rubin's eyes said he was very serious.

Winkelman had gotten to his new position circuitously. Born in the Netherlands, he studied economics at Rotterdam and then went to Wharton in 1971, having persuaded a Dutch company to pay his way in exchange for a ten-year commitment to work for the company after graduation. Before taking up that offer, however, he got a scholarship at Wharton, so he was able to cover his own costs. What's more, he recalls, "Even more fortunately for me, I met a girl in a very short skirt on my second day—and we are now married." After Wharton, Winkelman worked briefly for a small firm in Cambridge, Massachusetts, on bond-arbitrage software and then at the World Bank in the innovative finance unit run by Gene Rothberg.

Frank Smeal brought Winkelman—described by colleagues as brainy, rigorous, fair, and very Dutch—from the World Bank in 1977 to start a Goldman Sachs operation in interest-rate-futures arbitrage, a fast-changing business.[1] The key to success in the bond business had switched from service to disciplined risk taking, and each dealer had to figure out for himself how profoundly the markets had changed with derivatives and globalization. Winkelman's mission was to install and develop an options and arbitrage capability for the bond business and to work with the traders.

Five years later, "my switch into commodities looked like a fairly dumb move to most people," acknowledges Winkelman. Bonds were booming, and the big positive market trends seemed sure to continue. In contrast, gold—which was crucial to J. Aron's business—had peaked briefly at $850 an ounce when Russia invaded Afghanistan, the global political world seemed out of control, and Jimmy Carter seemed out of his depth. Fed chairman Paul Volcker's clampdown on inflation propelled interest rates and money-market volatility to record levels. Then, as calm returned to the markets, the price of gold came down—plunging to three hundred dollars. Gold's price volatility dropped even more than the price, evaporating almost all opportunity to profit from trading against changes in prices.

Because it was so obviously a career-risking move, Winkelman was advised by peers: "I wouldn't switch if I were you." But Winkelman had a private reason to switch: The competition between him and Jon Corzine in fixed income had become too intense. Winkelman's success was a persistent problem for Corzine, and their working relationship was increasingly strained. "At first, we were like two young bulls, pawing the ground and looking for ways to dominate," Winkelman recalls, though he adds that over time they made their differences mesh pretty well and became successfully interdependent.

Commodities were not entirely new to Goldman Sachs. In the late seventies, the commodities industry was enjoying the best and final years of a long-term cyclical boom in coffee, grains, silver, gold, and particularly oil, where prices were way up due to OPEC, while the securities business had been slowly going downhill for years; the Dow stood at 1,000 in both 1966 and 1982, sixteen years later. As an industry expert[2] observed, "Everybody saw opportunities in commodities." In 1980, Rubin hired Dan Amstutz, a grain trader, to develop a small agricultural commodities business within the arbitrage department, reflecting Rubin's considerable curiosity about how different money businesses worked.

Winkelman had been developing another small commodities-trading business at Goldman Sachs as one of Bob Rubin's R&D initiatives when he heard the November 1981 announcement of the firm's acquisition of J. Aron. He resolved to quit. How could he hope to make his career now, with six J. Aron people, all deeply experienced in commodities, suddenly being made Goldman Sachs partners and one even going onto the management committee? With that many partners competing with him, Winkelman saw his career as hopelessly stuck in a big traffic jam.

"Mark, don't be foolish," counseled John Whitehead. "You'll be part of the biggest and best commodities business in the world. Commodities are far more international than securities, and this whole firm is going international. You'll have a superb international perspective. J. Aron is a great platform for a rising young star like you, and this is a major strategic thrust for the firm, so you'll soon see we are doing you a favor. You can ride this big wave to great things. So roll up your sleeves and get to work."

John Weinberg was even more direct: "Don't be stupid! I understand that you're angry about this sudden change, and I can see why. We're not sure just how yet, but we're going to make something important out of this business."

"Sit tight. Let's wait and see," was Bob Rubin's noncommittal but encouraging advice. "The next election of partners is in just one year. How bad can it be to wait a year to see?" Winkelman decided to stay.

Then the Two Johns, Weinberg and Whitehead, made everything perfectly clear: J. Aron was an important opportunity—for Winkelman and for the firm. "You will go to J. Aron." Somewhat intimidated and yet pleased to be given this responsibility, Winkelman dove into every salient aspect of the operation. Two years later, he developed the budget he thought appropriately bold, the one that drew Rubin's astonishing response: "Tell us what we need to do to make a profit of a hundred million *this* year!"

"Bob Rubin had a very soft touch with words and as a manager, usually making his quiet suggestions by asking questions," recalls Winkelman. "His approach worked best with people who were personally modest, intellectually open, and comfortable with genuine doubt. If you weren't this kind of person—and many traders weren't even close—Bob would simply move on until he found someone he could really work with." Rubin set the right tone of understatement to make his challenge clear and compelling to Winkelman.

In his revised business plan, Winkelman took J. Aron aggressively into currency trading with the firm's capital at risk. With this change, the unit's profits in its third year as part of Goldman Sachs were actually well *over* one hundred million dollars—and a few years later, were well over one billion, no less than one-third of Goldman Sachs's total profits—with only three hundred employees in a firm of six thousand.*

The firm's eventual success in commodities was certainly not created by the acquisition of J. Aron. Success was achieved only through massive changes in every important dimension of the business *after* the acquisition. Most of the people and all the business leaders were changed, and the basic risk-controlled financial arbitrage business model was changed into a capital-at-risk proprietary business model. However, as disappointing and painful as the first few years' financial results were, the acquisition did bring to Goldman Sachs a cadre of traders and a trading culture that would become dominant in the firm—and the man who would become its CEO.

---

* J. Aron contributed an estimated 40 percent of firm earnings in 1990, roughly one-third in 1991, and 35 percent in 1992, primarily from foreign-exchange and petroleum trading. Though 1990 was a poor profit year in the securities industry, with the help of J. Aron, Goldman Sachs earned record profits. *Wall Street Journal*, November 9, 1992.

Still, the path from here to there would have to be figured out and major changes made. Over the next several years, even the markets in which J. Aron operated were changed as J. Aron moved boldly into foreign exchange and oil trading. These changes required reinventing the business and the business concepts. Profit opportunity in the gold-trading business was basically a function of bullion's price volatility and financial-markets arbitrage, so J. Aron had needed little capital and enjoyed a high rate of return on the capital it did invest.

As a matter of policy, J. Aron seldom went long or short on gold bullion or tried to profit on an inventory position. Profits were made principally by arbitraging the changing spread between the London bullion market and the new futures markets. Growth in these profits came from increasing market volatility and trading volume.

In a typical day as an independent firm, J. Aron had done one thousand trades in the morning and three thousand trades in the afternoon—carefully matching its long and short positions within *seconds* to be sure the firm was never much exposed to market risk. "Our plan of operation called for being long or short up to a maximum of twenty seconds," explained Jack Aron. If ever there was any serious doubt—once or twice a year—the whole firm would stop doing any business with a command like, "Okay, everybody! Shut off the phones immediately! We're doing a one-hundred-percent books-to-cards check to be *sure* we have absolutely no net positions." The complete analysis could take until nine or ten at night.

J. Aron began as a coffee trader in New Orleans in 1898 with ten thousand dollars in capital, prospered, and moved to New York in 1910. Jack Aron and Gus Levy were distant relatives who became friends in their early days in both New Orleans and New York City, and both were leaders at Mount Sinai Hospital and in the Jewish community. Their two firms did occasional business together, so Levy had been interested when Aron called on him in the late sixties to say, "Gus, I'm getting old. My two sons have no real interest in the business. Our two firms are both private. So if you'd like to buy, I'd like to sell."

After some discussions, a large tax liability on an unrealized gain at J. Aron got in the way, and Levy's interest in a deal quickly faded. Later, when Jack Aron took another tentative Goldman Sachs offer to his partners, the deal was voted down by the younger J. Aron partners in a move led by Herb Coyne. Coyne was shrewd, consistently pragmatic, and never sentimental, famously saying, "Honesty is *one* of the best policies" and leaving it to his listeners to guess which policies he might think were equally good. Coyne was an astute strategist focused on the goal of maximizing wealth. By then Aron was in his seventies and had moved away from the business to concentrate on his charitable foundation, so it was not hard for the two men to agree on an internal management buyout and arrange the sale of the firm to Coyne, his brother Marty, and twelve other shareholders.

George Doty had gotten to know J. Aron partners when he was working with them to create low-cost income-tax deferrals for Goldman Sachs partners based on "straddles" in commodities futures. He became a strong proponent of acquiring a commodities firm because he believed Goldman Sachs should get into the business, yet he didn't believe it had the necessary perseverance as a partnership: One group of partners would have had to make the several years of costly investment spending and building that would be needed to get established, knowing that any returns on those investments would go mostly to their successors. In any case, Doty would never have favored a "build our own" entry strategy because it would entail, as he exclaimed several times, "too much risk!"

In what must have seemed like a very lucky break, Herb Coyne approached Goldman Sachs just two years after the J. Aron partners had bought out Jack Aron and his two sons, and asked the firm to try to find a buyer. Before almost anyone else, Coyne had figured out the probable impact of the new futures markets on both the gold-bullion and the foreign-exchange markets. Almost simultaneously, another fortunate coincidence developed: In September 1981, Engelhard Minerals proposed—through Goldman Sachs—an acquisition of J. Aron, but the controlling partners of J. Aron refused. They were not interested in signing long-term employment contracts or being part of a public company.

J. Aron partners were unwilling to give up their cherished privacy—particularly when profits were spectacularly large. To avoid attracting competition, Coyne imposed specific rules of secrecy: "Don't tell *anyone* where you're going, who you're seeing, or what you've heard—ever!" His partners all agreed: "Never tell anyone how much money you make—just smile as you walk to the bank." As one J. Aron partner readily conceded, "The way we made money was so simple, anyone could do it—so we were sworn to secrecy."

J. Aron had expanded in the late sixties from coffee into precious-metals trading and began growing rapidly and very profitably. After a recapitalization shrank the partnership capital to four hundred thousand dollars, profits mush-roomed through the seventies and lifted the partnership capital to one hundred million dollars by 1981. That year, J. Aron made profits of sixty million dollars on its capital of one hundred million dollars—similar in ratio to Goldman Sachs's profits that year of $150 million on partners' capital of $272 million—but Goldman Sachs had earned its profits by taking much greater market and credit risks than J. Aron had taken.

The two firms were vastly different in style and culture. Coyne had recently begun hiring "top of their class" lawyers because the business had become so complex that only the most astute analysts could stay ahead of the markets through creativity, but J. Aron had for many past years promoted clerks with only high school education—including Herb Coyne's former driver—*not* Harvard MBAs. If they were smart, tough, and ambitious, lack of education didn't matter. J. Aron remained an autocratic, hierarchical pecking order, with recent hires ordered to fetch lunch for slightly more senior people. In contrast, Goldman Sachs was all about teamwork in a relatively flat organization that believed in at least fifteen preemployment interviews and thought graduate degrees from top-tier schools were essential. Goldman Sachs prized modesty, even humility. At J. Aron, the consensus was totally different: "We were convinced we were the smartest people in the universe because we were making all that money," recalls a former partner. "There was a hubris that just infected the place." Goldman Sachs investment bankers prized deferential client service and were always polite, but at J. Aron traders spoke just as crudely as traders always have about customers. While the larger accounts were accorded deferential respect, small accounts were assigned to juniors who could get them little more than price quotes and transactions.

J. Aron was in three different businesses, and acquisition advocates at Goldman Sachs saw opportunities in all three: first, gold, silver, platinum, and palladium, plus a range of small positions in other commodities; second, a small business in foreign exchange; and third, coffee, where it clearly ranked number one in the world as an importer of unroasted green coffee. As Whitehead recalls: "J. Aron was a unique opportunity with unusual attractions. In gold, J. Aron was a world leader. Gold trades in more daily volume than anything else—more than General Electric stock or General Motors stock, for example—particularly in the Arab world."

There were opportunities to expand in other agricultural commodities such as cocoa, corn, and other grains, building on J. Aron's strength in coffee, where it acted as selling agent for coffee growers and as buying agent for General Foods and Folgers, among others. And there were opportunities to develop the profitability of the business by engaging in directly associated activities such as shipping, insurance, and warehousing in Brazil and New York City—all without taking on price risk. As Whitehead saw it, "We could control the whole process—and if someone tried to compete on price in any one function, we could simply bring our pricing down below his for that particular function and move our profit making to another part of the chain. We would have complete control. And by selling to roasters at the same time we bought from the growers, we would have no price risk."

Interbank foreign-exchange dealing was another opportunity, but Doty had no interest: "Leave it to the commercial banks! They'll do FX for *nothing*. You'll never be able to make any real money in a business they'll always dominate." But J. Aron was already active in the fledgling currency-futures markets, which commercial banks were ignoring, and in arbitraging the fluctuating spreads between futures and the cash market.

During their two years of ownership, Herb Coyne and his group had built up the metals business and made three particularly clever moves. First, as an ever-curious intellectual who loved to figure things out, Coyne learned that the central banks of many nations kept their currency reserves in gold bars stored in the vaults of the Bank of England in London or the New York Federal Reserve Bank. Taken together, all this great wealth of nations had what Coyne saw as one fascinating characteristic: It earned zero return. It just sat in the vaults. But Coyne knew that the time value of money *always* figured into any futures contract and that the forward markets in commodities always reflected implicit interest rates, so he called on the central bankers in one country after another and made what appeared to be a generous and innovative offer: "Lend me your sterile bars of gold bullion and I'll pay you a fee of half of one percent every year!"

The banks were familiar with J. Aron's large business in gold and its reputation for absolute integrity and meticulous care, so they saw J. Aron as a no-risk counterparty and the 0.5 percent fee as found money. Even a small country would have two hundred million dollars in gold reserves, so Coyne's deal would take that country's annual income on its gold bars up from zero to one million dollars. The central bank of Austria, after a long series of meetings at which each aspect of the arrangement was carefully explained and pondered, finally signed up.[3] It was soon followed by the central banks of Hungary and Mexico. Others, like Portugal, followed later.*

Coyne knew what the central bankers did not know: J. Aron could create a near-perfect hedge by selling short the borrowed gold and buying gold futures (which incorporated the high interest rates of those years) for an annualized profit as high as 8 percent on the matched book.[4] That was 8 percent on a risk-free matched book that required almost no equity capital, so it produced a nearly infinite rate of return. J. Aron's strong relationships with many central banks were the keys to this magic kingdom of profits, because the central banks had virtually unlimited reservoirs of gold-bullion reserves and could keep supplying the market to match any volume of demand.

In a second clever innovation, J. Aron created and ran a highly profitable sideline business selling gold coins minted in Mexico, Russia, Canada, and South Africa—for which it sold over one million Krugerrands. The margins were not large, but J. Aron acted only as an agent: The governments owned and stored the inventory; there was no competition and virtually no costs of operation. Again, the return on capital was nearly infinite.

Coyne's third business strategy was particularly astute and venturesome. Driven by Herbert and Bunker Hunt's remarkable speculative efforts to corner the world silver market, silver bullion was selling at record prices in 1980, and people everywhere were responding by trying to melt down the family silver to make tradable bullion bars and capture the unusual spread in prices between silver in flatware and pure silver bars. But to do this required refining. Anticipating that demand for silver refining capacity would continue to rise, Coyne contacted major smelters, including Europe's largest,[5] and asked for price quotes on future capacity. Given a set price and anticipating strong demand, he signed binding contracts for virtually all the refiners' worldwide future capacity. This was a brilliant stroke and a masterful speculation on a grand scale. Since J. Aron had already prebooked the refineries, everyone had to come to it and pay a big premium to get scrap silver refined. J. Aron made another killing.

The profits from letting speculators pay up to buy scarce refining capacity

* An alternative arrangement for these central banks was to give them dollars—for ninety days—equal to the value of the gold turned over to J. Aron so they could invest those dollars as they wished.

and the profits from borrowing gold-bullion bars from central banks were rich, but that could not and would not continue forever, as Coyne fully understood. The short-run bonanza masked the major problem that was rapidly developing in J. Aron's basic business. Commercial banks were becoming increasingly active competitors in commodities, and they instinctively swept cash balances automatically every day to invest them at the prevailing 10 percent–plus interest rates. Most corporate and individual customers had instead let cash balances build up, allowing J. Aron to invest those cash balances in the money market and keep the interest earned for itself. At the same time, improved worldwide communications were taking the information-processing time required to complete a trade down from an hour for a cabled instruction to just one second for electronics—reducing uncertainties and squeezing core profitability. In addition, Paul Volcker's determined drive against inflation had pushed interest rates up to record levels, provoking a recession, which in turn calmed the market volatility in gold prices that had been so profitable for traders like J. Aron.

"The Coyne brothers knew their business was in trouble, but they could not see a way out. They didn't have a clue—not a clue—about how to get out of the trap they'd put themselves into," says Winkelman. "The profits of the physicals-versus-futures [arbitrage] business were evaporating. That's the only business they really knew. They had no understanding of how to shape their firm into a major risk-taking, capital-based business—and that had become the only way to go."

Coyne had seen other firms like his take capital risks and get wiped out. He knew his organization didn't have the ability to run an aggressive risk-based business; he and his senior partners were not up to date with new instruments, like currency options, that were just starting to trade and were major potential profit makers. So it was a good time for him to cash in, become part of a much larger business organization, and hope to find ways then to make even more money.

Coyne made his most important strategic move when he reinitiated merger discussions with George Doty at Goldman Sachs—just when Salomon Brothers was combining with the commodities giant Phillips Brothers, known as Phibro.[6] Through his work with Doty on tax shelters for Goldman Sachs partners, Coyne knew how very profitable the firm was. And he succeeded in selling J. Aron to Goldman Sachs at the absolute peak of its earnings.

Strong opposition to making the acquisition came from Goldman Sachs partners: "That's *not* our business"; "Commodities aren't securities"; "If they want to sell, why should we be their buyer? We'll just be patsies." But as debate within the partnership kept postponing the decision—and risking J. Aron's doing a deal with some other organization—the recognition of the moderate risk of loss if things went wrong became increasingly persuasive. With the agreed purchase price of $135 million offset by book value of one hundred million dollars—almost all in cash and cash equivalents—serious risk seemed small. "Since risky trading positions were minimized because traders simultaneously matched buy and sell interests," explains Whitehead, "the operation was virtually risk-free." Whitehead's strategic interest in internationalizing Goldman Sachs kept his focus on a macro vision—and away from the rigorous operational analysis for which he was well known. "Gold trading involves every country in the world, so it's the most *international* of businesses, and at Goldman Sachs we were expanding internationally." Whitehead was determined to acquire J. Aron as one part of internationalizing the firm and as a signature transaction that would permanently change Goldman Sachs.

"We had a terrible time getting the acquisition approved by our own people," recalls Whitehead, "so I assigned Steve Friedman and Ken Brody to study the merits of the acquisition, believing that since Steve worked for me and was ambitious to advance, his report would make a solid, positive case for making the acquisition. But he surprised me by recommending against acquiring J. Aron." But it really didn't matter what others said or thought, because Doty and Whitehead were determined, and they drove it through the all-powerful management committee in October 1981.

"I was never in favor of buying a business," says Friedman. "From my M&A experience, I knew that mergers are always hard and often don't work out. It's not that they actually fail financially, but they underperform and disappoint relative to expectations because the organizational cultures don't fit together. Conflicts and tensions are so easy to have and cultures are so very hard to integrate, and Goldman Sachs has a very strong, very different culture. We would always be better off building our own because the key to success is always people and we have the best people—*lots* of best people."* Ironically, given Friedman's observation, after the acquisition only one person—Mark Winkelman—was transferred from Goldman

---

* After the problems with J. Aron showed how difficult acquisitions could be, John Weinberg decided against acquiring any investment managers and said, "We'll build the investment business ourselves."

Sachs into J. Aron, while several J. Aron people would become leaders in Goldman Sachs and one, Lloyd Blankfein, would eventually become the firm's CEO.

A few weeks after the acquisition—while Goldman Sachs was striving to make the J. Aron people feel part of the family—J. Aron's CFO, Charles Griffith, went to see Doty to say, "George, I'm going to resign—unless I can become a partner." Doty and Whitehead quickly agreed that he would have to be made a partner. That certainly did not go down easily with all those who had been competing for years to earn a Goldman Sachs partnership—particularly after seeing six other J. Aron people made partners as part of the deal. One of the cardinal firm rules was that nobody should *ever* threaten to leave if not taken into the partnership. Partners were made only by the firm and only when the firm was ready.

These postmerger problems were disturbing, but certainly not as disconcerting as the core problems with the J. Aron business. Even though the deal was done, as more and more difficulties developed, opponents within Goldman Sachs were convinced that the acquisition of J. Aron was based on a collection of mistakes in both strategy and tactics. Some of the erupting difficulties were due to errors, even serious errors, but some were due to unexpected external problems. Most partners didn't bother to sort out the two kinds of trouble; the whole experience was too painful. As one partner lamented, "We made every mistake in this merger that we always worried clients would make in their mergers."

One mistake was to react to a competitor's move and impute a threatening reason for that move. Although some had seen Salomon Brothers's link with Phibro as a strategic master stroke, in fact that merger had not been driven by any grand strategy: It was really just a great trade—a chance for the partners of Salomon Brothers, a private firm, to sell out and get 100 percent liquid at a high price. Another mistake was for innocent observers to develop an almost romantic vision of another firm's having both low business risk and unlimited opportunity while seeing commodities as a hedge against the adversities inflation might impose on the securities business. Another was to assume that Gus Levy's interest in the J. Aron deal had been strategic when it was really closer to opportunistic. Another was not knowing how and where the profits were really being made and not realizing how serious the misunderstandings based on this innocence could be. The two firms' cultures, styles, and values were not only different; they would be in open conflict and would make integration difficult.

Mistakes would include losing key executives early on; not having a clear strategy for increasing profits after the deal was done; paying up front rather than obligating the sellers to an earn-out; and tying up precious capital and management time. The classic mistake was not understanding the true motivation of the sellers and not remembering that most "acquisitions" are not *purchases* driven by the interests of the buyer, but are *sales* driven by seller motivations that the buyers learn about only long after the deal is done. Misreadings were also important at J. Aron, where Coyne had somehow expected to become the leader of the combined J. Aron–Goldman Sachs organization and to have his partners in major leadership roles.

Goldman Sachs did not really understand the J. Aron business, but the sellers certainly did. As one J. Aron partner later observed, "It would have been a very difficult time if we had not sold the business."[7]

In less than a year, J. Aron's record profits were cut in half, and a year later there were losses. With tens of millions of dollars of Goldman Sachs partners' capital locked up in this one acquisition, the added opportunity cost of not using that money in the firm's own highly profitable proprietary trading businesses was over thirty million dollars a year.

Opposition to the acquisition was fanned back into flames. In addition to a major capital commitment, many Goldman Sachs partners had thought the non-financial cost of the acquisition was way too high: Many insiders resented Marvin Schur, who headed the coffee business, being made a member of the management committee and five "outsiders" suddenly being made full partners. It certainly didn't help that after a year of experience, as others soon found out, John Weinberg didn't much like the J. Aron guys. And they didn't like Goldman Sachs. One of J. Aron's seniors was explicit: "I don't really *want* to be your partner." He was being honest, but what a way to try combining two organizations! Then profits suddenly plunged because "soft" commodities like coffee were cyclical and commercial banks and other securities dealers moved into the hard-commodities business of gold and precious-metals trading just when market volatility dropped, taking margins down from 0.5 percent to just $1/32$ of 1 percent.

When Doty retired, responsibility for supervision of J. Aron passed to Bob Rubin, who made just one change in the J. Aron organization: He replaced Ron Tauber with Mark Winkelman as CEO. Rubin and Winkelman soon decided that

264 · THE PARTNERSHIP

J. Aron's COO, a lawyer, had to go and that overhead was way too large because many people who had appeared to be profit makers when gold volatility was high were not moneymakers in more normal markets. With help from the internal leaders they identified at J. Aron, Rubin and Winkelman cleared out the last of J. Aron's old guard—Aron's younger stars saw that as a breath of fresh air—and cut the staff by 50 percent. "J. Aron was in real trouble," recalls Winkelman. "Costs had to be cut back sharply, and cutting costs meant cutting people—something Goldman Sachs traditionally did not do." To control the pain, it was agreed to do all the terminations on one day—to get it over quickly instead of stretching it out—and that each person would be privately informed by his direct supervisor unless that supervisor was also being fired. "Because George Doty and the Two Johns were in a different building and J. Aron was still a separate organization, doing all those terminations was considered okay. We were fighting for our very existence and we had to cleanse the culture from a bootlicking family-run business," recalls Winkelman. "After half a dozen years at J. Aron, I still was known as the smart-ass that knows how to fire people."

While he was terminating many, many people—ultimately 130 of J. Aron's 230 employees were identified as redundant—Winkelman made one eventually crucial decision to go the other way and keep a young man who had already been turned away by Goldman Sachs. Lloyd Blankfein—son of a postal clerk, who went through Harvard College and Harvard Law School on scholarships—had been hired as a personal assistant by Herb Coyne in the summer of 1982. "The place was lousy with lawyers," recalls a J. Aron colleague. "Lloyd was hired because lawyers know how to work hard and could explain to clients new instruments like options and complex trading strategies. Lloyd was and is funny—one of the most naturally funny people in the world—warm and real. We all knew Lloyd was the guy, and Mark Winkelman soon had that figured out."

There were more departures. In less than a year, Marvin Schur and Herb Coyne both discovered—not at all surprisingly to skeptics within Goldman Sachs—that they had serious health problems. The day after the merger was completed, Coyne had complained of a pain in his chest. Within a year, Schur was not feeling well either. Soon both men retired. As Goldman Sachs partner Lee Cooperman says sardonically, "With chest pains and forty million dollars apiece in the bank, who wouldn't?"

Within J. Aron, which had had only six major owners, it had been under-stood for some years that share ownership was going to be redistributed so everyone in management would be an owner. But young, brainy natural lead-ers who were well trained and would become the real leaders of J. Aron under Winkelman—and ten senior people who had been promised a stake—were not included in the sale of the firm. Bitter people know little loyalty. People who were counting on that "share the wealth" proposition felt badly jerked around when the Coyne brothers sold the firm out from under them. A week after the deal, two key J. Aron employees left for Drexel Burnham Lambert and took with them their business—the business of renting gold bars from Central and Eastern Euro-pean, African, and Latin American central banks—determined to compete for the business aggressively in every way, including price. This quickly clobbered J. Aron's lush profits in the "gold loan" business.

Expectations of repetitive thirty- to thirty-five-million-dollar annual risk-free profits from J. Aron now seemed a chimera. "Internally the traditional J. Aron business was going through the wringer," recalls Winkelman, "and it looked as though profits would *never* come back." The prices of gold and sil-ver came down and kept falling. Competitors like Drexel Burnham cut into the central-bank gold-bar lending business by offering to pay higher interest rates and taking market share. As volatility subsided, commercial banks got into gold trading and cut the profit margins on that business. The pressure was really on.

The Two Johns made a very visible and personal pledge to the partnership: "We'll take care of this situation." They met every week with Winkelman, not to discuss trading but to explore possible business strategies and management deci-sions. "At first, I thought it would be difficult—a real punishment," recalls Win-kelman, "but soon I realized that it was a golden opportunity. First, I saw what a great strategic vision John Whitehead had and how important that was. Second, we got a lot of exposure to the firm's real leaders. They got personally involved to be *sure* we would eventually solve the many problems at J. Aron—and there were *lots* of problems." With low volume and narrow spreads, the real question was whether a commodities business needed the big overheads of a large organization or whether it could operate with a small group of skillful traders.

During that difficult period, the naysayers within the firm were having a field day. Not only, they told management, have you—apparently just to keep up with the Joneses at Salomon-Phibro—bought a business we don't understand and really don't need, and lost a pile of money and tied up a lot of capital, you now want to send good money after bad to build up a trading business by making markets almost none of us know anything about with customers we know very little about—and care less about. It's the wrong business, at the wrong price, done for the wrong reason at the wrong time. And now you want to build up an even larger risk exposure and capital commitment to do a bad business with the wrong accounts!

Whitehead and Weinberg understood what had to be done: a complete redesign of every aspect of the old business model. "In foreign exchange, J. Aron's business model was modest and deliberately cautious. This was all wrong for the market as it was developing, and we realized we had to start over," recalls Winkelman, who began asking himself a series of fundamental questions, including the one that led to a breakthrough: "What if we risk our capital and work as *dealers?*" Rubin and Winkelman agreed on that strategic imperative: The firm would have to commit substantial capital to the business and switch to boldly embracing risk in a capital-intensive, risk-taking principal business on a global scale. To make serious money, the firm would have to take serious risks, trading commodities for its own account.

When acquired, J. Aron was described as "a leading gold and commodity trading firm";[8] by the time, less than a decade later, that J. Aron was contributing one-third of Goldman Sachs's profits, it was making most of its money not in gold and general commodities, but in foreign exchange and oil trading. After twenty years coffee trading was closed. It required too many people to make too little in profits.

After Coyne left at the end of 1982, Blankfein was suddenly without a specific job. "But he was quite promising and wasn't paid all that much," recalls Winkelman, "so we moved him into sales in metals to see if he might work out. He was clearly bright and energetic, even dynamic and passionate." Blankfein demonstrated good sales talents in metals, so Winkelman gave him more responsibility in 1984 by putting him in charge of the six salesmen in foreign exchange. Winkelman had been advocating a sales effort to try building an advice-based business with corporations. Later he also put Blankfein in charge of foreign-exchange trading.

Winkelman was advised against that move. "Mark," cautioned Bob Rubin, "that's probably not the right thing to do. We've never seen it work to put sales-people in charge of trading in other areas of the firm. Are you pretty sure of your analysis?"

"Really appreciate your experience, Bob, but I think he'll do all right. Lloyd's driven, and he is a very smart guy with a very inquiring mind, so I have some confidence."

What Winkelman didn't know was that Blankfein was an occasional visitor to gambling casinos, fascinated by the discipline of poker and very used to win-ning. Blankfein was determined to learn all he could and surrounded himself with traders and economists. As Winkelman had advised him, he practiced by taking small trading positions to develop his skills in timing and his feel for the markets while working to learn, learn, and learn.

"Fortunately, the global commodities business was growing rapidly in vol-ume, and strategic changes are always easier to make in a growth situation," recalls Winkelman. Not only the scale, but also the very nature of the commodi-ties business was changing as derivatives kept displacing physicals and thousands of new participants came into the markets.

"We should do oil," announced Bob Rubin one morning in the eighties, having noticed Phibro's volume in crude oil and oil futures. The same sort of change was coming to oil trading that had come to foreign exchange in the seventies, as long-term fixed-rate contracts were displaced by markets in options and futures. "Phibro is big in oil, so let's look there for good people." But after looking over a few Phibro oil traders and deciding they'd never fit into Gold-man Sachs, Rubin decided to focus recruiting on traders working at major non-financial companies and hired John Drury, head oil-products trader at Cargill's European subsidiary. While he couldn't fit in culturally and was soon eased out of Goldman Sachs, before he left, Drury set up an effective organization, hired some good people, and brought others over to oil trading from the declining met-als business.

Oil is not completely fungible, like wheat or gold, so it can't be swapped or exchanged in the same way. Oil trading is operationally intensive because each forward contract is a specific link in a long chain of transactions involving one specific tanker load. Each contract is unique and has to be cleared, step by step, through that same entire chain. "We went into oil trading in 1983–84 with all the market-making and operational difficulties you might imagine," recalls Winkelman, "but we did better that year—instead of another loss of six million dollars, we made a profit of eighteen million. I was feeling pretty proud and confident in the future of the business and felt good about the approach we were taking. But I was only a second-year partner, so in preparing for the annual planning meeting of the partners in December, I turned to Bob Rubin for help, and he laid out his vision for the business and his expectations for the coming year or two."

Currency-options trading was just getting started on the International Monetary Market. With his early understanding of the equity-options market, Rubin pressed for more and more commitment to developing new currency-options instruments and making markets in them. He understood that while "early stages" volume would be light, margins would be wide and that the best time to establish Goldman Sachs as a major market maker was early—at the creation of the markets. Currency-options trading was still too small for the big commercial banks, and they had not participated in equity options and had no related business experience, so they stayed away, while Winkelman's J. Aron made ten million dollars in this niche business in 1984 and twenty million dollars in 1985. Winkelman wasn't satisfied. While it was fine to make six million dollars trading on the 1985 Plaza Accord, an agreement by the G5 industrial nations to stop the dollar's increasing in value against the yen and the German mark, he recognized that the firm could have made—and, he thought, should have made—sixty million dollars.

The metals-trading business model was also changing substantially, but it didn't really matter because overall market volume was way down, and, as Winkelman says, "It's hard to make large profits in a dying business."

After replacing eighty percent to ninety percent of management, J. Aron is in a very different business than the one we acquired," says a continuing skeptic. "The partners of Goldman Sachs would not say the acquisition itself was a good deal."

Whitehead takes a different view: "We never would have ventured into any of those highly profitable businesses without the J. Aron acquisition, and the worldwide nature of the commodities businesses contributed importantly to the firm's going global." Others go further and say it was the best acquisition the firm ever made—partly because of the profits, partly because of the people who became firm leaders, and partly for the firmwide commitment to proprietary trading and to an entrepreneurial trading style that blossomed under Winkelman, Rubin, and Blankfein. As pension funds expanded their investment in international stocks and bonds and became major buyers and sellers of currencies, as major changes in exchange rates wrenched the money markets, as oil prices and trading volume surged, as commodities moved to record prices on record volumes, each created a bonanza for J. Aron and Goldman Sachs.

Lloyd Blankfein came to believe that as the profitability of the traditional agency business faded away, the DNA of commercial instincts essential to risk-taking principal trading that were first spawned at J. Aron became vital to Goldman Sachs as it reinvented itself as a profit-creating, risk-taking global financial intermediary.

16

TENDER DEFENSE, A MAGIC CARPET

C all me as soon as possible—no matter how late—Bob Hurst."

When Steve Friedman got back to his apartment after a long dinner in 1974, he got the message and called Hurst, who had just joined the firm.[1] "Steve, opportunity is knocking if we act very quickly. When I was at Merrill Lynch before coming over to the firm, I covered Electric Storage Battery Corporation in Philadelphia and got to know their people and their business pretty well. They're being raided—by International Nickel. And get this: Inco's being advised by Morgan Stanley!"

"Are they asking for help?"

"They called me today. They may not realize it yet, but ESB is in real trouble, and they are going to need a lot of help from somebody. So let's make that somebody *us*. I called on their CEO just two days ago and warned him pretty bluntly that if he were in the UK instead of the U.S. he would get raided because his stock is selling at such a cheap price relative to liquid assets. Steve, I think we should be at ESB's office first thing tomorrow morning so they'll know we're really committed. They may not realize it yet, but they do need us—and will soon recognize their need. Can you go with me?"

"What time does the first morning train leave Penn Station?"

Friedman and Hurst were on that train and spent most of the next week in Philadelphia working with Electric Storage Battery, trying to find the best way out—and each day buying new sets of shirts, shorts, and socks at a nearby Brooks Brothers. "We couldn't protect ESB's independence," says Friedman, "but we could and did get them a much higher price and a friendly merger with a white knight."

The combination of many components into a new kind of business may look obvious in retrospect. And as the parts are actually coming together, the combination may look like just good luck. But for people with an entrepreneurial mind-set, putting different pieces together to gain a competitive advantage can become a habitual way of thinking. For Goldman Sachs, what became known as tender defense—and proved to be a major vehicle for the firm's strategic advancement in investment banking—combined several components: Whitehead's Investment Banking Services organization had become fully operational with a large, aggressive, and increasingly experienced sales force hungry for products and services to offer its clients and hundreds of prospective clients; the phenomenon of large corporations' repetitively acquiring other companies was accelerating and would become a major force in the nation's capital markets; institutional investors were ready to respond swiftly with large blocks of stock to attractive takeover offers; arbitrageurs were increasingly large, active, and forceful market participants; Goldman Sachs, thanks to the recent work of partners Corbin Day, Steve Friedman, and Geoff Boisi, was developing a credible reputation in mergers and acquisitions; and because of its long-standing policy against advising on hostile takeovers, Goldman Sachs had been building its skills, experience, and reputation for integrity as the one Wall Street firm that was always on management's side.

"Goldman Sachs's policy on no hostiles was based on the simple proposition that, in most cases, they just don't work," explains Whitehead. "The very act of a hostile takeover will alienate the management of the acquired company: Many will be embittered and will quit. Those that stay on will have gone through an unhappy, adversarial confrontation—in public, with real damage done. It usually begins with a meeting that comes as an unwelcome surprise. The target company's shares are almost always in a slump, usually selling for less than book value. The intended acquirer opens the initial meeting with a general observation that a combination of the two companies would surely be quite favorable for everyone and then proceeds to propose several specific actions to realize the fine opportunities for synergy and to increase profits. But of course, none of these actions or ideas appeals to the target company's management, so they decline the invitation to merge and the meeting breaks up."

But not for long. As Whitehead recounts it, "The very next day, in an obviously *previously* well-planned attack that is in clear contrast to the assertions of friendly cooperation made the day before, large advertisements appear in all the newspapers delineating the gross incompetence, strategic blunders, and persistent errors of the present management and offering to rescue shareholders with a bid some 20 percent over the current market price. Various judgmental comments are made in private and in public about the obvious inadequacies of incumbent management. Then the target's management responds in similar tones or worse—and the fight is on. And it gets worse and worse as time goes on. If the target company resists, the acquisitor will step up the pressure, usually disparaging the current management and its past record, sometimes quite forcefully and publicly. Vitriol comes easily. Things are said under pressure, some quite bitter and hurtful, that are very hard to forget later on."

After all that, what are the real chances of the two managements working well together? "Not very great," Whitehead says. "So most hostile takeovers do eventually fail. The act of taking over often does real damage. So we decided against being involved in hostile takeovers—partly as a matter of business ethics, but primarily as a matter of business judgment. And over the years, we earned a reputation as a firm that could truly be trusted and couldn't be bought and was, perhaps, more focused on ethics and judgment. So companies increasingly often came to us on their own initiative, seeking our advice and assistance. And quite a few chose to retain Goldman Sachs to advise them on the ways they could prevent, or at least greatly impede, a hostile attempt at takeover. Overall, it did work out very well: Goldman Sachs prospered commercially, and our reputation grew as a good firm to do business with."

The firm got paid its full retainer each year whether or not the client got raided. For a giant corporation, while a hostile takeover was clearly unlikely, the annual fee seemed so small and the subject so new and important that signing on was an easy "why not?" matter. As Fred Weintz recalls, "This business fit in with our image as a firm and our desire to be seen always on the same side of the table as our client, and it fit with the firm's long history of seller representation—helping owners whose companies were ready for sale decide whether to have a public offering or merge into a larger company." Friedman summarizes: "And it worked well as a business."

But not at the beginning. Even the name wasn't clear. Friedman favored—and still does—the more explicit and graphic term "raid defense," and others preferred "takeover defense," but Whitehead, ever the statesman in public, decided on using the softer, more mellow euphemism: "tender defense." At first Friedman argued that the firm could work on both sides, but Whitehead said no. Some were cautious at first because the mechanics could get pretty complex pretty fast and nobody in IBS wanted to be embarrassed by not fully understanding the complexities. But IBS guys loved to sell it. The fee was low and known up front. Every prospective client welcomed the offer. Many were scared that they might be next.

The firm's no-hostiles policy fit perfectly with its increasing emphasis on "exclusive seller representation," a business Whitehead had innovated and advocated as far superior to conventional business brokerage—both in business decorum and, even better, in profit to the firm—because it was not competitive and was fee-based, and because success could earn significant incentive fees. "Seller rep" was particularly well suited to Goldman Sachs's extensive relationships, created by its increasingly effective IBS business developers, with smaller and mid-size companies, often privately owned or dominated by an owner-manager. When leadership succession or business strategy problems were serious difficulties, it was not unusual for an owner to solve his business problem by selling. Goldman Sachs conscientiously developed a premier reputation for getting a higher than expected price—which the IBS organization would be sure to recount to its many future prospects. So Goldman Sachs was unusually well positioned to take advantage of opportunity when it came as a result of change in federal antitrust policy.

For Wall Street, the business of advising on mergers and acquisitions—"M&A" in the patois of the financial markets—for a large fee had begun to bloom at a very specific time: the day in 1981 when a Stanford Law School professor, William Baxter, told Ronald Reagan's recruiters, "I'll take the job as assistant attorney general, but only if I can change the basic framing of antitrust policy." His proposition was accepted, and six months later he put out entirely new policy guidelines on how markets and market dominance should be defined—guidelines that were much more tolerant of mergers. Then, in industry after industry, one company tried making an acquisition and then, when the Antitrust Division did not complain or intervene, another company would make an acquisition—and soon it seemed that everyone got into acquiring and merging. This led to giant fees for Wall Street for advising on mergers and acquisitions—and then to Wall Street's taking the initiative and proposing acquisitions and mergers to expansionist companies in one industry after another.

Serving too few of the nation's largest corporations had for years been a major frustration for Sidney Weinberg, whose strategic objective had always been to build Goldman Sachs into a leading investment bank—which ipso facto meant serving the largest and leading corporations. But Morgan Stanley, First Boston, Dillon Read, and Lehman Brothers were almost unassailable in their positions as investment bankers to most of the major blue-chip corporations, so Goldman Sachs would have to build most of its business with medium-size and smaller companies, and these companies were a lot more likely to be takeover *targets*. But now, with tender defense, what had been a problem suddenly became an opportunity. Since Goldman Sachs's clients were much more likely to be targets needing help with their defenses, the firm was much less likely than others to face conflicts of interest when offering advice on defense, because most of its clients were too small to be the attacking raiders. Goldman Sachs could make a virtue out of its competitive weakness and decided to make a major push in tender defense. Friedman says, "We had a bloodlust to go up in front of boards of directors."

The pathway leading to Bob Hurst's "call me as soon as possible" message began a few months before with a surprise. The Ronson lighter company, a well-established Goldman Sachs client, suddenly became the target of an unwanted takeover bid by a European conglomerate. This was a new kind of experience: new to Ronson, new to America, and new to Goldman Sachs. Scrambling to find a possible white knight that might outbid the European predator, one of the companies the firm decided to call on was Electric Storage Battery. As Hurst recalls, "My first call for Goldman Sachs was on Electric Storage Battery, one of my old Merrill Lynch clients: a sleepy midsize company with several fine products, including Ray-O-Vac batteries, and a stock price selling below net current assets. My main purpose in calling on ESB was to see if they might be interested in buying Ronson, but during that visit, I warned CEO Fred Port that his own company was vulnerable to a potential takeover because the share price was so very low."

Three months later, on a Thursday, International Nickel, one of Canada's most respected companies, with a fine credit rating, made a takeover bid for ESB through Morgan Stanley. This was America's first hostile takeover bid advised by a major "blue blood" investment banking firm. And coming as it did from Morgan Stanley, then *the* prestige firm in the business, it threw out the old rule book, which had said that respectable investment bankers simply did not conduct hostile raids on other companies. If Morgan Stanley could and would do a raid, all the old assumptions against raids were over and the gloves were off. From then on, any investment banker could advise any corporate client on anything and, with perfect impunity, *everybody* could do a raid.

In the mid-seventies, by law, a cash tender offer had to be accepted or rejected by the target company's board of directors in no more than eight days. This made time-urgency a major factor for both the raider and the target company. The laws would be changed, but in 1974 time pressure was very real, particularly for the unprepared—which is why cash tenders were called Saturday night specials.

"ESB was totally unprepared—and I was totally unprepared," recalls Hurst. "I'd been on vacation on Cape Cod in a little cottage with no electricity and no phone. On Thursday, I decided to walk into town, in shorts and barefoot, to mail a letter and call the office. By the end of that day, I was in Manhattan waiting for Steve to return my call." And early the next morning, Hurst was in Philadelphia with Friedman. They were closeted with the ESB people, trying to figure out ways to block Inco. Friedman recalls: "Blocking Inco meant blocking Bob Greenhill of Morgan Stanley and Joe Flom of Skadden Arps, two of the best talents in the business. We didn't know what to do. Inventing and improvising, we made it up as we went along. But we were committed, smart, and determined.

Fortunately for us and for ESB, as unprepared as we were, nobody else really knew what to do either, so there were no rules of the road."

Inco's initial offer was twenty-seven dollars a share. United Technologies—then still called United Aircraft—was brought in by Goldman Sachs as the white knight, and a deal was finally done. Inco prevailed but paid forty-one dollars, more than 50 percent above its initial "generous" offer. As Friedman says, "We may have 'lost'—although, ironically, that acquisition later turned out to be a real turkey for Inco—but our client won a major improvement in price and we got great press coverage for all the good work we'd done, plus a nice fee. And smart people in the marketplace got the crucial message: Goldman Sachs is a good firm to have in your corner when the going gets really tough."

A few weeks later, Houston's Apache Oil Company got raided. Friedman phoned: "Can we help?" "No need for any help, thank you. We'll be okay on our own." Wait a day and call again: "Can we help?" "No need, thank you." Then wait another day and call *again*. After being told "No, thanks" twenty times, the reply became, "Okay, come on over." Back to Brooks Brothers again—and again.

Friedman, Whitehead, and partner Jim Gorter were all sensing that a pattern was starting to emerge, and just possibly a new line of business could be developed. Sangamo Electric was an early tender-defense client. Arthur Highland, Jim Gorter's near neighbor, was son-in-law to Sangamo's major owner and president of the company—an ideal combination for getting the business. As Highland got off his plane one day, a raider handed him an envelope with the takeover "offer" inside. Highland called Gorter, explained the situation, said, "We've got one hell of a problem," and asked the obvious question: "What'll we do?" "Lots!" came the immediate and confident reply. Years later, Gorter reflects, "He was quick to see Goldman Sachs in the role of his defender. And we were ready to help. It was perfect."

Friedman flew to Chicago's O'Hare Airport and drove to Gorter's home on the North Shore. The two men sat by the pool to talk out what the real business opportunity might be and how Goldman Sachs could take full advantage of it. Could the firm develop a significant, profitable business? How could it best be done? "Strategically, we soon realized that we were seeing what could be the first robin of a major transformational change," recalls Friedman. "The game and all its rules were changing, maybe forever. We could tell that there would be more hostile takeovers bids—maybe *lots* more. So we knew we should get involved in a major way."

The two men began sketching out a business proposition, asking themselves: If a company has no ties to Wall Street, and management gets the call from a raider some Friday night, whom are they going to call? If they call their banker or lawyer and ask for a recommendation, whom will they suggest? Gorter and Friedman answered their own questions: If we're seen to be on the side of the angels, we'll get *all* those calls. As Whitehead later said, "Lawyers for a threatened company would certainly be encouraged to say, 'Why not retain Goldman Sachs—just for this one special service? They can be trusted.' So we got lots of mandates—often from companies we didn't know particularly well—and tender defense fit in with the firm's overall position of 'no conflicts with management' and the reality of Goldman Sachs's clients typically being smaller companies— and therefore acquisition targets. Tender defense worked out quite well as a business for Goldman Sachs. And our reputation grew as a firm that could truly be trusted and as a good firm with which to do business."

Late one night, Friedman and Boisi were at Joe Flom's law offices at Skadden Arps talking shop when an associate came in with an early copy of the next day's *New York Times* to show Flom a full-page advertisement they had placed on behalf of a client that was about to raid Garlock Paper of Rochester. As the lawyers talked excitedly about their ad and the deal, Friedman whispered to Boisi to call the IBS man who covered Rochester for Goldman Sachs: "Tell him to call Garlock and tell them two things: They will be raided tomorrow morning, and we are ready to help."

Geoff Boisi recalls the way the firm continued taking the initiative. From then on, he says, "at ten p.m. we'd jump in a cab and drive up Broadway to Nathan's Famous—not for hot dogs, but for the next day's *New York Times*, because we'd learned that a neighboring newsstand was the first place in the city to have tomorrow's *New York Times* for sale—and would quickly look for advertisements of tender offers. Then we'd call our IBS guy, any directors we might know, and the CEO. I remember calling the CEO of Hydro Metals in Houston—a company Goldman Sachs had never before called on—to tell him we would be in his office the very next morning to help him defend against a hostile takeover. He was stunned: He hadn't heard a peep about being in danger. Our call was the first he heard that he was in a crisis. He didn't know any of us, but he sure treated us like long-lost friends when we arrived in Houston that next morning. In a raid defense situation like this, we'd take one secretary and one associate and *live* with our new client."

In 1974 interest rates were at record highs and stock prices were seriously depressed, so the middle-market companies Goldman Sachs had specialized in serving were unusually vulnerable to takeovers. With the Antitrust Division taking a much more laissez-faire approach to mergers, most public companies were unprepared for anything like a hostile raid. "They hadn't even reviewed their own bylaws," says Friedman. "They didn't know the differences in the takeover laws and regulations or the judicial decision histories between Delaware and New York. There were no poison-pill provisions. Companies—even likely takeover targets—had no plans for their own defense." To Friedman, "For acquisition-hungry predator corporations, it was like being the fox in the hen coop."

It worked well for Goldman Sachs too. When the balloon went up—a hostile takeover, launched in a dawn raid—and the battle began, directors wouldn't have the slightest idea what to do, so they would call their lawyers, and soon realize that the local lawyers had no good ideas about what to do—other than scrambling around, looking busy. Recalls Friedman, "We organized all the best ideas for action we could come up with and enlisted the two best lawyers in the field—Joe Flom and Marty Lipton—and went around the country from one board meeting to another explaining what we knew was going on. It was just like Chautauqua."

After Electric Storage Battery, hostile takeovers went from being rare to being normal and frequent. Takeovers could be proposed at any time by any investment banker, accelerated by institutional investors, and decided by arbitrageurs. Goldman Sachs was in close and regular contact with all three groups and understood their motivations and their capabilities. And Goldman Sachs's no-hostiles policy positioned the firm perfectly to be the knight in shining armor rushing to defend the frightened target company from the hostile aggressor's sneak attack.

"We couldn't recruit outstanding people or attract top guys from other areas of the firm until we launched Tender Defense in the early 1970s and it took our

M&A unit from being a small, arcane backwater to being the number one profit contributor in investment banking," recalls Friedman. "Still, we got a lot of resistance from inside the firm. The IBS guys, having had to overcome lots of 'new idea resistance' themselves just a few years before, might have reached out to help us launch Tender Defense but were instead major resisters, protesting: 'How can you expect me to go to my client and scare him to death about being taken over and losing his job?' We wanted a fee structure that had no incentives for us to sell the company, so we worked out a way to win in any of three outcomes. First, we'd win if we beat the raider off. Second, we could win by getting the raider to pay a higher price. And we would win if the target company got sold to another company—a white knight. Sometimes, of course, we soft-pedaled Tender Defense, preferring to get in on the arbitrage business instead." Goldman Sachs's arbitrageurs, led by Bob Rubin, often gave important help with market intelligence on the risks of a raid's developing and how it might develop.

An important part of Goldman Sachs's arsenal was its skill and bold strategies in negotiating the terms—particularly the price—of final deals. Friedman was particularly effective in takeover negotiations—always working to maximize the client's interests, particularly when the client was being too cautious. The management of Chicago's LaSalle Bank had decided to sell and had agreed internally on their number—the share price at which they would sell. ABN-Amro, a high-grade Dutch bank, got interested in buying a U.S. bank and entered into negotiations with LaSalle, and everything was soon agreed—except a price.

The Dutch came in with a nice price: thirty-two dollars a share, more than two dollars over LaSalle's management's "number." Management was more than pleased and about to say yes when Friedman said, "No, there's more here." "But thirty-two dollars is higher than our target number. Let's not risk losing the deal at thirty-two dollars." Gorter recalls the situation: "Steve was as cool as could be, saying, 'There's more in it for you.' And sure enough, after some intense negotiation with the Dutch, that's just what happened: Steve got them even more."

When a raid began, if the firm wasn't already involved, it would decide, based on the profit potential for Goldman Sachs, whether to concentrate on the arbitrage opportunities or to get involved as an adviser on defense—advising management on ways to monitor purchases by potentially hostile investors, knowing how to react and respond to a hostile bid, and recommending that the target company retain as special counsel on takeovers either Skadden Arps or Wachtell Lipton. This, of course, did not go unnoticed by those two major law firms, so it was no surprise when they repeatedly recommended Goldman Sachs as the investment bank to use for this specialized service. The business soon began to pour in.

Goldman Sachs's offer to give a tender-defense presentation to a board of directors was easy for the management to accept. Declining was hard. Companies that worried about being raided and taken over were a lot more numerous than the companies that were actually raided, so with IBS advocating "at least give our experts one hearing" the tender-defense business expanded rapidly. Engaging the firm was made easy by the decision to price this new service at a modest annual fee of forty thousand to eighty thousand dollars. "We decided to charge a nominal annual retainer fee," recalls Whitehead. "We considered both twenty-five thousand and fifty thousand, but doubted we could get fifty thousand, so we went with forty thousand. And that's what the law firms charged, too. With fifty corporations as clients, we soon had a nice little business." The business required zero capital and little senior-banker time. With more than two hundred clients and annual revenues well over ten million dollars, the business was highly profitable.

Most directors of most corporations had little or no knowledge of any of the complex actions and possibilities for action that come together in a major corporate takeover. That might have seemed like bad news for Goldman Sachs—it meant the firm could have a fairly hard time explaining what it could do to help. But in fact it was great news, because Goldman Sachs would have every opportunity to be—and be perceived to be—real and compelling experts. Since hostile takeover raids were truly a life-and-death threat to executives' and directors' jobs, Goldman Sachs always got their absolute attention as it explained that any company with assets that were not carrying their own weight by generating adequate earnings was at real and very visible risk because a raider could sell off those very assets to raise money and pay a significant part of his purchase price with the target company's own assets. Several aggressive, change-minded CEOs had a special reason for inviting the firm to make presentations. They realized they could use the threat of a takeover to force through structural changes.

"Whenever senior management introduced us to a company's board of directors, either Marty Lipton or Joe Flom would present along with us," recalls

Friedman. "It was great. This was a subject on which we were suddenly experts, and it was a matter of actual life or death for the company. So we were in an ideal situation: Seen as experts on a crucial matter, we were clearly on the company's side, and we were talking to all the right people in each company. This automatically put us in the ideal pole position to compete for any future investment banking business and to develop a strong long-term relationship with that company. For investment bankers, it just doesn't get any better."

Goldman Sachs not only got paid its annual retainer fee for advising on tender defense, it won numerous mandates from its new clients to execute specific transactions because the best defense was often preemptive: Take the actions a raider might take *after* gaining control—such as selling off unrelated or unnecessary businesses—but do it *before* the raider made his first bid. If the value of a division was not reflected in the company's total market value, and a raider would probably sell it to raise money to help pay for the takeover, why wait? Sell that division *now*. The operations being divested were usually the result of a prior management's ad hoc or nonstrategic acquisitions, so selling was often painless. Of course, for every seller, there had to be a buyer, so many of these "clear the decks" divestitures earned the firm not one, but two fees—and often opened the door to another new corporate client relationship. M&A quickly went from being only incidental to a major investment banking relationship to being crucial. Geoff Boisi recalls, "Our total investment banking fees went up nearly a thousand times—from three million dollars to nearly two *billion*."

Over the next few years, Goldman Sachs enjoyed a decisive competitive advantage in developing new business relationships. With its refusal to take hostile takeover assignments—while its major competitors had all joined in that highly profitable business—Goldman Sachs repositioned itself as the trustworthy friend of corporations and management and established investment banking relationships with more and more of America's largest and most prestigious corporations. While competitors divided the lush fees for advising on individual hostile takeovers, Goldman Sachs was dominant in tender defense, developing relationships that would produce large fees for many years to come and would lift the firm to market leadership in investment banking. And that was not the end of it.

Inside Goldman Sachs, another major change was brought about by the tender-defense business. To organize and develop a proper defense for a corporate client, Goldman Sachs's tender-defense advisers drew on the expertise of sometimes as many as seven or eight different and previously quite separate and separately managed divisions of the firm: Arbitrage, Equity Research, Institutional Sales, Commercial Paper, Block Trading, Bonds, Options, Private Client Services. This kind of intense, multiunit cooperation in doing business was fairly new to the firm. In the past, each division had run its own business in its own way, reporting only final results to the management committee. How you ran your business was strictly your own business. Now, for the first time, teamwork within the silos would become teamwork across the silos, because tender defense called for and rewarded coordinated efforts across the several divisions. "Up until this time," says Friedman, "firmwide teamwork was honored more in the concept than in reality. As we struggled to gain recognition and competitive position, we built a tremendous internal team spirit, centered in M&A and fanning out to all areas of the firm. We called for help, insisted on getting it, and rewarded every part of the firm for helping us dominate the market. The time-urgency of tender defense forced us to work well together and rewarded working well together by our winning more often and getting paid more—and it was exciting, fun work. We realized we could be—and so we were absolutely determined to be—more expert, more experienced, and more effective than anyone else. When others were good, we drove ourselves to be better—and faster, more creative, and more hard-hitting. Just as Gus Levy wanted *every* block trade, our team wanted to be in on and win in *every* takeover."

Tender defense came at the perfect time for Goldman Sachs. The firm was ready to expand and upgrade its business from commercial paper and seller representation for middle-market companies. IBS was well organized and working effectively but was hungry for more product. Arbitrage and block trading were humming. Research was improving. If the firm hadn't made a bold and clever strategic move, it would have seen its mostly small and medium-size clients disappearing—one at a time, but steadily disappearing—but if it did make a bold and clever move, it could expand quite rapidly and profitably. When Goldman Sachs put together a "holistic" program of defensive tactics and strategies and went out on the road, tender defense became the firm's strategic magic carpet in investment banking—and eventually lifted Goldman Sachs above Morgan Stanley, First Boston, and Lehman Brothers. Part of the surge in competitive strength came from the effectiveness of Whitehead's IBS organization. Part came as a result of vigorous recruiting. Part came from the emphasis on teamwork. Part came from Goldman Sachs's new commitment to entrepreneurial innovation, and part came because so many companies had reason to be afraid of being taken over by a hostile raider.

Being in the flow and active in one deal after another proved crucial to the firm's rapid expansion in tender defense because it gave Goldman Sachs the chance to be in on all the details of recent transactions, and that gave the firm great credibility. Having done the latest merger in an industry and being able to tell the specific details of each losing bidder's tactics and how it all played out gave the firm a big advantage when competing for the next deal in the same industry. And if there were a third deal in the same industry, the momentum could be unstoppable. "In pitching for business," recalls Friedman, "we also learned to be careful not to be dumb—like asking a forest-products company what a cruise [an inspection to estimate a tract's lumber potential] was or not understanding the lingo of the oil industry and innocently asking a *really* dumb question—which I did during an eight-course dinner at Antoine's in New Orleans. And when we came out, I was hit on the head by a huge bird-dropping from an overhead pigeon. It was so symbolic."

17

~∽~

THE USES AND ABUSES
OF RESEARCH

The research operation whose strategy Gus Levy later redirected began informally in the fifties. It was a sideline for one man who occasionally helped salesmen and a few customers with the important financial information he packed into the pages in his midsize, three-ring black notebook—information on the companies where Sidney Weinberg was a director. Nat Bowen never gave anyone his little black book to read, but he would use it to check the facts before offering "guidance" on current developments at the three dozen companies he tracked very carefully. Having all the facts on those companies was essential to Bowen; his job as assistant to Sidney Weinberg was to keep all the important data on Weinberg's companies in one place for quick reference so he could brief "Mr. Director" on financial and operating details just before each of his many board meetings. Bowen's briefings helped Weinberg greatly as he built his reputation for being the best-informed director at the many companies he served.

For salesmen Bowen considered sufficiently serious, he was willing to answer questions and to meet occasionally with their more thoughtful clients. Of course, in today's more regulated market Bowen would have been doling out prohibited "insider information," but in the fifties the boundary lines were not only much less clearly defined, they were further apart on the behavior allowed. "Nat Bowen was a great help," remembers partner Bob Menschel. "We'd arrange quiet lunches with Nat and key accounts. While he wouldn't give away his little black book, he would consult the data he had packed inside and give broad indications of how a company was doing. Nat had all the facts, and the accounts knew it. So even though he said little, he knew his stuff and clients appreciated his perspective."[1]

Later in the fifties, the link between statisticians and sales began to be regularized, with George Boyer, a statistician, talking to the salesmen about companies and stocks in the late afternoon when there was no real business to be done because the stock market had closed for the day. Goldman Sachs still had very little franchise in underwriting or in research, so salesmen were always looking for an entry point with each institutional account. Superior research gave Goldman Sachs analysts and salesmen preferential access to the institutional analysts and portfolio managers who were making the decisions, and knowing in advance what stocks might be bought or sold helped Goldman Sachs increase its share of trading volume. Trading was where the profits were.

Research as a specific function at Goldman Sachs—and in Wall Street—developed slowly until the sixties. Security analysts—still called statisticians, many still wearing green eyeshades, and all relying on slide rules—were hired to provide useful data for investment banking and arbitrage. In the early sixties, as a series of research-boutique firms were formed to go after the rapidly expanding institutional stockbrokerage business, Bob Danforth agreed to organize a research department to provide research for institutional investors—but primarily to uncover attractive investment ideas for Goldman Sachs partners' personal accounts.* "The firm had only six or eight people in research," recalls Menschel. "Danforth covered paper, Nick Petrillo covered rails, and Lou Weston covered financials. We put out one four-page report each month: one page on rails, one on industrials, one on utilities, and one on financials." Since Danforth was far more interested in finding attractive personal investments for himself and the firm's

---

* Danforth was a canny stock picker who turned down a partnership invitation because he wanted to be free to invest his own account and use margin for leverage, which partners weren't allowed to do. After the boom years of the seventies and eighties, when Goldman Sachs was earning its reputation as Wall Street's most profitable firm, he acknowledged that the firm had done almost as well as he'd done on his own.

partners than in building and managing a business serving institutional investors, he concentrated on small, emerging growth stocks.

Promising as the potential price appreciation for these stocks might be, the big business of Goldman Sachs was not in *investing* in stocks. The firm's big and fast-growing business was in Gus Levy's business of *trading* stocks for clients and collecting commissions. Goldman Sachs could make much more money using its capital to finance a large, high-margin stockbrokerage business than it could ever hope to make through investing that capital in public stocks as a mere passive investor. (Similarly, the people who typically make the most money in the goldfields are not the miners, but the purveyors of blankets, food and drink, or mining tools.)

In 1967 a mathematician and computer whiz named Leslie Peck was hired to develop a mathematical model to predict corporate earnings. Peck had been head of operations research at Arthur D. Little, with tours at Los Alamos and the Institute for Advanced Study at Princeton, and had proved that most of the "technical" analysis then popular on Wall Street was useless hogwash. But building the model proved far too complicated, and the effort was given up. However, Peck did develop a simple computer model to predict changes in the prices of utility stocks based on a few standard measures of financial strength, such as the trend of earnings growth and a stock's customary dividend yield compared to all other utility stocks'. The reason his model worked was not rocket science but social science. In those days, new information in this slow-moving sector could take two or three years to be fully reflected in the stock prices, but the direction of change and an approximation of the magnitude of change were fairly easy to estimate because investors' evaluations were, eventually, consistent over time and across five dozen highly comparable regulated utilities.

The most effective research may have been done by Rudy Stanish, a Goldman Sachs dining room employee who, as a masterful crepes chef, was a welcome presence at all sorts of firm receptions and parties, preparing customized crepes for the mighty of finance and silently absorbing the names of specific stocks that smart, hardworking analysts and portfolio managers from all the leading institutions were most excited about. While waiting in line for Stanish to finish preparing their favorite crepes and omelets, investment experts from leading institutions, in an understandable effort to impress their friends, would describe to one another their favorite stocks. If you had served an average of a hundred crepes and omelets a day for thirty years, while listening to the nation's best investors; bought and sold stocks with the smart consensus; and acted on a few tips partners might pass along to a loyal retainer who was always respectfully appreciative and discreet, you too might have accumulated a personal portfolio worth over ten million dollars—while preparing crepes and omelets actually as a sideline.

Responding to insistent demands from his largest block-trading accounts in the early seventies, Gus Levy called for a firmwide refocusing from midsize companies and "small-cap" stocks to extensive research coverage of the nation's larger companies, the companies that dominated institutional investors' portfolios and their trading—the area where Goldman Sachs was the disproportionate leader. As usual, Levy was impatient to see results.

The partners of Goldman Sachs were divided as to the best strategy for building up a research department to cover large companies. Some wanted to acquire a research-boutique firm, while others wanted to hire away the research department of another major firm. Both groups worried that hiring a full team of analysts one at a time would be too slow. Others argued that with intensive, one-at-a-time recruiting of people who would fit well with Goldman Sachs's culture and organization, the firm could create an all-star research department and avoid the we-they conflicts that so often afflict firms after a major merger. They pointed out that securities firms are remarkably "tribal" and most mergers go through a costly tribal "fight to the death" until one culture or tribe eventually dominates—usually at great cost to the organization. Goldman Sachs decided to recruit individual analysts who could fit into the firm's culture and concentrated on hiring young analysts with rapidly developing "franchise reputations" for expertise in specific industries. Once the core group was established, the firm would revert to the "grow our own" policy that characterized Goldman Sachs.

In retrospect, even though the securities business was under heavy pressure in the early seventies, the strategic buildup in research came at an ideal time. Covering large-cap stocks in research protected Levy's block-trading profit cornucopia, and research was key to IBS's refocus on major companies. Moreover, the firm's steadily increasing profitability during the seventies—particularly in investment banking—made a major research organization affordable. "It was planned," insists Whitehead. "In a time of unsettled conditions on Wall Street, while others were economizing, we saw an opportunity to upgrade the quality of our research department. Our research was soon costing us about six million dollars a year, but we kept telling ourselves that our customers would find a way to pay us for it."

Deciding to hire franchise analysts and build the firm's own research department was one thing; actually doing it was another. Analysts are professional doubters and are particularly cautious about their own careers. The firm soon found that prospective recruits were asking skeptical questions about Goldman Sachs's true commitment to an institutional business—blunt questions like "Why should I trust you?" They pointed to other firms that had made large promises while hiring during favorable markets and had then fired all their newly hired analysts when the stock market and trading volume turned down and profits got squeezed. This concern was particularly strong when analysts were considering joining a firm that was, like Goldman Sachs, dominated by investment banking or trading, rather than agency brokerage. Analysts would have had their fears confirmed if they had heard George Doty say sardonically, "Research is like a parking lot for a movie theater. You have to have one, but it's not the business you're in."

Having decided that Goldman Sachs should have the best research on Wall Street, the firm's leaders gave partner Lee Cooperman the classic mandate: Do it! Cooperman, joined later by partner Bill Kealy, drove to get strong, independent thinkers and produce strong, independent research.

Partner Mike Armellino recalls, "With rising earnings, Goldman Sachs could and did stay with all its commitments to research, and fulfilled all its promises with regular actions." Each analyst was challenged to develop an innovative strategy that would make him or her distinctive—a "must" source of ideas and information. "The firm has always provided all the resources you need as an analyst," Armellino says. "Once each year, each analyst would meet with management and work out a compact. You'd explain what support resources you needed and why—and what your plan was for contributing to the success of the firm." Goldman Sachs encouraged each of the firm's research analysts to develop his or her own franchise and accepted that the resulting differences in style and content would lack the firm's traditional consistency and cohesiveness. "We told our analysts: Figure out your particular comparative advantage versus the competition, seize on it, and make your unique service truly *addictive* for clients," says Armellino. "Only *you* can identify what will distinguish you and your work. Find it, excel at it—and grow!"

Each analyst was expected and challenged to be an entrepreneur. For example, Joe Ellis made himself the leading retailing analyst on Wall Street. "We began the idea of conducting field trips for institutional analysts to visit retailers back in 1984," recalls Ellis. "Now other firms do similar things. So we've gone on to other things—like our annual conference on international retailing, where I give a slide show of pictures I've taken to show the best merchandising being done around the world."

As partner Steven Einhorn recalls, "Comparative advantage differed from analyst to analyst, but the firm also wanted enough consistency to create an overall brand for its research. Part of this was visual. So that Goldman Sachs research would stand out, research reports always had three sections: the investment conclusion, the reasons, and any risks. With this format, there were no structural surprises and the serious reader knew what to expect. The firm also used a consistent approach to valuation and identified the drivers in each sector. Professional editors were brought in to increase the clarity and consistency of the analysts' writing in research reports. "It was essential to find the balance between *individualization* to maximize the different strengths of different individuals and *teamwork* so we would collectively develop a 'bigger than any one of us' franchise. One thing was a certainty: We didn't want to homogenize creativity and entrepreneurial drive into 'blah.' "

The stylistic and analytical differences between analysts' coverage of their different industries were offset by a strong commitment to "framing" capabilities in macroeconomics and portfolio strategy. Both Lee Cooperman and Gary Wenglowski became partners because their work in portfolio strategy and economics was so strong and so well accepted by institutional investors all over the country. This acceptance did not come easily. Both men were highly visible on the institutional investor circuit—New York, Hartford, Boston, Philadelphia, Chicago, Minneapolis, Denver, San Francisco, Los Angeles, Houston, Dallas, Atlanta. They were on the road almost half their days and nights, with the local salesmen in each city running them through meeting after meeting, from an early breakfast right through dinner, and then a late flight on to the next city—and another series of meetings.

The research sales organization developed by Richard Menschel capitalized effectively on the rapidly developing research product and established Goldman Sachs as the most important provider of research services to the most institutional investors, developing a strong stream of revenues and earnings and the relationship network for success in underwriting. Another strength behind the firm's rapid buildup in research was economic: The department didn't have to rely entirely on institutional stockbrokerage to absorb costs. Investment banking helped in a major way. "We were the first firm to have banking pay for research," recalls Cooperman. "They paid fifty percent of the total cost because the relationship managers in banking were all generalists and they knew they needed to have research to have a competitive edge when making their calls on companies."

An obvious question was how the firm should handle conflicts when an analyst was negative about a major investment banking client. Would professional integrity or "he who pays the piper calls the tune" prevail? The answer to that question was clear from the beginning: "Goldman Sachs has always been first-class on integrity in research," says Joe Ellis.[2] "If you've done your homework and formed a judgment, you'll be supported in your decision. For example, Sears has always been a very important client of the firm. Back in 1974, after writing a positive report in 1972, I recognized that things were becoming terribly wrong in the way Sears was being managed and the way it was headed—and I became quite negative on the stock as an investment. While we didn't publish a formal negative report, everyone knew I was negative and they knew why. Even so, our firm's management was very supportive."

An analyst's career begins with mastering an industry, its major companies, and financial analysis. Then, if he or she has managed to develop a strong franchise with institutional investors, the analyst becomes a top-ranked "name" institutional analyst with a support team helping with client service and covering more companies in the industry. That industry expertise is then linked to investment banking. Working on deals with senior corporate management gives the industry analyst an opportunity to demonstrate knowledge of the industry and the major competitors and gives the analyst in-depth exposure to the operational realities of the firm's business, which helps professional growth. Says Ellis, "My advice to young analysts is always: Dedicate yourself to being number one in your research specialty and, if you're not number one, examine why you're not yet and what you must do to get there."

The analyst's job is hard and requires many different skills. As Ellis says, "You have to be very good on financial analysis *and* on interviewing *and* on business judgment and market judgment *and* able to work effectively with institutional investors and the sales force *and* with corporate executives *and* investment bankers. It's complicated. And it's very hard to serve all of them really well." Ellis worries that the firm missed an opportunity to be even more effective by developing one branding for Goldman Sachs rather than each analyst's developing his or her own brand.

Analysts initiate, develop, and maintain relationships with institutional analysts and portfolio managers through visits, phone calls, e-mails, and formal research reports, all of which are supported by salespeople who also call and visit, telling the latest news from the analyst. Merchandising an analyst's expertise as well as specific recommendations is nearly as important as research rigor in establishing an analyst's franchise with institutional investors.

By the eighties, the research organization had over seven hundred people—of whom half were line analysts—collectively covering sixty industries in every major country and doing macro research in every major nation on economics, currencies, and commodities. The total research staff would peak at nine hundred at the millennium. "Of our worldwide research department, fifty percent were in the U.S. and they probably produced eighty percent of the total global firepower," says Einhorn, who was research director.[3] "The number of analysts needed to cover all the major companies in all the world's stock markets became a managerial problem because it was so hard to integrate so many people into a coordinated whole that would make all their capabilities fully and consistently available to all clients."

The firm's successful drive to develop homegrown research talents made Goldman Sachs an obvious target for others seeking to recruit experienced analysts. In the nineties, a major problem developed at the top end of the spectrum: The most effective analyst-entrepreneurs started moving to hedge funds. Hedge funds could pay remarkably high compensation and free the individual from the structures of a large organization and, more important, the need to spend lots of time selling and servicing customers.

· · ·

I n the mid-nineties, Goldman Sachs's research budget was over $175 million, with analysts producing over 3,500 reports each year covering nearly two thousand companies in sixty-eight industries plus all the world's major economies, currencies, and commodities. Managing research on such a scale so integrity is always ensured is challenging. In 1999 an analyst named J. D. Miller was fired for plagiarism less than a month after he joined Goldman Sachs. In an eighteen-page report, he copied passages verbatim and misspelled names exactly as had a report from the Putnam Lovell investment bank, which protested after being tipped off by an institutional investor. Miller was summoned to a meeting in the personnel department for immediate dismissal and told, "Take your jacket with you."[4]

"Steve Einhorn was a superb professional to work with in the boom years when investment banking wanted to use economics as a tool," says partner Gavyn Davies. "He agreed that we would only publish what we knew to be true. Since Steve left, this rule has been less clear. Now it's a bare-knuckle fight."

In 2003 Goldman Sachs would be fined $110 million for violating rules of the National Association of Securities Dealers, the industry's self-regulatory organization, and of the New York Stock Exchange in an action brought before Judge William H. Pauley in U.S. District Court. The essential issue was that research analysts, at Goldman Sachs and elsewhere, while presenting their work as objective and unbiased, were in fact distorting their recommendations to help the firm win investment banking business during the dot-com bubble of 1999–2001.

The court found that the firm knew about the conflicts but failed to establish policies and procedures to detect and prevent the conflicts. In their individual plans, analysts had been expected to tell how they planned to support investment banking. Analysts were asked to identify companies where their relationship with senior management was stronger or better than the firm's investment banking relationship and how that could be used to enhance the firm's business opportunities.

In retrospect, the step-by-step process by which Goldman Sachs and others moved almost inexorably into misbehavior seems almost predestined. By the mid-seventies, investment bankers knew that superior research coverage of a client company was good for business. Corporations wanted to be covered and to be recommended by leading analysts, because that improved the market for their shares with institutional investors. Without research coverage by their firm, investment bankers would be seriously handicapped in developing a strong and profitable relationship. Since bankers wanted first-rate coverage of more companies, it made sense for investment banking to help pay the cost of research. Goldman Sachs was one of the first to do this: Banking agreed to pay half. Corporate executives enjoyed in-depth discussions with the leading analysts covering their industry, getting an objective, informed, outside view of their company as well as candid appraisals of key competitors. And analysts enjoyed the chance to test their thinking with industry leaders. Everybody saw benefits. By the early eighties, the best analysts knew that working with investment bankers and their clients on corporate financings and acquisitions helped make them accepted as experts by their colleagues in banking and by the institutional investors they worked with.

Naturally, if banking was paying half the cost of research, investment bankers wanted a say in how that money was spent: which industries and companies would be covered; which analysts were hired; and how analysts were rewarded. By the late eighties, leading analysts were earning substantial annual bonuses—sometimes in the millions—for decisive contributions to their firm's banking business. In the nineties, investment bankers were increasingly insisting that if they were paying more than half of analysts' total compensation, they had a right to expect favorable coverage of their clients—and certainly not negative coverage.

In the worst cases, highly favorable research reports were sent out to clients recommending stocks that informal internal e-mails proved were simultaneously being knocked as junk. The conflicts of interests were blatant when uncovered by New York State attorney general Eliot Spitzer and the SEC, with help from whistle-blowers and access to e-mails. There were alarming violations of NASD and NYSE rules against "acts or practices contrary to fair dealing."

During the first half of 2000, Goldman Sachs research analysts were involved in thirty-one mergers involving fifty-six billion dollars and financings for 209 companies totaling eighty-three billion dollars, and analysts helped solicit 328 separate transactions. Analysts' coverage was a regular item in "pitch books" seeking to win banking business. The combination of opportunity and motivation created an organizational risk that individual analysts would go too far, and soon analysts certainly did:

According to court findings, an analyst defined the three most important goals for 2000 as: "1. Get more investment banking revenue. 2. Get more investment banking revenue. 3. Get more investment banking revenue." An analyst decided not to lower a company's earnings estimates solely because it was too close in time to an IPO. Analysts published "recommendations and/or ratings that were exaggerated or unwarranted, and/or contained opinions for which there was no reasonable basis."

In April 2001 an analyst wrote to a supervising analyst, "In light of the fact that [the company] is worth 0, do you think we should adjust our rating on price target?" and got this reply: "Changing the rating now is probably not a good idea. . . ." In May 2001, WorldCom had the firm's highest rating when the senior U.S. analyst told his European counterpart, "Would have loved to have cut ratings long ago. Unfortunately, we can't cut [AT&T], because we're essentially restricted there. And without cutting [AT&T], there is no consistency in cutting WCOM [WorldCom]." WorldCom stayed on the firm's recommended list until July, but in April, when a hedge fund asked the research leader for telecom whether to buy, sell, or hold at twenty dollars per share, the reply was "sell."

Just *before* an important downgrade of Exodus Technology Corporation from "recommended" to "market outperformer," the analyst met with an institutional client and subsequently received grateful e-mails. One said, in part, "Fortunately, we were able to get out . . . and avoid the recent earnings in the shares." In a survey of the sales force about this analyst, one respondent commented: "His investment recommendations have been abysmal and while I understand he communicates what he really thinks to a sele[c]t few, his public ratings have been an embarrassment to the firm."

Goldman Sachs and the nine other defendants were required by the consent decree to separate research and banking into different organizational units with separate reporting lines; to prevent any input from banking about analysts' compensation; to prevent analysts from participating in new-business solicitations; to erect "firewalls" to prevent communication between research and banking about potential business; and to prohibit analysts' participating in road shows prior to an underwriting. The decree required a set of standardized disclosures of a firm's economic interests in each company being evaluated, and required each defendant firm to pay for and provide to its investor clients third-party research from at least three independent firms, to provide tracking measures of past research by each of the firm's published analysts, and to pay for an independent monitor to ensure compliance.[5]

Judge Pauley found, "In several instances Goldman Sachs issued certain research reports for companies that were not based on principles of fair dealing and good faith and did not provide a sound basis for evaluating facts, contained exaggerated or unwarranted claims about these companies, and/or contained opinions for which there was no reasonable basis."

Goldman Sachs and other firms were ordered to pay large civil penalties. It was clear that the penalties would be large. The question was how large, and the most important part of "large" was relative—relative to the other major firms that were major competitors. The most important competitor was Morgan Stanley, particularly in reputation, but also in research and in investment banking.

Chairman Hank Paulson called in Bob Steel, vice chairman and head of the equities division. "Bob, your job is to get a settlement that makes Goldman Sachs look okay—okay compared to Morgan Stanley. It may well be that our analysts did worse things than theirs did, so your job is clear: Make sure our firm [fares] no worse than their firm."

Steel "won." He got a fine of $110 million for Goldman Sachs, while Morgan Stanley paid $125 million.

Goldman Sachs had put itself in position to get relatively favorable treatment by taking remedial action in early 2002. It appointed new coheads of research, separating research from investment banking and from sales and trading operations to demonstrate that "research is a stand-alone independent operation." To clarify the independence, research analysts were prohibited from owning stocks in companies in the sectors they covered.[6]

While prohibiting the most egregious misbehavior by the small minority of analysts who were the worst offenders, the settlement cast a pall over investment research and created a field day in the realm of unintended consequences. Analysts' compensation—which had risen to highly attractive levels—fell off. Firms cut back their research organizations to save on costs. Bureaucratic requirements like having a chaperone sit in on conversations between bankers and analysts slowed down internal communication, only a small part of which, after all, had migrated into being "inappropriate."

Conforming to the series of organizational requirements imposed on the defendant firms, Goldman Sachs has codified the separation between research and banking. Analysts are encouraged to call it as they see it on earnings estimates and research recommendations. Every research report carries a declaration by the analyst that it is his or her work and believed objective and valid, and each report includes a statistical distribution of the firm's buy, hold, or sell recommendations. The firm requires all incoming analysts to take and pass the all-day professional examinations given over three years by the CFA Institute and provides time and resources for preparation.

Nevertheless, the consequences of the settlement were and continue to be disturbing. The firm still talks about the importance of research. "Research has always been important at Goldman Sachs," says partner Abby Joseph Cohen. "Clients are increasingly looking for new ways to look at investments, how to use options and other derivatives, environmental sensitivity, and other creative ways to develop insight. Our emphasis is increasingly on long-term thematic research." Yet at Goldman Sachs and other major firms, research has been damaged. The career trajectory of an industry analyst had once been viewed as a high-speed escalator to financial independence and professional stature. Bright, articulate, and numerate analysts willing to work hard analyzing companies and servicing institutional investors could earn upward of five hundred thousand dollars a year—sometimes even one million dollars—within five years, a much faster acceleration than in almost any other line of professional work. For the self-reliant and highly motivated, this opportunity rang all the right bells. But after the settlement, analysts' compensation fell by half or more. Many left the major firms and went to hedge funds, where creativity was treasured, there was no bureaucracy, and pay was high.

Institutional stockbrokerage as a business continued to suffer a grinding squeeze on profit margins, because mutual funds and pension funds, two major groups of customers, pressured stockbrokers for lower and lower fees. Low-cost brokers and electronic exchanges both gained increasing shares of the total business. For full-service stockbrokers like Goldman Sachs, profitability was drained away. Institutional stockbrokerage was no longer the rich business it had been since Gus Levy's triumphs. Cost discipline and cost reduction became important, changing the role of research and the career opportunities for research analysts. When combined with the changes imposed by the settlement, the change in the environment was profound. Research reverted from being a leading-edge part of the firm and its business to being only a necessary service accommodation. Capable, diligent professional analysts were needed, but their roles, like aging movie stars', shifted from romantic leads to supporting characters.

18

JOHN WEINBERG

With his abrupt, disarming candor, people of all sorts quickly learned to trust and like John L. Weinberg, the son of Sidney Weinberg and half of the Two Johns. Consistently unpretentious and surprisingly approachable for a Wall Streeter with nearly fifty years as a leading frontline investment banker and fourteen years as cochairman or chairman of Goldman Sachs, Weinberg would chuckle, "I'm here to help people. If they want somebody with gray hairs and scars, I'm their guy."

Weinberg's affable manner partly explains how he was able to contribute so substantially to the successful resolution of the tense, potentially confrontational situation in which Seagram and DuPont found themselves in 1995. Seagram was the unwanted largest—and potentially dominant—shareholder in DuPont, and had been since DuPont's "white knight" acquisition of Conoco for $7.8 billion in 1981. The confrontation was resolved when DuPont repurchased 156 million shares—over 24 percent—of its own common stock for an astounding $8.8 billion, by far the largest such transaction ever effected.

The scale of the deal was exceptional, but its successful execution was typical of the man: Both sides trusted John Weinberg. Those closest to the deal appreciated the sophistication of the technique used in the execution. Using derivatives, the transaction kept Seagram's *percentage* shareholding constant because while it sold 156 million DuPont shares, part of what it got in payment was an equal number of warrants to buy shares. While those warrants were deliberately priced high enough that they would never be exercised, their existence meant that the transaction between DuPont and Seagram qualified under IRS guidelines as an intercorporate dividend, taxable at just 7 percent, rather than as a capital gain at a tax rate of 35 percent.[1] The press release from Seagram specifically acknowledged "the contribution of Goldman Sachs and the unique role of John L. Weinberg."

Weinberg was the central playmaker. But in typical fashion, he credited others—particularly, in this case, the attorneys at Simpson Thacher & Bartlett—for doing an outstanding job in structuring the complex transaction and providing what he cheerfully recognized as "a lot of room for negotiating agreement." This may be one of the few billion-dollar understatements in financial history. In the terms on which they finally agreed, DuPont and Seagram effectively split a tax saving of nearly $1.5 billion.*

To appreciate Weinberg's performance in DuPont's massive repurchase, it helps to understand the background of the complex situation so decisively resolved. A bidding war for Conoco began in 1981 when Dome Petroleum bid for no fewer than fourteen million and no more than twenty-two million shares of Conoco at sixty-five dollars a share—30 percent above the market. Dome was intending to swap the acquired shares later for Conoco's 52.9 percent interest in Hudson Bay Oil & Gas, like Dome a Canadian company, saving Conoco the capital-gains tax it would have incurred in a cash sale. However, Dome's offer was fatally flawed because Dome's shares were owned by a subsidiary, not by Dome itself.

Meanwhile, Seagram had $2.3 billion in cash it had received from selling a large oil holding to Sun Company and wanted to invest this money. Learning in 1981 that 52 percent of Conoco's shares had been tendered—well over the 22 percent Dome had sought, and leaving 30 percent of the Conoco shares "unspoken for"—Edgar Bronfman Sr. called in Weinberg, a longtime friend, adviser to the

* The directors of DuPont did not expect their chairman, Edgar Bronfman Jr., to get IRS approval for his tax deal, even though he was a major political campaign contributor. His father and uncle both preferred to hold on to DuPont—whose stock price nearly doubled in the next few years under the rationalizing leadership of Edward Jefferson Jr.—but Bronfman wanted to try harder to do better by buying MCA.

Bronfmans, and a director of Seagram. A tentative accord was soon set: Seagram would buy 35 percent of Conoco and agree to a standstill agreement at that percentage. Soon thereafter, the situation was made much more complex by DuPont's white-knight purchase of Conoco for $7.8 billion. This left Seagram with over 24 percent of DuPont's shares, enough to be DuPont's controlling shareholder.

For more than a decade, DuPont management, understandably uncomfortable with Seagram's powerful position and the potential for future confrontation, wanted to buy out Seagram. Again, Weinberg would be the principal negotiator, this time working with DuPont's senior management. "Edgar and I courted our wives together," offered Weinberg as a typically matter-of-fact explanation of how he'd gotten to know the Bronfman family, the key to his ability forty-five years later to orchestrate the largest share repurchase in history.

Like every successful deal maker, Weinberg always looked for the "bond in common" and often found it on a personal level. DuPont's very British CEO, Edward Jefferson, seemed stiff and aloof—far removed from John Weinberg's gregarious, earthy informality. But Weinberg knew that Jefferson had also served in combat, and out of that common experience he quickly developed a friendly relationship and a channel of communication that facilitated a major transaction between distant and different organizations. As Weinberg later explained, "Back in 1981, when the Bronfmans bought their position, we had worked out a standstill agreement, including how many seats the Seagram group had on the DuPont board and on each of the key committees. So we got to know everybody pretty well over the years."

Typically, Weinberg left out any explanation of how he earned the respect and trust of both parties in a situation that just a few years before had offered little hope of an amicable resolution. "I just do my job," he said. Making no mention of the twenty-five-million-dollar fee he earned, Weinberg added that, while the high price DuPont had paid for Conoco back in 1981 may have looked like the top dollar paid at the top of the oil market, "when run *by* DuPont and *for* DuPont, it has been a big contributor." Nor did Weinberg mention that Goldman Sachs's policy of not representing a buyer in a hostile bid for a company had obliged him to resign from advising Seagram—and to pass up an eleven-million-dollar fee for managing Seagram's original hostile bid for Conoco. Weinberg was demonstrating the true test of a policy: You follow that policy through even when it's costing you real money. Goldman Sachs was the only major investment banking house in New York City that did not take in millions of dollars in payments during the Conoco fight as deal manager, arbitrageur, or adviser.[2] By the time the dust settled, Texaco, Mobil, and Cities Service, as well as Seagram and DuPont, had each been involved in what was then the largest takeover in history.

Over his many years, Weinberg, who was born in 1925, performed key roles in many other major transactions, including GE's acquisition of RCA, where Weinberg advised GE's Jack Welch on negotiations with RCA's top brass, and U.S. Steel's purchase of Marathon Oil, then the second largest acquisition in American history. One part of Weinberg's effectiveness was his ability to stay out of the newspapers and to work effectively within the Goldman Sachs organization. "The best work I do is anonymous," he observed. The *New York Times* noted that he had "achieved a privacy that would make any head of the Central Intelligence Agency jealous."[3]

Weinberg never took himself too seriously. "The boss needs to lose arguments—not all arguments, but enough to keep everybody honest and responsible for clear thinking. You can't micromanage this business from headquarters." About innovative ideas, of which there were a great many, he tended to be conservative. But if the young bucks were pressing hard, he liked to give way, saying, "I'm just an old guy, so I don't know all the ins and outs of this new stuff, so if you're sure it's right, let's go!" He could then observe with a knowing smile, "I can't lose now. If I *was* right, they'll soon be saying, 'Jesus, maybe the old guy knows the score,' and if *they* are right, they'll feel really good about themselves—and will work even harder."

Genially self-mocking in manner, Weinberg knew his business and knew how to get paid fully for his and his firm's services. "In 1986, after the RCA deal, he felt strongly that he and his firm had earned a fee of six million dollars," recalls Jack Welch. "Being always cheap, I thought that was too high. So John drove up to my home in Connecticut over the weekend and we argued for a while and then we had a heart-to-heart and then I agreed to pay the full six million dollars."

Welch adds: "At the final stages, we were absolutely divided. Felix Rohatyn was insisting on sixty-seven dollars a share for RCA, and I was adamant for sixty-five dollars. We were each in a separate room at the Waldorf. John asked for a few minutes alone and said, 'Everybody wants a victory. You'll be thrilled with all you can do with and for RCA, and RCA people will be with you for a long long time. Leave 'em with dignity, with a victory.' Final offer: sixty-six fifty. I never dealt with Goldman Sachs—I always dealt with John. It was a very personal relationship with John Weinberg. John was as good inside as they make 'em."*

Weinberg's major business responsibility at Goldman Sachs was doing large transactions for large clients, continuing to build up the client relationships Sidney Weinberg had developed over many prior years and adding important new clients. He adhered to his father's advice to leave internal management of the firm to others. "Delegate *everything* to others and keep close tabs on what they are doing," Sidney Weinberg had insisted, "but don't do any managing yourself. You may not be able to delegate everything, but remember: If you're really any good, the best work you'll do for the firm will *not* be in management."

John Weinberg's focus on transactions for clients goes back to the fifties. Howard Morgans, Procter & Gamble's CEO, was working in the early hours of a morning on the final negotiations in P&G's 1957 acquisition of Clorox, a relatively minor transaction. Weinberg recalled, "We learned that three Teamsters at a P&G plant in Oregon were about to go on strike. If they went on strike, all the other Teamsters in the P&G system, following the 'hot cargo' clause in their contract, would have to strike too." Morgans turned to Weinberg and said, "Procter & Gamble cannot take a strike now just because three guys in Oregon are up in arms. The only quick and sure way out of this mess is to have somebody else own that unit." And then he continued, "So here's what we're going to do: We are selling that plant to . . . you!"

Weinberg protested that Goldman Sachs couldn't just buy a food-processing business. Morgans insisted. "And pretty soon," recalls Weinberg, "I'm signing a one-page agreement to buy the Oregon business unit for $460,000. P&G never bought or sold *anything* without complete documentation, but here I am signing for nearly half a million bucks on a single sheet of paper! Next day, I arrive back at the office on the red-eye and, naturally, march right over to Pop's office, where I tell him the acquisition is all set—and then I own up that we had a little difficulty at the end and explain the Oregon business and that I signed the papers and that we bought the unit. Pop's reaction was fast: 'All right, shithead, you are fired!'

---

* When Jack Welch divorced his wife to marry a much younger woman after retiring from GE, Weinberg disapproved. Despite their long personal and business relationship, the two men saw much less of each other. "He and Sue and my former wife and I used to play golf together, but it's been difficult since my divorce," said Welch.

And then Pop launches into a ninety-minute reaming of me and my capabilities and my judgment, and *everything*. It was an amazing exit interview. It took two weeks before he would hire me back into the firm."

In what must be a governance record, John Weinberg's thirty-four years of service as a director of B.F. Goodrich and twenty-six years at National Dairy (today's Kraft) extended Sidney Weinberg's previous service of thirty-two years with each of these corporations to exceed half a century.[4] Weinberg also continued his father's custom of buying the products of the companies he served as a director: Ford cars, GE refrigerators, Goodrich tires. "I was brought up that way. My father always did it, and I got in the habit of doing it." Weinberg kept a plaque inherited from his father that enumerated the many setbacks suffered by Abraham Lincoln on his way to becoming a great president, with the message that enormous success does not come without setbacks. As part of training John to lead the firm, Sidney Weinberg had made a point of taking his son to observe and meet business leaders.[5] (Similarly, John Weinberg took weekly weekend walks with *his* son John to advise on how to do well at the firm.) Very much his own man, John Weinberg was proud to be his father's son but frank about Sidney's toughness. "He peeled you when you made a mistake. He was a great father, a great banker, a good teacher, but a very tough guy and very demanding, who said, 'I don't care how far you go, but you damn well better try *hard*.' . . . I first heard about Goldman Sachs in the womb! I grew up on it. My first job at the firm was in the summer of forty-seven. After three and a half years in the Marines, my plan for that summer was to relax and have some fun. 'The hell you are!' said Pops. 'You're going to work.' So I spent the summer with the old-timers in the cage, learning how operations really worked."[6]

John Weinberg was quite purposefully self-deprecating. He drove an old Ford, wore short socks with his calf showing, would casually scratch his shins, wore short-sleeved shirts in the summer, and described his cigars as "El Rope-O No. 2" in a *New York Times* interview, adding, "I don't let my ego get in the way."[7] Unlike any other prominent executive of his time, he was so very natural that he really didn't care about appearances. He never mentioned his membership in Augusta National or his service on the governing boards of all three of the prestigious schools he had attended: Deerfield, Princeton, and Harvard Business School. In contrast, he spoke about his service in the U.S. Marines hundreds of times.

"He knew exactly what he was doing," said an admiring partner.

Sometimes he got tested. "Rent a Royal" was a high-profile opportunity to entertain clients in London. The arrangement was simple. All members of the royal family are patrons of various arts organizations, so for a £25,000 contribution to "their" charity, Charles and Diana would mingle with Goldman Sachs's guests for a cocktail reception *and* again at the intermission *and* for a farewell reception at the evening's end. Goldman Sachs signed up for an evening with the royals at the London Philharmonic.

Weinberg was in London on business, so he sat in the royal box with Charles and Diana. Though as always he wore short socks, he was on his best behavior and keen to master the first rule of etiquette with the future king and queen: Never initiate conversation; wait until spoken to. Princess Diana, lovely in her green silk dress, was soon enjoying a conversation she initiated with Weinberg, but she had a problem—and that problem quickly became a test of Weinberg's resourcefulness. "Mr. Weinberg, my back itches—way up high. Could you do me a favor and scratch my back?" The royal box is in clear view of the entire audience. People were, of course, always looking. What to do? Fortunately, just then the house lights dimmed, Weinberg quickly scratched gently—and Diana gave him her warm smile of royal gratitude.

At the other end of the spectrum, Weinberg's capacity for folksy contact with "the troops" had many illustrations over his long years at Goldman Sachs. He was in his office on the eleventh floor at 55 Broad Street when one of several summer associates saw him and thought, *Why not introduce myself?* Weinberg was glad to chat with a new associate and wanted to know: "Where are you from? Where are you working? Where are you in school? Are you enjoying New York? Are we keeping you busy? Helping you with your questions?" Busy as he surely was, Weinberg was never too busy for individuals who worked at the firm. The associate, who stayed with the firm for a decade, recalled with appreciation, "I *still* got Christmas cards from John—twenty years after I'd left the firm."

Intent on protecting the firm's culture from emerging arrogance among young partners, Weinberg was consistently tough as he told offenders, "Knock it off or else"—clearly implying they might have to leave the firm. In fact, Weinberg didn't much like the term "culture," which he considered highfalutin, but he believed deeply in the concept, the commitment to shared values: "It's the glue that holds the firm together so we can all work together." More than any other firm on Wall Street, Goldman Sachs forged a set of shared values and beliefs: an emphasis on both entrepreneurial aggressiveness and self-effacing teamwork; never disparaging a competitor; having clear ground rules on the sorts of business it would and wouldn't do; having a strong preference for developing its own talent (almost all partners spent their entire careers with the firm), a tendency to insularity, and a strong, expressed determination to put clients' interest first.

Weinberg came into his own in the six years he was sole senior partner, the era in which heavy investment spending converted the concepts Whitehead had articulated in his vision of Goldman Sachs as "the first global firm" into substantial on-the-ground reality with experienced Europeans leading the business in each of Europe's major countries.

Weinberg would see the firm's commitment to those policies tested again and again in ways large and small. Fred Krimendahl, an exceptionally capable leader within Goldman Sachs, developed the corporate-finance unit into one of the best in the business. Bob Rubin and Krimendahl sponsored the launch of the Water Street Corporate Recovery Fund. Operationally, it was co-led by Alfred Eckert III and Mikael Salovaara, both partners of Goldman Sachs. Water Street was funded with $750 million, partly partners' capital and partly clients'. Water Street's strategy was to buy up controlling blocks of distressed high-yield junk bonds that could put the fund in position to control the terms of any subsequent refinancing. The bonds were often being sold at prices significantly below fair market value by institutional investors who did not want to get into all the work, time, and effort of negotiating an adversarial workout and did want to get the bonds off their books when reporting to clients. Buying those bonds from "highly motivated sellers" at very low prices, fighting the fights and forcing solutions, promised to be very profitable for Water Street and for Goldman Sachs.

The "vulture" business, as it was called in slang-prone Wall Street, is and was capable of forcing companies to accept harsh refinancing terms. It can be a rough business of confrontational power plays and often quite bitter fights in court and in the market. Executives at companies involved in fights over particular bond issues were soon getting squeezed by Water Street. Several complained to John Weinberg that Water Street's rough dealings were in direct conflict with the firm's vaunted no-raids policy and its carefully crafted franchise for having high "client integrity." Weinberg saw the conflict and promptly closed down the highly profitable fund. Later Eckert and Salovaara separated and got into prolonged, bitter arguments and more than a decade of angry litigation. Years later, Fred Eckert, who went on to establish a successful firm of his own, said, "I agreed then and now with [Weinberg's] decision. I had an impossible partner. Since that closing, no investment bank has tried the same sort of fund."

Weinberg also said no to bridge loans when they were a hot new product. In a bridge loan, investment banks lend as much as one billion dollars of their own capital to an acquiring company so it can finance a takeover, on the assumption—not always valid—that a public bond offering can soon be underwritten to pay off the loan. This stratagem was used only by borrowers with poor credit, and several bridge-loan financings collapsed before the investment banks' loans were refinanced—with obviously painful consequences to the firms. Partners admired Weinberg's ability to make such difficult decisions. (Years later, the firm returned to bridge loans and developed a large business.)

S ome of Weinberg's judgment calls were on much more personal matters. Sex and sexuality have always been part of the scene on Wall Street, just as they are in Washington and Hollywood. The people attracted to all three need to connect with other people; they all live lives that are detached from reality, and they are constantly engaged in one way or another in seducing other people. Many are young, live "gee whiz" lives, and have money to spend. Flirting comes easily. So does going further. For those engaged in the excitement of the experience, knowing where the invisible boundary lines are is not a priority.

In the January 8, 1990, issue of *New York* magazine, a seven-page article described the events leading up to an unusually brief memorandum to the whole firm from John L. Weinberg announcing that a rapidly rising partner was resigning.[8] Weinberg had a clear code of moral behavior based squarely on all-American core values. He'd been around and was realistic about how other people—in the Marines, at Princeton, and in Manhattan or on the road—were behaving. But there were boundaries and limits. As he would say to a large group at the firm, "You can, if you want, do every sheep in Central Park . . . but leave our girls alone!"

In August 1989, two New York City policemen in uniform had gone to the twenty-ninth floor at 85 Broad Street to serve partner Lew Eisenberg, respected co-head of the equities division, with a criminal harassment complaint filed by his former assistant. Called on the carpet by Weinberg, Eisenberg told Weinberg that her boyfriend, an NYPD cop, was attempting blackmail and blowing an old affair all out of proportion. There was nothing to her accusations of abuse or pressure: The relationship had always been entirely consensual—and it was over; there was no truth to the rumors.

Anyone who has ever made a serious mistake knows how easy it is to keep pretending it hasn't really happened. It's hard to stop at the moment of confrontation and say, "What you're saying is accurate. I've made a terrible mistake and done something wrong. I'm truly sorry and am stopping *now*."

Then, on a business trip, Weinberg read the real story in the newspapers— particularly the *New York Post*—and blew his top.[9] At first, he thought Eisenberg might not have told the whole story. After that storm cleared and Weinberg's composure returned, most partners carefully avoided the subject. Eisenberg was strongly advised by his seniors to close the case down and pay the cop the half million he was after. But Eisenberg felt he couldn't do that. Given that decision—and the firm's determination to contain and stop what it saw as embarrassing publicity—Eisenberg would be given a "choice": resign or be forced out. He resigned and took his case to court, where he eventually won. Guilty of extortion, the accuser was thrown off the police force and the media printed retractions. But by then it was way too late for retraction to matter. (A dozen partners invested with him, the firm became his prime broker, and Rubin and Friedman wrote him a warm letter of appreciation for his leadership in building the stockbrokerage business to record levels.) Eisenberg was immediately banished from the firm. Weinberg accepted the "realities" of affairs in the office, even between partners and others. Weinberg could have accepted the affair, even when parts of it made the papers, but he would not accept anything short of the whole truth when any situation required his asking questions. Believing that the maxim "Much is expected of those to whom much has been given" applied directly to partners of Goldman Sachs, when Weinberg was told less than the 100 percent truth he always required, the partner had to go. Later Weinberg told his partners that if anyone entered into an affair with a subordinate, one or the other must request a transfer so the partner would not be supervising a lover.

· · ·

Weinberg's own adventures were in the corporate world with his many clients. When Sir James Goldsmith made his massive twenty-billion-dollar raid on the United Kingdom's British American Tobacco Company in 1989, it was the largest hostile bid in European history. An urgent call went out from CEO Patrick Sheehy in London to John Weinberg in New York—at least in part because Goldman Sachs, under Weinberg's direction, had three years previously defended Goodyear Tire & Rubber from a prior Goldsmith raid. Weinberg took the next flight to London to lead the successful defense, helping establish Goldman Sachs as one of the principal investment banks to British industry.

Weinberg clearly took pleasure in helping to work things out. In 1993 he was an adviser to Eastman Kodak's board of directors and to the committee of the board in charge of the search for a new CEO for the company. He and Coca-Cola CEO Roberto Goizueta had agreed that the right man to take the helm at Kodak was George Fisher of Motorola. They went to see Fisher together and, as planned, hit him with both barrels. First, they argued that a great American corporation was floundering, and Fisher, with his leadership qualities and his understanding of technology, was uniquely qualified to be CEO and to accomplish something of great importance for this major company and for America. Second, they laid out an incentive package that would make Fisher a wealthy man if he succeeded.

The two men were playing to win. But they were not making much progress and certainly were not getting to the close. During a lull, Weinberg was alone with Fisher, who said, "John, it's a great job and a wonderful offer. I know that. But I'm not going to accept it—even from Roberto and you—and I want to tell you why. My wife, Anne, has been wonderful to me, and I owe her the time and the fun she's clearly entitled to, but she would lose out on this if I took the job and embarked on a major new challenge at Eastman Kodak. I'm just not going to do that to Anne."

Weinberg replied warmly, "That's wonderful, George, truly wonderful."[10] Then he asked gently, "Would you mind if I were to give Anne a call?" With Fisher's assent, Weinberg was on the phone in a few minutes, explaining the Kodak opportunity and its importance and saying, "But, Anne, George won't take the job at Eastman Kodak." Asked why, he explained with innocent appreciation, "Because he loves *you*." Anne Fisher asked for twenty-four hours, and well within the time limit, George Fisher was on the phone to John Weinberg. He and Anne had discussed it all and had agreed he should move to Kodak. Once again, Weinberg had done his job for a client.

He also did his job for Goldman Sachs—sometimes parlaying a lucky break into a significant advance. During the 1980s, the major investment banks needed huge amounts of long-term capital to finance global expansion and, particularly, the enormous increases in their dealer inventories as they made markets in debt and equity securities all around the world, often in tremendous amounts. Goldman Sachs continued its tough capital-retention policies and arranged a series of private-placement debt financings with major insurance companies, but these were not enough to meet the firm's mushrooming need for equity capital—the same need that was driving competitor firms to merge into major commercial banks or go public and lose the cachet of being private partnerships.

Morgan Stanley had gone public. Salomon Brothers had gone public by merging with Phibro, and DLJ was public through an IPO and might combine at any time with a major underwriter. Bear Stearns was public and building out its banking business. In a major report he prepared for Rubin and Friedman, partner Don Gant explained the problem with the partnership. Sure, the firm had much more capital than it had ever had before—nearly $1.8 billion—but six hundred million dollars of that belonged to the retired or limited partners and was scheduled to be paid out to them over the next several years. The other two-thirds belonged to the active general partners, but those with the largest percentages were almost certain to be retiring over the next few years, and each would be taking half his capital out of the firm on the day he went limited. Realistic projections showed that just when the firm needed much more capital to support its expanding and increasingly capital-intensive business activities, it was almost certain to have less equity capital on its balance sheet.

All the big commercial banks were not only public, they were armed with potent balance sheets, many corporate relationships, and strong international networks. They were trying to expand into investment banking and securities underwriting. Several banks had bought into securities dealers in London. The big banks all had ambitions to expand into securities dealing, and it was clear they were prepared to extend large loans and cut prices to gain market share in the investment banking business. The consensus among Wall Street's leaders was clear: *Those big, dumb banks will ruin our business!*

To get more capital, Goldman Sachs identified four possible solutions: Lock in partners' capital when they went limited—a major change in the partnership compact that the major partners and all limiteds were sure to oppose; go public—which the newer partners would clearly oppose; somehow increase the firm's profitability—a lot; or find some sugar daddy who wanted to make a large equity investment in the firm despite all the competitive uncertainties.

Of the four choices, Friedman and Rubin, widely recognized as the firm's next generation of leaders, championed an IPO. Having permanent capital and access to the public markets fit with their strategic interests, which would all require capital: investing firm capital in much more proprietary trading, investing in private equity and real estate, and expanding internationally. The management committee—dominated by senior partners who would soon be retiring and would, individually, be the major beneficiaries of an IPO—agreed unanimously to go along, and John Weinberg acceded to the consensus. At the next partners' meeting, Friedman and Rubin presented the case for an IPO but somehow did not project real conviction. Moreover, the partners had not been prepared in advance for such a profound change in the basic nature of their firm. The slide presentation showed what each partner would take home and, emphasizing how stretched for capital the firm was already, explained how and why the needs for capital would increase steadily as the firm took advantage of its growth opportunities. Then, turning from carrots to sticks, they reminded the group that any one or two severe problems—like Penn Central, a large, sudden trading loss, or any of the many different kinds of trouble that could easily be imagined or conjured up—could suddenly do great harm to the firm and its partners.

The presentation was unconvincing. To some, it seemed inconsistent in several ways. The thirty-seven new partners would have none of it: An IPO did almost nothing for them and would preclude their building up their capital positions over the next several years. They had not begun to build up their capital accounts, so even though partnership accounts were valued at three times book value, three times zero was still zero. Partnership decisions were not weighted by shares of partnership capital—they were one partner, one vote—and all the new and most of the nearly new partners were opposed. That meant that while Rubin and Friedman could bring it up again, the idea of an IPO was pushed off for at least a year.

Then, on February 13, 1987, partner Bob Freeman was arrested in the office and charged with multiple counts of trading on inside information. In all the emotional and legal confusion, one thing was clear: There would be no IPO for Goldman Sachs. But the firm still needed capital, particularly since major competitors had gone public and now had substantial permanent capital. Goldman Sachs was competing in fast-changing markets with one hand tied behind its back.

Happily, the problem was solved in a most unusual way that began with a most unusual visit to John Weinberg. Earthy John Weinberg was no dreamer; he never expected to come up with big new ideas. But all of a sudden, in 1987, the least likely solution to Goldman Sachs's need for a large capital infusion presented itself to Weinberg. The solution would be a huge investment in Goldman Sachs by one of the world's largest banks—a gigantic Japanese bank with no prior experience in investment banking. The president of Sumitomo Bank, Koh Komatsu, arrived at Weinberg's office wearing dark glasses so he would not be recognized, having traveled by a deliberately circuitous, deceptive route: Osaka to Seattle, Seattle to Washington, DC, and then the shuttle to New York City. "I had to tell him," said Weinberg, chortling, "that taking the shuttle from Washington National to LaGuardia was no way to hide. Those planes are full of guys from Wall Street—and reporters!"

Komatsu-san, accompanied by Akira Kondoh,[11] explained that Sumitomo Bank, Japan's most profitable commercial bank and the third largest in the world, with nearly $150 billion in assets, had a strategic interest in developing its capabilities as an investment bank and had retained McKinsey & Company to advise on the best way forward. During the postwar occupation of Japan, Douglas MacArthur had mandated a separation of commercial and investment banking along the lines of Glass-Steagall, but that law had been changed recently to allow Japan's commercial banks to provide investment banking services through subsidiaries. McKinsey had recommended a major capital commitment to one of the foremost American investment banks and suggested Goldman Sachs as the industry leader. Felix Rohatyn of Lazard Freres had been chosen to act as an intermediary to make the initial contact with Goldman Sachs. Sumitomo wanted to send two dozen young officers to the firm's New York office for training and indoctrination in the American ways of corporate finance.

Sumitomo's proposition seemed almost too good to be true: It wanted to invest up to five hundred million dollars in cash for an equity interest in the firm. While open to negotiating terms, Komatsu explained that if Goldman Sachs would not agree to the five-hundred-million-dollar amount, the proposition would really not be worth pursuing. As negotiations would later determine, Sumitomo acquired a one-eighth interest in the firm that valued Goldman Sachs at a multiple of 3⅜ times book value—four billion dollars.[12] After generations of Goldman Sachs partners had patiently built up the firm's capital over nearly a hundred years, Sumitomo's proposition would, remarkably, increase the capital overnight by 38 percent.

The firm's need for more capital—long-term, permanent equity capital—had been the most important argument for an IPO. But when the IPO had been scuttled in 1986, Weinberg had certainly not been unhappy. He believed strongly in the partnership, just as he believed in its client relationships, and he knew his father would have opposed public ownership. He also believed in Goldman Sachs becoming the leading firm on Wall Street and knew that was going to require more capital than the partners could retain out of current profits. Weinberg could barely contain himself, because Komatsu's visit was so improbable and could be so important. "You won't believe this—not in a million years—but I've just had the most amazing visit!" he exclaimed over the phone to Don Gant.

Gant and Weinberg had first met at the firm twenty years before and had always hit it off. Gant is taciturn and tight-lipped and can be trusted with anything. In maintaining the Ford Motor Company relationship, working under Gus Levy, Gant had proved that he could handle matters that were complex and sensitive and required on-the-spot good judgment. In addition, he had done all the detailed financial analysis and documentation for the recently failed proposal for an IPO, so he knew all the numbers. Weinberg, cautious and deliberate, wanted to check out every aspect of Sumitomo's amazing proposition, which is why he turned to Gant. "Don, this may be nothing, but if it does work out, it could be very, very big. Come over to my office right away so I can fill you in. We've got work to do!"

When Gant arrived at his office, Weinberg was grinning widely. "Felix Rohatyn came in this morning with two Japanese guys wearing dark glasses. One guy speaks only Japanese, but is obviously very senior. The other is his translator. The senior guy explains that he doesn't want to be recognized by any newspaper reporters or Wall Streeters, which is why he was wearing dark glasses and why he had come by such a screwball route." Weinberg laughed over the memories of the human foibles as much as over the strategic triumph the opportunity presented. In an industry where equity capital can be leveraged fifty times over by firms with high credit ratings, half a billion dollars of fresh equity capital could be a mighty powerful infusion. Still laughing, Weinberg, as usual, got quickly to the point with Gant: "Don, give Felix Rohatyn a call right away to see how serious this guy is about what he said to me—that Sumitomo Bank wants to be a partner in Goldman Sachs. See if they're really serious." Then, chuckling, Weinberg said, "Who knows? We may soon be Goldman Sake!"

Gant knew Rohatyn from working together on deals with 3M, so they talked candidly. Gant then reported back to Weinberg: "John, Rohatyn says Sumitomo is absolutely for real on this. We can't just dismiss it. They have the money and want to be a silent partner. If we negotiate this the right way, Rohatyn says we can write our own ticket."

"Are you ready to take the lead on the negotiation, Don? Knowing the Japanese, it could take a *lot* of time!"

"I'll be okay."[13]

"Lucky they didn't come when Gus was still here," observed Weinberg years later. "He hated the Japs. And didn't like the French much either. Never had any interest in international—not even for five seconds."

At first, the Federal Reserve Board of Governors rejected the application for Sumitomo to invest. Institutionally, this made Sumitomo very unhappy; the bank felt "set up." On a personal level, this rebuff hurt the career of Sumitomo's key man in the negotiations because in Japan, anything so important would have been carefully precleared with the Ministry of Finance to prevent just such surprises.

When Sumitomo Bank was attempting to make its huge investment in Goldman Sachs, there was a lot of easy talk in the United States about the Japanese buying up America, and there were specific concerns about any foreign commercial bank owning a piece of a major American investment bank. To head off political interference, partner Bob Downey arranged a meeting between John Weinberg and Representative John Dingell, chairman of the House Energy and Finance Committee, to fill the congressman in. As Downey recalls, "John Weinberg was quite ready to explain that Sumitomo had paid three and a half times book value and that they wouldn't have a voting interest in the firm and all that, but he seemed quite reluctant when I suggested he mention to the congressman that he had had experience with the Japanese all the way back to the 1940s. That's why I was so surprised when John started right off with saying, 'Congressman, don't ever forget that in the war, we fought those bastards.' Dingell cut in: 'Now, John'—but the point on our protecting our independence had already been made for certain. We had no trouble with Congress after that."

After months of discussions and three formal hearings, the Federal Reserve agreed to consider the application but set strict limits to protect Glass-Steagall: Sumitomo couldn't own more than 24.9 percent of Goldman Sachs, and its partnership interest must be nonvoting.[14] The agreement was limited, at Goldman Sachs's initiative, to a five-year term, with either party free to opt out at the end of five years if notification was given at the end of four years. If Goldman Sachs should ever go public, Sumitomo's partnership interest would convert to 12.5 percent of the common stock.[15]

Insisting on secrecy, Sumitomo Bank sent a team of eighteen executives to conduct the negotiations. They all expected to remain in New York City for several months while working with Lazard Freres. (One member of the Sumitomo team met a Japanese woman who was living in New York City and married her—with Gant escorting the bride in the wedding ceremony.) Gant soon understood that Goldman Sachs was in a strong negotiating position.[16] In Japan, Sumitomo Bank was known for being a maverick and boldly innovative—and proudly from Osaka. With a successful resolution of negotiations, Sumitomo would win great prestige, but failure would mean a serious loss of face. Understanding this, Gant was able, whenever necessary, to unwind potential deal breakers simply by assuring his counterparts that a particular demand simply would never be acceptable to Goldman Sachs's management committee.

Initially, Sumitomo thought it would want to have all sorts of trainees at the firm, but Weinberg and Gant explained that to "protect your investment" it would be important to avoid the perception that Goldman Sachs was too close to the Sumitomo Group. The Fed decided that Sumitomo could send two—not two dozen—interns, and they could not remain in New York City for more than twelve months before rotating home. Sumitomo was not at all comfortable with these restrictions, so negotiations continued to be, as Gant later recalled, "touch and go." One problem for Gant was finding partners willing to train a Sumitomo intern, knowing he would not be staying more than a year.

Sumitomo would just be a silent partner and not have a vote. Again, Weinberg explained, "It was to protect their investment." In fact, it was the best investment Sumitomo ever made, because the bank could fund its whole commitment in the Euromarkets at a net cost of just 1 percent. With characteristic genial understatement, Weinberg observed, "It's worked out well for everyone."

As background to the Sumitomo story, Weinberg would later explain that he had lots of close friends in Japan, saying, "I've been going there for twenty-five years." He was diplomatic in understating the reality that he'd actually been going for more than *fifty* years. His first mission was as a Marine, to liberate POW camps in the early stages of the U.S. occupation. As he said, "I'd seen a lot and heard a lot about POW camps—but nothing like what I saw in Japan."[17]

To get into the Marine Corps, Weinberg had lied about his age: He was only seventeen. Since no good deed goes unpunished, nearly a decade later he was called back for a second combat tour, as a platoon leader in Korea.[18]

He would regale friends with stories about events of the war and postwar years—like the day his life was threatened by a Marine captain who accompanied him on a work party at a former kamikaze launching station in Kyushu to reorganize a brothel the Japanese army had maintained for the young pilots going out on their "final mission." The group's assignment was to clean out the facility before reopening it so the same tough White Russian women—who knew how and when to use their fists to maintain order—could service the GIs. The captain called it a "recreational facility." He didn't want young Weinberg telling tales that might tarnish his promising back-home career in medicine, so he made himself menacingly clear: "If anybody *anywhere ever* hears about what we're doing here, I'll find you and I *will* kill you!"

In the year Weinberg received the Harvard Business School's prestigious Alumni Achievement Award, Bristol-Meyers CEO Richard Gelb, Weinberg's HBS classmate, good-naturedly referred obliquely to Weinberg's occupation experience converting the brothel. Gelb noted slyly that Weinberg's assignment had "presented unusual challenges" but provided "rich experience in retailing" that was "characterized by being labor-intensive with a high cash flow." Weinberg's friends and classmates in the audience of dignitaries loved the mercifully cryptic remarks because they knew the real story.

In the few years after Sumitomo's investment, Goldman Sachs's profits

316 · THE PARTNERSHIP

increased substantially, and the firm could readily have bought out Sumitomo's stake at the already agreed rate of one hundred million dollars a year over five successive years but didn't, because the capital was employed so profitably. During John Weinberg's fourteen years as managing partner, Goldman Sachs's earnings multiplied ten times and equity capital soared from sixty million dollars to $2.3 billion. With the IPO, Sumitomo's return on its investment was astronomical. Ironically, however, Sumitomo did not achieve its strategic objective, which was to develop and use a new expertise. It never did investment banking business in Japan.

As an intense competitor against other Wall Street firms, Weinberg placed an urgent call to Fred Frank at Lehman Brothers about an underwriting Lehman Brothers was about to do without Goldman Sachs. "We brought that company public, so it would be a great embarrassment to our firm—and to me personally—if we aren't involved as a major underwriter in this offering. So, Fred, I'm asking you." Frank arranged to have Goldman Sachs reinstated, simply saying to the client: "You can't drop Goldman Sachs—because it's such a strong firm that everyone on Wall Street will think *they* dropped *you*."

A few years later, on a different topic, Frank was back on the phone with Weinberg, describing overly aggressive behavior by a Goldman Sachs banker. "Gee, Fred, that's awful," commiserated Weinberg, asking for time to look into the situation and promising to call back. Frank expected Weinberg's contrition to result in a satisfying business change. So when he next spoke with Weinberg, he asked: "Well, then, John, will you be able to take care of this and put a stop to it?"

"Oh. No, Fred, certainly not," came the surprising reply. "That would be micromanaging." Always an unrelenting competitor, Weinberg was not about to squelch his aggressive colleague. As Frank observed, "For Goldman Sachs, it's not just that they must win—but also *you* must fail."

Long-term relationships were particularly important to Weinberg, and he clearly felt most comfortable where the loyalty went both ways and was equally strong. Loyalty up, loyalty down, say the U.S. Marines. When a relationship was not working, he would work hard to get it right—as illustrated by his work with

General Electric. Weinberg explained: "My father had been a longtime director of GE, and we were all disappointed that after his death Goldman Sachs was not invited to continue the relationship as co–investment banker for GE, a traditional relationship the firm had enjoyed." GE turned to Morgan Stanley to serve as its lead investment banker.

Weinberg decided to see what could be done and made a point of showing up at GE's corporate offices in Fairfield, Connecticut, every month over twelve long years, meeting with people, particularly the new people being brought into the senior management group.[19] "I've always gotten along pretty well with regular working people, so one day I'm there and it's pretty quiet, and one of the secretaries I knew—she typed all the superconfidential executive-performance evaluations—said to me, 'There's a new executive you should see,' and in another minute, she ushers me into the office of this guy I'd never heard of before: Jack Welch."

Welch had never heard of Weinberg either, so he asked, "What's on your mind?" Weinberg had to admit, "I really don't have anything particularly on my mind," and asked Welch what his responsibilities would be at GE. Welch grinned and made a sarcastic observation about the value of really doing your homework before calling on busy people and then explained he was now sector executive for several business units, including GE Credit. Weinberg asked how Goldman Sachs could help, and Welch grinned again, commenting about the importance of coming prepared with specific, documented proposals and action recommendations, and asked, "Don't you *ever* do *any* homework?" As Weinberg perceived, however, "Somehow we were actually getting along pretty well on a personal level, and the next thing I know, he's saying how he hopes to become GE's CEO one day and asks me how Goldman Sachs can help him do a great job for the corporation. We talked about various things, and pretty soon things seemed to come together for us both."

Over the next several years, despite starting out so awkwardly, the two men worked together in many ways. For example, the steel industry needed huge investment in continuous-casting equipment, and the IRS allowed a transfer of the investment tax credit if the equipment was leased—and that's where GE Credit could come in. Since the steel companies had little or no profits and few taxes against which to take the tax credit, Weinberg worked out a way for GE

Credit to buy the equipment, take the tax credit, and then lease the equipment to the steel companies. Weinberg's summary: "Naturally, everybody was happy."

His engaged, no-pretenses manner left Weinberg open to good-natured ribbing from his many friends—sometimes in public, sometimes in private one-on-one fun. When Jack Welch called his friend several years later to divulge something big happening at General Electric, he began the conversation in a personally affectionate way that anyone on Wall Street would die for: "You're dumb. You're ugly. And . . . you're oh so very lucky!" And then he continued, "I'm about to be asked to go into the boardroom. When I come out, I'll be CEO—and you and Goldman Sachs will again be our lead investment banker."

Weinberg was not in his office. He was in Midtown taking his turn at a series of physical examinations at the Life Extension Institute. As Weinberg liked to tell the story, he was sitting in the waiting area with Morgan Stanley's then managing partner, Robert Baldwin, who was waiting to be called for a proctoscopic exam. Grinning, Weinberg would end the story by explaining that just when General Electric's outgoing CEO, Reginald Jones, called Baldwin to explain that Morgan Stanley would no longer be GE's lead investment banker, the attendant came to say it was time for Baldwin's examination.

During the late seventies, those equipment-leasing arrangements helped Welch's GE Credit bring in nearly 75 percent of GE's total reported earnings, making it the earnings engine for GE as a whole. "Over the years, Jack and I developed a good understanding and a lot of respect for each other," said Weinberg. "We became great friends and saw a lot of each other. He's an extraordinary human being." Welch reciprocates: "I could talk for a week about him. I'm really a fan. John was wise, practical, and unpretentious, with extraordinary common sense. He had a great nose for value and never depended on all those spreadsheets other guys insisted on. He was a great judge of character and represented Goldman Sachs at its best. The thing that distinguished John was that he was not just a deal maker for the deal's sake. He was interested in what was right for both parties. He cared about his clients and his own people in as sensitive a way as anybody in business."

While most of his time was spent outside the firm with clients, Weinberg made sure his clients regularly got the very best talents of the firm working on their deals. He also took major roles inside Goldman Sachs. In 1990 the *Economist* credited Weinberg for his leadership: "His mix of warmth and toughness has guided Goldman Sachs though an unparalleled expansion and to higher profits over the past fourteen years. His cautiousness kept the firm from making bridge loans, from putting its own capital into takeovers, or from buying the junk bonds that have so tripped up rivals. 'We watch our eggs very carefully. Because they are our eggs—and everything we have.' "[20]

Weinberg combined deliberately abrupt and unpolished personal ways with quick recall of names, dates, and other details. He was always ready to deal directly with problems and almost instinctively recognized what was right for each person in a difficult situation. This combination enabled him to move directly to pragmatic resolution of matters large and small to the repeated satisfaction of clients and colleagues, and often vaporized the inherent conflicts within Goldman Sachs between talented, hard-charging individuals with different objectives and different perspectives. Weinberg's self-imposed mission was to achieve harmony between two goals that others often found contradictory: cooperative teamwork and aggressive individual initiative—and to do so quickly, decisively, and fairly, with no hard feelings.

Within the firm, Weinberg's approach was simple, direct, and effective. He would take the antagonists aside and, moving up very close and lowering his voice, would lay out exactly how the problem would be resolved: "Now, I'm going to decide this thing once and for all—by noon tomorrow. So each of you should think very carefully about what you really want most included in my final decision and then tell me the exact decision you'd like me to make—a decision you can and you will live with. Make it just as fair as you can to the other guy because he'll be giving me his best and fairest final decision too. I'm going to pick just one of those recommendations and that will be that—and then we'll all get back to work."

Weinberg's strength with the people of Goldman Sachs was matched by his strength with clients, old and new. Always the Marine, he was aggressive and kept moving up, was never a "showboat"—and was loved because he lived and breathed the core values of Goldman Sachs. "I really love this place," he explained quite openly and naturally. "You want people to feel good about themselves and about the firm." His sincerely innocent assumption was that what was so naturally obvious to him must surely be equally self-evident to others. It often *was*—once he'd put it into words. "People want to be treated well, and I don't see any reason not to," he said. On the other hand, Weinberg quickly deflated others' self-importance, observing from experience, "After they get promotions, some people really grow, but others just swell."

Weinberg was direct. Advising a young partner who was bringing a proposal to the management committee, he said: "I want you to have a very successful meeting, and I'll want to contribute directly to your success. So, just as I tell everyone else, I want to have *all* the materials to be discussed forty-eight hours before the meeting. I *will* read it, and so will everyone else. The meeting will begin with questions—and I will ask the first question."

In the decade following his retirement as a partner, Weinberg continued to be a busy man, laughing, "I've been bringing in more business than when I was there." Deals included Chemical Bank's takeover of Manufacturers Hanover Bank and GCA Corporation's $2.3 billion merger with Columbia Healthcare and their combination into Hospital Corporation of America. At seventy-five, as a Goldman Sachs adviser, Weinberg received a huge raise: five million dollars annually under a new two-year contract, up from two million dollars a year under his previous contract. According to a letter from Hank Paulson, Weinberg would receive an additional five million dollars when his contract expired or was terminated. The contract stayed in force until Weinberg's death at eighty-one on August 7, 2006.

While Weinberg was best known for his success in managing major corporate client relationships, that was not his highest priority. "John's greatest pride was not in recovering the GE relationship or taking over as successfully as he did Sidney Weinberg's many major corporate relationships—the backbone of the firm," says his brother Jim, who had a closer relationship with John Weinberg— three fathoms down—than most people realized. "These and other achievements were all *external*. What John cared most about were the many ways the firm was strengthened internally." Weinberg worried that Goldman Sachs's culture, a primal strength in America, would be in conflict with the cultures of other countries. He was delighted to see that the values and work ethic he believed in seemed universal. As one partner observed for everyone: "He was the soul of the firm."

19

~

INNOCENTS ABROAD

Getting out of a London taxi he and a partner had taken from the City of London out to Heathrow—which in the early sixties was a ten-pound fare— Ray Young, head of securities sales, gave the driver a tip of one hundred pounds. At the prevailing exchange rate of $2.80 to the pound, that was $280. Young's startled Goldman Sachs companion was aghast: "Ray! You can't *do* that. It's *wrong*."

"Why? That's what I always do wherever I go: a hundred lire in Italy, a hundred yen in Tokyo, a hundred francs in France—always a hundred, whatever the local currency."

Young had no thought of the substantial differences from one currency to another and no idea that he had just tipped his cab driver more than the average worker in England earned in six *weeks*—or that in Rome, his standard hundred-lire tip was worth about sixteen cents. Goldman Sachs had a lot to learn before it would become the leading investment banking and securities firm in Europe and Asia.

Urbane Stanley Miller had been in Wall Street before the war. He came to Goldman Sachs from the State Department because Sidney Weinberg

knew him; he was recruited to develop international business—not in investment banking, but in trading. To cultivate opportunities for block trading, he
would travel twice a year to call on institutions in Europe. Back in New York
City, he supervised a few elderly European stockbrokers who sold to wealthy
individuals, a Belgian arbitrageur, and a few young Yanks who covered institutional investors in American shares. To make an overseas telephone call, the
caller had to get Miller's permission, partly because calls were expensive and
partly to protect against innocents' forgetting the five- or six-hour time differences and calling customers at a boorishly inappropriate hour of the night.
Miller was shocked to find the firm served neither wine nor aperitifs at luncheons
in the office. He knew better: He had come to build an international business,
and international visitors would surely expect a "libation" at such luncheons; if
nothing was served, prospective clients simply would stop coming. But at Goldman Sachs, there was no drinking—period. It took several days to find a compromise: Miller could offer sherry, but only in his lunchroom. Later, luncheon
guests at the firm would generally be offered sherry, but the people of Goldman
Sachs would *always* pass, and the rumor held that one bottle of sherry lasted
for many years.

International business at Goldman Sachs can be traced back to 1897, when
a profit of four thousand dollars was recorded. Profits increased to $250,000 in
1903 and peaked in 1906 at just over five hundred thousand dollars. But during
the Depression and the Second World War, most American investment banks,
Goldman Sachs included, dropped their international business and closed any
overseas offices. After the war, major firms like Morgan Stanley, First Boston,
Lehman Brothers, and Kuhn Loeb took the lead on international financings for
the European Coal and Steel Community, the Japanese government, and other
major organizations in a series of large and prestigious financings. Goldman
Sachs, still stigmatized by the failure of Goldman Sachs Trading Corporation,
was not included. Its overseas offices stayed closed.

Goldman Sachs's modern international expansion began—slowly—after the
Korean War. As Whitehead explains, "Other firms were well ahead of us with what
were then called foreign offices. Goldman Sachs had no international offices and
really no interest. If a Goldman Sachs client made an acquisition overseas, it would
use another firm—usually one in that foreign country, but sometimes an Ameri-

can competitor like First Boston or Morgan Stanley. To protect our client business, we knew we had to get into the international side of the business, but our first attempts, particularly looking back from today's position, were pretty feeble."

Charles Saltzman, who had been a vice president of the New York Stock Exchange before becoming deputy secretary of state under George Marshall, joined the firm as a partner and was interested in Japan, so he took an annual trip to Tokyo. "He was well respected, but he never asked for an order," observes Whitehead. In 1974 Bill Brown came over from McKinsey, where he had run a one-man office in Tokyo, and did the same for Goldman Sachs for a decade.[1] "He didn't know much about investment banking, but he did know Japan," recalls Whitehead, who notes the defensive roles governments then played effectively against outside financial firms: "The Japanese Ministry of Finance had always blocked us in Japan. They were just as tough and just as effective as we and our Federal Reserve were at blocking them in America. And in the United Kingdom, the Bank of England was clearly our major problem. They were *very* slow to approve the things we wanted to do—just as our government was very slow to approve the initiatives our European competitors wanted to take in America."

International efforts began to accelerate slightly in 1969 when Sidney Weinberg and Gus Levy brought in Lyndon Johnson's secretary of the Treasury (and Roy Smith's father-in-law), Henry Fowler, as a partner and chairman of Goldman Sachs International Corporation. Fowler, careful not to overwork his government-initiated relationships, described his international role as "less that of a director and more that of an ambassador."

The firm's buildup in Asia began with a small thread of opportunity. In 1969 a trainee from Nikko Securities arrived and sat near Roy Smith. Partner Fred Krimendahl had worked with Nikko on an issue a few years before and had stayed in fairly close communication, so when Nikko wanted to ask if Goldman Sachs could take on an associate to get some experience, the request went to Krimendahl and he made the arrangements. After a few months of licking envelopes, the associate walked to Smith's desk and said, "So sorry, but I have something to say, please."

"What's that?"

"Our firm believes your firm doesn't do enough to promote Japanese securities business, but all your competitors do."

324 · THE PARTNERSHIP

"Why do you tell *me?*"

"Can't tell Mr. Krimendahl. He's too senior. You must tell him."

"But I don't know much about Japan or why we should do more business there. And what's more, Fred knows all this about me."

Nikko's man understood Smith's problem—and had a solution. "We will prepare a written report for you to give to Mr. Krimendahl."

The report was produced, and after going back and forth with Nikko's people several times to get it right, Smith took it to Krimendahl, saying, "Nikko prepared this report on why they think we should be promoting more business in Japan and asked me to bring it to your attention—so you would decide to read it."

The report made an impression. A few months later, Krimendahl called Smith into his office to say that "because of your strong interest in Japan"—which was all news to Smith—"the management committee has decided you should go to Japan for a while to see if we should be doing any business there. Henry Fowler and Charlie Saltzman will go with you to open doors."

As Smith recalls, "At first, it was *my* trip with them coming along to help me, but soon it reversed and became me accompanying them on *their* trip. We spent three weeks in Japan during that 1969 trip and saw a hundred different companies. Not much investment banking or securities business was being done in Japan in those days, but the firm's major competitors were all active in anticipation of business somehow opening up—business that might be done, of course, by Goldman Sachs if it did all the right things." Shortly after returning from this initial trip, Smith was told, "Because of your great interest *and* your great skills and expertise in Japan, we want you to be our man in Japan, but don't spend more than a quarter of your time on this important responsibility."

For the next several years, Smith made five two- to three-week trips a year to Japan. His major work continued to be in New York, serving John Weinberg's clients. In Japan his "office" was his hotel room, and he called on companies, banks, and securities firms—without a translator. "Most firms had either native speakers or translators, but we had neither, which limited the substantive content of our meetings." The Big Four Japanese securities firms controlled all the business, so all the foreign firms beat a path to their doors." Smith recalls, "It was *very* competitive."

One day John Weinberg, believing Smith was either spending too much or too little time in Japan, told him as bluntly as usual, "Shit or get off the pot." So in 1971, Smith went full time in the international business, concentrating on Japan.

Competitor firms all relied on the relationships they'd begun by getting an introduction through a Japanese securities firm, but Smith understood that these introductions often result in pointless meetings with "face men." "I believed it was better to be known as the smart people from New York with good ideas that would be interesting to the Japanese, so they would see me and then I could play, 'Who do you know,' making reference over and over again to Henry Fowler." Smith made appointments with senior executives through those earlier contacts whenever he could, and, as he recalls, "sent a lot of letters."

Those early days were never easy, and some of the difficulties were quite remarkable. For example, there usually were no street numbers on Tokyo build-ings, and any numbers that were there were not in numerical sequence along a street, as in the West, but in the chronological order in which the buildings had been constructed. So to keep from getting lost, Smith had to get a taxi with a driver who spoke some English. Language was a persistent problem. During an initial sales call, Smith might say, "Thank you for seeing me. I am from Goldman Sachs"—without knowing that "zachs" in Japanese is the word for condom.

Smith decided not to live in Japan, believing that the business-development effort would collapse if he wasn't based in the New York office, networking and lobbying with partners and then going back to Japan with the newest and freshest ideas. "If I'd been in Tokyo and out of touch with key people in the firm, we'd never have gotten Japanese business accepted by the management committee in New York, where everyone seemed to think that Japanese business was really just junk-bond business."

Issuing commercial paper for Mitsui—a three-hundred-year-old company where Henry Fowler had a friend from his time as treasury secretary—promised to be the firm's first breakthrough in Japan. But the U.S. commercial-paper market wouldn't accept Japanese paper. Smith's solution was to arrange a U.S. bank letter of credit as backup, an innovation that reassured investors about the credit quality. Once Mitsui's paper had been accepted in the U.S. market, Smith went to every major Japanese company he could identify, "marketing the pants off the idea of issuing commercial paper as a low-cost way to raise money," and got several other Japanese companies to issue U.S. commercial paper. "It was an opportunistic time," he remembers, "and we would try anything that worked." A year later, Goldman Sachs did a convertible bond for Mitsui, and this significantly increased the firm's stature in Japan.

An early Japanese equity offering by Goldman Sachs was for Wacoal, a brassiere maker. Smith pointed out that Wacoal made more bras than anyone else in the world. This was a surprise to the New Yorkers, since Japanese women were not as "endowed" as American women.

"Who are you going to sell this to?" asked John Weinberg.

"Institutions," replied Smith.

"You'll have a lot of explaining to do," said Weinberg with a grin.

Wacoal wanted to be certain the shares would get the firm's support in the aftermarket. As Smith later explained, "Before we could get the assignment, we had to promise we would do the underwriting successfully, and then, after we got the mandate, we had to study the data to see if and how we could actually do the underwriting." The deal was successful and made a nice profit.

Goldman Sachs's first office in London was opened on Wood Street in early 1970 by Powell Cabot, a son of Sidney Weinberg's great friend Paul Cabot. He was succeeded for a while by Sape Stheeman, a Dutchman hired from S.G. Warburg who built the staff to two dozen. In 1970 Michael Cowles, who had just become a partner and was trying to pull all the international business together, was sent to London to run the office.[2] "Nobody told us what to do," recalls Smith. "Nobody supervised our work. We were out of sight, out of mind, and free to figure it out for ourselves. I called on an awful lot of people to introduce myself and to talk about the firm."

Goldman Sachs was virtually unknown in corporate London, so it had to have a demonstrably superior "wedge" product to break into the market. "Fortunately, we had just such a product in commercial paper," recalls Whitehead. "Our unique product gave us an effective way to get started." Commercial paper was almost unknown in London, and there was no commercial-paper market on the Continent. As the leading commercial-paper dealer in America, the firm had a clearly deliverable and clearly differentiating product. With commercial paper, it could raise working capital for a major corporation at significantly lower interest rates than the British banks were charging on commercial loans. As Whitehead explains, "The big breakthrough for commercial-paper business in Europe came when Electricité de France became a major issuer [through Goldman Sachs] in the early 1970s."

Whitehead tried to provide leadership to the fledgling international effort. "I'd go to London two or three times a year," he recalls, "and travel around Europe, committing one full day with each man on our investment banking team, which included Ted Botts, Jean-Charles Charpentier, and Bob Hamburger. Naturally, they made sure that these days were as fully packed and productive as possible. I wasn't just looking for mandates to sell commercial paper. I was always looking for some other things we could sell."

A decade later, Roy Smith was sent to cover Europe while continuing his work in Japan, where Gene Atkinson had become head of the Tokyo office. One week each month for three years, Smith was in London, where the firm had a staff of sixty—mostly securities salespeople—in a building on Queen Victoria Street that also housed a representative office of Chicago's Continental Illinois National Bank.[3] The Bank of England, the principal regulatory authority, insisted that all significant banks and brokers locate inside the City of London financial district and thus within easy walking distance, but the firm was not considered important enough to be required to get space within the Square Mile.

With exchange controls—until Margaret Thatcher abolished them in 1979—British investors were particularly cautious about investing in American stocks, and trading volume was low. Indeed, investors had four levels of uncertainty when they purchased American stocks:

- How would the company do as a business?
- How would the stock price do on the NYSE?
- How would the dollar-pound exchange rate change? There had been some devaluation. And . . .
- How would the "dollar premium" change? Because British subjects and institutions could not convert pounds into dollars and so had to buy dollars to invest from other Britons, dollars were sold in London at a premium that fluctuated around 30 percent and was subject to sudden and significant change.

These multiple uncertainties greatly limited American-share activity and Goldman Sachs business in London, as did the prospect of exchange controls being abolished and the 30 percent premium being eliminated. The firm's small brokerage business was unimportant to London and unimportant to Goldman Sachs. It had also been doing a minor export business in investment banking, helping British companies buy American companies, and, in its work as "seller rep," finding British buyers for U.S. companies that wanted to sell. The firm also sold some commercial paper, a few private debt placements, and the occasional U.S. tranche of an international securities syndication, but it was primarily a broker of American stocks to British institutional investors. All trading was still done in New York so it could be controlled and processed by New York's back office. Middle Eastern brokerage accounts were also covered out of London. Smith's mission was to build up these businesses and to see if the firm could develop some indigenous investment banking business in the UK and on the Continent. Eurobonds were one possibility, but bidding by competitors was so aggressive that, as Smith explains, "winning these mandates could also be an easy way to lose a lot of money." In late summer of 1982, Goldman Sachs acquired the London merchant-banking arm of a U.S. bank to help in financing J. Aron's global commodities business and renamed it Goldman Sachs Ltd.[4]

In the early 1980s, international business represented 20 percent or more of the firm's bond and M&A businesses and a bit less than 20 percent in stockbrokerage, but still only 10 percent of the firm's total revenues—and it was losing money. But by the late 1980s, International would contribute 20 percent of the firm's profits. Transforming Goldman Sachs into an international powerhouse would require great changes in both substance and perception inside the firm and among thousands of clients and nonclients. From 1921 to 1984, Lone Star Gas had used only two firms for its many transactions: Goldman Sachs and Salomon Brothers. Lone Star was the ultimate "loyal client." Sanford Singer, the CFO, really liked Goldman Sachs and Salomon Brothers, and he knew the firm was doing great work for him in America, but when he had a small piece of business to be done in Europe, he never even thought of calling Goldman Sachs. "Here was our most loyal client simply *assuming* we had no capabilities and no interest in things international," says Smith. "Obviously, if our *best* clients won't call us, we must be very vulnerable with all our other clients."

Thinking back on the disruptions of May Day, which ended fixed U.S. brokerage commissions in 1975, Smith said, "If we'd known what lay ahead for the stockbrokerage business, with its drastic collapse in commission rates, we would have been very tempted to close up shop. Fortunately, we had the leadership of Gus Levy, who was unafraid, as was John Whitehead. 'You can do *anything*,' they said—and they meant it. 'Go out and call! We have the capital and we have the people.'" So in the eighties, while competitors softened and slowed down their international efforts, Goldman Sachs toughened up and accelerated.

B ill Landreth noticed a line on the list of occupants of offices in a large London building that read, "Football." A bit homesick and an athlete, he hoped it might have something to do with the American football he knew, but soon realized it was really about soccer, the game the British call football. Then he noticed another name: Kuwait Investment Office. He certainly knew what investing was and had some free time, so he decided to check it out. Getting off the lift at the appropriate floor, he asked the receptionist with whom he might speak about investing in stocks and was told to talk to a Mr. Buchan. David Buchan came out, they talked, and they almost immediately hit it off, starting an important new client relationship.

Salomon Brothers, which had hired the son of a senior KIO official, was already doing substantial business with KIO, the Kuwait government's investing arm. So was Merrill Lynch. But the Goldman Sachs relationship developed quite rapidly, and soon Buchan was sharing his investment objectives with Landreth. Kuwait wanted to invest for safety and liquidity in the U.S. market. Its plan was to buy shares in a diverse group of American corporations. The total investment would be substantial. "Would Goldman Sachs be interested in helping to get this done—very quietly?"

"Sure."

"Since the SEC requires reporting any ownership position as large as 5 percent, there will be a limit on how much we can buy," cautioned Buchan. Buying almost 5 percent of a long list of major companies' stocks was certain to be very big business for the executing brokers. Even as extraordinarily low-key a man as Bill Landreth must have been working hard to maintain calm as the biggest account he'd ever heard of was steadily moving toward being *his* account. Landreth managed to say almost matter-of-factly: "That's okay."

Very discreetly, Kuwait would soon place the largest orders ever: Buy a major position in each of America's fifty largest corporations.

Stockbroking in London was still a small business but was beginning to show promise. The firm was concentrating on selling British securities to British institutions in the morning and then, when the New York Stock Exchange was open, selling them American securities all afternoon. "We were ballsy, and nobody in New York was checking us out," recalls Smith. "All my international days were frontier days—before the sidewalks were laid down." To get a private placement done for a Danish company, even though the issue wasn't fully taken up when the closing date came, the unsold balance was positioned—bought and temporarily held—by the London office, something the firm would never do in New York. Smith recalls, "We made our first million-dollar loss on a trade we did for Imperial Chemical Industries—after snatching it away from S. G. Warburg. They thought we'd made a profit on ICI and wouldn't talk to us for a week."

After exchange controls were removed in 1979, demand mushroomed for American securities, particularly those of technology and pharmaceutical companies. Talk of the European Union and a single multinational currency were in the air. Prosperity was quite clearly returning to Europe and promising opportunity. Sales volume in securities had been going up, thanks to the leadership of security sales manager Bill Landreth.

Given these positive changes, increasing numbers of partners were becoming interested in capitalizing on John Whitehead's international vision and making a major commitment to expansion in Europe—and even Asia. Not every division head was in favor of this commitment, and some were strongly opposed—the opportunities available to Goldman Sachs in Europe looked small, and the costs that would have to be absorbed by the firm were surely large. Even more important, opportunities in the United States were large and obvious, and incremental business fell directly to the bottom line as pure profits that the partners could take home. The argument illustrated the conventional problems of partnerships making long-term strategic decisions: Consensus is needed, and each partner frames the issue in terms of his own particular business and experience. These conflicts are compounded by the economic reality that while a particular commitment might achieve substantial, long-term benefits and profits for a *future* group of partners, it would impose large and certain potential short-term costs and difficulties on the *present* partners, who will be making the decision on whether or not to absorb the costs and make the investment. It is a testament to the strength of the Two Johns' leadership and their long-term vision that the large investment in International was made and sustained over many years.

As a trader who always had to worry about the very short term, Bob Mnuchin might have been expected to resist a large long-term strategic investment, but he was strongly in favor of the commitment to building the firm's international business. "We know capital markets and trading in ways the Asians and Europeans may never know. They don't understood how to use capital in trading. It takes years to learn block trading—and they may never figure out how to do it properly." As so often before, Menschel and Mnuchin did not agree.

Richard Menschel was skeptical of a major international expansion. "We have great opportunities right here in America. We know how to win this game; we know we have the people who can do it; and we know we can make lots of money—*now*." Menschel was not alone. Many partners took a similar view: Making a big push to go international would be a waste of time and a waste of opportunity to make money. "We can make much more profit by building up our already strong domestic business," ran their arguments. "This is no time to pull our best young lions and tigers—who are rapidly building up the business they generate right where they are—off the line in big markets to redeploy them into markets like London and Paris, which may have famous names but are really very small business opportunities and even smaller profit opportunities. If Europe or Asia-Japan really is a major long-term business opportunity, we can go after it in five years or even ten years. It will still be there. Let competitors bash their heads against the walls of regulation, different cultures and languages, entrenched nationalistic relationships, anti-Americanism, and all that stuff while we build up our profits and our capital and our organization in our huge home market, the biggest, best market in the whole world—and with five more years of doing what we know we can do, we'll own the essential market, our market. Let's not risk losing this once-in-a-lifetime opportunity when, by just waiting, we'll soon be able to launch an international expansion from a position of great strength. We'll be unbeatable."

Change could create opportunity for Goldman Sachs internationally if the firm could find the right point of entry. So acquiring a strong local firm was an obvious possibility. Wood Mackenzie, one of London's leading brokerage firms, had been doing stockbrokerage business for Goldman Sachs. Because it made every effort to give excellent service, that business had grown until Wood Mackenzie was doing virtually all of Goldman Sachs's agency brokerage and all the trading for partner Bob Freeman's international arbitrage business—making Goldman Sachs its twelfth-largest account. At a luncheon to get to know Goldman Sachs's branch manager, Bob Wilson, John Chiene of "Wood Mac" explained, "We have no U.S.-share business to send your way, so we can't reciprocate directly, but there must be other ways we can be helpful." Wilson knew that Freeman wanted badly to meet with a key European Union regulatory official in Brussels who was proving completely unavailable, so he asked Chiene for advice on whether it would be possible to arrange such a meeting.

"Whom do you wish to see?" asked Chiene.

"Christopher Tugendhat. We can't seem to get through at all."

"I'll see what we can do and will call you back. When would you most like to meet if it can be arranged?"

No need to tell Freeman that he had known Tugendhat for years, had retained him as a consultant to Wood Mac, and, out of friendship, had been one of his initial financial backers when he wanted to run for a seat in Parliament. Tugendhat took Chiene's call, of course, and said he would be delighted to meet at any time on any day. In less than ten minutes, the inaccessible and essential official had an appointment with Freeman at just the right time, and Chiene had made a vital point: Wood Mac was good at getting things done.

The partners of both Goldman Sachs and Wood Mackenzie were beginning to think of a possible combination. The conclusion of Wood Mackenzie's annual partners' business-planning weekend was that the future would bring transatlantic ownership of securities firms. But by whom? Not knowing the answer, Chiene went across to New York and called on every major firm. After meeting Dick Menschel and others, Chiene concluded, "It's a no-brainer. Goldman Sachs is clearly number one." After Britain's Big Bang in 1986 brought deregulation and

substantially opened up the firms of London—previously closed by law to outside ownership—Goldman Sachs was interested in acquiring a 14.9 percent stake
in Wood Mac, the largest amount then allowable, so a full day of discussions and
a dinner were arranged in New York City. Chiene prepared a thirty-page "tell
all" memo on Wood Mackenzie, and discussions during the day were so candid
and forthcoming that Dick Menschel said, "We've told you more about our firm's
operations and profitability than we've ever told anyone else." The discussions
went smoothly; goodwill was steadily increasing on both sides. After a short
break, the discussions were to be picked up again during dinner.

The purchase price—set at $350 million—was too much for Goldman
Sachs's management committee to pay for a strictly agency broker in the UK, but
if American-style block trading could be added, perhaps a deal could be struck.
Bob Mnuchin would be critical to any major move based on the potential profitability of block trading, because that was clearly his business.

As the fifteen Wood Mackenzie partners and their counterparts from Goldman Sachs sat down for dinner, the day's open cordiality was displaced. The
evening's discussion was dominated by Mnuchin's increasingly aggressive questioning about how Wood Mac was organized for trading, particularly block trading. As Mnuchin's manner became more and more belligerent, Mnuchin's partners
recognized alcohol as the probable cause, but the Scottish visitors didn't realize
what was going on. While Chiene and others tried to clarify politely that in London, a firm was either an agency broker *or* a market maker and could not be both,
Mnuchin didn't get it and persisted in pressing his tougher and tougher questions
in an increasingly argumentative way. The meeting rapidly deteriorated until it
could continue no longer. As the evening broke up, Mnuchin and Chiene took a
cab uptown together. As Chiene observed years later, "It was a *long* cab ride."

The next morning, Chiene got a call from a Goldman Sachs partner: "We're
told Bob really bombed last night's meeting."

"Yes, he did."

The discussions were over—forever—and another way would have to be
found to build a significant business in London and Europe.[5] As Steel later explained:
"You could argue that the buildup would have been faster with an acquisition, but
most of such combinations have proved to be costly disappointments—usually
within just a few years' time."[6] Big Bang in 1986 not only allowed agency brokers

to combine with market-making dealers, gilt (British Treasury bond) dealers, and merchant banks, it allowed foreign banks and firms to buy into British firms. In a flurry of activity, over twenty combinations were effected in just two years. Almost all were soon failures.

After substantial debate and disagreement, the strongest leaders prevailed— particularly John Weinberg and Jim Gorter, head of the Chicago regional office and one of the real powers in the firm. The decision was made in late 1986 to build, not buy, and to build as quickly as possible. As David Silfen recalls, "We could see the first indications of major change developing in Europe—change that was coming our way. So we made the decision to pull some of our very best young people out of their positions in Chicago, Los Angeles, and New York, and send them over, saying, 'You have two responsibilities. First, figure out how to build a significant and sustainable business over there and build it! Second, find your successor—somebody with a local passport—and show him or her how to be very successful. After that, you can come back home.'" For those who were successful, the promise of a partnership didn't need to be spelled out.

Bob Steel remembers Dick Menschel saying to him, "Some clown will call you and give you a song and dance about going to *London*, for God's sake." The message was clear. "Don't be a fool and don't be a sucker. Going would *not* be good for your career." The next morning Steel got a very different call from Jim Gorter: "Bob, this is probably the most exciting moment in your life and the best day in your career. You have done very well at Goldman Sachs, so now you'll have the chance to go to *London* and show us all how very good you really are." Similar calls went out to all the chosen. Steel went to Terry Mulvihill for advice, ready for his "uncle" to try to keep him in Chicago, but the reaction was completely different: "This is your great opportunity, Bob, so you just get the hell out of here, go to London as fast as you can—and make us all terribly proud of you and what you can do."[7]

Gene Fife, Bob Steel, Jeff Weingarten, and Pat Ward were among the pride of ten young lions who went to join Bill Landreth and John Thornton in London and Henry James in Tokyo to transform those offices from remote overseas outposts into major international centers and to take the profits from marginal to major. The talent infusion comprised some new partners still determined to prove themselves and some almost-partners with at least equal determination, all believing they could certainly do good and maybe great business by selling sophisticated services—services they knew well from experience in America—into European markets where the local bankers and brokers had had no experience with many kinds of transactions. The pan-European market was just developing, so no indigenous firms and no international competitors had entrenched positions.

"In the early years the firm rarely sent over its best people," acknowledges Thornton. "Predictably, in those circumstances, the most outstanding European professionals were not going to join the firm either. Just saying 'We want to be global and excellent' was not enough. Even after the firm started to invest seriously in Europe, most of our best people chose to stay home, focus on U.S. clients, and do familiar transactions with well-established strategies, with assured high-margin revenues and profits. So in Europe, we decided to take the hand we'd been dealt and do the best we could through intensity of focus and effort. Our recruiting and business development had to be done country by country so as to build critical mass in each market. Once you succeed in recruiting one outstanding European, it is easier to get a second and a third and so on. We started in the UK and expanded to France and Germany and then the other major economies."

When Steel arrived in London from Chicago in February 1987, assigned to build a large, profitable stockbrokerage business based on trading and arbitrage, Goldman Sachs was doing only a modest twenty-million-dollar annual business selling American shares to British and Continental institutions in roughly equal proportions—along with a few tired brokers peddling British shares. It was clearly not an important business, but Steel's mandate had been made clear to him: "If you make this business important to the firm, the firm will make you a partner." That was not going to be easy. The British-share business was large in volume, but very low in profit margins, while the American-share business was growing in volume, but margins were shrinking as commissions were negotiated lower and lower. The best hope was to convert a low-profit agency business into a profitable proprietary dealer business with arbitrage primarily in two dozen dual-listed stocks—including BP, ICI, Royal Dutch Shell, and Tokio Marine—that had shares in London and American Depositary Receipts in New York, where an American firm had a comparative advantage.

"We realized that with Big Bang, institutions would soon be dominating the stock market, and their demand for liquidity would increase a lot," recalls partner

Peter Sachs. "This meant block trading would come to London, and this would change the market so much that the whole process of corporate deals would speed up. With Big Bang, bankers, dealers, and brokers would be combining, and markets were sure to move upstairs and require huge capital bases. The London brokers and merchant bankers had little capital, so not only were they unable to defend their home turf, they couldn't attack ours. It was classic Clausewitz! We knew from our U.S. experiences with May Day just what kind of future London was moving into with Big Bang, so we knew we could create a major business. But first we had to become a strong indigenous firm or merchant bank." Though the stockbrokerage business usually ran at or near breakeven on routine business, a skillful and committed trading firm could see most of the trading possibilities, so it could pick and choose the best opportunities for profitable trading. On top of this base business, any underwriting business a firm did would bring in almost pure profits. The last thing London's established firms wanted was to share those limited revenues with newcomers and outsiders like Goldman Sachs. "The British firms wasted no love on Americans trying to muscle in on their business," remembers Steel, "particularly since it really wasn't a very big business. Offices were shabby, trading was all agency business, and there was too little business to share—and yet, there we were!"

Steel decided to reconnoiter the situation by calling on major clients to see how the firm was perceived and how it could increase its business. "I went over to King William Street to see Mercury Asset Management, by far the largest account in London and in all of Europe, to see what our strategy ought to be and how we could build on the base of our U.S.-share business, where we knew we were getting ten percent to twelve percent of their brokerage business." The first thing Steel learned was that Mercury's U.S.-share business was just a tiny fraction of its total brokerage-commission volume. While Goldman Sachs had an okay competitive position in American shares, that business was really unimportant to Mercury—and, as just an American-share broker, Goldman Sachs was unimportant too. The fact that Goldman Sachs was doing pretty well as a broker in U.S. shares did not matter one iota to the people at Mercury who were doing the really big business in British shares, Japanese shares, German, Dutch, French, or Italian shares. Finally, every investment group—domestic British or Japanese or Continental—was on a separate floor of Mercury's building; every group made investment decisions and allocated brokerage commissions in its own particular way. To be important *overall* to this very important account, Goldman Sachs would have to build relationships on each and every floor—almost always starting near zero and competing against formidable, established competition.

"So that's what we set out to do," says Steel. "I went to the management committee and said we should hire two and a half *times* as many people as we had. The management committee said 'Go!' and we hired twelve people that first year. We hired people with talent, drive, and skill—thirty- to thirty-five-year-olds who knew their business and were ambitious—by offering them the chance to work with the big accounts they would have had to wait ten or twenty years to take over at their old firms. We had zero turnover in our people, while other firms suffered twenty percent to thirty percent turnover. And we added three percent to six percent through new hires each year—all MBAs—and focused on the discipline of going for dollars. In the recruiting interviews, we learned a lot about how the City really worked and how the game was really played. For example, we learned that senior people of [the patrician London brokerage firm] Cazenove would give research insights first to favored clients who were insiders in the old-boy network, so they could get invested ahead of the other institutional investors. We didn't think that was an ethical way to do business."

Fortunately for Goldman Sachs and the other American invaders, the established British firms made serious strategic mistakes. Some joined with commercial banks to get capital, but along with the capital they got stultifying commercial-bank management and commercial bankers' concepts of compensation and risk taking, which soon smothered the acquired brokerage units. Some brokerage firms combined with other brokers to get scale but did not get the capital they would soon need for market making. S.G. Warburg, then Britain's strongest merchant bank, dispersed its once-formidable strengths with an unfortunate acquisition strategy of buying up one of the two or three leading brokerage firms in each country on the Continent. That strategy would doom the once-great firm to a business model with a high cost structure but only mediocre revenues, and to strategic sclerosis, with proud local executives, experienced in their own national markets, holding on to their familiar strategies and their own senior management positions while trying to protect their local people from the disruptive impact of the drastic changes that were required for an integrated firm to become cost-effective.

Cost-effectiveness was clearly the strategic imperative as the business went from closed and protected national markets to open markets with intense international competition steadily eroding the commission-pricing structure. Most Continental stockbrokers tried to combine with brokers of other countries, which made them, like S.G. Warburg, high-cost, rigid-structure outfits. This unfortunate strategy made it almost easy for the Americans—particularly Goldman Sachs, Morgan Stanley, and Merrill Lynch—to break through with aggressive speed and flexibility. While S.G. Warburg bought the firms of the past and imprisoned itself in an inflexible, balkanized, high-cost organizational structure, Goldman Sachs began recruiting one by one the best individuals for the future while keeping costs under control and maintaining flexibility. Equally important, Goldman Sachs appreciated the inevitable direction and formidable magnitude of change that lay ahead for every firm, having just experienced the same revolutionary market transformation to institutional dominance in America.

The most important objective, particularly in investment research, would be to shift the firm from being perceived as the risky, here-today-gone-tomorrow American firm that nobody who was really any good would feel safe in joining to the powerful, here-to-stay global leader that understood the future and knew how to succeed in the new era. To establish unusual, visible strength in research, a few key hires were essential. At this juncture, the firm got lucky because, as always, chance favors the prepared mind.

After growing up in Rhodesia, reading economics at Oxford, and completing his doctorate at Cambridge, Gavyn Davies went to No. 10 Downing Street with the Labour government of James Callaghan. He then joined Phillips & Drew, a well-regarded research and investment firm where he worked with David Morrison for a few years before they went together to Simon & Coates. "With the looming prospect of Big Bang, we felt it necessary to upgrade our employer," says Davies. "We decided in 1985 to investigate the Wall Street firms and thought Morgan Stanley or Goldman Sachs would be right, but we didn't actually know anyone. We knew that Goldman Sachs had no international economist, so I called Lee Cooperman in New York and he passed me on to Gary Wenglowski, who was the firm's chief economist."

Wenglowski was brusque: "Never heard of you. Why do you want to work for Goldman Sachs?"

"We've identified you as a firm that can *win*."

"Well, I've no idea who you are or what you can do, so I can't give you any encouragement." And that was effectively the end of that.

A year later, Goldman Sachs was expanding in fixed-income dealing in a series of markets straight across Europe—gilts in the UK, Bunds in Germany, and others. As an ambitious but novice bond dealer in Europe, the firm needed an economist to cover these new markets. "They did a search," recalls Davies, "and found . . . David Morrison and me."

"Why should we go there now?" asked Morrison cautiously. "They didn't hire us when we offered ourselves to them a year ago."

But a year had passed, and they could now credit Goldman Sachs with being committed to developing strength in research and having some basic knowledge of the major economies of Europe. Davies was increasingly confident that Goldman Sachs was a winning firm and that he and Morrison could be winners within Goldman Sachs, a double multiplier. They became the European economics team at Goldman Sachs and then expanded their international coverage to include Japan and Asia while Bob Giordano built up the U.S. economics operation, which Davies and Morrison then integrated into a whole—not as U.S. economics with an international adjunct, but as international economics *including* the United States. Their timing was perfect.

The markets, particularly the currency markets and the debt capital markets, were being integrated worldwide, and institutional investors were expanding their international commitments. So everyone was suddenly looking for a global-economics context for decisions, and the traders at Goldman Sachs were looking for helpful guidance on where to avoid troubles and where to look for profit opportunities. Recalls Davies, "Clients saw Goldman Sachs taking the *world* seriously. The U.S. was the elephant, but that was not the whole story."

Because David Morrison enjoyed the debt markets even more than he enjoyed economic theory, all their work on economics and currencies got integrated into the trading operations of the firm and made serious money for Goldman Sachs. The firm's traders found his help valuable because Morrison had a keen eye for short-term anomalies in the market as well as the long-term political policies of various nations.

Davies concentrated on the central banks and forecasting interest rates and changes in exchange rates. "We did a lot of writing and personal presentations using charts to make things understandable. Institutional investors found all this quite useful to them. We were in the right place with the right information at the right time, and in less than two years we each gained a partnership—partly because the firm knew it needed to have highly visible European partners in order to overcome the rampant local prejudice against flighty, unreliable American outsiders who don't understand our ways and our values." This xenophobic but widely held view of American firms would have to be changed if Goldman Sachs was going to recruit the best and brightest Europeans to combine with the group of young firm leaders sent over to Europe by Gorter, Rubin, and Friedman.

"Next came a major money-spinning success in the currency markets," recalls Davies. "We called two major devaluations. Also, the firm was keen to be a government bond dealer in the UK and Germany, and our work on those two economies was quite helpful." Inside the firm and in the markets, it was soon recognized that Goldman Sachs was serious about being international. "God damn!" said Leon Cooperman. "I never would have believed we'd have a partner who was an international economist—and never *ever* that we'd have two!"

Davies and Morrison started Goldman Sachs's research in each new market by establishing the visibly best economic research product. They were determined to avoid two critical errors: having too short-term a focus on the vagaries of any specific business, and having a single worldview; intellectual competition within the firm was encouraged. A third factor crucial to their success and their credibility with clients was their evident independence. "We were independent of any inappropriate pressure to act on behalf of the House," says Davies. This would be proved by a dramatic confrontation.

Analyzing their data on the French economy and the French franc, Davies and Morrison came to a strong conclusion that the franc was seriously overvalued and sure to be devalued. The finance director of the French central bank, a Monsieur Stan, came to Davies's office one day in 1993 waving Davies's report that

France would probably devalue the franc. "What *is* this report? Do you *dare* to believe what you have written?"

"Yes," said Davies calmly, "I do."

Stan was indignant and left quickly, giving assurances that more would soon be said.

Two days later, Jean-Claude Trichet, Stan's superior, insisted that Steve Friedman come to his office at the Banque de France. He was in a rage. "You are ignorant! You do not know France! You are ignorant! We will *never* devalue!" The whole weight of a major nation's central bank was projected—at the highest level—directly at forcing Friedman to fire Davies. "You are useless and your firm . . . your, your Goldman Sachs . . . will never earn another sou in France unless you fire the person who did this awful thing!"

Having checked out Davies and Morrison with others in the firm, Friedman carefully drew the line in the sand: "Mr. Davies is a fine economist. He has earned the respect of our many clients through the care and rigor of his analyses on currencies. His professional independence is essential to our clients and, therefore, to our firm. So, with all due respect for you and your position, sir, I have no intention of telling him what to say or what to do." In less than ninety days, France devalued the franc.

Davies and Morrison concentrated their analysis of currencies on trying to develop just three or four major opinions a year. For each major opinion, Goldman Sachs was able to create significant, highly leveraged trading positions. About two-thirds of the time, Davies and Morrison were correct. For skillful currency traders, these very favorable odds were an enormous advantage. Big money was made over and over again.

Tim Plaut, S.G. Warburg's stellar auto analyst, understood the strategic realities of the revolution coming to London but could not get his alarming view of the future recognized at his own firm. So, thinking *if you can't beat 'em, join 'em*, he contacted Davies. They discussed the outlook, and Davies lured him into Goldman Sachs as one of the first of a pan-European all-star research team—all located in London—that would be a strong third leg of an integrated multinational research-banking-trading triangle with powerful competitive advantages. With its multinational organization, Goldman Sachs would steadily gain dominance over the country-by-country brokers, particularly at the larger institutions where the best brokerage business was concentrated.

With this "first robin," Jeff Weingarten, who himself had been a celebrated analyst in America, launched a one-by-one recruiting campaign and steadily built a strong research team. His strategy was to probe the major British institutions' analysts in each industry for the names of "promising but still too young" analysts with a strong commitment to client service and unusual drive, offering these comers a chance to move up faster than their current employers would think appropriate. As an "analyst's analyst," he was a convincing recruiter and soon made Goldman Sachs a career-destination firm.

On many occasions in its long, competitive struggle to market leadership, Goldman Sachs made large, sudden advances or ducked large, sudden losses. Sometimes it was by being lucky; sometimes it was by being astute. When David Mayhew, head of Cazenove, wanted a meeting with Goldman Sachs's senior management, Pat Ward took over for Bob Steel, who was in New York for meetings. A South African who had been working out of the Tokyo office, Ward was new to London and had not yet met Mayhew, who was coming to the firm to discuss a bid for a large block of newly issued Daily Telegraph Company stock.

Mayhew arrived at Goldman Sachs's London headquarters at five in the afternoon. To greet his guest, Ward put on his suit jacket, because Cazenove was recognized as the queen's stockbroker and held a special and carefully nurtured prestigious position in the City. Going to Room F, Ward greeted his guest and introduced his trader, Mike Hintze. Mayhew took out a cigarette, lit it, and, in a gesture asserting control, pulled the heavy glass ashtray toward himself so he could reach it more conveniently. Ward detests smoking and doesn't like the residual smell of smoke in his clothes, so he took off his jacket. Mayhew, clearly expecting to dominate the meeting, spoke with assurance: "The decision maker for this transition is in In-dyah. I spoke to him today and told him that with the market at 513p, the right price would likely be 503p."

Hintze, a six-foot-three Aussie trader who specialized in bidding on large blocks of stock, sat looking vaguely at the floor, rolling a ballpoint pen back and forth between his palms, his hands moving faster and faster.

Ward rose, walked behind Mayhew, began stretching gently to ease a pain in his back, and, carefully avoiding formality, spoke: "David, thank you for coming and thank you for your preliminary thoughts." Then turning directly to his Aussie trader, he continued: "Mike, you've heard one opinion. You know that this trade is very large—approximately £180 million—and the trade can only be done, can only be *considered*, because of our firm's large balance sheet. It can't be done without us. So, Mike, *you* will decide the price you will pay—and when you have made your decision for our firm, that decision will be final."

Goldman Sachs bid 493 pence. It took two full days to complete the resale—and then, just twenty-nine days later, the market price plunged, dropping over 40 percent to less than 300 pence because Daily Telegraph, worried about faltering sales, had cut the retail price of its newspaper, which was sure to cut deeply into earnings. As Wellington said of Waterloo, "'Twas a damned near-run thing." And as the Sopranos would mutter: "It's not personal. Just business." Welcome to London.[8]

Important as the stockbrokerage business clearly was for Goldman Sachs, it would be even more important for the firm to develop a strong international business in investment banking—partly for profits and partly for prestige. Many UK corporations were worth more than their current stock market value, so the firm soon focused on becoming defense advisers to companies threatened by takeover raids and at least participating in, if not winning, every deal it could. As the leader in takeover defense in America, Goldman Sachs had special expertise in this compelling new aspect of corporate finance and a favorable reputation as the trustworthy friend of management.

The "dance of death," as John Thornton called it, was the process by which a company with no escape would go inevitably and eventually into *somebody's* hands. "You could influence the outcome and you could often select the eventual acquirer, but you could rarely prevent some sort of takeover from happening. The worst choice was for a management to believe such head-in-the-sand foolishness as: 'Those *idiots*. We'll soon be rid of them!'"

Imperial Group, formerly Imperial Tobacco, bought Howard Johnson in the United States via Goldman Sachs's Bob Hamburger. Then Hanson Trust raided Imperial—and won. Goldman Sachs had been on the raid-defense team, backstopping Imperial's traditional merchant banker, but an acquisition was eventually inevitable. After it was all over and the acquisition was about to be formally implemented, all participants went around to Imperial's offices for a "funeral" luncheon, which lasted almost until the three o'clock moment of official closure on the takeover—after which the Imperial executives were sure to be tossed out of their jobs. Conversation turned to what each man would do next. One said he was off to India; one was going to tramp Hadrian's Wall for two weeks. The pair from Goldman Sachs, sitting at the lower end of the table, said they had to leave for a four o'clock appointment at Woolworths, which had hired Goldman Sachs the day before to defend it against a raid by Dixons, the electronics retailer. Goldman Sachs was focused on the next business transaction.

Intensity of commitment and very long hours differentiated Goldman Sachs. An American got into a London cab at the Savoy Hotel at seven one morning and gave his destination to the driver, who turned and asked another cabbie: "This gentleman's going to the City. Can you guess which address?" The answer seemed obvious to both: Goldman Sachs—for breakfast.

The CFO of Vickers told a partner, "If a British merchant banker were up all night working to complete a transaction, he would never tell anyone for fear he would look inadequately skillful. But if an American pulled an all-nighter, he would make certain to tell me—as proof of his commitment."

From the beginning," Thornton recalls, "we decided to focus on two groups of potential clients: the leading blue-chip companies which we knew would take a long time to win over and companies which were in difficulty and were, therefore, more likely to be open to fresh thinking and new advisers. We believed that we needed to advise one consequential person or company in one significant transaction, and then a second and a third, until one day we would have a compelling record of distinctive advice and impressive results. In 1986, after three years of quietly building the business—almost invisibly—exactly this began to happen. That year we defended four of the five first ever one-billion-pound hostile takeovers and were successful in keeping three of the target companies independent."

Thornton explains: "In a situation like this, at the very beginning, you, as an individual, *are* the 'brand.' You have nothing to carry you and nothing to fall back on. Going from an initial meeting and general discussion to specific, nuanced advice that is listened to and accepted is a transformation that's completely dependent on you—what you say and do, how you develop each relationship, how you build up the prospect's confidence—not just in your *firm*, not just in your *advice*, but in *you*. And that confidence has to be strong enough to prevail against the tide of general opinion and natural resistance to change, which is particularly strong in major financial transactions. The typical CEO is sixty, and I was twenty-eight—a kid! How could I persuade the CEO to trust me and decide to rely on me? The answer seemed obvious: Be distinctive so you can't be replicated by others. And in doing so build the necessary personal trust and confidence. Eventually, of course, this would translate into respecting and trusting the firm—but it takes a long time."

Another obvious answer was to get help from New York. Peter Sachs, grandson of Harry Sachs, brother of Marcus Goldman's first partner, was assigned to provide senior coverage with Thornton in leading a sea change in London. Sachs recalls: "We went to school on the UK market to learn the business drivers. Press coverage was crucial. Our PR adviser was very helpful to us—and we to him because we brought him in on many deals. The Sunday papers were key to our whole public relations program. We were also the best clients of the law firms that worked with us, and they naturally told their clients how they saw us, our commitment, and our capabilities. Using lawyers, we had both the legal and financial sides covered. With our repeating big fees, we soon became the lawyers' best friends. Our question for lawyers was always the same: not *can* we do this deal, but *how* can we do this deal? We used a lot of lawyers—and taught the British merchant banks to do the same. We brought the 'indemnification letter' to London, whereby the corporation pledges, if a deal fails, to cover Goldman Sachs's costs and losses—unless we were terminated for negligence. For five months, I flew to London every Sunday, came back Thursday night to spend the day in the office on Friday and a Saturday with my family, and then back on the plane on Sunday, headed to London."

Personal commitments such as Peter Sachs's were, like the first few robins of spring, an early indication of the commitment of American firms like Goldman Sachs—where the London organization went from 120 people to 880 in just four years. Such commitment would bring major, disruptive change in the London market and make the rapid rise of Goldman Sachs inevitable.

20

~

BREAKING AND
ENTERING

Eric Dobkin's big break came in 1984, but at first he certainly didn't recognize it when Jim Gorter, as co-head of investment banking, called. "We just had the first meeting of the investment banking strategic planning group and, Eric, here's what we found: Goldman Sachs ranks first in institutional research, first in institutional sales, first in block trading—all the important *parts*—but when you put it all together in equity league tables showing where firms rank in common-stock underwriting, Goldman Sachs ranks . . . only . . . ninth! Eric, *we* have a problem and *you* have an opportunity. Go figure out how to fix it! In equity underwriting, with all our strengths, Goldman Sachs should rank *first!*" Gorter gave Dobkin one key advantage: freedom to pick his own team.

After Gorter hung up, Dobkin, forty-two, was worried, really worried. "I had *no* idea what to do," he recalls. "The next day I had no idea what to do. And the *next* day I had no idea what to do *and* I'm starting to lose sleep. Finally, on the fourth day, I'm standing in the shower when I have an 'aha!' and realize what we have to do: Turn the whole syndicate business on its head."

For decades, the underwriting business had been organized around the traditional critical need: to get *distribution* for the new issue when a corporation needed to raise capital. Retail brokers had the accounts with individual investors, so syndicates of retail brokerage firms were organized to gain access to the many thousands of individual investors that were, realistically, unknown to the major underwriters who originated issues; as wholesalers, the underwriters traditionally focused on their clients, the corporate issuers. This system worked when the business was dominated by retail investors—but by the early eighties, the securities business was dominated by institutions. For an institutional market with professional investors making all the decisions, the old syndicate business was completely obsolete. It added little value because it required no understanding of each investor's portfolio strategy, how he made investment decisions, why he might or might not buy a particular offering, and the role his research analysts played. Old-line underwriters had no understanding of the new world of institutional marketing and distribution and didn't know how to craft a strong sales pitch or organize an effective road show for audiences of experienced, professionally skeptical institutional investors. "They didn't even know enough to rehearse their presentations," marvels Dobkin in retrospect.

In his shower-stall epiphany, Dobkin realized almost immediately how Goldman Sachs could easily outflank such out-of-date, out-of-touch, ossified competition: "All we had to do was take the skills and strategies we'd developed while serving institutions in the *secondary* market and apply them to doing business in the *primary* market. We'd need salesmen who could really sell the fact that Goldman Sachs has the best institutional relationships *and* the best access to the best institutional shareholders *and* that we know how to merchandise interesting investment ideas to the most attractive institutions."

Establishment firms all have the same priority: Protect their old business— the business senior executives know best and are best at doing. Often, that's also the business with the highest-profit history, cloaked in the folklore of the organization. But business models don't work forever. As clients change and clients' needs change, any intermediary needs to change. A once-great business model can become a dangerous sacred cow when it gets old and tired and profits start fading. Yet change is difficult. Hardly anyone wants to wrench away from the traditional, comfortable way of doing business simply because the traditional way is not fulfilling client needs or preferences.

Wall Street's traditional underwriting syndicates were elaborate expressions of just such legacy issues. The rules that governed syndicate participation were more like those of a fraternity than those of a hard-nosed, pay-for-performance business. The major underwriting firms cared deeply about maintaining their "traditional" positions in each company's underwritings. Because the leading investment banking firms that originated the corporate stock and bond offerings did not have retail distribution, they needed the "wirehouse" retail stockbrokers for distribution, so the wirehouses were powerful—powerful resisters of change.

With retail brokers talking only to individual investors and underwriters talking only to corporate issuers, nobody was organized to serve *both* sides. So Goldman Sachs positioned itself right in the middle of the action. The major changes on the buy side that came with the strong growth of institutional investing created a vacuum. Institutional investors wanted new services that met *their* needs, which were quite different from individual investors' needs and were not being met by retail brokers. Institutions didn't want to buy a hundred shares, they wanted *a hundred thousand* shares. Institutions didn't want the one-page reports used by retail customers, they wanted twenty- to fifty-page analyses produced by industry experts who really knew the companies and could give well-documented advice on which were the better investments and why. The stock market was moving away from retail toward institutional investors, and a local retail brokerage office in, say, St. Louis or Indianapolis couldn't possibly meet the service requirements of institutional investors—in-depth company and industry research, large block transactions, direct access to corporate management.

Goldman Sachs organized itself to sell very large amounts of stock in an underwriting by developing a rigorous sales and marketing plan for each transaction before the underwriting came to market. If Federated Department Stores was the issuing company, then Goldman Sachs's retail-industry analyst, Joe Ellis, would go out and visit with the major institutions: one day in Los Angeles, one day in San Francisco, one in Minneapolis (mostly at Investors Diversified Services), two days in Chicago, three days in Boston, three or four in New York City, and one in Philadelphia. At each institution, Ellis would review the retailing industry with the institution's retail analyst and one or more portfolio managers; define Federated's competitive position, its strategy and its prospects; cite the key data for the current year; explain the prospects; and answer any and all questions.

The salesman who went with Ellis to make all the appropriate introductions would focus on gauging the depth and degree of interest, sizing up potential demand, and planning the best way to get a major order from each institution.

"If we had the time, we did all the same work when the firm had a big block of stock to sell," explains Dobkin. "So none of this was new to us—or to the accounts. First, we had to recognize that in an institutional market the biggest difference was the number of zeros—and the amount of time we would have to organize and execute effectively. Order size was larger, time to execute was shorter. Plus, in the equity capital markets business, we were working in the primary market, so unlike with everyday new issues, we now had [the issuers'] corporate management on our side, actively working with us, and we seldom had to risk our own capital. Our equity capital markets underwriting business was similar to the old system in only one way: We had an SEC prospectus. Because those were the SEC's rules, we did not issue a *written* research report during the selling period. But we did send our 'rainmaker' analysts around the circuit to lay the groundwork for the actual offering. Besides, just because there was no formal written research report, that didn't mean our salesmen couldn't recite the key facts and tell the story as our industry analyst saw it. At the same time, the firm would identify the probable major buyers, work with corporate management to craft the right story, and set the right price."

The firm could custom-tailor selling to the institutional market—institution by institution—because Goldman Sachs knew from all its day-to-day work with the institutions what each institution wanted and how it made its investment decisions. Dobkin and his team would sit down with the key corporate executives and say, "Here's the right way to merchandise your company's stock to each of the specific institutions we know you really want as investors," and then demonstrate that they knew the institutional market at every level—portfolio managers, analysts, and traders—and knew how to employ Goldman Sachs's investment research and how to deal in blocks. Dobkin recalls: "The corporate executives found it all quite fascinating, and this gave us an edge. We also showed the corporate executives that we were real people—not stuffy, pompous investment bankers like those from other firms who didn't really know either the corporation or the institutions. We put a wedge in between the issuers and old-line underwriting houses like Kuhn Loeb, Lehman Brothers, and Dillon Read because we knew the institutions inside out—and they really didn't. Then we put another wedge versus the retail stockbrokerage firms because the corporations believed that with increasing ownership among high-quality institutional investors, their stock's price-earnings ratio went up—because we were creating demand for their shares through good marketing."

The old way of underwriting was basically adversarial—and one-sided at that, because the underwriting syndicate always lined up with the corporate client issuing the stock and then pushed the shares through the retail system to individual investors. But Dobkin said, "Wait! We do this kind of selling to these institutions every day. It's not a 'once in a great while' special event." He showed anyone who would listen how his new approach could be made a win-win, with the corporate issuers and the institutional buyers *both* benefiting by working together and developing a shared understanding. "Fair pricing was mandatory, and that was fully understood by both sides. Both the corporations and the institutions got engaged. *That* was the secret sauce!"

With this reconceptualization of the underwriting business and its intensive implementation, Goldman Sachs quickly became a major participant in more underwritings, increased its share of each underwriting, and even ran several major underwritings as the sole distributor. "Profits multiplied," notes Dobkin. From 1985 on, Goldman Sachs was number one in the equity underwriting league tables—except for one year. "As my grandmother always said, 'It's not a perfect world.'"

Developing the equity capital markets business in America was a triumph, but since at Goldman Sachs no good deed goes unpunished, Dobkin had to re-create his stateside success in Europe, starting in the United Kingdom. In the early 1980s, as Margaret Thatcher launched her Conservative revolution to privatize British industry and make voters owners, Kleinwort Benson quickly established itself as Her Majesty's Government's leading merchant banker by winning the bids to arrange the stock-market flotations of British Aerospace, British Telecom, and British Gas. Unfortunately for Kleinwort Benson, its triumph in winning the mandates as adviser to the government and lead underwriter was a classic Pyrrhic victory, one it really could not afford to win. Those mandates required so much senior-level time to execute that while Kleinwort Benson got the prestige and the gross volume, they tied up its organization so much that it could not compete for important and much more lucrative corporate mergers and underwritings. As a result, Kleinwort Benson worked exceedingly hard for little profit during a challenging era of turbulent change in the City of London when every merchant bank needed extra profits to retain or recruit talented bankers to protect its traditional corporate clientele. Preoccupied with early privatizations like British Telecom, Kleinwort Benson found itself unable to fend off recruitment of its best young professionals—particularly by the more aggressive and profit-focused American firms like Goldman Sachs.

HM Government, while naturally preferring a British firm, took the broader view that American firms might offer particular comparative advantages in fresh ideas and new techniques—crafting a convincing story, rehearsing the presentation to perfection, knowing how to organize and run a road show—that could change the basis on which the enormous privatizations were done. Sir Steve Robson at HM Government and Sir John Guinness, the senior civil servant at the Department of Energy, were personally interested in opening up, if not breaking up, the close-knit oligopoly of the British firms in the City. Without considering other firms, HM Government turned to Morgan Stanley, the British government's traditional North American banker since the days of J.P. Morgan. This so infuriated Eric Dobkin at Goldman Sachs that he resolved to engage, swiftly and vigorously, with each and every senior HM Government official he could identify.

Then Goldman Sachs got lucky—very lucky—and Morgan Stanley could not have been more helpful to Goldman Sachs. British Telecom's privatization got badly screwed up—starting with the Morgan Stanley syndicate head's arrogantly telling the British government that Morgan Stanley absolutely would *not* accept the United Kingdom's traditional two-week exposure to underwriting risks. In the UK, most stock offerings were done by well-established corporations whose shares had long been listed on the London Stock Exchange. Underwritings of common stock—usually 10 percent to 20 percent increases in total shares—were done as rights offerings, with most of the shares taken up by institutional investors that were included in the offering syndicate as subunderwriters when they agreed to take an agreed amount of stock at an agreed price. In addition, the underwriting syndicate's offering price was fixed on "impact day" and then held for two weeks to provide enough time for individual retail investors to read the full-page newspaper ads offering the shares, clip the order form at the bottom of the page, and mail in their purchase orders. In the usual UK rights offering, this leisurely and gentlemanly way of raising moderate increments of equity capital had been satisfactory for both issuers and investors, but Margaret Thatcher's enormous privatizations were different—radically different in scale and in structure.

In scale, privatizations were huge—many times larger than the traditional, incremental rights offerings—and were initial public offerings in a market with few IPOs. As IPOs they had no price history and no established group of share-holders. This meant that the risk involved in underwriting—and holding to one fixed price for two long weeks—was much greater than the risk in an American-style underwriting, where the whole transaction, after several weeks or days of informal prearrangement, is formally completed in a few minutes or seconds. So Morgan Stanley balked and the Bank of England agreed to take 100 percent of the market risk by underwriting the U.S. placement and thereby guaranteeing Morgan Stanley against loss.

Then everything went wrong. The UK underwriters badly misjudged both the pricing of the offering and the aftermarket demand for British Telecom shares. Investor demand from both institutions and individuals was *very* strong. A particularly insistent demand for shares came from the large index funds because the *Financial Times* had decided to include British Telecom in its widely used "FTSE" stock-exchange index, known as Footsie, on the day of the offering. Every index fund felt compelled to buy British Telecom. However, the index weighting of British Telecom was calculated as if 100 percent of British Telecom shares were publicly owned, while the initial offering was only for 25 percent of British Telecom shares. As a result, supply was far too limited to meet the index funds' requirement, so the stock was bid up in price an astounding 100 percent on the first day.

That was bad underwriting in the UK, and the impact in the United States was worse. Despite the British government's policy priority of establishing a broad retail investor base, Morgan Stanley sold most of its part of the offering to a few favored institutional clients that quickly sold the stock to take their quick profits. All the stock that was supposed to be held by long-term investors in North America got on the supersonic Concorde and flew straight back to London even before the ink could dry to meet the demands of the index funds. The reflow was terrible. None of British Telecom was still held in the United States! It was a disaster. Morgan Stanley got blamed in the press. This made it politically difficult for HM Government to select Morgan Stanley for the next big privatization.

That's when Dobkin, seeing his major competitor blocked so he had an open field to run in, began commuting to London every week, sometimes taking the morning Concorde over and the next Concorde back and sometimes staying several nights in London. His focus: Win for Goldman Sachs the mandate as lead underwriter for the next privatization. British Gas would be the largest IPO in the world; all institutional investors would be keenly interested; the competition to be North American lead manager would be intense; the manager would be selected strictly "on the merits"; and Morgan Stanley, the British government's traditional underwriter, was almost certainly out of the running with its handling of BT. Dobkin was playing to win on a grand scale.

"Intensity was Eric's middle name," says Bob Steel. "He called me to say we would meet Sunday at noon at the Dorchester. So off I went, telling my wife I should be back in less than two hours. Not even close: We went—intensively— that Sunday from noon until midnight. One morning, I got a call from Eric at three a.m. Struggling awake, I couldn't help asking: 'Eric, do you know what *time* it is in London?'"

"Of course I do," came the reply. "I'm here too."

Tony Ault of N.M. Rothschild & Sons, a tall, lanky chain-smoker, was appointed as HM Government's adviser for the privatization of British Gas. Dobkin was glad to have Ault playing this key role, partly because he had made his own way in life and was bright and direct, but particularly because he very clearly, like Dobkin and Dobkin's colleagues back at Goldman Sachs, had *not* gone to Eton. Ault would not be influenced by old school ties; he had made his own way. "Tell me what you're thinking about," began Ault. Dobkin, aggressive as usual, moved in quickly. "Cut the crap, Tony. Tell me what we need to do to win British Gas."

"Will Goldman Sachs accept the traditional UK underwriting risk?"

"Yes."

"Will you put that in writing?"

"You bet."

354 · THE PARTNERSHIP

"You'll need to be prepared to put that commitment in writing."

Once again, Dobkin was out on a limb, committing the firm. Now, he had to get Bob Mnuchin's okay right away. Since Mnuchin had no way of knowing that Dobkin's call was urgent, it took three calls to get through to the Coach. Mnuchin had one question: "Will they price it to sell?"

"Absolutely. There's no way the British government is going to let retail get hurt; they're all *voters*."

Silence.

"Tell 'em we'll take one *billion* pounds."

"That's great, Bob. Absolutely great! Of course, you should sign the letter since you're the key decision maker."

"No, *you* sign. You're a partner."

"Seriously, you've gotta sign. You have the global stature."

Dobkin drafted the letter and faxed it to New York, where lawyers made minor changes and the letter was retyped, signed by Mnuchin, and faxed back to Dobkin, who went immediately to see Tony Ault at Rothschild. "I came to see you to present something very special. Here it is for your eyes to read."

Ault read the short, bold letter and, putting it down, said it all in just one word: "Wow!"

"Do I have the business?"

"Forget about *that*, Eric! This is just the first round in a very careful and quite deliberate selection process. The process cannot be rushed—even with this letter. It will take about a year." So for a year, Dobkin was on the Concorde almost every week—usually having five or six meetings, but sometimes only one.

A year later, the formal "beauty contest" was held to evaluate prospective underwriters. The adviser to the government, Ault, greeted Dobkin as a friend: "Hi, Eric." But this would not be a meeting of friends. Dobkin would be making his presentation to a review board composed of senior partners of London's major firms—the "great and good" of the City, serving their patriotic duty on behalf of Her Majesty's Government. The preliminaries were over; a final decision on the lead underwriter for the crucial, large North American market was on the table, and the question was put: "Mr. Dobkin, on behalf of Goldman Sachs, what is your price recommendation?"

Dobkin was determined not only to win the North American mandate for

British Gas, but to do all he could to force a revolutionary change in the way underwriting was traditionally done in London. In his answer, Dobkin attacked established tradition directly—on every front. If British firms traditionally kept secret which institutions were cooperating as subunderwriters, Dobkin would show all his cards, and promptly passed around an outsize multipage spreadsheet listing the institutional investors down the left-hand side and, across the pages, showing specific data for each institution in a series of columns with such headings as "Total Assets," "Equity Assets," "Comparable Stocks Owned," "Price Acceptable," "Required Number of Shares," "Number of One-on-One Meetings Held," "Research Contact," and so on. Total disclosure was Dobkin's objective. And that wasn't all. "For each institution, if you care to know more, we have in the large binders beside me a complete dossier—one page per institution—on our firm's evaluation of each aspect of that institution's decision making on British Gas." Then Dobkin asked for a much larger allocation of shares to North America, where institutions aren't interested in holding small amounts of a stock: "To do our job well for HM Treasury, we'll need more shares so we can meet the real demand among institutional investors in the U.S.—so they will get enough to have positions large enough to keep and then buy more."

Then he turned specifically to the question of price. "You ask what is our recommendation as the proper offering price for British Gas. In our judgment anything less than 125 pence would be wrong for Her Majesty's Government and wrong for the British people. Anything less and, candidly, I'll be personally insulted because both the Crown and the British people deserve full value. One other commitment: Goldman Sachs promises it will buy five hundred million dollars of British Gas shares up to a price of 135 pence."

Silence.

"Thank you, Mr. Dobkin. Would you please wait outside?"

Dobkin rose, collected his papers, looked slowly around the panel of judges with all the gravity he could muster, and left the meeting room, walking with as much formality and dignity as he could manage, and sat down quietly in the anteroom. After half an hour, he expected some sort of response. After an hour, he was unable to imagine what might be going on. Had he overstated his case? Had he left anything out? Were other firms making equally strong presentations? Could *any* firm possibly be even stronger? After two hours, Dobkin's sangfroid was giving way to real concern. Something, somehow had gone wrong—perhaps very wrong.

After two and a half hours, the door opened. It was *not* Tony Ault. It was John Guinness's secretary. "Be patient, please, Mr. Dobkin." A while later, John Guinness, chief of staff of the Department of Energy, came out to say, "Following your presentation, the *good* news is that on the strength of your argument, a larger proportion of the British Gas underwriting will be allocated to North America. The *bad* news is we cannot allocate to North America as much stock as you had recommended. But there is one more piece of good news: Your allocation [for North America] *has* been increased . . . to a substantial degree. Further good news is that your advice to price the issue at 125 pence versus 120 has required an interruption of the minister's luncheon and, as you have seen, this has taken some time."[9]

The British government announced Goldman Sachs's selection as lead international underwriter on Monday morning, and Sir Evelyn de Rothschild, acting as the government's adviser, called John Weinberg in New York. Weinberg had to come out of a management committee meeting he was chairing to take the call and get the exciting news.

Weinberg called Dobkin: "Congratulations, Eric. You've just won the largest and most important privatization in history. This is very good news. We're all very proud of you and what you've done—so far."

Then, in the typical Goldman Sachs manner, his tone hardened: "Eric, don't screw this one up. Don't make *any* mistakes. We'll all be watching you—and counting on you to do everything just the right way."

21

HOW BP ALMOST
BECAME A DRY HOLE

On Friday, October 16, 1987, a sudden strong storm with winds of nearly one hundred miles per hour slashed across southeastern England to London, uprooting dozens of century-old trees in St. James's Park—trees that would take over a year to cut up and burn or haul away. With broken trees blocking trains and roads in the surrounding commuter towns and villages, many commuters couldn't reach the City, so the stock exchange would have stayed closed for days even if it hadn't been a weekend. When the exchange did reopen on Monday the nineteenth, the extraordinary event of nature was followed by the worst-ever single-day drop in London share prices, with comparably sharp declines hitting stock markets all around the world. In New York, the Dow Jones Industrials plunged 508 points, or 22.6 percent—a record for a single day's fall.[1]

Several months before, the British government had chosen that very Monday for the sale of an enormous block of stock: its remaining 31.5 percent shareholding in giant British Petroleum.[2] For the BP offering, each underwriter would have a defined role. Goldman Sachs's strategy had been typically direct: Make application to be appointed the government's adviser on the large tranche of shares to be placed internationally, for which the firm's well-known strengths in America would give it a major advantage. And then, as was customary practice, Goldman Sachs would appoint itself to be a leading distributor and underwriter when the issue came to market. BP also planned to sell £1.5 billion of new shares, so the offering would total a record £7.25 billion (over twelve billion dollars at the 1987 exchange rate). "By a malign coincidence," wrote Nigel Lawson, chancellor of the exchequer, "the world's largest-ever share sale collided with the world's most dramatic stock-market crash."[3]

U nderwriting practices in the United Kingdom were then very different from those in the United States. These differences would matter greatly in the BP offering. American underwriters are at risk with their own capital for all the shares they underwrite, and everything is organized to minimize, usually to minutes, the length of time over which they are exposed to the vicissitudes of the market. In the traditional British system, which was well suited to modest increases in equity, a group of institutional investors would serve as subunderwriters. For a share of the underwriter's fee, institutions would buy large, specified amounts of stock at the agreed-upon price, so the merchant banks acting as the primary underwriters would have only a small exposure to the major risk facing any underwriter: owning unsold shares that are declining in market price. Since the British economy had few technology or other fast-growth companies, IPOs were a rarity. Most public offerings were modest increases in the equity of established corporations at well-established valuations. Most institutional portfolios were either indexed or quasi-indexed, so institutional investors participated in most underwritings. The British system was based on the concept of preemption—that current investors had preemptive rights to protect their percentage ownership by buying an equal proportion of new shares being offered. It was almost leisurely. The system comfortably suited all parties—corporations, institutional investors, and merchant-bank intermediaries. It assumed that already-public companies would be raising only moderate increments of equity capital and that a slower process would suit all participants well. The American system of underwriting assumed instead that speed of execution would protect the underwriters by keeping their exposure to market risk very brief.

Under the British system, individual investors would have the assurance that well-informed professionals, having had ample time for objective analysis, had determined that the offering price was fair and reasonable, since they were committed to pay the same price for their shares. As part of Margaret Thatcher's "people's capitalism," several unique inducements were added in the BP offering to broaden participation by individual investors. An unusually simple order form was developed, and small investors were assured of receiving their first one hundred shares, and proration on additional shares, if they were willing to accept whatever price "cleared the market." Small shareholders willing to hold for three years would get another 10 percent "share bonus" after the three-year holding period. What's more, buyers of BP shares would not need to pay in full on the date of purchase. Far from it. In this underwriting, they would receive the full dividend per share but pay only £1.20 per share "on application," with two other installment payments spread out over twelve months. Finally, the price to the public would be set at a slight discount to the prevailing market price. As was the custom in the United Kingdom at that time, the underwriters would work over the summer at building up investor interest and at forming the underwriting syndicate—including lining up the institutional subunderwriters and preparing all the necessary documents for the offering. Under British rules, the price at which the shares would be offered would be published in the major newspapers well in advance of the actual offering and maintained by the underwriters at this price for two consecutive weeks, with actual payment settling two weeks later.

In America, by contrast, the price was set only on the day of the offering, and institutional investors were not committed until the last minute (though they might indicate the size of their tentative interest, which could result in a penciled "light circle" on the underwriters' order sheet). For the few minutes that typically fell between the SEC's approval of the underwriting and the formal confirmation of the purchase of shares by both institutional and individual investors, the underwriters owned the whole offering, paid for by signing a purchase agreement with the issuing company.

To protect London underwriters against the risk of a totally unexpected, unmanageable, and uninsurable risk, such as the outbreak of war, British underwriting agreements usually had a force majeure provision. If an unforeseen event of great importance occurred, there would be no obligation to plunge stubbornly ahead: The issue could be delayed until normal conditions returned.

Privatization—though never featured in any of her statements before she led the government—was the dramatic and radical initiative by Margaret Thatcher's Conservative government to transfer ownership of over two dozen major businesses employing nearly a million people from state ownership to the private sector by selling shares to large numbers of individual investors. Her Majesty's Government felt no obligation to protect preemption and knew that the major corporations it intended to privatize would almost automatically become part of the *Financial Times'* FTSE (Footsie) market index. This meant that British institutions, to maintain market-matching portfolios, would surely be reliable buyers of each offering, as they had been with British Gas. The government also knew that the London market could not readily absorb large IPOs; access to the international markets—particularly the American market—would be crucial. Since British merchant banks were not powerful distributors in North America or Japan or across Europe, international distributors would be central to underwriting success.

Mrs. Thatcher had become convinced that the British government owned far too much of British industry; that service by government-owned companies was poor and getting worse; that the companies were not well run or efficient; and that the whole British economy was stagnating because those large government-owned companies were far too risk-averse, afraid to take chances or innovate, and had no appetite for hard decisions that might upset voters. Mrs. Thatcher insisted that to justify taking entrepreneurial risks for growth, British managers needed to have the freedom to fail. Her solution was to separate British industry from the British government and the stifling "compact of politics" by selling off the nationalized corporations, starting with the telephone company British Telecom, followed by British Gas.[4] Privatization was a remarkably successful program that revitalized many major companies, greatly broadened British share ownership, broadened and strengthened Thatcher's Conservative political party, and reversed decisively the postwar global trend toward increasing nationalization.[5]

However, these massive sales of common stock from the government to private investors were orders of magnitude larger than the underwritings for which the British system of underwriting had been designed. Since the nationalized companies were typically owned outright by the government, there was no current market valuation of the shares before the offerings. The privatizations were IPOs, so the price would be determined by supply and demand for shares, with the large institutional investors that served as subunderwriters having the dominant voice.

In planning the privatization of British Telecom, HM Treasury had structured the underwriting group with both domestic and international underwriters—with separate groups for the United Kingdom, continental Europe, Japan, Canada, and the United States. The telephone giant had been ideal for Thatcher's privatization program because everybody used telephones. Kleinwort Benson had been retained by the government to advise on the November 1984 sale, which totaled £3.9 billion for 25 percent of the equity, and the privatization doubled the number of share-owning Britons as two million people bought shares, half subscribing to four hundred shares or less. Next, in December 1986 British Gas was privatized in a flotation raising £5.4 billion, and British Airways was sold to the public for nine hundred million pounds in February 1987. Following these successes, the major stock markets of the world were all unusually strong during the first three quarters of 1987. By September the NYSE was 44 percent higher than it had been in early January. The London market peaked in July, up 46 percent, and Tokyo was up 42 percent. Market conditions appeared ideal for further privatizations, and BP was in the queue and proceeding smoothly.

BP was different in advantageous ways from prior privatizations. It was already a publicly traded company. While the British government owned a large part of the giant company—obtained when Britain took over Middle Eastern oil fields—BP had always been run as a private-sector corporation. And the political-party politics that might be troublesome over the sale of a valuable property owned by the British public had been neutralized. The Labour Party, which would vigorously challenge other privatizations, could not easily oppose the BP sale because a Labour government had sold BP shares as recently as 1977—and the Conservative government had sold another £290 million block of shares in November 1979 without any political protest. The government and the British stock market both had every reason to expect a quiet and orderly reception of the giant offering of BP.

On the advice of his appointed adviser, N.M. Rothschild & Sons, Nigel Lawson decided that it would be wise to appoint two major international underwriters. As it had with the British Gas privatization, the Treasury conducted a "beauty contest" examination of non-British underwriters. This time it chose Goldman Sachs, not Morgan Stanley—the U.S. firm traditionally used by the British government. (To manage its own £1.5 billion simultaneous share offering, BP chose S.G. Warburg.) For Goldman Sachs, this was a major breakthrough, confirming the success of years of building up its stature in the City.

A few people at Goldman Sachs had special reasons to feel proud of the firm's selection. Eric Sheinberg had been developing Goldman Sachs's London market-making operation, which helped the firm's winning presentation to the British government. The firm's UK oil analyst had well-recognized expertise on BP as a company and would perform an important role in distributing the shares to institutional buyers. Eric Dobkin, who had developed the equity capital markets division in New York, had led Goldman Sachs's campaign to be a major underwriter of privatizations in the UK, stressing the firm's distribution experience in major global industries like telecoms and banks and its strength as a leading underwriter in America, the world's largest securities market. In distributing British privatizations, particularly outside the UK, Dobkin's drive to win business was increasingly effective. The firm's campaign was strengthened by BP's desire to increase its shareholder base in the United States significantly.

Discussion of the enormous BP underwriting began with private meetings between HM Treasury and the leading underwriters in early January 1987. A public announcement of the intended offering was made in March, and the traditional process of organizing all the many parts of the underwriting process culminated at 11 a.m. on October 14 in a meeting at the Treasury called to specify the price at which BP shares were to be underwritten. Michael Richardson of N.M. Rothschild & Sons, acting as official adviser to the government, indicated he might not get agreement among the underwriters for a price of £3.50 per share but would try his best. A few hours later, Richardson returned to No. 11 Downing Street to say that as shares were already trading at £3.50, £3.30 was the best he could do; a noticeable price discount would be necessary for a successful offering. Contrary to the usual expectation of protracted back-and-forth negotiations between the seller, which would want the highest price, and the underwriters, which would want the lowest price to facilitate an easy, riskless sale, Chancellor of the Exchequer Lawson surprised everyone in the room by declaring: "Done!"

The next step was to set the fee concession to compensate the subunderwriters, using competitive bidding. The normal concession was 0.5 percent. The average bid to underwrite BP—with its broad, deep market already well established— was much lower: 0.18 percent, or £1,800 for each one million pounds of shares placed with subunderwriters. The next morning—Thursday, October 15—more than four hundred investing institutions signed up as subunderwriters.

The public market price for shares in BP closed at £3.47 on Thursday. Most London merchant banks, sensing easy profits on a well-known, highly regarded corporation's straightforward underwriting, decided to keep more than the usual proportion of their participations on their own books rather than arranging larger subunderwritings with institutional investors.[6] While they were now more than usually exposed to underwriting risks, the magnitude of their exposures, while significant relative to their equity capital, was still moderate—typically ten million pounds for a major UK underwriter, not the bravura exposures of fifty million to one hundred million dollars taken on by each of the U.S. investment banks, led by Goldman Sachs.

Then came that unprecedented market drop on Monday, October 19. And on Tuesday, the London market plunged again. BP had been underwritten at £3.30. With £1.20 paid in cash and the rest deferred, meaning that buyers would be responsible for the deferred payments, the partly paid shares were suddenly selling at only seventy-five to eighty pence. Obviously—and ominously—investors would not buy from underwriters *above* the market, and the British government rightly feared "tagging" (harming) individual investors—and voters. Unless the BP issue were called off, which would require "unwinding" or nullifying the sales already made to investors at prices as high as £3.30, the underwriters—particularly the Americans—would take substantial losses. The total loss for London underwriters and subunderwriters would be seventy million pounds; while divided among over four hundred participants, the two largest City losses would be ten million pounds each for Rothschild and S.G. Warburg.

The drop in BP's price could cost Goldman Sachs, Morgan Stanley, Shearson

Lehman, and Salomon Brothers nearly one hundred million dollars apiece—and this was in addition to the heavy losses they had each taken in their regular block-trading businesses during the stock-market plunge. The American underwriters had serious arguments among themselves because they had sharply different views of their financial and reputation risks, but they didn't break ranks in public. In meetings on Friday, October 23, and on the following Monday, they asserted that the week's market trauma was exactly what the force majeure provision was all about. They insisted that the enormous, sudden drop in *all* the world's stock markets was indeed a force majeure event that clearly justified withdrawing the offering and waiting for better and more normal market conditions.

The collapse of world markets was certainly a major force, unexpected, unmanageable, and uninsurable. But was it sufficient to declare force majeure? Should the BP underwriting be delayed and the underwriters absolved of their obligations and their sudden losses? "Within the City of London, the initial consensus was that the BP issue should not be reversed, and the City firms agreed to take their losses as part of the nature of the business and to protect the traditional pricing system," explained Sir Win Bischoff, chief executive of Schroders. "We thought that that was a rational business decision—for the long term." Market drops, even very large ones, were not part of the understood reason for force majeure. So at first the British underwriters quietly agreed to carry on.

The American underwriters—Goldman Sachs, Morgan Stanley, Salomon Brothers, and Shearson Lehman Brothers—saw things differently. In America, there were no subunderwriters. These four firms had taken 480 million BP shares onto their books and were now facing up to $330 million in sudden losses. For each of them, the loss on BP would be the largest loss any underwriter anywhere had ever experienced.

While the Americans claimed the right to call the whole thing off, the force majeure escape provision could only be triggered by a claim by the leading *domestic* British underwriters in London. The decision centered on clause 8, the force majeure clause that explained under what circumstances underwriters could request a release from their obligations. Because the British underwriters were so numerous and the percentages they had underwritten themselves (versus passing on to subunderwriters) were relatively small, their individual exposures to loss were much smaller than the Americans'—typically only 10 percent as large—so some of the British firms continued to feel that the October market break, while clearly very unusual, did not trigger force majeure. But eventually a majority of the twenty-two major UK underwriters voted to recommend to HM Treasury that force majeure should be declared. If the Treasury agreed, the underwriting would be off.

Exposed to much larger losses, the Americans were initially unanimous that the BP underwriting had to be postponed. With the sudden drop-off in share price, swallowing the losses would cut deeply into each underwriter's equity capital. Eric Dobkin *assumed* that the market drop was a force majeure event and said that it would be dumb to go ahead with the underwriting. Dobkin flew to London to plead with HM Treasury officials to pull the BP issue. Archie Cox for Morgan Stanley and Bill Landreth for Goldman Sachs went to the Bank of England to call on Eddie George, the deputy governor of the bank. Their mission was to strongly recommend that their firms be released from their underwriting commitments because of the largest market break in history, which they declared triggered the force majeure provision.

Governor George refused. They were underwriters. They had won the mandate precisely because they guaranteed the contractual price to the British government. A guarantee was a guarantee.

Similarly, Chancellor of the Exchequer Lawson said he was "not impressed and certainly not convinced," but the underwriters' opinion did trigger a careful process of formal review by the Bank of England, the Treasury, and Parliament— with the Bank of England staff siding with the underwriters' concern. The bank's staff proposed to guarantee a stock buyback at £3.10. If effected, this would have saved the three groups of underwriters £750 million and resulted in the Bank of England's owning most of the BP shares. Chancellor Lawson quickly rejected the bank staff's idea.

On Tuesday the four American underwriters went to U.S. Treasury under secretary George Gould, pleading for help. He agreed to see what might be done. On advice given in clear and emphatic terms by Gould's British counterpart, it was decided not to have President Reagan call Prime Minister Thatcher: "No! Absolutely do *not* have Mr. Reagan call Mrs. Thatcher. She'll do anything he asks!" Instead, James Baker, secretary of the Treasury, reached Nigel Lawson— in full evening dress at eleven in the evening after a Mansion House banquet—to plead on behalf of the U.S. underwriters in what Lawson later called "the strongest possible terms." A senior White House staffer tried to persuade Mrs. Thatcher to intercede with Lawson. And BP management joined in calling for a postponement. Lawson refused, and Thatcher backed him. Because Alan Greenspan was only two months into his job as chairman of the Federal Reserve, his predecessor, Paul Volcker, was asked to call the four U.S. underwriters to assure them that the Fed would flood the banking system with liquidity.

Later in the discussions, it was agreed that a buyback floor of £3.10 would be put below the market price to reassure the 270,000 small investors; the floor wouldn't apply to the underwriters. It was put in place, but no investors chose to use it. After frustrating delays caused by the slow production of the Bank of England's advisory report, Chancellor Lawson told Parliament at 10:05 in the evening of Thursday, October 29: "I would like the House to be quite clear about the objectives of my decision: first, and most important, to allow taxpayers to secure the full proceeds of the BP sale to which they are entitled; secondly, to ensure that there are orderly aftermarkets in BP shares; thirdly, to make quite sure that the sale does not add to present difficulties in world markets. It is *not* my objective in any way to bail out the underwriters, whether in this country or elsewhere. By proceeding as I have indicated, the City will uphold its reputation as the world's leading international financial center."[7,8]

Everyone now knew that Goldman Sachs and the other major American underwriters owned enormous blocks of BP shares that they would have to sell at whatever price they could get. There was a "buyer's strike" by institutional investors, particularly in London. Hedge funds in New York and other dealers began to drive the market price even lower by selling BP stock short, knowing they could easily cover their shorts by buying shares from the major underwriters. Worse, short sellers could sell *lots* of shares because the underwriters had such huge amounts of stock they would sooner or later have to sell.

At Goldman Sachs, one of the most important units, and the least known externally, is the commitment committee. Its focus is on making certain that the firm never makes a "life-threatening bet." It works to ensure that all the risks in every capital commitment decision are fully identified, fully discussed, and fully understood before any significant commitment of the firm's capital. As Bob Rubin once explained, "I can see for myself what could go *right*. Concentrate your analysis on what could go *wrong*. That's where you can really be most help-ful." Eric Dobkin and Bob Steel had been responsible for writing the twenty-page memo on the BP underwriting for the commitment committee, and they both knew the rules: Cover *every* risk; 100 percent candor; no selling or advocating; explain *all* the worst-case possibilities of what could go wrong; specify how much the firm might lose. Dobkin and Steel had followed the rules all the way, so, as bad as BP clearly was, their worst-case estimates were at least accurate—which helped the firm's decision makers stay focused and rational.

The American underwriters scrambled to find a legal basis for asserting force majeure. "Sue them!" was the reaction at Morgan Stanley. "Sue the British government?" "Absolutely!" John Weinberg didn't join in the complaints and legalisms. Knowing how enormous the loss could be, he said, "We bought it and we own it." He knew the loss was painful. He also knew how much Goldman Sachs had invested in the past few years to establish itself in London and that it would cost the firm even more in loss of business momentum and morale to drop out. Making a strength out of a horrendous loss—the largest underwriting loss the firm had ever taken—Weinberg, like the decisive Marine he'd been, decided, "Take it!" This was the cost of establishing the firm's position for the long run, just as the costs had been high at Iwo Jima and Okinawa. As so often before, Weinberg was blunt and earthy: "If we cut and run away on BP, we won't under-write a doghouse in London."

The British were suitably impressed, particularly at the highest level, where it mattered most. Weinberg's intuitive judgment was later proven right when Morgan Stanley pulled back from large privatizations because of the British sys-tem for underwriting. Goldman Sachs was able to push ahead, underwrote giant privatizations for British Steel and British Electricity, and was soon established as the leading investment banker to the British government and to British industry.

When the New York stock market crashed, large investors scrambled for safety and liquidity. They rushed into bonds, and the Federal Reserve flooded the financial system with liquidity, so bond prices, particularly government-bond prices, surged. As a major market maker, Goldman Sachs held huge bond inventories and made enormous gains in bonds on the same day that the stock market crashed. The losses in BP and other stocks were only part of the firm's total portfolio. Big profits in fixed income largely offset the big losses in underwriting and in block trading that could have opened up serious wounds within the firm. The firm's net loss in October was thirty million dollars, pretax. John Weinberg declared that the charge for the BP loss would be made in the firm's P&L below the line that showed profits division by division.[9] This way, there would be no politics; the entire cost would be charged to the firm as a whole, and not to a particular division, where it might become a political football.

Within the firm, BP gave the remaining "nationalists" one last open shot to strike back at the "internationalists." With Goldman Sachs still in the first year of its major strategic drive to establish a strong beachhead in London, the large loss in BP provoked again the familiar internal arguments against going global: Europe was a well-protected market; volume was mediocre; profits were low; each country had its own rules and practices in underwriting; it would take far too long to become profitable; important opportunities—larger, more profitable, and much easier to exploit—were in America; and on and on. Besides, BP "proved" two points: The firm would never lose that much money on one deal in North America, and Goldman Sachs was clearly being "stuffed by the Brits," who refused to invoke force majeure. The internationalists argued that many more privatizations were coming—in the UK and in several other countries— and that American concepts and practices in underwriting were sure to dominate, which would give Goldman Sachs and other U.S. firms important competitive advantages. As always, the question was asked: How much should *current* partners spend on building the business when the profits—if there ever were any— would only come after they had gone limited, so they would enrich only *future* partners?

"The BP offering was the very worst experience of my whole career," says partner Bob Conway. As London branch manager, he got a call from Reuters: "We understand on good authority that Goldman Sachs will be filing for protection under the laws of bankruptcy. Would you care to comment?" In Canada the BP deal had blown away *all* the capital of Wood Gundy, one of that nation's leading securities firms, and forced it to merge abruptly with a major commercial bank. Still, for Conway, explaining to a newspaper reporter who thought he had a prize-winning scoop that the rumor of bankruptcy at the leading U.S. firm was untrue was almost easy compared to going around to each and every bank to insist that Goldman Sachs was financially strong. "Every night," he recalls, "I called our CFO, Bob Friedman, in New York to review the details of every banker's call. That week was the longest week of my life."

Eric Dobkin also got a call from a newspaper reporter: "You will know this is a very sensitive call, which is why I'm calling you personally. I have it on very good authority that your firm has taken a major loss in BP shares and that Goldman Sachs may be in serious financial difficulty at this very moment. Can you verify this—or can you assure me that it is not true?"

Dobkin responded: "I have not spoken to New York for three hours, so it's always possible that something has gone wrong that I don't know about, but I very much doubt it. Yes, we have taken a big loss on BP—as much as seventy million dollars—but BP is not our only position. Our largest positions are not in stocks at all—they're in bonds, where we've become a major market maker, and prices of bonds have gone up a lot. Goldman Sachs has made a lot more money in bonds during the past days than it has lost in BP—a *lot* more."

Dobkin knew he had created an opening and knew how to use it: "Now you owe me one. Where did this rumor come from? Who's saying Goldman Sachs may be in trouble?" It turned out to be the charming, patrician Simon Garmoyle— then Viscount Cairns, later an earl—who was head of Scrimgeour Vickers, a leading London stockbroker, and later chief executive at S.G. Warburg. So Dobkin, who is five-foot-six, went to see Cairns, who is six-foot-two, and gave him a blunt and memorable "don't ever try that again" warning. Both men knew that leadership in the City was changing.

Goldman Sachs partner Bill Landreth called his friends at the Kuwait Investment Office: "British Petroleum is clearly solid value. The price was set at a very attractive level a week ago, before the offering. Now, after the big market break, the price is even more attractive—and there is very good 'buyer's liquidity,' making it easy to buy a major position in a great company at a price certain." The KIO agreed to acquire a significant part of Goldman Sachs's block and kept right on going with open-market purchases. BP chairman Peter Walter warned in late October that "an unwelcome buyer could obtain a major stake in

BP for a very low initial cost."[10] On November 18 the Kuwait Investment Office announced it had purchased 10 percent of BP and was still buying. By year-end, the KIO owned 18 percent of BP, and in March 1988 the KIO owned nearly 22 percent, acquired through a series of major block purchases arranged by Goldman Sachs and other firms.

While the KIO is a strictly commercial operation, it is owned by the Kuwait Investment Agency, which is responsible for advancing the strategic and political interests of the Kuwaiti government. On the basis of KIO's large share ownership, Kuwait had demanded a seat on the board of directors of Daimler-Benz and might now do the same at BP—even though BP was a direct competitor of Kuwait Petroleum Corporation (brand name: Q8). When KIO ownership reached 22 percent, Margaret Thatcher and Nigel Lawson referred the matter to Britain's Monopolies and Mergers Commission. The KIO stopped buying and announced it would reduce its ownership to 20 percent and voluntarily limit its voting to 15 percent. That was not enough for the Monopolies and Mergers Commission, which ruled in September 1988 that the KIO's ownership would be limited to 10 percent and set a one-year time limit—later extended to three years—for the KIO to conform.

Over the next several years, the Kuwait Investment Office's remaining shareholding in BP kept increasing in value. The market price tripled during the 1990s, and securities firms, sensing the opportunity for large, profitable trades, kept in contact with the KIO. The Kuwaitis chose to work through Schroders, and just before five in the afternoon of May 14, 1997, Schroders called Goldman Sachs, Salomon Brothers, and UBS—which had all known for a few weeks that a very large trade was coming—and gave them one hour to make their bids for the biggest block trade in history.

Goldman Sachs was ready. In April 1996, Gary Williams, with no prior experience in trading European stocks, had moved to London to head equities trading in Europe. During his first week in his new role, a senior partner in corporate finance got a hint from another client of a possible sale of KIO's BP. Williams and Wiet Pot, co-head of the European-shares business, called David Silfen in New York, who suggested they offer to bid for the whole five-billion-dollar position to make a powerful, memorable proposition.

As soon as a meeting could be arranged, David Silfen, Pat Ward, Williams, and Pot met with the KIO and made Goldman Sachs's bid: a 5 percent discount off the prevailing price for the KIO's entire five-billion-dollar stake in BP. The KIO seemed impressed but gave no indication that it might sell. Both sides agreed to stay in touch. The group from Goldman Sachs met again a month later with the KIO and were introduced to Philip Mallinckrodt of Schroders, which was advising KIO "on various matters." Over the next several months, they met several times to explore various alternatives to maximize KIO's proceeds, but no specific plans were ever acknowledged by KIO. "The KIO and Mallinckrodt were most professional," recalls Williams. "They gave away nothing but were completely honest in what they did say."

Pot and Williams had many discussions over the next several months. They agreed they should do all they could to be fully prepared, because they knew from experience that very big trades could be time-pressured, leaving too little time to get approvals, design hedging strategies, check legal questions, and develop a specific strategy for reselling. By resolving all these aspects of the trade well in advance, they could concentrate on making the "right" bid, given liquidity, risk factors, and current market conditions. One thing they would not do: talk to any potential buyers or even to anyone who would be talking to clients. Over a full year's gestation of the trade, there were zero leaks from Goldman Sachs, but there were occasional hints from other firms. So Williams and Pot grew to expect that if they ever did get a call, it would probably be in competition with other dealers.

When Schroders phoned on May 14, 1997, Williams was at a scheduled meeting at Britain's Financial Services Authority. A colleague got a call on his cell phone from Williams's secretary—because Williams didn't own a cell phone: "Wiet says the trade is on and wants to know how soon you can get here." The trade would be two billion dollars, not the five billion dollars originally considered but still by far the largest ever.

Williams excused himself from the meeting and, borrowing the cell phone, went looking for a cab, but no empty cabs were to be found shortly after five, so he started walking in what he hoped was the right direction. He called Pot, who was organizing a conference call with Roy Zuckerberg, Eric Dobkin, and Bob Steel in New York and John Thain in London. (Silfen had retired at the end of 1996, so he was not included.) Finding a cab at last, Williams returned to the office, participating in the transatlantic phone call while riding through the City.

Williams had an advantage: He had a feel for how traders make pricing decisions in blind competitions because of his experience with similar trades in convertible securities. BP shares had closed in London at £7.44. The group settled on a reoffering price—the price at which Goldman Sachs would offer the shares to investors if it won the bidding—of £7.15, a discount of 4.2 percent. Williams then suggested that £7.16 would be seen as virtually the same. So they increased it to £7.16. Then Williams said, "If we all thought 715 [pence], we must assume our competitors will too. If it's 715, the natural bid would be 710. But experienced dealers know not to bid round numbers, so the guy who'll bid 710 will add a 'tail'—he'll actually bid 710.10, or maybe 710.20 to be really clever. So, if we're going to die with this trade, let's go down in flames. Let's bid 710.50—so we won't be edged out by a fraction of a penny." Dobkin had been thinking the same way, so the extra tail was confirmed.

Forty minutes after getting Schroders's call, they were agreed on a price of 710.50 for 170 million shares. Pat Ward, who knew Philip Mallinckrodt and Dr. Yousef Al-Awadi, who headed KIO in London, called Mallinckrodt with Goldman Sachs's bid. After nearly an hour, which seemed a very long time, Ward called Mallinckrodt again, hoping to gain an insight into what might be happening. Mallinckrodt's guarded response: "Pat, are you calling because you want to raise your bid?"

A few minutes later, Mallinckrodt called back. Goldman Sachs's bid had won.

"What was the cover?" asked Ward. The next highest bid is customarily disclosed to the winners.

Mallinckrodt responded: "I've never seen anything this close. Are you sure you didn't collaborate?" Goldman Sachs could not have colluded because it did not know which other firms were bidding. The next highest bid was . . . 710.10— a gap of less than one-tenth of 1 percent on two billion dollars!

Now that it owned 170 million shares of BP, worth over two billion dollars, Goldman Sachs did . . . practically nothing. The position was far too large to hedge. The only way to protect against market risk was to sell well. That's why the firm planned to tell clients about the trade only after the 4 p.m. close of NYSE trading. U.S. clients would be solicited immediately after four, Asian clients would be contacted overnight, and UK and European clients would be approached the following morning—before the London opening.

The carefully developed plan took a detour, however, when at 3 p.m. a senior partner in New York, uncomfortable with the market risk, phoned Pot and Williams and proposed a launch as soon as possible, saying that some of the decision makers at big U.S. clients would be leaving early for the day. Pot and Williams felt they had to follow his lead, so they did. It might have been possible to appeal to a higher authority—but Williams and Pot limited themselves to one more recitation of their reasoning. When that brought no change, they accepted that there was no time for a full debate. Now they had a problem. Although sales to clients would be an "off board" (non-NYSE) distribution, regulations required that when clients were solicited prior to the 4 p.m. close, the specialist's book had to be "collapsed" after the close down to the distribution price and that all higher public bids had to be filled at the distribution price. This would make the discount look less attractive. Furthermore, a preclose announcement would give market opportunists the chance to "shoot against" the price for the rest of the trading day. All of this raised the risk of something going wrong.

As directed, a few substantial sales were executed in the United States that afternoon and evening, and the balance was sold to UK, Continental, and Asian clients the next morning. Before it was over, Goldman Sachs resold the shares to more than five hundred institutional and individual investors worldwide at £7.16 (or $11.77 for an American Depositary Receipt representing one BP share and an allowance for currency conversion). Inside the firm, traders were professionally proud that there had been zero leaks and that BP was the largest block trade ever done by a single firm as a pure blind bid, where the bids of others weren't known.

Goldman Sachs made a profit of seventeen million dollars—and demonstrated that massive transactions could be executed at a very low cost relative to the assets involved. It was a triumphant trade, but with two billion dollars at risk, seventeen million dollars of profit was tiny—hard evidence that in the block-trading business, the margin of profit had become far too low to justify the market risk.

22

CHANGING THE GUARD

I n the quiet, walnut-paneled dining room at London's Connaught Hotel, John Weinberg was in a candid discussion with Lord Weinstock, the CEO of GEC, the British General Electric Company. Their subject was succession. Weinstock, apparently unconcerned about nepotism, said he was doing all he could to arrange it so his son would be chosen to lead GEC. Weinberg said he was committed to meritocracy but wasn't finding it easy. "I spoke with the one guy I really wanted, but he said he didn't want to take the job as sole CEO, so I'll have to appoint two as co-heads."

Developing his successors was a high priority for Weinberg, and he would soon position Steve Friedman and Bob Rubin, his chosen heirs apparent, by pairing them as co-heads of the fixed-income division. Rubin and Friedman had enjoyed a special relationship from their first meeting. "As lawyers, Bob and I had a lot in common," says Friedman. "Lawyers learn to ask lots of questions and learn to think systematically. We first met when a friend called me to say he had a pal who was leaving the practice of law and wanted to introduce us." Despite their differences—Friedman would bore down into the detailed data to master all the evidence while Rubin looked for large governing concepts—they were very much alike: Besides sharing training as lawyers, both inspired unusual personal loyalty, each liked and trusted the other, and both took a cerebral view of business decisions. Both were determined to accelerate the firm's pace to make it more entrepreneurial, more creative, and more profitable. Over many years of working together, they developed an unusually close and deep friendship that continues to be important to both men to this day. As they bonded together, more and more people within the firm saw them as the obvious heirs apparent.

Rubin could cheerfully spend several hours analyzing different possibilities and working out his understanding of the nature of a complex problem. Friedman was superb at quickly establishing rapport with a new client's key decision makers, particularly if they felt under pressure. His intensity showed clients how deeply engaged he was in solving their problem or their crisis. Rubin was good with clients partly because they recognized how smart he was, partly because he had no visible ego needs, and partly because he saw events and personalities within a broad context.

They were and had always been primarily individual contributors. While both were outstanding at relating to individuals or small groups, neither man was a large-group "people person" by nature or training, and neither was widely experienced at working with and through large numbers of other people in managing the different and often competitive groups that make up large, complex organizations. For most of their careers they had both been inspiring leaders, usually of small, close-knit teams, not large groups of five or six hundred or complex organizations of five or six thousand. Appropriately, Bob Rubin's sole acknowledged extracurricular passion is fly fishing, where the secret for success is learning to think like a fish.

As several partners observed, Rubin and Friedman had been insiders focused on a series of specific transactions, with little responsibility for developing long-term relationships. Both men excelled at finding creative solutions to hundreds of individual problems. But like most of their predecessors and peers at other firms, neither had needed to develop the skills of building consensus across large groups—skills needed for integrating very different kinds of businesses and different groups of people into a coherent organizational strategy.

Still, the two men differed greatly in managerial style and in ways of operating. As they prepared to take the lead in restructuring the bond business, Friedman gathered up more than a yard-deep pile of computer printouts and financial reports and dove in, working on his own through page after page of specifics, often making careful notes of questions to examine with extra care as he developed factual mastery to assure himself that he had a thorough understanding of every aspect of the bond-dealing business. Then he would cross-examine the unit heads—asking, as always, *lots* of questions—probing more and more deeply to develop a bottom-up understanding. In contrast, Rubin invited unit leaders to meet with him and explored with them each of the concepts and business models that seemed most important, and particularly those that appeared to be gaining importance, so he could understand the way the business might develop and where the firm would have the most interesting challenges and opportunities—and the risks in each case. As a result of his learning strategy, Rubin got to know the managers as individual people, and how they thought and understood their business, in ways Friedman never could.

Friedman almost instinctively thought in the terms of a wrestler: Speed, agility, initiative, and strength were important characteristics, but his focus was on defending against his competitor—one on one—and on winning each match. As Friedman says, "I like to argue—vigorously—as a test: Can you change my mind?" Rubin was in a different arena: He had no more interest in winning a discussion than in winning at Frisbee. As a result, they could see things differently. For example, while both men joked about having to wear kneepads, because, on behalf of one area of the firm or another, they so frequently had to get down on their knees in apology to outraged clients, they reacted very differently on the day that a distressed partner pleaded: "This is a major client and the guy is *really* angry. And he's demanding an apology—at *least* an apology."

"He's *wrong*," insisted Friedman. "And we know we're right. There's no need to genuflect to the SOB—no matter how big a client he thinks he is."

"I'll go," offered Rubin quietly. "His office is uptown. I'll stop by this afternoon on my way home. No big deal."

When Rubin got to the client's office, it was clear that the client was *very* angry—and he said so in no uncertain terms while Rubin listened. For emphasis, the client made his point again as Rubin listened. The client continued to vent his frustration as Rubin listened. The client explained why he felt so upset as Rubin continued to listen. The client said he hoped Bob understood and was glad he was listening. The client said he recognized he might have overreacted, but appreciated that Rubin had come to his office to listen. The client hoped that now that the matter was out in the open, now that there was a realistic understanding, they could get back to their old working relationship—maybe even better. Rubin listened and the client said he really appreciated Bob's dealing so quickly and thoughtfully with a situation that could cause some people to overreact and blow things out of proportion. Rubin continued to listen. A little later, as Rubin listened, the client paused and then reached out to shake Rubin's hand, saying; "Thanks again, Bob. Thank you for coming to hear my side. I really appreciate what you've done today, coming and hearing me out. I'm glad all that's behind us now and we can get right back to doing good business together. Bob, I really owe you one for what you've done today to restore our fine relationship. You're a prince." Shaking Rubin's hand, warmly, he walked his guest to the elevator and, smiling as the doors closed, said, "Thanks again, Bob, you're the best."

The next day, Friedman asked: "Bob, I know we joke about 'creative groveling' and having to kiss all four cheeks in our jobs, but don't you *ever* tire of having to listen to all that blustering bullshit?"

"He was upset and needed to have a chance to have his say—to get it out and be heard by one of us," Rubin explained. "So while he was going on and on, certain that I was listening to his every word, my mind was on what I'll be doing tomorrow. Being there, letting him talk it all out, was no problem for me."

M*anagement* in a continuous-process business (and every professional service business is continuous) involves all-day and every-day nurturing of better and better performance, and carefully reducing or removing errors. *Leadership* concentrates on decisive acts and decisions. Bob Rubin was unusually good at both leadership and management.

"Frank, could I see you for a minute?" Rubin had followed partner Frank Brosens out of a management committee meeting. The meeting had been a triumph. Brosens had presented a compelling case for a bold commitment to arbitraging Japanese equity warrants, and the committee had strongly agreed with his recommendation. Brosens had made the entire presentation, but, as a learning experience, he had invited Zachary Cuberinick to sit in on the meeting as an observer. Brosens knew he'd had all the bases covered and all the facts clearly in hand, but he could hardly believe Rubin had been so impressed that he would leave the meeting to compliment him immediately. Brosens was right; Rubin was not rushing to compliment him on his performance.

"Frank," said Rubin in his soft, relaxed voice, "you and I both know that, as young as he is, Cuberinick knows all that you know about Japanese warrants and he could have made the case equally well. You really should have let him make the case—and get the experience of coming before the management committee. By not taking the credit, you become *more* effective. If you do right by people, *they* win *and* you win. Frank, always go out of your way to share credit."

"Bob Rubin was my best boss ever," says Tom Steyer. "He always listened to you, really *listened*, to get a full understanding of all your information and your best ideas. He was clear, absolutely clear, on the plan of action. He was *always* calm—incredibly calm—and never flustered or put off by markets or by the sometimes truly outrageous behavior of individuals, which never, ever got to him. And he was decisive on action plans." Rubin's response to everyone who asked his opinion was always the same: "What do *you* think?" This obliged others to do their homework and offer their best judgment. It also gave Rubin a little extra time for thought and a "first approximation" estimate of what might be the right way to frame the question or understand the problem.[1]

"Whether Bob agreed with you or not, he made it so clear that he really understood the point you'd made or the view you held that you didn't feel any personal loss if he made a different decision, because you knew he knew all you knew—and must know more." One thing Rubin did *not* do was change a well-reasoned, fact-founded plan of action. He would get annoyed, even angry, with anyone who wanted to reopen a discussion he thought was closed. He always stayed with the agreed plan unless the facts changed significantly.

When Brosens had first been put in charge of arbitrage, he had one exciting talent in the division—Eric Mindich, a man in his early twenties whom he wanted to put in charge of risk arbitrage for the firm's own account. Silfen and Zuckerberg wondered about assigning so much responsibility to such a young star. "Last year was a tough year in arbitrage. Shouldn't you focus more on this area yourself?"

"I believe with a hundred percent of his time, he can do better than I can do with forty percent of my time."

Rubin joined in: "Age is irrelevant. By expanding his responsibilities now, you may keep a real star that you might otherwise lose."

Mindich soon became the youngest-ever partner of Goldman Sachs, at age twenty-seven.

In 1984 Goldman Sachs's rank among corporate bond underwriters had dropped from first in mid-1983 to fifth as market share fell from 11 percent to 9.6 percent, while a more aggressive Salomon Brothers's market share had shot up from 16.2 percent to 25.8 percent.[2] Apologists within the firm pointed with pride to the fact that the fixed-income division had gone in less than fifteen years from breaking even—and that only because payouts to salesmen had been shaved— to being the firm's most profitable division. Realists, however, showed that too much of the apparent gain in profits was misleading. The "gain" had come from two seriously wrong sources: milking the firm's business by not being fully competitive as a dealer and losing to competitors the bond-underwriting business of longstanding clients like Sears Roebuck. Rubin and Friedman were determined to make major changes: "We see where the markets are going, and we're going to adjust." That was an understatement: They were determined to revolutionize the bond business and change everything, beginning with the business concepts or model and the leadership.

Bob Rubin and Steve Friedman had an agenda. They were convinced— just as convinced as the Two Johns had been during their sandwich lunches at Scottie's—that Goldman Sachs had to change. The firm could prosper as a small boutique *or* as a large multifaceted organization, but it could not succeed for long as a midsize firm "stuck in the muddle in the middle," which is where they thought it was. As they pointed out, it was already too late to choose the boutique option. The strategic imperative, therefore, was to expand in services and products, and particularly in markets, by going international. They wanted change both in course direction and in pace of process, and they wanted to move away from limiting the firm to Whitehead's and Weinberg's focus on client service by adding increasingly bold use of capital in disciplined, risk-taking, proprietary businesses. Competition was accelerating, particularly from large international rivals and emboldened commercial banks using capital more aggressively, taking more risks. This meant the firm risked being, relative to the best competitors, too slow, too siloed, and too cautious about new ideas and new business. They believed that the firm's "every tub on its own bottom" tradition of divisional independence made Goldman Sachs as a whole less effective than it could and should be. They worried about the implicitly cautious incrementalism of being only "fast followers"—and not always being even that. They argued that the pace of competition and the markets had accelerated so significantly that in addition to being fast followers, the firm had to be more creative, more aggressive, and better coordinated. As Friedman said, "If we're not leaders in innovation, we won't be fast enough to reap the really good profits that the innovators get—and deserve." Firmwide strategic planning was needed to identify new business opportunities, like seller-rep and tender defense, early so the firm could get out ahead of the competition.

The first step toward firmwide cooperation was for the individual departmental barons to give up their customary focus on what was best for their own separate units. "I give Bob a lot of credit for self-denial," says Friedman. "Over and over again, when we discussed how to play particular takeover battles, he *always* came down on the side of 'What's best for the firm?'—*never* on what's best for arbitrage or for him personally. He couldn't have been more partnerlike."

To Rubin and Friedman, even Goldman Sachs's traditionally great strength in nurturing client relationships could be used as an excuse for not innovating, which could hold the firm back from being fully competitive. Too many people, particularly senior people, were reluctant to upset old-time relationships or, as they saw it, tarnish the firm's sterling reputation by getting into high-profit areas like unsolicited takeovers, high-yield bonds, mortgage-backed and asset-backed securities, derivatives, and all the other rapidly emerging ways that the firm's steadily accumulating capital and its capital-markets expertise could be used aggressively to make money with money by deliberately taking informed risks. This was the origin of the transformation of Goldman Sachs from a service firm acting as *agents* to a formidable organization of capitalists acting as *principals*.

"I got caught up in a mission to fix the place," recalls Friedman. "The firm was seriously underperforming, so it was clear that there was an awful lot of work to do, but I never had a focus on becoming managing partner the same way I had dreamt of winning the national wrestling championship or a law-school prize for earning top marks or becoming a partner of Goldman Sachs. Those three were truly burning ambitions, but doing the work that had to be done at Goldman

Sachs was just an obvious responsibility. Being managing partner was a means to strengthen the firm and a responsibility, not an end."

Rubin and Friedman were right about the risk that being wisely conservative can deteriorate into defensive caution and about the importance of the firm's becoming more aggressive. John Whitehead had seen it, and it was an important factor in his decision to retire. But the obvious irony was that the cautious, conservative style Rubin and Friedman found so constraining had been at the core of the strong, team-centered culture, the reputation for integrity at every level, the consistent service to corporate and institutional clients, the strong earnings and solid financials, the persistent and skillful recruiting, the superior management, and the consistently disciplined execution upon which their more aggressive business strategies could now build. In many ways, Friedman and Rubin managed to carry these traditions forward while making Goldman Sachs an increasingly unified "one-firm firm" by reducing divisional separations, having annual reviews done by people in other departments, explicitly recognizing and rewarding cross-departmental teamwork and cooperation—and penalizing those who did not "get it."

The changes Rubin and Friedman wanted—bolder use of capital, more risk taking, rigorous evaluation of individual performance with more differentiated compensation of both employees and partners, more coordination and interaction between business units, more computerization of operations, and centralized strategic guidance—would require important changes in organizational structure and decision making. Building a strong bond business was one major reform, but only one. The totality of change they wanted amounted to a transformation of Goldman Sachs.

The kind of coordinated acceleration Friedman and Rubin sought was already taking place in mergers and acquisitions and across the investment banking division, often the incubator and beta testing site for new initiatives. The firm's key player in M&A was a young, charismatic partner, Geoff Boisi. Jesuit trained and by nature intensely committed, Boisi had come into the firm at flank speed searching for a place to make a total commitment. He started in M&A in 1971 and then ran the department informally from 1977 on and officially from 1980, a period of rapid growth and high profits. Boisi has a powerful capacity to solve problems by analyzing complex, interactive developments, evaluating all the alternatives, and, like a chess master, projecting the outcomes many moves ahead with remarkable rigor—rigor that some would see as inspiring but others would see as leading to views so strongly articulated they could appear impervious to argument.

Boisi at his best had been on display in 1984 when Getty Oil stock jumped 38 percent from $80 to $110 on a takeover bid by Pennzoil. Goldman Sachs was retained to defend Getty from the unsolicited takeover. Conflicting interests and factions within the Getty estate and its representation on the board complicated the situation. Gordon Getty, one family representative on the board, had worked with Pennzoil in developing its unsolicited offer. Influential Getty directors were in agreement that this generous and surprising offer should be accepted. Boisi, much the youngest man in the room but one of the most experienced M&A bankers in the country, took a different position that was vintage Boisi. Getty had retained Goldman Sachs to protect the shareholders' interests, and Boisi was the representative of the firm's careful, comprehensive work on the range of prices that Goldman Sachs would consider fair. So young, so analytical, so tough—and so confident he was right because he was sure the team working on the question back at the firm had rigorously examined every facet of every possibility and come to a carefully reasoned conclusion—Boisi explained that the breakup value of the company's assets was demonstrably higher than the offer. While Pennzoil's was the only offer then on the table, he insisted that an even higher offer was highly probable if Goldman Sachs was permitted to explore the merger market; so the rational decision was to reject Pennzoil. But being so very rational came across to some of the conflicted parties as unrealistic, given the time constraints of the Pennzoil offer. He was increasingly alone as one after another of the directors—some thirty years older, some forty years older—challenged his judgment and the analysis behind it. But Boisi would not be moved.

Tension mounted. Voices rose. But Boisi would not be moved.

Finally, Larry Tisch—new to the board, but experienced in business and particularly in takeovers—rose in anger: "You young guys—guys with *no* stock and *nothing* at risk—don't know what you're talking about! You don't know anything at all! You're all wrong! This is a *great* deal! This deal should be accepted—now!"

Boisi would not be moved. He was representing the careful judgment of Goldman Sachs.

Time was getting short: Under the law, Boisi and his team from Goldman Sachs would have only ten days to obtain an even higher takeover bid. But Boisi held firm. Then, four days later, after Goldman Sachs found several potential bidders, Texaco bid $130—adding nearly 20 percent more for shareholders. At eleven billion dollars, it was then the biggest acquisition in history.

A t sixty, John Weinberg was at the height of his powers as a relationship banker, enjoying substantial personal success, doing some of his most impressive deals with major clients, earning large fees, getting increasing recognition for his accomplishments, and enjoying the admiration of both clients and partners. Having devoted all his time and energy to Goldman Sachs, he had no major outside interests and almost no friends outside his business friends, so Weinberg was understandably in no hurry to leave his beloved firm or his position as its head. As Weinberg saw it, he was carefully bringing along his chosen successors, making sure Rubin and Friedman proved themselves as capable, strong organizational leaders both to the partners and to the firm's many major clients. This would take time, and there was plenty of important work for them to do in the meanwhile as they got some seasoning.

Weinberg was still leading the firm in its fast-changing business and making important strategic decisions, often "not" decisions—*not* to do the bridge loans that wreaked so much havoc at other firms, *not* to change the firm's policy against lucrative hostile takeovers, and *not* to continue the Water Street "vulture" fund. While many of Weinberg's decisions were wisely conservative, as markets changed some later appeared *too* conservative. Experienced in an era when bonds were divided into the three broad categories of high grade, medium grade, and junk, Weinberg was traditionally disdainful of dealing in junk bonds—later called high-yield bonds; he was understandably slow to recognize the rapid changes in the debt capital markets and in corporate finance that were coming because insurance companies and bond-oriented mutual funds were accepting greater credit risk in individual bond issues in their continuous search for higher bond yields for their well-diversified bond portfolios.

Weinberg believed that ensuring orderly leadership succession would be an important capstone for his career. He thought he had it all worked out and was proudly bringing along his heirs at what he saw as the right pace, schooling them to be co-leaders. When he announced in early August 1985 that Rubin and Friedman would co-head fixed income from December 1, Weinberg said, "They are very capable, very talented people, but we have a lot of talented guys around here." Weinberg was not ready to retire and not nearly ready to anoint successors, despite the widely held expectation that Rubin and Friedman would eventually be chosen. (Rubin had been with the firm for nineteen years and Friedman for twenty.) Weinberg continued with his deliberately restrained praise: "Steve and Bob have not been in the fixed-income business, but they are good organizers and will be there long enough to give the talent we have in that division some time to grow so future leaders could come from within the division."

Weinberg saw the announcement as a clear step in his long-term plan to bring them along and was proud of having given them more and more authority over the preceding five years in a progression-transition that affirmed the special quality of Goldman Sachs's thoughtfully planned leadership. But Rubin and Friedman saw it differently.

They believed that as an intermediary in an intensely competitive market, Goldman Sachs would need to expand the range of services provided and establish leadership in major regional markets around the world as the markets globalized. As Goldman Sachs expanded, it would simultaneously move in stages up the economic and profitability ladder from agency broker to underwriter and dealer to managing agent to managing partner to independent, capital-strong, risk-embracing principal. The ceiling of one stage became the floor for the next stage. As leaders, Rubin and Friedman were determined to provide the conceptual framework, and they stimulated and rewarded entrepreneurial leadership to increase the organizational drive that would make serial transformation possible. "John Weinberg was not much interested in strategy and planning," explains John Whitehead, "so Steve Friedman and Bob Rubin inherited the budgeting and planning side of the business *and* running the firm on a day-to-day basis."

"Nobody chose us or assigned us to take over the bond business," says Friedman, somehow misremembering John Weinberg's key role. "No one appointed us: We were really *self*-appointed as we worked at solving problems. Nobody chose us to lead the firm. We just led. We could see the job that needed to be done, so we just did it. We were de facto COOs of Goldman Sachs several years before we got those official letters, and Bob and I became co-heads of the firm by self-selection. For the bond business, we just started marching to the sound of the guns and improvising as we went along. While we were never thwarted and wanted to be sure we understood everyone's opinion and perspective, it took way too long to get action, particularly when we sometimes had to go back over everything to include in the loop all the other people John Weinberg felt should get a hearing." Rubin and Friedman were convinced of a need for radical organizational and strategic change, but Weinberg was not so sure, particularly as he saw other firms absorb large losses on "imperative" innovations.

Every fully developed organization is hardwired, and it's a challenge to rewire that organization to recruit and train people who are really different, particularly if the objective is to make the new organization both different and better. Doing that implies upgrading the quality of the people already in place. Friedman and Rubin had no time for patient gradualism: They wanted major change now, particularly in fixed income.

Abrupt changes, transfers, and demotions were new to Goldman Sachs, so it was striking to many when two senior partners were abruptly transferred. Eric Sheinberg, a fourteen-year partner, was switched out of his position as head of corporate bonds and soon linked up with Robert Maxwell in London, and John D. Gilliam, a twelve-year partner who headed corporate underwriting, had his position taken by two-year partner Nelson Abanto. Sheinberg was shocked and said only, "I would rather not comment." Others thought, *It's about time!* As Friedman puts it, "What's so fair about keeping tired older partners when that means blocking the best young people and violating our commitment to meritocracy?"

When the firm won business by bidding too boldly against Salomon Brothers and had to carry hundreds of millions of dollars in unsold inventories, Gilliam observed sardonically, "History tells you that we were too aggressive." An unrepentant Abanto would say, "I plead guilty to being aggressive." As Rubin and Friedman had intended, the firm's concept of the bond business soon changed from risk-avoiding, minimal use of capital and extensive customer service to boldly risking the firm's own capital to make much larger profits.

Revolutionizing the bond business was matched with important internal changes. For example, the back office was not up to date and not well integrated into the firm's operations. Information Technology would get a request for a new subsystem, go work on it for a year, and come back only to be told, "We can't use that. Our business has changed. We don't do our business the same way anymore." Friedman took the lead in rationalizing the firm's enormous expenditures in IT—nearly five hundred million dollars a year. He started by interviewing a lot of IT managers about management and quickly concluded, "It was pretty obvious and took no great genius to recognize that IT had to be integrated directly into operations and that Goldman Sachs needed to work out the costs versus values right at the line-manager level so that when a manager decided what *value* he wanted, that automatically meant the *costs* were his too."

Friedman took responsibility for dealing with complaints provoked by the incentive compensation system he and Rubin had inherited in fixed income and were determined to make more effective as a way of making the unit more competitive. Bond salesmen could—when they got everything right—make a lot of money compared to investment bankers, so some bankers went to Friedman to complain. They got this response: "Yes, the bond salesmen make more money than you do, and some make a *lot* more. That's because of two things. First, they're very talented in their work and they work very hard. Second—and this may be far more important to you—they are on a different career path with very different prospects of ever becoming a partner. So don't bitch to me unless you really think bond salesmen have a better overall career situation. If, after serious consideration, you really think theirs is better, let me know and I'll arrange an interview in bond sales for you right away." Complaints vaporized.

Friedman and Rubin pressed Weinberg more and more explicitly to turn the firm leadership over to them, but Weinberg started thinking he might stay on a while longer as senior partner. Agreeing that they would have to force the issue of Weinberg's passing the baton, Rubin and Friedman went to see him. "I told him then and there," recalls Friedman, "that if he was thinking of making a decision to stay, he had to know he'd also be deciding that it was time for me to go because I'd always said I wanted to retire young enough to have a second career. I wouldn't wait around until he was seventy and then take over the leadership for another ten years after that. That would be taking up too much of my time."

In December 1990, Rubin and Friedman officially became co–senior partners and co-CEOs, and Weinberg became senior chairman and continued working on megadeals for major clients. Rubin and Friedman would serve as co-CEOs for just three years.

They pressed ahead with organizational changes that matched their strategy. Departmental silos had to be removed and different units of the firm much more fully coordinated and integrated. The departmental barons' independence had to be reduced in favor of a firm-first orientation with far more accountability both for planning and for the results produced. "It's easy to have a strong, consistent culture when only a few people are involved and they all grew up in the same business with the same objectives, same standards, and same economic interests," says Friedman. "As the firm grew in numbers of people—and particularly in variety of allegiances, experiences, and priorities—the whole concept of teamwork became more and more important and more and more challenging."

To accelerate the dynamism of the firm, a change they believed necessary, Rubin and Friedman identified talented people who were impatient for constructive change and promoted them into key positions where their demonstrated talent and impatience would help pick up the pace in their whole unit. To preclude "too easy" acceptance of their ideas, Friedman and Rubin insisted on talking it all out and promoting debate—asking the junior people to speak first so they would not be disputing their seniors, and so seniors would have the insights of younger people before expressing their own views. They also believed that full and open discussion would result in stronger commitment to what was decided.

They intended to lead, direct, and control through the management committee—and to lead that powerful committee by consistently thinking through and agreeing on decisions in advance, which meant they were taking and holding the initiative. They would get together and work their way through each complex problem on each meeting's agenda, clarify the essence of an idea or decision, and then try to develop the best strategy and the most effective implementation. "We would work out our agreements in private and then take them forward," recalls Friedman. "If either of us felt strongly about any decision, we would defer to that strong view. If we both felt equally strongly about something, we would take the more conservative way. Bob and I never had an argument. I do not recall ever being upset with Bob. We were always asking one core question: How can we advance what's best for the firm—and make more money?" At the same time, recognizing that all members had useful information and insights to contribute "even though not all were equally valuable," they worked hard at making the committee a forum for discussion and *decisions*, not merely approvals.

However, while Friedman and Rubin believed that they never pushed things through and always thought others had useful insights, and that discussion flushed out all the key variables, other management committee members began to feel that they really brought issues to the committee just for ratification. Friedman and Rubin were determined to raise the bar: If a presenter was taking too long or repeating himself, he'd be cut off with a comment like "We heard you the first three times you made that same point." The rigorous questioning of division heads was seen as a radical change from John Weinberg's open, laissez-faire style of trusting and empowering the unit heads in the different lines of business and in different geographic regions. Some participants felt it was not the right process in a true partnership.

Rubin and Friedman would signal their disciplined focus on decision making by declaring, "There'll be no presentation. Assume always that we have all read your memo of recommendation with care." This put some investment bankers off their usual game plan of starting every discussion with crisp, energizing presentations that would frame the decision and dominate the meeting.

"Bob and Steve agreed on one dominating factor—brains," recalls Bob Steel. "They always went with the smartest guys." But this focus on brainpower was not always the right way to go. As another partner recalls, "Steve and Bob were so rational, they ignored some of those human aspects that are also very important." The intellectual rigor of the meetings increased and then increased again as Friedman and Rubin drove for what Friedman calls "strategic and tactical dynamism" and zero defects. Silfen remembers, "As the management committee took up very complex issues—and only the really hard ones go to that committee—Bob Rubin time and again would ask the deeply insightful killer questions, the ones you had been hoping nobody would be asking. With his enormous range of knowledge and amazing processing and conceptualizing capability, that was Bob's real specialty. It was uncanny. He had a tremendous grasp of what really mattered and why. Very rational, but not necessarily so good on emotional intelligence or working with other people."

Friedman mixed outward self-confidence with indications of inner uncertainty. For example, he could worry over the slightest details, even the phrasing of a simple thank-you letter after a client visit. One partner, in frustration, blurted out: "Steve, Goldman Sachs is a big firm. You have important work to do. Sign the damn letter!" Others on the management committee were amused by one member who seemed too obvious in his frequently stated admiration for Friedman's comments and opinions during and shortly after meetings. "The management committee of twelve," recalls one partner, "divided into Steve, Bob, nine others for Bob, and one for Steve: Hank Paulson," a fast-rising investment banking partner in Chicago. Friedman saw Paulson's agreement with him as demonstrating their similarities in objectives, similar experience as bankers, and similar thought processes. They had almost always already discussed the agenda items; Paulson made a practice of calling Friedman at home over the weekend. These conversations brought the men closer together on substance and, increasingly, as friends.

As Friedman and Rubin looked ahead, they agreed that with globalization, big opportunities were opening up for Goldman Sachs, but bold action would be necessary. Otherwise the best business would be taken by the firm's many smart, tough domestic competitors, like Morgan Stanley, Salomon Brothers, Lehman Brothers, First Boston, and Merrill Lynch, and by international firms like S.G. Warburg, Morgan Grenfell, Schroders, and Nomura, plus the best of the big banks, like Citibank, J.P. Morgan, Deutsche Bank, Sumitomo, HSBC, and the large Swiss banks—and a hundred other contenders. While most commercial banks would probably find a way to fall short or blunder, some were sure to get it. With their powerful resources—big balance sheets, well-established corporate and government customer relationships, and armies of people, plus the advantages of local-market national pride—they could only get stronger as competitors. Caution, delay, and half measures by the firm would be dangerously part of the problem.

While Friedman and Rubin felt frustrated by what they thought was slowness on strategic decisions, their drive to break siloed separations between divisions helped internal communications within the firm to accelerate and become a phenomenal competitive strength. This transformation depended on a combination of individuals' driving commitment to both send and receive actionable information quickly for all who might be concerned; the power of the organization's "no secrets" culture of lateral sharing and communicating widely; the flattening of hierarchy during Gus Levy's era; and the communications technology that the firm provided everyone. Even on Saturday and Sunday, a hundred incoming and a hundred outgoing messages every day would become normal for every partner—with immediate response common and same-day response mandatory, no matter where in the whole world the sender and receiver might be.

Friedman and Rubin were particularly proficient at communicating with each other. Like Whitehead and Weinberg, they were determined to prevent the obvious problem of having people play one of them off against the other, so they set out a clear policy: "If you talk to one of us, you've talked to both of us. It's our job to keep each other fully up to date." A late-night policy question to one of them might be answered with a specific decision early the next morning by the other. As Friedman recalls, "We didn't want any chance of anyone getting one inch of water in between us. We were tenacious because we had to be, but I felt badly when people thought we were too aggressive and called us the Doberman pinschers."

As managing partners, Rubin and Friedman had to be actively engaged in the firm's major client relationships globally and had to understand the market risks being taken worldwide. So both had huge travel obligations and each had key clients to cover. "We adopted an effective one-here-one-traveling coordination, recognizing that when two people coordinate *and* focus, their impact on an organization can be truly formidable," explains Friedman. He then smiles as he adds mischievously, "We split countries and client coverage as evenly as possible. Bob got Moscow, so to be entirely fair, I graciously took Paris."

Rubin and Friedman wanted to differentiate Goldman Sachs in the breadth and intensity of service received by the firm's clients and prospective clients, so they drove for a superior level of coordination across the whole firm through "360-degree" personal-performance reviews based on evaluations collected on each person by everyone he worked with, in and out of his department. They also established "cross-roughing" reviews in which people were evaluated by managers from other units to ensure consistent firmwide objectivity. "With three-sixty reviews, everyone knew they had a real say in one another's evaluations and that everything was put out in the open once each year," recalls Friedman. "Everyone was taught to play to their strengths and not to expose the firm to their weaknesses." Taking control of performance appraisals and compensation—which traditionally had been left to the different unit heads—was important to Rubin and Friedman. Centralization facilitated consistency, rewarded firmwide teamwork, and reduced the powers of the divisional barons. As Friedman recalls, "We needed control of the personnel review process to drive cooperation through."

Friedman believed there should be much more differentiation in compensation, to achieve more discipline and accountability—and more control by the firm as a whole rather than by the separate divisions. Explains Friedman, "On compensation, the firm had become more interested in maximizing social harmony than in rigorous evaluations, so actual payouts to individuals were closer than might be expected, and they were converging." As Friedman identified one source of the problem, "If a reviewer had fifty reviews to do—which was not unusual—it was awfully hard not to start skipping and skimming to get the task out of the way, even though people's careers were at stake. But this was not fair to the careers of the individuals. We owed them accurate feedback." Friedman and Rubin were prepared to force objective discrimination to prevent cronyism. Every unit head was required to evaluate all his people twice a year, divide them into quartiles, and reflect those rankings in compensation—even unit heads who protested sincerely, "But I don't have *any* fourth-quartile performers!" Anyone in the bottom quartile was likely to get fired. If someone was in the fourth quartile for three or four consecutive years—sometimes called the "fifth quartile"—he was almost sure to get fired.

In the past, most members of a partnership class had traditionally held the same percentage of the partnership for many years. No more. After the second two-year review, performance-based differentiation took hold—and the partners knew one another's percentages. The differentiation in partnership percentages became increasingly significant. If they were not continually strong performers, partners were, with increasing frequency, taken out of the partnership and obliged to go limited.

Friedman was convinced that principal investing was a highly profitable opportunity and that Goldman Sachs was in an ideal position to move boldly into the business by combining its own capital, its expertise in corporate finance, its many corporate relationships, its research knowledge of companies and industries, and its access to institutional investors and, through Private Client Services, to wealthy individuals. Through its extraordinary relationships with senior executives at thousands of client companies that might be open to considering spin-offs and divestitures—as many did as clients for tender defense—Goldman Sachs would have the valuable competitive advantage of getting the first call on potential deals. But launching principal investing was not easy.

"It was a bitch to get the firm to make the first principal investments," recalls Friedman, who wanted to put five million dollars into the first KKR fund to get a window on how to succeed in private-equity investing. Resistance was strong, with comments from partners like "We don't work to support other people's business" and "Go start your own fund." (Earlier, Friedman had been tempted to resign from Goldman Sachs to do private equity on his own, and after eventually leaving Goldman Sachs, he did go into private equity.) To one complaint, "KKR will see us as *competitors*," Friedman replied: "Yes, but they'll get used to it." And then he got an okay for a starter deal with KKR. "Eventually," he says, "for four million, we bought a small paper business from the Rockefellers. At least it got us started."

As Friedman recalls, "For private equity, the ultimate key was to get Hank Paulson—a one-hundred-percent-certified investment banker and co-head of IBS—to oversee and take the lead and head up that unit and incorporate its results into investment banking's P&L.[3] If we were okay on our skills as investors and we had the best deal flow, we would have a clear competitive edge overall. But we needed the superior deal flow that could only come from our many corporate clients, and that meant we needed the IBS guys out there working for *us*. Once we got the system going properly, it was clear that we would often be the preferred investors."

Friedman got little active support and considerable resistance for his private-equity initiative, confirming his observation that "it's harder to get a good idea accepted than it is to get a good idea." But with fund-raising help from PCS salesmen and a three-hundred-million-dollar commitment of capital by the firm, Goldman Sachs raised one billion dollars for GS Capital Partners I in 1991. With another three-hundred-million-dollar commitment, the firm raised $1.75 billion for GS Capital Partners II in 1995. As investment results confirmed the firm's capabilities, even larger funds would be raised, and Goldman Sachs became increasingly prominent in private-equity investing. In 1994, 28 percent of Ralph Lauren's private company was acquired for $135 million, and that investment more than tripled in value to $578 million in an IPO three years later. Understandably, enthusiasm for private equity increased.

As his interest in real estate led him to study the driving factors in that business, Friedman was told by the firm's experts in real estate that the key to success with an important office building was getting the prime tenant. "As a major firm with a large number of employees, lots of equipment, special spatial needs like a large trading floor plus attractive space to accommodate numerous visitors, Goldman Sachs was clearly a prime tenant," Friedman recalls. "So why give that economic advantage to a developer when we could, instead, keep it and use it ourselves? Since we knew we could deliver the prime tenant—ourselves—we should own our own building." This thinking was behind the firm's acting on a recommendation by George Doty that it buy and complete the large headquarters at 85 Broad Street being constructed by a Columbus, Ohio, developer. Upon completion, it was sold as a fully rented building to MetLife and then leased back for the firm's use on terms that gave Goldman Sachs 100 percent control of all operating decisions, plus a tidy profit.

In the early nineties the firm also took a hard look at Canary Wharf in London. Commercial-property leases in London are traditionally long term and "marked to market" every five years. The only way out of risking these escalations was to buy a building. As the managing partner charged with all sorts of administrative responsibilities, Fred Krimendahl bid—but was outbid—on two City properties. Then the *Daily Telegraph* moved its huge printing presses to the London Docklands, and its cavernous building on Fleet Street became available during Christmas week—if a deal could be closed by year-end. The vacated space was ideal for constructing a major new office building in a fine location now known worldwide as Peterborough Court. Krimendahl quickly organized a Channel Islands company for tax reasons and bought the property—only to be criticized for not clearing it with the management committee. The move was a great success.

The alternatives remained unattractive. As Friedman recalls, "I could see that by 2010 Canary Wharf would be a superb property, but back at the time of decision, there were way too many problems: None of the stores or apartments you see now were there, transportation was awful, the location was completely unfamiliar, it took too long to get there because the tube and light-rail lines were not yet installed, and, as a partnership rather than a corporation, we'd have had all sorts of significant tax problems. So we passed on that particular project." However, the commitment to capital investments, and not just in buildings, was gaining momentum at Goldman Sachs.

Bob Rubin saw numerous opportunities to commit capital in high-profit principal trading and knew that since the greatest risk in trading is *time*, traders must have long-term, patient capital that can wait for results; as Keynes observed, markets can stay "wrong" longer than a dealer can stay liquid, causing "gambler's ruin." If the firm was to pursue its most profitable principal trading opportunities, Goldman Sachs would have to accept abrupt, irregular gains and losses and would need very patient capital.

As a principal investor, few other financial organizations in the world had so much going for them. The firm's network of agency relationships was a powerful advantage. But one big ingredient was wrong for principal investing and acquisitions: Goldman Sachs's partnership economics. Great investments could take many years to mature fully, but partnership accounting measured everything annually. The risks on a principal investment would usually concentrate during the early years, but the payoffs would usually come in later years—off cycle with a partnership. One solution to this mismatch would have been to use dated accounts, under which the partners who made the investment would reap the returns no matter when they came.

But that approach wasn't Friedman and Rubin's. Both were skillful and experienced defensive players, watchful to identify risks and uncertainties and to protect against them. The combination of more capital commitments and the need for more liquidity was a straightforward management problem to Friedman and Rubin, and there was a better solution: public ownership, originally suggested long before by Fred Krimendahl.

With more and more firms talking about going public, or taking action, cagey John Weinberg had been ready to explore the question for Goldman Sachs but made no explicit commitment: "Do you think I want to go public?

Not me!" Weinberg and others spent years of off-site meetings pondering an IPO and how to maintain the spirit of the partnership, and Friedman and Rubin had quickly championed the idea. In December 1986, they had made their ill-fated presentation to the partners on behalf of a unanimous management committee of a proposal to take Goldman Sachs public. At the Saturday morning meeting, Rubin and Friedman, who were already widely accepted as the next generation of leaders, gave their vision of the future opportunities that were opening up for the firm as a trading powerhouse and as a private-equity investor and why an important pathway to becoming that higher-profit firm was public ownership.

Looking back, those who were there say the Saturday morning presentation was not successful because it was surprisingly weak and amateurish. An important problem was that almost no time had been given in advance to preparing the partners' thinking about an IPO, so the partners had not thought enough about the complex subject or its many implications to agree to such a major organizational and cultural change. The partnership had always been considered almost sacred to the people—and especially the partners—of Goldman Sachs. Most had assumed the firm would forever be a private partnership, and most believed the partnership had been and would always be the vital engine of the firm's continuing success.

Everyone could see that an IPO would make senior partners suddenly wealthy, but it was also clear to the thirty-seven new partners—twice as many as in any prior class—who had become partners only one week before, that they would be frozen at small percentages, getting only a very small part of the wealth they could expect to accumulate over the next ten or fifteen years as active partners. (Rubin, given his cautious outlook for the business, had actually thought even the new partners would be better off with an IPO.) Senior partners tended to be in favor, but were silent. Various groups raised questions. Some expressed concern about the loss of privacy regarding their accumulating wealth. Investment bankers had no need in their business for large amounts of permanent capital and were unenthusiastic about making major capital commitments to support trading. As the meeting continued, partners spoke with increasingly strong feelings and sometimes in loud voices—even with tears—about the risk of losing the spiritual values of a partnership that had been nurtured for many years by their predecessors and that would, they hoped, be strengthened and passed on to worthy successors. Resistance was so strong that it was back to the drawing boards for an IPO. But both Rubin and Friedman were determined to change Goldman Sachs in structure, strategy, operations, incentives, and controls, and to commit to international expansion, embracing risk, using technology, increasing discipline, and deploying capital. Permanent capital—going public—was key.

Perhaps symbolically, John Weinberg had taken a seat on the dais somewhat physically separated from the management committee and expressed no support for the proposal, even though partners in the audience knew that his share in a public offering would be worth well over one hundred million dollars. No decision was made on Saturday, and the traditional partners' dinner dance was held that night at Sotheby's.

Sunday morning, before the meeting reconvened, the new partners gathered together. They could, if they agreed, vote as a block of thirty-seven. Then Steve Friedman arrived. He was angry and insisted there be no block voting by any interest group—everyone should think for and vote for the firm as a whole. "You don't have to be Mother Teresa, but vote—individually—with only half being what's right for you and at least half what's best for Goldman Sachs." The new partners were daunted: They knew Friedman was strongly in favor of an IPO, and they all knew that future changes in their partnership percentages would be made by the management committee.

Jim Weinberg, who for many years headed up IBS and provided invaluable informal counsel to his younger brother John, rose to speak for faithful stewardship and the partners' responsibilities to the next generation. In his view, the proposal just didn't make any sense. The heritage that had been entrusted to the current partners as stewards brought with it a responsibility to make the firm stronger and pass it on to the next generation. Besides, he had no interest in reading in the newspapers about partners' earnings. This signaled for many that John was not really in favor of an IPO. As Jim Weinberg often did, he had caught the consensus of the partnership. No vote was taken or needed.

Some believed that with the consensus not to go public, the traditional values of the partnership were reaffirmed and the partners were rededicated to building the firm. Some believed the business strategy of going global was agreed. Others worried that the genie of greed was out of the bottle. For many, the infusion of equity capital from Sumitomo showed that an IPO was not necessary to obtain the capital needed for a strategy of growth and expansion abroad. It didn't really matter. The partners of Goldman Sachs were not psychologically ready to be a public company.

After the silent decision not to go public became clear to all, Bob Rubin spoke to the whole firm: "As partners in this firm, we are not the owners of the firm. We are closer to being fiduciaries and caretakers of the culture. We really believe we don't have the right to sell Goldman Sachs."

On December 11, 1992, an impromptu meeting of the available partners was called via e-mail and held on the thirtieth floor of 85 Broad Street. The partners of Goldman Sachs had expected five or ten years under Rubin and Friedman. Nobody had expected Bill Clinton to win the presidency. Ten days before, Warren Christopher, soon to be named secretary of state, had called Rubin, sounding him out about becoming secretary of the Treasury, but Rubin said he was too new to Washington and felt that Lloyd Bentsen was the best candidate for Treasury because he had the right experience. Then Christopher and others pressed Rubin to take a new economic-policy-coordinating job at the White House.

"Can I talk to people outside the government to get their judgment?"

"Can you give me an example?"

"Well, I'd always want to get Steve Friedman's thoughts."

After a long meeting in Arkansas, Rubin—who had not expected to go to DC and had not known Clinton well—would be going to Washington. When he returned to New York early the next day, he went directly to Goldman Sachs to meet with his partners and tell them of his plans. He was obviously tired and hungry. On the plane from Little Rock to New York, he'd made some notes of what to say, and he spoke to the group as he ate some breakfast. He talked informally and emotionally about how much he treasured his experiences and his friendships at Goldman Sachs. But it was clear to his partners that he was already relocating his personal center of gravity to Washington.

Steve Friedman would now be alone. Partners would urge him to appoint strong people to share the burdens of global leadership. For many, the loss of Bob Rubin was far more than the loss of a unique business leader. It was spiritual.

"For me," recalls Styer, "the defining picture of what it really meant to be a partner of Goldman Sachs is the picture etched into my mind of Bob Rubin and Bob Mnuchin, each with a Styrofoam cup of coffee in his hand, standing together in the trading room, quietly chatting—chatting about the markets and some ideas of what they might do—and it's only seven in the morning! Why so intensely engaged so early in the morning *every* day? Because that's what they truly wanted to do and where they wanted to be. And that's the way it was all the time for everybody at Goldman Sachs. At Morgan Stanley, where I also worked for a while, people saw their work as personally defining—it was what they could do and did do—but at Goldman Sachs, it was much more: It was *life*."

In the past, the firm's career compact with its professional staff had been clear: almost no lateral hires, so those who had made a commitment to the firm had no worry about competition being brought in over them. The longer people work together, the better their understanding of one another and the better their communication. Over the years, however, this policy has been diluted by so many exceptions that it's no longer a policy. International expansion was a force for the change, as were the move into bonds, the acquisition of J. Aron, and the expansion of Goldman Sachs Asset Management.

When there were no strong internal candidates, key people had been recruited from other organizations. George Doty came from Coopers to head internal administration. Claude Ballard came from Prudential Insurance to lead a new effort in real estate. And Jim Weinberg joined the firm after fifteen years at Owens-Corning Fiberglas when John Whitehead called to say: "We're hiring good people to join us in investment banking and developing our corporate-client relationships. This could be just your kind of work." Mike Mortara came from Salomon Brothers to lead in mortgages; Simon Robertson came from Kleinwort Benson; Sylvain Hefes came from Rothschild to develop investment banking in France. In 1993 E. Gerald Corrigan, who had just completed nine years' service as president of the Federal Reserve Bank of New York, joined the firm at fifty-two to chair its international advisers group.

Lateral hiring is not as easy as it may at first appear. As a banking partner explains, "When you are growing too rapidly to develop all your own people, and start hiring people laterally, you *will* make mistakes—hiring wrong people and promoting wrong people. Those people can become the organization's enemy within—people other people don't want to help, do want to avoid, and will even risk hurting the firm just to penalize the bad guy. You try to hire only very strong outsiders, but they usually have to unlearn the habits, practices, and ways of doing things that worked very well for them in their old place. This almost assures they'll be different. Combine this with their not knowing most of our people and our ways of doing things, and the odds of disruption are high. The odds go up again when they come as strong individuals to a culture that depends upon teamwork and interchangeability and commitment to the group and the firm—to *we*, not *me*."

"Transferring into Goldman Sachs from other firms is usually quite difficult," says partner Jun Makihara. "Having learned how to succeed in other firms, lateral transfers typically reach for P&L authority and accountability, but that would conflict with Goldman Sachs's concepts of teaming." Ken Wilson, who came in laterally, makes telling comparisons: "If you try a solo hero deal and fail, you're in double jeopardy—once for failing and once for trying to go it alone. At Salomon Brothers, it was hard to get the right analyst or product specialist to schlep all the way to Asia, but at Goldman Sachs, it's easy. 'On the next plane' is SOP. This firm plays to win—as a firm."

23

❧

TRANSFORMATION

For many years, Wall Street traders and academics were worlds apart and each group was proud of both not respecting and not liking the other. Each group was articulate in dismissing the other as knowing nothing of importance, understanding nothing that mattered, and doing nothing of great value. But in one of history's great intellectual revolutions, the rigorous quantitative models of academic finance, bolstered by powerful computers and extensive databases, came into a powerful coherence with the creativity of Wall Street's highly motivated traders. That combination changed everything.

The primary change-making factor was the development of financial derivatives. Trading in derivatives grew exponentially in a profusion of variations. In a single decade, derivatives grew to dominate the traditional cash markets in value traded. Moreover, they created bridges between previously separated markets and currencies that "connected all the dots" into one massive, interconnected global market for all securities in all currencies over all time spans.

The first linkup between academics and traders occurred in the seventies in a small "skunk works" unit at the World Bank. Led by Eugene Rotberg, an iconoclastic innovator who served as the bank's treasurer, the unit made the bank one of the world's largest and most creative borrowers. Rotberg's objective was to minimize the bank's cost of borrowing. His strategy was to minimize cost by maximizing innovation. That's why Rotberg hired bold creative rationalists like Mark Winkelman into his skunk works of creativity.

In 1977 Mark Winkelman was recruited from the World Bank to Goldman Sachs by Victor Chiang to set up a business within Fixed Income to trade financial futures versus Treasuries. (T-bill futures began trading on the Chicago Mercantile Exchange in 1976 and Treasury-bond futures began trading in 1977.) No one in Fixed Income at Goldman Sachs understood futures, so Winkelman was joining others who were leaving the World Bank to make real money in this new business, which seemed certain to grow rapidly. But even the most enthusiastic optimists would be astonished by the explosive growth that developed quickly and continued to compound for several decades. Growth in futures exceeded all expectations and created an expanding series of profit-making opportunities for Goldman Sachs.

Being new and poorly understood, financial futures—whose true value was hardwired to the price of the underlying Treasury security, which had no credit risk—were often substantially mispriced. This created opportunities to go long or short futures and short or long the underlying Treasuries in a wide variety of riskless arbitrages of the frequently mispriced spreads. With half a dozen different and interchangeable government bonds, Winkelman had ample trading options to work with, so—with very little real risk—he made substantial and steadily increasing profits. Chiang was also interested in "rolling down the yield curve"— exploiting mispricings between, for example, three-month Treasuries and six-month Treasuries. But the magnitude of these mispricings was much smaller and the arbitrage less perfect than when working with futures versus Treasuries.

In 1978 "interest rates went completely crazy," recalls Winkelman. The main causes were political. To have both guns and butter—to pay for both Vietnam and his Great Society commitments without raising taxes—Lyndon Johnson had produced a delayed tsunami of inflation, which surged under Jimmy Carter until Federal Reserve chairman Paul Volcker slammed on the brakes. By forcing interest rates to record highs, the Fed opened up a rich variety of highly profitable opportunities for cash-versus-futures arbitrages for Winkelman's unit to exploit.

Chiang understood the academic theory of fixed-income arbitrage, but he was much too theoretical for Goldman Sachs's traders, wasn't a trader himself, and was, unfortunately, a poor presenter—particularly to rough-and-tumble traders and the men on the management committee, who were unfamiliar with futures and options and still held the prejudices of traders about academics. When Winkelman began meeting with the management committee to explain what he was doing and how it worked, the reaction was, "Thank goodness you finally made this stuff all clear and understandable!" The management committee's increasingly favorable reaction, and the increasingly impressive profits Winkelman produced, encouraged Jon Corzine to use the new techniques on the government-bond desk. After Henry Fowler joined the firm, Goldman Sachs had become a registered dealer in U.S. government bonds, but Corzine agreed with Winkelman that "you'll never make any real money as a routine dealer in Treasuries." Corzine would make substantial profits for Goldman Sachs in risk-embracing trades based on long-maturity Treasury bonds.

As a long-bond trader in governments, Corzine was in a very different business from Winkelman as an arbitrageur, and their styles of thinking were divergent. Winkelman was rigorously analytical, stayed close to market specifics, and was careful. Corzine understood concepts, had a sensitive feel for the markets, was intuitive, and boldly took substantial risks. Their fundamental differences in concepts and approach to trading would spring to the surface when both men— for different reasons—wanted to hit the same major bid or offer, putting them into direct conflict for a profitable trade.

Friedman and Rubin went looking for people who could make Goldman Sachs at least fully competitive with the two leading bond dealers, Salomon Brothers and First Boston. Their first approach consisted of promotions and transfers within Goldman Sachs. Rubin knew Winkelman was a good manager of people and a smart leader with the power of disciplined determination. Winkelman was rational, dry, a bit formal, and a loner. Corzine was a strongly intuitive risk taker and a relentless trader. With his warm teddy-bear personal touch, he was unusually well connected within and without the firm. Winkelman was not willing to come into Goldman Sachs as a subordinate of Corzine's—which was what Corzine clearly expected. After some awkwardness, the two men agreed they would share an office on the fifth floor as equals. When Friedman and Rubin were appointed co-COOs, Corzine and Winkelman were made co-heads of fixed income. Again, Corzine was disappointed not to be in complete control. Later Corzine would see all too clearly the drawbacks of divided executive power, but once Friedman and Rubin made it clear that Corzine and Winkelman had to work together, they worked at it with reasonable success. "Once we developed an understanding that we would have to work together," says Winkelman, "we developed a sensible structure and soon found working together was pretty easy." But their differences in personality, ways of doing business, and strategic concepts could neither be hidden nor fully harmonized.

When Friedman and Rubin had taken over the division in the early eighties, they identified Salomon Brothers as the business pacesetter and the firm to beat. In a deliberate break with the firm's traditions, they hired in several Salomon people, who jump-started the buildup in the mid-eighties. In a few years, most of the imports from Salomon Brothers had left, but they had made an important impact on the firm's strategic change from service and accommodation to a profit-focused, risk-taking, principal and proprietary trading dealer.

With considerable help from the powerful imports from Salomon Brothers, Goldman Sachs deliberately and conscientiously transformed the bond business from the old business of making judgments and taking risks on interest rates and bond maturities—which had proven too difficult as savvy institutions became increasingly dominant in the bond markets—to a business that concentrated on managing spreads and arbitrages in deliberately crafted portfolios across markets and between different types of securities in markets all over the world. As partner Rick Garonzik explained with evident satisfaction, "Now, it doesn't really matter whether interest rates or markets go up or down. We're organized to produce profits on a regular basis, and this stability of earnings is important to our cost of funding our very large dealer positions. The complexity of operations in a modern bond dealership, thanks to computer systems and sophisticated risk controls, is awesome. Our bond business is so complex now that it is very hard to explain. While the guys in the business have much more understanding of their business situation and what they can do as managers, it's *really* hard to explain to people outside the business—and even harder for them to understand."

Taking deliberate risks and managing those risks had long been central to the way business was understood and conducted at Goldman Sachs—particularly under Gus Levy and Bob Rubin, who both came out of arbitrage, where they developed a way of thinking about using risk productively to make profits. Explains Garonzik, "We make every effort to know and understand each risk and the interconnectedness of all the different types of risks, and then build a *portfolio* of business risks that is profoundly different from a simple sum of the parts."

In one area after another, Friedman and Rubin made simultaneous changes on many dimensions in the strategy and structure of the firm's bond business. The accelerating speed of innovation and the faster maturation of the proliferating new bond markets—which brought new-product profit margins down—was a fundamental change in the character of markets. It brought changes in the competitive strategies of firms and in the pace of competition. No longer could Goldman Sachs afford to follow Whitehead's careful strategy of letting the competitor firms develop new products and services and then figuring out the best feasible design enhancements and rolling to market dominance through its well-established network of corporate relationships. "That strategy was too slow; any firm following that strategy implementation wouldn't get to the market until the best part of the profit party was all over," recalls Steve Friedman.

A series of strategic initiatives were launched to capitalize on market developments or catch up with competitors. Steve Friedman brought over Arthur Walter from First Boston to develop an interest-rate swaps business, but his operation was limited by credit concerns, particularly on "long tail" swaps that didn't fit at all comfortably into partnership accounting. For many years, the firm would do swaps only on an agency basis, but Corzine and Winkelman campaigned for and finally did get approval to act as principals in the swaps business.

Joel Kirschbaum was charged with developing a fixed-income capital markets group to work with bond issuers to create transactions by showing investors ways to create tactical gains by making market-sensitive trades at rapid-fire speeds. This replicated much of what Gus Levy and Bob Mnuchin had created in block trading for the institutional equity market.

In bond research, a rapid buildup reached one hundred people in short order. In mortgages, Salomon Brothers already had a bear hug on the business by the time Goldman Sachs got going. It would take five or six years of slugging it out without profit for Goldman Sachs to establish a major market presence—too long a time in a partnership. Other firms, like Salomon Brothers and First Boston, already had the high ground and could dictate the terms of competition from positions of great strength in the markets. But Rubin and Friedman were determined. Goldman Sachs resolved to absorb several years of losses to muscle its way into the business.

International bond dealing surged in the late seventies and early eighties as Eurobonds, for which all trading had to be executed overseas, became an important part of the international financial markets. But Goldman Sachs was slow internationally and executed poorly. As Garonzik recognized in retrospect, "In the mid-eighties, when I went to London, we were losing a lot of money. Part of this was not having the right people. It was chaotic, a real mess."

Rubin had initiated futures arbitrage as part of his experiments in potential new markets and wanted to build a small commodities business. He had started a small foreign-exchange business and was considering trading in gold when the purchase of J. Aron overwhelmed those nascent strategies.

As commercial-paper spreads shrank, Friedman and Rubin recognized that adjustments would not be enough: The firm's longest-running business needed a total reorganization. Recognizing the difference in approach to business problems between Winkelman and Corzine—analytical versus intuitive and objective versus people-sensitive—Friedman and Rubin assigned Winkelman to reorganize not only commercial paper, but the whole money-market business. This would include T-bills and federal-agency securities, which intruded into what Corzine saw as part his territory as head of Governments. As Winkelman recalls, "The firm's commercial-paper business was run pretty much the same way it had been run for thirty years, even though, with commercial banks forcing their way into the business by cutting prices, spreads were collapsing. Risk-adjusted, the business was no longer profitable. It was dumb to be making markets in commercial paper, but we did it to support the guys in investment banking. We made no money, but at least it helped start relationships with corporations, relationships the firm could build on."

Winkelman quickly saw the only realistic way out of the box: Cut costs so much more than any competitor possibly could that profits would come back. The only way to wring out costs was to automate and computerize all but the most unusual or difficult orders.

· · · ·

I nconsequential as it may have appeared to them at the time, the decisive moment in bringing academics and traders together was a phone call in the mid-eighties from Bob Rubin to Professor Robert Merton. While living in traditionally separated worlds, both men were exceedingly bright and quietly charming, and each had enjoyed their recent first meeting. Rubin was looking for leads on unusually talented people who might be able to help Goldman Sachs develop a new kind of business based on an intriguing cluster of insights being developed by financial economists at a few universities. Searching, as usual, for extreme brainpower, he asked Merton, "Do you know anyone who is really good at quantitative analysis and sophisticated models?" Merton suggested talking to a young MIT professor, Fischer Black. "He's very good—a serious prospect for a Nobel Prize—and he's getting a divorce so he may be looking for a real change in his life situation. He's unusual in several ways. Even spells his name differently: It's F-i-s-*c*-h-e-r. I think he's special."

Increasingly fascinated by the profound changes he saw coming with the development of the Chicago Board Options Exchange, where he had gotten involved from the beginning, Rubin was interested in the potential of capitalizing on the new mathematical concepts of market behavior coming from leading academics, particularly the "quants" at MIT, Chicago, Harvard, and Yale. As Rubin would soon learn, the creative leader of this group at MIT was in fact Fischer Black. He taught a rigorous course on capital-market theory and liked to begin classes with descriptions of anomalies—observable market behaviors that did not seem rational.[1]

"The Value Line index trades on the Kansas City exchange," announced Black as he began one of his classes. "The individual stocks represented by the index trade on the New York and American stock exchanges. There appears to be a mispricing here because the share-weighted price of the index is not an identity with the sum of the prices of the shares taken individually." Students had heard things like this before. To most, it illustrated how predictably arcane the finance classes could be at MIT, particularly with a professor as extraordinarily intelligent and classically "ivory tower" as Fischer Black, who was already becoming famous for coinventing the Black-Scholes options-pricing model. While students admired Black's brilliance, most thought his odd fascination with recondite anomalies was surely a useless waste of time, meaningless in the *real* world where they hoped to be heading: Wall Street.

In physics, the concept of equilibrium, where two opposing forces cancel each other exactly—for example, when the heat flowing into a body cancels exactly the heat flowing out—is formidable in its applications. Black believed that market prices were determined by similar cancellations by opposing forces, so equilibrium was at the center of his research. In Black-Scholes, the value-determining equation assumes that a stock and an option on that stock will be in equilibrium, and since their prices will provide investors with the same expected return per unit of risk, a rational investor will be indifferent between buying the stock and buying the option. When written out mathematically, this produced the original Black-Scholes equation, but solving the equation took several more years. Robert Merton, working in parallel to Black and Scholes, developed a rigorous understanding of the logic behind Black-Scholes. He showed that the value of a stock option can be replicated with a "simple" dynamic blend of cash and shares of stock by continually exchanging shares for cash or cash for shares until the investor winds up with the same payout as the option; so the value of the option is always exactly equal to the cost of buying the correct initial mixture of cash and shares at their current market prices. Merton's approach was more formal and hence more powerful, so it became the standard approach for users, including Fischer Black. Before Black-Scholes, each trader had to have his own way of estimating the correct price of each stock option—estimating only approximately and never accurately enough to commit significant money to making good markets based on small apparent differences. Because it provided the exactly correct prices traders needed to make reliably profitable markets, the Black-Scholes model went directly from an academic journal to the floor of the Chicago Board Options Exchange and the trading desks of all major securities dealers.[2]

After the introduction of Black-Scholes, the markets for options—and an exploding proliferation of other derivatives—mushroomed from marginal importance to global dominance, transforming corporate finance and all financial markets, particularly the options-dealing business. Options changed from a business with high risks of capital losses for the dealer due to mispricing to a business with virtually no dealer risk of mispricing. Through "dynamic replication," a dealer could create his own options by continually changing the mix of cash and stock, and therefore would always know the exact cost of doing so. With mispricing risks to dealers expunged, the premium costs charged to option buyers shrank greatly and the pricing of options became standardized. As a result of these three major changes, options came out of the closet and trading volume took off. Before Black-Scholes, options dealers were always at risk as principals on every option they wrote, so they wrote options in small amounts on special terms and at high costs to the buyer—which, of course, kept demand low. But now—after the insights of Merton, Black, and Scholes—dealers could use the model's recipe to mix up their own calls out of cash and shares and easily and accurately estimate their costs. This meant they could price their homemade options correctly to make a profit while taking zero capital risk. As the costs fell, creativity on Wall Street flourished. All sorts of new kinds of options were developed and traded, including options on interest rates, credit ratings, weather, energy and commodity prices, and all sorts of other futurities.

In 1971 America had followed Germany and Japan in leaving the Bretton Woods system of fixed currency-exchange rates, and exchange rates floated, set by supply and demand. In 1972 the International Monetary Market opened for trading in Chicago, and in 1976 the ban on commodity options was lifted by Congress. In 1982 the Chicago Mercantile Exchange would begin trading a new "commodity": futures contracts on the S&P 500 stock index. And in 1983 it began trading options on S&P futures—setting off the chain reaction of the derivatives revolution on Wall Street and in global finance. By the 1990s, the underlying value of CBOE options would exceed the value traded in the NYSE cash market. In the current decade, derivatives volume worldwide has ballooned to a total value estimated at $150 *trillion*—many, many times larger than the volume of all the stock, bond, and currency markets.

A member of the Chicago Board Options Exchange since 1973, Rubin understood the Black-Scholes formula, which he'd been using since before it was published. Rubin and a few others at Goldman Sachs recognized the potential profit power of coordinating and even integrating the brainpower of a Fischer Black with the firm's trading operation, where a new kind of trader was learning to understand the importance of having rigorous analytical models to determine the correct way to hedge against each risk exposure.

Rubin was clear in his reasoning on hiring quants: "They see and think about things outside the range of our thinking. That appears to be a difference that might work. And if it does, it's so different that it could make us a lot of money. And if it doesn't work, we can easily kill it."

In December 1983, Professor Black met in Cambridge with the partner in charge of the most "real world," profit-focused, pragmatic business unit at Goldman Sachs: risk arbitrage.[3] Black was favorably impressed with the caliber of Rubin's analytical mind, and Rubin sensed that there was an opportunity to engage Professor Black's conceptual and analytical brilliance with the data-processing power, trading know-how, and risk capital of Goldman Sachs.* After several hours of mutual probing, they each knew the other was a very special thinker and believed they could work well together. Rubin soon offered Black a job as an "experiment"—an experiment that would work remarkably well. Black was surprised by the amount of pay Rubin offered "for starters" and agreed to consider it. Two months later, Black left MIT and moved to Goldman Sachs.

For Black, the lure of an academic life had been the freedom to think new thoughts. Now, Black would find Goldman Sachs even "better for learning than a university, partly because the firm's business required continual learning as it adapts to new conditions."[4] Explained Black, "One of the things I like about doing science, that is the most fun, is coming up with something that seems ridiculous when you first hear it, but finally seems obvious when you've finished."[5] He believed that fundamental discovery could come only from challenging conventional wisdom and that the ultimate test of any theory or innovation was its practical usefulness.

At Goldman Sachs, Black found not only high rewards and the freedom to think new thoughts, but also, given Rubin's strategic drive, a truly compelling need to think still more new thoughts. Just as Black believed that in all investing, the biggest source of risk is time, Rubin believed it was important to have few *beliefs*, because the markets are uncertain and always subject to change; the secret to successful adaptation was mental agility and flexibility. Rubin was experienced in uncertain markets and skilled in the disciplines of arbitrage, so he knew that taking on risk as a measured part of the skilled, intelligent use of capital was vital

---

* Technology development at Goldman Sachs was profit driven, so it could be very advanced where profits were to be made and archaic in nearby areas. For example, even in 1990, the Goldman Sachs payroll system could not cut checks for more than one hundred thousand dollars, so if a bonus was one million dollars, the recipient got a stack of ten envelopes, each with one check for one hundred thousand dollars inside—just before Thanksgiving.

to the firm's future. He turned to David Silfen, a sophisticated and serially innovative trader: "You'll be the one to amalgamate Fischer into the firm"—and left
the two of them to figure it out. As Black would soon recognize, "flow trading"—
knowing all about the many sources of supply and demand—enables traders in
the middle of all those flows to anticipate price movements.

"Bob had the vision to appreciate how the guys with the academic theories
and quantitative models could work with the traders and add substantial value,"
recalls Silfen. "He was clear that the only guys who could really cut it were the
guys with the very high candlepower—real intellectual talent." Rubin quietly
and quickly made it clear that every division head should focus on recruiting,
on getting the best brains. "Bob's a democrat, both personally and politically,"
explains Silfen, "but in business, he was consistently and insistently interested in
one thing—excellence."

Rubin wanted Black to help in two ways. First, use computers and finance
theory to make money trading stocks and options for the equities division, where
Black organized the quantitative strategies group.[6] Second, apply financial theory to identifying the underlying source of profit making in *any* area of the firm's
business, generalize that source of profit, and suggest how it might be increased
or applied in other parts of the firm.

One of Black's early subjects for examination was the risk of going long, a
European-style put option—which can only be exercised at the end of the option
period—and short, an American-style put—which can be exercised at any time
during the period.[7] Black's work was to be part of Rubin's overall strategic drive
to develop innovative market powers that could transform the firm into *the* leading investment banking and market-making organization worldwide. "We will
learn from Fischer and he will learn from us" was Rubin's assurance to his partners.[8] Working together, Black and Rubin launched an intellectual revolution
within Goldman Sachs.

Black was one of the first of the quants to arrive, but others came in rapidly
increasing numbers from the physics, math, computer sciences, and economics
faculties of America's leading universities, and from aerospace and computer
companies and Bell Labs. Their challenge was to create analytical computer programs that would enable traders to combine the rational consistency of advanced
mathematics with their street smarts and market experience to produce profits

again and again—on numerous occasions, very large profits. Black was used by the firm to vet other candidate quants. If he had any doubts about a candidate, those doubts were usually decisive.

After Fischer Black, Rubin recruited professors Richard Roll from UCLA and Steve Ross from Yale and a series of other brilliant, innovative thinkers in markets and finance. Roll set up a mortgage research group that would enable Goldman Sachs, with its powerful, persistent sales organization, to race from far behind to well ahead of the initial innovators at Salomon Brothers. The traders were often impatient for answers and often could not explain their real problem clearly. The quant experts' first task was to understand the question behind the question when traders came to them with one of their problems.

While some quants were attracted by the paychecks, most came to Wall Street because that's where they found the most interesting and intensive intellectual action in finance. In a few years, hundreds of quants were working their hypothetical, innovative ways of thinking and analyzing into the fabric of Goldman Sachs and profoundly changing the firm.

Black, whose office was specially soundproofed to keep out the clamor of trading, never did a major transaction or "bellied up to the bar with the boys." He fit into Goldman Sachs in one, but only one, way: He believed he could change the world—in his case, by changing the world's ideas about how the world itself actually worked. Black understood that his ideas could change the world only by changing the way people looked at it. If they resisted, he did not take it personally. He learned that the way to change any business practice was not by sudden revolution, but by proposing small changes to those who were both directly engaged and emotionally and intellectually ready to embrace change.[9]

Black was a remarkably organized filer. In addition to seven three-drawer paper files, he created a twenty-megabyte database comprising the summaries he typed up of every conversation he had and everything he had read or thought. Deeply introverted and shy, he seemed remote and aloof to others. This set him apart from the guy-bonding so common in an intense trading environment like Goldman Sachs's. Black's office on the twenty-ninth floor had on the wall a large Nike poster showing a long country road with this caption: "The race is not always to the swift, but to those who keep on running." In his contract with the firm, he had one day a week for his own research—plus Saturdays and Sundays.

He may have thought he had an ideal situation: Wall Street compensation, no classes, and ample time for research, but others resented it. Most of the people at Goldman Sachs didn't understand and didn't see how Black could be adding much value, because there were no trading coups or corporate transactions with his name on them. Black was never part of the firm's culture in many other ways. He interacted with several hundred people, but only to the extent that their interests overlapped with his and he was learning from them. Without Rubin's sponsorship and guidance, he would no more have become part of the firm than oil mixes with water. A loner, he never could join in the intense collaboration that was so central to Goldman Sachs's operations. He was certainly not a team manager, and he had no selling skills and no interest in developing client relationships, particularly outside normal business hours. Worse, using Black with clients could backfire on a salesman because Black always spoke as he thought at a particular moment; he was not predictable. Even more clearly and significantly, in a firm where making money was the common denominator, Black did not consider money a particularly useful measure of success. For some, this wasn't all bad: As Jon Corzine recalled, "He was the easiest partner in the world when it came to discussions about money. Basically, he didn't care."

Devoted to simplicity and clarity when giving directions, Black was precise and expected all others to be precise too, so he forbade taking decimals beyond the "significant numbers." Steve Ross, a Yale and MIT professor who often consulted with Goldman Sachs, recalls: "Fischer Black looked like an academic should look, and when he talked, he sounded like an academic should sound. Fischer also had a few quirky academic habits like going silent for as long as a minute on the phone while thinking about the right way to answer your question." After studying his options pricing model and his articles, the Japanese and many Europeans revered Black. To them, his long pauses and rigorous manner showed he must be a genius.

While the capabilities of traders and quants might be integrated, their payouts could differ markedly. If a quant developed a new idea for a money-making trading model that could be used by a trader, the quant might get $150,000 for a year's work, while the trader using the model and doing what it told him to do and how to do it might get ten times as much. The quants developed sardonic ways of explaining this reality: "There are form guys and substance guys. If you're all substance, you're actually of *no* value because nobody will use your ideas. And if you're all form, there *is* no value." One quant unit had a chart on the wall, trying to plot where the optimal position would be—and where an individual would get paid the most.

Black was quantitative to a fault. The rigor of his logic and his inability to be anything but entirely logical led him to state some positions that were so perfectly rational that they were really very irrational. For example, one day he stopped everyone's clock with his conclusion that Goldman Sachs should go short—ten billion dollars short—in financial futures. "If we are intellectually honest with ourselves, we will go short futures by enough to fully hedge our exposures to the cash markets, instead of always being net long. That way, we will be operating the firm with zero net exposure to market risk."

"Any idea how much that would involve?" asked David Silfen.

"Yes, I've examined the market-risk exposures of every unit in every division. On average, the firm is long—every day—by ten billion dollars. So to expunge those collective exposures to market risk, we should simply short financial futures by ten billion dollars."

" 'Simply' was the key word," recalls Silfen. "For Fischer, it was completely rational." But that was theory, and the pragmatists of Goldman Sachs—with less than one billion dollars in total capital—simply couldn't imagine establishing a "simple" short position that was ten times as large as the firm's total capital. For them, Black's idea might be academically valid, but it was so totally irrational that it was insane. Besides, for a real-world firm like Goldman Sachs, a rising market—rewarding long positions, not short—was vital to M&A, underwriting, Goldman Sachs Asset Management, and virtually every other aspect of the business.

In sharp contrast to the frenetic energy displayed in Goldman Sachs trading rooms, Black was always calm and in personal equilibrium. For Black, models brought with them systematic disciplines that helped prevent operational errors by traders and would augment a trader's intuition by enabling experimentation. The real world, in Black's view, differs from the idealized world of the capital-asset pricing model in three ways. Costly information, costly management, and costly selling were all frictions that caused the real world to deviate from the ideal.[10] And every deviation offered an opportunity for traders to profit.

Black held the view—a superbly profitable view when put into action by Goldman Sachs's traders—that central-bank interventions were never made to

414 · THE PARTNERSHIP

earn profits, but were often made to move interest rates or currency exchange rates in ways that free markets would not, and that these not-for-profit moves could create large profit opportunities for astute, rational traders. Black argued that central-bank interventions were usually *not* rational and so were wrong, and that traders could take the other side of central-bank distortions at significant profit. Those profit opportunities began increasing almost exponentially in the 1980s.

Within months of his arrival, Black began building a large arbitrage position on that same Value Line index mispricing anomaly he had presented to his finance class at MIT. The futures contract had been trading—at the wrong price—on the Kansas City exchange since 1982. The Value Line index was a geometric average, not an arithmetic average, and since a geometric average is always less than an arithmetic average, the futures contract was always overpriced.[11] So the appropriate action was to go long the stocks and short the futures—a nightmare to implement unless it could be automated. Fortunately, the DOT (direct order trading) system that Goldman Sachs had recently introduced was automated, so the firm put together a large matched-book position: Long all the stocks in the Value Line index and short the futures. This position made many small arbitrage profits—so small they never disturbed the market. During the spring and early summer of 1986, this long-short position was steadily expanded until it represented a full one-third of the open interest in the Value Line index. This meant that the local Kansas City market participants were indirectly and unknowingly providing the other side of the firm's huge arbitrage position. The largest position on the other side was held by a group of finance professors who were trying to exploit the "January effect," in which small-cap stocks often make excess returns in January. The professors were long Value Line and short the S&P 500. They thought they were information traders but were actually no better informed than "noise" traders who act on tips, rumors, and the like.

Rubin looked into Black's office one morning with a question: "What would happen if all those counterparties in Kansas City failed and went bankrupt?"

Black, as so often with his hand on his chin, raised his eyebrows rather obviously but remained silent as he waited for one of his quant colleagues in the room to answer. Since no one spoke, Black did: "If that happened, Bob, we'd be screwed."

"But what are the odds that that would happen? Could you work on it?"

This same question soon caught the attention of the management committee when Rubin asked his standard question: "What's your biggest risk—and can you quantify it?" Satisfied with the answer, Rubin let the Value Line position continue. When closed out later that summer, it had made Goldman Sachs twenty million dollars risk-free. It earned a partnership for Black in 1986 and opened a new line of business in basket trading—where a package, or basket, of five to fifty stocks is sold as a portfolio, and another basket is purchased—and a new category of arbitrage opportunities.

Over time, Black's disciplined analytics became part of the fabric of Goldman Sachs—partly because Rubin was Black's sponsor and partly because in many respects Black was the very model of what Goldman Sachs wants its people to be: unselfish about credit, honest, client-focused, and intellect-driven. For his part, these requirements were exactly what Black liked about the firm: It hires talented, driven people, but only if they are ready and willing to work for the good of the whole firm.

24

~

FALSE STARTS
IN INVESTMENT
MANAGEMENT

J ohn, we need your help. We've got a major problem that must be solved quickly, and there's a lot at stake." In 1981 John Whitehead received that concerned call from Paul Nagle, the senior financial officer of Chicago's Household Finance Corporation, on whose board of directors they both served. Nagle was a trustee of a mutual fund that invested in a narrow spectrum of short-term debt instruments for a unique clientele: For smaller banks, insurance companies, and corporations, it had been one of the first of the now-numerous "money market" funds that guaranteed institutional investors full liquidity via unlimited redemptions at par value. Named Institutional Liquid Assets and called ILA, it had a portfolio of five hundred million dollars.

ILA had been operating successfully for years and, with increasing institutional acceptance, its assets had grown substantially. But recently, Whitehead was told, Salomon Brothers, as investment manager, had tried to increase the fund's yield by lengthening portfolio maturities. Just then, interest rates rose sharply, so market prices of debt securities fell, reducing the portfolio's market value and "breaking the buck" by taking the fund's share price below its mandatory stated par value of one dollar. While Salomon Brothers was ready to put up the three million dollars needed to restore the fund's net asset value to one dollar, ILA's trustees just as quickly agreed they wanted to get a new investment manager. So Nagle called Whitehead to ask: "Would Goldman Sachs be willing to take over and manage ILA?"*

Whitehead recognized a real opportunity and expressed appreciation for the compliment to Goldman Sachs of being asked—but he was still cautious. As he explained, Goldman Sachs had long avoided going into the investment-management business. The reason: It wanted to avoid any conflicts with its institutional clients, and several of the firm's most active block-trading customers—including Dreyfus, Morgan, and Fidelity—had been particularly vocal on the matter. Still, since Whitehead recognized opportunity in ILA, he went on to explain to his caller that most of the expressed concerns related to managing *common-stock* portfolios—a much higher-fee business. Because the ILA fund invested only in money-market instruments and charged a low fee, it might well be okay. Nagle said ILA's trustees were hoping to have a decision made over the weekend. Saying he could make no promises, Whitehead offered to see what, if anything, might be done and agreed to try to get a formal commitment from his partners that same weekend.

But some of his partners surprised him with strong resistance. Nobody at Goldman Sachs seemed to focus on what Whitehead thought was the obvious profit opportunity for the firm, as a dealer in all sorts of money-market instruments, to work closely with a large and regular investor in those very same instruments. In a classic case of looking a gift horse in the mouth, skeptical partners raised a series of cautious questions, including concerns about the sophisticated back-office operations that would be required of a large money-market fund and the cost of clearing dozens and dozens of short-term trades. "This should be of no concern," soothed Whitehead, "because all clearing and other back-office operations will continue to be provided entirely by Continental Illinois National Bank."

George Doty was interested in going ahead with the deal because ILA had developed computer technology that enabled real-time recording of transactions, a capability he believed had applications across the firm. Other factors helped:

---

* Salomon Brothers alumni offer a different history: Continental Illinois National Bank & Trust made the classic error of selling what was supposed to be purchased, and as the market moved, this error "broke the buck." Salomon Brothers could have put up the three million dollars, but because it was having a bad earnings year, Salomon refused, knowing that the decision would end the business. "We gave it away—and eventually, Goldman Sachs was smart enough to accept the gift," says Tom Brock, former partner of Salomon Brothers.

It was "only" a money-market fund serving "only" financial institutions, a low-margin, niche-market part of the investment business. Even so, after Goldman Sachs agreed to take on the ILA management assignment, Howard Stein of Dreyfus, a major block-trading account, called to complain about business "encroachments" and, to make his point perfectly clear, stopped doing any stock-brokerage business with the firm for several months.

After three long weeks of partners' carefully pondering every tooth in this gift horse's mouth, Whitehead finally got the go-ahead from his partners to do a favor for Nagle, a corporate client's senior executive; enter into the one area of the investment-management business thought to involve no direct conflicts with the firm's large block-trading customers; and manage the ILA fund. Twenty-five years later, the assets of ILA and other money-market funds offered by Goldman Sachs would be two hundred *times* larger: over one hundred billion dollars.

The main reasons for taking over ILA were economic. In the short run, managing ILA made it easy for a major commercial-paper and money-market dealer like Goldman Sachs to do quite profitable incremental business. ILA would earn the firm approximately five million dollars in annual revenues with virtually zero capital commitment and only minor incremental costs. And while any hint of self-dealing must be avoided, there would surely be profitable ways to coordinate the firm's dealing business with this investment-management business. Over the intermediate term, the Goldman Sachs sales force could surely build up the assets under management and increase management fees through their extensive, regular contacts with major financial institutions and corporations.

The hopes that ILA would be the cash cow that might finance the buildup of a major asset-management business were soon dimmed when Dreyfus and Fidelity, the two major competitors in money-market funds, cut their fees in half—from forty basis points to eighteen—forcing ILA and all other competitors to follow. Profitability was clearly deferred. This was not the firm's first disappointment in investment management—or its last.

Before taking over ILA, investment management at Goldman Sachs had had a desultory and disappointing history. An investment-advisory department was organized in the early 1960s under Arthur Altschul, who had been made a partner years before mostly because he could contribute capital the firm needed badly as it struggled to recover from the losses of Goldman Sachs Trading Corporation and the lean years of depression and war. Altschul's business model was impressively unimpressive: Fees were low because the service was an obsolete, nondiscretionary "advice only" service, with clients making each individual trading decision; the people in the unit were old and tired; and there were few prospects for growth. The main hope for this dull business was that the old retainers in this low-margin, go-nowhere unit would not make mistakes that would embarrass the firm with clients for its other lines of business.

Goldman Sachs partners were settled in the conventional view that, as a leading institutional stockbroker, the firm should stay away from institutional investment management. They had several strong reasons. The firm's Investment Banking Services men wouldn't want to risk an investment-advisory portfolio manager's having poor performance—even for a year or two. Everybody knew that even the best investors had "dry" periods of poor performance and that overall relationships, particularly with corporate clients, could easily be soured by such an experience. If Investment Advisory used the firm's research ideas, how would it manage the obvious conflict of who goes first—institutional clients or advisory clients? If the advisory unit bought shares in a company that was or might become an investment banking client, wouldn't the firm find selling that stock later on "difficult"? As an underwriter, the firm's primary client loyalty had to be to the issuing corporation, so buying any shares in a firm underwriting would be risky. If the stock price went up, questions would be raised: Was the offering price too low? If the price went down: Was the firm "stuffing"? The obvious policy was to stay out of that whole business. Brokerage was brokerage and investment management was investment management—and never the twain should meet.

Anyway, the traditional fees for investment management were so low that the business was not very profitable. And others of Levy's major block-trading clients were as clear spoken as Dreyfus had been: *If Goldman Sachs wants to continue to be our number one stockbroker, do not compete with us in our investment-management business.* Finally, everyone at Goldman Sachs remembered the financial losses and the reputational harm to the firm coming out of the Penn Central fiasco, and everyone had heard about Goldman Sachs Trading Corporation. The perceived risk of "you should have known" lawsuits loomed large in the minds of older partners, particularly managing partner Gus Levy.

"We really bought into the idea that you should never compete with your customer," recalls Jim Gorter. "We believed it—and believed *in* it. That was certainly right at one time. But just as certainly, we stayed with that policy way too long, which is why we didn't get into the investment-management business in a timely way on a major scale. We would not let the investment-advisory division recruit anyone from our institutional clients. We did not want them to take business away from institutional clients or compete with them for new accounts. Investment management looked like a very low-margin business—particularly if you deducted whatever business you were afraid might be lost in another division." In discussions, lots of hidden risks were linked to the possible harm coming from highly visible investment performance—particularly *under*performance. Investment Advisory was thought of as group of second-rate people doing a third-rate business, crystallized by that ultimate put-down question: "Would you put your mom's money there?" The decisive answer was the same for many years: "No!"

The firm's policy of preventing the investment-management unit from competing with good customers in profitable businesses went way back. Levy, Menschel, Mnuchin, Whitehead, Weinberg, and others had all agreed in the 1960s to stay out of investment management to avoid conflicts with stockbrokerage clients. Some were concerned about corporate clients' being upset about performance problems in their pension funds. Others didn't want to have conflicts with their brokerage clients, particularly while building up block trading. But, as Gorter conceded years later, "At Goldman Sachs, we bought the importance of not competing, not conflicting with our clients. But even the guys at Capital Group, one of our largest clients, never paid up for our 'integrity.'[1] No institution every paid us *more* because we had integrity and therefore we did not compete. It didn't pay to be good boys—but it sure cost us a lot to play that way. Our decision may have been one hundred percent right in 1970, but the world keeps changing and the decision was never revisited. So what had probably been a correct decision became the *wrong* decision. And that was a tragedy. We could have built a fine, big business in asset management."

Goldman Sachs's main underwriting competitors—Morgan Stanley, First Boston, Salomon Brothers, Merrill Lynch, Blyth, and Dean Witter—were definitely *not* in the investment-management business, and they were, back then, explicit that being in investment management would be a clear conflict of interest.[2] But that simple "stay out of the other guy's yard" policy could not hold up once Wall Street discovered how very profitable the asset-management business really was. One of the first to see how profitable the business could be was Gus Levy. What transformed his skepticism into enthusiasm was a single document.

"We gotta get in on *this!*" exclaimed Levy after reading the IPO prospectus for Donaldson, Lufkin & Jenrette, the first securities firm to file for a public offering with the SEC. Levy was astounded by the scale of that upstart firm's investment-management business and how amazingly profitable it was. Fees were not low; they were high: A full 1 percent of assets—cleverly offset by rebating 50 percent of commissions generated. With high portfolio turnover, this meant that net fees were actually *zero* to the client, but income to the manager was huge because portfolio turnover and fixed brokerage commissions were both high.

No wonder Levy wanted to get into that high-profit business right away. Wasting no time, he put Arthur Altschul out to pasture, changed the unit's name to Investment Management Services, or IMS, moved Bruce McCowan over from research, where he had been the partner in charge, and gave him instructions to build the business—quickly. McCowan pulled together a team of young investment managers and salespeople and went to work on developing a strategy to develop business.

McCowan focused on investing in mid-cap stocks with "growth at a reasonable price," or GARP, and early results were good. The new team won a few corporate accounts such as Heublein and, thanks to recommendations by selection consultants at Cambridge Associates, which was just getting started, mandates to manage pension funds for Diebold, Crompton & Knowles, and Bulova Watch— all mid-cap companies. But disappointments soon intruded. The original strategic concept was to get major sales leverage through IBS's great relationships with corporations—and their pension funds. As partner Denis Turko later explained, "We needed leverage to get up over all the ingrained prejudices—earned prejudices, of course—against broker-related investment managers for churning accounts and buying deals they couldn't sell and all that jazz. We thought all we had to do was hitch onto the IBS powerhouse and the rest would be a sleigh ride into the big time." But the leverage IMS hoped for did not come through. Only Gus Levy, in his role as a corporate director, delivered a pension account.

Then the long bear market of the early 1970s put a stop to any thought of business development. "In that fierce bear market, our stocks got clobbered," recalls

Turko, "and the IBS guys were all saying: 'Jesus! I worked for ten years to build up a good relationship with that company, and we were about to do some great, high-fee investment banking business and get a good return on all my efforts, when, wham! you guys butcher a tiny piece of their pension fund that I helped you get and everything I've ever done for them for *years* is completely ruined. So no, not a chance: I'm never going to help you screw-ups ever again—ever!' " Nobody could blame them, but it meant IMS would get no leverage from the firm.

Without the support of IBS and *with* a hangover of disappointing investment performance, the best IMS could hope for would be a year or more of "consolidation" and then several years of competing for new accounts—one at a time. It would be as hard as pulling up tree stumps, and the firm would never be satisfied with a slow "one step at a time" buildup. McCowan and his team knew they would need to find a way to accelerate their progress, ideally an imaginative "break the conventional rules" way. They needed something new and different, a truly clever breakthrough marketing strategy—ideally something, recalls Turko, "comparable to MacArthur's landing at Inchon." International investing might do the trick.

International investing was just getting started among American pension funds. To get a piece of the action, a few U.S. investment managers, accepting their lack of foreign experience, had begun linking up with London firms that had a long history of international investing. Maybe Goldman Sachs's IMS could try that same strategy. For Goldman Sachs people, the obvious international firm to link up with was the asset-management division of London's Kleinwort Benson, since ties between the two firms went back over seventy years. Kleinwort Benson could use help managing its U.S. investments, and it had hopes of developing an international investing business with American pension funds that were starting to diversify their portfolios. The McCowan team thought Kleinwort Benson's stature and assets would give them just the extra credibility they needed. Gus Levy made the appropriate introductions, and both parties agreed on a combination of the two investment units. Goldman Sachs would own 20 percent—the limit allowed a NYSE member firm—and Kleinwort Benson would own 40 percent; those doing the actual work, including McCowan and Turko, would own the other 40 percent. A contributing factor was a miscall on the ERISA pension legislation then pending in Congress. Goldman Sachs expected securities firms to be prohibited from managing pension funds, but the final bill went the other way, making an asset-management unit even more valuable—but by then the deal with Kleinwort Benson had already been made.

Despite all the high expectations for the combined unit—Kleinwort Benson McCowan—it didn't work. Kleinwort Benson never moved much of its U.S. business over to the joint venture and, with typical British distaste for anything as crassly commercial as serious institutional selling, it *didn't* sell.[3] The joint venture labored along for a while, but could never get up much steam. In 1980 the American managers bought out Kleinwort's 40 percent and renamed the firm McCowan Associates. Troubles continued. As Turko recalls, "Bruce always thought he was the king and the firm was his kingdom—not a partnership—so in 1983 we split up." Bruce McCowan left McCowan Associates. That split-up was done very quietly because Goldman Sachs still owned its 20 percent and McCowan Associates reported to George Doty. "We knew there must be no adverse publicity about our going separate ways or Doty would kill us. He always kept us on a very tight leash. Besides, we had too much respect for the partners of Goldman Sachs to create any difficulties." A partner says, "Bruce was disappointing as an investor because he didn't know what he didn't know, so he made way too many mistakes. Beautiful to look at and a great relationship salesman, he was *not* a great investor." Soon McCowan Associates bought out Goldman Sachs's 20 percent, taking the firm out of the investment-management business—except for Whitehead's Institutional Liquid Assets, which by then had grown substantially from five hundred million dollars to thirteen billion dollars.

One strategic solution to the problems that had plagued Goldman Sachs's efforts to make a mark in investment management would be to acquire a small firm with a strong investment product and smart leaders who could jump-start the business. In 1987 Friedman suggested to Steve Ross and Richard Roll that Goldman Sachs could buy their investment-management firm, Roll & Ross, and put them in charge of the firm's investment business, assuring them Goldman Sachs partnerships. Friedman knew both men well. Ross, a brilliant economics professor at Yale, originated arbitrage-pricing theory and developed a model for pricing derivatives; he had consulted with the real estate division's management committee. Roll, equally brilliant, was a professor at UCLA who had very successfully created Goldman Sachs's research organization in mortgage-backed bonds. Both had demonstrated their flair for things entrepreneurial by creating their hot investment-management firm. Acquiring Roll & Ross could jump the firm ahead in the institutional market with a distinctive "quant" product.

Fischer Black wasn't so sure: "We should test their model rigorously to ascertain that it is actually superior to the models we already have." Ross replied: "It doesn't really matter which is 'best.' What the firm needs is a broad portfolio of investment products. It would be a mistake to bet the future of the business on any one product. Ours is a proven winner and would have an important role in any array of offerings— and *that's* what's needed." As he thought about the combination further, however, Ross realized he really didn't want to work for a large firm: "I treasure my independence. I've made my fortune. Why give up my freedom for 'more'?" No sale.

Another possible effort to get a toehold in investment management had come and gone in 1974 when Congress passed ERISA. Turko had been sure such major legislation would create real opportunity, so he teamed up with Peter Hager in corporate finance and went looking for ways the firm could help corporations deal with all those new rules, doing all the homework on everything they could think of. They went to Washington to sit in on Senator Kennedy's hearings; they studied the rules and regulations; they talked to key people in the Department of Labor; they studied every aspect of all the financial questions. Finally they developed what they thought was a business plan and took it to George Doty. After reading their plan, Doty said: "Sounds like a good idea. But let me tell you something: In my past career, I've worked by the hour, and whatever the field is, it's a shitty way to do business. I like to sell *money*. Go ahead with this plan if you want to, but be advised: If you get as far with it as the management committee, I'll be there—and I *will* vote against you!'" The idea died.

For nearly a decade, Lee Cooperman had campaigned for major change. As head of research and in frequent contact with the leaders of the country's major investment-management organizations, he saw others grow rapidly and profitably. "We're really missing the game here. We should make a big commitment to investment management. It's a very big, fast-growing, and hugely profitable business—a business that's really right for us, and Goldman Sachs is really right for it: We have all the right skills in investing *and* in sales."

In 1989 Bob Rubin and Steve Friedman went to Cooperman with a proposition: "You've been arguing and agitating for a decade that we were missing the boat and should make a major move into investment management. The firm has always said no. Well, you were right and we were wrong. We now accept that institutions will accept our going into the business if they know we're competing on a level playing field: paying full commissions, no special access to research or underwritings, charging reasonable fees, and all that. We want you to build the investment-management business you've been saying all along the firm should have." Cooperman agreed to leave his position as head of equity research, where his work had won him a long string of firsts as the institutional investors' favorite portfolio strategist. He was tiring of constantly being on the road giving seminars and speeches, meeting day after day with one after another institutional investor, and always being challenged by hopeful competitors from other brokerage firms to be original, fully documented, decisive—and always interesting, engaging, and charming. Cooperman was increasingly confident that he was as good as anyone at portfolio strategy and stock selection. He was already managing a few accounts for friends and felt ready for a new challenge. He was sure he could build a profitable investment-management business in hedge funds based on a combination of his investment capabilities and the reputation he had worked so long and hard to build for himself. And hedge-fund economics would make the division profitable.

The investment-management division's assets—mostly ILA's low-margin money-market assets—had increased to twenty billion dollars, but total earnings were only twelve million dollars. "Relative to the earnings of the whole firm, it was just a rounding error," recalls Cooperman, who went to Rubin and Friedman with his proposition to establish a hedge fund. It would change the economics completely. With five hundred million dollars of assets, a 20 percent gain with a 20 percent carried interest (the general partners' share of a hedge fund's gains) would produce twenty million dollars profit, far more than doubling the division's earnings contribution to the firm. Friedman and Rubin agreed, and because the firm recognized the need for a major change, a new division was launched named Goldman Sachs Asset Management, or GSAM (pronounced "gee-sam"). It needed just what Cooperman offered, so he moved over with his new strategy. Rubin and

Friedman wanted none of the aggressive action of the more notorious hedge funds, so they told Cooperman to work out controls and procedures with general counsel Bob Katz until they felt truly comfortable. They were halfway through this work when the troubles of Water Street Recovery Fund burst on the scene.

"All would have gone fine until the flak over Water Street," recalls Cooperman. Water Street Recovery Fund, launched by Goldman Sachs in 1989, was in the business of buying junk bonds of companies in financial distress and forcing the issuing companies to negotiate more favorable terms. Some of the companies getting pressured by the fund had been the firm's clients, and some of these protested that they didn't think this behavior fit with the firm's claim of always being on the side of its corporate clients. Then, in 1990, junk-bond investor Bill Huff claimed publicly that Goldman Sachs was improperly using proprietary information gained when it wrote the indentures in its role as bond underwriter; he organized a boycott of Goldman Sachs by high-yield-bond investors. In combination, the corporate protest and the boycott worked: John Weinberg closed down Water Street and returned the investors' money, a full one billion dollars. All Cooperman could do was to protest that the business he had had in mind was entirely different: "But I'm *not* in a zero-sum game like Water Street was!"

Weinberg was unmoved: "Who're you kidding? Say you have a big hedge fund and someday decide to short the stock of one of our investment banking clients. There could be big trouble, and you will *never* explain it away."

The Water Street crisis frightened Rubin and Friedman. "If 'unknowns' like those who launched Water Street can cause the firm that much trouble," said Friedman, "with your strong name recognition your hedge fund might short the stock of an important client and cause us all sorts of trouble. We want you to build up GSAM's business as a business—just as you did in Research. Do us all a favor. Forget about managing money as a star portfolio manager with a hedge fund and build us a major money-management *business*—as a business manager. You built Research up from nearly nothing. This is the same kind of challenge. It should be a natural for you."

The strategy Cooperman developed was to downplay the institutional business. Institutional clients demanded a manager with a well-established track record of superior investment performance over at least three years, and direct competition with institutional block-trading clients would be inevitable. Cooperman would focus instead on building a mutual-fund business and selling to *individuals*—including the customers of Private Client Services. The key to this strategy's success would be superior investment performance, which Cooperman saw playing directly to his own strengths as a leading investment strategist and stock picker who was well known and highly regarded by the PCS brokers. The best part of Cooperman's strategy was that he had to win only a fair share of the money flowing into mutual funds. "It's a huge potential market," said Cooperman. "All you need is a thin sliver to make a very profitable business."[4] Strong investment performance would pull money into the new unit and quickly make it very profitable. Now, instead of needing five million dollars to invest with Goldman Sachs, an investor needed only $1,200. Cooperman put two million dollars of his own money into the first mutual fund and encouraged other partners to invest their personal capital too.

To get salesmen in PCS to sell the new funds to their clients, an effective financial incentive would be needed. The management fee was set at 1 percent, with part to be paid out each year to the salesmen who put their clients' money into the fund. Recent investment results reinforced Cooperman's confidence: Recommendations from his research department had bested the S&P 500 by 5.4 percentage points during the prior year.[5] To dramatize the level playing field, the eighty-person GSAM division moved out of Goldman Sachs's offices to a new facility in lower Manhattan. To avoid client conflicts, Cooperman's hands would be tied with tough restrictions imposed by the firm. No investment professionals and no mutual-fund wholesalers were to be poached from any clients. And John Weinberg declared, "I'll be goddamned if we'll use the name Goldman Sachs after all that my father went through with Goldman Sachs Trading Corporation." He insisted that "Goldman Sachs" could not be used in the names of any mutual funds—yet he accepted the use of the initials GS as the first two letters of every fund's name, so the connection to the firm was certainly no secret. GSAM's first fund, GS Capital Growth Fund, was launched on April 9, 1990. It sold well, with a substantial fraction of the buying coming from PCS, where salesmen were strongly encouraged by management to put their clients' money *and* their own money into the new mutual fund.

Cooperman, ever the portfolio strategist, was cautious about the market, saying, "I don't see the overwhelming, compelling case for investing fully in this stock market." Of the money raised, he invested only one-third in stocks. He was right in that the S&P rose only 2.5 percent that year. But after a 6 percent sales load, the fund's net asset value was 12 percent below its offering price. This shortfall was clearly a disappointment; clients, partners, and PCS men were not amused. In 1991 the market was up over 30 percent, and Cooperman's fund did slightly better. But after the first year's results many PCS brokers had decided "never again" on selling GSAM funds to their clients. (Another reason was that once put into those funds, the assets were no longer available for other kinds of transactions and the commissions that could be generated.) Naturally, brokers at other firms had no interest, and no incentives, to sell funds managed by a competitor like Goldman Sachs.

A quant product came next in 1991 in a mutual fund named GS Select Equity Fund, which was managed by Robert Jones, head of GSAM's quantitative stock-strategies unit. Jones focused on "more timely names which have favorable price momentum and better values,"[6] which really meant research-department stock selections sifted through a quantitative screen. Given the frustration with the first fund, it was no surprise that Jones said, "The new fund will be fully invested in equities at all times and have a less contrarian, out-of-favor approach with more mainstream growth kinds of names." After raising only $120 million, GS Select Equity was closed to new money, at least temporarily. Since management fees, trading costs, and 5.5 percent sales charges would offset all or most of the nearly 2 percent rate-of-return advantage that Goldman Sachs's research-recommended list had enjoyed, Jones's computer model was expected to add the value that would attract investors. His quant model used twelve computerized screens to rank recommended stocks on such criteria as P/E ratios, dividends, price volatility, and market capitalization, plus five broad investment characteristics. Fortunately, first-year investment performance was strong—nearly twice the average gains made by comparable funds.

"Leon Cooperman saw himself as a master investor, which he was," says Steve Friedman, "and expected performance to pull in assets like a powerful magnet. But the job as head of GSAM was not really to pick great stocks; the job was to build a great investment business, and the key to business success would have to be excellence in gathering assets even more than investing. In a strategy based on building assets through selling, a superstar investor was sure to be a problem, not a strength, because too much would depend on that one superstar. He'd be a bottleneck on selling new business to those who believed in him, because he couldn't be everywhere, and for those who didn't believe he could continue shooting out the lights, they'd stay away because they'd think he couldn't keep it up. Leon didn't understand this at all."

When Bob Rubin said, "Lee, you'll have to delegate more," Cooperman turned to Friedman and said, "Bob doesn't understand investment management. He's never had to pick great stocks. He doesn't understand investing. Picking stocks is the core of the business, and that can't be delegated."

Friedman and Rubin came to believe that Cooperman, knowledgeable as he was about investing, did not understand that building the business would require him to focus on gathering assets, or "distribution." The problem Cooperman faced—in addition to the constraints imposed by the firm—was that while long-term investing is in theory what mutual-fund investing is all about, in practice, short-run performance dominates mutual-fund sales, particularly for organizations that are new to the business. Cooperman's early results had been below market because he was a "value" investor, and value stocks had performed poorly. Investors who bought in on the expectation of great results didn't want explanations: They wanted the great performance they felt they'd been promised. As Wall Streeters observe, investment managers who rely on achieving superior investment performance live by the numbers and die by the numbers. After the first mutual fund faltered, Cooperman got almost no help at all in selling the other mutual funds, either from the PCS salesmen or from IBS relationship specialists who might have introduced him to corporate pension-fund executives. Cooperman was struggling with a stock market that was going against him and a senior management that expected a quick fix while not giving him the financial support he'd like and imposing on him a hobbling set of constraints—no competing with firm clients, no recruiting from firm clients, no advertising, and more.

"Lee Cooperman's thesis was that he was an investing expert," recalls a partner, "maybe another Warren Buffett. So, as his client or as his manager, you could and should just close your eyes and wait twenty-five years while Lee did great things. And if you'd only leave it to him, he would give you great results—if you stayed with him for twenty-five years."

Michael Armellino, who had succeeded Cooperman as research director, was brought back from early retirement to succeed him at GSAM in 1991. GSAM's strength in the marketplace during its early years was in fixed income under partner Alan Schuch. While assets continued to build, the hope for a major success would still depend upon developing a strong equity business where fees were higher and profit margins wider. Armellino knew he needed a new strategy to gather assets, and he knew he would have to build a record of at least three years of superior investment performance to be "qualified" for that market. All this meant that he had to succeed in the retail market and do so with mutual-fund distribution through brokers without depending on PCS. Armellino's new strategy for building GSAM's business was to concentrate on developing strong mutual-fund sales, overcoming the major firm-imposed handicaps. "No poaching" meant no hiring experienced portfolio managers or analysts or salespeople from any institutional client—including experienced mutual-fund wholesalers, the key to success in mutual-fund sales because there are so many funds and past investment performance is so unreliable as the basis for selecting funds. Armellino was left to do the best he could to build a mutual-fund business with the management committee having tied one arm behind his back. He recruited MBAs who were new to the business and worked hard at developing "favored firm" acceptance at major regional firms, like Edward Jones, that had strong distribution but did not manage investments. Armellino's first move was to broaden GSAM's product line. Retail sales of GSAM funds increased, and new funds were added in international emerging markets and currencies to provide a full spectrum of offerings.

Other mutual funds soon followed: GS Small Cap Equity and GS International Equity were introduced in 1992, followed in 1993 by a government-bond income fund and an adjustable-rate-mortgage fund. Virtually all fund sales were made through the firm's PCS brokers to their customers. By mid-1993, Capital Growth Fund was again performing well—up 60 percent, well ahead of the S&P 500's 49 percent.

Unintentionally, Cooperman could have done real harm to GSAM had he taken out the man who would, a few years later, figure out a winning strategy for investment management and get senior firm management to accept and commit to it. As Friedman explained the next steps to get good business management in GSAM, "We drafted John McNulty to work with Lee—no, *under* Lee because Lee never worked *with* anyone. McNulty lasted one month before he came to me insisting on reassignment."[7] After just four weeks in GSAM, McNulty, who had come from PCS, had decided that his views on the business were so at odds with Cooperman's strategy that he should leave GSAM and transfer to another division. Seeing any move to transfer out of GSAM as an act of personal disloyalty, Cooperman, as McNulty remembered years later, said, "Nobody *ever* leaves working for me. If you do leave, wherever you go within Goldman Sachs and whatever you do, I'll be looking for you and I'll be absolutely against you."

McNulty transferred anyway. Several months later, he asked to have lunch with Cooperman. "Lee," he said, "you know we've disagreed in the past, but I've said nothing, ever, to anyone else about our differences. Now I need your help, because I'll be coming up for partnership." Cooperman knew what he had said and knew what he could do, but he decided to relent: "I won't vote *for* you. That's not something I can ever do. Still, I won't hurt you. I won't vote *against* you." So McNulty made partner. He would soon be essential to GSAM's eventual great success.

Cooperman loved investing and had only reluctantly given up plans to leave Goldman Sachs and start his own hedge fund, so when his wife of twenty-five years said, "I've never told you what to do and never will, but how old will you have to be before you do what you really *want* to do?" he went back to Rubin and Friedman. "I'm the fifth-largest percentage partner, so I obviously want the best for the firm. I'll give you two full years. Then let me retire and set up my own hedge fund outside the noncompete provision. I'll consult with you for a year and launch my own hedge fund." Recognizing that Cooperman's mind was made up, Rubin pragmatically said, "We hope you'll use us as your prime broker." And Cooperman replied, "Of course." The firm offered him five hundred thousand dollars for the consulting work. Today fifteen of the twenty largest investors in Cooperman's Omega hedge fund are Goldman Sachs partners.

Progress was being made when Armellino's efforts got hit with another blow: false accounting. Assets had been accumulating, primarily in GSAM's

fixed-income unit. Michael L. Smirlock, then the thirty-six-year-old chief investment officer of that fourteen-billion-dollar unit, had joined the firm after achieving academic distinction as a young professor at Wharton. He had just recently
been named a partner and was hiring a cluster of able people that included Cliff
Asness, who later created Global Alpha, a triumphantly successful hedge fund.
Then, suddenly, Smirlock was fired in March 1993 for deliberately misallocating
cash inflows among different accounts by "reassigning" some five million dollars
of securities from one account to another, apparently to make investment performance look better. Smirlock's irregularities were discovered on a Friday, and that
Saturday he was suspended.[8]

"It's so hard to understand," commented Armellino. "He was young, brilliant, articulate, and he didn't take any money doing it. But he sure ruined his
career." The speed with which Smirlock was dismissed and the irregularity
reported to the regulatory authorities was considered appropriate for a firm that
held itself out as an ethical leader, but the event reminded all too many prospective GSAM clients of doubts about any Wall Street brokerage firm's being trusted
as an investment manager. And put a stop to fixed-income business development
at GSAM.

Another blow came later. After a fast start, GS Small Cap Equity Fund finished three mediocre years with a return of only 11 percent in the twelve months
to March 1996, when the median small-cap fund produced 31 percent. This
fund was in the bottom 5 percent of funds for the three-year period. Worse, the
thirty-three-year-old fund manager, Paul Farrell, was clearly not using the firm's
research recommendations and had concentrated investments in small specialty-
retailing stocks.

While Cooperman and Armellino had both enjoyed important prior successes, neither succeeded in the asset-management business because, in addition
to firm-imposed constraints, their experience and their managerial instincts were
not in harmony with the special needs and rhythms of the institutional asset-
management business, a problem that was neither new nor limited to GSAM.
Notoriously, executives and organizations that had been successful in insurance or commercial banking failed when they tried to apply the lessons learned
in "their" financial service to an apparently similar financial service: investment
management. While all involve money and service, the particulars are very

different; what works well in one financial service can fail in another. Even "obviously" similar *investment* services, such as mutual funds and institutional separate accounts, involve significant differences in selling, marketing, reporting, and client service. Incompatibility at the operating level was one of the reasons most banks and insurers failed in their efforts to develop investment-management businesses—even with their own good customers in banking or insurance. Another reason was strategic conflict; each organization's strategic priority was protecting the current strengths of its historic businesses—just as Goldman Sachs had protected stockbrokerage by restricting GSAM.

In retrospect, the best and boldest strategy for GSAM would have been to jump-start the investment-management business by making one or more major acquisitions—as Morgan Stanley, Credit Suisse First Boston, and Lehman Brothers all eventually did. But this was prevented by a major problem for most major firms, including Goldman Sachs: a misunderstanding by senior management of the value of the asset-management business. Not understanding how to value asset-management businesses, they couldn't accept the pricing. Acquisitions to make a strategic entry into the business and get up to scale seemed far too costly.

For years and years, senior management at Goldman Sachs failed to understand the asset-management business as a business, so they made mistakes—major, repetitive mistakes. And because they were smart, rigorous, disciplined thinkers, they made their mistakes with conviction. Not understanding the right way to evaluate the business or do the accounting, firm management didn't understand the asset-management business.

Most partners thought about investment management as a personal-service business, way too dependent on key individuals. They did not recognize how persistent or "sticky" institutional account relationships really were—even as key people came and went—and said, "The real assets in the investment business—the investment professionals who are essential for success—go up and down in the elevator every night. That's not a real business, and it would be impossible to evaluate or put a fair price on it."

The skeptical partners sounded astute and rational, but their conclusion was based on a misperception. Sure, some investment managers do believe they are the be-all and end-all, but as Charles de Gaulle so shrewdly observed, "The cemeteries of the world are filled with indispensable men." The relationships between institutional clients and investment-management organizations continue on and on even as the specific individual representatives on both sides of major institutional relationships come and go. So the individuals who ride elevators really are all replaceable. The secret to business success in investment management is not so much investment results as it is asset gathering through distribution and sales.

Not seeing this, senior management did not understand how profitable and steady a business asset management could be, particularly if it could be well connected to an asset-gathering juggernaut like Goldman Sachs. As senior executives saw the modest profits reported by Armellino's operation, several frustrated members of the powerful management committee gave serious consideration to shutting it down altogether. GSAM was running at or near breakeven until the accounting was changed and partnership charges were allocated to it. Recalls McNulty: "This put GSAM in the red—big time. That's when powerful people again started asking questions like: 'Do we really need an *institutional* investment business?' They didn't appreciate how long it takes and how much investment spending is needed to build a really strong, sustained profit-making investment business." As advocates of closing down saw the situation, GSAM was not making money; it exposed the firm to all sorts of business and perception risks; asset management was too different from a securities business; nobody had come up with a strategy for substantial success; and GSAM's history was a history of failures. Unless basic changes were made, GSAM would continue laboring along, making modest losses or modest profits, unable to afford the investment capabilities or products that would earn substantial profits and reflect favorably on Goldman Sachs as a total organization. GSAM was late to the market, had little or no brand or franchise strength, and was too high-cost in its operations. It was, in brief, just a bolt-on to a broker-dealer. So long as it stayed that way, GSAM could never become important to the firm, either professionally or economically. During this dark period, Steve Friedman and others advocated getting out of the asset-management business, but Bob Rubin supported Armellino's pleas to stay the course. That would pay off in a major way.

The best acquisition opportunity for GSAM was an easy layup—or could have been. In 1994 Miller Anderson & Sherrerd was a prestigious Philadelphia manager of large institutional accounts that had built a good-size, well-balanced business investing in domestic stocks and both international and domestic bonds;

it also had an international-equity joint venture with a powerful Japanese institution. Assets under management had grown to thirty-six billion dollars—a solid base upon which to build an institutional business because it would instantly establish GSAM as a leading asset manager. In addition, the name principals, Paul Miller and Jay Sherrerd, and their partners were widely regarded as "cream of the crop" in investment management and had attracted a stellar group of young professionals who worked well together and with clients and had a strong track record of investment performance. Even better for Goldman Sachs, with its hundreds of strong corporate relationships and great strength in sales, the investment professionals at Miller Anderson had done little marketing because they believed business development conflicted with their priority as professional investors. They were reluctant to spend much time or energy prospecting for new business, preferring to let clients and consultants come to them. They went out on business development calls only when invited. As IBS and PCS had proved, Goldman Sachs could sell good product very well, so the combination of the two firms seemed to promise wholesale synergy, a very effective win-win proposition.

In approaching Miller Anderson, Goldman Sachs had an "unfair competitive advantage." Richard Worley, the leader of Miller Anderson's booming bond business and for the prior five years managing partner for the whole firm, was known there as "the man from Goldman Sachs." He had been an economist in research at the firm, knew and liked everyone, and was best friends with David Ford and Jon Corzine. Corzine and Worley lived across the street from each other in Summit, New Jersey, and for several years drove in to work together most days and went out with their wives most Friday nights. Ford, who had recently agreed to become co-head of GSAM and very much wanted to build GSAM's business with a major acquisition, told partners: "I said five years ago that we should have made a major commitment to build GSAM quickly, either by acquisition or by multiyear 'investment spending' to build from within." Ford saw a natural strategic fit between Goldman Sachs and Miller Anderson & Sherrerd, so in one of his regular conversations with his friend and neighbor, early in the morning on a lovely spring weekend in 1993, he raised the possibility of a combination: "Could we do something together?"

Worley and his firm had been approached about an acquisition six or more times before. In the 1980s George Russell of Frank Russell Company had come with a two-hundred-million-dollar offer from Lloyd's Bank. Chubb Insurance made an approach but was waved off for lack of fit. Swiss Bancorp and ING were two other suitors. Worley recalls an observation by the man who did the most acquisitions of investment-management firms: "Norton Reamer once said investment firms only sell when they're scared. Well, we weren't scared and knew we had a good thing going." Worley said Miller Anderson was not for sale but acknowledged that global distribution was becoming increasingly important and that he recognized this was an area where Goldman Sachs had proven strengths. Discussions quickly accelerated. As Worley recalls, "If we were going to be acquired, we should select the right partner ourselves, and if the basic terms of a deal were okay, it would be better to be in a truly global organization like Goldman Sachs."

Merger negotiations went forward rapidly and easily. Everyone could see the compelling advantage: Miller Anderson had the product while Goldman Sachs had the delivery system. Then obstacles began to surface. Miller Anderson people wanted to stay in Philadelphia and run their own show, not move to New York City. With no difficulty, that was agreed. Could Miller Anderson partners *all* expect to be made partners in Goldman Sachs? That would be too many: There were nearly two dozen Miller Anderson partners. Goldman Sachs proposed three partnerships; Miller Anderson asked for twelve. A specific problem for Goldman Sachs was that the name founders and a few others, as part of their partnership agreement, were legally entitled to a substantial "annuity" payout until their deaths. Nobody knew quite how to value this obligation; one proposal was to cap the payouts at current levels and limit them to five years, but this was a far cry from the perpetual share of rising earnings that the partnership agreement had carved out of Miller Anderson. Nobody at Goldman Sachs had ever had a comparable arrangement, and nobody at Goldman Sachs liked it. Miller Anderson wanted a partnership within the Goldman Sachs partnership so it could have its own independent compensation arrangements based on a share of the profits it generated; it also wanted its own decision-making process. For the partners of Miller Anderson, an earn-out was particularly important. Worley proposed that Goldman Sachs buy a large percentage, but not 100 percent, of Miller Anderson's future earnings so there would be strong incentives for future investment professionals. However, that was not the Goldman Sachs way.

In the end, the decisive problems were both financial and perceptual. In one four-hour talk, Corzine and Armellino explained why, given the Goldman Sachs culture, only a few partnerships could be made available—and that limit put stress on the deal, even though both Corzine and Armellino wanted to make the deal work. In addition, Steve Friedman—still thinking "the assets go up and down in the elevator"—could not commit to the $350 million price that Miller Anderson's partners believed was their firm's true market value. An important part of the financial problem was that a partnership has great difficulty making a large investment and fairly distributing the costs and benefits to the ever-changing partners. Friedman decided to lowball the bid and offer just two hundred million dollars. That final offer was made during a luncheon in New York City with Worley and four partners from Miller Anderson—not by Friedman or Corzine, but by Dick Herbst, a lieutenant of Friedman's who had been acting as the banker on the transaction.

The barriers to a successful deal were not all financial. The two organizations had real cultural differences and very different partnership expectations. At GSAM, the culture was to start work before seven each morning. Most people were going full tilt by seven and many were in the office every Saturday. There was a lot of travel too. The senior professionals at Miller Anderson had not been working nearly this hard—and got paid several times as much as GSAM partners. So there was a real miss on cultural fit and compensation.

In January 1995, Friedman had retired. Corzine and Ford came back to Miller Anderson & Sherrerd, but a deal was still unworkable. When they got wind that Miller Anderson was in early negotiations with Morgan Stanley, they were upset and called Worley. As a public company, Morgan Stanley had a convenient currency in its stock and was willing to design the specific deal terms to suit Miller Anderson. Worley spoke directly: "We've been friends for a very long time, and I certainly expect to remain friends. Let's agree on a fair price—fair to our retired partners and fair to our younger partners. You understand fair value in the asset-management business. If Goldman Sachs wants to make a fair offer, tell me and we'll call off our discussions with Morgan Stanley." But Worley's invitation was not one Goldman Sachs was ready to accept. As Worley observes with a knowing smile, "Any deal Goldman Sachs wants to do, you don't want to be on the other side." A year later, Miller Anderson was acquired by Morgan Stanley for $350 million.

25

❧

ROBERT MAXWELL,
THE CLIENT FROM HELL

obert Maxwell was found dead in the water off the Canary Islands not
far from his yacht, the *Lady Ghislaine,* on November 5, 1991, nude and
apparently a suicide.[1] If, as most observers believed, the bizarre British publisher and high-profile Goldman Sachs customer had committed suicide, it
was the one last way for him to escape years of public humiliation and condemna-
tion for piling up unpayable bank loans of $2.8 billion and plundering five hun-
dred million dollars from two public companies and the pensions of thirty-three
thousand British workers.

Some suggested that Maxwell, who suffered from prostate constriction and
was seriously overweight, simply fell overboard while struggling to urinate after
having too much to drink. Others, noting that the sea was unusually calm that
night and that the railing on the *Lady Ghislaine* was three and a half feet high—
and claiming inside knowledge—said Maxwell's death was not suicide. It was,
they insisted, murder by Mossad, the Israeli secret service, for which Maxwell
allegedly had long been an agent. Why kill him? Because given his severe financial failures, he was no longer "reliable."

The initial pathologist's report by Dr. Carlos Lopez de Lamela said death was due to a heart attack, but Maxwell's own doctor said he was not suffering a heart condition. He did not think death was due to natural causes.

The far more realistic and credible explanation is that Maxwell knew he was in an unwinnable confrontation with Goldman Sachs, to which he owed a huge debt and which was insisting on immediate payment. Maxwell had also just been told by Lehman Brothers of its intention to sue for payment of his large debts to that firm, and Credit Suisse First Boston was demanding payment of a big loan too. Maxwell knew that the amazingly complex, many-layered game he had been playing with increasing desperation was now over. He was sure to be bankrupted, jailed, and humiliated publicly—in a very short while. He had nothing good to live for, so why continue? Suicide was Maxwell's last way to control events, as he had done so often before, but he could not control everything. In the cruel way that securities traders make short, crude jokes of the calamities and failures of others, Maxwell was swiftly renamed Captain Bob-Bob-Bob.

Robert Maxwell was born a Czechoslovakian pauper named Jan Ludrodrik—or was it Jan Ludwig Hoch?—on June 10, 1923, and became Juan de Maurier, then Leslie Jones, and then Ian Robert Maxwell. He spoke nine languages, had nine children, stood six-foot-five, adored being important, had a Gulfstream IV and suites in the Helmsley Palace and Waldorf Towers in New York and the Ritz in Paris, entertained celebrities often and lavishly, and knew Margaret Thatcher, Ronald Reagan, Mikhail Gorbachev, and senior officers of the CIA, the KGB, the Soviet military-intelligence agency GRU, and Mossad. For some or all of these agencies, his accusers even claimed that he did what is known in the espionage trade as "wet work" because it can be bloody.

On November 10, 1991, Maxwell's funeral took place on the Mount of Olives in Jerusalem, the resting place for that nation's most revered heroes. It had all the trappings of a state occasion, attended by leaders of both the government and the opposition. No fewer than six serving and former heads of the Israeli intelligence community listened as Prime Minister Shamir eulogized: "He had done more for Israel than can today be said."[2] President Chaim Herzog said: "He scaled the heights. Kings and barons besieged his doorstep. Many admired him. Many disliked him. But nobody remained indifferent to him." Former prime minister Shimon Peres said: "Here on the Mount of Olives eternity will absorb one of its greatest sons. He deserves not only freedom, but rest."[3]

In the twenty years from 1951 to 1971, Robert Maxwell had gone from obscurity to affluence and prominence and then back down to severe public criticism by an agency of the British government; he was declared unfit to manage a publicly owned company and sent into apparent financial exile. But then, in the twenty years from 1971 to 1991, he rose all the way back up to wealth and power and then, despite both great determination and skillful deception, went all the way back down again to financial ruin and death.

Goldman Sachs—through a long-serving partner, Eric Sheinberg—unintentionally became Maxwell's "principal financial enabler"[4] during the later years. As a result, Maxwell's disaster was also a disaster for the firm. Eventually Goldman Sachs paid a settlement of $254 million—the largest in the long history of the City of London. Bad as it was, the cost of the firm's affair with Maxwell could have been much worse. Goldman Sachs had actually feared an even larger settlement, so partners were relieved that the loss was "limited." As managing partner, Steve Friedman decided to settle rather than prolong the pain in hopes of a somewhat smaller penalty.

Like individuals, securities firms are known by the company they keep, and Goldman Sachs had clearly been keeping intimate company with a man one of its own British partners had correctly warned was "very bad news." Partner Gavyn Davies was equally clear: "He damages our reputation. Doing business with the likes of Maxwell is *not* why I joined Goldman Sachs."

Maxwell's had been a long, complex story. After service with the British army during World War II, Robert Maxwell decided to settle in the United Kingdom. He launched Pergamon Press in 1951 and built it up as a highly profitable specialized publisher of scientific journals. In 1964 he was elected Labour MP for Buckingham. Then in 1971, a formal inquiry by Her Majesty's Government into Maxwell's conduct at Pergamon Press Ltd. criticized his business methods and concluded in its considered judgment that Maxwell, "notwithstanding . . . his acknowledged abilities and energy is not a person who can be relied on to exercise proper stewardship of a publicly quoted company." Maxwell was censured by the Department of Trade and Industry (DTI) in a careful report of its investigation. It would not be the last time.

By the early 1980s he was again a recognized force in the United Kingdom through aggressiveness wrapped in the bluff and bluster of a master showman. He used every handle within reach to gain leverage—including Goldman Sachs, then an ambitious "outsider" securities firm determined to make its way to the top ranks in the City of London, the financial capital of Europe. Maxwell knew how to exploit the ambitions of the expansionist American firms. Once, he arranged simultaneous meetings with three firms—Goldman Sachs, Merrill Lynch, and SG Warburg—in one hotel but in separate rooms, so he could go from room to room carrying a magnum of rare Dom Pérignon pink champagne, advising each firm how the others were planning to bid on his offer for ten million shares of stock in a closed-end investment company, and encouraging each to offer terms more and more favorable to win.

Maxwell did not "walk" his companies, he *ran* them in a most imperial way through a series of complex interconnections that he kept so secret that he alone wielded the second most powerful tool of control: information. And he exercised nearly as total command over the *most* powerful means of control: money. He retained sole signatory authority over all the bank accounts and, except for some U.S.-regulated pension funds, all the investments of Mirror Group's and Maxwell Communication's pension funds. While those who have money generally have great power, there are two decisive exceptions: Borrowed money belongs ultimately to the banks that lend it, and the money of public investors, particularly when placed as retirement savings in a pension fund, is supervised by government regulators. In the United Kingdom, the supreme regulatory power is Her Majesty's Government—as Maxwell and Goldman Sachs were destined to learn.

By 1974, despite the Department of Trade and Industry's negative reports, Maxwell had regained control of Pergamon Press and proceeded to build up its profitability aggressively. Then in 1980 he acquired control of the nearly bankrupt British Printing Corporation, made himself CEO, and renamed it Maxwell Communication Corporation. The night the acquisition became final, Maxwell went to the offices at midnight and commanded that a board meeting be held right then and there. This was done at 2:45 a.m. with nine directors present and then repeated the next afternoon at 2:45 p.m. with eleven directors present. At these meetings, Maxwell demanded and got authority to make transfers from the companies' bank accounts on his sole signature and for any amount.

Maxwell exercised voting control of the two public companies and several private companies and trusts through a Swiss lawyer named Dr. Werner Rechsteiner and a series of Lichtenstein entities with confusingly similar and often changing names of which the main entity was called, after four name changes in just six years, the Maxwell Foundation. In 1984, through the numerous private companies he secretly controlled, Maxwell acquired, for £113 million, Mirror Group Newspapers, which he subsequently made profitable by introducing modern technology, stopping restrictive work practices, and increasing cash flow. Soon he announced his intention to build a major international communications complex and compete on a global basis with Rupert Murdoch by making numerous acquisitions in Europe and North America.[5]

Typical of his complex dealings and his repetitive, complex links to Goldman Sachs, Maxwell got the Mirror Group pension fund to buy Strand House, next to the Daily Mirror in Holborn—the only building in the area that had a flat roof and was tall enough to land a helicopter—on the understanding that Goldman Sachs would lease substantial space. (Tenants complained because diesel fumes from helicopters were sucked into the air ducts of the building.) There had been no firm agreement, but in time Goldman Sachs took a five-year lease. The building was bought for seventeen million pounds and sold less than two years later for thirty-six million pounds, but only a small fraction of this profit went to the pension fund: Most of the profit went to Pergamon Press—which held a secret option on the property.

Maxwell was a showman in crude and obvious ways. With several telephones on his desk, he would interrupt meetings to take or dismiss what purported to be urgent calls. "No, Golda, we do not think this is the right time in the market." "Oh, Helmut, you are too kind and too generous. Thank you for saying such a very nice thing, but, no, we cannot accept such generosity." "Tell Maggie that I'm too busy to talk with her just now." Maxwell sought public attention in many ways: hobnobbing with politicians, movie stars, and moguls; traveling to central London by helicopter; hosting large, noisy parties with champagne and caviar; and obtaining extensive press coverage of his own and his companies' exploits. In a 1986 publicity coup, Maxwell Communication Corporation's stock was included in the FTSE 100 Company Index. In public perception this was like being included in the Dow Jones Industrial Average. Combining charm, flamboyance, intimidation, and ambition, he entertained and was entertained by leading executives, financiers, and politicians. His star, shining steadily more brightly and strongly, was rising. Perceptions of people change when they have a lot of money, and Maxwell had or appeared to have billions. He certainly had connections, panache, a forceful personality, and lived on a very grand scale.

Maxwell ran the companies and the pension funds as "best suited his overall interests" within a complex empire of concealment.[6] He stage-managed the multiplicity of interrelationships between public and private corporate entities, using confusingly similar names for various entities and disclosing as little information as possible to bankers or investors. He had audits of his various business units done on different dates so he could move money in and out of the different entities to "dress up" their financial reports serially and followed a fully developed practice of being "very economical with information."[7] The appointed auditors, Coopers & Lybrand Deloitte, were paid large fees to provide advice on numerous acquisitions and not look too closely at Maxwell's many secret maneuvers. All of this made it very difficult for his bankers to know or find out what was really going on.

Maxwell's financial practices ranged from unusual to inappropriate. When he needed to sell investments to raise cash, he directed the captive pension funds to buy them and hold them for him—even including large investments in the shares of Maxwell Communication. In 1985, to finance his various businesses, Maxwell began borrowing large sums from the pension funds of both Maxwell Communication and Mirror Group—unsecured and without the trustees' knowledge.

In 1987 Goldman Sachs helped arrange a syndicated bank loan of £105 million secured by a series of Maxwell-related properties. In 1988 Maxwell Communication borrowed three billion dollars to acquire Macmillan, the book publisher, and OAG, publisher of the Official Airline Guide—both in one week and both at inflated prices; the bid for Macmillan was ninety dollars per share, when its shares had been trading at forty dollars. Taking on this large debt would eventually prove fatal to the empire, given Maxwell's swashbuckling ways. By 1989, Maxwell Communication shares were being pledged as collateral for nearly another one billion pounds of bank loans. When commercial banks balked at accepting those shares as collateral for loans to Maxwell's private companies, he began using as collateral shares he simply appropriated from the pension funds.

The appropriation was disguised as stock lending "to make it appear to be the legitimate practice of [furnishing] securities to market makers as part of ordinary share dealing activities."[8]

Largely because serious British investors knew enough about Robert Maxwell to know not to trust him, Maxwell Communication common stock did not perform well. As Maxwell's company's stock price drifted down on the stock market, he started supporting the price with the resources at his command: open-market purchases by the company. The next incremental decision was to turn to the company's pension fund and command it to buy shares.

Maxwell was obsessed by the Maxwell Communication Corporation share price because the shares were the principal collateral supporting the enormous bank loans he had taken out to pay for his corporate wheeling and dealing. Over 50 percent of Maxwell Communication shares were held by Maxwell's private entities, both his companies and his foundations. As part of his scheme to support the market price, he continued to buy shares through his private companies and increasingly though the public companies' pension funds. From January 1988 to October 1991, the proportion of Maxwell Communication's shares owned by his private companies increased from 52 percent to 68 percent—and shares owned without immediate disclosure by the pension funds brought that total up to 85 percent. As the DTI report stated: "From May 1989, he manipulated the market, principally by buying shares secretly through overseas entities. The investment bank with whom he principally dealt was Goldman Sachs."

Using pension-fund assets as collateral, Maxwell continued to borrow substantial sums for his own purposes. By any standards, the abuses were flagrant. As the DTI report explained in rigorous detail, the major abuses were these: One hundred million pounds in cash loans was taken from the pension funds; fifty-five million pounds of the pension funds' large holding of Maxwell Communication Corporation's shares was secretly sold, which should have been fully disclosed in the prior year but was not; and £270 million of the pension funds' stocks was used as collateral for Maxwell's bank loans.[9] Mirror Group Newspapers, which was presented to regulators and the public as an independent company, was "inextricably" tied to Maxwell's private companies, which owed banks one billion pounds. Eventually, Maxwell decided to float 49 percent of Mirror Group Newspapers on the London Stock Exchange to raise money to repay bank borrowings and to have a second listed stock to use as future collateral for still more bank loans.

In the summer of 1990, when the UK economy turned down, Maxwell's weak financial situation quickly became a crisis. Large bank loans were coming due; market prices for businesses that might have been sold at high valuations had fallen sharply; one hundred million pounds was borrowed from the pension funds, so repayment required the sale of shares; and companies within the group had already borrowed heavily from banks to lend to other companies in the group that were even more in need of funding. Under these large and increasing pressures, someone like Robert Maxwell would turn to expanding deception.

As Maxwell Communication Corporation shares declined in price, Maxwell effectively bought shares worth £130 million. However, these transactions were not reported as purchases, but only as options to purchase. On examination, they were not really arms-length options: With a premium of only one-third the norm, the "options" were really deferred-payment purchases by Maxwell. Two such "option" transactions were arranged through Goldman Sachs as the counterparty. In November 1990, Maxwell sold Goldman Sachs another "put option"— also unrealistically priced—for thirty million shares. The transactions cited are only a few of the large number executed with Maxwell by Goldman Sachs.

Like the American wheeler-dealers that Gus Levy had made lucrative clients for the firm during the conglomerate era—combining trading, arbitrage, underwriting, and M&A—Maxwell was active, imaginative, responsive to ideas for action, personally engaged, very ambitious—and no Calvinist about rules or regulations. As the Department of Trade and Industry report put it, "We have not discovered any evidence that Mr. Robert Maxwell had 'changed his spots' as regards his stewardship of publicly listed companies. Maxwell continued to shuffle large sums between public and private entities he controlled [upwards of an amazing four hundred] and to borrow heavily from the pension funds, including a transaction that was not properly reported in London: the sale in April 1991 of two overseas entities for £55 million through Goldman Sachs in New York. The manipulations and deceptions increased in size, frequency, and complexity with Mirror Group pension funds used to finance other Maxwell businesses. Mirror Group newspapers was not suitable for listing, and the prospectus was inaccurate and misleading."

Maxwell had agreed with the underwriters at the time of Mirror Group Newspapers's flotation not to buy or sell shares without their specific permission. When the shares fell in price, he requested permission to buy shares—obviously to support their price and equally obviously in retrospect to protect their value as collateral for his extensive disclosed and undisclosed bank borrowings. Permission denied, he went ahead anyway, using two overseas entities to buy shares secretly in May and June—the twenty-six million pounds of secret purchases were made through Goldman Sachs—but he was unable to stop a price decline of 25 percent over less than ninety days. Later that year, still trying to keep the share price from falling, Maxwell bought another seventy-five million pounds of Mirror Group shares via Goldman Sachs, bringing the total to £344 million.

A 51 percent holding of shares in Mirror Group Newspapers was pledged to banks to secure loans to the "private side" companies—but the market value of these Mirror Group shares continued falling. By late October, the private-side companies had sold off all available assets except shares in Mirror Group Newspapers and Maxwell Communication Corporation. Observed the DTI investigators in formal British understatement, "At that time the pressures became severe. Maxwell was instructed to repay two loans to Goldman Sachs, but Maxwell was fully margined and had no way to repay those loans." Lehman Brothers also instructed Maxwell to repay loans—and also received no payment.

As Goldman Sachs began selling the Maxwell Communication shares it held as collateral into a declining market, according to the DTI, "the imminent collapse of the empire was inevitable."[10] It came just seven months after the flotation, and Mirror Group Newspapers suddenly had to obtain loans from its bankers because so much money had been taken out of it by Robert Maxwell. Employees were laid off. Pensioners suffered losses. "Goldman Sachs . . . bears a substantial responsibility in respect of the manipulation that occurred in the market."[11]

While the whole of Maxwell's story is, in its own tawdry way, quite fascinating, the crucial question that emerges for Goldman Sachs can be tightly focused: How did the firm get so far off the straight and narrow that it preferred to pay a quarter of a billion dollars rather than risk a public confrontation?

Events that don't seem to make sense can sometimes be explained by recognizing the importance of antecedents. Dick Menschel "went limited" and left Goldman Sachs in 1988, and Bob Mnuchin did so in 1990. While both men were remarkably capable, Mnuchin and Menschel did not like each other and could not work together, so the two parts of the stockbrokerage business—sales and trading—were, for many years, run quite separately. After they left, the two separated parts were combined into a unified equities division under the leadership of Roy Zuckerberg and David Silfen.

Over the years since Gus Levy's death, Mnuchin had been recognized as Eric Sheinberg's "rabbi," the powerful senior who would watch out for and protect him. Mnuchin respected Sheinberg's skills as a trader who was good at working a market and who would always keep his mouth shut. And in a firm whose organizational fibers were "family" loyalties, Mnuchin and Sheinberg had both been "sons" to Gus Levy, and Mnuchin instinctively knew the duty of sibling loyalty. Sheinberg was absolutely loyal to Mnuchin. There was something else: Sheinberg was intensely committed to Goldman Sachs. As one of the partners explained, "The firm was Eric's first love."

As he was going limited and leaving the firm, Mnuchin spoke to Silfen, who was taking over as partner in charge of trading: "Eric made partner before you did, so try to be sensitive that he won't feel right about reporting up to you. He's very good at trading difficult blocks and international stocks. Don't make the reporting relationship too hard for Eric. Give him some room to do his thing his own way—and to feel good about his situation. Always remember: He was senior to you."

Indeed, Sheinberg had introduced Silfen to L. Jay Tenenbaum, who had hired him, so on a personal level it wasn't easy for Sheinberg to report to Silfen now as his supervisor. Silfen set the guidelines that Sheinberg and other trading partners could work within with the understanding that Sheinberg would always call if ever he had need or reason to go beyond those guidelines. Then Silfen said: "Eric, we go way back together—back to the sixties. So no surprises, okay?"

From New York City, Sheinberg had been supervising a group of Eurobond traders he had hired in London. Once a month, he would fly to London, take his traders, who had come from working-class families, out at night, get them drunk enough to loosen up, and learn all he could about what they were doing and how they were doing it. During this period, Goldman Sachs was invited to compete with nearly a dozen other dealers—some British and some American—on a large trade for the £331 million stock portfolio held by Phillip Hill Investment Trust. The competition included the who's who of London finance, so a winning bid, if it was also profitable to the firm, would be a highly visible signal that Goldman Sachs was on the scene and a factor to be recognized. Sheinberg worked hard on pricing the numerous individual stocks in the portfolio, made his bid—and won.

Robert Maxwell called the New York office from London to congratulate Sheinberg, who modestly offered to visit when next in London. With gusto, Maxwell urged him to do so and suggested they could do much more business together. Maxwell soon began placing orders with Sheinberg, always calling personally and talking about markets and prices. Sheinberg enjoyed being the expert, and Maxwell enjoyed sharing views on trades and trading strategies. They were both markets-and-trading junkies and were soon speaking on the transatlantic phone two or three times a day. When the management committee decided to move a cluster of smart, young up-and-comers to London, they decided that Sheinberg, while older, would be included.

Sheinberg's special interest and expertise was in trading convertible bonds. Gus Levy and L. Jay Tenenbaum were both "convertible guys" and appreciated what Sheinberg could do as a convertibles trader. Because trading spreads were narrowing in New York and the business was getting less profitable, Sheinberg's plan when he moved to London was to work the European markets where spreads were still wide and good profits could be created at low risk. He had made major money for the firm in the past, but his stature in the firm and his percentage of the partnership had both been significantly reduced. Sources report that Sheinberg would have been squeezed out of the firm if John Weinberg had not personally intervened. Now, Sheinberg wanted to make a major comeback and was determined to do the same "money spinning" in London that he had done elsewhere—this time by making American-style markets in British stocks.

If he could find the opening, Sheinberg knew he had the skills to make a major impact. He could even be the one to help Goldman Sachs establish itself as a major factor in the City—and then across Europe. As he took up his new position in London, a series of subtle factors came into alignment whose composite danger would become clear—but only in hindsight. He arrived in London when Goldman Sachs had not yet developed the necessary experience as an international organization, and nobody had had much direct experience in the London market from which to appreciate the clues and subtleties that experts might pick up.

Always clearly on the make, Maxwell was keen to do business. So was Bob Conway, a young Goldman Sachs investment banking partner who was new to London and unusually good-looking, engaging, and bright—but not protected by skeptical instincts. Transferred to London in the early stages of the firm's buildup there, Conway's nearly impossible mission was to break into investment and merchant banking in a market that was already overserved and had neither interest nor appetite for new "alternative" bankers, particularly Americans. Realistically, Conway would have to find the unusual company or unorthodox executive to get a start on making a breakthrough.

Conway "found" Maxwell the same way a raccoon "finds" a trap or a fish "finds" a hook. Conway wanted to please others, and when he helped in Dun & Bradstreet's sale of the OAG airline guide to Maxwell, Maxwell was pleased and said so. Maxwell, who was always doing deals, began courting Conway, inviting him to glamorous parties and events—and all the while, Conway was courting Maxwell as a potential breakthrough client. When the management committee voted "no" on doing investment banking business for Robert Maxwell because he had a reputation of not living up to his commitments, Conway was looking for someone to take over the relationship and see if other kinds of business could be developed instead.[12] He spoke to Peter Spira, who had just joined the firm from S.G. Warburg. As Spira recounts, "Mindful of the report by the Board of Trade in 1972 castigating the gentleman in question, and also benefiting from the sense of smell acquired at Warburg's, I refused point blank. On the following day, Bob Hamburger put his head round my door to say that he had been asked the same question and what should he do? My reply was unequivocally that he should not touch the account with a barge pole, either proverbial or otherwise."[13]

Conway encouraged Eric Sheinberg to develop his relationship with Maxwell, and soon it was Sheinberg's turn to be invited into the glitz and glitter of Maxwell's parties. Like every new entrant to an already established market, Sheinberg had no chance, of course, of waltzing into the most prestigious, most dignified accounts and persuading them to change the way they did their business or the firms they used. He knew he would have to get started as best he could, working with innovative products, disruptive initiatives—and marginal customers. In the firm's still "stovepipe" reporting structure, operational units in London did not report to a locally based executive in the City, where a sense of the market might have warned a manager of potential trouble. Finally, Sheinberg was a loner—he even played golf alone—and the London partners didn't care for him as a person, so they quietly went their separate ways. None of the other London partners wanted to work with Maxwell—and they felt they didn't need to compromise, because Goldman Sachs had already won the big British Gas privatization and was confident it could win British Petroleum. Maxwell, however, really needed Goldman Sachs to legitimize himself.

There were other factors too—some within Sheinberg and some within Goldman Sachs. In one unusual habit, he checked all trading tickets every day, saying, "There are no friends in the business and I don't trade on the basis of friendship." With his penchant for secrecy—he often retreated to a private office and closed the door, speaking over the phone with accounts in a hushed, confidential way—Sheinberg was unusual, particularly within a trading organization that emphasized teamwork. Routinely avoided by the firm's other traders, isolated and opaque, he was often cantankerous and made it immediately clear to everyone to stay out of his way and leave him alone. When Maxwell called, Sheinberg insisted everyone leave his office and then closed the door.

The firm was rapidly getting larger and larger, doing business in numerous different countries, and becoming more formal and systematic. Goldman Sachs wasn't the same anymore: The firm was going through a period of major multidimensional change and moving rapidly away from the small, close-knit family unit that Levy had created and Sheinberg had known and loved. But some of the old habits of personal loyalties, rabbis, and leaving partners free to build and run their own businesses persisted, particularly among the old-timers. Sheinberg had been passed over in favor of the young MBAs and PhDs who were using increasingly sophisticated computer models and were part of a technology revolution moving toward modern Wall Street. They looked down on Sheinberg as just another out-of-date, over-the-hill "intuitive" trader. Sheinberg resented those self-confident, well-educated, socially adept young traders who were moving up into positions of power within the firm and taking up responsibilities greater than his. Now he had to get approvals from people who were really his juniors. He hated it—but quietly.[14]

Sheinberg was glad to be asked to develop the firm's London trading operation. He was always interested in figuring out new markets, and not only was London a new market for him, there was lots of talk about a major restructuring—known as Big Bang—of the securities markets in the City. Such major change would disrupt established relationships and established ways of doing business, giving new firms like Goldman Sachs a unique opportunity to break in and build up. Sheinberg and others anticipated that London would go, as New York had gone in the 1960s, from a pure agency brokerage business model to a mixed market with both agency and principal trading. To the extent the "mixed" market developed, it played right into Goldman Sachs's strengths: extensive experience with block trading; deep understanding of how to take risks; knowledge of how to coordinate sales and trading; and plenty of capital. Best of all, if everything went right, London could be the chance Sheinberg had been looking for. London was his chance to make a major personal comeback. If he made a real success in London, he'd be back on top.

He was on to something. Before Big Bang allowed British brokers and dealers to combine, all listed securities trading was pure agency execution of orders, with no capital at risk in market making. Brokers in London did not make markets—only jobbers did and only on a modest scale—so the brokers had almost no capital and no experience with making markets as risk-taking dealers. Even after Big Bang, British firms were cautious about block trading. But Goldman Sachs and the other American firms took the initiative, committing substantial capital and taking deliberate, managed risks to make markets in listed and over-the-counter stocks. London's institutional investors soon learned the considerable convenience of executing large orders through experienced market-making dealers who were ready to risk capital in all sorts of markets to facilitate large block trades at specified prices.

"Eric did a lot of trading when and where he could," recalls Bob Steel. "When he got to London, we were small and outsiders. In those days, people in the City cared a lot about where you went to school and how you got there. And they wasted no love on Americans trying to muscle in on their business, particularly since it really wasn't a very big business. Offices were shabby, trading was all agency business, and there was too little business to share—and we Americans were there! So Eric nosed around, looking for people who might like to do business. He particularly looked for ways to break into the British-share business, and maybe into Continental shares." One way to break into the London market was to do portfolio trades, which Goldman Sachs understood well from years of experience in New York, but portfolio trading was entirely new to the Londoners. That's how Eric Sheinberg had met Robert Maxwell.

Where Sheinberg was cautious, Maxwell was charismatic and larger than life and made things happen. Sheinberg checked him out and found he was doing business with Cazenove and all the other establishment firms, but his contact at Cazenove said something that later proved prescient: "We do business with Maxwell, but not *risk* business where we would be dependent on his judgment of a situation. It's dangerous to have clients who could be adversaries."

Sheinberg had gone to London at the same time as the "A Team" of strong, young leaders who were determined to break into that very establishment market as the strategic salient from which Goldman Sachs could then expand onto the European Continent and realize John Whitehead's vision of being a global investment bank. The campaign would begin with stockbrokerage, and stockbrokerage would be led by institutional block trading. Sheinberg's mission would be to build up block trading—using as little firm capital and taking as little risk as possible. The best way to do this had already been demonstrated by Gus Levy and Bob Mnuchin: Link institutional trading with the transactions of corporate wheeler-dealers; get in the middle of the action; and "let the games begin." Block trading as a business to pursue was new to the City and familiar to Goldman Sachs. Sheinberg saw Maxwell as his "elephant"—a major account that would make his comeback within the firm.

"We were infatuated," remembers Steel, who shared an office with Sheinberg. "Maxwell was our ticket of admission to the party. We knew we were good at trading, and Eric knew he was very good at trading. The big trading accounts are often 'unusual,' and they're never Girl Guides. The more business Eric did with Maxwell, the more interesting it was to all the rest of us—all except Gavyn Davies, Goldman Sachs's chief economist for Europe, who knew how to read people like Maxwell and who would have nothing to do with him." Simon Robertson, who had many years of experience before joining the firm from Kleinwort Benson, had the same view: "That man is bad news. Diesel-fume him!" Sir Win Bischoff, then head of the leading London merchant bank Schroders, recounts a similar view: "In our morning managing committee meetings, we took the view that if one of our eight members said no and the others yes, we would go ahead. But if *two* said no, *we* said no. Maxwell came up three times, and each time, we had a majority in favor, but two or more opposed, so we would not act for him."

Sheinberg shared Maxwell's interest in Israel and was delighted and dazzled by the glitter that Maxwell always showered around himself in London: movie stars, champagne, big cars, helicopters, politicians, fancy dinners. During an evening at Sotheby's for a charity auction of Ronald Reagan's doodles, Sheinberg's guest posed to a newspaper reporter as a Goldman Sachs economist and, continuing the bluff, agreed on the spot to do an informal interview on the UK's economic outlook. "Eric was an accident waiting to happen when he crossed paths with Maxwell," explains Steel. "Eric saw Maxwell as his ticket back to significance in the firm and told others to 'stay away from *my* account,' even though everyone at Goldman Sachs knew the policy was that all accounts were always the firm's accounts." Sheinberg and Maxwell developed a separate relationship—dealing on their own.

Sheinberg often dealt directly with clients who particularly liked to trade—people like Robert Maxwell, who enjoyed the excitement of making large trades in public markets and regarded themselves as quite skillful. While Maxwell might have several others involved with him in setting up a particular trade, he would not consider himself committed to a trade until he personally said the decisive words, "You've dealt."

Sheinberg set up large margin loans against Maxwell's stock and then more loans against the pension funds' stock, getting authorization to do this by arguing that with six-day settlements, "if the stock collateral starts to go down, we'll sell the stock. There's no exposure to Maxwell. We get to shoot first!" With a margin account, the firm would always be in control, so trading for Maxwell would be okay even though underwriting was not.

Sensing opportunity, Sheinberg became a market maker in Maxwell Communication Corporation (MCC). Sheinberg and Maxwell each believed he would always be controlling the other. Sheinberg should have understood that Maxwell was a clever and experienced customer dealing in large size and operating at the edges of legality, but he just *knew* that as smart as Maxwell might be, he was even smarter about trading and markets, and was certain he would always be in control. Meanwhile, Maxwell respected Sheinberg's trading skills but also knew that he was not telling Sheinberg everything—and some of his secrets were crucial. Skillful and experienced as he was in trading, Sheinberg's excessive self-confidence made it possible for Maxwell to out-trade him.

Sheinberg was making good profits trading in MCC shares and was steadily developing the firm's reputation as an effective institutional block trader. With his skills and connections, he was establishing Goldman Sachs as a clear leader in bringing large-scale, American-style, capital-at-risk block trading to London. And his largest account was with Robert Maxwell, whose declared intention was to buy companies and build up a global media business. Things were going well. "Everyone wanted to meet Maxwell," recalls Steel. "We all wanted to get admitted to the party too." Maxwell could be the key client for the firm as it tried to build up its investment banking business.

Bob Conway was ambitious to build up Corporate Finance, so he urged John Thornton, already a stellar vice president, to work with Maxwell on taking the Berlitz language schools public. "Maxwell gave us the Berlitz underwriting," recalls Conway, "a very big deal and a landmark for us: a UK share underwriting for a British company with most of the stock taken up by London-based institutions." Like crossing the equator, this was a signal event in the firm's recognizing that it could make it in London.

The partners of Goldman Sachs thought they knew enough about Maxwell to protect themselves. "We knew Maxwell had been declared—in public by a British supervisory body—as unfit to manage a public company," recalls Peter Sachs. "We knew he was comparable to Victor Posner," the acquisitive American who was eventually barred by the SEC from serving as an officer or director of a public company. Conway was confident the firm could safely take Berlitz public for Maxwell for two reasons. First, taking it public would remove Berlitz from Maxwell's direct control, and second, with some care, Goldman Sachs could insulate itself from Maxwell. As usual, hope was father to the thought and, as usual, the linkage was mostly imaginary.

In early 1991 Maxwell bought another £105 million of Maxwell Communication Corporation shares—largely through Goldman Sachs, which was then doing over half the trading in MCC shares. In April 1991, fifty-five million pounds of MCC shares held by the company's pension funds were sold to two offshore units controlled by Maxwell. The sale, which was not properly reported in London, was executed in New York through Goldman Sachs. During 1990–91,

Maxwell bought an astonishing four hundred million pounds of MCC shares—largely through Goldman Sachs.

In April 1991 Maxwell turned to outright theft—and got Sheinberg's unwitting help in return for a relatively small £110,000 commission on an agency trade, with no questions asked. Goldman Sachs bought twenty-five million shares of MCC from two Maxwell-controlled pension funds on April 26 for £54.9 million and, with financing through Bishopsgate Investment Management, Maxwell's private company, they were bought the same day by two Lichtenstein trusts—secretly and indirectly controlled by Maxwell—so they were now available as collateral for desperately needed bank loans.

Maxwell arranged an IPO of 49 percent of Mirror Group Newspapers for April 30, 1991. This was accompanied by extensive marketing in America and on the Continent, where Maxwell's unsavory reputation was less well known. The funds raised were used to pay down bank borrowings. Knowing that more than two-thirds of Maxwell Communication Corporation shares were owned by the Maxwell entities (the legal limit was 70 percent) and that a total of 80 percent was owned by investors who would not sell, Sheinberg believed he could catch short sellers in a serious lack of liquidity and then squeeze the bears—making a major killing for Goldman Sachs. When Maxwell reached the 70 percent limit, he guided Sheinberg to other "friendly" buyers acting for trusts in Lichtenstein through Dr. Rechsteiner in Zurich. Again, Sheinberg—proud of being Brooklyn-born and streetwise—did not ask key questions even though a market-savvy observer could have intuited that the buyers were controlled by Maxwell.

Goldman Sachs continued to act for Maxwell in the spring of 1991, and MCC's share price rose as the planned IPO was done through "advisers of the highest reputation."[15] The firm's exposure to Maxwell was for a total of $160 million in shares, foreign exchange deals, and a holding of OAG preferred. This was so large that David Silfen told Sheinberg he had to reduce the exposure.

In August, Sheinberg offered Maxwell another large block: 16.7 million shares. Maxwell balked at an outright purchase, but made an attractive counterproposal: He would buy those shares at a large premium over the current market—but only months later. This offer became a Goldman Sachs put option to sell 15.7 million MCC shares at £2.03, well above the current price of £1.71.

The put option had one particularly significant feature: It expired on November 30, only two days after the two-month period in which Maxwell was not allowed to buy shares—and the very day that was the end of Goldman Sachs's fiscal year, when all positions had to be marked to market. During the life of the option, MCC shares declined to £1.39, giving Sheinberg and Goldman Sachs a powerful incentive to buy shares they knew they could sell to Maxwell at £2.03. The put option was at such a low premium that it was clearly just a deferred purchase—assuming Maxwell had the money to honor his commitment. Sheinberg should have known that Maxwell was propping up MCC's share price. Goldman Sachs could, of course, threaten Maxwell that if he didn't buy the shares, they would be dumped on the market, reducing their price and value as loan collateral.

Meanwhile, Maxwell owed Goldman Sachs ninety million dollars in a margin account. But he didn't have the money and couldn't borrow it either. In New York, three Goldman Sachs partners who were chosen because they were independent, fresh faces and outside the chain of command—Ken Brody, Bob Katz, and Bob Hurst—went to see Maxwell at his penthouse suite at the Waldorf Towers to tell him in no uncertain terms that he absolutely had to pay up. Maxwell took them out onto the roof terrace, where they explained what he must do: Reduce the exposure *now* or we will reduce it for you by selling the collateral. The wind was howling, so voices could hardly be heard. Maxwell looked straight at the trio and said, "If you must shoot me, shoot me!" On the way down in the elevator, Hurst asked: "Why do you suppose he wanted to go out on the deck?"

"So whatever he said could not be picked up electronically," said Katz. "He must have thought we were wired!"

On October 22, 1991, Maxwell urgently requested a meeting at Goldman Sachs, but Bob Katz, general counsel, says, "We were not interested in a meeting. The only thing we were interested in was getting paid. The deadline had passed. There was nothing to discuss."[16] Desperate, Maxwell walked unannounced into Goldman Sachs's New York office, where he met with Brody, who reminded Maxwell of the story about the sultan's dog being taught to talk *if* execution were deferred one year.* Maxwell was given one more week, but could not deliver the money.

---

* The condemned man promised the sultan he could teach the sultan's dog to talk. Asked by a fellow prisoner why he had made such an outrageous promise to such a cruel and vindictive sultan, the man explained: "Well, in a year, I might die anyway or the sultan might die . . . or that dog might talk!"

Inside observers were surprised that Goldman Sachs, which is usually so strict about documentation, had accepted merely verbal assurances from Maxwell that the secretive trusts were independent of his control. Realistically, Goldman Sachs could have been sued as a conduit, if not as a coconspirator, when Maxwell embezzled the pension funds, because Maxwell sold Mirror Group's pension fund's shares via Goldman Sachs and directed where the proceeds were to go.

Maxwell was guilty of market manipulation and artificially supporting the share price of Mirror Group through purchases by the Lichtenstein trusts he controlled. Sheinberg was accused of enabling fraud: He either knew or should have known that the trades he was executing for Maxwell were part of a scheme to deceive investors by supporting the stock price to protect the market value of the shares being used as collateral for bank loans. Either Sheinberg was negligently abetting a fraud or he was a victim. If Goldman Sachs did not know or guess what Maxwell was doing, it was, to quote Sidney Weinberg's comment in a different context, "not very bright"—or as current partners said, *stupid!*

On Monday, November 4, 1991, Gene Fife of Goldman Sachs called Eddie George, the deputy governor of the Bank of England, to inform him that an announcement would be made on the fifth that Goldman Sachs would be selling Maxwell Communication Corporation shares to liquidate the loans. Goldman Sachs was, at long last, closing out its complex financial dealings with Robert Maxwell. The next day, Robert Maxwell would be dead.

G oldman Sachs finally negotiated a civil settlement with the liquidators representing the pension funds three and half years later in which, without the firm's admitting guilt or liability, $254 million was paid into the pension funds. (Another $156 million was paid by Lehman Brothers and the accountants.) The negotiations that concluded with this better-than-expected result were handled by Gene Fife, the partner in charge of the London office who, with quiet West Virginia charm and considerable time and attention, had developed a wide network of friendly, respectful relationships throughout the British government and British industry.

Recognizing the importance of expert advice, Fife retained as his public relations adviser Peter Gummer of Shandwick Consultants. Gummer advised that

Goldman Sachs should contribute two million dollars to a public-interest group that would study all aspects of the matter. Far more important to the final outcome, Gummer—whose brother later served in John Major's cabinet and who had useful contacts at all levels of government—helped advance the selection of an unusually widely experienced, careful, and objective public servant, Sir John Cuckney, as the principal investigator. Cuckney had been knighted for his career in intelligence in MI6, Her Majesty's secret service, which reports directly to the prime minister.

Fife met with Cuckney many, many times. While it was always "Sir John" for Fife, what began as "Mr. Fife" for Cuckney eased over a year's time into "Gene" as these two men sized each other up, learned to understand each other, made careful appraisals of each other's values, and jointly explored the information that was becoming increasingly available to them. Each meeting began with a quiet admonition: The rules must be clearly understood; no notes are to be taken—and this meeting never took place. Each time, Cuckney paused until Fife had nodded. The central question on their agenda was easy to say, but hard to decide—partly because the consequences of getting it wrong were enormous and enduring, partly because any decision would be final and irreversible, and partly because the basis for judgment would necessarily be entirely qualitative.

Fife's goal was clear: Avoid a prolonged public flailing of Goldman Sachs and reach agreement on the size of a financial settlement that would not cripple the firm. Avoiding an indictment was paramount. The consequences of a criminal indictment and conviction would have included suspension from trading, grievous losses of business in the United Kingdom and around the world, large penalties in numerous additional civil suits, investigations by the SEC in America, and an albatross of shame with all sorts of "pariah" consequences for the firm.

Fife's objective was to build the evidence and understanding in Cuckney's mind that would enable this experienced career intelligence professional to make the objective judgment that Sheinberg's behavior was an aberration—not at all representative of Goldman Sachs as a firm and in no way indicative of the way Goldman Sachs would behave in the future—and that both the United Kingdom and London's market would be far better off to have Goldman Sachs "wounded, but not killed."

Like a father's evaluation of the character of a prospective son-in-law, the process would take time and repetitive exposures. Their discussions fit no particular pattern, often revisiting familiar ground and sometimes turning quickly to new topics. They were always probing for greater understanding of each other, of the facts, policies, and practices of Goldman Sachs, and of the people. All their meetings were in person; they never discussed matters by telephone.

While Cuckney and Fife were meeting over more than a year, Sullivan & Cromwell, the firm's principal U.S. law firm, and in-house counsel were gathering facts. In the end, they came to a definitive conclusion: Goldman Sachs should settle. The case must not go to trial.

Knowing time was running out, Fife and Cuckney met yet again, hoping they could come to closure. Both men were acting on their own. Neither would or could go back to his principal for any approvals. Both men knew before their meeting began that the money involved in a settlement would be very large—surely record size. Both men were pleasantly surprised by the brevity with which they reached their accord. In the end, Cuckney trusted Fife and decided Goldman Sachs was more valuable to Britain alive and chastened by a major civil penalty than mortally wounded by a criminal conviction. Goldman Sachs would contribute $254 million to the Maxwell-plundered pension funds. Large at it was, the penalty could have been much larger. The management committee was braced to accept anything less than five hundred million dollars as generally acceptable for Goldman Sachs.

As they shook hands warmly, Sir John smiled and said, "Gene, I think you might be interested in this document," and handed Fife a formal criminal charge. "Had we been unable to agree to terms as we have just done, it had already been decided that our negotiations would have been terminated completely and Goldman Sachs would have been formally charged this day."

New trustees were appointed for the raided pension funds, which had lost approximately six hundred million dollars due to Maxwell's maneuvers. They promptly launched a major lawsuit against Goldman Sachs, Lehman Brothers, and the accountants who had represented Maxwell, seeking an enormous recovery. The firm was in the worst of all possible situations as foreigners—all too easily accused of greed-driven market manipulation at the expense of thousands of now-impoverished pensioners. Partners of Goldman Sachs could easily imagine the scene outside the Old Bailey courtroom: pensioners on crutches and in wheelchairs being photographed and giving statements for the front pages of London's sensationalizing newspapers. As today, newspaper coverage in London could be relentless, with seven morning papers and two evening tabloids that followed up on the stories featured in the morning. The competition was vigorous. The Maxwell story and the firm's involvement could sell a lot of papers. As it was, the aroma from Maxwell noticeably hurt the firm's business in the UK and across Europe over the next year or so.

Through it all, the partners were deeply embarrassed by their own question: "How could we have let that happen?" The lesson was clear: Nobody can ever be allowed to operate outside the clear reporting lines of decision or the chain of command. The firm had stayed far too long with the old ways that might have sufficed several years before for a much smaller "family" firm in a slower-paced market. For a major firm dealing in the fast, global capital markets, formal risk controls were mandatory, and the real test of a risk-control system would be that it caught not only what you would not expect, but also what you would have thought not possible.

"With Robert Maxwell, supervision was lax," acknowledges Jim Gorter. "We didn't have the necessary checks and balances. A trading relationship that started out okay got bigger and bigger and became so different in composition that it was not okay. In the end, it cost us a lot of money. Ours is a very complex business. When it surges forward in volume—*and* speed *and* complexity—the business can suddenly outgrow the control system. And when that happens, mistakes get made. Not all of them are caught, and some of these mistakes really bite you. We were lucky to be caught out so few times. The two major dangers that come from within a firm are arrogance—and counting the profits."

So the Maxwell fiasco had one good result: much stronger and more rigorous risk controls—and *no* exceptions. It also strengthened Jon Corzine's case for public ownership because in a public company, those heavy costs absorbed painfully by the partnership would simply be written off as a mere "stroke of a pen" accounting charge. The Maxwell affair soon led to the partnership being converted to a limited liability partnership or "LLP"—another rung on the ladder to an IPO.

Partners had mentally reserved for the Maxwell settlement, but the amounts had been based on estimates. With the settlement, estimates would shift into hard numbers. Inside Goldman Sachs, the immediate next question was which partners would pay the $254 million. The settlement was treated as a "dated account," and partners from prior years got hit with a "chargeback" requiring them to contribute to the settlement.

Jim Gorter and Fred Krimendahl negotiated on behalf of the various partnership classes. Throughout April 1995 input was sought from general partners, limited partners, and retired partners. The management committee decided to allocate 80 percent of the settlement cost to those who were general partners in 1991, 15 percent to those of 1990, and 5 percent to those of 1989.[17] In a memorandum to 164 partners, the management committee took the position that "this decision, in our judgment, should meet the appropriate expectations that anyone who has been a general partner should have developed regarding how a matter such as this would be handled if it ever arose."[18]

It was, and could only be, rough justice. Getting past a settlement and 100 percent back to business was particularly important because at that time Goldman Sachs was making a huge commitment of talent and treasure to its international expansion. A persistent Maxwell cloud would have been a costly burden.

The $254 million settlement was not the end of the costs of Maxwell. Accountants and lawyers were sure to bill substantial fees for their services in sorting out the details of Maxwell's depredations, and the Financial Services Authority fined Goldman Sachs £160,000 for violating financial reporting requirements on three transactions.[19, 20] The firm also lost more than ninety million dollars in loans to and unsettled transactions with Maxwell, and was excluded by HM Treasury from the third round of privatization by British Telecom, known as BT3. The total cost to Goldman Sachs was on the order of five hundred million dollars.

At the end of November 1995, Eric Sheinberg, then Goldman Sachs's longest-tenured partner, went limited. He had joined the firm in 1960 and had become a partner in 1971.

H er Majesty's Government, through the Department of Trade and Industry, published findings of fact in 2001. Among them: Maxwell "parked" controlled investments by selling them to the MCC pension funds. Some of the transactions were so complex and numerous that even with 20/20 hindsight, the diligent DTI investigators were obliged to acknowledge: "We have been unable to obtain a rational explanation for these sales and purchases."[21] In 1986–87, pension-fund money was fairly regularly lent by the pension funds at Maxwell's command without any form of security. Maxwell would decide the price and timing specifics of a transaction with Sheinberg and then instruct Sheinberg to call Dr. Rechsteiner and pretend to arrive independently at exactly the same terms. In placing thirty million Maxwell Communication Corporation shares in Japan via Nikko Securities in October 1989, a series of obfuscating transactions enabled Maxwell to avoid disclosure. A key step in the process involved Goldman Sachs. Six months later, Sheinberg saw that the shares Nikko had placed were coming back into the London market and, knowing Maxwell "had a fixation about the price of shares," saw a trading opportunity: He could buy on dips in the market knowing that Maxwell would buy any large block he assembled at a higher price and thus at a good profit to Goldman Sachs. One sizable block was accumulated in early August 1990 and then sold by Goldman Sachs. On two occasions Maxwell sold large put options to Goldman Sachs—for over thirty million shares—which enabled the firm to accumulate shares in the market with the certainty that it could sell the shares to Maxwell at above-market prices, a stratagem to support the share price. In September large share purchases were made by the pension funds. By far the largest, for seventeen million pounds, was done though Goldman Sachs.

Goldman Sachs's considerable ability to put a less negative spin on newspaper stories was demonstrated by its initial public statement after the DTI investigative report was released: "A spokesman for Goldman Sachs in London said Friday that the report 'correctly concludes that Goldman Sachs wasn't acting in league with or on the basis of any agreement with Robert Maxwell.' He added that Mr. Maxwell 'intentionally and successfully deceived' the firm. We deeply regret this and with the benefit of hindsight, and with the information now available to us, we would have acted differently."[22]

Noting that Maxwell's son and others were acquitted after a long trial, the DTI inspectors said, "In view of the acquittals in the criminal proceedings, we decided we would proceed in a manner that did not, and would not be seen to, call the acquittals into question. Nonetheless, conduct can be blameworthy without being criminal. We do not make legal determinations. . . . Where, therefore, we attribute responsibility, we do so in that context, and in terms of blame . . . the primary responsibility rests with Mr. Robert Maxwell. Goldman Sachs were the Investment Bank with whom Mr. Robert Maxwell principally dealt when purchasing . . . shares and bears a substantial responsibility in respect of the manipulation."

Kevin Maxwell testified that Goldman Sachs had advised his father to conduct a multimillion-pound share-support operation to boost MCC's share price, but apparently the firm made the operation ineffective by conducting its own trading operation.[23] Sheinberg's testimony to the DTI inspectors often differed significantly from comparable testimony by Kevin Maxwell and others involved in the particular trades. Usually, the key difference was whether or not Robert Maxwell was the decision maker. Sheinberg often said Maxwell was not involved. The others repeatedly said he was the *only* person involved. Either way, a Goldman Sachs partner was intimately involved, and both Sheinberg and the Goldman Sachs partners in supervisory roles should have known better.

As an informed partner summarizes, "The final number may have seemed large to many, but those on the management committee were all relieved that it was finally settled. Gene Fife did an outstanding job of managing that potentially explosive and hurtful issue." Still, since virtually none of the partners had had anything remotely to do with Maxwell, they understandably were upset at having to ante up millions of dollars— and some were somehow angry at Fife.

Years later, Gene and Anne Fife were in London, catching up with friends, seeing shows, and enjoying a vacation. Staying at the Cadogan Hotel, they received an envelope with an invitation to come for tea at the House of Lords the next day at four o'clock—from J. Cuckney, who by then had been elevated to a life peerage. Arriving at the House of Lords, they were surprised to be greeted by former Labour cabinet minister Frank Field and his staff of six as well as Lord Cuckney. After warm greetings, the group went into the drawing room for tea, and Lord Cuckney said, "We gather together to say to you that the Maxwell matter is now closed—and to thank you, Gene, for the very fine way you conducted yourself through what must have been for you a most difficult proceeding. We shall always be grateful. Thank you, Gene."

26

MAKING ARBITRAGE
A BUSINESS

Risk arbitrage is based on the simple idea that if there are two market prices for the same thing or two equivalent things, they will converge at some point as though pulled together by a rubber band. Arbitrageurs take disciplined actions to create profits by capturing differences in prices for the same item in different markets or of different but interchangeable items in the same market. The price differences they exploit are caused by market inefficiencies or mistakes caused by imbalances of supply and demand due to differences between *uncertainty* and *risk*, which differ in ways only experts usually care about. Arbitrageurs increase market efficiency and—indirectly and unintentionally, as Adam Smith famously explained in *The Wealth of Nations*—they increase the consistency and fairness of markets and therefore the confidence investors have in markets; that helps improve overall economic performance. Arbitrageurs are working in free, competitive markets that are open to everyone, so to earn profits they need to see what others do not see, to see more clearly than others do, or to take actions others would not have considered.

For example, in 1988 Equimark, a small Pennsylvania bank holding company with ten million shares trading at $6, issued an equal number of rights to buy ten million shares at $4. The stock quickly dropped by one-third to $4, and the market price of the rights—which were offered to shareholders without cost—dropped by half, from $2.50 to $1.25. Reading the prospectus carefully, Frank Brosens made an interesting discovery: Shareholders were not limited by the number of shares they owned, but could apply for as many rights as they wanted. All the other shareholders applied for sensible amounts, for a total of 8.5 million new shares—less than one new share for every old share. Brosens did not. He submitted a very different application. Working with lawyers to be sure of every step, including setting up a new corporate entity so that the bid would not be directly by Goldman Sachs (which would have violated the Glass-Steagall Act then restricting interactions between investment banks and commercial banks), he entered a bid for rights to buy all ten million shares. Of course, the total bids far exceeded the total available, so the firm's bid was prorated back down. But with zero market risk and virtually no capital tied up, the firm collected a $1 million profit on this one position—and made a nearly infinite rate of return.

Clarifying the separation between risk and uncertainty is important to understanding arbitrage. With a large enough population of independent events of the same kind, a risk analyst theoretically knows the odds of each possible outcome with what is correctly called "actuarial accuracy" before having to make his decision. And given a table of possible payoffs and the probability of each, a decision maker is conceptually able to calculate the probabilities of all possible specific outcomes. That's why actuaries can, for a large population, predict patterns of mortality with such precision and accuracy. Given enough independent events, a rational and informed decision maker can virtually predict the future. Uncertainty is different: While you may have plausible expectations, you really don't know the odds and you may not know the payoffs, and while you know both are probably changing, you usually don't know the speed or sometimes even the direction of the change. Uncertainty, like the probable mortality of an individual, is greatest for a sample of one—or any unique occurrence.

Understandably, most investors dislike uncertainty so much that they try to avoid it or protect themselves from it, particularly with one-off disasters like a major fire, a serious accident, or an early death. So it can be profitable for those who are well informed, skillful, and broadly active in the risk markets to absorb all the specific uncertainties investors so dislike. Insurance companies earn profits by making a market between an individual's uncertainty and a population's true risk. In the capital and money markets of the world, risk arbitrageurs provide liquidity for investors who are reluctant to hold on to an investment that obliges them to accept uncertainty such as whether a proposed merger will or will not be consummated at a particular price on a particular date. Arbitrageurs earn high returns on their capital because the work is so difficult to do well on a scale that involves enough independent events to enable the arbitrageur to profit reliably on the gap between uncertainty and true risk. Potential competitors are discouraged because, while profits come in small percentages most of the time, losses can be sudden and awful. Skeptics liken it to picking up nickels and dimes in front of a steamroller.

Three factors are crucial for success in arbitrage: extraordinary, unemotional rationality or objectivity in all decisions and actions; superior access to information; and the ability to understand that information and think unconventionally and rigorously about it. Arbitrageurs live in a sea of changing information, estimates, rumors, fears, and hopes that drive markets and change prices, amid which they make bold decisions with tens of millions of dollars at stake.

Risk arbitrage, a specialty within arbitrage, centers on making rational judgments of the appropriate prices of the securities to be offered in a takeover if and when it actually goes through, knowing that deals sometimes get rejected as inadequate by the target company or its shareholders, and that deals may get broken up by antitrust lawsuits that are sometimes contested successfully, by competing offers (sometimes from "white knights" brought in by the target company), or by adverse changes in market prices. Individual transaction profits are often rather small—because markets are not *that* inefficient—but the best arbitrageurs earn a high rate of return on their capital by rigorously avoiding mistakes, running a diversified portfolio of commitments, and moving capital from one situation to another, always striving to maximize current-period returns. "Arbitrageurs need to be totally rational, have no ideology, be dispassionate, and have a team that is balanced, thoughtful, and decisive—changing their actions as the facts change," says Frank Brosens. Arbitrageur Dinakar Singh adds, "The only things that count are the specific facts on the yellow pad and logic. Emotion is in the market, waiting to be discovered by objective analysis."

Mergers, particularly contested takeovers, are unique events dependent on human judgment and frailties. They are replete with legal, financial, and competitive problems and consequent market uncertainties. The risk arbitrageur is always dealing with uncertainty and never dealing with actuarial accuracy about risk. While there may be general patterns, each situation is unique. Fortunately, over time, many unique situations—if correctly analyzed component by component—can be understood as part of a universe in which, although each merger is unique, there are patterns of repetition in some of the components. Experienced arbitrageurs can increase their average profitability by increasing the depth and detail of their knowledge of each specific situation in the search for exploitable patterns. Arbitrageurs do not strive to be right so much as to be more nearly right—or less wrong—than the informed consensus represented by market price.

In the 1980s, Goldman Sachs would have a portfolio of eighty to one hundred arbitrage positions. Some would be held for as little as three or four weeks, and others for a year or two. With five or six people in research and three or four in trading, the arbitrage unit was closely knit. Now the unit has over twenty people. Every position is regularly reviewed and evaluated in the context of the whole portfolio of arbitrage positions. About 5 percent of positions result in losses. Rates of return have been substantially reduced by competition—from 25 percent annual returns in the sixties and seventies to 18 to 20 percent in the eighties and then, in recent years, to less than 15 percent. If the market is 85 percent "right" about prices and an arbitrageur—with more or better data and better insight or greater objectivity—can be 90 or even 95 percent "right," that comparative advantage will be his source of hard-earned profit.

Nothing is known or certain in risk arbitrage. Everything is estimates and probabilities, and stock market prices are determined by the always-changing estimates of the unfolding future as perceived by many different kinds of investors, each with different objectives, skills, and information. All the moving parts are changing—sometimes significantly and suddenly. Information, insight, and perspective are vital to successful arbitrage operations, and all arbitrageurs are in competition will all other arbitrageurs. Since information is useful only when fresh or unique and therefore not already reflected in the market prices, arbitrageurs are in frequent contact with many, many potential sources of information by making dozens of calls every day. Useful, original information, which is essential to making money, is never just given. It is *exchanged* for other valuable information in a fast-paced bartering process; each side in a relationship keeps a running mental estimate or record of value given versus value received.

Merger arbitrage is dominated by uncertainty: How will the market today and tomorrow value a variety of unusual, newly created debt and equity securities? Will the government try to disallow a merger? Will it succeed? Is the accounting correct? Will ABC Corporation issue a competitive bid? How might XYZ Corporation respond? Are other arbitrageurs or hedge funds—often the major short-term market movers—favoring ABC or XYZ? In merger arbitrage, the stakes are large, the profit margins are thin, and the market reactions to small changes in perceived probability come quickly. Arbitrage always requires a style of detached intensity because it requires making many specific decisions after appraising the risk-adjusted, anticipated future market values of publicly traded securities. These estimates depend on gathering, sorting, and appraising incremental insights on many, many dimensions. Arbitrage situations are never in black and white, but rather in subtle shades of gray that are always changing. Nothing in arbitrage is ever both highly profitable *and* simple and clear—or easy.

During the postwar years, securities arbitrage came in three main categories. First was pure arbitrage, where two markets for exactly the same security or commodity differed temporarily because of local supply-demand imbalances. This enabled an arbitrageur to make a small but certain profit by selling short in the higher-priced market and buying long in the lower-priced market in equal amounts. The classic illustration: The shares of Royal Dutch Shell trade on both the Dutch and British markets and the prices might differ slightly, creating a pure arbitrage opportunity to sell in the higher-priced market and simultaneously buy in the lower-priced market. J. Aron conducted pure arbitrage in gold when the price in London or New York City differed slightly from the price in Tehran or Baghdad or Singapore.

The second type of arbitrage—Gus Levy's specialty—was based on the breakup of public utilities and railroads emerging from bankruptcy. Arbitrageurs made markets in "when-issued" securities—securities that were announced but not yet issued. There were inherent uncertainties in any yet-to-be-issued security's market reception, and uncertainties cause price discounts. Arbitrageurs could make markets in these when-issued securities and profit from their willingness to put their capital at risk while estimating—hopefully accurately—the fair market prices of the future securities. This was not a big business, but it could be quite profitable for the few skillful arbitrageurs who specialized in it.

During the Depression, most railroads went into bankruptcy. Then, with all the profitable traffic volume of World War II, they piled up huge cash positions, and many railroads filed plans with the Interstate Commerce Commission to come out of bankruptcy. But since they'd been in bankruptcy for many years, there were only limited markets for their common or preferred stock or their bonds. Similarly, when the 1937 Utility Holding Company Act limited utility holding companies to owning properties in contiguous states, the larger utility holding companies had to break up. But nobody knew for sure what the parts were really worth; a valuation was needed for each separate security on a when-issued basis. This uncertainty gave market makers and arbitrageurs like Levy many opportunities for profitable trading.

The key to success in arbitrage is unemotional detachment in evaluating each alternative. What are the regulatory hurdles? How will each regulator frame its questions? Into what context will the regulator put this particular issue? Which are the best lawyers for advice on regulatory actions or antitrust? The answers will differ according to the industry involved. Goldman Sachs had an advantage in retaining the best lawyers. It was large enough as a fee-paying client on a regular basis to get attention from the very best.

If the market estimates the probabilities at 93 percent and the firm accurately estimates them at 97 percent, it can profit on the 4 percent difference. Such small differences do not explain the emotional roller coaster that can hit arbitrage. In 1997 risk arbitrage at Goldman Sachs made $75 million in two months, increased that to $400 million, then went to zero followed by a loss, and then rebounded to end the year up $50 million. The group agreed: *Lock it in and count your lucky stars!*

The third type of arbitrage—merger arbitrage—began to become important in the sixties as the conglomerates bid against one another for corporations to take over. Merger arbitrage was a small business in the fifties because there were few mergers and most were friendly deals in which the principal uncertainty was how the Antitrust Division of the Justice Department or the Federal Deposit Insurance Corporation would react. Gus Levy had a network of Wall Street pals who would take arbitrage positions when a merger situation offered attractive prospects of profit. They exchanged ideas and information regularly, particularly during weekend get-togethers at the Century Country Club in Purchase, New York. But for them, arbitrage was never more than an interesting sideline. They relied primarily on scuttlebutt, tips from friends, and what would today be called inside information. In those days, using such information was still considered okay. The boundary line defining what was inside information moved and would move again as markets changed, business practices changed, and risk arbitrage changed in volume, complexity, and pace.

O nce a successful securities salesman, or customer's man, L. Jay Tenen-baum had concentrated on selling securities to Jewish refugees in New York. He soon became the number two "producer" at Goldman Sachs, behind only Jerry McNamara, a Catholic who worked the Catholic community. Tenen-baum began working in arbitrage part-time and proved he had a flair for engaging anyone in conversation, often leading corporate executives to say more than they probably should and to provide more useful insight than they may have realized.

As his block-trading and corporate-finance activities grew larger and faster, Levy needed help. Never easy to work for, he was particularly hard on Tenen-baum and demanded action.

"L. Jay, did you see that merger announcement in the morning paper?"

"Yes."

"Well, what are you *doing* about it?"*

Tenenbaum was soon in charge of the trading room, where block trading was one important unit. Other units included arbitrage, over-the-counter trading, retail brokerage, and convertible bonds. Levy saw arbitrage as an opportunity to build a regular business. He focused on organizing it as such, and built arbi-trage into an important business for the firm. Goldman Sachs had strengths that could be marshaled. Increasing skills in investment research meant Tenenbaum could quickly get up-to-date, experienced insight into the business strategy of

---

* Levy wasn't the only one telling Tenenbaum what to do. Levy had invited Tenenbaum: "L. Jay, if you ever need anything, just tell my secretary," Charlotte Kamp. When Tenenbaum first tried to take advantage of Levy's offer by asking, "Charlotte, will you take a letter?" he got an immediate response: "Will *you* take a *walk?*" Tenenbaum typed his own letters.

MAKING ARBITRAGE A BUSINESS · 471

a company that was suddenly put in play. The firm's institutional sales force was in constant contact with portfolio managers at all the investing institutions and could quickly find out what each institution was doing about a proposed merger, or thinking it might do. In trading, the firm had strong connections with all the major institutions and was seeing more order flow than any of its competitors. Finally, the firm had an extensive network of corporate contacts—competitors, customers, suppliers, former executives—and was developing a reputation for being, more than most, on the side of corporate management. So if Company A was being pursued by Company X or Company Y, Tenenbaum had many ways to make contact and start a conversation with knowledgeable people, develop that conversation to increasing specificity on important aspects of a deal, and keep it going as more and more aspects of the deal's possibilities came into focus. While separated, arbitrage became the Goldman Sachs trading department's single largest and most important account, providing valuable order flow because Levy had established himself and his firm at the crossroads of the acquisitive conglomerates, institutional investors, and arbitrageurs.

The major participants in the stock markets of the sixties and seventies—performance-driven institutional investors—were larger, faster, and more aggressive in both buying and selling than any investors ever seen before. But the biggest change was in the corporate world, particularly the conglomerates—multi-industry corporations whose business strategy was to buy low-priced companies, restructure their operations, spin off some parts, and refinance other parts to drive reported earnings per share higher and higher. With rising earnings, the acquiring conglomerate's stock's price-earnings ratio would stay high enough to enable the conglomerate to buy still more companies. Conglomerates were frequently in competition with one another to acquire any company put in play by another conglomerate's initial takeover bid. On the prowl for takeover targets, Litton, Teledyne, Studebaker-Worthington, LTV, Gulf & Western, NL Industries, CPC International, United Brands, Norton Simon, and others retained smart, creative lawyers, hired "innovative" accountants, used publicists, and hired the most skillful and aggressive investment bankers. At the peak of takeover activity, several new acquisitions were announced every week and changes in deal terms of one or more contested acquisitions were daily fodder for the newspapers.

Because merger activity was subject to antitrust regulation and the government's antitrust policies were far more restrictive than they are now, Tenenbaum developed a network of experienced lawyers, particularly those who had previously served in the Antitrust Division or on the staff of the Federal Trade Commission, and would war-game the possibilities and probabilities with them, striving to get an edge or insight. Antitrust law could be interpreted differently by the Justice Department, the FTC, or the FDIC, and court rulings could differ from one court to another. Small differences in facts or in ability to interpret facts could be worth millions. As Tenenbaum explains just one of hundreds of factors, "The Antitrust Division had injunctive powers, so they could stop a deal for as long as a year with an injunction—and no deal can wait a whole year. But the FTC did not have injunctive powers, so it really mattered where the government would put the responsibility for each proposed merger."

Tenenbaum developed a highly profitable business with 20 percent average annual rates of return, limited only by the amount of capital that a midsize, capital-constrained firm like Goldman Sachs could commit to arbitrage. Partners learned to respect Tenenbaum's moneymaking capabilities even if they never expected to understand them fully. "I told L. Jay I couldn't fathom or understand the way he thought," recalls partner Fred Weintz. "But I knew he was brilliant, and so I said, 'If I ever start a new firm, I'll want *you*!' He thought so differently. I told my [client] companies, 'I don't know what he's talking about, but *he* does—and you should do what he says.'"

The capacity to encourage others to talk is essential in arbitrage, where every competitor is always looking for incremental information and assessing the probabilities of deals going through *or* being delayed *or* being blocked. An arbitrageur might start by saying, "I've read your public announcement and want to be sure my understanding is correct." Then, as the conversation develops, he might ask about various aspects of timing or specific features of the deal, increasing his knowledge and understanding of the always-changing situation. The key to success in merger arbitrage is the ability to find out significant information so that you *know* you are the best informed factually, and then to combine subtle clues into an actionable perception of reality.[1]

Tenenbaum could pick up some additional commission business by showing his hand to institutions that would be discreet and would do all their arbitrage trading with Goldman Sachs—outfits like Irwin Management, which managed the family fortune established by J. Irwin Miller, the chairman of Cummins Corporation. Tenenbaum built a network of two dozen like-minded institutions that did arbitrage trading in the hundreds of thousands of shares. At a commission of 40 cents a share, these institutional co-investors generated significant incremental commissions and added substantial throw weight to Tenenbaum's positions, increasing the odds that the acquirer he favored would prevail in contested takeovers—which increased his profits as an arbitrageur.

When Bob Lenzner, who worked for Tenenbaum in arbitrage, left Goldman Sachs in the late sixties, Tenenbaum needed an assistant and had just started looking when the great investment manager Marty Whitman called: "L. Jay, I know you're looking for an assistant. I do business with Alex Rubin, who has a son at Cleary Gottlieb who wants to leave the law and is having serious talks with Felix Rohatyn over at Lazard Freres. You should meet this kid."

Over lunch, Tenenbaum asked Robert Rubin: "Are you serious about your career? Because if you're serious, you'll want to come to Goldman Sachs. Felix Rohatyn is a big shot—and that means you'll just carry his briefcase. I'm a *little* shot—with no briefcase. I've got more deals than I can possibly handle, more than four hundred this year, so you'll soon have deals that are your own—and you'll be working with . . . Gus Levy." Rubin joined Goldman Sachs in arbitrage with the clear understanding that he could and would manage his own account on the side.[2]

The volume and complexity of mergers were not the only changes affecting merger arbitrage. The rules on what was okay and not okay had been changing too—partly through legislation, partly through regulation, and partly through judicial decisions. The direction of change was consistently toward requiring more disclosure to ensure more fairness to all investors. In addition, there were major changes in the chances of violators' getting caught as regulators developed increasingly complete electronic access to data on who bought or sold what and when. But while the rules were clear and the transparency high in such areas as public offerings, retail stock brokerage, and government-bond dealing, they were still unclear at the other end of a very wide spectrum—risk arbitrage.

Bob Rubin was perfectly suited to arbitrage as it developed in the sixties and seventies: increasing scale, increasing numbers of deals and deal makers, increasing complexity in the terms of offerings, and increasingly frequent changes in terms as competing potential acquirers tried to outmaneuver one another. While Rubin was clearly brilliant, conceptual, and numerate, his greatest strength was an almost eerie calm under pressure. As the pressures intensified—provoking others to tension, angry outbursts, and mistakes—Rubin's calm rationality kept increasing. Under the pressures of a market that was going against him, Rubin seemed to gain focused concentration and to achieve an extradisciplined rigor and objectivity in his reasoning. If the markets went even harder against him, he simply took his calm, coolness, and rationality up to an even higher level. The more intense the pressure, the more calm and rational he would be. "Rubin was the coolest cat in the whole world when the market was going against one of his positions," recalls Bob Steel. "Where everyone else saw nerve-racking chaos, Rubin recognized opportunity to create new order and saw where to take specific action. He was often in very insecure situations, but he showed no personal *feeling* of insecurity. There was no sign of fear, just cool analysis and deliberate action."

Rubin brought disciplined probabilistic process and later sophisticated "quant" analytics and mathematical models to Goldman Sachs, developing risk arbitrage into a repetitively very profitable proprietary core business. This business was passed on to Bob Freeman, Frank Brosens, Tom Steyer, Eric Mindich, Eddie Lambert, Danny Och, Dinakar Singh, and others who expanded the firm's capacity, extended into options and then all sorts of derivatives, and took risk arbitrage international, starting in London.

Rubin was not a quant and never studied advanced mathematics, but he had a fine intuitive, almost aesthetic sense of the concepts. He genuinely liked solving puzzles and managing problematic new things like options, convertible securities, and risks. He was actively involved in the early days of the Chicago Board Options Exchange. Robin also had strategic vision and a keen sense of people.

As mergers and acquisitions activity accelerated during the late 1970s and through the 1980s, Rubin understood the strategic importance of detached, rational analysis and the ability to take decisive action based on it, so he recruited several key people with that same calm, analytic detachment. Arbitrage became known as the area where the very brightest people worked together. It developed into a power node of creativity and profitability within the firm.[3] "Most of the information that risk arbitrageurs work with is not hard information," says Tenenbaum. "It's all *soft*—changing estimates of changing probabilities." That's why people like Marty Siegel of Kidder Peabody built networks of contacts to exchange information and why Bob Freeman participated in some of those exchanges—exchanges that, as we shall shortly see, proved disastrous.

Arbitrage people are—and are known to be—Wall Street's most capable people, but what really differentiates arbitrage is that it's dignified. There's no shouting. The very best people work very hard without any flash and in flat organizational structures. The facts are king. You always start with the facts—all the facts you can possibly get—and then you develop a logical line of reasoning or argument, and then—and only then—do you develop an opinion. Opinions always come last. Facts, analysis, and logic matter. Ego has no role in analysis or in developing an opinion. Age and experience do not matter—once you're on the team.

When William F. Baxter, a Stanford law professor, agreed to become the head of the Antitrust Division under Ronald Reagan in 1982, he did so on one important condition: that antitrust regulation be based on market economics rather than legal precedents. This change greatly increased the size of the "relevant" markets that merging companies were considered to compete in and greatly reduced the risk that the Antitrust Division would declare a merger in restraint of trade. This change led to an enormous increase in corporate merger activity, particularly hostile takeovers. The increase in the volume of takeovers was more than matched by the simultaneous increase in the complexity of the securities offered and by the probability that whenever a target company was put into play by an initial acquisition attempt, one or more other acquisitive conglomerate corporations would make a competing offer for the same company.

Rubin's calm rationality became increasingly important to the firm as pressures intensified in many ways. With an enormous increase in both the number and the scale of mergers and hostile takeovers, and in the intensity of competition between aggressive conglomerates, the opportunities and the challenges for risk arbitrageurs expanded substantially. So did the firm's capital commitments and risk exposures—exposures to major gains *and* to major losses. The deals done were not just larger than before but also far more complex as two, three, or even more competing corporate acquirers offered competing packages of cash, stock, convertible preferred stock, convertible bonds, or bonds with warrants attached. Each of these complex securities required sophisticated credit analysis to determine how it would be evaluated and priced in the future, as circumstances changed and then changed again. Adding complexity, the preferences and valuations of major arbitrageurs and institutional investors and their probable votes on proxy issues all grew increasingly important. Institutional investors not only held major share positions and had so lots of votes but could also add to or buy new shares if they believed ABC Corporation was making what would be the winning offer. So the institutions' investment decisions would affect both the market valuations of specific securities and the probable outcome of the final shareholder vote on the competitive offers. That's why the leading conglomerates designed their offering packages for their multiple acquisitions to please the institutions and the major arbitrageurs. As John Maynard Keynes memorably explained, in guessing who will win a beauty contest, a smart man does not pick the girl *he* thinks prettiest, but rather the girl *others* will think prettiest.

Bob Rubin wanted to find great moneymakers and develop them into great leaders. He and Frank Brosens were happiest when younger, newer people thought they were wrong (or not quite as right as they might be) or had a better idea. Encouraging or even requiring open debate as a way of developing each person's maximum growth is clearly not as efficient as issuing orders, but in the long run will encourage creativity and be more effective at protecting against loss—particularly the cataclysmic loss that could have gone unforeseen.

On the day of the October crash of 1987, Goldman Sachs's risk arbitrage unit took substantial losses, eliminating most of its year-to-date gains.* Rubin stopped by and asked quietly: "How'd you do today?" The only answer was obvious: "Terribly! We lost a fortune!" After all that day's market punishment, the arbitrage unit had taken its losses, cut in half the size of its positions, and was hunkering down, wondering what might come next.

Rubin smiled and continued: "In today's meeting, the management committee agreed unanimously that we have 100 percent confidence in you as a team and

---

* A competitor, Smith Barney, to avoid flowing its own losses through its income statement, fired *everyone* in its risk arbitrage business that very day so it could avoid showing the loss as a charge against earnings in its income statement. Accounting rules allowed a company to tuck away the results of "discontinued operations" in a footnote.

in the way you run your business. So, if you want to double up on your positions, go right ahead."

Rubin was saying, *It's your call*—that the people who had just lost a fortune were trusted to do what was right for the firm. Rubin's message and the importance of his getting full approval from the management committee were important.

"After that," recalls Frank Brosens, "we didn't hesitate to take action when we saw an attractive opportunity. We were bold while people at other firms were getting caught in the trap of worrying about the impact of their trades on themselves as individuals and on their careers—and staying worried for months and months. With our aggressive stance, we produced a record year in 1988!"

After several years of increases, by the late 1980s Japan's Nikkei stock index had developed a price momentum of its own that could not be justified by earnings fundamentals. Goldman Sachs, a few other dealers, and several large hedge funds believed that the Japanese stock market was seriously overpriced. Deciding to take a hedge position in favor of the inevitable correction, Goldman Sachs went long the S&P 500 and short the Nikkei index on the proposition that sooner or later, the remarkable spread in valuation would have to narrow substantially. The world's two largest markets just could not really be so different indefinitely.

However, markets are not always rational, and instead of making the "inevitable" profit, the firm—and all the other rational bettors—took serious losses during the 1987 crash in American stocks. Inexplicably, the Nikkei declined much less than the S&P and then rose much more rapidly—as though it had escaped economic gravity. As a free thinker with commercial instincts, persistently searching for profits, Rubin asked his favorite question: Why? Rubin's further questioning went something like this: Assume the Nikkei *was* overpriced at 26,000. Did that mean it couldn't go even higher—even a lot higher? And wasn't it impossible to *know* how far up its price might go? So even if the Nikkei appeared badly overpriced now, that didn't mean it couldn't get *more* overpriced for reasons that strictly rational Westerners might never understand.

In this cross-cultural context, it made little sense to bet heavily against such a possibility. *But* if you made your bets with put options—instead of simply going short the stocks in the Nikkei average—you could limit your potential losses, and this could change the risk-reward balance significantly. Eureka! Inventive Bob Granovsky was asked to develop the required put options by creating a new kind of derivative security through the firm's equity capital markets operations.

Japanese insurance companies were buying twenty-year notes to get their slightly higher yields and, in exchange, were giving up some principal at maturity equal to any loss they might have taken in the Nikkei; they accomplished this by writing "European-style" puts—in yen—on the Nikkei average at the price on the date of issue. (European-style puts can be exercised only on the last day of the put contract, while "American-style" puts can be exercised at any time during the life of the put option, which is often a year and sometimes even a decade. With an American-style put option, if the price of the underlying security goes way down early in the option's life, a dealer can buy the stock, locking in his profit on the option and simply holding it to maturity.) In 1988–89, Goldman Sachs established a position of more than $300 million in Nikkei puts. As the Japanese market declined—eventually falling from 36,000 all the way to 12,000—the value of that position rose exponentially.

The arbitrage group decided to look for a way to list an options-based instrument that could be sold to U.S. retail customers. Goldman Sachs was not yet a public company, so to list the options on a stock exchange, another creditworthy institution would be needed to stand behind and guarantee the offering. This was arranged with the Kingdom of Denmark providing the backstop, and Goldman Sachs issued American-style puts denominated in U.S. dollars.

Recognizing that Merck produced an extraordinary series of major new drugs during the 1970s and 1980s because it institutionalized creativity as a deliberate part of its organizational strategy, Goldman Sachs wanted to do the same thing in risk arbitrage and then in other areas of trading—to make it normal to be abnormally creative. Frank Brosens knew that if you could, either solo or in teams, see something that was new and different or recognize a real change in the way something worked, it would probably be feasible to find ways to make a profit. And if the change was significant, the profitability could be dramatic. If you created or exploited change in an imaginative way, you could move a "commodity" business into a "specialty" product with stunning profitability during the period of early change—the period of change before others caught on to it. Into the 1990s, the firm risked its own capital only on the two main kinds of arbitrage—risk arbitrage and fixed-income arbitrage. Then the foreign-exchange department started taking risks with firm capital. Now every area of the firm does.

"Bob Granovsky was a key player in this," recalls Brosens. "An unusual character at only five foot seven, with a big Afro-like head of hair, a beard, and a nasal voice, he was incredibly creative. He could take any analysis of a new product idea right through big brick walls. He was unstoppable on the mechanics of making things work. However, on selling his ideas to others, he had problems, so that's where teamwork came in again and again." The people in arbitrage who are really effective commercially—and make the most profits—clearly have flair. Arbitrage now makes profits averaging $1 billion a year.

The best arbitrageurs can zero in on the key drivers with no pride of authorship, always asking the right questions and triangulating to the most useful and relevant answers, gathering and sorting the insights and information from others. What are the key players in the deal really like? Will they draw a line in the sand or are they pragmatists who can be flexible in developing a solution, able to differ on the "right" price and get past roadblocks to do a deal? How can we think differently about what could go wrong? Each deal is unique; what risk is not included in your own thinking? If ABC Company is making a hostile tender now, what are the odds of a different, competitive offer being made?

Into this swirling storm of competition came a new kind of organization—leveraged buyout (LBO) funds, organized for the purpose of executing leveraged buyouts, takeovers, refinancings, and restructurings. They raised capital—billions of dollars from large investing institutions, particularly public pension funds. The senior partners of Kohlberg Kravis Roberts, one of the leading buyout firms, came well versed in the ways of Wall Street, having worked together at Bear Stearns. They knew they were on their way to creating great personal fortunes, and they knew the best way to get the most help from Wall Street—by interesting the best people at the best firms in going all out for KKR. This was easily done. Every senior in Wall Street knew that KKR would be a highly profitable client, so when Henry Kravis called the head of any firm to say, "Your man Jack Smith is doing great work for KKR, and we want him to continue working closely with us," this was virtually a command, and Smith's firm would be very well rewarded. Moreover, Smith knew about the call from Kravis to his boss right away and knew how much it could accelerate his career, so Smith went all out for KKR. And so did his colleague Jones, who was also ambitious to succeed and hoped to do so well by KKR that his boss would also get called. So did all the other young stars at all the major firms; as a result, KKR continually got—and gets—the best of the best and the first call with investment information.

Creative moneymaking ideas will always find a home. For example, if a company's management, working confidentially with an investment banker as adviser, almost did a management buyout (MBO) and then decided not to proceed because arranging financing was too difficult, that idea for a possible MBO could easily become an idea for an LBO. That could be passed along by the knowing investment banker to active conglomerates or LBO firms like KKR that might decide to take action, spewing big fees and lots of business to the originating firm. It's only natural that every Wall Street firm is always looking for ways to serve KKR and Carlyle, Clayton Dubilier, and other private equity firms. And the arbitrageurs at every major Wall Street firm have every incentive to know, understand, and work closely with the major buyout firms, making sure they have close, frequent contact—closer and more frequent than any other arbitrageur, so that they have greater access and an information edge.

Legal espionage is central to everything arbitrageurs do: going right up to the legal limit to learn more sooner than the market knows, to get a competitive edge. Superior information and evaluation are the only legitimate advantages they can ever have when betting tens of millions of dollars that their estimates are better than the market's. The boundary line on inside information for arbitrageurs has always had two problematic characteristics. First, the line was never clearly delineated, and, second, the line was never fixed or constant. As Steve Friedman often said, "The sidelines of the playing field—the boundaries—keep shifting inward: You never move, but suddenly you're out of bounds."

Rules were not the only things that changed. Volume, pace, and scale were all changing, and new people with different attitudes and values were coming into arbitrage. One of these was an arbitrageur named Ivan Boesky who ran a fund that did nothing but merger arbitrage. Boesky was different.

As an experienced arbitrageur who was there at the time said, "Back in 1984, Bob Rubin told us: 'Nobody's to talk with Boesky—period. That guy is trouble.' Bob Freeman would not have been capable of making that call."

. . .

Complicated problems occur in all markets, so while the number and size of U.S. arbitrage operations has increased enough to dilute the possible rate of return, outside the United States the arbitrage opportunities increased even more rapidly," says Eric Mindich. "Markets opened up in Europe, Asia, and Latin America *and* in new instruments: derivatives, complex debt securities, currencies, and more, in every market area. The growth in the supply of opportunities has outpaced the growth in arbitrage assets."

27

J'ACCUSE

At 10:30 on the morning of February 12, 1987, in a light snow, Special Deputy U.S. Marshal Thomas Doonan and two armed postal inspectors went to the twenty-ninth-floor trading room of Goldman Sachs, located partner Robert Freeman, the firm's head of arbitrage, and told him to go to his glass-walled office, where they pulled down the blinds and announced, "You are under arrest" on charges related to insider trading. They searched his desk and files and confiscated his Rolodex. Federal marshals roped off the trading area and began carting away documents. "Everyone was in total shock," recalls partner Geoff Boisi, who was there.

Freeman called Lawrence Pedowitz at Goldman Sachs's law firm to tell him. Pedowitz did not believe what he was told. "Bob, I'm about to go on vacation, skiing in Utah. This *is* a joke, right?"

"No, Larry, I'm serious. There's someone from the U.S. Attorney's Office named Tom Doonan. He's here to arrest me."[1]

"Let me speak with Tom." Pedowitz and Doonan were friends from their time together in the U.S. Attorney's Office.

"Tom, Bob is a really fine person. You don't need to put handcuffs on him."

Freeman was led out to the elevator where, despite Pedowitz's request, he was handcuffed and taken to a waiting car while Doonan remained to search Freeman's office. Freeman was arraigned at the federal court in Foley Square. Goldman Sachs's chief of security, Jim Flick, drove there, arriving in time to toss a raincoat over Freeman's handcuffed hands as TV crews, photographers, and newsmen rushed in. Freeman realized how distressed he was when asked his Social Security number: he couldn't remember. His passport was confiscated; he was fingerprinted and photographed, and bail was set at $250,000. He was then released. Asked why Freeman had been handcuffed, John Slavinski, a senior investigator with the U.S. Postal Inspection Service, seemed surprised by the question and said it was standard practice in a field that sometimes included arresting violent criminals: "We have to protect our agents at the time of arrest."[2]

A block and a half away from Goldman Sachs's headquarters, Richard Wigton had the same experience at Kidder Peabody. Wigton, known to his friends as Wiggie, could not believe what was happening to him and thought it must be some kind of a bad joke. He had never even heard of postal inspectors, so he told the federal agents to get lost. They promptly handcuffed him. A Kidder colleague, Tim Tabor, was also arrested—so late in the day that he had to stay overnight before posting bond.

After being booked, Freeman returned to Goldman Sachs and went directly to the management committee meeting room where Bob Rubin, Steve Friedman, and Pedowitz were waiting. "That liar!" he exclaimed. "That liar! I didn't do anything wrong." And to Rubin, his mentor, he said, "It's not true, Bob. It's just not true."

In Tokyo, Goldman Sachs partner Jim Gorter was asleep in his hotel when Hank Paulson called him and said he had to go out to Narita Airport to meet a jet-lagged John Weinberg as soon as he got off his plane from New York and tell Weinberg that his partner Bob Freeman had been arrested and charged with insider trading. Twenty years later, Gorter would say, "I remember that as clearly as the day Sidney Weinberg called me at the Chicago Club to tell me I was being made a partner."

Freeman, forty-eight, was formally indicted April 9 on federal charges of conspiring to violate securities laws.

Immediately after Freeman's high-profile arrest, Goldman Sachs retained outside lawyers to conduct an internal investigation. All trading records were examined, and Freeman was interviewed for eight weeks about every aspect of his trading to reconstruct the past two years—all with particular attention to trades and calls to or from Martin Siegel of Kidder Peabody, his accuser.

The theatrical arrests and dramatized bookings were trademark methods of New York's politically ambitious U.S. attorney Rudolph Giuliani. As a prosecutor, Giuliani had been an unusually visible law-and-order associate attorney general in the Reagan administration. He then advanced in 1983 to become U.S. attorney for the Southern District of New York. Determined to make that office far more aggressive and attract much more media attention, he never seemed to worry about losing that office's carefully earned and widely respected reputation for integrity and diligent, first-quality investigations. In addition to changing basic policies and procedures in the U.S. Attorney's Office, Giuliani strategically focused his staff and the resources of his office on organized crime and narcotics—two very visible areas—made high-profile arrests, and got extensive media coverage. Quickly breaking with the publicity-avoiding policies of his recent predecessors, Giuliani actively sought press coverage and mastered the skills of using well-timed leaks to favored reporters to get the most impact and the most personal attention—and get articles published that could burrow inside a suspect's mind and mess up his thought process. Other ways to get inside a suspect's mind were also used by Giuliani's organization, including anonymous phone calls and letters.

Prosecutors negotiate. Most prosecutions never get to trial; they are settled out of court. Working with limited resources, prosecutors know they can usually accomplish more by negotiating settlements than by going through expensive trials. Giuliani based his own preferred style of "negotiation" on confrontation, surprise, and intimidation, believing that people move and can be moved further when they are surprised or scared. A prosecutor exercises substantial public power and can have an important, even dominating private agenda, particularly if the personal objective is to win an important public office.

. . .

The curious series of events and motivations that led to the specific charges against Bob Freeman developed over more than two years. In 1985 Beatrice Companies' senior management, frustrated by the lack of investor interest in their food and consumer products conglomerate and the resulting lackluster market performance of Beatrice's common stock, decided to "do something." They held exploratory conversations with Goldman Sachs about a possible leveraged management buyout. During these discussions, Beatrice stock was "gray-listed" at Goldman Sachs—put on the firm's rigorous restricted trading list. When nothing developed from these exploratory talks, Beatrice was taken off the gray list.

Then, on October 16, 1985, Kohlberg Kravis Roberts & Company, having retained Marty Siegel of Kidder Peabody as investment banker, offered nearly $5 billion for the company—then the largest-ever LBO bid—and Beatrice was suddenly in play. On October 20, Beatrice's board of directors met and rejected KKR's offer as inadequate.

On October 29, KKR raised its offer from $45 to $47 per share. As arbitrageurs normally do, Freeman moved quickly to establish a significant position, knowing he could develop a specific strategy as he studied the situation. He bought Beatrice stock aggressively—for his own account (to a total of $1.5 million), for family trusts, and for the firm's arbitrage account. The firm's account soon held a whopping 1,360,100 shares of stock and 4,074 March call options.

On October 31, reports in the press indicated that KKR would not increase its offer, and there were rumors that KKR's offer might even be withdrawn. Freeman called Henry Kravis of KKR that day and was told, "Everything is fine. We're not pulling out."[3] Freeman quickly bought another ten thousand shares of Beatrice for his personal account at $41.60.*

On November 12, KKR increased its bid to $50—$43 in cash and $7 in securities—an offer the Beatrice board of directors accepted on November 15.

On December 20, KKR announced that it had arranged financing, and the

---

* Arbitrageurs traded not only for the firm's account but for their own personal accounts as well, often in the same securities. Gus Levy and L. Jay Tenenbaum did. Bob Rubin did, quite profitably for several years. And Bob Freeman did. When Rubin and Friedman went to reorganize and run the fixed-income unit, Freeman and Rubin continued to exchange ideas on trading as they had been doing for years. Changes had been coming to the markets and in the laws against trading on insider information—and further changes have been made in the years since Freeman was arrested.

market price firmed. In private, however, KKR became convinced during the first week of January that the price was too high to finance the enormous total package. Freeman was still buying Beatrice: He held 1.4 million shares and call options worth $66 million for the firm's account as well as 2,500 shares and call options for himself. These amounts were large; the Beatrice position for Goldman Sachs exceeded the firm's $50 million limit on "friendly" takeovers, and Freeman's personal positions in Beatrice were 40 percent of the family assets he was willing to put at risk.

On January 7, Freeman bought 22,500 shares—shares he had just sold—in order to maintain position in his own account.[4] Trading volume was heavy: Beatrice was the second most active stock that day on the NYSE, but despite the volume, the price edged down. As Beatrice's stock sagged in the market, Freeman started making phone calls. Dick Nye, the respected arbitrageur at First Security Corporation, who the day before had sold—through Goldman Sachs—a block of 300,000 shares of Beatrice, offered his reasoning: no hard news, no specific reason, just a little nervous so a little cautious; the deal was close to closing, and the remaining spread between market price and deal value was pretty small, so the risk-adjusted return on holding until the deal closed just didn't look all that great.

Freeman called Henry Kravis, who gave no indication of problems, but his tone of voice made Freeman suspicious: "He was very abrupt and appeared anxious to end the conversation quickly."

During the morning of January 8, Freeman decided to close out his personal position in Beatrice and to cut the firm's holdings down to the $50 million limit. Then he spoke with Bernard "Bunny" Lasker, who was a longtime floor trader on the NYSE; a permanent member of the exchange establishment, well connected socially and politically; and an active participant in risk arbitrage. Lasker's view: The deal could possibly be in some trouble.

Finally, Freeman focused on Marty Siegel, who was a star in M&A at Kidder Peabody. Freeman and Siegel had met in person only once, but they spoke by telephone almost every week and were used to contacting each other for useful information and insights. Siegel was truly unusual: movie-star good-looking and remarkably articulate and charming. He could sell almost anything to almost anyone. One of the youngest in his class at Harvard Business School, where he cheated unnecessarily at touch football, he was one of the top graduates.[5,6]

As Freeman would later recount, "I told Mr. Siegel that I had heard there was a problem with the Beatrice LBO. He asked from whom I had heard this and I answered, 'Bunny Lasker.' Martin Siegel said, 'Your bunny has a very good nose.'"

Freeman thought that was a curious semiconfirmation of an unknown difficulty, perhaps a delay in the deal's closing date. For the next half hour, he and his colleagues in arbitrage exchanged possible interpretations, trying to figure out what Siegel's cryptic remark might mean. The conclusion they came to was not correct. It was what scientists call a false positive.

Knowing that KKR had carefully developed a Street reputation for always completing its takeovers, Freeman and his colleagues in arbitrage figured KKR must be delaying the closing date. After all, it was an enormous LBO and KKR may have decided to take more time in arranging the very large bank loans.

Freeman felt that, if what he thought Lasker meant was correct, postponement would spread the expected gain out over a longer period of time, which would reduce the daily rate of return. He decided the resulting expected rate of return would now be too low, so he chose to sell the calls he had bought for the firm, and left in effect his earlier sell orders.[7]

At 1:45, KKR announced that its offer was being changed—not in timing, but in structure—to $40 in cash and $10 in securities. This was a different action than Freeman and others had expected. Beatrice common stock dropped sharply to $44.25, down $4. Even though his conclusion had been wrong, by trading that morning Freeman had avoided personal losses of $93,000 and an estimated loss for the firm of $548,000.[8] Ironically, even if Freeman and his colleagues had understood Lasker's remark correctly, they would have gotten it wrong again. Once they heard how the deal structure had actually changed, they estimated that the change would cause the stock to drop by only 25 to 40 *cents*—certainly not by four dollars a share—not enough to justify selling the Beatrice stock or calls.

The government would argue that after hearing Siegel's "bunny" comment, Freeman should have known he was now legally an insider—even though he seriously misinterpreted the information—and pulled his order to sell.[9]

The usual test of insider information is whether an informed investor who gets that information would know how it would affect the market price, giving him an unfair and improper advantage over the company's other investors. If it took Freeman and his colleagues half an hour to decide—incorrectly—what Siegel's comment probably meant, was the information sufficiently informative to be illegal insider information? If the interpretation that Freeman and his colleagues made was wrong, and if they would not have taken any action if they had gotten the likely price change right, can they still be guilty of a crime of trading on inside information? Did it matter that Siegel never remembered the bunny comment?

Goldman Sachs would defend Freeman. He was a partner, a member of the firm family, and had made a lot of money for the partners. Other reasons for defending Freeman were important too. If Freeman was found guilty, the firm's reputation could be hurt badly, and reputations matter greatly on Wall Street. (Later Long-Term Capital Management and Bear Stearns would be wiped out because the confidence of others fell away.) The fines and penalties coming from civil suits could be enormous. A public offering of Goldman Sachs shares that had been very much under consideration was impossible with a major risk of legal liability unresolved. Licenses to operate a securities business could be suspended or revoked. Recruiting could be impaired. New-business and client relationships—particularly internationally—would be handicapped at best, and hurt badly at worst.

Since anyone could be subpoenaed and deposed about what he had said or heard or thought, it was better to overcontrol contact with Freeman. Weinberg, Friedman, Rubin, and Pedowitz ran a tight strategy on defense, reporting every week to the management committee but limiting discussion to a small circle of people and minimizing the number who had any direct communication with Freeman.

Context is important to understanding specific events, particularly events involving ethical judgments. With the explosion of takeovers, mergers, divestitures, and financings that increasingly flourished during the 1960s, 1970s, and 1980s, the world of arbitrage changed so much that it got destabilized. New people came into the business, the economics changed considerably, the pace of action accelerated, huge personal profit-making opportunities came within easy reach, and the old rules were bent or pushed aside. Another important change was an influx of independent arbitrageurs. As a competitor reflected years later, "Everyone in arbitrage was in a situation you could only appreciate if you were there at the time to see it and feel it yourself. Everything was changing: Solid corporations were coming apart or being taken apart, companies in very different businesses were combining together or forced together, every retail broker was talking up what he'd heard might happen, and otherwise sensible people were believing all sorts of stories. Everything seemed in flux. You'd have to understand the context to understand any specific situation."

In the late seventies and the eighties, substantial changes in corporate financial strategy and substantial changes in the capital markets combined to create a continuous Chinese firecracker of serial takeover explosions. Institutional investors, already the dominant forces in the stock market, competed aggressively to achieve superior investment performance, because recent performance attracted lots of new business. With many institutions holding large blocks of stock in most public companies and quite ready to sell at a profit, conglomerates whose main business was buying, reorganizing, and selling smaller companies could win a takeover competition simply by offering to pay 20 percent or 30 percent above the market, often financing all or part of their purchases with low-cost debt.

As the best arbitrageurs must, Freeman was always looking everywhere for insight or perspective—for an edge. As one partner recalls, "If Bob Freeman called me and asked me to check with a particular institution to see how deal X was being seen at that account, I knew that 'my' fishing line was only one of twenty or thirty or more lines Bob would have out in the water—all being worked very carefully."

As more and more companies got involved in takeovers—often in competition with other conglomerates and often with complex packages of common stock, preferred stock, convertible preferred, convertible bonds, bonds, and cash—the volume of offerings created a smorgasbord of new securities that the markets did not immediately price correctly. This produced a rich array of opportunities for arbitrageurs to make significant profits, so the number of arbitrageurs and the scale of their operations mushroomed. Arbitrageurs became an important force in the market and altered both corporate finance and institutional investing; they connected two dynamic groups that had been separated into one complex, interactive, interdependent new business with unfamiliar players, few reliable rules or codes of behavior, and lots of intensive competition—all at faster speeds and on a larger scale than ever seen before. Fortunes were rapidly made or lost. Deal makers went from obscurity to notoriety, and new players quickly became forces to be reckoned with. As so often in such revolutionary situations, hard prices dominated soft values—soft values like integrity, quality, and trust.

Trading spreads are widest and profit opportunities greatest near the edge that divides activities that are okay from those that are not okay, an edge that moved and then moved again, as laws, regulations, and judicial decisions changed the boundaries of what is and is not inside information. Ivan Boesky was known on the Street to be very close to the edge or just over it. In time it would be shown that he was way over the edge and a serious, repetitive criminal. Rubin and Freeman agreed well before Boesky got into trouble that while Goldman Sachs would continue to execute orders for Boesky, it would not discuss arbitrage situations with him.

"Everybody does it"—second only to "This time it's different" as an escape from reality—spread its tentacles wider as rules and regulations got tested again and again by clever, highly motivated people seeking incremental competitive advantages. Established norms of conduct got rubber legs. If knowing the price of everything and the value of nothing defines cynicism, Wall Street was becoming a crowd of cynics. Two who demonstrated how cynical and then criminal some could be were Michael Milken and Ivan Boesky, leading figures in the web of scandal that finally enmeshed Robert Freeman.

On May 25, 1985, a letter from a jilted woman in Caracas, Venezuela, arrived at the office of Richard Drew, vice president in Merrill Lynch's large compliance unit. The letter accused two Merrill Lynch brokers in Caracas of insider trading. An internal investigation showed that the pair were mimicking the trades of a third broker, who had been in their same 1982 Merrill Lynch training class but had moved over to Smith Barney. The Caracas brokers were paying the third broker a percentage of their profits, and *he* was mimicking the trades of his largest account: Bank Leu International's branch in the Bahamas. Sharing profits was not allowed at Merrill Lynch, so the two Caracas brokers were terminated. At Smith Barney, where supervision and compliance were not so strict, the third broker was merely informed that he had been reported, and the matter was dropped. As a Swiss bank subject to Switzerland's strict secrecy laws, Bank Leu would insist on ensuring absolute confidentiality for its clients. Bank Leu was sure to do nothing. The story could have died then and there if Drew had not taken an extra initiative.

Merrill Lynch takes compliance quite seriously, so Drew passed the information to Gary Lynch, who, at only thirty-five, had just become the SEC's director of enforcement. Lynch had been concerned about an increasing epidemic of trading on insider information that was causing stock prices to run up just before corporate takeovers were announced. Most inside-information abuses involved just one stock, but this time was clearly different. Lynch was particularly impressed by the large number of stocks showing the suspicious trading pattern: twenty-eight. He decided to investigate.

The trades certainly indicated illegal use of insider information, but to get to the original source the SEC staff would have to break through the cordon of secrecy at Bank Leu. The Smith Barney broker had been in frequent contact with a specific Bank Leu officer who handled the secret account of a certain "Mr. Diamond." The SEC would later learn, after careful investigations and difficult, complex negotiations over many months, that "Mr. Diamond" was Dennis R. Levine.[10]

Dennis Levine was on the make. He wanted to have all the usual external signs of success, but he had neither the talent nor the drive to do the work that might enable him to earn what he wanted to have. On the other hand, he had enough low-level charm to ingratiate himself with some, particularly those who were not paying close attention, and an ability to objectify others, including his wife and closest associates.[11] Levine was clever enough to identify sufficiently gullible young professionals he could seduce into joining his network, and clever enough to set up and operate a system for twelve years that might never have been uncovered if only each person in the network had followed his explicit instructions. But they were all human and they didn't. As a result, instead of "No one will ever know," the network and Levine were discovered—but only just barely.

Contrary to Levine's instructions, there being no honor among thieves, most trades had been executed through just one broker at Smith Barney. That broker saw how consistently and quickly "Mr. Diamond's" stock picks went up, so he decided to mimic them in his own account and to share in the profits made on the tips he passed along to his two training classmates at Merrill Lynch's office in Caracas.

When he first heard about the SEC's inquiries, Levine was unshaken. He advised his account officer at Bank Leu to parry the SEC's request for an explanation with a simple cover-up statement that he was basing all the decisions on available investment research—research that Levine would now provide retroactively. While initially intimidated and frightened, Bank Leu's officer agreed to the plan. Shrewdly, Levine also advised the bank to retain the services of Harvey Pitt, a former SEC general counsel now in private practice, to represent it in any legal or regulatory confrontation with the SEC.

Bank Leu's officer went, he thought secretly, to New York to meet Pitt. However, U.S. Customs, alerted by the SEC, recorded his entry into the United States and his intended address: the Waldorf-Astoria Hotel. When SEC agents suddenly accosted him in his hotel room and handed him summonses demanding his personal trading records and Bank Leu's records, he was frightened. He called Harvey Pitt, asking what to do. Pitt took over, telling the SEC that Bank Leu would produce documents showing that trades were made in dozens of accounts. Pitt then flew to the Bahamas to get the supporting records from Bank Leu, but they could not be produced. Learning this, Pitt nearly quit; however, he agreed to continue if Bank Leu stopped all trading for the "Mr. Diamond" account. Pitt urged the bank to try to offer up Levine's still-secret identity in exchange for immunity for the bank and its officers—if the SEC would agree.

Pitt contacted Lynch at the SEC and told him that what he had previously asserted as fact was not true. If a "status player" on Wall Street—not Bank Leu's officer—had initiated the trades, would the SEC accept his identity in exchange for immunity for the bank and its officers? If so, the bank would seek permission from Swiss banking regulators to disclose the status player's name. Of course, the Department of Justice and Rudy Giuliani would have to agree too, so that both civil and criminal cases would be combined. After discussion and consideration, the SEC agreed. Now it would be essential to gain agreement with the U.S. Attorney's Office.

In Giuliani's office, Charles Carberry was new to the fraud unit and not very interested in cases of trading on insider information; he thought such arcane matters should usually be left to the SEC. However, Carberry also thought the Bank Leu situation was so systemic and different that it threatened to corrupt the whole stock market. After listening to Pitt and the SEC lawyers, he agreed to go along with granting immunity for Bank Leu in order to focus faster on the status player.

To penetrate Bahamian secrecy laws, a delegation of SEC and Justice Department lawyers called on the Bahamian attorney general, argued that securities transactions were really not "banking," and got his okay. On Friday, May 19, 1986, Pitt reported to Gary Lynch at the SEC that the status player was Dennis Levine. A warrant for Levine's arrest was immediately made out.

Over a dozen years, Levine had recruited a circle of junior associates at prominent law firms and investment banks into a loose network of informants. Trading on the insider information filched by these associates, he parlayed his secret account into trading profits that had accumulated to $10.6 million. That's not all. He gained a reputation for somehow having a special feel for the market during corporate takeovers. In just nine years, Levine's annual income had multiplied more than a hundredfold, from $19,000 to over $2 million.

Levine had recruited his clandestine network of associates partly by selecting and enticing weak, susceptible young people; partly by using secret bank accounts and coded messages that lent their activities an air of mystery, adventure, and gaming the system—a big change from the inherent boredom of their routine daily work; and partly by assuring them that they, like him, would make millions and never get caught. Increasingly ensnaring them as they went further and further down the primrose path, Levine was also showing and describing to them the obvious benefits: his handsome apartment, his luxury cars—a BMW *and* a Ferrari—and his fast-growing bank account. To young, impressionable, naive, and struggling associates, it must have seemed like a sure thing, fascinating, lucrative—and safe.

All that changed suddenly at 7:30 on the evening of May 20, 1986, when Levine turned himself in and was formally arrested and incarcerated in the Metropolitan Correction Center in a cell with two drug dealers. Next day, he posted bail of $5 million and retained Arthur Liman as his defense attorney. Still detached from reality, Levine somehow thought he would find a way out. He was wrong.

Liman negotiated a plea bargain with Giuliani's Carberry and got Levine's charges reduced to four felonies, including two counts of tax evasion, with a maximum of twenty years in prison, in exchange for full cooperation in convicting his four co-conspirators and—far more important—for information that would lead to the conviction of a much bigger figure, a prominent arbitrageur who was extensively engaged in trading on insider information. Carberry agreed, and during interrogation Levine identified Ivan Boesky. As a result of his remarkable cooperation, Levine's sentence was reduced to only two years in prison and a fine of $362,000 in addition to his SEC fine of $11.6 million.

Ivan Boesky was not a nice man. He was a demanding bully in his office and over the telephone, bought and sold boldly and in bulk, and ran a $700,000 loan from his mother-in-law into a fortune. He enhanced or fabricated his education, most particularly leading people to assume he must have gone to Harvard because he used the Harvard Club of New York City extensively. (Actually, he was a member because, after making a large gift to the Harvard School of Public Health, he was taken onto its board of advisers, which, as he probably knew before making the gift, qualified him to apply for club membership.) He did go to law school—at the seldom-heard-of Detroit College of Law—and graduated five years later in 1964, but couldn't get a job in any law firm. Susan Silberstein, daughter of a wealthy Detroit developer who owned the Beverly Hills Hotel and other properties, married him. The couple moved to New York and Ivan worked in arbitrage for several different firms before setting up Ivan F. Boesky & Company in 1975. Seeking public recognition and approval, Boesky published a book on arbitrage, *Merger Mania;* was the subject of a feature article in *Fortune;* became an adjunct professor at Columbia and NYU; and was identified as one of America's richest people by *Forbes.*

In May 1986, Boesky was chosen by seniors at the University of California, Berkeley, to deliver their commencement address. He flew out in a private plane, arrived late for the precommencement festivities, and left abruptly right after speaking. Most of his address was boring, but he got applause for saying: "Greed is all right, by the way. I think greed is healthy. You can be greedy and feel good about yourself."

On June 10, 1986, in a highly unusual memorandum to Goldman Sachs employees, John Weinberg said, "We normally don't respond to newspaper articles, but this morning's article in the *Wall Street Journal* deserves an exception. You should know that we have no knowledge that anyone at Goldman Sachs is being investigated by the government in connection with insider trading or any other matter. Neither the SEC nor the U.S. Attorney has contacted us in connection with such an investigation. Based on our enquiries, we have not uncovered any facts that would warrant such an investigation."[12]

People at the firm began to wonder: Even at Goldman Sachs, if there was smoke, could there also be fire? Less than a month later, on July 3, David S. Brown, a thirty-one-year-old lawyer and vice president in the firm's mortgage-backed securities department, resigned from Goldman Sachs in a letter delivered by his attorney. For $30,000 cash, he had sold information about pending take-overs to a college friend, Ira B. Sokolow, formerly of Shearson Lehman Brothers, who, for a total of $90,000, had sold tips on fourteen takeover bids to Levine, who made $1.8 million on them.

Goldman Sachs said it was "shocked and dismayed at this development,"[13] which made it the fourth Wall Street firm—after Drexel Burnham Lambert, Lazard Freres, and Shearson Lehman Brothers—to be caught in the largest-ever insider trading scandal. Sokolow and Brown both pleaded guilty to two felony counts apiece, with each count carrying a possible fine of $250,000 and five years in jail. Brown paid $145,790, but kept his Ninety-fourth Street home, $65,000 in cash, and a $10,000 IRA. He was sentenced to thirty days in jail, three hundred hours of community service, and three years of probation. Newspaper articles noted that "a senior figure in the arbitrage community was also being investigated."

In late August 1986, Boesky's trading records were subpoenaed by the SEC and Boesky too retained Harvey Pitt as counsel. Pitt pleaded with Gary Lynch for a bargain, asserting it was not in the government's interest simply to prosecute Boesky. There was a much more important opportunity. Pitt proposed the fol-lowing grand bargain: no criminal prosecution in exchange for Boesky's paying a major fine, leaving the securities business, and fully cooperating in revealing a complex and extensive pattern of behavior and relationships that was equivalent to the nefarious scheming revealed by the legendary Pecora Hearings, which had led to the 1933 and 1934 Securities Acts and the establishment of the SEC.

Since no deal with the SEC would succeed without Giuliani's agreement, Pitt put the same question to Carberry on the Tuesday after Labor Day. Carberry took it to Giuliani, who could give him only five minutes because he was pre-occupied with a high-profile case on political corruption that he had decided to prosecute himself. Carberry explained that without a bargain, it would take two years to investigate and then try Boesky, and even then a conviction was uncer-tain, but Boesky's cooperation could lead to "interesting" possibilities. Giuliani and Carberry quickly agreed to negotiate a plea, but it would have to include at least one felony and a giant fine. Carberry suggested a record fine of $100 million, partly because it was a big, memorable number and partly because it was close to the SEC's total annual budget.

As negotiations approached a conclusion, Pitt refused to provide names. Then, after the government broke off negotiations in frustration, Pitt did give names: Michael Milken of Drexel Burnham Lambert; Martin Siegel, who by then had moved to Drexel Burnham; and Boyd Jefferies of Jefferies & Company. On September 10, the SEC approved the bargain, and a week later, after he signed his plea agreement, Boesky was enrolled as a U.S. government agent. His debriefing lasted several weeks. Secrecy was vital if Boesky was going to obtain incriminating evidence. Wearing a wire, he went to Los Angeles to meet Milken and tried unsuccessfully to develop a conversation with him that would include incriminating information. Boesky made it clear to investigators that he was dependent on Milken, and said he also suspected others on Wall Street of insider trading.

On Friday, November 14, at 4:30 p.m., U.S. attorney Rudolph Giuliani in New York and SEC chairman John Shad in Washington held simultaneous press conferences to announce the investigatory success of the decade. Estimates of Boesky's illegal trading profits rose to $300 million. Press and TV coverage was phenomenal—but not always triumphant. Many complained that Boesky had been punished far too lightly for what he had done and the way he had done it. When told the government had given Boesky two full weeks before making any announcement so that he could liquidate his arbitrage positions and raise the money to pay the fine without disturbing the markets, arbitrageurs were angry: Boesky's massive liquidation was, to them, the largest insider-information trading ever done.

I n November 1986, Martin Siegel got a mysterious call about "the letter." Puzzled at first, he realized he had not been out to his Connecticut home for two weeks, drove there, and found the mystery letter, which declared the writer "knew" and demanded money. Siegel consulted a lawyer and soon heard that the U.S. Attorney's Office knew all about Siegel and Boesky.

Siegel broke down, saying he was guilty and wanted to do right. That day he told his wife and retained Ted Rakoff, who had headed the securities fraud section at the U.S. Attorney's Office. He also heard the reports of Boesky's plea agreement. Siegel told Rakoff he wanted to plead and make amends.

The SEC insisted on a tough financial settlement, apparently chastened by the press's reaction to its previous "leniency" with Boesky. Siegel decided to move his family to Florida, where homestead laws prevent creditors from seizing a debtor's home; he bought a $3.5 million house in Ponte Vedra and a two-million-dollar pre-paid whole life insurance policy from First Colony Insurance Company, from which he could draw $180,000 annually tax-free for spending. Rakoff and the U.S. Attorney's Office agreed to a reduction from four felonies to two in exchange for Siegel's producing the head of arbitrage at a major firm.

Freeman was an easy mark. He and Siegel had spoken often; Freeman was habitually helpful and generous with his time, spending long hours with investment bankers at his own firm—and even at other firms—discussing how arbitrageurs would most probably evaluate alternative deal structures and terms. In the complex takeover battles of the era, understanding how arbitrageurs would evaluate different packages of securities would often be decisive in a tightly contested takeover battle. Freeman's insights and advice were highly valued, particularly since he was head of Wall Street's largest arbitrage operation, with up to $1 billion of committed capital. Other arbitrageurs had been distancing themselves from Siegel and not returning his phone calls. They were uncomfortable about working with someone who was so obviously interested in exchanging sensitive information, repetitively offering "something juicy" now in informal exchange for "being helpful" in the future.

Siegel's decision to finger Freeman was easy. He didn't really know Freeman. They'd met only once briefly. Their phone calls—three or four a week—were about trades and deals and markets. Friendly, but nothing personal. Siegel always had many contacts and acquaintances but had never developed true friendships and had no personal loyalties. His focus had become entirely on making more money. He wasn't about to have everything he had always wanted taken away from him now. The guy he needed to accuse had to be in arbitrage, so an arrangement to swap inside information on deals would have been both possible and believable. Freeman was a big fish in a big pond as head of arbitrage at Wall Street's biggest arbitrage department in one of Wall Street's most prestigious firms. Nobody else came close.

Bob Freeman going to prison versus Marty Siegel? Easy call. Better him than me.

Investigative reporters for the *Wall Street Journal* projected the distinct possibility that Freeman and Siegel had been participating in an extensive pattern of conspiracy, feeding each other sensitive inside information and making substantial profits—with Beatrice being only the tip of a large iceberg.

But were some or many of the "revelations" just clever plants by Siegel to help him plea-bargain? "It seemed to those of us who were involved," recalls a retired Goldman Sachs partner, "that James Stewart, who wrote a series of apparently well-informed articles for the *Wall Street Journal*, was reporting the story the way Siegel would want and had become, effectively, Siegel's mouthpiece." Or were the leaks coming from Giuliani to increase the pressure on Freeman or to garner more publicity for his campaign against insider trading or to build his public recognition for a political future?

As a team player, Freeman would be expected to advise Goldman Sachs bankers on how arbitrageurs would react to various hypothetical moves and terms of offer in a contest for control of a target company. Did Freeman cross over the ill-defined line between legal and illegal? "Clearly *not* okay today, but rules and standards about what's okay change over time, particularly in arbitrage. Bob Freeman is exceedingly rational and objective, well suited to the constantly changing set of probabilistic judgments needed for success in merger arbitrage. I spoke with Bob almost every day. In deals where Goldman Sachs was the investment banker, if I hadn't formulated my own view on what to recommend to a CEO and Bob asked me for my perspective on the deal, anything I said would be absolutely hypothetical, but it would help him see how other people would reason when given a particular set of facts," explains a partner.

Outside lawyers were retained to conduct an audit for Goldman Sachs, but the firm's records and recordings could show only one side of thousands of trades—what *was* done, but not *why* it was done—and arbitrageurs were always dealing in shades of gray. In meetings between lawyers for the firm and Freeman and lawyers for the government, Goldman Sachs's lawyers focused on the firm's long-standing reputation for integrity. As Pedowitz explained, for every allegation by Siegel there were highly credible alternative explanations.

In February 1987, the New York Stock Exchange required its members to tighten internal controls and report quarterly that employees' personal trading had been legal.[14] Goldman Sachs and other firms sharply restricted personal-account trading, barred short-term trading in stocks and options, and required employees to hold purchases for at least thirty days. Rubin and Friedman had attorneys and auditors evaluate every division's practices to be certain that all systems precluded improper conduct.

The government immunized Goldman Sachs arbitrageur Frank Brosens, but his testimony before the grand jury was yielding little when the prosecutor asked if he could remember anything else. Brosens repeated the bunny story. This made absolutely no difference, because the story had been known by both sides for two years. Still, government lawyers would focus here, asserting that when Siegel, who was clearly an insider, confirmed Lasker's estimate, Freeman should have instructed the firm's traders to stop selling Beatrice, because from the moment he got Siegel's confirmation, Freeman had legally become an insider too.

In a memo to the staff, the management committee explained that "our lawyers tell us that the law underlying this charge is exceedingly technical, and that while there is a factual and a legal basis for Bob to plead not guilty, the facts are very unusual and very unlike any other criminal securities case that has previously been brought." If Freeman fought the lawsuit all the way, he ran the risk of several years in prison among hardened criminals. Moreover, he would be putting his family's fortune at risk because civil suits could follow any criminal finding, and the awards for damages in a civil suit, though difficult to predict, could be very large. As Freeman later said, "The atmosphere was extremely poisoned for anyone who had anything to do with the eighties. There was no sympathy."[15] If Freeman insisted on going to trial and the jury found him guilty on a criminal count, that could immediately put the firm at risk for civil suits.

Since complexity characterizes arbitrage as a business, it is perhaps poetic that complexity came to characterize Freeman's prosecution and defense. The complexities went beyond those expected of negotiations between government lawyers and former government lawyers now in private practice. Giuliani's young, relatively inexperienced lawyers were dealing with ill-defined laws; they were understaffed and overwhelmed by work. They had thousands of documents to study, knowing that important parts of any firm's arbitrage operations would deliberately not be documented and that some of the documents may have been planted after the fact to give an appearance of careful research that might divert investigators' attention from decisions that might actually have been made on privileged information.

It took two months to go from Freeman's arrest to an indictment. As Paul Curran, counsel for the firm, noted with deliberate scorn, "It would appear the government is now doing an investigation *after* his arrest." On May 12, 1987, the government requested a two-month delay in the trial date, admitting it had proceeded too quickly and pleading for more time to prepare its case. This request was refused by the court, so the government pleaded not that it had too *little* information, but that it had too *much* in the fifty cartons of documents and transcripts of sixty interviews, and maintained that it was on the verge of breaking a major insider trading scandal involving nine megadeals in 1984–85—if only it had more time. Again the judge refused. Then on May 13, Giuliani's staff lawyers asked that the case be dismissed without prejudice and promised to seek a new indictment based on an eighteen-month conspiracy between Freeman and Siegel. Giuliani spoke of "the tip of the iceberg."

Dick Rosenthal, Salomon Brothers' partner in charge of arbitrage, called Freeman to volunteer as an expert witness: "I can explain it so clearly to the jury that they'll know they understand." In yet another ironic twist, a month later and long before the trial, Rosenthal was killed while flying his own airplane.

Another complexity was Giuliani's adroit use of the media to build pressure on Freeman and Goldman Sachs by trying the case in the papers, particularly the *Wall Street Journal*. James Stewart and Daniel Hertzberg, both Pulitzer Prize–winning reporters, who had been out in front of the story all along, alleged a "detailed catalogue" of misdeeds by Freeman in relation to Siegel. Freeman countered by taking—and completely passing—an all-inclusive lie detector test including that he had not known Kidder Peabody did any arbitrage.

Goldman Sachs would surely benefit from a change in the way the case was proceeding. "An idea came to me in the middle of the night," recalled John Weinberg. "Who could better represent the best of Goldman Sachs in a private conversation with the federal attorneys?" Who better, that is, than John Weinberg? Chairman David M. Roderick of U.S. Steel had done something like this when

Carl Icahn was threatening a takeover raid on Big Steel. Roderick invited Icahn to come for a meeting once a month for several hours of high-level talks. During those talks, Roderick went on and on about all sorts of things for hours, until one day Icahn called to suggest they meet not monthly, but every two or three months—and then even less and less.

"I asked Larry Pedowitz of Wachtell Lipton what he thought," recalled Weinberg. "He wasn't enthusiastic because he could see the risks, but he agreed it was an interesting idea. So I went alone to see Rudy Giuliani at the DA's office—after asking that he invite all his group heads to be there too. What a break! Here were eight guys—all from Brooklyn. So I told them about the history of the firm as a family firm and about my dad and the troubles we had dealt with and what the firm meant to us, that we care very greatly about integrity and doing the right thing and accepted no hanky-panky. And after an hour and a half about the firm, its history and values, I laid it on the line. 'If you can write out on a piece of paper something I can believe makes a real case that Bob Freeman did anything really wrong, I will personally *kill* him—and I'll bury the bones so nobody will *ever* find them.'"

Trying to calm Weinberg , Giuliani quickly cut in: "That's okay, Mr. Weinberg. That's okay." Then Giuliani left the meeting, and the U.S. attorney's lawyers began to shift from concentrating on a prosecution to arranging a settlement.

A careful review of actual trading obliterates the "case" against Freeman. It was, apparently, contrived by Marty Siegel and, thanks to his remarkable skills of presentation, accepted by both James Stewart and Giuliani, who became parties to a sad and painful injustice to Bob Freeman. Stewart is a wonderful writer and anyone reading *Den of Thieves,* his 1991 book on these events, would find it convincing. To the extent that he was relying on Siegel as his source, Stewart was depending on a spellbinding storyteller with a compelling ability to recall names, dates, numbers, and other facts. Apparently Siegel was feeding the same story to the U.S. Attorney's Office, which in turn was "independently" confirming Siegel's story to Stewart.

The most important and distressing allegation against Freeman was that he was supposed to have engaged in an eighteen-month conspiracy with Siegel to exchange insider information. Siegel's story was accepted by the prosecutors without an independent investigation of trading records or crucial telephone calls and became the core of the government's case. Before looking into the alleged components, some background will be helpful. Siegel was one of the era's most blatant abusers of insider information, taking hundreds of thousands of dollars in briefcases filled with cash and using secret passwords in exchanges with Ivan Boesky, the felon who would pay the record $100 million fine. Siegel was not recognized for what he really was by anyone at either Kidder Peabody or Drexel Burnham[16]— except in retrospect, when he would be seen as a con man of enormous charm. With major prison time in prospect, Siegel was highly motivated to be, and, particularly to be seen to be, an unusually cooperative government witness.

Given his extraordinary ability to recall specific names and dates, his charm, his motivation, and his amoral indifference to the consequences for others, Siegel was in a good but imperfect position to invent and articulate a believable alternative reality. His main problem was that he had no access to hard data on trades. He had left Kidder Peabody and was attacking that firm and Goldman Sachs, so they obviously would not help him in any way.

Siegel had an important advantage going for him. For years, he had been a major source of information and insight for James Stewart and Daniel Hertzberg at the *Wall Street Journal* and had developed an unusually close relationship with Stewart, who wrote not only a series of articles that seemed wonderfully on top of the whole seamy story of insider trading, but also the best-selling *Den of Thieves*. The book told the story in considerable and convincing detail—with one major problem: For the section on Freeman, Stewart apparently relied heavily on Siegel and on Rudolph Giuliani's office, which in turn relied on Siegel as a major source. A careful review of the trading records clarifies the major problem: Siegel's story was a string of lies.

The "conspiracy" was supposed to consist of several parts, each based on a different corporate takeover. The first and originating phase of the supposed conspiracy involved Walt Disney Company. Corporate raider Saul Steinberg had acquired a position and was rumored to be about to bid for a takeover. According to Siegel, Freeman told him in June 1984 that he liked the stock. Siegel, who was managing a secret arbitrage account as well as leading an M&A unit—a combination never allowed at other firms—claimed he called his Kidder Peabody colleagues and told them to load up on Disney stock.[17] When rumors circulated that

Disney might pay "greenmail" to Steinberg, Siegel allegedly consulted Freeman, who supposedly assured him that that would never happen. But then Disney did pay greenmail, and its stock fell, causing a major loss for Kidder Peabody. This supposedly caused Siegel to be angry with Freeman. When he called Freeman, Freeman allegedly said he had sold his own stock before the announcement. Supposedly this made Siegel furious and so embarrassed Freeman that he began supplying Siegel with insider information on other deals to make amends.

Unfortunately for Siegel's conspiracy allegations, Freeman and Goldman Sachs owned no Disney stock in June 1984. At least as important, trading records show that Freeman and Goldman Sachs did not expect Steinberg to succeed. On June 6, to block Steinberg, Disney agreed to acquire a company called Gibson Greetings. Here the two Wall Street firms' actions diverged: Kidder Peabody aggressively bought Disney stock while Goldman Sachs bought Gibson Greetings. Kidder Peabody expected Steinberg to prevail; Goldman Sachs expected him to fail. Since Freeman would not have had any reason to see Disney stock as a "buy," he would have had no reason to suggest it to Siegel—so there would be no remorse for Freeman and consequently no motive to start a conspiracy.

Another chapter in the "conspiracy" involved Continental Group, a Goldman Sachs client, which was the target of a June 1984 takeover bid of $50 per share by Sir James Goldsmith. Accepting Siegel's recollection that a call from Siegel to Freeman was on a Friday several days after Disney announced it had paid Steinberg greenmail, the actual date must have been June 15. Allegedly, Freeman told Siegel, "They'll sell the company [Continental] anyway," and then Siegel told Wigton and Tabor to buy Continental. However, by June 15, Kidder Peabody already owned 20,000 shares of Continental, and a broad search for a white-knight bidder had been in full swing for more than a week—with one of the candidates a major client of Siegel's. It's not plausible that an M&A maven like Siegel would not have known that Continental was for sale.

In Stewart's book, one alleged conversation is highly dramatized. Starting with Freeman allegedly saying, "It doesn't matter. They'll sell the company anyway," the book continues, "Siegel was astounded. Coming from a partner in the firm representing Continental, this sounded like inside information. He hung up the phone and gazed out over the late-spring panorama of the Connecticut coast. He knew that, in his conversation with Freeman, they had just crossed an unspoken line . . ." Nicely told, but since Siegel had to know—one of his major clients had just signed a confidentiality letter with Continental—he could not have been astounded. More important, Continental Group was gray-listed at Goldman Sachs by Investment Banking and any inside information would certainly have been kept from Freeman in Arbitrage.

By the NYSE close on June 25, Kidder Peabody had gradually accumulated 299,400 shares of Continental Group (not 2.5 million as Stewart's book says), and it later bought another 70,600 shares. For a major firm's arbitrage unit, this is not the urgent pattern of buying that would indicate the use of insider information. More important, Freeman did not get involved until *after* June 25. In Stewart's book, Siegel claimed that Freeman assured him that West Coast financier David Murdock would top Goldsmith's bid, but this doesn't compute because Murdock did not decide to bid until early on June 29, the day *after* Kidder Peabody's final purchase.

In Siegel's version and in Stewart's book, a takeover battle for SCA Services, a waste management company, appears to be an alarming example of a conspiracy, but the detailed trading records contradict that appearance. Siegel claimed that Goldman Sachs had taken a "massive" position and that Freeman was worried about possible antitrust problems and insisted that Siegel provide helpful information. Siegel reluctantly said talk of antitrust was just a ploy to get a higher price and encouraged Freeman to increase his position. In contrast, records show that Goldman Sachs never held a "massive" position, but rather bought only 10,000 shares for $208,000—less than half of one percent of the firm's $50 million policy limit—and only bought that small position five days *after* the press reported that four different companies were interested in bidding for SCA. Finally, there was no basis for an antitrust problem: Thousands of companies are in the waste management business, and all the public companies combined held only a tiny market share.

In August 1984, the battle for SCA heated up, and Goldman Sachs bought shares on August 9, 10, and 13—after SCA said on August 3 that it was considering all options to "maximize shareholder value." Waste Management Inc. announced a tender offer at $28.50, and Goldman Sachs bought another 123,500 shares. Specific details matter. The critical conversation described in Stewart's book—on the basis of which Freeman allegedly made a quick profit using Siegel's insider information—supposedly occurred on August 13, before the announcement later that day that, Stewart writes, "sent the stock price roaring, just after Goldman Sachs acquired another 57,000 shares." But trading records show that Goldman Sachs did not buy any shares between the time of the alleged conversation and the announcement. Interestingly, Boesky *was* buying a massive position in SCA. He brought 395,000 shares in fifteen minutes before the announcement, paying just under $23.50 per share, or $4 less than Goldman Sachs paid when it bought shares *after* the announcement.[18]

St. Regis comes next. Stewart writes that Kidder Peabody was buying the paper company's stock based on leaked information from Freeman and that David Murdock, Freeman's friend, represented a new threat to the company. Actually, it was Rupert Murdoch, not David Murdock. Since Freeman had never met or spoken with Rupert Murdoch, the name switch is significant. (Curiously, Stewart got the right Murdoch in his own February 12, 1988, *Wall Street Journal* article.)

At the time, St. Regis was on Goldman Sachs's gray list of restricted stocks, which is controlled by partners in investment banking to be certain that no inappropriate trading will be done. Stewart mistakenly attributes control of the list to a "low-prestige compliance officer . . . who wouldn't dare challenge the trading of a powerful partner like Freeman." In the book, he goes on to say that Freeman did trade anyway. But under Goldman Sachs's strict internal controls, that would never have been permitted. (When St. Regis was not on the gray list, Freeman did trade for the firm and for his own accounts—in compliance with firm rules.)

Storer Communications was rumored as a likely takeover candidate in early 1985, and on March 19 Coniston Partners filed an SEC 13D report showing it held more than 5 percent of Storer's stock and declaring that it planned to wage a proxy fight for control of the board of directors as part of its plan to liquidate the company. Freeman *bought* Storer shares, believing Coniston would win a proxy fight and liquidate at $90 to $100 per share. While Goldman Sachs bought, Kidder Peabody *sold* Storer. Siegel immediately began representing Florida Power & Light in a possible white-knight acquisition of Storer, and Kidder Peabody arbitrage subsequently accumulated a sizable stake in Storer while Siegel also had inside information from his client KKR, the eventual acquirer.

In Stewart's book, Siegel claims that he asked Freeman's permission on April 15 to mention Storer to KKR. But this was two weeks *after* Siegel, representing

KKR, had held meetings with Dillon Reed, the firm that represented Storer. (Of course, in M&A, investment bankers do not ask each other for permission to talk to their own clients.) In another date switch, Stewart's book has Siegel telling Freeman secret information on April 20–21, 1985, that caused him to go on a buying spree on April 17. If true, this would have Freeman buying on insider information several days before he received it.

More interesting is that during the week of April 22 Freeman and Goldman Sachs were *buying* stock and calls—exactly opposite to Kidder Peabody's *selling* and *opposite* to what he had alleged in the complaint. On Monday, Kidder Peabody held Storer stock worth over $25 million, all of which was sold that day and next. This 180-degree difference makes it hard to believe there was any collusion or "tipping." Siegel was right to sell and capture profits—if he could be legally or ethically right to sell when, as KKR's investment banker, he had insider information about KKR's strategy—while Freeman would lose money on his trading.

Unocal was put in play on April 8, 1985, when T. Boone Pickens made a hostile tender offer to pay $54 cash for 50.1 percent of the company's stock and, if he got that done, $54 in high-yield bonds for all the rest. Unocal, which had been selling below $35 a share, jumped to nearly $50. To ward off Pickens, Unocal offered on April 16 to pay $72 for 50 percent of its own stock, or 87 million shares. The government's complaint against Freeman alleged that Freeman told Siegel in April that Unocal would announce a partial buyback of its own stock and that the offer would exclude Pickens, and that he specified how many shares Unocal would offer to buy. According to the complaint, Siegel used this information to craft a clever trading strategy: Buy enough put options to cover the shares in Kidder Peabody's position that would not be accepted in the buyback and would therefore trade at a much lower price than it had paid.

Actually, from April 16, when Unocal announced the repurchase plan, to April 24, Kidder Peabody did not buy it. If Siegel had been tipped about Unocal, the correct strategy would indeed have been to buy Unocal puts before April 23. Actually, Kidder Peabody *sold* Unocal puts and bought 150,000 shares—its largest purchase—apparently believing that Pickens would prevail.

Ironically, Stewart observes that "Unocal showed how important seemingly arcane details of financial transactions can be" but 130 pages later minimizes the significance of an error in the government's affidavit in which Doonan, transcribing a colleague's notes, said the Unocal information was passed in April rather than in May. Stewart sees the damage to credibility that the senior people at Goldman Sachs claimed this difference of a month created as "all out of proportion to the degree of the inaccuracy," but the shift from April to May takes all the excitement out of the information being "inside." By May, Unocal's defense strategy was completely public, and all Kidder Peabody's trading was done after the April 16 public announcement.

Not only was the percentage-proration factor not known to Freeman before it was publicly announced, but this information was public before Kidder Peabody traded. The proration factor was announced before the market opened on April 20, and the settlement between Mesa Petroleum and Unocal was announced later that day. During the next two days, Kidder Peabody sold 46,600 "when issued" shares of Unocal.

Beatrice was the only deal where Siegel's allegations could not be directly refuted. Curiously, Siegel never recalled the bunny exchange. If there had been a conspiracy, it would have made no sense to be indirect. It was standard practice for M&A bankers to confirm those aspects of a story that were favorable to their clients' interests, and KKR would have wanted Beatrice's price to fall.

On *Face the Nation* on February 22, 1987, Giuliani said, "We wouldn't go with a case unless we obviously had confidence in it . . . I'm saying that I don't know of a case where you rely on just one witness and really expect that you are going to be able to win it so I think you can be confident that there's more than just one witness."

Five days earlier a *Wall Street Journal* article by Stewart and Hertzberg had said, "It is known that Mr. Siegel is not the principal witness against Mr. Freeman." Three and a half years later, the U.S. Attorney's Office would inform the court that Siegel was indeed the only witness.

A retrospective study would describe the situation this way: "Never well conceived to begin with, the case against the trio began to crumble as soon as defense lawyers got a look at its details. Here was a virtual conspiracy of strangers: Tabor didn't know Freeman, and Freeman didn't know Wigton. Moreover, instead of subpoenaing the men's trading accounts to see whether Siegel's assertions were true, the prosecutors had simply arrested the men. When they finally did get around to checking the documents, the information in them proved nothing."[19]

Siegel *was* a gifted story teller, he *was* speaking to prosecutors who had recently been uncovering conspiracies in the Mafia and in drugs. Once the prosecutors had accepted the conspiracy story, they were committed to a very cooperative witness and to a compelling story that fit with Boesky and Milken and Levine, and looked like a straight shot at a prosecutorial success ideal for launching a political career.

Freeman and his lawyers had to prove a negative and show that the Goldman Sachs trading was not triggered by inside information, not illegal, and not based on Siegel's alleged tips, but rather on astute analysis of public information, a much less interesting and often more complicated alternative.

Freeman clearly got too close to Marty Siegel. If other arbitrageurs saw Siegel for what he was, why didn't Freeman? To be fair, why didn't Siegel's colleagues at Kidder Peabody or Drexel Burnham Lambert, who saw him much more often—both on stage and off? He was that good at being convincing.

Compared to Boesky and Siegel, who both deliberately, frequently, and knowingly violated the spirit and letter of the law, the worst that can be said about Bob Freeman is that he went too close to the edge when he called Marty Siegel looking for extra insight on Beatrice, that like many others he was fooled for years by Siegel, and that he was a target of opportunity for an ambitious prosecutor in an era when Wall Street was under dark suspicion.

A t five o' clock on a morning in December 1987, a task force of fifty federal marshals, heavily armed and wearing bulletproof vests, with helicopter searchlights overhead, raided the Princeton, New Jersey, offices of a small hedge fund named Oakley Sutton (taking the middle names of its two principals, James "Jay" Sutton Regan and Edward Oakley Thorp, the latter the author of a classic book on how to win at blackjack).[20] The marshals collected three hundred boxes of files and records, apparently hoping to determine whether the firm "parked" stocks for Milken or traded inside information with Freeman in its investment unit called Princeton/Newport Partners.[21] Sutton was a Dartmouth friend of Freeman. They had continued their friendship.

Regan and colleagues at Princeton/Newport were convicted on sixty-three out of sixty-four charges—after only two days of jury deliberation, clearly indicating that other juries wouldn't be intimidated or baffled by complex financial cases. This convinced Freeman to agree to negotiate a settlement. Said one of his lawyers, "When Bob heard the Princeton/Newport decision, the fight just went out of him." While almost all of those convictions were later reversed on appeal, Freeman did not know what would happen.[22]

The U.S. Attorney's Office began the case with understandable conviction. Just as had happened in its narcotics and Mafia prosecutions, each falling domino of insider trading pushed over the next domino: Levine, Boesky, Siegel, and then Freeman. As the case against Freeman got weaker and weaker, the political need for closure got stronger and stronger. Giuliani was running for mayor of New York City as a law-and-order candidate and, knowing his case against was not strong, needed a settlement before the November election. This added time pressure. In the end, both sides wanted to put the case behind them; both needed a pragmatic way to close the issue. The talks were accelerated when the Princeton/Newport defendants were convicted because of Freeman's immediate reaction to this news. In August 1989, to limit his losses, Freeman pleaded guilty to one count. The original seventeen charges were all dropped back in May 1987. He would be sentenced the following April 17. Freeman's maximum prison term could be five years.

In November 1989, U.S. district judge Pierre N. Leval refused to accept the government's 120-page sentencing memorandum (in which prosecutors wanted the judge to consider other instances of alleged insider training in Storer Communications, Unocal, St. Regis, and Continental Group) and Freeman's lawyer's 800-page response.[23] He asked both parties to confine any reference to insider trading to the one instance on which Freeman had pleaded guilty.

Citing sentencing guidelines that had been put into effect *after* Freeman's events, prosecutors said Freeman should have to serve thirty to thirty-seven months and pay a heavy fine to reflect "the magnitude of the crime and the absence of any excuse." Freeman's attorneys, Robert Fiske and Paul Curran, argued that his "crime" did not warrant *any* time in prison and, further, that leniency was appropriate because Freeman had suffered from the government's "precipitous and highly publicized arrest."

Judge Leval said, "Arbitrageurs who disregard the law and their practices undermine the integrity of the marketplace. It is precisely because of these facts that the court cannot treat the matter as one of small importance."[24] He continued, "I have received scores of letters that speak very eloquently in favor of a man who is obviously a human being of value. The particular crime was a matter of temptation, an indiscretion, all of which took place so far as I can see in a matter of minutes."

In imposing the sentence, Judge Leval described Freeman as a "very chastened person," noting that letters to the court described him as "generous, responsible, and honest." The judge said Freeman did not require "punishment of a serious nature." Still, Leval felt he was compelled to look beyond Freeman's character and assess what impact the sentence would have on preserving the integrity of the financial markets, and for that reason he believed incarceration was necessary. Reading slowly from a yellow legal pad, Judge Leval said, "It has astonished me to read in the press that conduct—illegal conduct, criminal conduct—of the nature before me should be condoned or treated as a trifle because it's done every day." Calling Freeman a man of "eminence, power, and wealth," Judge Leval said, "I cannot pass a sentence that would give the world a message that when people in those positions violate the law, the court would treat it as trivial whereas when a common thief steals a few dollars, that calls for jail time."

Because it was limited to the single Beatrice case, Freeman's lawyers described the settlement as a "vindication," but an SEC official retorted: "The guy is a convicted felon. We obtained full injunctive relief against him and a ban for three years from the industry. That doesn't sound like vindication to me."

On August 17, 1989, Freeman had resigned from Goldman Sachs after nineteen years and pleaded guilty to a felony—not insider trading, but mail fraud. The Supreme Court's fairly recent decision in *Carpenter v. United States*, 484 U.S. 19 (1987), had established that anytime an employee or agent deprives his or her employer of exclusive possession of confidential business information, an embezzlement in violation of the federal mail-fraud statute has been committed if someone somewhere uses the mails even in only an incidental way. Under this interpretation, Siegel and Freeman had in effect embezzled a form of property—confidential information—from a client: Beatrice. A charge of mail fraud gives the prosecutor a tactical advantage because the materiality of the information is no longer as relevant; it's enough that the information constitutes "property." The mail-fraud statute now has a civil injunction provision that would give the prosecutor an alternative to criminal indictment.

Freeman paid $1.1 million (twice the losses avoided by his trades plus seven years' interest) to the SEC and agreed to stay out of the securities industry for three years. After nine months of discovery and pretrial, Freeman was sentenced to four months in prison—he was actually sentenced to one year, with eight months suspended—and a fine on a nolo contendere plea with a prearranged agreement to leave the securities business and perform four hundred hours of community service.[25] (Other "insider" convictions had resulted in lifetime prohibitions.) Freeman was not obligated to cooperate in the government's investigation and was understood to deny any other wrongdoing.

Freeman's prosecution showed the degree to which the line between what was civilly actionable and what was criminal was rapidly disappearing. The case was never criminal until Freeman and Giuliani's office needed a way out. The plea bargain accomplished that.

Martin Siegel was designated a "very cooperating witness" who "spent countless hours" and was identified as a "credible and reliable" witness. Siegel's lawyer, Ted Rakoff, made a case for leniency, and Assistant U.S. Attorney Neil Cartusciello made an unprecedented, even stronger case for leniency. Judge Robert Ward spoke at length about the importance of Siegel's cooperation and the importance of such forthrightness for successful law enforcement. Adding a statement about the importance of deterring white-collar crime, Ward said he had considered a sentence of eighteen to twenty-four months, but had concluded that Siegel must serve time—though less than Freeman. He settled on sentencing Siegel to two months in prison, five years on probation, and community service at a computer camp.

Bob Freeman served out his four-month sentence (with time off for good behavior, it came to 109 days) mostly mowing the grass on the golf course at Pensacola Naval Air Station, during which time he lost the thirty pounds he had gained after his arrest. "Saufley [a federal prison at the naval facility] was small and did not have the same homosexuality and violence that higher-level prisons have," said Freeman. "But it was not a country club, and this was not a country club experience." Freeman did his four hundred hours of community service and then spent two years settling his civil suit with the SEC. In the summer of 1993—six and a half years after his arrest—he was legally free of suspicion and accusation.

As it turned out, Freeman made a mistake in calculating his odds. Like any good arbitrageur, he calculated the odds and decided on the facts and probabilities as he saw them to plead and settle for one year in prison. His calculation was accurate but not right. Had Freeman waited another year, he would almost certainly have been let go, and all charges would have been dropped—as happened to Kidder Peabody's Wigton and Tabor, who had been accused by Siegel of trading on inside information from Freeman.

Freeman's real penalties were the distress imposed on his family, the cloud of suspicion that would hang over him—*Oh yeah, Freeman. Isn't he the guy who got caught trading on inside information?*—having to leave a high-paying job at Goldman Sachs and not participating when the firm went public.

28

~≈~

BUILDING
A GLOBAL BUSINESS

"Most of us really didn't know much of anything about Europe or the UK or London," recalls Gene Fife, who was going to London from San Francisco in 1985, only a few months after triple bypass surgery and in the first year of a second happy marriage.[1] Fife had no budget and no authorization to hire people, didn't know Europe, and didn't know any partners who spoke a language other than English.[2] No division head in New York had any international experience, so Fife would have no knowledgeable supporters. Fife was chosen, according to Jim Gorter, because in establishing the firm's investment banking business in California, he had demonstrated the ability to build business almost from scratch with little help from headquarters in New York—and that was what he was expected to do in Europe from a headquarters in London. It would be challenging.

"Goldman Sachs was not Goldman Sachs in London," recalls Fife, in his understated West Virginia way. While John Whitehead had made an articulate conceptual case for international expansion, the firm seldom sent top people overseas because the management committee didn't believe in the business potential and didn't want to incur more cost than necessary.[3] With a few stellar excep-

tions—particulary in stockbrokerage, where strong leadership was already showing what could be accomplished—the firm had two kinds of people in London:
people it couldn't or didn't want to fire who had been told to move there or leave
the firm, and people who were content to work with second-tier people.[4] London
was considered just a cost center, so the strategic objective had been clear: Keep
the costs low enough that London's losses would be tolerated. This, of course,
produced a strategy designed for—and doomed to—only very limited success.
The London office had had no overall vision beyond simply selling American
stocks, U.S. government bonds, and some Eurobonds for U.S. corporations like
Ford. None of this was, or was even hoped to be, more than marginally profitable, and it led nowhere. It was clear to Fife that massive change was needed,
particularly in investment banking. "Our challenge was to replicate Goldman
Sachs in London and across Europe so the firm looked, felt, and tasted like Goldman Sachs as much as McDonald's is McDonald's in Frankfurt, Germany, or
Toowoomba, Australia. To do this global branding, we had only one choice: Our
standard must always be excellence." The firm would have to become truly international in capabilities and commitments.

This meant, first, that many people in the London office would have to go
and, second, that it would be nearly impossible to recruit people with the expertise the firm would need to make consistently astute moves and avoid "outsider"
mistakes. In addition to these strategic challenges, Fife would also encounter specific problems. Shortly after his arrival in London, he got a disturbing call from
the manager of Claridge's Hotel: "Two of your young people who have stayed at
Claridge's for some weeks have this day been required to leave our hotel. They
have made a deliberate shambles of the room in which they have been staying,
and they have been intolerably rude to our staff. We will not permit such arrogant
behavior. From now on, Mr. Fife, they are persona non grata at Claridge's. This
hotel is *not* a playground." Nor did it fit with Fife's mandate.

In 1986 the management committee made a major strategic commitment to
Europe, sending ten top performers to develop a comprehensive strategy for the firm's
business in London and across Europe. Each New York division had its own "strategy" for London. Fixed Income was selling U.S. government bonds and Eurobonds
to Europeans—at very low profit margins. Investment Banking and Debt Capital

Markets were selling sovereign bonds "won" by competitive bidding against Japanese firms that cared only about volume. Goldman Sachs bankers were pleased when the firm won a Eurobond mandate for an important U.S. client and "only" lost $300,000. Goldman Sachs was losing $100 million annually in London, and all the other U.S. firms were losing money too. But change was in the air. So was opportunity.

Turning to the first of his challenges, Fife could have fired everyone, but that would have been unnecessarily hurtful for the individuals and for the firm, so he developed a different plan. Meeting privately with each banker, he said, "Not a word will be said here or anywhere, but you need to find another job that really suits your capabilities and interests much better than your present position. Take the time you need to do it right, and in not more than six months be sure you have completed your search so you can resign from the firm and move along with your career. We'll help you, but your next job is your choice to make and it's your responsibility to make it—just as it's our choice to do this with dignity and consideration for you as a person."

Fife's gracious way of dealing with people paid off: There were no unpleasant stories in the London newspapers about massive layoffs at Goldman Sachs. And one of those obliged to leave would call Fife a few years later to say, "A newspaper reporter is trying very hard to get some dirt—*any* dirt—on Goldman Sachs." The caller gave the reporter's name and paper so the firm could preempt the adverse story before it got printed—a lesson for Leo Durocher that nice guys sometimes win.

In late 1985, Woolworths UK was being raided by another retailer named Dixons. Goldman Sachs had signed a contract with Woolworths to keep that company's stock price up at an agreed level, and Woolworths had agreed to indemnify the firm against any losses. This agreement was customary practice in London at the time—but the provision for reimbursement was illegal. When Fife found out, he called Woolworths' chairman to say, "This agreement is against the law, and we as a firm will not do what we have agreed to do. We urge that you should not either." People at Goldman Sachs were angry: They knew this change meant they would lose money if they continued to support the market price of Woolworths' stock. The chairman agreed with Fife, and Goldman Sachs kept the Woolworths account. A year later, one of London's storied merchant banking leaders—Morgan Grenfell—was stunned when caught in the same sort of illegal operation in the Guinness affair, a scheme to prop up the price of the brewing company's shares; with this violation, that firm was on its way to being out of business, and its CFO was sent to prison. Fife explains, "Leaders should always set the bar high—very high—and then find the way to meet that standard. Trust and consistent execution make you the preferred supplier. Any compromise on standards, and you're sowing the seeds of your own destruction."

In London, Fife insisted, "We need strong people in each line of business—bonds, stockbrokerage, banking, and M&A—strong, experienced young stars." Easily said, but certainly not easily done. It was a fight for every person and for every dollar to pay salaries. Jim Gorter was, for a brief period, the firm's designated "international coordinator," so Fife went to him with his problem. Gorter agreed that Fife could cherry-pick his people. Knowing that Bill Landreth wanted to return to the States after ten strong years in London, Fife asked for a suggestion to head European equity sales. Gorter proposed Bob Steel in Chicago as a guy with the guts to go—even though his wife was pregnant. For Fixed Income, Fife tried Rick Garonzik, but he said, "No, thanks." So Fife asked Jon Corzine if he could have John Farmer, who was working in California for Corzine. Corzine had already tried to get Farmer to move to New York and was sure he would never move, but Fife knew that Farmer's wife treasured summer vacations in France and, while not interested in New York City, was far from parochial. The Farmers were delighted with the chance to live in London. Farmer's commitment convinced Garonzik to change his mind a month later and agree to go too. For banking, Fife wanted Peter Sacerdote, but Geoff Boisi vetoed that and instead offered Don Opatrny, who proved effective and a strong team builder. Fife recalls, "Each man was a true culture carrier, and all were prepared to make a serious commitment and talked openly about staying ten years—a crucial difference from the prior two- or three-year tours. This small group of strong performers gave me the nucleus we could build from."

David Fisher, a leading analyst at the world's leading international investment manager, Capital Group, was guest speaker at Goldman Sachs's equities divisional conference in 1985. Richard Menschel asked him, "So, David, if you were going to build a strong research effort in Europe, what would you do?" Fisher had no trouble with that question: "Send some guy like Jeff Weingarten to

Europe and let him figure it out." Weingarten, an all-star beverages analyst, had had a fight with research director Lee Cooperman, so he was eager for a change. He was soon on his way—with some advice from Cooperman: "Hire a few high-profile superstars and cover the rest with smoke and mirrors."

Weingarten knew recruiting in London would be hard: If, by analogy, S.G. Warburg came to New York and offered him a position, why would he leave Goldman Sachs? His case for joining an American firm would have to marshal a series of strategic reasons that astute analysts would find compelling. Fortunately for Weingarten, Big Bang had the City of London in turmoil, and mergers were making—or threatening to make—some talented analysts redundant. So analysts were looking for strong firms—firms like Goldman Sachs.

Leading British firms expanding onto the Continent invariably thought of having two separate research departments: one covering companies in the UK and another covering Continental companies. This gave Weingarten a decisive opening: His strategy would be pan-European. Investors wouldn't care about geography: They would want the best ideas industry-wide. Another advantage that Weingarten had going for him: Goldman Sachs analysts could link with investment bankers, which would enrich their expertise and their career opportunities. Weingarten's strategy was to concentrate on the very best analysts and to focus within this group on those who liked to work hard and would get excited about building something new and different as part of a winning team committed to building a strong European presence. Within a few years, Goldman Sachs was the first American firm to break into Europe's top ten in research.

"Our first priority is to generate significant profits," said Fife. "After that, our priority will be to elect partners so we can make the decisions and the moves that will enable us to continue earning profits." He knew he would need support, so to show the still skeptical management committee that Europe represented large opportunity, Fife went to the Guildhall Business Library, took *Fortune*'s list of the world's largest corporations, and showed how, over the years, European corporations had kept moving up in the rankings and how rapidly they had grown. Fife also knew he could sure use a local, experienced guide for the climb.

Realistically, the people of Goldman Sachs were so far out of touch with the British market that they didn't know the white hats from the black hats, or which lawyers were best at which legal issues, or how the British government worked. "We were in London physically," recalls Fife, "but we were clearly outsiders and certainly not part of the City or even knowledgeable about London. And none of the established firms had any interest in our ever finding out how the City really worked." His first challenge would be getting accurate information and reliable understanding of London's realities. His second challenge would be in recruiting. Fife was determined to build for the long term—a major change in strategy.

Not only was Goldman Sachs almost unknown in the UK, but most of the people it already employed there were not going to attract outstanding new people—quite the opposite. Adding to the problem facing Fife, Americans had a reputation as short-timers who visited fairly well but had no intention of staying for the long term. A *Euromoney* cover caught the prevailing feeling in London by showing young, arrogant American investment bankers streaming off the Concorde, planning to stay for only a few days before flying back on the Concorde. They were known as "pigeon bankers," investment bankers who "fly over, dump crap on us, and fly back."

Salomon Brothers had recently terminated a large group of London employees, almost all of them British subjects, so Britons whom Goldman Sachs might want to recruit would ask, "Why should I join you, knowing that promotions, particularly to partnership, will mostly go to Americans, but that if you ever have poor earnings, you'll sack the English like me and send the Yanks safely home to New York?" Not an easy question to answer. Titles might help; since partnerships were hard to earn and "vice president" was so widely used that it meant little, a new title—executive director—was invented. To get an objective, external appraisal of why stellar university graduates were not willing to join Goldman Sachs, Fife retained a UK consulting and search firm.[5] Its report was blunt: American firms were seen to "hire up and fire down"—adding people in good times and dismissing them in cyclical downturns. In addition, American firms filled their key positions—department heads and partners—with rotating Americans, not local Britons. The search firm's report explained that Goldman Sachs could change these perceptions and establish trust only by recognizing that "people won't believe what you say—only what you *do*, and exemplary behavior will be crucial." Mere words would not suffice; the only way to counter such worries was to use convincing symbols and take action. So Fife never even considered living in a rental flat or in the firm's handsome apartment on Chester Square.[6] He sold it and bought a substantial house in London where he frequently hosted dinners for clients and others, including Margaret Thatcher. The symbolism was powerful in England, where "home" has such great meaning. It told everyone, *The people of Goldman Sachs are here to stay.*

Fife knew he needed strength at senior levels all around Europe and was unwilling, as other firms had done, to hire "ornamentals." But he also knew it would be impossible to hire partner-level people with real ability. Moreover, each country in Europe was different in culture, business norms, politics, and customs. In France, the top graduates of the *grandes écoles* went into government for twenty years before being placed in the top executive positions of major French corporations. "We wanted to know the minutiae of how French clients saw each of Goldman Sachs's French people," says Fife. "Frenchmen who went to Harvard for their MBAs are considered 'different'—very able, but *outsiders*. The true French will be wary of them." He knew that he didn't know the inside rules and customs in each country in Europe and that he needed a way to make judgments on social, political, ethical, and cultural dimensions. He needed somebody he trusted to keep him out of trouble. In Italy, for example, bribery was endemic, and Fife was determined not to compromise Goldman Sachs's standards. Only by understanding the most subtle characteristics of each national system and the complex strengths and personal priorities of the key players—a richness of understanding that would take a lifetime to master—could Goldman Sachs compete with local banks. Fife could not afford to spend a lifetime getting going; he needed to make visible, strong progress and significant profits soon. He was trying to figure out what to do when he got a helpful call from New York City.

Eric Sheinberg was on the phone, "I know someone who's leaving the Spanish government who might be interesting for you to meet. His name is Guillermo de la Dehesa. He's a cabinet minister, and he might be interested in a job after he leaves the Spanish government."[7] Fife called de la Dehesa, liked what he heard, and arranged a meeting on his next trip to Spain. In a series of meetings over several months, the two men developed a good personal relationship and established the basis for a constructive working relationship. De la Dehesa would not be asked to open doors or make contacts, and his name would not be bandied about by the people from Goldman Sachs.* As Fife explained, "We need you as our coach, to show us how things are really done in Spain. Be critical of every aspect of our plans and, most particularly, of our executives. Help us learn what we need to learn. We don't know the personalities or the objectives or the beliefs and prejudices of the key decision makers. We don't know the code of conduct— who really counts, how to act, what to say, or when to say it. We don't even speak the language."

Serving as a country adviser for Spain—and later Latin America—de la Dehesa would be paired with a senior investment banker. Not a mere door opener, he would provide expert advice on Spain's laws, national customs, and practices; coach the firm's bankers on social, political, and commercial dos and don'ts; and identify people to be wary of and people to focus on because they were rising in stature within the nation's inner circle. He would advise on how to develop trustworthy relationships for the long term; on how best to position Goldman Sachs over the years ahead as an important firm to do important business with; and on which law firms and accounting firms to use in different situations. And he would critique Goldman Sachs's performance and suggest changes.

Fife and de la Dehesa worked out the appropriate terms and conditions. Great men would be unwilling just to be advisers—a term that suggests mere show horses—so Fife had Sullivan & Cromwell organize a new company: Goldman Sachs International. He would be the chairman, and country advisers would be vice chairmen and be paid $100,000 a year—soon raised to $150,000—with the opportunity to earn bonuses upto $1 million based on how helpful they were to all divisions in getting new mandates and completing transactions.[8]

For each major country, Fife identified and recruited an expert adviser. "These men had distinguished careers behind them and extensive connections in government and in major corporations," he said. "To say the least, they were initially skeptical. Knowing we had very little presence in Europe or in their home countries and naturally worried that we wanted them only to take advantage

---

* Both men knew of several firms that had decorative but never really satisfying international advisory boards— including Goldman Sachs, where such luminaries as Henry Kissinger and Robert McNamara gathered to exchange Olympian views. These decorative advisory boards never connected to the real business of the sponsoring organization, and the experts contributed little of substance and gained little insight or understanding that was valuable or meaningful to them.

of their connections and relationships (and perhaps even drop them once we'd gotten connected), they were sensitive to the reputation—fair or unfair—that the Americans come and then go if and when the market cools." So early on, Fife emphasized that the firm was not simply looking to exploit their relationship: "We needed to know how people in each country would think and feel about different questions. We wanted people who would know when we were wrong or about to be wrong—and would tell us bluntly. While not opposed to their help on specific transactions, what we really needed and wanted was their important help on understanding, in their particular country, just how to do each part of our work correctly so we could and would become one of the truly leading investment banking firms in their country."

The country advisers—soon called international advisers—became a loose-knit group and a sounding board on business-development strategies as well as on changing economic and political environments in an integrating Europe. The country advisers would meet quarterly for two days: one day for briefing Goldman Sachs bankers on the most important developments in their countries, and one day for being briefed by the firm's bankers on the firm's latest developments—particularly its new capabilities in investment banking—with detailed insider explanations of specific transactions and the lessons learned.

Fife recalls that two years later, Jean-Charles Charpentier—"a really nice guy who had been covering France for Goldman Sachs but just wasn't right for investment banking" and had been gently let go—called him to suggest three names to consider as country adviser for France. Of the three, one was truly outstanding: Jacques Mayoux.[9] In France, the elite *grandes écoles,* established by Napoleon nearly two hundred years ago, graduate small numbers of carefully selected, brilliant students. The best of these gain the title Inspecteur de Finances, which marks them for life as great men. Valéry Giscard d'Estaing was proud to have graduated third in his class, a ranking that would be respected all his life—and all his life he looked up to the man who graduated number one: Jacques Mayoux. Having been the youngest CEO of any French bank at thirty-nine, Mayoux was now the retired CEO of Société Générale, France's leading corporate bank. Mayoux knew his rightful place: at the very top of the French power pyramid. His agreement to work with Goldman Sachs was a breakthrough, and he proved remarkably effective.

When Total, France's giant oil company, was to be privatized, Total's CEO had decided on using Morgan Stanley. Informed of this on a Sunday, Mayoux was indignant. "What? Morgan Stanley? This cannot *be*!" He instructed his driver to take him immediately to the home of Total's CEO, where he sputtered: "You dishonor me! This underwriting will *not* be given to Morgan Stanley! This underwriting will—*bien sûr, monsieur!*—be managed by the one correct firm which is, of course, Goldman Sachs! See to it—*immédiatement*!"

Next day, it was announced that Total's giant privatization would be managed by Goldman Sachs, and Total's CEO won recognition for his astute good judgment among France's business elite. If he had not made that decision, Mayoux had made it clear that he would be marked for life as an incompetent.

"Jacques Mayoux spent 150 percent of his time on commercial cut and thrust," recalls John Thornton. "Nothing that happened anywhere escaped his attention. To call on companies he had known, we went to Tokyo, a market he knew well from many years of regular visits." One evening in Tokyo, Thornton went to Mayoux's hotel room to give him a document. The door was open, so Thornton knocked and walked in. On the floor were a dozen books on Japan that Mayoux—in his seventies—was studying so that he could, as he explained, "help prepare the ground" and develop a multistage strategy of competitive battle for business. Explains Thornton, "To develop a distinctive position, you have to get inside the system. Being well liked is just not the same thing as being really respected and on the inside."

Romano Prodi—later the prime minister—became country adviser for Italy, saying behind the scenes, "Don't do this piece of business that way; do it in the following way."[10] When it appeared that the only way to land one major transaction was to pay the customary bribes, Prodi advised Fife, who insisted that Goldman Sachs would *never* pay bribes, on a series of moves that not only led to the bribe-seekers being so boxed in politically that they couldn't block Goldman Sachs's getting the mandate but also had important observers applauding the firm and the decision to award it the mandate. Recalls Fife, "After we won that mandate, we did a *ton* of business."[11]

N othing was obvious or straightforward about getting fully accepted at the highest levels in all those different countries," remembers Fife. Brian

Griffiths was the next to last in the first group of eight international advisers. He had served as Margaret Thatcher's chief domestic adviser and became the only Thatcher cabinet minister to be made a lord. For Goldman Sachs, he may have been somewhat less commercially oriented than others, but he knew all the ins and outs in the British government and was crucial to Fife's understanding the British context during the complex and difficult Maxwell affair.

The circle of international advisers was built one by one over three years into a formidable force. Victor Halberstadt of the University of Leiden, with an international career in academia, government, and business, had a strong "make it happen" way of working around the world. Rounding out the group was Peter Sutherland, who had recently been recommended by Thornton. As luck would have it, Sutherland, the head of the World Trade Organization and former director general of GATT, and Fife were soon seated together on a transatlantic Concorde flight and had ample uninterrupted time to develop rapport. Sutherland soon agreed to join.[12]

As Fife notes, "The more we invested in our country advisers, the more we got back from them." International advisers counseled Fife and were effective mentors to Goldman Sachs's country and product specialists. They paved the firm's way at many major companies, and when paired with an outstanding senior banker, they soon learned to become very effective commercially.

I n Germany, the firm had two international advisers: Hans Friderichs, who had served as minister of Economics and as Helmut Schmidt's key adviser, and Klaus Luft of the Nixdorf computer firm. At Davos, Switzerland, Fife met Richard Breeden of the SEC, who wanted great companies like automaker Daimler-Benz to list in the United States. Breeden would help with regulations if Fife could create interest. Friderichs was close to Edzard Reuter, Daimler's CEO, and arranged a meeting in Stuttgart with him and his CFO. Fife proposed a listing on the New York Stock Exchange. When the CFO, surprised and miffed, doubted that Goldman Sachs had the necessary stature to represent mighty Daimler, Reuter bluntly instructed him: "Starting now, this and other important business will be done with one American firm: Goldman Sachs!"

Within Goldman Sachs, there was plenty of opposition to making a major commitment to Germany. As Bob Mnuchin saw it, "The markets are too small and too controlled by the locals to make any trading money." Steve Friedman said, "The big German banks have everything all tied up. We'll never break in." Opening the Paris office had been easy; Fife simply did it. Opening an office in Frankfurt met specific resistance, particularly among some Jewish partners. John Weinberg understood. Direct as always, he said, "I was there right after the war, and saw and heard things you can't even imagine."

But Fife was determined to find a way. Mark Winkelman and Jon Corzine recognized the importance of Germany for bond dealing and foreign exchange, so those divisions committed before security sales did. Fortunately, Bob Rubin was supportive and put the question in his usual probabilistic, risk-reward analytical way: "If it fails, so what? The cost will be small. We can close it off at any time. And we're big enough as a firm to try to push the envelope." Arthur Walter, a German-speaking lateral transfer from First Boston, opened the office in Frankfurt. After the Berlin Wall came down in 1989, Goldman Sachs handled many transactions involving the rationalization of industry following Germany's unification.

Fife had yet another problem—a structural problem in the way Goldman Sachs was organized. "As head of the London office, I had all sorts of responsibilities, but *zero* authority." All real power was with the division heads in New York City. If Fife had any authority at all, it came from the soft powers of communication and persuasion or was derivative—derived from making the divisional heads look good.

Challenges within the firm were at least as daunting as those external to it. On a trip to Spain in the mid-1980s, Fife learned that Telefónica, the national telephone company, would be privatized. Telefónica was so large that it would require global distribution, a task clearly beyond any Spanish organization. This may have seemed a major opportunity for the firm, but Fife's initial probing found that Telefónica's CEO held a negative view of Goldman Sachs. The feeling was mutual among many within the firm. Learning that Telefónica's financial vice president would be coming to New York City, Fife contacted New York for help. No interest: "Gene, are you sure Telefónica is a company we want to work for."

Then Fife got a lucky break. In 1987 Bob Rubin called Fife on a personal matter: "Judy and I always leave New York during Christmas, and this year we plan to go to Spain. Can you suggest the best hotel and a couple of first-rate restaurants in Madrid?"

"Sure, Bob. The best hotel is the Ritz, and I'll get you the names of a few special restaurants. While you're in Madrid, could you spare one lunch for an important prospect?"

"Gene, this is a holiday!"

But Fife persisted, and Rubin relented. In Madrid, he met first with a Spanish cabinet minister to discuss the first partial privatization of Telefónica. Later a private dinner was arranged for him and the CEO and CFO of Telefónica. It did not go well. As Rubin reported to Fife, "Gene, all he did all evening was to throw sand in my face because we do no research on his company." But Rubin had made a strong impression, and Eric Dobkin, the partner in charge of common-stock offerings, agreed to organize the syndicate and document Goldman Sachs's record of achievement in telecom underwritings. Over the next several months, the firm developed the basis for taking the mandate away from First Boston—which planted stories alleging bribery—and earned a fee of $13 million, equal to the total international revenues of Fife's first year a decade earlier. Two more large privatizations of Telefónica were underwritten, in 1995 and 1997, with Tom Tuft in charge for Goldman Sachs.[13]

To teach his colleagues in London the realities of their challenges, Fife organized a panel consisting of the CEOs of British Petroleum, Unilever, and BAT Industries to articulate how they saw Goldman Sachs's strengths and, particularly, its weaknesses relative to the competition—with special emphasis on their specific reasons for not choosing to use Goldman Sachs. It was devastating. The cold summary: When visited by Goldman Sachs bankers, the British executives limited their thoughts to just their U.S. activities, because they had learned that that was really all Goldman Sachs bankers would talk about. While they enjoyed those conversations, their most interesting and most important business challenges were spread all over the world: a financing in Indonesia, an acquisition in Argentina, a real estate lease in Hong Kong, and so on. All these business challenges were beyond the capabilities or knowledge of One-Track

Charlie, the banker from Goldman Sachs, and only a small fraction of the total fees they paid for investment banking services were for services in North America.

After jump-starting M&A successes in the United Kingdom, John Thornton was promoted and put in charge of the Investment Banking Services relationship bankers for the continental countries. "The formula we used in the UK was the right formula for country after country," recalls Thornton. "Each country had *one* main city—at most two. The pecking order is unspoken, but known to everyone—like in a small town or a secret society. Reputations are formed by actions, and people make judgments. Concepts are not complicated, but execution is, so execution is always more important than strategy in building a reputation." But when strategy is wrong, it will dominate.

During the same years, the strongest British merchant banks made an organizational and strategy blunder. While Goldman Sachs was expanding its strategic options and adding substantial, deployable resources, S.G. Warburg boxed itself in strategically by acquiring small, go-nowhere subsidiaries in Spain, France, Germany, and other countries, draining and dispersing its capital and its managerial talents.

When Thornton took over IBS in Europe, the unit had twelve people. Knowing the key to success is not only to have people who are high in both energy and ability but also to focus them on the most important people at the most important prospective clients, Thornton decided to reorganize each salesperson's efforts. "In Finland, we had a good man, but he was 'covering' 120 companies and spread way too thin. I asked him to make a list of the twenty most important people in the country and focus all his time on those twenty people. He and I both knew that would create a problem. If he focused on just twenty and any of the other one hundred did a transaction, someone at the New York divisional head office would surely be quick to demand to know why we had missed that piece of business. So I said I'd take the heat on those complaints."

Thornton sat down with each IBS man to review his list and the frequency of his calls on each key prospect. He was looking for each of his twelve people to make one or more significant calls every week. Of the 240 "priority" prospects—twenty for each of the twelve—only twenty-six had been called on even once during the past three *months*. After that first review, the number of calls drifted upward, but still only one-third of the prospects were getting periodic visits, while one-third were getting occasional visits, and one-third were getting none. But Thornton stayed at it. After nine months, all 240 prospects were getting calls or visits *every week*. And those calls kept shifting toward more and more senior executives. Thornton kept reminding everyone, "Sure, the treasurer is important, but the CEO is more important." Thornton summarizes, "The goal was to be able to make significant calls three to five times a day—*every* day. We wanted a disciplined, systematic way to insinuate ourselves into the power structure."

Thornton joined in the hunt and aimed for an elephant. "We were doing little business with BP.[14] I figured out that John Browne was, in time, going to be really important—probably CEO—so I started calling on him. In my first visit, I realized he was brilliant, shy, and reserved. We got nowhere. In thirty minutes the meeting was *over*.

"On the second call, I took Mark Winkelman. Zip. Nothing.

"Then I invited Browne and his mother to dinner with my wife and me. Both women were sick that evening, so Browne and I were alone. I decided to open up to him, making myself vulnerable. That's when everything changed, because he saw he could trust me. The dam broke—for me. But for competitors, the barriers were at least as high as ever, and maybe even a little higher because now I was on the inside."

Browne soon advanced to CEO, and BP became a major client of Goldman Sachs.

Thornton adds, "After building the requisite relationships of trust and depth, our long-term goal was to do consequential transactions for the market leaders. You worry about what drives your client and where you can be indispensable. This takes time. Meanwhile, you have to pay the light bill. It's easy to get a mandate to sell a U.S. business for a UK company, but this proves almost nothing. The proof comes in doing real work on really key matters."

Goldman Sachs's business-development strategy was to build out in larger and larger rings, starting with U.S. transactions, such as acquiring U.S. companies for European corporations, issuing commercial paper, or selling European stock and bonds to U.S. investors. The next round of expansion was based on helping German or French or Dutch companies do deals in Europe outside their national borders. And the highest level of business development was to win mandates for purely domestic business inside the company's own country against the leading local competition. This was done in one country after another by winning international mandates and then overservicing each client company until it decided to use Goldman Sachs for domestic business.

In Germany, Deutsche Bank was so dominant in every way in financial markets that great firms like S.G. Warburg willingly confined their German banking business to specialized one-off transactions or studies for smaller companies that Deutsche Bank really did not care about—the proverbial crumbs off the high table—always being careful not to challenge or offend the giant. Goldman Sachs took the opposite approach. It had a shocking, almost ludicrous ambition to which it was absolutely committed: *We are number one in America, the world's largest and most sophisticated market, and we* will *be number one in each major country in Europe—including Germany.*

Phil Murphy, a rising star and a strong leader, went to Germany and learned in a crash course to speak German. Good enough when working directly with clients, he was superb at organizing and motivating the people of Goldman Sachs from within—and swore and drank like the unabashed Irishman he was. Open to new ideas and new people, he was absolutely committed to the mission of establishing Goldman Sachs as the leading investment bank in Germany. However, determined resistance by the established banks was certain.

"When I was at S.G. Warburg," says Tim Plaut, who took over the firm's German business in 1999, "we won a small mandate to sell bonds with warrants as a result of several years of work with the finance director of a major German corporation. Deutsche Bank got wind of it and sent a very senior man to meet with the corporation's CEO and say, 'There has been a mistake by your finance director, who apparently did not check with your CFO and has made a very foolish suggestion to do a financing with some foreign firm. This cannot be. It would be entirely inappropriate. We share this work with only one bank—Commerzbank—and it is their turn to do the next transaction. So please make all necessary arrangements immediately for this transaction to be done with Commerz.' We were promptly excluded and, of course, the transaction was done by Commerzbank. And that same thing will happen again and again."[15]

Murphy would not listen to such advice. Murphy had a plan: Identify the thirty biggest and best investment banking prospects and make them clients of Goldman Sachs. Make a list, get everyone together, and figure out who at each giant corporation really decides which investment banks to use and which products to use. Then figure out how to break through and get to him, and decide who at Goldman Sachs can and would do it.

This, of course, was absurd, except for one reality: No firm had ever tried it. Monopolists and oligopolists are so sure they control their markets that they sometimes make mistakes. They don't always do everything right; they can get too confident, sometimes even sloppy or arrogant. They might leave openings without realizing it. They get so used to having all the business that they don't work hard enough for the *next* piece of business. And the world keeps changing—in technologies, in ideas, in priorities—and companies keep changing as people come and go. Some have new priorities, some have new ideas, some have new relationships, and many want to make their mark by doing new things. As Plaut explains, "These people are curious enough to give any interesting firm—even ones they've never seen before—at least *one* short, introductory meeting. If you tell them something new and do it effectively in a way they find interesting, they will see you again."

Murphy put one name at the top of his list—and the room full of German nationals burst into laughter. Outrageous! Never! Not a chance—*ever*. The name: Daimler-Benz.

Murphy then added another name: Siemens. More nervous laughter.

Then one of the German bankers stood to remonstrate: "You start your list with Daimler-Benz and Siemens, so I'll start with these two as representative of the realities you must learn to understand and accept. Daimler-Benz is 30 percent owned by Deutsche Bank. Deutsche Bank has always done *all* their financing—and Deutsche Bank is a jealous guardian of its business. Siemens is another example on your list. It was started in 1885, over a hundred years ago, and was actually created by Deutsche Bank. Today that bank always provides the Siemens chairman."

The Germans at Goldman Sachs were not the only ones who thought Murphy was crazy to be so audacious and presumptuous. Morgan Stanley and Merrill Lynch executives were delighted to learn that Goldman Sachs was going down the wrong road in the wrong direction, so they would have no need to worry about *that* competitor—at least not in Germany, and probably not in all of Europe.

The German bankers insisted that John Thornton's one-on-one focus on *the* decision makers—a focus that worked so very well in the United Kingdom and Scandinavia—couldn't work in the structured bureaucracy of a large German corporation, where the CEO usually knows nothing about finance and even the CFO is not much involved in capital raising, relying instead on the finance direc-tor. And all three of those senior executives and all the directors each have a veto. So for the finance director, there's serious career risk in using a new firm for any investment banking service—particularly a foreign firm like Goldman Sachs.

Murphy wouldn't listen. He was determined.

Weekend after weekend, Goldman Sachs's investment bankers in Germany, like their peers in France, Italy, and the United Kingdom, gathered together in quasi resorts for strategic planning sessions, striving to identify the most important corporations and the best way to get to them. In these sessions and back at the office, there was no talk by any of the group about Gold-man Sachs's traditional first priority: profitability. The focus now was on becoming first in the "league tables," based entirely on volume of business done, to establish Goldman Sachs as number one in Germany. Victory first—profits would come later. Corporate prospects were separated into three groups—super league, major, and important—according to how much they paid or would pay in investment banking fees on a rolling three-year basis.

Siemens was one of the first major German corporations to pay fees for investment banking services, and soon became quite a large fee payer.[16] Goldman Sachs worked with Siemens in its acquisition of Westinghouse. It took Siemens eighteen months to agree to sign the firm's fee letter, with the CFO protesting to the very end: "We will sign if you insist, but you will be off the list if you do insist and we'll never do banking business with you again." Any other investment bank might have become discouraged. Goldman Sachs got lucky. The investor relations manager soon took over as CFO. He was a man Tim Plaut had grown up with. Corzine called Plaut that day to acknowledge: "You are taking over Siemens."[17] He added: "I learned a long time ago that when somebody spits in your face, if you're really any good, you do three things: One, declare it must have been a rain drop. Two, wipe it off. And three, renew your determination and commitment."

The next major target was indeed a giant: Deutsche Telekom. In the run-up to the selection of lead underwriters for Deutsche Telekom, international adviser Hans Friderichs quietly arranged a private meeting with Chancellor Helmut Kohl for Goldman Sachs. Later, at a special meeting of the Bundestag, Goldman Sachs bankers gave legislators a detailed briefing on every aspect of the complexities involved in the Deutsche Telekom privatization. This created the solid political base that enabled Goldman Sachs to win the mandate as the lead international underwriter for the privatization, which became a dramatic demonstration of Goldman Sachs's ascendance in Germany.

Deutsche Telekom was a stunner: the largest-ever IPO in the world, with Goldman Sachs coequal with Deutsche Bank as lead underwriters. This triumph for Goldman Sachs came after six years of persistent hard work and an important lucky break: Deutsche Telekom's capable future chairman, Ron Sommer, had previously been an employee of Klaus Luft, Goldman Sachs's other adviser in Germany. Luft had the guts to insist on coequal underwriters. "If that transaction had been Luft's only major contribution—and it could not have been done without him—it was plenty," says Steve Friedman.[18]

Chairman Hilmar Kopper of Deutsche Bank paid the firm a high compliment by saying, "Nobody irritates me like Goldman Sachs. You get mandates we have not expected you to be even *considered* for!"

Thornton's ability to conceptualize audacious business-development strategies, which worked so well in the UK and then across Europe, would be tested successfully again—this time in Asia. When he arrived, Goldman Sachs Asia had about one thousand people—and was losing money. Thornton had a key advantage: Corzine had agreed to let him select his two top people—Phil Murphy for Hong Kong and Mark Schwartz for Tokyo. "We met for three days and made a list of the ten most important things we wanted to get done," Thornton recalls. "China was central, and since we had almost nothing there it would be hardest—so I took China."

Thornton was central to the rebuilding of Goldman Sachs's Hong Kong operation. "He took charge and set high goals," remembers partner Dinakar Singh, "and then challenged us to figure out the strategies that could and would take us there. Then he told us to go out and get the people we would need. Fortunately for us, since we had already cut back earlier, we were hiring just when competitors were firing, so we had lots of choices and could hire the very best." Thornton wasted no time following his own instruction: "On a twelve-hour flight, I sat beside a real star from Morgan Stanley. By the time we landed, he had agreed to come over to Goldman Sachs."

After leaving the firm in 2003, Thornton was an outside director of Industrial and Commercial Bank of China, by far the largest bank in China.[19] At his first meeting, the CEO proposed ratifying a business agreement with Goldman Sachs. All the bank's other directors were Chinese government officials who asked tough, critical questions: "Exactly what is the strategy?" "What is the fee arrangement?" "What are the profit shares?" And a string of others. As the questions poured out, it soon became clear that Goldman Sachs was proposing to tie up all the bank's future business without making significant reciprocal commitments to ICBC. The chairman asked Thornton to meet with him privately outside the meeting. He wanted Thornton's advice on how to salvage the deal. Thornton suggested that ICBC should renegotiate the price-to-value relationship. "For example, ICBC can get substantive, explicit commitments like having Jerry Corrigan [a Goldman Sachs partner and former head of the Federal Reserve Bank of New York] come several times a year to do seminars on risk management. Do the same in ten other areas where Goldman Sachs has expertise you can really use." Goldman Sachs was soon delivering particularly valuable services to ICBC, and the working relationship between the firm and the bank would prove to be highly beneficial to both.

Still, the experience at ICBC highlighted long-term policy and practice decisions that the firm by then confronted as a public company. Should it have separated its roles as adviser versus investor? More important, the firm would need to develop the right policy on personal investing. As individuals, Goldman Sachs partners bought shares in ICBC that they believed were sure to double— and double again. If this were ever interpreted by the Chinese as an indicator of opportunism, it would show the firm was unworthy of trust over the long term. Members of the Chinese governing elite are all about long term. As an old China hand advises, "They'll find out who you really are and will treat you that way."

Markets are anonymous, so firms can trade bonds, commodities, and foreign exchange anonymously. You need A-plus people to succeed, but you don't need to care about who loses or gets hurt. Nobody even knows you were ever there. It's an anonymous world. Relationship banking is entirely different. The record is cumulative, and clients have long memories and make choices.

29

STEVE QUIT!

I n February 1994, Steve Friedman asked partner Bob Katz, Goldman Sachs's general counsel, to stay for a brief one-on-one conversation after the weekly meeting of the management committee. They went to Friedman's office, where Friedman closed the door and took Katz into his very private confidence. For the next several months, hardly anyone else, other than Barbara Friedman, would know what Friedman was telling Katz. (A month later, Friedman met Bob Rubin at the Jefferson Hotel in Washington for another confidential briefing on the same subject.)

"Bob, at the partners' monthly meeting in September . . . I'll make an announcement . . . which I'm going to share with you and you only, but first you must promise me absolute confidentiality, that you will never, ever even mention this to anyone."

Katz understood. When he came over from Sullivan & Cromwell, he had assured Friedman their conversations would always be confidential—with just two exceptions: something criminal, of course, and anything that could seriously harm the firm.

"I'm going to retire from Goldman Sachs later this year, probably in

September." He paused. "And, Bob, you have given me your word to keep this absolutely private—just you and me."

If Friedman or Katz had known what troubles lay ahead for Goldman Sachs, both would have known this would put Katz in an untenable position. As general counsel, his first loyalty was to the firm and not to any individual, even the senior partner. But coming off a great 1993, both men expected 1994 to be another strong profit year. Neither had even an inkling of how badly 1994 would unfold. Friedman believed the firm's strategy was in place. Trading wasn't where it needed to be, but it was clearly progressing. Most of his work had been done. The Maxwell matter was virtually resolved. He felt he had stayed on an extra year already to manage those issues. And he obviously had his mind made up.

Katz asked if he was certain.

"Absolutely certain. I've promised Barbara. This job is a killer, and it'll kill *me* if I stay in it—and she knows that."

Weeks later, in the early spring, Friedman and Katz had dinner together so they could talk through the specifies of transition. They chose an Italian restaurant south of Fourteenth Street that specialized in Tuscan cooking, hoping to avoid people from Goldman Sachs whom they would probably run into on the Upper East Side. No such luck. Mike McCarthy, head of municipal bonds, came over to say hello. A few days later, ironically on April 1, the firm took a major trading loss: $300 million.

After Bob Rubin's 1992 announcement that he was leaving to join the Clinton administration, David Silfen had gone to Steve Friedman to urge him to appoint another partner to co-head the firm.* "No offense, Steve, but leading this global firm has become a huge job—too big for any one person to do alone. You can't possibly be in Singapore and in Frankfurt at the same time. If you think it's too early to name successors, take Roy [Zuckerberg]. He has all the stars and bars you need, and he's great with clients. Let him help you cover the bases. Because as it's structured now, it's a killer job." Frank Brosens, the partner in charge of arbitrage, made a similar suggestion. Friedman had refused even to consider such an idea. "I was never interested in running the firm," says Silfen. "You have to subordinate your whole life to doing that job, which I would not do. With his comple-

---

* Michael Carroll's October 1994 article in *Institutional Investor,* "Inside Goldman's College of Cardinals," was particularly helpful for this chapter.

mentary capabilities, Roy could have taken up much of the load Steve had been sharing with Bob. And Roy was of an age that made him no threat to Jon [Corzine] or Mark [Winkelman] or any of the other aspirants." Years later, still puzzled by Friedman's rejection of the need for help, some partners speculated that he may have wanted to get out of Rubin's shadow and prove something to himself.

Friedman had already decided who should be his successor, but as he told Rubin during their dinner at the Jefferson, "I can't sell him yet to the others on the committee." Nor could Rubin persuade Friedman to stay longer at the firm. Friedman's hope had been to "give others time to prove themselves," as he said, so he had assigned tasks "to test their leadership and managerial capabilities in different ways." Winkelman and Zuckerberg were to look for ways to upgrade the firm's technology, and Corzine and Paulson were assigned to work together on Asia.

At Cornell, Steve Friedman had won the All-Ivy, Eastern Intercollegiate, and national championships in wrestling, very individual demonstrations of physical prowess and disciplined determination. Similarly, law is not usually a teamwork profession. And M&A centers on intense direct competition against specific adversaries. Successful performers are almost necessarily self-reliant loners. As the pressures and demands of his job mounted to unbearable levels, Friedman relied more and more on the one person he knew he could really trust: Steve Friedman.

Timing matters in championship wrestling and in M&A—and in changing organizational leadership—and his timing would go against Steve Friedman in 1994. Without intending irony, Friedman says he couldn't spare the time and energy during his final year to develop an effective working relationship with another firmwide leader—somehow not recognizing how much harder it would be for new leaders to achieve rapport with each other with no time for developing understanding. Given only seven or eight months, and no warning of what was going on, a "natural" succession solution was unlikely. Friedman's intention to prevent divisive politics by confining the succession selection to just one week at the end of summer would compel a decision, but not necessarily a sound, well-accepted solution. And in February, nobody had anticipated how harsh the markets would become during 1994, especially toward the end of Goldman Sachs's fiscal year in November.

Understandable as it may have been, his determination to go it alone would eventually force Friedman into a corner. He convinced himself that it would be politically too difficult to pick one or two people to work with him; he worried that underlying individual frictions and chemistry issues would fester with a long interregnum. The firm had never had a nonobvious leadership transition before, and Friedman's priority became avoiding a long horse race. But even while accepting that conviction as plausible, almost nobody believes his decision was wise or right. Not right for the firm and not right for Steve Friedman, particularly as the fourth quarter developed.

Goldman Sachs had made a killing in foreign exchange in 1993 by betting heavily against the British pound and had a fabulous earnings year that appeared to prove Friedman right. He really could do it all alone. Friedman's pay was $46 million. But as market-savvy people know, if you live by the sword, you can get whacked by the sword. Great as 1993 had been for profits, 1994 would be just the opposite: it was awful.

"By the end of 1993," explains Friedman, "I was tired—really tired—and decided that December that I would have to quit. Both Freeman and Maxwell were serious problems that took up a lot of my time. Bob Rubin and I had split the long-distance travel, but now I had it all. As interest rates went up, our risk controls proved that we could get all the ratios and correlations right—but even so, the individual traders did very badly, and we had to instruct specific traders to cut back their risk positions. We were afraid of getting caught with a high cost structure worldwide *and* too low a trading volume *and* too little investment banking business—and, consequently, seriously inadequate profits. We had to cut costs a *lot*."

In the spring, Friedman suggested cutting fixed costs, but the management committee, believing the trading problems were only temporary, voted not to cut back. After earning $375 million in December, the first month of its fiscal 1994, the firm incurred a series of poor months—even losses—as markets went against its positions. Maxwell's margin loans were still open, and the settlement was sure to cost the firm a bundle—and meanwhile was taking a lot of management's time and energy. Corzine had raised another $250 million of equity capital from the Bishop Estate, a large Hawaiian endowment fund,[1] but the trading losses dominated everyone's thinking. Large trading positions in Treasuries and the yen were hurting, and a position in gilts in London could go either way quite suddenly.

Friedman was warned that he risked being tarred forever as the guy who quit and ran when the going got really rough, but he had made his decision and was known for persistence. In August 1994, the pressures of managing a global securities business that was struggling financially were spoiling a retreat by the Friedman family to their vacation home in Jackson Hole, Wyoming. Up since 4 a.m., Friedman was working the telephones to the major debt, equity, and corporate markets of the world; absorbing the spot news that the firm's traders in London had just taken another loss of $50 million; and receiving an indignant call from an executive at John Hancock Mutual Life who told him that the insurance company was so angered by the firm's poaching one of its people that he was cutting off all its very modest-volume business with Goldman Sachs and wanted Friedman, as managing partner, to hear directly and personally of this *major* decision. Friedman had never heard the man's name before, and the insurance company wasn't even close to being among the firm's one thousand largest clients, but taking the call, and the heat, was all part of the job—and the immediate reason for Friedman's blunt summation, as a visiting partner recalls: "This job *stinks!*"

"I was never driven to get the job as managing partner," reflects Friedman, who says he had always expected to retire early enough to have a full second career. "I was driven by the mission—the need for change—and that mission was clearly being completed. Actually, back in 1990, we could see the strategic horizon: Fixed Income, while still not great, was clearly getting better and better; the global organization was in place and getting good traction in all the major markets; the culture was transformed with a new strategic dynamism; and the principal investment business was well launched—although the old guard continued to worry and fret over conflicts with clients even though we explained to them that there are always conflicts, but you could manage the conflicts with full disclosure and making the right choices. And we were making money—profits were at a new and much higher level. I had no problem running the firm except one: I was not enjoying it. Client-relations meetings were everywhere and all the time. I'd get back from a hard trip to Europe and have three different client meetings—all of them urgently needed—on *Sunday*."

As the *Wall Street Journal* blandly noted, "Like its Wall Street peers, Goldman was hurt when the yen rose against the U.S. dollar and interest rates rose around the world. [The firm had been betting heavily against the yen's rise and was carrying huge bond inventories that plummeted in value when interest rates shot up.] Mr. Corzine concedes that Goldman 'fell prey' to the sudden shift in interest rates earlier this year. 'Like a lot of other firms, we were not fully attuned to the market,' he says."[2]

Jon Corzine and Mark Winkelman had agreed to establish two large arbitrage trades in the firm's proprietary trading account. One was a municipal-bond arbitrage. The other was in London. Both positions had been established too soon, and the markets were still going massively the wrong way on both. Corzine knew what to do: Buy more! "The worse it appears," he said, "the better the reality. The probability is strong that if we hang on, and even increase our position, this can be a real winner." Corzine wasn't listening to doubts or doubters. *But Jon, strong as that may be in theory, in the real world we could run out of capital or run out of liquidity or run out of time before your "sure thing" comes home and pays off.* As losses piled up in the fourth quarter, liquidity wasn't threatened but the firm's capital fell nearly to the minimum required by the SEC. Bob Hurst recalls, with admiration, "Jon had brass balls, and plenty of guts." But Corzine was a partner, and many other partners—including Steve Friedman—did not have his market experience, his trading expertise, or his ability to maintain calm. They saw the large, repetitive losses, and they were deeply concerned, even frightened.

"Steve was suffering from the grinding stress and strain of the job," recalls another partner. The markets were unusually difficult, and Friedman was not a deeply experienced risk manager, so he wouldn't understand how to deal with uncertainty the way Rubin always had. Where Rubin would create trust and calm, Friedman's habit of asking many challenging questions could make tensions worse. Some worried about Friedman's health. People could see that the pressure was getting to him and were saying, "You look green," or "Steve, you look gray and ashen." Others found it hard to believe he had a health problem at fifty-six. Recalls one of the partners, "No way! Steve's always worried about his health. There's not an ounce of fat on him. Steve always took special care of himself physically. I remember a dinner our key partners held at Primavera for the CEO and senior management of Sears, our oldest and one of our best clients. Steve comes—forty-five whole minutes late. Why? Because he had insisted on going to the gym first for his daily workout!"

During the first and second days of September 1994, Bob Katz called all the members of the management committee to remind them that the weekly meeting usually held on Monday would that week occur on Wednesday, September 7, because Monday was Labor Day and Tuesday was Rosh Hashanah. Attendance, as always, was mandatory. "Whatever your plans, wherever you are, whatever your commitments, *be* there!" This absolute insistence seemed unusual, particularly since, with so many people just coming back from summer vacations, the period around Labor Day was usually a quiet time of year. Bob Hurst called his friend Steve Friedman to ask what this was all about, but he could get no insight—just that it was a mandatory meeting. "Be there!"

On Sunday, Friedman told John Weinberg over lunch and then called John Whitehead to give him a heads-up. Some partners believe he also called Jon Corzine and Hank Paulson. Weinberg said the partners would live through it okay, but not the employees. As an ex-Marine, he kept his true feelings in check that first day, but later his outrage would again and again break loose in angry invective: "Yellow-bellied coward!"; "Abandoning his post and troops in combat!"; and "Cowardice in the face of the enemy!" were toward the gentle end of the spectrum of hostility Weinberg poured out at every provocation for many months. He could not contain himself. He simply could not believe that anyone would care so little for the firm or its partners as to just cut and run. Of course, Weinberg felt double-crossed too. He had identified Friedman and Rubin as his successors, and felt he had carefully brought them along so that they would have the right experience and the right recognition both inside and outside the firm. Smooth succession was an important capstone on Weinberg's own career. Now he was outraged by what he saw as the violence done to the whole concept of loyalty—to the partners, to the people of the firm, and to the ideals of his beloved Goldman Sachs.

Members of the management committee met as usual on September 7. As the firm's leaders took their seats for the meeting, everything appeared normal. As usual, Steve Friedman had his jacket off and his sleeves rolled up. Then, just as he had told Katz eight months before, Friedman delivered his bombshell to the members of the all-powerful committee: "I'm retiring, at the end of November, as senior partner. This is an absolute and final decision."

Silence. Not even a pin drop.

Then Friedman said: "This must be kept absolutely secret for all this coming week—one day per person in this group is the longest we can keep the secret. Next Monday, the twelfth, is the monthly partners' meeting. It will be mandatory attendance, so every partner will get told at exactly the same time. Between now and next week, all this must be kept absolutely secret." Friedman went on to explain that he had promised his wife that he would leave because he was suffering from serious heart palpitations: "I had heart fibrillation at 160 beats a minute and once spent nine hours on a gurney at New York Hospital with fluid dripping through a tube." He and his wife feared he might be dying, and both agreed that if he did not stop, the job would certainly kill him. Friedman did not say that he had made that commitment to Barbara Friedman nearly a year ago, or that he had told Bob Katz back in February.

The speed to decision now required was completely foreign to a firm that had always been slow, deliberate, and methodical about changes in leadership, even at the departmental level, so that everyone could adjust and get comfortable with the change. Five days was terribly fast. Such speed assumed everyone knew everything he should be considering. Committee members recall feeling that it was not respectful of the importance of the decision, the committee, or the firm. Being rushed by an artificial time schedule felt humiliating.

Friedman broke the firm's pattern of identifying and developing future leaders well in advance, at all levels, and carefully establishing successors. No plans had been developed in the industry's most methodical firm for the most important change that could be made—the change in firmwide leadership. There would be no time for discussions of policy or strategy as context for leader selection. No time for Friedman to overlap with successors. Friedman says he chose to keep the time pressure on the group to "keep politics in the bottle," knowing the usual frictions between bankers and traders. But speedy change was foreign to the deliberate, carefully planned process of continuous adjustment that had been so important to Goldman Sachs's sense of itself and its carefully nurtured image.

Some immediately began to wonder, *By what right does the SOB quitter have any right to say anything—or be listened to?* Friedman, however, confidently expressed clear views on what should and should not be done now and, particularly, on how to decide who should succeed him. Three main questions needed resolution: How would the new "transition" leadership be decided? Internally, just how would the changes be explained to the partners and the employees?

Externally, how would the changes be explained to corporate and institutional clients?

Roy Zuckerberg, the urbane, genial, always articulate, smoothly composed senior partner and member of the management committee, was completely undone. Zuckerberg captured the way everyone felt when, an hour later, he telephoned Silfen (who had had to detour to his local hospital because a family member had had a severe allergic reaction) and exclaimed: "I'm so totally surprised, I can hardly get the words out. Steve has just *quit*. The guy came to our management committee and—with absolutely zero warning or anything—Steve *quit*!"

Friedman did not try to dictate his successor, saying, "I'm leaving. You'll be the ones working with the leader you select, so this has to be your choice. To get started, here are three questions you'll need to ask: (1) Who would you pick to lead the firm? Pick one. (2) Who do you want to work with that one leader? (3) Other than that specific number two, who would you pick as an alternative?"

Only later, as discussion developed, would Friedman's views become clear as he blocked some candidates and assisted others.

Looking back, Friedman still offers a favorable view of his thinking at the beginning of the fateful week: "I wanted to avoid anything that was political, and I wanted to give myself and other management committee members the opportunity to continue to evaluate how different people worked together. We had seen numerous firms in which the succession process dragged on and was the cause of politics and divisiveness—or a long, drawn-out transition with too many hands on the steering wheel. We were convinced our firm could avoid that." In retrospect, Friedman cites the procedural difficulty of not having a board of directors that would, in a corporation, make the decision. After his surprise announcement, the management committee spent Wednesday through Friday at the firm's headquarters at 85 Broad Street. In an endless series of tense meetings, the firm's titans—most of them wholly unprepared, though Corzine and Paulson may have been warned—tried to reach a decision on who would be their leaders.

For the first time in over half a century, the firm did not have a strong, well-accepted leader in control. Signs of politics and personal ambitions quickly began to show as individuals were looking out for their own personal interests, quickly making and remaking alliances and commitments to position themselves advantageously. Everybody knew that the financial stakes were huge and that the firm—if it did not get too badly hurt by the persistent trading problems—was almost certain to go public: While everyone's focus was on what was best for the firm, everyone understood that when it did, those in the best positions would each be worth well over $100 million. This was no ordinary time.

A week after Friedman's surprise announcement, the firm suffered a major trading loss in UK gilts when the chancellor of the exchequer raised interest rates, foreshadowing the painful fourth quarter.

Looking back years later, Friedman is still convinced he handled the change in the best possible way: "There was no point in talking to anyone on the management committee in advance of the decision. That would have unleashed a torrent of politicking: 'I'll support you, but you're gonna need an experienced vice chairman,' or 'I'm really interested in heading up investment banking,' or any of a whole slew of deals. You'd be amazed how many people have hopes, even expectations, of getting to the top."

David Silfen was clear: He strongly wanted a successful process and transition in leadership, but he was not a candidate. He was quick to admit, "I'm really upset—not at what is being decided, but at how important partnership decisions are being made in a compressed period of time."

Roy Zuckerberg had aspirations, but he was older—a senior statesman to his friends, but perhaps too old and neither an investment banker nor a trader. He was the ultimate relationship manager—or to his detractors, merely a salesman—seen as more diplomat than leader. Some doubted he could handle the tough calls that always had to be made, but maybe he would serve as a placeholder for three or four years until John Thain and John Thornton would be ready. Bob Hurst was too young, not well-enough known across the whole firm and too new to the committee. Besides, his stature had been hurt by dismissive locker room nicknames. Worried that the job demands would imperil his already strained marriage, Hurst had effectively taken himself out of consideration when he said to Friedman a month earlier: "Why would *anyone* want your job? It's no way to live!"

Friedman blocked Mark Winkelman, saying he was "too independent" from the firm's norms. He could have meant that Winkelman was a loner, but being Dutch, Winkelman heard it as "foreigner." The easy reason for avoiding Winkelman was that Jon Corzine, the major contender, was a bond trader—and so was Winkelman. Not experienced with the markets' complexities or understanding Winkelman's particular brilliance, Friedman did not fully appreciate Winkelman's skill or his leadership style, which had so inspired others. Winkelman was so rational, logical, and quantitatively proficient that he somehow never recognized Friedman's discomfort with market-dependent decisions. Winkelman's native Holland is a nation where people accept blunt, confrontational disagreement, believe deeply in "loyal opposition," and enjoy stone-faced teasing and mockery—none of which were comfortable for Friedman. As some of their colleagues sensed, he and Winkelman seemed almost destined to be on different railroad tracks.

At a management retreat that Friedman had organized earlier that year, Winkelman had been asked to give a presentation on a subject that was important to Friedman. After the presentation, Friedman had repeatedly asked him the same leading question, knowing that Winkelman knew exactly what answer Friedman wanted. But Winkelman did not think that was the right answer, and would not bend. Friedman got increasingly frustrated and showed it. In addition, Winkelman had always focused on doing his work; he had not made time to become a member of the firm's social core. On the management committee, he had no devoted friends or allies.

In contrast, Corzine seemed a sure bet. He was co-head of fixed income, the firm's biggest business. He was also co-CFO, so he knew the numbers. And he was an engaging, natural leader, popular and smart.

Corzine had been on the management committee longer than any other serious candidate, and as CFO he had the broadest and best understanding of the whole firm and each division. He was close to the Bishop Estate and knew the key people at Sumitomo. He was recognized as a great bond trader who had made a fortune for the firm in 1993. And while the huge losses were in positions he had instituted, he understood them better than anyone else. "We all pretty much agreed on Corzine," recalls Silfen. "He was co-head of fixed income, which was becoming the powerful profits engine for the firm and key to overall risks, and he was CFO—clearly not an appropriate separation of powers in a line versus staff structure, but that's the way it was." At the first count, while not unanimous, Corzine had the most votes.

Friedman positioned himself to broker the final decision. Despite having stunned the group with his counterculturally abrupt leaving, he still had personal momentum from past years as senior partner and a large reservoir of goodwill from his many years of hard work and dedication to the firm. In a series of private one-on-one meetings, Friedman worked to gather a consensus. Because all were so taken by surprise, nobody had had time to pair up into alliances the way Friedman and Rubin had done. Firm leadership was too burdensome for just one person; everyone agreed on that but Corzine. If Corzine were to be chairman, the next question was who could work with him, most likely as vice chairman. Almost everyone favored himself for number two. Friedman recommended Hank Paulson as cochairman. Others were opposed. Then Zuckerberg, Winkelman, and Paulson were suggested as a trio of vice chairmen, but Paulson said he wasn't prepared to move to New York from Chicago just to be a co–vice chairman. He had agreed with his wife that they much preferred the values and the people of the Midwest and so would raise their family there.

Friedman met individually with each member of the management committee, working through the "If not you, who?" question and getting views on the optimal management structure. Then he asked that each member put his thoughts—briefly—in writing and fax it to him. While each man on the management committee may have thought or dreamed privately that he should or could be chosen, as the discussions went on and on Friedman pushed harder for "a banker" to work with and balance Corzine the trader.

The choice of Corzine as a consensus candidate provoked Winkelman to say he couldn't, after years of working as co-heads of fixed income, where the two men developed a high degree of trust in each other and shared a small office, agree to suddenly being subordinate to Corzine. "I couldn't do that," Winkelman said, even though he believed that Corzine would certainly be acceptable and could well be an excellent chairman—and that Corzine would be far more successful as chairman with Winkelman as vice chairman. Mark Winkelman and Jon Corzine knew all about each other—all the good and all the bad. "Besides, with the committee having agreed on Corzine, Mark really didn't have a chance of being chosen," recalls Silfen, "because we wouldn't want two people from the same line of business even though Mark was both rational and disciplined."

The choice of Corzine was not so much an absolute vote *for* Corzine as a relative preference for Corzine over others. Corzine, but not the other candidates, was at least acceptable to everyone. "What we didn't recognize at the time was that Jon had always wanted to be senior partner of Goldman Sachs and that that driving ambition had defined the way he built alliances and loyalties inside Goldman Sachs as a natural politician. It was in his blood," says Winkelman. Later others would wish they had asked Winkelman for more information about his difficulties in working with Corzine, but those questions were not raised as the meetings continued at the UN Plaza Hotel and at Friedman's home at One Beekman Place.

Friedman made an increasingly explicit case in one-on-one meetings at his home for selecting "a banker" to work with Corzine. He never had to be specific because, by simple observation, that somebody would have to be Hank Paulson, who was already the person most often chosen as number two. Friedman felt that only Paulson was strong enough to balance Corzine. Such a pairing recalled the success of Whitehead and Weinberg, and fitted the firm's traditional focus on being a leader in investment banking. Almost inevitably, the consensus jelled on Paulson as number two to Corzine.

However, this power pairing faced one major problem: Corzine and Paulson did not get along well, and some of their partners doubted they *could* get along well enough to succeed as co-leaders. Friedman had attempted to develop their rapport by assigning Corzine to oversee bond dealing in Asia while Paulson supervised Asian investment banking, but that had been a nonstarter because the two men found it difficult even to coordinate their schedules. They each went to Asia many times, but they did not go or work together. In addition, some worried that Paulson spoke too bluntly, too quickly, and too often to be put in a top position. For his part, Paulson still had doubts about relocating his wife and family to New York City for just a number two job.

During a meeting at Friedman's apartment on Beekman Place on Saturday, September 10, Corzine and Paulson seemed at an impasse, but Corzine, the people person, always believed he could work with anyone—anyone who would make the commitment to work with him. So he reached out: "Hank, let's go for a walk—just the two of us—and see if we can't find the common-ground basis for an understanding." During their walk, Corzine said warmly, "Hank, nothing could please me more than to work closely with you. We'll work closely together. We'll really be *partners*." Corzine knew that was what Paulson needed to hear. They came back in an hour with what they thought was an agreement to work together.

While several different structures had been considered, Friedman made it clear in public statements that the enormous demands imposed on the firm's leadership ruled out a single stand-alone chairman such as he had been. Putting the best possible interpretation on the situation a few weeks later, Friedman said, "We were sorting out how we would work together and came to believe [Corzine's and Paulson's] chemistry would be very good, and we had a sense of optimism about it. They wanted to work together." But the compromise, like so many compromises, was inherently unstable: not one CEO and not two equal co-CEOs, but Corzine as senior partner and chairman of the management committee and Paulson as vice chairman.

On Sunday, when the management committee reconvened at the UN Plaza Hotel, Friedman formally nominated Corzine and Paulson and suggested that each man say a few words, answer a few questions, and then leave so that the others could have a discussion. (The two men went to watch the U.S. Tennis Open men's final on TV: Andre Agassi versus Michael Stich.) Approval was unanimous, even though several committee members, particularly Zuckerberg, had strong reservations about the ability of Corzine and Paulson to work together. The decision was still secret. On Monday partners were informed; on Tuesday it was made public.

Corzine and Paulson were vastly different people with different work experiences. While notoriously not a careful dresser, Paulson, forty-seven, was tightly self-disciplined in his work habits. Corzine, forty-eight, was relaxed and informal, knew the firm's operations cold, loved markets and understood taking large positions with managed risks. Paulson worked hard to control or eliminate risk and didn't understand or enjoy markets with all their uncertainties. Corzine *appeared* very open and candid; Paulson *was* open and candid, even outspoken. While both are earnest Midwesterners, Paulson is a traditional Republican, Corzine a liberal Democrat. They thought differently on almost everything and felt uncomfortable with each other's working style. Coming up in very different divisions, working with very different disciplines, and living and working in very different cities, they had never worked together, traditionally the best bonding experience in a professional firm. Corzine had been elevated to the management committee several years before Paulson, and his fixed-income division had recently been outpacing Paulson's investment banking division in magnitude of profit contribution.

Corzine was great with people but had an awful time telling anyone any bad news. If he was supposed to tell Joe that it had already been decided that Joe was out as a partner, Corzine would call Joe, explain he'd really like a chance to talk, ask if it might be possible to get together for dinner, wonder when might be convenient, and then be deeply appreciative of Joe's making the time on his busy calendar. After their dinner, Joe would know that Jon admired and liked him a lot, and would think it was probably going to be time for him to leave the firm in a few years but that it was a decision on which he would control the timing.

Paulson would call Joe, tell him the decision was final, specify Joe's last day at the firm, and ask Joe what he would like to see included in the official announcement that would be going out on Monday.

Peter Sutherland, remarkably credentialed when he joined the firm as chairman for Europe, wanted very much to be a member of the management committee. Paulson understood that Corzine was to tell him this would not be possible. But after Corzine spoke with Sutherland, that clear, simple message had become transmuted into an assurance that Sutherland would be named to the committee after one more year. When Corzine's partners expressed their dismay, Corzine multiplied their distress by warmly saying, "Not to worry, guys. A lot can happen in a year."

At the partners meeting on September 12 Friedman made his announcement that he was retiring—not quitting, retiring. In a memo to employees the next day, Friedman wrote, "At the end of last year, I promised myself and my family that I would fill my role for one more year and then pass the baton to younger successors. When the job is done with maximum intensity, it can be more than a little tiring. . . . 1994 has been a frustrating year for all of us." In an interview, he conceded, "Yeah, I would have preferred record profits, but if you take '93 and '94 and you average them, you get a record."

"When Steve quit without doing either of two things he could have done instead, he threw open the door for any partner to quit, and several did, on very short notice—some with only a week or two's notice. Steve had two easy and far better choices," says Lee Cooperman. "First, when he told his wife, he could easily have told his partners—so successors could be chosen and work together for six months or so, and then he could say, 'These guys are so great, I'm proud to say we can turn to them even now, so I'll be leaving earlier than I'd planned. Carry on!' Or, he could have told the management committee he had to quit, picked his successors, and then overlapped with them for six months or so, and then given the same speech—'They're great; they're ready; they're the leaders'—and left early. Steve Friedman had a great career, but what he did in 1994 was wrong—wrong for Steve and wrong for the firm."

"Steve's action in suddenly leaving the firm is not at all consistent with the Steve Friedman I knew and admired," recalled partner Bob Conway. "Intellectually honest to the first degree, great mental candlepower, always seeking input from everyone and acting as 'decision central.' In my first year, I remember working on a valuation fairness-opinion and needed someone to check out my reasoning and my analysis. I asked Steve, even though he was not involved, to take a look. He closed the door behind us and spent the next hour and a half going over every aspect of the valuation with me. I learned a lot about valuations in that one and a half hours, a lot about teamwork and commitment to the firm, and a lot about Steve."

The *Wall Street Journal*, in an understated articulation of the Wall Street community's surprise, put it this way: "Goldman Sachs had long prided itself on a tradition of carefully orchestrating the leadership succession process by naming heirs apparent and grooming them for a few years before they acceded to the top jobs."[3] The firm had had no experience with a forced transition—particularly when it was losing money—since the days of Waddill Catchings. This time nobody had had time to prepare for the enormous question of succession, and the firm's business was clearly in serious trouble, with those bigger and bigger trading losses. With Friedman's sudden departure, partners began to perceive a real risk of the firm's coming apart or even being torn apart by heavy financial losses and sudden defections by partners. The two main challenges were clear: to hold Goldman Sachs together, and to reassure all the firm's clients.

What does Friedman know that I don't know—yet? was the question many partners were asking. Silfen recalls, "Many partners came into my office to sit on the couch." Despite the best efforts of John Weinberg and many other senior partners to persuade them to stay with the firm, partners' defections accelerated, setting a grim record in 1994: Thirty-four partners up sharply, from thirteen the year before, quit. Each additional partner's checking out increased the pressure to leave on the other partners. Some simply caved in. Many decided for the first time to take the calls that came with increasing frequency from headhunters. Investment bankers, perhaps because they didn't really understand how markets could take money away and then later bring it back, didn't know what to think or how to think it out. Since the year's earnings were sure to be unusually low, those who were thinking of bailing knew one certainty: They would be leaving little money on the table if they did decide to go.

In late 1994, as serious trading losses suddenly accumulated, retirements by partners accelerated. Friedman never recognized that his abrupt, unilateral retirement broke the covenant and made it socially acceptable for other partners to leave. Some gave only one or two weeks' notice. Leaving out of fear for the future and personal financial losses, they went limited. That froze the amount of their capital for the six-year payout. *What does he know that I don't know—yet?* A partner who was considered an expert on the firm's finances said, "With things going the way they are in bonds, in just six more months, Goldman Sachs will be bankrupt and *over*," and then told Bob Hurst that he had decided to quit.

Hurst countered, "But if you do that now—and others do that now—it won't take twenty-eight days. Realistically, the firm is over *now*."

Friedman, of course, would have disagreed: Fundamentally, the firm was in good shape, the strategy was clear, and liquidity was good. There was no systemic problem. On the other hand, Friedman did not recognize how close to panic many partners were. The fear might have escalated more if hadn't been for John Weinberg's going from partner to partner urging them to stay, and from office to office around the globe telling groups with pugnacious good humor, "Well, we are not going broke today—or tomorrow," and reminding everyone that the firm had always come through the toughest times stronger, more focused, and more effective.

Notwithstanding the firm's reported 1994 earnings of $508 million, partners suffered reductions in their capital accounts after payments to retired partners,

Sumitomo, and Bishop Estate were netted out. While other parts of the firm continued to thrive—the merger business, for instance, was booming amid the frenzy in mergers and acquisitions activity—the firm had taken serious losses in trading. Partners' incomes fell by one-third. The fourth quarter was the worst. Japanese yen and Japanese government bonds both lost money, and the London proprietary trading desk was incurring serious losses. Hundreds of people were suddenly laid off. Even worse than this abrupt break with the firm's long-established understandings of "loyalty up, loyalty down" was the rough, negative way some people perceived their terminations were executed. Gone were the nice words about past efforts or achievements. As one of those terminated said, "People were just trashed." The immediate challenges were to reassure clients, continue projecting the image of a controlled process in changing leadership, cut costs, and hold Goldman Sachs together as financials hemorrhaged and partners quit.

Paulson, in interviews, generally deferred to Corzine, although he did note, "There will be a natural tendency early on to work on the things we already know. We're not locked into any pattern. I am very, very comfortable with this."

Corzine ventured: "I would say Hank and I would like to see our leadership evolve to where we could both have a meaningful view and a participatory role in the breadth of Goldman Sachs's activities. But we want to evolve to that point instead of forcing it on day one or year one or year two."[4]

Paulson had agreed to work with Corzine—in what he had heard was to be an equal partnership—but general counsel Bob Katz told Paulson: "No, Hank. Jon's offer is one and a half." Paulson chose to ignore or overlook this. He didn't want to be number two. But Katz was accurate. Corzine saw Corzine as CEO—period. He had bold ideas of what could and—having decided that Goldman Sachs was not big enough—what should be done in major strategic moves. Corzine had the "I want it" determination to be CEO *and* senior partner. He was exceedingly confident in his own decisions, as a great bond trader should be, but he didn't listen to others once his mind was resolved. This wasn't always a negative. It enabled him to stay on course during the firm's most turbulent times. In the dangerous crisis Goldman Sachs was in, Corzine would show great—and necessary—strength and courage, including the courage of his convictions. As Winkelman said, "Jon showed incredible courage and capability. He was a perfect fit to the need of those turbulent awful times."

Estimates of the equity capital that would be withdrawn by partners leaving in 1994 centered on $400 million—$150 million more than the new capital obtained from Bishop Estate. Few organizations ever survive such catastrophic losses, particularly when they come so abruptly. On the Tuesday before Thanksgiving, Peter Weinberg, Jim Weinberg's son, told partner Chuck Davis in the car going home to Greenwich how sad he was to see partners quitting. The next day, Davis went to Peter Weinberg's office: "I've just spoken to John Weinberg to tell him what I couldn't tell you first. I'm resigning."

That may have been the nadir.

In his plea bargain, Freeman—who had never thought he had done anything wrong and certainly nothing criminal—was required, under oath, to say he knew at the time that his trading in Beatrice was illegal. Because he swore that in court, Freeman will not now deny it, making him a public captive of his own sworn statement.

On the Friday after Thanksgiving, partner Tom Tuft went to Peter Weinberg's office to exclaim: "Those guys are making a terrible mistake! We'll show 'em!" That exchange between two young partners came at what may have been the turning point. One after another, partners banded together, committing themselves even more strongly to the partnership and to Goldman Sachs. As partner Peter Fahey observed, "Steve's quitting actually solidified the partnership. The guys who stayed felt challenged to prove they could make it work. This was a big positive."

Giuliani never offered anything resembling an apology, but he did tell a reporter in an informal walking interview that the arrest was "probably a mistake."

30

COLLECTING THE BEST

Robin Neustein, who would later become a partner at Goldman Sachs, knew she had to change jobs when she was told in 1982 that her employer, one of Chicago's leading commercial banks, required that all after-hours typing be submitted by 5 p.m. so it could be delivered to an outside typing service that would return it the next morning at nine. To Neustein, that measured pace was not even nearly competitive. Explosively talented and ambitious to achieve, Neustein had earned both JD and MBA degrees at Northwestern, plus a CPA, and, having suffered as her father went bankrupt and died while she was a student at Brown, she was focused on earning a significant nest egg as quickly as possible: "I barely breathed until I had saved $1 million."

A friend said, "Go to Wall Street!" So she called New York City information and got the telephone numbers for the top investment banking firms on a list she'd seen in a magazine. Salomon Brothers' operator switched her to personnel. "Sorry, this year's recruiting has been completed. Call again next year." The second firm was Goldman Sachs.

"Be on my side, *please*," she pleaded to the firm's switchboard operator. "I need to talk to someone—a real person—in investment banking. I'm looking for a job. *Please* don't send me to personnel." The operator took the initiative to connect her to an investment banker, who answered, "Tom Shattan."

"Tom, I was told to talk to you. I'm looking for a job. I really want investment banking, and I really want to work for Goldman Sachs."

"Faith Rosenfeld is managing our investment banking recruiting. I'll transfer you to her."

"Faith, this is Robin Neustein. Tom Shattan asked me to speak with you." After half an hour's conversation, things were looking good, but the bank where she was working was a Goldman Sachs client, so the firm's banker covering the account had to approve. He said no.

Then Bob Conway looked at Neustein's résumé and was interested enough to launch her into a round of interviews with twenty Goldman Sachs people in private placements and real estate investment banking. Gene Mercy made her an offer of $90,000. That was more than she had expected, but Neustein still said, "Not enough. I need more. I've been out of school for two years."

"How much do you need?"

Pulling a number out of her hat and hoping it wasn't enough to queer the deal, Neustein said, "105."

"I'll get back to you."

After two days of anxiety for Neustein, her offer was accepted.

As we've seen, the preeminence of Goldman Sachs has been built out of a multiplicity of skills, ideas, and world-changing ambition and drive. At the heart of it all has always been the ability to attract and keep extraordinary people. Of all the firm's competencies, recruiting must be the most consequential. As John Whitehead says with serene conviction, "If you don't have the best people, you can't be the best firm. But if you do have the best people and you train them rigorously, organize them effectively, and motivate them to do their best work consistently, you will inevitably become the best firm."

In most ways, all the major investment banking competitors are equals. All firms strive to serve the same customers; all firms use the same computers, telephones, markets, databases, airplanes, hotels, and office buildings; all firms are subject to the same regulations; and they all know each other and can quickly copy each other's newest services. So with all these equalizers, how can any firm get out ahead—and stay out ahead? There are only four ways to gain and keep a significant competitive advantage: more effective recruiting, a stronger culture, a better strategy, and greater intensity of commitment.

When Neustein arrived at Goldman Sachs the norm was at least a dozen or more interviews, and many would have to be with partners. A generation earlier, recruiting had almost always been improvisational. L. Jay Tenenbaum, later one of the firm's most influential collectors of talent—he recruited such future leaders as Bob Rubin, Roy Zuckerberg, David Silfen, Bob Mnuchin, Bob Freeman, and Steve Friedman—came to Goldman Sachs in a most haphazard way during the 1950s. Tenenbaum's father had been a customer's man in a two-man securities firm in St. Louis. His father knew Gus Levy through their work together in railroad and utility holding company securities arbitrage. After Edgar Baruc's death, Gus Levy was playing golf in Boca Raton, Florida, and lamenting to his friend that Sidney Weinberg's son John had just turned down his offer to take him on as his assistant. "Why not my son L. Jay?" Why not, indeed? After serving in the 10th Mountain Division, the six-foot-one young Tenenbaum had sold ladies' dresses in Iowa, the Dakotas, and Nebraska and was a municipal bond salesman in Arkansas. Leaving for an opportunity in New York City would not require much consideration, so when his father saw him, he just declared, "Pack your bags, L. Jay! You're going to Goldman Sachs!" Tenenbaum was soon working for Levy in arbitrage.

Recruiting, particularly at senior levels, is as much about not making mistakes as it is about bringing in great contributors. When David Silfen declined an offer to head up the firm's planned effort to build a junk-bond business, Tenenbaum knew where to turn: "When Bill Bozniak in the bond department refused to have anything to do with our reselling to good customers those junk bonds we sometimes had to take into inventory to accommodate a client, we had to turn to Michael Milken of Drexel Burnham to find a market, just like everybody else." With all Wall Street dealers going to him, Milken soon had control of the market in all junk issues—and Milken knew that anyone wanting to sell junk bonds needed him and his bids. So, at twenty-four years of age, using the techniques of analysis invented by one of his professors at Wharton, Milken would call into a firm like Goldman Sachs and say, "I know you have a big position you want to sell—and we both know you can't. So I'll buy half a million at $70." Milken knew his offer was way below the market because he *was* the market. He set the price because there was no other dealer. As Tenenbaum reflects, "Milken showed brilliance in how well he knew his market and how it worked—and how and when to be very bold."

Tenenbaum invited Milken to breakfast. But first he checked with I. W. "Tubby" Burnham, Gus Levy's old friend and the longtime head of Burnham & Company (which, after two mergers, would become Drexel Burnham Lambert). Burnham reported his considered judgment on Milken: "He is very smart, but he has larceny in his soul. If he's watched, he can be a real winner. Are you *sure* you want to offer him a position at Goldman Sachs?"

Tenenbaum said, "We can watch him over here," to which Burnbaum replied, "Well, you better watch him very carefully." Tenenbaum arranged to make Milken a compelling offer: The firm would put up the capital, and he would get a good salary plus participation in profit sharing, whereby selected nonpartner employees got to participate in the firm's profits plus a 15 percent "carried interest" in their bottom-line profits *and* a special bonus. For a young man joining the firm as a lateral hire, this was an unusually powerful offer.

"No deal," said Milken. He insisted on two things: First, he wanted his own *independent* department, and, second, he wanted to pay himself 30 percent of his profits.

"No way would we do that," said Tenenbaum. "The payout was way too big—and we knew from prior experience with an insurance-stock trader how many issues and arguments there would be over cost allocations."* Milken stayed where he was, built a spectacularly profitable business, got paid over a billion dollars, drove Drexel Burnham Lambert into a notorious bankruptcy, was convicted of breaking several federal laws, paid a record fine, and went to prison.

"No matter how carefully you screen when recruiting, some people that just don't belong will get into the firm," laments partner Joe Ellis, for many years the dominant analyst in the retailing industry. "I'm glad to say we've lost some bad

---

* Years later, when Tenenbaum's son called on Milken—looking for a job and armed with his father's introduction—Milken was at the top of his career in junk bonds. Milken began the conversation directly: "The job is yours if you decide you want it. I owe that to your father. If you take the job, for the next five years you'll start with me every morning at four a.m., which is seven a.m. in New York, and work until five or six p.m. Day or night, seven days a week, you're on call if I want you. I'll *own* you. After that, you'll know the business cold and will have made some real money." Young Tenenbaum did not take the job.

people, and there's nothing that strengthens the good in a firm quite like removing the not-so-good." Or avoiding the wrong people entirely. The true cost of a bad senior hire is ten to twenty times the pay package. Partner and former research director Steve Einhorn says, "Recruiting people of exceptional talent and character—good moral compass, decency, and integrity—is vital to the success of any professional firm and yet is always underestimated. We wanted to give our analysts the opportunity to succeed, and we attracted talented young analysts by showing them how they could become the number one analyst in their sector by staying here. We had a compact that if they worked hard, knew their industries really well, and gave great service to clients, the firm would never bring in a lateral hire on top of them. They knew they could go all the way if their talent and drive would take them there."

Einhorn illustrates the importance of this policy by explaining how the firm dodged a bullet in the dot-com bubble market. Jack Grubman—who shortly after became the poster boy for investment banking abuses by securities analysts—was being courted by investment bankers at Goldman Sachs as a lateral hire to cover telecom companies and do deals in that fast-changing industry. Grubman had an investment-banking-deals focus and a detached view of compliance. He wanted to be free to operate outside the organization of the research department and did not want to be accountable to the research director, and said so. Einhorn recalls, "Bringing him in over our existing analyst in the telecom sector instead of advancing the man we had trained there seemed unfair to me. Besides, he was *not* nice to work with."

Einhorn explains why he himself joined Goldman Sachs: "Niceness, intensity, and integrity are the three key words to describe Goldman Sachs—and why I joined the firm. I really didn't consider any others. It can sound almost trite, but really respecting and really liking the people you work with—not just a select few, but *all* the people you work with—is so important. Good people attract good people and very good people attract very good people and make them want to stay. I had a wonderful twenty-eight-year career at Goldman Sachs."

Hank Paulson, Bob Hurst, and others insisted that the firm should hire Grubman. Jon Corzine didn't want to confront the issue, so he withdrew from the recruiting process, and Einhorn was able to block an offer. But the second time around, Einhorn got overruled and the firm made Grubman a big offer: $25 million. Citigroup's CEO, Sandy Weill, topped the firm's offer significantly, and Grubman, fortunately for Goldman Sachs, stayed where he was. Soon after, his employer, Citigroup's Salomon Smith Barney, paid a civil penalty of $400 million—by far the largest penalty paid by any firm in the "analysts case," where serious conflict-of-interest transgressions were uncovered.

Convinced that recruiting the best people was strategically the only way to become the best professional firm, Whitehead had set out long ago to systematically recruit the men with the greatest promise of becoming the best investment bankers. To be sure of success, he did the on-campus interviewing himself, striving to add one or two stellar people each year. In the late 1950s and early 1960s, few Wall Street firms interviewed MBAs, so Goldman Sachs had little direct competition. Determined to develop intense commitment within the Goldman Sachs system, Whitehead recruited "intensity" people who gave out clear signs of hungering for achievement. Selection was to be based on three equally weighted criteria: one-third on intelligence as measured by grades and SAT scores, one-third on leadership as shown by roles in extracurricular organizations, and one-third on ambition to achieve.

The recruiting net was thrown wide; the firm interviewed almost everyone who was interested because some might become clients in the future. On purpose, the firm's offer was—in comparison to today's $150,000-plus offers—stunningly small at $3,600, even if adjusted for inflation. Whitehead was determined never to pay more than other companies and preferred to be known to pay *less*, because if the firm could get the best for less, that sent a message that there must be something special about Goldman Sachs. Whitehead insisted on truly outstanding people, but he had no interest in egotistic "stars"—he was looking for team players who would stay for their careers. Many interviews—some deliberately tough, some deliberately easy—were used to give the candidate a cross-sectional view of Goldman Sachs and to assess whether he would be satisfied with the team concept that was rapidly becoming the required distinguishing characteristic of Goldman Sachs people.

As Bob Conway recalls, "John Whitehead *knew* that recruiting was the most important thing we could ever do, and that if we organized sooner and better and worked at it harder and with more skill, we could identify and attract better people more often. And if we did this consistently, we would build a better and better organization and could become the best investment-banking firm in America—and in the world. As John put it—and he really meant it—'Recruiting is the most important thing we can ever do. And if we ever stop doing recruiting very well, within just five years, we will be on that slippery down slope, doomed to mediocrity.' "

Conway got memorable proof that Whitehead meant what he said. Scheduled to go with the recruiting team to Stanford Business School when an urgent matter came up with Ford Motor Company, then the firm's most important client, Conway didn't know what to do, so he went to Whitehead. "John, I'm not omniscient and I'm not able to be omnipresent. Which do you want me to do? Stanford or Ford?"

Whitehead didn't even think about it. His immediate answer, "Go to Stanford! I'll cover for you at Ford."

As Conway says, "It's choices like that that show you what a leader really believes in. And it was decisions like that that made Goldman Sachs such an effective recruiter." A vital factor in the firm's commitment to recruiting was its use of partners to do the work. When Conway was out recruiting, he always checked the other firms' sign-up sheets to see who was there to represent each of the firms. "Every time, it was the same: Goldman Sachs *always* sent the more senior team." Goldman Sachs doesn't look for top-quartile—or even top-decile—MBAs. Convinced that over the long term there is inevitably a major difference between the top 5 percent and the second 5 percent, the firm focuses on recruiting only the very best young professionals, selecting carefully for such characteristics as leadership, drive, and appetite for hard work. Starting with the 5 percent most qualified and capable, the firm proceeds to sort out the most effective team-playing contributors—initially through fifteen to thirty interviews and then through actual work experience and direct observation to find the very best 1 or 2 percent.

Methodical recruiting for Goldman Sachs began at Harvard Business School when Donald David, who had known Sidney Weinberg during World War II, became dean and joined with Paul Cabot, Harvard's powerful treasurer and Weinberg's great friend, in urging Weinberg to recruit at Harvard.[1] Weinberg quickly agreed to take one MBA each year. An early result was the hiring of John Whitehead, who was then put in charge of recruiting stellar young people for investment banking. Whitehead concentrated on Harvard Business School, partly because he had gone there, partly because it was the leading business school, and partly because public-school dropout Sidney Weinberg was a convinced "Hah-vahd man."

Goldman Sachs concentrated on outstanding students, and within this group looked for team captains and leaders of organizations because they must have had something special that resulted in their being chosen by their peers to lead. After a few years, while Harvard would always be the firm's most important source of talent, Goldman Sachs's recruiting expanded to twenty-five additional business schools.

The team intensity of recruiting at Harvard, Columbia, Wharton, Chicago, Stanford, and Northwestern was an order of magnitude stronger than any other firm's. For every one of these schools, teams of twelve to fifteen people—always led by partners—every year organized ten different visits with the faculty members who knew the students best. Over time, this consistent engagement accumulated powerful momentum.

One of the best indicators of importance within the firm is the stature of the person given leadership responsibility for the effort. In his day, John Whitehead ran recruiting. When Fred Krimendahl ran corporate finance, he also ran recruiting, and it was the same with Peter Sachs. At least as important, there was *no* delegation of recruiting responsibilities to juniors or Human Resources. At each business school, Goldman Sachs recruiters would work with the professors and with the firm's own prior-year hires from that school to identify the very best candidates to invite to initial half-hour screening interviews. Interviewing continued all day. At the end of the afternoon, the Goldman Sachs team would group together to identify the best candidates so that everyone knew which candidates to focus on when the students got to the firm's cocktail reception that evening at the best downtown hotel. During the reception, the top candidates were carefully introduced to the senior partners who had flown in for the occasion. After the two-hour reception, the team from Goldman Sachs huddled again over dinner to decide which students should be invited to the firm for more interviews. Invitations to visit Goldman Sachs's office went out the next day.

Offering salaries were carefully calibrated, based on each school's graduates' average starting salary for the year before. The firm stuck to that conservative barometer and hardly ever made an exception. For the people Goldman Sachs hired, it was rarely the highest salary they were offered. Always stressing the long-range opportunity of a career with Goldman Sachs, the firm wanted recruits to weigh other factors, believing that those who accepted jobs because of salary were more inclined to leave later for a higher offer from somewhere else. The worst thing the firm could do was hire someone, train him for a few years, and then have him go elsewhere for more money.

Goldman Sachs was one of the first Wall Street firms to focus on recruiting carefully selected MBAs from leading schools as securities salespeople. This worked for the firm and for the recruit because at Goldman Sachs, experienced salespeople earned several times the average for salespeople on Wall Street. Recruiting for securities sales was led and carefully controlled for many years by Richard Menschel, who explained, "The secret to success is always the same. Carefully hire very good people and let them grow." Menschel devoted considerable time and care to selecting individuals who had unusual drive but would also be team players. The right people would respond well to the exacting discipline with which he managed each person's professional development, creating loyalty to him and loyalty to the firm.

Menschel was always the final interview for anyone coming into securities sales. This was his way of asserting complete control over all hiring decisions, and he made it clear that he, unlike some other department heads, had no patience for campaigning: If anyone promoted a candidate for security sales, Menschel would be sure to reject that candidate. To show job candidates just who was in charge, he would make the candidate wait—sometimes for a long time. And his decisions were as absolutely final as a papal election. When hiring picked up in London, Menschel still insisted on making all the hiring decisions, so candidates would be flown to New York, ostensibly for a day or two of interviews, but really for just that one hour with Menschel. In one peak-volume year in the 1980s, Menschel interviewed nine hundred candidates from thirty-five business schools and selected just twenty-three. His only comment: "Better people and better training mean a better product."

George Ross, the regional office manager in Philadelphia, was an accomplished talent spotter. He focused on Wharton and developed a close relationship with the dean, who gladly told Ross who were his school's best people. Ross then focused on recruiting those "high potentials," including Eric Schwartz, David Ford, Eric Dobkin, John McNulty, and Jon Corzine from Chicago.

After earning a BA at Dartmouth, Lew Eisenberg did his MBA at Cornell. Soliciting Gene Mercy for United Way in 1966, he was asked if he'd like to talk with Bob Menschel about a possible opening in securities sales in Chicago or St. Louis. Having grown up in Chicago, Eisenberg was interested. The financial arrangement was careful: a salary of $6,200, the potential for earning a 20 percent year-end bonus, and—since he would be a "visitor" in New York City who would later be assigned to work elsewhere—an extra Manhattan cost-of-living allowance of $75 per week. When Eisenberg later agreed to stay in New York, Menschel arranged to have that $75, which by then had been used to pay off $2,000 in school debts, subtracted from Eisenberg's paycheck—a pay cut of 25 percent. Such tightfisted cost discipline was pervasive at Goldman Sachs in the sixties and seventies.

Extensive interviewing was becoming a firm tradition. Even in the sixties, Bob Menschel had interviewed with *every* partner because, as a "family firm," that was the Goldman Sachs way. It gave the firm multiple opportunities to assess a recruit's capabilities, interests, and personal fit with the firm and it gave the recruit an informed basis for deciding whether to make the commitment. As Conway says, "You could, of course, say that our commitment to interviewing was carried through to a fault. We took so long to make decisions with our multiple interview process that some people were lost to other firms, particularly those firms offering 'exploding' offers where the offer blows up if not accepted in a specific, short period of time." Interviews were deliberately varied in topics, tone, and content; assessment of capability, personality, and fit was cumulative.

Like everyone else who was new to Goldman Sachs, Peter Sutherland was surprised in the 1980s by the extensive interviewing process. "I learned that as international chairman, I was the thirty-second person to interview a new hire who came to us without experience and that all the e-mail campaigning I had experienced about this absolute tyro was all part of the process of, by far, the most aggressive recruiting I'd ever seen. Even more surprising to me: That extreme behavior was *normal* at Goldman Sachs. An unrelenting drive to get *all* the best people."

Partner Michael Evans adds, "Where we differ most from other firms is in the attention we pay to retention. Goldman Sachs's standards of care for its professionals are simply the best in the industry. We hire the best and work hard year round to retain them through intensive training and mentoring." Recognizing the firm's unusual emphasis on teamwork and fitting into a consistent pattern of unrelenting work, Evans identified the potential problem: "The one possible negative of our approach is that the firm has less tolerance for nonconformist behavior."

Goldman Sachs has long understood the strong power of attraction that the most highly talented and interesting people have for each other, how engaging it can be for unusually capable people to know they'll be on a steep, challenging learning curve, and how motivating and energizing it is to be part of a winning team. Of course, large financial rewards are motivating too, and for many years Goldman Sachs has paid its people better than other firms as they develop and perform. Goldman Sachs soon learned that being explicit about its high standards, hard work, long hours, and extensive travel can be a powerful positive magnet that attracts top people with ambition and the will to excel, particularly if they believe the competition to get ahead is and will always be fair. In its annual review for 1990, the firm wrote: "We will continue aggressively to recruit the best people, to ensure that they are well trained, and to work hard to maintain a culture that both supports and motivates them. We are committed to advancing our people solely on the basis of merit. This is a major investment in terms of time and energy, but it is an exceedingly productive one."

Of course, there is a flip side, as the 1990 *MBA Career Guide* noted: "While we think we give people outstanding opportunities, we also demand much from them. Our people work long hours and weekends, sometimes in very pressured situations. Many of them travel a great deal. The demands of the job often require them to make personal sacrifices. We believe we get an unusual degree of commitment from our people because they attach a great deal of importance to our firm's shared values."

Partner Peter Fahey recalls, "We recruited intensely because we were determined to be the very best firm—*and* have some good fun. We had the process down pat." In the 1960s, the process started with recruiting the best first-year students at Harvard Business School for summer jobs at the firm. This provided the opportunity to observe each summer associate closely for aptitude, attitude, and ambition. Starting with two "summers" each year, the firm increased the number to several dozen in the eighties. Recruiting summer associates gave the firm a low-cost option on potential hires and an effective way to evaluate each person as a longer-term candidate. All those who worked at Goldman Sachs and then returned to graduate school become part of the dragnet set to find other talented, personable, driven team players who might qualify for career opportunities at the firm.

In the late seventies, recruiting was extended to include college graduates without graduate training. "Goldman Sachs has a fixation on the accuracy of data," says Fahey. "We simply do not trust the publicly available data from sources like Compustat, so we decided we needed bright beginners to do data-entry work. That's when the associates program began. We brought in very bright graduates of the top colleges to do this work—and soon learned they could do lots of other things that were even more valuable."

As the competition for talent intensifies, recruiting is extended even further and now begins with college juniors looking for summer jobs between junior and senior years. The best of these are invited back for the three-year associate program designed for college graduates expecting to go to business school. The best of these, based on direct observation of their skills, drive, and commitment to the firm and its culture, are invited back as MBA associates. And the best of these are advanced to greater and greater responsibility. Those who do not keep up are let go in a repetitive Darwinian process of selection. The very best leadership performers, after extensive and intensive evaluation of their capabilities, drive, and commitment, become partners and take the lead in the rigorous, disciplined recruiting process. With all the evaluation and peer reviews, and direct observations, errors are few and the success rate very high. This systematic process produces 75 or 80 percent of all recruits, but room is also provided for 20 or 25 percent of recruits to "come in from left field" each year—people like Robin Neustein.

At Goldman Sachs, college graduates typically work from 8 a.m. to 6 p.m., break for a quick supper, and then work until 9 or 10 p.m. At midnight—even at 2 a.m.—the floor will still be busy. Workaholics are normal.

College recruiting is much riskier than MBA recruiting, where today most candidates have already had three years in the firm's associate program before going to business school and many have worked at the firm one or two summers while in college. Even then, Goldman Sachs spends an unusual amount of time interviewing and evaluating each candidate. When new recruits get to Goldman Sachs, their indoctrination into the firm's culture and principles begins immediately and is seen by everyone as a high priority.

Developing senior people from within the firm has long been part of the compact at Goldman Sachs and central to the culture of teamwork; loyalty up, loyalty down; firm first; and staying at Goldman Sachs for a full career. No matter how skilled the individual performers, an all-star team is never as strong as an excellent experienced team. Performing well as a team takes time and practice, learning who does each function particularly well and who is best at helping each individual do his best and enabling the group to do its best. "Losses of strong people are very disruptive," explains Richard Menschel, "partly in the interrupted relationships with clients, but even more seriously in the internal loss of the closeness, trust, and superb teamwork and coordination that characterize the very best-performing firms." People of ability and ambition need to know that if they make their career commitment to the organization, the organization will protect them from the dreaded career-breaking risk of an outsider being brought in over them. Deep commitment comes when three levels—mental, intellectual, and emotional—combine both for each individual and for all the individuals who comprise the organization. With few exceptions—and only in unusual circumstances such as a major, rapid expansion in a new market or a new business—Goldman Sachs has almost always promoted from within.

I ntensity of commitment can spill over into offensive behavior, and it did so more than once. While interviewing at Stanford Business School in the late seventies, a Goldman Sachs recruiter asked a woman candidate: "If it was important to your career—say you were working on a long, complex deal—would you get an abortion so you could stay at work at the firm?" The fury unleashed among the Stanford MBAs by this crude question was exceeded in only one place: John Weinberg's office at 85 Broad.

"But, John," said Bob Rubin, "he's so young. He's only twenty-five. He made a mistake."

"Yeah? When I was twenty-five, I'd already been leading a Marine platoon in combat. You're not too young at twenty-five to have enough decency and judgment to know a lot better than to say something as dumb as that!"

That incident was unusual but not unique. In 1970, also at Stanford, James E. Colfield Jr. was advised that his candidacy could not be considered because he was African American. Colfield sued the firm and received an out-of-court settlement. The firm was banned from recruiting at Stanford for a year.[2]

As with any strength, consistent success can harbor a weakness or a problem. John Whitehead had a grave concern that he decided to emphasize at the annual investment banking planning conference in the late seventies: "There is one thing on my mind tonight. It worries me and I'm not quite sure what, if anything, to do about it. It has done great harm to some of our competitors and could do serious harm to Goldman Sachs. What worries me is the early indications of a serious disease that can be quite destructive in a professional service firm. We must all be diligent to prevent and eradicate it here at our firm. And that disease has a name we don't like to use, but we must. It's . . . arrogance. If any of you has *any* suggestions at *any* time on how we can prevent arrogance, you know I'd appreciate your help. Who would like to start this important discussion?"

One hand went up. Whitehead turned and looked toward the young banker. "And what can you suggest we do?"

"John, there's one really effective way to put an end to what you're worried about."

"And what would that be?"

"Hire mediocre people."

31

~∾~

JON CORZINE

Many people at Goldman Sachs enjoyed Jon Corzine's easygoing, unpretentious ways and saw his unusual thick beard, habitual sweater vests, and interest in pick-up games of basketball or knockin' 'em back with the boys as confirmation of the genial good guy they liked so much.[1] Corzine could put anyone at ease. Now, as he took his new position in 1994, his friends would learn that Corzine had long wanted to be senior partner of Goldman Sachs. He had an agenda and was determined to put it through. Going public was Corzine's strategic imperative as Goldman Sachs's new senior partner. Having served as the firm's chief financial officer, he knew it could not succeed in the global financial markets that were developing rapidly without change, and as a successful bond dealer—who says, "Personally I never had an unprofitable year"—he understood how profitable a risk-controlled, diversified proprietary fixed-income operation could be *if* it had a strong capital base.

Without the substantial permanent capital that public ownership could provide, the firm he loved would be outgunned by competitors, particularly the giant commercial banks and foreign "universal" banks that were aggressively expanding into the underwriting and securities-trading businesses. In addition, the firm would always be exposed to the unanticipated catastrophic risks that had been the final experience of so many once-famous firms. If it had substantial permanent capital, Corzine knew from experience in the markets that Goldman Sachs could create its own profits—and plenty of them—through the proprietary trading, for its own account, that it now knew how to do worldwide. Without permanent capital, reaching for those remarkable profit opportunities would increase the risks unacceptably. Thorough examination led to one inevitable conclusion: The firm's future—grim or great—depended on substantial permanent capital.

To prepare Goldman Sachs for an initial public offering, Corzine's first priority had to be to save the firm and rebuild profitability by cutting costs. Ominously, the fourth quarter of 1994 showed a major loss. But actual results were even worse: The active partners suffered a net loss for the whole year after their draws and the mandatory payouts to retired partners and to Sumitomo Bank and Bishop Estate.

Corzine understood his mission: Get Goldman Sachs back to financial health and full strength. With the comfortable confidence in him and his values held throughout the firm, his in-depth grasp of the financials, and his recognized prowess as a trader, Corzine had a lot going for him as the firm's crisis leader. Some of his great strengths were personal: a voracious appetite for work; a "patriot's" deep commitment to the success of Goldman Sachs; and an unrelenting, "don't bother me with any distractions" focus once he had decided on his main objective. His strengths were also his weaknesses.

To increase profits, Corzine's obvious first steps were working out of the accumulated losses in proprietary bond trading—losses totaling $2.5 billion— and getting the firm's regular operations and finances back under control; he set out to remove at least $1 billion of the $3.6 billion in operating costs that had accumulated like Topsy in the drive for geographic and product-line expansion and market share. During the prior two years, staffing had increased by more than one-third—from 7,200 to 9,400. Cutting costs meant cutting people and cutting compensation—hard work for anyone anywhere, but particularly hard at Goldman Sachs, which had a long tradition of protecting employees from layoffs and was already distressed by Steve Friedman's leaving, the departures of forty other partners, and the collapse in earnings. By early October 1994, commitments had been made to terminate 450 employees—5 percent—with particular emphasis on cuts at J. Aron and Fixed Income, where the 70 percent drop in nine-month earnings had been concentrated. Terminations were soon increased to 10 percent of staff, or nearly one thousand people. Professional pay was cut in half, and year-end bonuses were cut from 30 percent of salary to just 8 percent—the lowest in twenty years.

But Corzine was far from being just a cost-cutter. He was a dedicated expansionist, determined to create the opportunities for personal growth that would attract and keep outstanding people. In October, fifty-eight people—by far the largest group ever and two-thirds more than in the biennial class of 1992—were added to the 151 partners who had stayed with the firm. The large number elevated to partnership helped offset the negative impact of the year's much lower cash payouts and helped keep stellar people from defecting to other firms. All new partners were paid bonuses of $500,000 without regard to the performance of their divisions.

Corzine advocated restructuring Goldman Sachs and expanding the organization substantially. As he explained, sustaining the firm's growth could take the profits to new highs before the decade was over. To dramatize his point at a firmwide planning session, he put up a slide that showed just one number: $10 billion. Many were, of course, skeptical at the time. But in a decade Goldman Sachs reported its profits: $10 billion.

In addition to cutting costs, Corzine had another challenge: establishing himself as senior partner with clients, partners, and the powerful management committee. The management committee traditionally had one representative from each major division. But even though membership had been expanded to a dozen, the committee no longer covered all the important business units and, some argued, was too slow in approving divisional initiatives. To increase efficiency, Corzine made two changes. To signal its decision-making power and move toward corporate nomenclature, the management committee was renamed the executive committee and cut from twelve members to six: Corzine, Hank Paulson, John Thain, Roy Zuckerberg, David Silfen, and Bob Hurst. (A year later, when Silfen went limited, Corzine appointed John Thornton.) This leaner group soon proved itself able to make faster decisions. Thornton and Thain had worked well together in London and tended to bond together, as did Silfen and Zuckerberg, who co-headed Equities so effectively.

To broaden participation in governance and leadership, Corzine simultaneously established two new and larger committees—each with eighteen partners, including a few from the new executive committee. Corzine would chair the more introspective of the two new groups, the partnership committee, to oversee partnership policies and partner-selection practices and to review and evaluate the firm's capital structure. Paulson would chair the other new group, the operating committee, which was to focus on facilitating communications among partners and between divisions to increase operational coordination, develop annual budgets, approve plans for new business initiatives, and ensure "strategic cohesion with an external focus." Corzine explained that he hoped the broader participation among partners would help spread the firm's culture and mission more widely. Members of all three committees were instructed to represent the interests of the whole firm, not just their own divisions. Skeptics expressed doubts about the real purpose and actual power of Corzine's two committees.

Since he was a bond trader, it might not be surprising that at first Corzine had little interest in developing relationships and rapport with unfamiliar corporate clients, but since he was always an astute politician, it is surprising that he gave so little thought or attention to the new executive committee or to its members, particularly president Hank Paulson. After a satisfactory first year, the strains between the two men were becoming increasingly obvious. "Corzine had to elevate Paulson to equal stature or one of them was inevitably going to have to leave," explains John Thornton. "The structure was inherently unstable, especially given their personalities. His decision to move him up but not as an equal just set the stage for an unhappy outcome."

No formal announcements were needed; everyone knew Corzine was moving the firm toward an IPO.* He was obviously making the moves that would make it easier to get there. Unlimited personal liability was eliminated by creating a limited liability corporation (LLC) as the sole general partner of Goldman Sachs. This meant that the liability of individuals, Sumitomo Bank, and Bishop Estate was limited to assets already committed to the organization. (Homes and personal investments would be safe, but since many Goldman Sachs people had over 85 percent of their total assets invested in the firm, it would not really matter

---

* Friedman had wanted to do an IPO in late 1993, but fortunately Corzine blocked it. To have had an IPO on peak profits, largely from trading, and then to have reported almost zero profits in the first year of public ownership would have been cataclysmic.

much for most partners.) The length of the capital-payout provision for partners going limited was extended, and in good years part of each partner's earnings would go into long-term capital accounts with an eight-year duration followed by a three-year payout. Corzine never took his eyes off his primary goal of taking Goldman Sachs public. He pressed the case for an IPO with partner after partner in a sustained campaign to accumulate votes for the action he *knew* was right—for Goldman Sachs and for Jon Corzine.

Corzine also made changes in titles. He started referring to himself, particularly externally and with reporters, as the firm's CEO. The most important change was to drop the term "partner" and convert all partners and many experienced vice presidents to managing directors (MDs)—the designation being used by competitors that had already gone public. The firm had long had complaints from the older investment banking vice presidents that in meetings with clients, the title "vice president" was less impressive than "managing director" and that they and the firm were losing business unnecessarily. With the MD title, selected vice presidents would get higher salaries and some perks: offices as large as partners', access to what had been the partners' dining rooms, and attendance at partners' meetings. In the annual report, managing directors would now be listed alphabetically, whether or not they were equity partners, and all would be offered participation shares in firmwide profits. Internally, the new title was mocked as "partner lite," but it was accepted as a pragmatic move because the firm was getting larger, going into more lines of business and more geographic markets, and so required more capital and more organizational formality. (Managing directors were divided internally into two categories: "participating" MDs were partners; "executive" MDs were not.) The MD title would also help with lateral recruiting: It was easier to offer a candidate an MD title than a partnership, and MDs at other firms wouldn't want to step down to a mere vice presidency.

By 1995, partners had become well informed on the issues involved in going public and, more important, had gotten used to the idea. Several competitors had gone public, and Morgan Stanley, Merrill Lynch, and Salomon Brothers all seemed to be gaining competitive strength. The strategic rationale for permanent capital was steadily gaining converts. Among the business reasons for going public—and during this era, they kept gaining in importance and persuasive power—were the size of the partnership and the increasing need for permanent capital to finance proprietary trading, expensive computer systems, and large, long-term principal investments. Position sizes in dealing were getting so large that the risks were much higher than they had been in the past. The time horizon for payoffs on large principal investments was being pushed further and further out—so the time between risk-taking investment and distribution of rewards was getting further out of alignment with the steady turnover among partners. As profits rebounded in 1995 to $1.37 billion, morale was also rebounding. Partners and staff believed they had weathered the worst, knew they were making progress, and believed more confidently in their future opportunities. The main question increasingly was whether Goldman Sachs had enough capital to finance its expansive ambitions and opportunities.

As the partnership got larger and the business of Goldman Sachs became more diverse and geometrically more complex, partners saw or worked with each other less. The close personal ties of the old "family" partnership attenuated to less and less importance both personally and organizationally. "After large layoffs and then big hiring, a *lot* of people were new to the firm, new to each other, and new to our culture," recalls partner Robin Neustein, who, hoping to bridge the gap, made speech after speech about the firm's past and its values. A partner in Frankfurt wouldn't really know a partner in Singapore and couldn't know much at all about what he did or how well he was doing for the firm. The many newer partners understandably had less attachment to the mystic cords of partnership than the longer-serving partners who either had retired or were retiring. Other changes were powerful: the departures of so many partners, particularly the loss of John Weinberg, Bob Rubin, and Steve Friedman; the emerging politics at the top of the organization; the acquisition of J. Aron, which brought in a very different and unfamiliar business and several new and different partners; and the large capital infusions from Sumitomo in 1987 and Bishop Estate in 1989.[2] The nature of the business and of competition continued to change in major, consequential ways. The business was going global in customers, competitors, and markets, and big balance sheets were increasingly necessary. Restrictive regulations were disappearing, technology was linking once-separate markets, and the "right size" to be a viable competitor was increasing rapidly.

The reasons for going public included both providing the firm the capital required to act swiftly as principals and the increasing importance of capital for defensive or protective strength: protective against groups of partners going limited in a hurry when times were tough, protective against the balance-sheet power of big competitors, and protective against the risk of a major accident such as a big loss in trading or a J. Aron–chartered tanker creating a disastrous oil spill. The large Maxwell settlement—and how it could have been much worse—was cited as instructive, as were the multibillion-dollar trading losses of 1994.

Corzine spent hours and hours week after week during 1995 trying to persuade individual partners of the importance of an IPO and lining up support. As a result, all partners knew where he stood. In January 1995, Corzine and Paulson met with the combined operating and partners committees to formally propose an IPO. Surprisingly, that meeting was a dud. Even though these senior partners would have the most to gain financially, they were still opposed. Without their support, an IPO would never be approved by the whole partnership. But in his drive to take the firm public, Corzine had already put an IPO on the agenda for the forthcoming meeting of all partners, which was now only two weeks away at Arrowwood in Rye, New York.

As Arrowwood approached, Corzine faced impressive opposition from within. His successor as chief financial officer, John Thain, highly respected within the partnership for his rational brilliance and his unemotional, objective judgment, was clearly opposed to an IPO. Paulson and Thornton supported Thain's position, so the executive committee was split three to three. This was not a good sign. In addition, Eric Dobkin, the firm's expert on pricing large global equity underwritings, said he believed that because so much of the firm's profits came from trading, an IPO would be priced at well under two times book value—a big discount from Morgan Stanley's market valuation at nearly three times book value. While others, including members of the executive committee, sharply disagreed, Dobkin held his ground. His low estimate was decisive in deflating the motivation for an IPO among the partners and leaving too little pressure to help Corzine override the traditional "spiritual" concerns about protecting the soft values of the partnership that were important in recruiting exceptional people, ensuring clients' confidence, and governing operations.

Still, Corzine plowed ahead when the firm held its annual two-day meeting at Arrowwood in January 1996. On Friday he presented a detailed capital-structure analysis and the logical case for an IPO. He intended to put the decision through at the Saturday session and was laying the groundwork for the "Let's go!" presentation he would be giving. Exceedingly political—an apt adumbration of his second career as senator and governor—Corzine pulled literally *every* partner aside for private, personal politicking for an IPO and made a continuous point of knowing the pulse of the partnership all the time. Through dinner and after dinner, he worked to connect with partners, particularly those from overseas offices that he didn't see so often.

As the partners' discussion of an IPO continued, it was increasingly clear that Corzine, while working hard to develop support all day Friday, would not have as much as he needed on Saturday. This was confirmed when the executive committee held a long meeting Friday night. After the committee meeting—at nearly 2 a.m.—Corzine, who enjoys relaxing with a drink, went to the bar, where a crowd of bankers were gathered. Having already had plenty to drink and being all fired up, they expressed a clear consensus on doing an IPO: *No way!*

Just a few hours later, at seven Saturday morning, Bob Hurst knocked on Robin Neustein's door, filled her in on the Friday night happenings, and asked her to go meet with Corzine. The Saturday agenda, already printed and distributed, had Corzine scheduled to speak that morning. But he knew he couldn't simply advocate going ahead with the IPO. That would not fly. So what could he say and do to strike the right tone? Corzine and Neustein quickly discussed what to say, how to say it, and what *not* to say. On a yellow legal pad Corzine wrote out an outline for his talk with a few key phrases, an introduction, and a closing line.

When he got to the meeting room, Corzine found that the young partners had organized their opposition. One after another, they spoke out against an IPO. After an hour, Corzine went to the podium and delivered the astonishing message he and Neustein had crafted, saying: "There will be no IPO. The IPO is off the table. It's over!"

He got it right. For the first time in the firm's history, the partners all rose and gave their managing partner a standing ovation. In the days that followed, congratulatory letters poured in: "We're so proud of you!" "I never felt more committed to the firm than I do now, thanks to you." "You were—and are—a great leader."

But those who knew Corzine best knew the IPO was not over. Although he couldn't force the issue, he wasn't about to give up. Corzine may have lost that particular round—even without a formal vote—but in his long-term campaign, he had made important gains. And almost everybody came to sense it. "Everyone wanted to be certain to stay for the big bonanza, to protect their own position in the firm—and get rich," explained one of the older partners. "Everyone went on the defensive. The whole firm seemed to slow down while everyone rubbed everybody's back and held on to their positions. This was terribly frustrating to the lower-ranking people who wanted to get ahead."

While failing to win a commitment for an IPO, Corzine had successfully changed the topic of public ownership from "not discussable" to openly and fully discussable. This had an accumulating influence in favor of going ahead because more and more partners were recognizing the importance of permanent capital for the firm and because, on a personal level, the dual desires, once unleashed, for greater wealth and for the power that comes with greater wealth compounded at an accelerating pace. At the same time, the strength of the forces in opposition waned. The old camaraderie among partners, which had been so strong, steadily dissipated, and the power of tradition became less and less meaningful. The fact that a partnership structure had worked so well in the past with a smaller, closer-knit firm with far less capital at risk—and with strong memories of building Goldman Sachs from insignificance to global leadership as a private partnership—carried less and less weight as the firm grew and as more partners worked in London, Paris, Frankfurt, Tokyo, Hong Kong, Singapore, and many other local markets with important local clients that were largely unknown to most of the other partners.

Some older partners argued that what would be sold in an IPO was something special that didn't really belong to those who would get paid the most. A big part of the value was the *past*—and another big part was the *future*. Past partners had created the stature, reputation, and franchise of the firm and most of its business and most of its clients, building the strong foundation for the present profits. So it really wasn't fair or right that all that IPO reward should go to the current—and only temporary—seat holders who were, realistically, just passing through.

Others argued that the *future* earning power of the firm was what IPO buyers were really buying. Bestowing all that wealth on current incumbents meant taking something away from the partners of the future. It would weaken the incentives the firm would need to attract and keep the very best people in the large numbers Goldman Sachs would require to lead a worldwide organization driving for leadership in all the many businesses that were now so important to its success. To those who felt this way, an IPO would inevitably rob the future. It might not show right away, but it would surely do irreparable harm.

John Whitehead and John Weinberg wrote a carefully crafted, several-page letter to the partners, making their case for not going public. Corzine read their letter aloud to the partners. It was obviously deeply felt and they were both highly regarded, but their era had passed. They were no longer the powerful leaders they had once been. Realistically, the center of gravity of their argument was already behind the firm—and every month, that reality was becoming clearer to more partners. Whitehead was asked years later why he and Weinberg, as experienced investment bankers who must have seen many other long-established business partnerships sell out, had not modified the partnership argument to ensure fairness in any possible future public offering when they had the power. Whitehead replied, "At the time of the IPO, there were 108 retired or limited partners. Back when I retired in 1984, there were eighty active partners and only twelve retired or limited partners, so the situation was very different. That's why we had never seriously considered predetermining the division of a hypothetical IPO."

With the prospect of an IPO deferred but still looming on the horizon, young people eager to become partners before the big payday realized they had an urgent need to find their mentor-sponsor-rabbi, develop their supporters, and make no mistakes and make no enemies. Those aspiring to become partners developed political skills, political alliances, and political capital. Politics takes time, energy, and attention—the same limited resources needed to build or maintain important client relationships and create new businesses. Throughout Goldman Sachs, time, energy, and attention went from being focused 100 percent on clients to being split fifty-fifty: half on clients, half on advancing everybody's own political position. "It was more important to focus inside the firm than outside with clients," said one knowing partner. With an IPO expected to produce a hundred, two hundred, or three hundred million dollars per senior partner, they all knew the stakes were enormous.

Tensions developed between partnership classes, or vintages, as issues clarified. Long-serving partners who had gone limited would get much smaller payouts than the successors they had trained up and to whom they had only recently turned over firm leadership. The forces behind the drive for going public were, as they always are, partly business strategy and partly personal and financial. It's important to keep them separate. As J. P. Morgan famously observed, "A man always has two reasons for doing anything: a good reason and the real reason."

The sensible business arguments in favor of an IPO added dignity to the pervasive personal fascination of seeing how much each partner's net worth would leap forward. Another strong motivator was the crude but effective "reality" proposition: *If we don't do it, the next group of partners, facing exactly the same question, will do it. So be realistic; all you're deciding when you say no is to hand those guys the same fortune on the same silver platter that you and your family could have enjoyed. Nothing else changes. And ten—no, just five—years from now, nobody will give a damn except you, your family—and, maybe though very unlikely, the guys you'll be giving all that money to.*

Corzine would wait for another time to bring an IPO to the partnership, but he would not wait quietly. He persistently urged partners to support an IPO, typically in one-on-one meetings. "Corzine bought votes one by one," recalls a partner, "taking each guy into his office and showing each how much money he would make." Corzine made lots of calls, went to many meetings, and talked the IPO up in every way he could. He did a lot of arm twisting, and he said to many partners, "We'll both be around for a *long* time after the IPO, working together." Corzine's words more than implied the importance of cooperating in support of him as the senior partner—but he never made explicit quid pro quo deals or specific promises. Still, politics flourished. "I told Jon Corzine that it would take ten years to evaporate the internal politics he generated by his drive to go public," said John Weinberg. "We had lots of time-dated greed." Forces in favor of an IPO continued to increase. The magnitude of profitability, plus an increasing view that the strength of the firm's earnings would command a higher price-to-earnings valuation, suggested that individual partners would be getting more if the firm went public—or leaving more on the table by refusing.

During 1997, other investment banks enlarged, broadened, and combined their operations, seriously challenging Goldman Sachs. Morgan Stanley merged with Dean Witter, a major retail stockbroker with strong distribution. Salomon Brothers merged with Travelers—and a year later combined with Citibank to create Citigroup. For $5.2 billion, Merrill Lynch acquired London's Mercury Asset Management, the largest investment manager in the United Kingdom and one of the largest and most prestigious in Europe with $175 billion in client assets, establishing a "high ground" base from which to build across Europe. Switzerland's UBS acquired S.G. Warburg. Deutsche Bank made a series of tactical acquisitions, recruited senior talent boldly, and expanded aggressively into investment banking and securities dealing; its powerful financial resources—which included over $25 billion of undisclosed reserves—could easily absorb large "investment spending" losses. Global banks were moving with their huge balance sheets into the investment banking and securities business, and regulatory restraints were coming down everywhere. Competition's center of gravity was moving inexorably toward permanent capital and big balance sheets.

"Heightened competition," Corzine observed, "will put a premium on cutting-edge technology, up-to-the-moment intelligence on global market opportunities, the development of innovative products and services, and a redoubled dedication to the customer. Competition will also require a renewed emphasis on risk management and financial soundness if firms are to survive the inevitable cyclical downturns, like the one from which the industry is even now emerging.[3] Striking the right balance between entrepreneurial initiative and financial prudence will be the fundamental test of success."[4]

The competitors were changing and the industry was changing—becoming more global, requiring major capital commitments for trading and information technology, increasing financial risk—and the business of the firm and its earnings were changing from agency-advisory investment banking to capital-at-risk proprietary trading and dealing. By many steps and stages, one partner after another moved from opposing to favoring an IPO. Fifty years before, the firm had had only one partner in the bond business; when an IPO came to a vote in 1998, there were fifty-three partners in Fixed Income and they voted 51 to 2 in favor of an IPO. Immersed in a trading culture, living in a mark-to-market world where everything was for sale, they had learned to be realists and were less enamored of traditions.

Good as 1996 had been in the firm's business, 1997 was even better. Goldman Sachs played key roles in Deutsche Telekom's gigantic $13 billion privatization, the privatization of China Telecom—that nation's first—and the largest industrial merger up to that time, and the $38 billion combination of Chrysler into Daimler-Benz. Profits exceeded $3 billion, taking return on equity capital up over 50 percent—well above the industry's 36 percent average.

As usual, Corzine was deeply and personally engaged in the global markets at any time of the day or night, checking the major markets every morning: a 6:15 call to Lloyd Blankfein in New York, a 6:30 call to Pat Ward in London, and at 6:45, a series of calls to offices in Asia. In addition, if needed for an important decision, Corzine gladly took calls at 2:30 a.m., again at 3:00 a.m., and again at 4:15 a.m. Naturally, more and more of the calls from those who needed a decision went to Corzine, increasing his operational expertise and his leadership strength within Goldman Sachs.

Not all the calls came from people trading in the markets. In 1996, Corzine got an angry message from Christopher Gent, the CEO of Vodaphone, a major client in the United Kingdom. Their business relationship could be terminated because the firm had underwritten a $1.2 billion IPO of Orange, a competitor, without first conferring with Vodaphone. Corzine quickly called Gent to apologize and, as Gent later recalled with characteristic understatement, "We came to an understanding early on of what was expected of them. I expected them to commit to us."[5]

While a partnership is a legal structure, the effectiveness of any partnership depends on informal bonds between partners. As partnerships get larger and larger, the person-to-person connectedness declines and the dynamic of the group changes. Intimacy fades into mere acquaintance; communication losses clarity, subtlety, and effectiveness; and personal warmth and affection decline. While the legal structure of partnership continues, the personal connections dissipate. Into all those spaces can slip tensions, misunderstandings, hurt feelings, and disagreements. Corzine believed he would outlast all the others; he compared himself to Sandy Weill of Citigroup and was determined to be the recognized king of Wall Street. "It's not that he always *thinks* he's right; it's that he *knows* he's right," said Bob Hurst. "That's dangerous."

As Corzine settled into his position as senior partner, the consensus jelled within the firm that he would be there for a long time. Partners agreed: *Jon Corzine will be picking his team for the next decade during the next few months*. Corzine would have good reason for thinking he was in a strong position. Profits had increased substantially; he had secured another major equity investment from the Bishop Estate; and increasing numbers of partners were recognizing the strategic importance of having permanent capital plus stock to use as currency in acquisitions and to reward strong contributors without having to offer a full partnership. With higher earnings from the rising importance of GSAM and strong trading profits—and the higher price-earnings multiples accorded competitors, the compelling power of great personal wealth was pulling increasing numbers of partners to support an IPO. And the objective case for an IPO was gaining power.

Corzine was increasingly popular within the partnership. But within the executive committee, important changes were coalescing toward confrontation.

"Jon thinks *big*," recalls Bob Hurst. "He had decided that Goldman Sachs was not big enough."

Declaring "I'm an expansionist!" Corzine wanted to do a string of small "shock absorber" acquisitions in investment management and initiated talks with several firms, including Robeco, Wellington, and Grantham Mayo Van Otterloo. Anticipating the inevitable collapse of Glass-Steagall, which had separated commercial and investment banking since the Depression, Corzine initiated talks with the CEO of J.P. Morgan, the CEO of Chase Manhattan, the CEO of U.S. Trust, and the CEO of Mellon Bank.[6] Having initiated a conversation about getting together with a major bank, Corzine would sometimes "adjust reality" and tell his partners that the initiative had actually come from the other party. Seeing himself as CEO, Corzine considered these strategic initiatives appropriate to his position and the powers he wanted, but his partners—particularly those on the executive committee—strongly disagreed. As they saw it, *they* were the ultimate power in Goldman Sachs because they represented the partnership, and within the committee they were all "one man, one vote" equals.

Corzine was off the ranch, as others saw it, going around to firm after firm and bank after bank to "get acquainted" and raising questions with several about possible working relationships or even mergers. His independent strategic initiatives paired in the minds of others with his informal, ad hoc way of making operational decisions. Corzine was often intuitive and seemed to others improvisational and undisciplined, while Paulson was all about careful plans and always had everything worked out in advance. "Corzine kept making seat-of-the-pants decisions and improvisations," recalls Bob Steel. "He was not buttoned up and had way too many things on his to-do list—way too many to get them all done."

Corzine's discussion with Mellon Bank provoked an especially negative reaction within the executive committee. When he came back from a weekend of unannounced talks with Mellon CEO Frank Cohuet, a partner said he was astonished that Corzine would do such a thing—partly because he didn't have the authority and partly because he was proving how naive he was about the dance of M&A. Thornton recalls saying, "As CEO, you should *never* initiate such a discussion. That's simply very bad tactics. Instead, you should carefully create a set of conditions so the other guy comes to *you*—and comes as a supplicant. The *last* thing a skillful CEO would ever do is go out courting a refusal all alone.[7] You are too inexperienced and you don't know how to play the role of a CEO in doing a merger deal. You have to be disciplined and self-aware. You don't know the rules. And, Jon, you're *not* a CEO; this is a partnership. You are our senior partner, Jon, but you're not our CEO. The management committee—all the way back to Gus Levy—is the responsible party in this firm's partnership. You can't go off on your own doing deals or raising possibilities of merger with others. Besides, you really don't have enough experience in M&A to know how to manager high-level exploratory talks about getting together."

John Weinberg warned Corzine to stay away from a merger with Chase. "Corzine was looking at merging with Chase Manhattan and I told him: 'If you join [CEO] Billy Harrison, he'll tell you he has to retire in a year because he has prostate cancer and will indicate that you can look to become CEO after he's gone in a year or so. But you'll be only one of five guys with the same come-on promise, and the other guys will all know all about commercial banking—about which you know *nothing*. Since that's the core business and since you don't know that business, they'll kill you. Besides, with a big outfit like that, they'll move lots of Goldman Sachs guys into various positions and milk the best of Goldman Sachs away, and then dilute the rest. You'll have no base of support. Commercial banking will be the combined organization's biggest business, so the next CEO will have to be chosen from those who know the main business—commercial banking—and it won't be you!'"

The balance between building the best firm and making the most money had changed a lot," explains a senior partner. "Twenty or thirty years ago, we all knew that if we built a great firm, the profits were sure to follow. We *knew* that if we were the best firm with the best people, we couldn't miss making big profits.

But with a public firm requiring quarterly earnings reports, the focus could shift."

Silfen leaned toward an IPO as a way of adding flexibility to compensation arrangements. "Reward the very best very well," he says, "but you need to find the balance that also holds the very good *and* motivates and rewards the very, very best, who are the decisive value-adders on crucial business transactions or the development of significant new ways of doing business. That's why I was one of those who favored going public—so we'd have the currency of a public stock and a way to tie everybody together with a common interest."

Much as he loved the firm, Silfen knew that being co-head of a major division and a member of the management committee was as far as he could go or wanted to go. He had made more money than he had ever dreamed of, and at fifty he still had ample time to do whatever he wanted in a second career. As a realist who understood markets, he felt comfortably objective about his career decision: It was time to go.

Silfen went to Corzine and laid it out quietly and clearly. The two men had never been particularly close. They had not worked closely together—one was in Equities and one in Fixed Income—and their personal styles were dissimilar. Silfen was careful, focused, and exact while Corzine was open, comfortable with ambivalence, and a risk-taker. Silfen may have had some hopes that Corzine would ask him to stay and perhaps even offer him a special incentive to do so, but Corzine didn't rise to the opportunity. He simply said he understood. "You've had a great run, David. It's your decision to make, of course. Not a problem." Silfen's parting would have little immediate significance to Corzine, but it would lead almost inevitably to Corzine's being forced out as managing partner of Goldman Sachs.

The initial public offering would position Goldman Sachs as an industry leader and make the partners rich, and the members of the executive committee very rich. The irony would be that the stresses generated by Corzine's unrelenting drive to complete the IPO were a significant factor in his approaching downfall. As Corzine said later, "It would've been a lot easier not to get into the fight about going public. I could've just stuck it out another fifteen years and accumulated a much bigger net worth."

LONG-TERM CAPITAL
MANAGEMENT

E xcepting that annus horribilis of 1994, 1998 was as bad as it gets. Goldman Sachs lost hundreds of millions of dollars in proprietary trading and very nearly lost hundreds of millions more in a major hedge fund's collapse. It simultaneously missed—by minutes and a few key words—an opportunity to pull off a moneymaking coup that could have *made* hundreds of millions. As a result, as the stock market declined, Goldman Sachs had to postpone indefinitely its on-again, off-again plans for an IPO, on which Jon Corzine had expended much of his personal political capital. This would hurt his credibility as the firm's leader.

In a longer-term context, 1998 was a time of significant change in the partners' consensus view of Goldman Sachs. The year's events would be seen as forceful evidence of the importance of securing permanent capital by going public. It also showed the increasing importance within Goldman Sachs of proprietary trading, which was on its way to taking precedence over what had been the firm's long-standing, nearly sacrosanct strategic priority: earning trust and recognition among corporate clients as the premier service and relationship investment banker. With its accelerating drive into trading, Goldman Sachs was reinventing itself as a major market-making, risk-taking financial intermediary—the revolutionary shift away from service-based *agent* to capital-based *principal* and toward becoming one of the most powerful financial forces in the world.

Goldman Sachs was becoming the quintessential capitalist organization, making aggressive capital investments and using highly sophisticated computer models to embrace and manage all sorts of risks—many previously unknown—to extract risk-controlled trading profits from capital markets around the world. The firm would profit from its creativity, its access to information, and its ability to organize transactions. Deference to clients and a strong commitment to nurturing relationships, valued as important strengths, would be balanced by and even outweighed by bold use of capital. They would be recognized as potential impediments and possible signs of weakness. One of the first major manifestations of the firm's emerging strategy was seen in its way of dealing with the threatened collapse of a giant, high-tech hedge fund called LTCM.

LTCM—Long-Term Capital Management—appeared to have discovered or invented a wonderful new way to manage a massive hedge fund with a low-risk, high-return portfolio. Only certified financial rocket scientists could really understand the details of how it worked, but everybody knew that LTCM—a mysterious, glorious, golden money spinner—produced spectacular results. The fund was launched in 1993 by John W. Meriwether, known to admirers as J.M., the quietly charismatic leader of Salomon Brothers' justly fabled and notoriously profitable proprietary trading unit. At LTCM, fewer than two hundred people, including two Nobel laureates and a host of brilliant Wall Streeters, managed a huge, private, and very secretive model-driven hedge fund for a partnership of fewer than one hundred large investors. In an era of financial creativity, it was truly outstanding. Four aspects of LTCM were large: the assets, the leverage, the egos of the principals, and the profits.

LTCM's portfolio appeared to be extraordinarily diversified because it was constructed of thousands of diverse, small, "perfect arbitrage" paired positions selected with the aid of advanced computer programs that identified thousands of anomalies, or market imperfections, in bond markets around the world. LTCM selected the most attractive opportunities for profit and constructed a portfolio designed to squeeze out or neutralize every identifiable specific risk and pile up the profits. While LTCM's individual positions were far larger than other investors', relative to its enormous total size they seemed small, and the profit on each paired position seemed very small. The overall strategy was to vacuum up nickels, dimes, and quarters all around the world in such repetitive, wholesale volume and with such great leverage that cumulative portfolio profits would be huge and almost actuarially certain.

The LTCM strategy worked beautifully for a time. LTCM was demonstrating extraordinary success, compounding profits at over 40 percent a year. The fund's disciplined moneymaking machine relied on two interdependent systems. One was the brilliantly designed computer system for scouring the markets of the world to find an extraordinary number and variety of attractive component parts for its portfolio of thousands of paired positions. The other was a secretive and complex system of borrowing from banks and broker-dealers around the world. LTCM used such enormous leverage that while its investors' *equity* was $3 billion, its *portfolio* totaled a gargantuan $100 billion. Beyond that, it had derivatives contracts with virtually every Wall Street bank and dealer, for a total market exposure of more than $1 trillion! The secret to this extraordinary leverage was the lenders' confidence that LTCM's portfolio was shrewdly diversified against *all* risks.

But unknown to both LTCM and its lenders, there was one risk against which it was not diversified: the risk that somehow all the many different markets around the world would all react the same way to a specific, important, very unlikely, and very distressing event—such as a sudden devaluation of the Russian ruble.

At LTCM, instead of the usual hedge fund fee of 1 percent of assets plus 20 percent of profits, the fund's management got a 2 percent fee and 25 percent of the profits. LTCM investors didn't really care that the fees were so high because they too were doing very, very well. After a 28 percent gain in its first year, LTCM produced a spectacular 58 percent gain in 1994. (Actually, given the huge payments to the general partners for managing the fund so successfully, the net gain to limited-partner investors was "only" 20 percent in 1993 and "only" 43 percent in 1994.) By the end of 1995, with annual "2 and 25" payouts accumulating—which they kept investing in LTCM—the general partners running LTCM had amassed $1.4 billion in their personal accounts in the fund. The general partners' position was up nearly ten times from their initial investment of $150 million in just two years. And more good news was coming.

In 1996, LTCM gained an astonishing $1.6 *billion*—57 percent, or 41 percent net to investors after paying the general partners. If $1.6 billion sounds very big, there was an even more significant number that sounds very *small:* The real return on the total portfolio in LTCM's great year was actually only 2.45 percent. As we shall see, the crucial factor in the giant gains to investors—and to LTCM's general partners—was leverage, *lots* of leverage.*

In addition to those two divergent numbers—$1.6 billion and 2.45 percent—another annual number mattered greatly. LTCM's large-scale and hyperintensive portfolio turnover generated a huge volume of business for Wall Street. Paying fees, spreads, and commissions that totaled well in excess of $100 million annually made LTCM one of the world's largest customers for the securities industry. While investors wanted to get in on the LTCM gravy train, their enthusiasm seemed almost restrained compared to the intensity with which the world's major banks and dealers scrambled to be helpful to LTCM. They all wanted more of that rich annual flow of $100 million. Goldman Sachs was not only one of the major dealers, but Corzine's "prop" (proprietary) desk was making similar, even identical "arb" trades, so it was also a competitor.

Not only was LTCM designed brilliantly, but it was operating supremely well too. LTCM was a spectacular multiple success: success for investors, success for banks and brokers, and success for LTCM's managing partners. Incredibly, however, spectacular success was becoming a problem, a large problem: LTCM had too much money to manage. Compared to the market's liquidity and trading volume, the partners decided LTCM had become *too* big. By 1997, investors' equity capital in LTCM was $5 billion. And it kept rising. At $7 billion in 1998, LTCM had more equity capital than Merrill Lynch, Wall Street's largest firm. Size was a problem because LTCM's buying or selling was moving prices and shrinking the profit opportunity in each market imperfection.

So LTCM did something unusual for a hedge fund or any other type of investment manager: It obliged investors to take back $2.7 billion of their invested capital. And LTCM's general partners did something else that was unusual: While returning so much capital to outside investors, they deliberately did *not* reduce the size of LTCM's portfolio. Instead, the general partners chose to borrow more and

* Roger Lowenstein's wonderful study *When Genius Failed* (New York: Random House, 2000) provided much of the detail used in this chapter.

increase the leverage so they and their investors could make even more money on their equity capital. LTCM's general partners were already rich, but now, with the increased leverage, they would be on their way to being superrich, making *really* big money. And this they did . . . but only for a few months.

A further problem was that LTCM was clearly not alone—the fund had too many imitators. Astute traders at the prop desks at major investment banks and at the big hedge funds had studied together at the same business schools, trained together at the same Wall Street firms, and used the same sort of quantitative models and computer programs. They were out looking for the same trades, and talked with each other all the time, comparing notes and sharing insights and facts. Enjoying their rivalries in discovering new things, they were more than glad to steal or copy each other's ideas—including the best ideas of LTCM. LTCM was the biggest and arguably the best, but many, many other smart quant traders were putting together the same perfect arbitrage pairs for the same reasons. And more and more bond-arbitrage funds were being formed to exploit the small niche anomalies in which LTCM specialized. It could never be proved, but many on Wall Street believed that the dealer most actively engaged in trading against LTCM was Goldman Sachs.

The markets in which LTCM operated were about to change dramatically and prove once again that leverage cuts both ways—sometimes suddenly. In June 1998, LTCM had a bad month: It lost $500 million. But investors knew "things happen," and Meriwether was candid and specific about the loss and the reasons for it. Overall: not a problem—yet.

Then, in August, Russia abruptly defaulted on its debt, and that changed everything.

In a massive flight to quality and liquidity, frightened investors everywhere scrambled to sell out of unusual and illiquid securities—exactly the securities LTCM was holding—and buy into the higher-grade, more liquid securities that LTCM had sold short in its perfect arbitrage paired positions. Getting hit both ways—longs being sold *down* and shorts being bought *up*—was obviously bad for LTCM. Now Meriwether was not entirely forthcoming: Performance disclosure was selective—and performance was far worse than most LTCM investors realized. Goldman Sachs realized it, though, because its own proprietary trading gave it unusual access to crucial market information.

Longer-term rational market behavior was being pushed aside, and the unexpected, unpredictable, and often irrational short-term market was being driven by anxious investors, dealers, and hedge funds fleeing to quality and liquidity. The spreads between LTCM's carefully matched long-short pairs were not closing as LTCM's models said they should; they were opening up wider and wider. Suddenly, LTCM was not making profits; instead, it was losing on thousands of pairs. And every time LTCM traders wanted to unwind a paired position, so too did many like-minded hedge funds and dealers.

Market liquidity depends on differences of opinion among many different buyers and many different sellers: the more differences, the better for liquidity. When investors agree, whether rationally or emotionally, on what is the "right" market direction, liquidity quickly evaporates. Strong agreement on market direction, particularly strong emotional agreement, can produce a stampede that quickly destroys liquidity. LTCM's computer models made no provisions for changes in market liquidity—particularly a sudden and unexpected evaporation of liquidity.

Volatility, or market risk, is roughly the opposite of what the most active investors and traders usually mean by "quality." Most investors dislike price volatility, so they would prefer to offload it. They can—for a price—and others will, for a price, accept or "buy" volatility. Volatility cannot be bought or sold directly. But volatility can be bought or sold *indirectly* by selling short or buying stock-index futures or, to get even greater leverage, buying or selling options on stock-index futures. Volatility is usually mispriced because, since most investors dislike market risk, they are quite willing to sell volatility at less than its mathematical fair value, because they are effectively buying insurance against market risk. Futures and options on futures will usually move away from their normal trading range when investors collectively either fear a market decline or hope for a rise. The more pervasive the hope or fear, the greater the distance from normal pricing for market volatility—which traders call "vol." LTCM could therefore effectively buy or sell vol by trading in stock-index futures, and this became a major part of its portfolio operations.

As investors, reacting to the surprising Russian default, scrambled out of the unusual, illiquid securities that LTCM specialized in, they sold what LTCM owned long and bought what LTCM had sold short. That drove market prices further and further away from the normal price correlations that LTCM's computer models had used to identify the anomalies that LTCM had been so successfully exploiting in its highly leveraged portfolio. Suddenly, everything was different. Now the market was going strongly against LTCM, and while its portfolio was wonderfully diversified in many, many ways, it had *no* diversification against the one risk of a worldwide, simultaneous flight to quality, with investors shunning more speculative securities—and that flight to quality was becoming a stampede and trampling LTCM.

Corzine knew that the traders at Goldman Sachs had large exposures to the same kind of complex, derivatives-based portfolio positions that Meriwether and his crew at LTCM had been establishing in recent weeks. Corzine also knew—because Goldman Sachs was believed to watch LTCM closely and allegedly often matched LTCM's trades in the firm's own proprietary portfolio—that the "spread" trades LTCM always liked to do had been going very much in the wrong direction. Corzine knew too about LTCM's large leverage. Bold investors might borrow half the money they invest, so they would have 50 percent leverage and 50 percent equity. Hedge funds often borrow more, reaching as much as 80 percent or, very temporarily, even 90 percent leverage. But at LTCM, Meriwether and his group were borrowing much more: The equity wasn't 50 percent or even 10 percent; it was a mere 3 percent. LTCM was using leverage with a vengeance. With 3 percent equity, a loss of just 3 percent in its total portfolio would completely wipe out LTCM.

Phenomenally secretive, LTCM had irritated Wall Street in its first few years of operation by refusing to inform its investors or its lenders about *any* of its internal operations. In a world that increasingly insisted on transparency, LTCM arrogantly insisted on being opaque. So when Meriwether had a "serious markdown" and felt obliged to step outside his closely guarded realm of secrecy to call one of his major dealers and financial backers at home early in the morning, Corzine knew that the situation was serious, no matter what verbal assurances J.M. was giving.

If he'd known at the outset that Meriwether was calling from Beijing, where he had excused himself from a dinner party to make the call and had just booked himself on the next flight home, Corzine would have known that the situation at LTCM was *very* serious.

As the worldwide flight to quality gained momentum and spread to more and more markets, arbitrage traders, who worked in the same market "space" as LTCM, got increasingly aggressive at cutting back their positions, particularly those positions that traders knew were similar to LTCM's and so wanted to get out of *first*. Some were acting on their senior managements' orders to cut back, and some had to reduce their positions because they were receiving margin calls from *their* banks. Suddenly, all the sophisticated traders wanted to sell. None wanted to buy. And they were selling their better-quality, more liquid positions, not because they wanted to—they didn't—but for one decisive reason: They *had* to sell the quality stuff to raise cash because nothing else *could* be sold into that suddenly anxious market.

In a normal, rational market, LTCM's highly diversified, carefully hedged positions *would* have been smart bets against a series of temporary pricing anomalies. In a normal, rational market, LTCM would have gone right on making millions by vacuuming up all those nickels and dimes. But LTCM's portfolio had two eventually critical problems. In every long-short pairing, LTCM always owned the lower-quality securities and was short the higher-quality securities. And most of its pairings involved complex trades in small, unusual markets where liquidity was always limited and could, as was now being proved, be *very* limited. Against the one specific risk of investors everywhere driving their portfolios toward higher quality and going against LTCM's clever positions, there was no hedge and no useful diversification. Instead of superb diversification in LTCM's portfolio, suddenly everything was strongly correlated.

Suddenly there was virtually no liquidity for the unusual, lower-grade securities LTCM owned most. Of course, given sufficient time, the market and its prices would eventually and inevitably become rational, but as John Maynard Keynes had warned long ago, "Markets can remain irrational longer than you can remain solvent." When they really *need* to sell, sellers don't choose the price, buyers do. A buyers' market was exactly what LTCM did not want.

When things go badly, the smart borrower doesn't wait for the lender to call. The smart borrower always makes the first call. So John Meriwether called his major banker: Jon Corzine at Goldman Sachs.

"We've had a serious markdown . . . but everything is fine with us." The words were reassuring. So was the tone of voice. But they always were when the very calm, understated, and self-contained and private caller was John Meriwether. J.M. was *always* calm and *always* understated, so his calmness this particular morning meant absolutely nothing. Corzine had enough experience and ample reason to know better than to feel reassured by Meriwether's call. First, the early morning call was not to his office; it was to his home. Second, it was starkly out of character for the secretive Meriwether to say *anything* about LTCM's portfolio, particularly anything as blatantly negative as "We've had a serious markdown."

As a long-experienced bond dealer who had made a career of buying billions of dollars of bonds that other people didn't want, Corzine was sensitive to signals, particularly any unusual or unexpected signal, and Meriwether was sending a soft, subtle, but very unusual, very unexpected—and therefore clearly significant—signal.

Corzine and Meriwether were contemporaries, knew each other well, had great respect for each other as major dealers, and understood markets and dealing in similar ways. They held similar beliefs about the changing nature of the world's capital markets and the increasingly attractive opportunities for highly profitable principal, proprietary investments, particularly in fixed-income arbitrage operations. Both men were unpretentious Midwesterners and comfortable within themselves—and both men were determined to win on a giant scale.

Corzine called Meriwether back because he wanted to know more—a lot more. He matched Meriwether's calmness with his own. Instead of saying, "J.M., you've been way too secretive. I know you're in a major jam. So you've got to come completely clean with us now or we'll cut your credit lines way back," Corzine simply cautioned: "We aren't getting adequate feedback. It could hurt your credit standing."

Corzine and Meriwether both knew the essential reality of the situation: LTCM was no longer in control. It would have to change its ways. Arrogant secrecy was over, a thing of the past. Now LTCM would have to share important information with its creditors, and that meant the creditors would learn things their traders could use to trade against LTCM, inevitably making the problem, however serious it proved to be, that much worse.

Given its extraordinarily high leverage, the adversities facing LTCM had developed rapidly. Calm as he seemed, Meriwether was quickly and quietly exploring extraordinary moves, searching for the best way to go. Possibilities ranged from raising a huge capital infusion from investors to selling LTCM to a "white knight."

Early Monday morning, Warren Buffett of Berkshire Hathaway turned down an invitation to take over LTCM's entire portfolio. Later that same day, George Soros agreed to invest $500 million in LTCM at the end of August *if* Meriwether could raise another $500 million from other sources in those two weeks. Meriwether's negotiation with Soros was a dance of opposites. Meriwether was casual, Midwestern, and pragmatic while Soros, an Eastern European, was formal and conceptual. Meriwether's investing was rational and based on precise, predictive mathematical models, while Soros saw markets as organic, "reflexive," and unpredictable. Still, Soros and Meriwether had one thing in common: Soros's funds had just lost $2 billion in Russia.

J.P. Morgan & Company was ready to invest $200 million, and some bankers thought Merrill Lynch *might* come in with $300 million. But on Wednesday, Merrill Lynch called to say no. Because of the need for a swift decision, LTCM went back to Buffett, offering to cut its management fee in half if he would make a major investment in the fund. Again, Buffett said no.

The tension of the situation can best be appreciated if the reader assumes he or she was one of the LTCM general partners who had been experiencing this series of extraordinary moments:

- On the same Thursday that Buffett said no, LTCM lost $277 million. Only one prior day had ever been worse.
- Banks to which LTCM owed $167 million demanded repayment, saying the fund's poor results were a "default event." But the management company could not meet the demand; it had no ready money. And, as "insiders," the partners certainly couldn't make withdrawals—even to pay off their personal loans—when results were poor and they were asking others to increase their investments.
- Rumors flew through Wall Street that Goldman Sachs traders were selling what LTCM held in its highly leveraged positions. So were other dealers.
- During tough, sometimes confrontational negotiations with its crucial clearing broker, Bear Stearns, LTCM had refused, as a negotiating tactic,

to sign a formal clearing agreement. So LTCM had never gotten a signed guarantee from Bear Stearns to clear its trades. This meant Bear Stearns was free to stop clearing at any time—and if and when Bear Stearns quit, nobody would rush in to take over LTCM's complex clearing business.

LTCM partners were able—just barely—to persuade another commercial bank to take over a nearly $50 million bank loan that had just been called. Far more significantly, the partners, as individuals, had borrowed $38 million against their own investments in the fund so they could pay large year-end staff bonuses. Mechanically clever and technically legal, borrowing from already leveraged accounts was highly unusual and clearly whispered that the LTCM partners were skating into a very gray zone. Rumor on the Street was that the partners were feeling trapped. If the management company went into default, trading counterparties could claim immediate payment in cash. And if several counterparties tried to settle quickly, they would precipitate a ruinous run on LTCM.

Meriwether, twice cautious after having been burned a few years before for not informing the Federal Reserve Bank about Salomon Brothers' embarrassing involvement in a Treasury bond scandal, called New York Federal Reserve president William McDonough to advise him that LTCM would need more money.

Corzine got another call from Meriwether on Friday, the 11th—in Vienna, Austria, where Corzine was on vacation. LTCM's "assets in the box" had dropped below the $500 million minimum Bear Stearns required to continue clearing LTCM's transactions, so Bear Stearns had called LTCM: Its inspection team was coming to examine LTCM's books—on Sunday. Unless fully satisfied, Bear Stearns would immediately stop clearing LTCM's trades. Without a clearing broker, LTCM would be out of business. Period. To keep Bear Stearns, LTCM needed more equity capital. That's why Meriwether called Corzine: LTCM needed big money in a big hurry.

One billion dollars would be too little. LTCM needed $2 billion—and it needed it *now*. Corzine and Goldman Sachs were the best chance, and maybe the only chance, of finding a savior that would put up that kind of money that fast.

Goldman Sachs's overall business strategy had been shifting, in response to changing markets and business conditions, toward capital-intensive, risk-taking proprietary trading. That's why Corzine had been increasingly interested in developing the kind of high-tech proprietary trading business that had been so profitable for LTCM. Now he recognized a major opportunity to move the firm decisively in the direction he believed best—a move that would also consolidate his position as the firm's undisputed leader.

Corzine knew his negotiating position vis-à-vis Meriwether had suddenly become very strong. Dealing from strength, he now offered Meriwether a proposition that was clearly tough, but just as clearly reasonable, given LTCM's grievously strained circumstances. For half ownership of LTCM, Goldman Sachs would provide $1 billion—partly from the firm's own capital and partly from its clients—and commit to raise another $1 billion from outsiders. With the money would come the intangible but obvious advantages of LTCM's having Goldman Sachs's strong, explicit, public support. In exchange, Goldman Sachs would not only own half of LTCM's management company but also set limits on LTCM's trading exposures (tantamount to taking full control of the fund's portfolio structure) and get complete knowledge of LTCM's investment strategies and analytic models, which Goldman Sachs could then use in its own proprietary trading operations.

The deal was conditional on Goldman Sachs's delivering the capital infusion and on an examination of LTCM's books, so both sides began working through LTCM's files immediately. Any deal involving a major commitment of the partners' capital would, of course, require approval of the newly formed successor to Goldman Sachs's management committee, the executive committee, but Corzine was increasingly thinking and acting not as a senior partner, but as the dominating CEO he envisioned himself to be.

As part of its insistence on maximum secrecy, LTCM had kept its long trades and its short trades at separate banks. Since the banks could not be sure the hedges were correctly paired, they had required somewhat more than the absolute minimum margin. If the hedges could each be paired up at the same bank, that extra margin could be released and the financial squeeze would be relaxed. Fine in concept, but as always, the devil would be in the details. LTCM did not run a simple business; it used extraordinary diversification to minimize the risk of any one position or specific group of positions going sour. As a result, LTCM had thirty-eight *thousand* different paired positions—with every pair carefully separated and each side housed at a different bank. Matching up all those pairs would take a lot of time. So LTCM was not only short of cash but also short of time.

The major irony was blatant: LTCM desperately needed *now* the $2.7 billion it had insisted that investors take back just months earlier. A Street-savvy guy at Bear Stearns gave a cold, blunt appraisal of LTCM: "It's all over. When you're down by half, people won't refinance your trades. They'll push the market against you. You're *finished*." LTCM's partners, sensing that LTCM might not make it, scrambled to protect their personal assets. One partner, recently worth half a billion dollars, was reduced to paying for work on his expensive new home out of his wife's checking account. Meriwether quietly put his own real estate in his wife's name.

Later some observers said Goldman Sachs's traders, working out of London and Tokyo, were selling short the positions they knew LTCM held and then, to cover those shorts, were offering to buy them from LTCM at depressed prices. Goldman Sachs was certainly trading actively, but if its traders were front-running LTCM, other dealers were surely doing much the same. In the global bond markets, the squeeze was on LTCM—particularly in volatility—and all the major dealers knew LTCM, with massive positions outstanding in futures and options, was massively short volatility. They knew LTCM would get increasingly desperate to cover its short positions, would have to come to them, and would have to pay up, greatly increasing their profits. Dealers all understood the rules of the market: if they knew enough about the way institutions were moving their portfolios, they could and would profit by using this market information in their proprietary portfolio operations. That profit opportunity was why Goldman Sachs had decided to get into proprietary trading in a major way and, as advocates told their partners, "learn to live with the conflicts of interest."

The month of August was cruel for hedge funds. Most lost serious money. But LTCM did far worse—its equity capital was cut down by 45 percent, or $1.9 billion, in that single month. August was the worst month ever for credit spreads. Irrational as it may have been in the long run, in the short run credit spreads expanded to record levels and moved strongly and "irrationally" against the historically "normal" assumptions so essential to LTCM's sophisticated market models. With the severe lack of liquidity in the market, LTCM couldn't sell portfolio positions to raise capital. It lost nearly $2 billion. LTCM also lost all hope of George Soros's delivering a major capital infusion.

Meriwether's regular monthly letter, containing some of the troubling news, was faxed to LTCM's investors early in September. Leaked to the press, it caused traders at other hedge funds to sell out any positions they thought LTCM might hold and would now have to try to sell. During September, the spreads that LTCM had confidently expected would *shrink* instead kept *expanding* as other dealers and hedge funds made increasingly large bets against LTCM, knowing its positions were huge and that sooner or later LTCM would have to come to them.

LTCM's portfolio was still huge: $125 billion—and now fifty-five *times* its shrinking equity capital. In addition, it held a large package of high-octane derivatives. With another portfolio loss of less than 2 percent, the management company and the partners would be wiped out. In mathematical theory, the odds of such an event actually happening had been nearly impossible just a few months before. But in real markets, traders say bell-shaped curves have "fat tails"—events that are very unlikely but do happen and cause great damage, recently popularized as "black swans." The highly improbable was now threatening to become grim reality.

Corzine's concerns about how to deal with the accelerating problems at LTCM were magnified by large losses in Goldman Sachs's own proprietary trading portfolio. Because they used similar models and similar data, the firm's traders had been taking positions similar to LTCM's. Losses in the proprietary bond-trading portfolio were losses that came right out of Corzine's partners' pockets. And he knew that the last time Goldman Sachs had come close to an IPO, it had been stopped by, among other adverse events, losses in the firms' proprietary trading portfolios.

Goldman Sachs's long-planned IPO was due to come to market the very next month. For Corzine, the IPO was by far the most important trade in a lifetime of trading—the most important test of his professional career, particularly since he had become managing partner, and also the most important for him personally. While Corzine never seemed to care about wealth except as a convenience, if the IPO came off as hoped, his personal stake would be worth over $250 million. He would be a very rich man with massive liquid assets and, at fifty-two, the personal freedom to stay or to leave the firm.[1] But if the IPO was put off—perhaps for several years—Corzine's percentage stake in the firm would decline, perhaps significantly. And if the firm did not go public now, it could be years before another opportunity could be found to ensure permanent capital. During those years of deferral, partners' shares were sure to change, particularly for senior partners who went limited and retired—a group that could include Corzine himself. Corzine was highly motivated to find a way to solve LTCM's problem, which was now the linchpin to launching the IPO.

Corzine understood that the major investors Goldman Sachs would be asking to join in a rescue had already been called—often several times—by LTCM itself. One specific possibility, already called several times, was obvious to everyone: Warren Buffett at Berkshire Hathaway. Buffett said he might be interested in buying LTCM's entire portfolio at its depressed market valuation, but he wanted no part of LTCM's management company or the LTCM partners.

Derivatives added a whole new dimension of pyramiding to the situation at LTCM. They had real potential for a disaster. LTCM had arranged seven thousand different derivative contracts with several dozen counterparties. Default on any *one* derivative contract could throw *all* those contracts into technical default. Their total notional value was spectacularly large—nearly $1.5 trillion, or $5,000 for every man, woman, and child in America—and they involved almost every major financial institution in the United States in the complex spiderweb that now had LTCM at its center.

Meanwhile, during the second week of September, trading losses kept hammering LTCM:

- On Thursday, $145 million was lost.
- On Friday, another $120 million was lost.

And during the third week of September, while initially less severe, LTCM's losses continued:

- On Monday, $5 million was lost.
- On Tuesday, $87 million was lost.
- On Wednesday, another $122 million was lost.

A tiny profit on Thursday was no help: Cumulatively, LTCM had lost over half a billion dollars in less than two weeks. In one month it had lost nearly 60 percent of its equity capital. And volatility spreads kept rising from one record level to another, driving still more LTCM losses.

Goldman Sachs was LTCM's only hope—and the capital gap it needed to cover had now jumped from $2 billion to $4 billion. John Thain, the firm's CFO and an increasingly central member of Goldman Sachs's senior management—a rational market technocrat with direct experience in the bond business—was moving into a key decision-making role. He didn't see a way to raise that much money for LTCM, but the firm would keep trying.

Another possibility was floated past Warren Buffett: a joint bid, perhaps with AIG, the giant and innovative insurer that had extensive experience with derivatives, for LTCM's whole portfolio *without* the management company. Buffett wasn't interested.

Corzine briefed president McDonough at the New York Fed, and McDonough called the other major banks. All agreed that an LTCM failure would seriously disrupt the nation's and the world's financial markets. Given the Fed's long-standing hands-off policy toward the capital markets, McDonough wanted to have a Wall Street leader take up the task of privately organizing a cooperative. But he and John Whitehead, Goldman Sachs's former managing partner and now chairman of the New York Fed, quickly agreed that no one person had the necessary stature or clout to do the job. McDonough accepted Corzine's offer to brief the Fed on LTCM's portfolio on Sunday, but fearing that any sign of urgency could upset the sensitive money markets, stayed with a previous plan to fly to London and sent his deputy instead. Before leaving, McDonough called Fed chairman Alan Greenspan and Treasury secretary Robert Rubin in Washington to warn them that LTCM probably couldn't raise the necessary capital.

Corzine was still hoping to find a solution, but he was hitting walls. Making contact with UBS's derivatives expert, who happened to be in New York that week, to ask if UBS would help, Corzine was surprised to learn that UBS was already LTCM's largest equity investor. Corzine was naturally angry about being underinformed or even misled—again—by LTCM. He would have to focus on Buffett.

As it happened, Buffett was with Bill Gates on a vacation float-trip in Alaska's fjords, where the sonic shadows of the steep mountains would break up cell-phone calls for more than an hour at a time. Buffett told Corzine it was okay for Goldman Sachs to work out the specifics of a Berkshire Hathaway takeover of LTCM so long as the management company and John Meriwether were specifically excluded. Such a takeover would require $4 billion to $5 billion. Only Berkshire Hathaway had that kind of money on hand *and* a decision maker like Buffett. Even so, Buffett would probably insist on a co-investment by Goldman Sachs.

Realities were now slamming hard into LTCM from several directions. Reality one: Awareness was spreading that LTCM had not hedged its highly leveraged portfolio against the specific risk of market volatility and a flight to quality. Reality two: LTCM's major counterparties on derivatives trades were now about to lose $2.8 billion even if the market calmed. Reality three: The global markets were *not* calm, so derivatives counterparties' losses might *double* to $5 billion. Fed executives worried that the markets, which were sure to drop sharply if LTCM went into default, might not be able to trade at all. This could create a dreadful fourth reality: loss of order and even panic in the nation's and then the world's capital markets.

On Sunday, Corzine spoke again with Buffett in Alaska. Corzine was still unable to make a firm commitment of Goldman Sachs capital. His partners—particularly investment banking partners—were outraged by the losses already taken and the real danger that Goldman Sachs might be saddled with more risk, have its capital tied up for months or years, and might even lose it all. Corzine called the Treasury Department to caution against expecting a private-sector bailout. He encouraged the Treasury to arrange an emergency bank consortium.

In markets around the world, dealers complained that other dealers were trading against LTCM's positions. In those complaints, Goldman Sachs was cited for being particularly aggressive. On Monday, September 21, LTCM lost $553 million—over one-third of its remaining equity capital. With a $100 billion portfolio, this put LTCM's portfolio leverage up to an extreme level: Debt was one hundred times its equity capital. Even a tiny hiccup could now be fatal.

Bear Stearns insisted on $500 million in coverage capital, essentially a security deposit, and Chase accepted its obligation to provide that amount based on a previously negotiated loan agreement. LTCM actually got $470 million—not the full $500 million—from Chase and its syndicate of twenty-four banks because Crédit Agricole, the French bank, refused to honor its part of the commitment.

As a bond dealer, Corzine kept his options close to his vest while working to develop others. He had been working with Merrill Lynch's brainy president, Herb Allison, on the design of a collective approach involving Wall Street's leading banks, but was still hoping he would be able to preempt the collective bailout with a Goldman-Berkshire bid for the whole LTCM portfolio.

At 7:30 a.m. on Tuesday, September 22, the New York Fed hosted breakfast for Corzine and Thain of Goldman Sachs, Roberto Mendoza of J.P. Morgan, and David Komansky and Herb Allison of Merrill Lynch. Allison lacks a commanding physical presence, but his rational brilliance was clear to everyone. To survive, LTCM needed $4 billion. If allowed to fail, the losses to the group could total $20 billion. Allison summarized: "We're all in this together. This is a *very* complex problem and we all know that in order to work, a complex problem *must* have a simple answer. In addition, as the nation's leading financial institutions, don't we have an obligation to the public?"

The global context for LTCM's crisis was deeply concerning. Russia and South America were both moving toward recession. The Fed would not protect the banks that had lent to LTCM. Its proper position was that, as free-market participants, they should absorb the losses of roughly $300 million apiece. But the problem might not be confined to LTCM. Corzine, who got almost no sleep for four days, says today, "It scared the hell out of me." After two hours of discussion, the bankers agreed to explore a clever proposal developed by Mendoza of J.P. Morgan to divide LTCM's positions into two baskets—one of debt securities and one of equities—and then sell the securities back to the issuing corporations at discounts that would make the offering a proposition they could not refuse. That would leave the bank consortium to swallow a smaller, known, and limited loss. But the implementation details couldn't be worked out in the time available, so the group turned to their one remaining alternative: Allison's proposal for a consortium investment by all the major banks.[2]

Corzine was now engaged in a two-front strategic battle. On one front, LTCM was in extremely serious trouble and a solution, not yet in place, was urgently needed. On the other front, Goldman Sachs's own proprietary trading losses in just the past two months had totaled a stunning $1.5 billion. This huge loss, combined with falling equity prices, would oblige the firm to postpone the IPO on which Corzine had expended so much of his personal leadership capital. Moreover, the firm's losses were concentrated in Corzine's overseas bond positions, so he was losing personal stature within the firm. Those losses were now *partners'* personal losses. A few months ago, each partner "knew" what wealth he might have with an IPO; now the partners faced real money losses. The double whammy concentrated their minds on Corzine and his adventurous trading. Understandably, they did not like what they were seeing.

That Tuesday, LTCM lost another $152 million. Now, with no alternative approaches, everyone focused on Allison of Merrill Lynch and his consortium strategy. The only way to achieve the necessary cooperation among so many banks and firms on such short notice would be for the Fed—even though it would not be proper for it to support any specific plan—to call a meeting of all the banks. This was agreed late in the afternoon, and a dozen major banks were informed that an emergency meeting would be held at the New York Federal Reserve Bank that very evening at eight. The four largest banks agreed to meet at the Fed an hour earlier. Merrill Lynch's plan would have sixteen banks each invest $250 million to reach the $4 billion capital infusion that John Thain had specified was necessary. If the group put up less than $4 billion, speculators would be too tempted to try to break the bank, as a decade before they had broken the Bank of England, forcing a devaluation of the British pound.

The four major banks were still arguing terms. Would the $4 billion be entirely a loan, or would some part have to be equity? Would LTCM's partners stay? Who would have control? On the last, Corzine was insistent: LTCM could *not* be in control. When the arguments went on past 8 p.m. without resolution, the other bankers, who had been cooling their heels, were brought in and told that while the Fed would maintain strict neutrality, it expected the private sector to find a workable solution to protect the integrity of the system.

Allison summarized Merrill's plan on one sheet of paper. Lehman Brothers objected to each firm's having to put up an equal share of the reserve fund; it proposed scaling contributions to match each firm's exposure. Others cut in saying that would be too complicated because each bank had its own risk model, so valuations—and "fair shares"—would differ way too much for resolution, given the shortness of time. Three hours later, at 11 p.m., the bankers' formal meeting was adjourned until 10 a.m. the next day. But informal work on specific terms continued until 1 a.m., when Corzine was briefed. Allison's plan could work—if everyone cooperated—and if it did work, it would be the first $4 billion fund-raising ever done in a single day.

At ten the next morning, forty-five bankers assembled at the New York

Federal Reserve Bank. Bear Stearns's CEO, Jimmy Cayne, began with this blunt warning: "If you want this to work, don't go alphabetically"—don't start by asking Bear Stearns.

New York Fed president McDonough, who had just flown in from London, quickly postponed the meeting for three hours, saying only, "Not all avenues have been exhausted." He did not say that Corzine and Thain had just taken him aside to whisper that Warren Buffett was ready to bid for the whole portfolio. McDonough called Buffett and got his confirmation. Instead of feeling relieved, when the bankers learned of this, most were angry that Corzine was playing games with them behind their backs.[3] Such solo initiatives by Corzine had already angered the partners of Goldman Sachs.

Buffett's bid—joint with Goldman Sachs and AIG—came in at 11:40 on a single page: $250 million to buy LTCM, with $3.75 billion more to be invested in the fund immediately to ensure stability. (The $4 billion was just over 5 percent of the value of LTCM's portfolio only ten months before.) Of the total, $3 billion would come from Berkshire Hathaway. Buffett's bid was good until a 12:30 deadline—just fifty minutes away.

It didn't matter. The deal couldn't be made. There were too many different parties at interest with dozens of counterparties to derivative contracts, plus a series of hub-and-spokes partnerships. It would be impossible to reset all their different contracts. And unfortunately, the Goldman Sachs investment banker covering Berkshire Hathaway had misunderstood the complex structure of LTCM, so he had not given Buffett the specific guidance that would have been necessary to formulate a correct bid. Once again, the devil was in the details. Buffett's bid as written was for LTCM, the *management* company, not the LTCM *portfolio*. Even so, there was a chance: If the Goldman-Berkshire-AIG bid were converted into an investment in the fund, as opposed to the management company, it might work because Buffett's group could still fire the LTCM partners. But just then, Buffett's boat went behind an Alaskan mountain and he could not be reached by cell phone. Minutes ticked away. The time limit on Buffett's bid was fixed. The clock kept ticking, and in half an hour the time ran out—before contact could be made.

The only option still viable was the bankers' consortium bid developed by Merrill Lynch's Allison. Even though he was not sure they would all come, McDonough called in the banks. They did all return, but their mood had been soured by the morning's events. Bear Stearns refused to participate, just as it had said it would. It already had more than enough exposure as LTCM's clearing agent. After a brief recess during which urgent pleas were made to it, Bear Stearns did agree to say to all the banks that it had no special knowledge causing it not to participate.

Tensions continued to rise as one after another banker got petulant and self-protective. Chase Manhattan's CEO, William Harrison, was furious: "Goldman Sachs is trading against the Street!" Morgan Stanley's Phil Purcell was in the consortium—and then out—until Allison said, "Call your capital-market traders and ask *them*." Purcell was told: "Herb's right. If you guys don't do this, and do it damn soon, it'll be a fucking catastrophe!" Then the French took a walk—followed by Bankers Trust's CEO, Frank Newman. During those tension-packed hours, it seemed that every bank was out of the deal at one point or another. As Allison recalls, "They were not seeing the big picture—how Wall Street would look to the whole world if the deal fell through and we failed."

Corzine insisted on signed contracts to lock in the LTCM partners, so they could be told exactly what to do or not do—a major change, of course, from his previous goal of partnering with Meriwether. Corzine called Meriwether to confirm that there would be full acceptance by LTCM of his tough terms. Nobody in the room at the Fed knew or suspected what lay ahead for Corzine, except Thain, who was taking calls in the conference room on his cell phone. Thain was speaking so quietly he couldn't be heard, but his facial expression signaled that he was struggling with grave concerns. He was *at* the meeting, but not *in* the meeting. He was providing updates on the negotiations to three other members of the Goldman Sachs executive committee. Those four would soon complete a coup d'état and oust Corzine.

The Merrill Lynch consortium plan assumed that sixteen banks would each commit $250 million, but when several banks refused to go that high, it was clear that the majors would each have to go up even higher—to $300 million apiece. Corzine, the only CEO who was also an experienced bond trader, had wanted to play the essential leadership role, but his partners were less caught up in the time urgency of endorsing the consortium strategy and were much more concerned about the potential costs and risks to Goldman Sachs. They made this clear in messages via Thain's cell phone, which Thain then whispered to Corzine. Hank Paulson said it all: "Get the hell out of there!"

Corzine couldn't go above $250 million without the approval of his executive committee, which had only *very* reluctantly authorized $250 million. He certainly didn't have his partners' authorization for an additional $50 million.[4] Considering himself essentially the CEO of a major firm and an expert in bonds and bond trading, Corzine found it embarrassing to need his partners' permission. But he knew that preparations for the IPO, the large, recent bond losses, and the accumulating issues surrounding the firm's leadership made it doubtful that the partners could absorb yet another stress. Given the stupendous personal financial stakes involved, political alignments within the firm were still in play as individuals counted up "their" IPO wealth. Even Corzine, politically sensitive as he had always been, really didn't know now just what his partners would say and do. But he did know most would be enraged, and many disgusted, with a jumbo capital commitment to bail out LTCM.

With the table stakes now at $300 million, Allison was going around the huge table, calling out each bank in turn for its commitment. If Goldman Sachs and the other major organizations came in at $300 million each and a few smaller banks came in for less, the consortium would—just barely—have the necessary $4 billion, including what equity capital remained at LTCM. Lehman Brothers couldn't do a whole unit, only $100 million. Bear Stearns refused to participate at all. And everyone knew that Chase didn't want to participate.

As Allison continued around the table, collecting commitments from most of the banks represented—including Chase—Corzine turned to Sandy Warner, chairman of J.P. Morgan, who was sitting next to him. They had become friendly during recent talks about possibly putting their two organizations together, so the basis for man-to-man candor had been established. Corzine whispered: "My partners *really* don't want to do this. And if I do, I'll have a massive need to persuade—and I'll probably have to leave Goldman Sachs."

One bank after another committed to $300 million. Only two banks had not yet been called: J.P. Morgan and Goldman Sachs.

Suddenly it was Corzine's turn. "Goldman Sachs?"

Corzine, the cool trader, never blinked. As though it were the most ordinary item of an ordinary day, he said, "Goldman Sachs is in for three hundred."

Morgan too was in for $300 million—and the deal was done.* Herb Allison later estimated the potential losses throughout the financial system of a failure to solve the problem presented by LTCM at an astounding $50 billion.

Many details still had to be resolved. Goldman Sachs insisted that its lawyer, John Mead of Sullivan & Cromwell, had to participate in the follow-on negotiations, representing only Goldman Sachs, while the consortium would be represented by Skadden Arps. An oversight committee was established to supervise LTCM's portfolio. The consortium would get half the management company for $1. LTCM's partners were obliged to sign employment contracts, with compensation for the group fixed at $250 million, with no bonus or incentives—a drastic pay cut for that supercompensated group. Goldman Sachs's lawyer insisted that LTCM's partners give personal guarantees of the accuracy of LTCM's financial statements and that the new money invested by the consortium be guaranteed absolute protection from any future lawsuits stemming from past actions.

Sunday evening, September 27, Robert Katz, Goldman Sachs's chief counsel, startled the negotiators by stating that the firm would not stay in the consortium unless Chase agreed not to require payment on its $500 million loan to LTCM. Chase, which had already made several concessions, was not prepared to go that far. When Corzine confirmed Goldman Sachs's hard line, Chase's man exploded with expletives—and then, very reluctantly, agreed to leave Chase's $500 million with LTCM.

Goldman Sachs's executive committee would meet at 6:30 Monday morning for a final decision. But knowing that the consortium could not wait for such a critical decision, Corzine checked with some of his partners and got their okay to say Sunday evening that Goldman Sachs was definitely in the consortium for $300 million.

During the first two weeks of the new arrangement, LTCM lost another $750 million—and then it stabilized. Over the next two years, LTCM's positions were gradually liquidated—at a modest profit to the consortium—because, as markets became rational again, the portfolio of perfect-arbitrage paired positions proved that Meriwether and his Nobel laureates were, as they always knew they were,

---

* This was almost certainly the largest-ever rescue effort by U.S. banks. The best-known previous bankers' pool, organized by Thomas W. Lamont of J.P. Morgan on October 24, 1929, during the Crash, began with $20 million (approximately $200 million in today's dollars) and was increased the next day to $40 million per bank. Over the next five weeks, the pool bought $129 million ($1.3 billion in today's dollars) of such major stocks as U.S. Steel, AT&T, General Electric, and American Can.

very right. But Keynes was right too: "Markets can remain irrational longer than you can remain solvent." And bell curves do have fat tails.

Still, Corzine was not a corporate CEO, and he had clearly not gotten partners' approval in the only way major decisions, particularly decisions involving the partners' capital, had always been made since Sidney Weinberg set up the management committee as a governor on Gus Levy. Capital was the scarce resource at Goldman Sachs, and Corzine had committed a big chunk of the firm's capital at a time when his own area of the firm, fixed income, was incurring major trading losses. Capital would now be tied up in a deal that at the time seemed likely to have low returns, particularly in comparison to other choices available to the firm, and quite possibly the LTCM capital commitment would incur losses.

On Monday, September 28, after twelve years of preparation, Goldman Sachs canceled its public offering. Sure, an IPO could be brought forward at some time in the future, but fourth-quarter earnings were seriously disappointing. It could easily be several years before the market would again be right for a Goldman Sachs IPO. And for senior partners who wanted to go limited, deferring the IPO was tantamount to taking money right out of their pockets—money they'd so recently thought was as good as theirs. And they knew the man to blame.

33

COUP

I n October 1998, Jon Corzine agreed to have breakfast with another partner at the Savoy Hotel, where he was staying in London. Two things made
it unusual: It was seven in the morning—on a Sunday. And an article in the
business section of London's *Sunday Times* carried a story that Corzine would be
pushed out of Goldman Sachs by John Thornton and John Thain.*

"Have you seen the story in this morning's paper?" the colleague asked on
the way to the dining room.

"Yeah, I saw it."

"What are you going to do about it?"

"I'm not sure."

"You should be sure, Jon. Since you're wearing a business suit, I assume you
have another meeting scheduled this morning, so here's what you should do:
Cancel any other meetings you've booked. Go directly to Heathrow and fly back
to the States. Before you take off, call Roy Zuckerberg and Bob Hurst and tell
them to meet you at your house in New Jersey today and make it absolutely clear

---

* Only the first edition carried the story, which apparently was quashed in all subsequent editions. But other newspapers carried references to the original article later that day.

to everyone that before the executive committee meets Monday morning, both Thain and Thornton are out—fired for playing politics and doing it in public so that it hurts the firm.

"If you do this immediately, everyone will understand and will back you. And if you don't, you'll be in real trouble, because in six months *they* will force *you* out."

"I couldn't do that," replied Corzine. "It would hurt the firm."

In iconic symbolism, Corzine and his partner could not even have their breakfast in the Savoy. The dining room was closed. It was never open as early as seven on a Sunday morning.

In four months, Jon Corzine was forced out by four members of the firm's executive committee—John Thain, John Thornton, Hank Paulson, and Bob Hurst. Many small parts came together like the pieces of a jigsaw puzzle to complete the picture that Corzine had to go.

Corzine had offended the firm's investment bankers by unilaterally committing $300 million to bail out Long-Term Capital Management when he was authorized to commit no more than $250 million—and getting approval even for that had been a struggle. Bad enough to make huge capital commitments to proprietary trading activities they didn't fully understand, but bailing out another firm with such enormous amounts of their precious capital was going way too far. His various independent and secret sorties into merger discussions rankled, particularly his approaches to Chase Manhattan Bank, Morgan Bank, and, in early 1998, Mellon Bank. Corzine's informal, intuitive, undisciplined way of making senior-level executive decisions would not fit with the responsibility of a CEO of a publicly owned corporation. And his unilateral strategic thrusts were completely at odds with the "one man, one vote" tradition and structure of the management committee, as was his unbridled style of trading. Corzine was too unpredictable. Examples were numerous. The case against him had accumulated steadily over his four years as chairman. As one committee member explained, "Corzine made freestyle decisions on important questions again and again—literally hundreds of times." Another committee member recalled, "It was Jon's attitude and the way he did things—too solo, too sloppy, too unpredictable—and not appreciating or even recognizing the importance of the executive committee." Another committee member concludes: "The code of conduct at Goldman Sachs was based on absolute candor and straight talk, but from day one Jon was not always straight or consistent, particularly with the people he worked with most closely."

The single most rigorously disciplined management process in the firm was the selection every two years of partners. It took a lot of everyone's time, and everything was done very carefully over several months. Still, there were always last-minute changes to the list, both additions and deletions. One year, as the executive committee was putting the final list of new partners together, Corzine exclaimed, "Oh, Jesus! I forgot so-and-so! Help me out, guys. I'm pretty committed and need your help on this one. I had a long dinner with him in Tokyo and pretty much promised him then that he would make partner this year. He's doing great work, and we've got to make him a partner. Please, guys, just one more!" Corzine may have been comfortable with improvising to circumstance—a necessary skill for traders—but to professionals experienced in the rigors of investment banking, improvisation was just being sloppy.

Paulson and Corzine were never good at working together. They didn't really like each other, didn't really respect each other's ways of leading or managing, and their businesses were completely different. At the weekly executive committee meetings, they didn't just disagree, they increasingly squabbled and bickered. "They were like teenage kids," recalls Zuckerberg, who had warned his friend Corzine during those UN Plaza meetings. To others on the executive committee, it seemed that Paulson and Corzine argued all the time, often quite bitterly. Partners went to Zuckerberg and said, "Can't you help? You know both guys and they both trust you." During one executive committee meeting, it got so bad—close to throwing punches—that Zuckerberg decided he had to do something, so he made Paulson and Corzine stay behind, closed the door, and said firmly, "You *must* work this out! It will hurt the firm if you keep it up." Paulson's accumulated frustrations were so wide and deep that he nearly left in late 1997 but was persuaded to stay. The committee spent one whole weekend trying to find ways to work it out.

In May 1998 Corzine offered that they should work as co-CEOs after all. Zuckerberg said tartly, "You two show you can really work together—for just six months—and *then* I'll support your idea." Looking back, Zuckerberg laments, "Corzine as senior partner and Paulson as president—one a partnership title and the other a corporate title—made no sense. It was cockamamie. When Corzine said, 'Let's go co. It's fine with me. I don't give a damn,' he was wrong—wrong to think they could work together and wrong about Paulson." Still, the committee decided to accept Corzine and Paulson's commitment to try to work together.

That same spring, the firm decided to launch the initial public offering in the fall. But market turbulence originating with Russia's financial crisis compelled a postponement.

The conclusion that Corzine had to go was not based on any one thing. One part of the jigsaw puzzle was structural: Corzine's decision to maintain a six-member executive committee rather than a larger management committee and then, ignoring advice, to let Silfen and then Zuckerberg go limited without adding strong, loyal supporters of his own choosing onto the committee. Another was his treating the executive committee as not all that important and acting like an all-powerful, freewheeling CEO; the others on the executive committee believed the committee was the ultimate power in the partnership and that all decision making rested with that committee on behalf of the partners. A third piece of the puzzle: Corzine was so confident of strong support across the large partnership that he somehow didn't recognize that broad support could be trumped by the small executive committee. He had been losing support in the committee and should have known it had the power, if it wanted to, to take him out—not simply out of being senior partner and chairman of the management committee, but right out of the partnership itself.

Aborting the IPO in September after announcing it just three months before had been embarrassing, particularly to the firm's investment bankers. More pungently, postponing the IPO—after showing individuals exactly how much money they would make—was certainly disconcerting to the 200 owners, 345 additional managing directors, and 16,500 employees who would each have benefited. Moreover, for Goldman Sachs to have lost nearly $1 billion in trading, often in positions similar to those that took down LTCM, was professionally humiliating to many at the firm. Tension between the firm's bankers and traders was heightened when trading losses suddenly wiped away the distributable profits of a record surge in banking fees.

An important component of the case against Corzine came from the personal decisions of individual committee members. In 1996 David Silfen, having decided he wasn't going to be made managing partner and wasn't really interested in the job, felt he'd already done all he could do to build trading into a highly profitable power center. So other than loyalty to the firm and to individual partners, he saw no real reason to stay. As a trader, Silfen had an understanding of the business that was similar to Corzine's, so even though they had limited personal rapport, the two men usually had similar views on key decisions and Silfen almost always voted with Corzine.

Similarly, Zuckerberg enjoyed close rapport with Corzine and regularly supported him on decisions. As co-heads of Equities, Silfen and Zuckerberg shared a personal as well as professional understanding; they had worked together on an extensive and successful reorganization and a major strategic repositioning. Elevated to vice chairman in early 1997, Zuckerberg had built two strong businesses, had also gone as far as he could hope to go in stature and share ownership, was getting older, and was exasperated by the bickering at committee meetings between Paulson and Corzine. On November 27, 1998, Zuckerberg went limited—with an agreement that protected his ownership interest even though nobody thought an IPO could be relaunched in less than a year. He also offered some advice: "Jon, we've been friends for a long time. Please take some advice from a friend: You need to put some of your own people on the executive committee—people you can work well with and who will work well with you."

"Appreciate your thoughts, Roy, and really appreciate our friendship and how supportive you've always been, but I don't see a big need for change just now. We'll be okay."

"Jon, you really should think about it. They could bury you."

When Silfen retired, his seat on the committee was taken by John Thornton. Corzine's appointing Thornton indicated to some a good relationship, but the reality was more complex. Thornton opposed an IPO, which he saw as "only one hand clapping"; he felt that going public would inevitably lead to a megamerger with a major commercial bank and that the firm would be falling into the old trap of taking bold action before it had developed an overall strategy.

When Zuckerberg retired in 1998, his seat was left vacant and the executive committee was down to five members: Corzine Paulson, Hurst, Thain, and Thornton.

Other personal developments contributed to the growing opposition to Corzine. Thain had been posted to London for a year in 1995 before succeeding Corzine as chief financial officer. Corzine had known Thain well from their years as leaders in Fixed Income. They respected and appreciated each other and each other's skills, particularly in Risk Management. It was natural for Corzine to trust Thain and to send him as "one of my guys" to London. But Thain was not one of Corzine's deputies. Thain had always seen himself as independent and had always thought for himself.

In London, Thornton, a master of creating remarkable closeness in personal relationships with senior executives, bonded with Thain, an exceedingly numerate and rigorous analyst. Both men excelled at conceptual understanding and macro strategy. As a duo, Thain and Thornton were clearly stellar: an expansive "blue-water" conceptual strategist and creative top-level relationship banker paired with a computer-savvy CFO with highly successful leadership and managerial experience in Trading, Fixed Income, and Risk Management. Both had great experience and maturity, and both were young: Thornton was forty-one and Thain was thirty-nine. Neither was devoted to Corzine.

In 1994, Brian Griffiths, the firm's country adviser for the United Kingdom, had called Thornton to say, "John, have you heard the good news?"

"No, what have you heard, Brian?"

"Jon Corzine has been chosen as the firm's new senior partner. He's a real man of the people!"

"Damn! That's bad news, Brian. We don't need a man of the people. The firm needs a real leader."

Thornton had never met Corzine and had no opinion of him personally, but the firm was in crisis, and he felt the first priority in selecting a new senior partner should be strong leadership above all else.

Later, as a new member of the executive committee, Thornton quickly set the boundaries by telling Corzine: "Jon, you're in charge, so on ninety-nine percent of the issues that come to the executive committee, I'll give you my advice or volunteer my opinion but you'll make the ultimate decision. But one percent of the time—on the really big issues—I'll insist on the formal governance mechanism in the partnership agreement and vote as one of six—as we all should. Okay?"

"Understood. Not a problem."

For a firm whose previous senior partners had been so dedicated for so many years to developing relationships with major corporations, Corzine's proprietary trading priorities were surprisingly different. His focus was on markets, not on client corporations. Walking along Park Avenue after a dinner, Gene Fife, who'd just spent several hours with IBM's CEO, Lou Gerstner, bumped into Corzine and asked, "Do you know Gerstner?"

"No."

"Would you like me to see if I can arrange a meeting for you?" Anticipating that the managing partner of Goldman Sachs—or any other investment bank—would jump at the chance to spend quality time with the accomplished CEO of one of America's great corporations, Fife was startled by the response.

"Why would I want to do that?" The obvious implication: Such a meeting would be a waste of valuable time. Corzine was still thinking like a proprietary bond trader. Later, as Corzine had more opportunities to meet one-on-one with corporate CEOs, he found he enjoyed it and—with his warm, avuncular, unpretentious style and open manner—was effective. He steadily increased his time commitment to corporate clients overseas.

Corzine repeatedly had "private" conversations with other partners—private from Paulson. "Don't say anything about this to Hank. We'll just keep it between ourselves—where it belongs for now."

As the pieces of the puzzle came together, a consensus developed among the members of the executive committee: Corzine was not the right man to lead Goldman Sachs—particularly as CEO of a publicly owned company—and he was not going to change. He would always be too sloppy and unreliable for the giant, fast-changing, complex business organization that Goldman Sachs had become. The organization needed discipline at the center.

With Silfen and Zuckerberg out, Paulson, supported by Thornton and Thain, needed only one more vote. Thornton and Thain understood Paulson to be planning to stay only two transitional years before passing the baton of leadership to them. Hurst now became the key man. He had been unhappy with Corzine for a long time and had co-led banking with Paulson. Some thought it helped that

Hurst, unlike the other three, was Jewish, which could be silently important at what had once been known as a "Jewish firm." While Corzine and his family were skiing in Telluride, Colorado, over Christmas break, Paulson, Thornton, Thain, and Hurst worked out an agreement: Corzine would have to go.

Timing matters. Within a few weeks the executive committee was sure to be expanded from its unusually small size when Zuckerberg was replaced. And once the firm went public, changes in CEO would be made by the board of directors, not by the executive committee. If they were going to push Corzine out, it had to be now. Decisions on who was brought into or taken out of the partnership had long been with the committee. According to the revised partnership agreement, to terminate Corzine as senior partner they needed an 80 percent majority of the five remaining active members of the committee—or four votes. With Hurst, they *had* four and 80 percent. Paulson, Hurst, Thain, and Thornton met and agreed to vote to remove Corzine as senior partner.

When speculating about the way the coup was organized, some partners point to early meetings held at Bob Hurst's apartment; others emphasize John Thornton's extraordinary skills at "blow your mind" strategizing; and others say, "Never underestimate Hank Paulson." Insiders see Thain's decision as a switch from supporting the man he knew and liked to a man he thought better qualified to head a public company.

Thain, who had known Corzine longest and was trustee-designate for the Corzine children's trusts, was chosen to tell him this cold-steel deal: Corzine would serve until the IPO was completed—to ensure at least the appearance of stability—and then would have to fall on his sword and leave the firm. He had to accept. They had the votes—and they had the power to reduce his shares *before* the IPO if he resisted.

Corzine had no accessible group to appeal to except the full partnership, and there was not enough time for that. As one partner explained, "If the decision had been put to the whole partnership, Corzine would never have lost his position; he was too popular and had too many loyal friends. But in the small group, when he wasn't looking, he could be—and was—blindsided. It was like living the history of imperial Rome."[1]

Corzine had tears in his eyes when told the surprise of a lifetime, but he played it out like a man, calling key clients and the president of the New York

Federal Reserve Bank, William McDonough, to say he had decided to relinquish being CEO but would still be co-chair.

While all the turbulence at the top was going on, the day-to-day work of the firm continued just as strongly and steadily as ever. Corzine insisted that renewing detailed plans for the IPO should be a decision of all two hundred voting managing directors, but Paulson and Thornton believed those decisions should be made by the executive committee.

Blithely calling the notion of a palace coup "inaccurate in every respect," Paulson went on to say to the press, with practiced air-brushing for public perception, "This is an evolutionary transition in management and governance, something that made long-term sense for the firm. The firm is doing very well and we thought it made sense to put these changes in place before the public offering. This was an evolutionary transition in management and governance."[2]

The IPO was completed on May 9, and on May 18 Jon Corzine's resignation was announced. Corzine was in a bizarre situation, and while he dealt with it straightforwardly, bizarre stores sprang up quickly. For example, Corzine's limo took him one day from his home in Summit, New Jersey, to Goldman Sachs headquarters in lower Manhattan. He did not get out. Being in the middle of an important call on his cell phone, he continued working from the limo's rear seat. While he continued his phone call, his driver called Corzine's secretary to bring some papers. A writer from *New York* magazine converted this brief happenstance into the core of a feature story saying that Corzine did this every day—working all day from his limo parked on the street next to Goldman Sachs's downtown headquarters.

While he focused on the IPO, Corzine also came close to organizing a group of investors to take over Long-Term Capital Management. But in early February 2000 New Jersey senator Frank Lautenberg announced he would not run for reelection. This gave Corzine the opening he needed—in a new field. As he explained, "I like to compete, and I like to win. Being in a campaign is the most competitive thing I've ever done." Corzine spent $60 million and won the election. He served part of a term in the Senate and then successfully ran for governor of New Jersey.

34

GETTING INVESTMENT
MANAGEMENT RIGHT

One of the most profitable discussions in the history of Goldman Sachs took place over several weeks in 1995 between Hank Paulson and John McNulty. The essence of the strategy that they developed can be evoked by a simple analogy: The lovely eight-to-ten-foot trees we use to decorate our homes at Christmas would take twenty years to grow from seed, but the ones we buy are only six or seven years old; young sprigs are grafted into stumps with extensive, well-established root structures that provide so much nutrition that the sprouts develop and grow super-rapidly into full trees. McNulty—who had been consulting with Goldman Sachs Asset Management while on leave from the firm to recover from an early-age heart attack—convinced Paulson that grafting GSAM's investing onto Goldman Sachs's powerful distribution would produce rapid growth in assets managed and strong, almost riskless growth in profits.

Paulson assigned McNulty to work in GSAM with his friend David Ford. Things changed quickly at GSAM because Ford and McNulty were given important advantages compared to their predecessors. A decisive advantage was an agreement that their business success would be measured on the basis of the market value of assets brought under management—that is, on GSAM's *capacity* to generate future earnings, not on current *reported* earnings.

"I had an epiphany," said McNulty, "that the correct way to measure the economic value of GSAM was *not* current profits, but accumulated assets under management—from which future profits and future growth in profits could be harvested." Traditionally at Goldman Sachs, each line of business, no matter how complex its inner workings, was always evaluated on a simple standard: Did you make money today for the partnership? That's the way it was and had always been with traditional Wall Street partnerships. But that's not the way it is in other businesses, such as oil and gas exploration, life insurance and annuities, and investment management. In each of these businesses, the first year of a major success appears to be a loser. The only way to understand these businesses is to use managerial accounting that recognizes the present value of the long-term increases in the economic value of drilling holes, creating customers, or building a franchise that will produce many years of *future* earnings.

Fortunately for GSAM and for Goldman Sachs, Paulson liked and trusted McNulty enough to listen carefully to his reasoning. Having watched M&A bankers sell asset-management firms to financial behemoths for surprisingly high valuations relative to earnings, Paulson was ready to recognize that McNulty and Ford had come to a crucial understanding about the best way to manage GSAM. GSAM's value was not current profits, but the accumulation of assets under management.

Changing the whole concept of how to measure success got strong confirmation from an unlikely source: the investment banking division. Goldman Sachs had been involved as adviser and banker in acquisitions of several asset-management firms and had learned how and why the market valued them so highly. This understanding was key to the transformation in measuring results and accountability that would enable McNulty and Ford to transform GSAM and its business. It meant that there would be no basis for complaints—and it might even be best for the firm in the long run—if the GSAM business was run at only breakeven for several years, provided it was adding substantial assets under management. With profits coming from a captive fee-based business, the stock market and debt-rating agencies would value those reliably recurring profits far more highly dollar for dollar than trading profits or banking fees.

When they took over from Steve Friedman in 1994, Jon Corzine and Hank Paulson were determined to decide once and for all what to do with GSAM—and how to do it. By agreement, Paulson would concentrate on improving internal operations while Corzine focused on making acquisitions. Paulson liked and trusted McNulty and listened carefully to what he had to say because he knew McNulty was a smart, conceptual, aggressive entrepreneurial realist. McNulty said of Corzine and Paulson, "They didn't really understand the investment business, but they asked all sorts of questions and their focus gave us energy for success." After starting out in Private Client Services, McNulty had moved from division to division, consistently in management and consistently successful. He spent hours and hours with Paulson, explaining the nature of GSAM's business and how it could be converted into a real success. The argument that the rating agencies were more interested in a million dollars of fee-based income than an equal million dollars of income from trading carried special weight with Corzine and Paulson since, as a private partnership without permanent capital, Goldman Sachs had a lower credit rating than its major investment banking competitors.

An expert observer of firm politics, McNulty viewed his career with engagingly sardonic good humor. "This is our last job at Goldman Sachs, David," McNulty warned Ford. "We are pioneers. And you know what they do: They fight the Indians, clear the land, and take all the big risks. Years later, folks build statues to celebrate the pioneers that nobody can remember by name—and the pigeons come and shit all over them. So, David, that's our destiny: pigeon shit."

Behind the banter were two successful partners with every intention of converting GSAM from perpetual widow-maker into another big Goldman Sachs success. As Ford and McNulty saw things, if the fee-based investment-management business could be built up substantially, GSAM could become important strategically to the firm and particularly to Corzine and Paulson, who were focused on launching the firm's IPO at the highest possible valuation. Paulson and Corzine had put Ford and McNulty in charge of GSAM with a clear mandate: "Build up the asset-management business so it at *least* moves the needle." McNulty told Paulson, "I'll stay until GSAM is profitable"—and he did stay until July 2001 and the first surge in profitability.

With Corzine and Paulson as sponsors providing air cover to protect GSAM from internal challenges from other divisions, individual partners, or even the management committee, Ford, McNulty, and their team were off and running. Suzanne Donnahoe transferred in from Investment Banking, and David Blood and George Walker came over from the bond unit led by John Thain.[1]

McNulty and Ford were in a hurry to catch up with GSAM's opportunity. McNulty convinced Paulson that, to achieve success, the firm would have to hire top people from competing asset-management firms, which were also major customers of the other divisions, even if it hurt the firm in those other business lines. That's when Corzine and Paulson took the competitive gloves off by removing the constraints that had hindered predecessors. Not only could Ford and McNulty hire people from competitors, but they could now invest firm capital in building the GSAM business through acquisitions. In addition, GSAM was now free to compete aggressively for new business even though that business—new as it might be to GSAM—could be taken away from a firm that was an institutional client of Goldman Sachs's securities business. Paulson said he'd take the heat from other partners when their clients complained or punished the firm. He kept his promise to provide both air cover and capital.

Encouragingly, the firm soon learned that the institutions' bark was worse than their bite. While major stockbrokerage clients would threaten to cut off the firm if GSAM competed with them, with very few exceptions, the threats—no matter how loud or explicit—were just threats. The institutions needed Goldman Sachs and the liquidity the firm provided more than Goldman Sachs needed any one of them. And not only were the people making the threats a small minority among the institutional investors, but most of them did not and could not speak for their whole organizations. The institutional traders who cared most about doing block-trading business with the firm cared the least about competition at "bake-offs" for new pension accounts. With dozens of competitors vying for each account, they weren't about to stop or cut back on using their most important block-trading firm to reduce the competition by just one investment manager. And their senior executives, when push came to shove, would not ask or tell them to do so. So they bluffed and issued warnings, but the penalties rarely came through and never lasted.

The firm had always treated a dollar earned in asset management as no better and no worse than a dollar earned in trading, underwriting, arbitrage, or stockbrokerage. Yet even investment-management firms that earned only moderate profits had market valuations twenty to twenty-five times their earnings, while trading businesses were worth only five or six times current earnings. In other words, the market value of a dollar of earnings in asset management was four or five times the market value of the same dollar earned in a trading business. The obvious imperative was to get control of assets, ideally by acquisition of capable investment units, and then apply the firm's power in marketing to gather in even more assets as rapidly as possible.

McNulty, who was never unnecessarily modest, acknowledged that he had great ability in recruiting strong people: "I believe in my nose for talent." In 1996–97, GSAM added two hundred new people, doubling its size and adding many needed skills, but taxing the infrastructure. Many new arrivals found there were no phones or desk space for them.

McNulty's team, with Walker focused on strategy, came up with a truly audacious plan, particularly for a business that seemed to be going nowhere. As McNulty put it, "We have to mirror Goldman Sachs's footprint. We have to be global *and* multiproduct. If we are only a U.S. manager, we'll never be right for Goldman Sachs's strategic vision of the future. We *must* catch up and match the size of our ambition to size of our opportunity."

The proposition was so bold that it was either a bad joke or it was brilliant. Paulson decided that McNulty, Walker, and two others just might be right. For his part, Corzine was already out looking for asset-management acquisitions. As McNulty observed, "Jon Corzine couldn't wait to buy an asset-management business—or two or three—and the bigger, the better." He tried Robeco and then Mellon. Serious merger discussions were held over several weeks with Wellington Management in Boston, and discussions with T. Rowe Price were initiated but never got beyond the preliminary stage; T. Rowe Price wanted only an investor, not an owner. Corzine nearly acquired Grantham Mayo Van Otterloo (GMO), a successful quantitative manager in Boston, at a price that would have made GMO's Jeremy Grantham the largest Goldman Sachs IPO shareholder—but Grantham broke off the discussions. (Later, taking a strong position that the Internet boom *was* a bubble despite clients' optimism, GMO took a very conservative stance in investing; it missed the dot-com millennium market, and its assets fell from over $80 billion to $20 billion but then—after GMO was proved very right—zoomed rapidly to more than $150 billion.) Partners Pat Ward and John Thain contacted

Stephen Zimmerman and Robin Jeffrey about buying their employer, Mercury Asset Management, the leading UK investment manager, for a suggested price of $5 billion. But they got little encouragement and probably would have encountered strong opposition within GSAM. While Corzine drove to acquire established management firms to get control of more assets, those closer to the business had a different focus; to them, the smarter buy would be a smaller firm with managers capable of handling much greater assets. "Buying on assets is buying the past," says Blood. "The smart buy is to lift out the top people and then help them build up the assets under management."

The strategy McNulty, Ford, Donnahoe, and Blood developed was almost as simple in summary as it was grand in scale of ambition and scope of imagination: "3 × 3 × 10"—three continental markets, three marketing channels, ten investment "products."[2] Their strategic summary was simple, but their ambition was no less than the total transformation of GSAM in just one decade of repetitive entrepreneurial innovations into a global asset-management powerhouse spewing profits like a lawn sprinkler.

In retrospect their multimarket, multiproduct strategy may be seen as a sure winner, but at the time the case for going ahead was not easy to make, particularly to that vortex of power, the management committee, where the dominant metric had always been current-year profits. When McNulty, Ford, Donnahoe, and Blood laid out their vision for the next ten or fifteen years, most partners scoffed that the ambitions they were discussing made no sense at all. *Those GSAM guys were actually advocating deliberately taking losses for years!*

The partners of Goldman Sachs had fought their way to the top of tough businesses, and the real power in the firm had always been the power of current profits. Instead of talking, as everyone on the management committee had always talked, about current profits booked and taken to the bank, McNulty & Co. were actually advocating accepting *losses* in GSAM for *at least* several years. To those on the management committee trained up in a cash-profits culture, it all sounded like smoke and mirrors. Losing money on purpose over a whole decade for something as abstract as "franchise building" in a business they really didn't know and understand made no sense at all—not any more than calling losses "investment spending." Losses are *losses*.

GSAM's business was still struggling with trivial profitability and had zero stature within the firm or in the outside markets. Could it possibly be developed into a global powerhouse as one the world's largest, most profitable, and most rapidly growing asset-management businesses, delivering substantial, repetitive profits to Goldman Sachs? Brazen as they were—especially to those who had wondered "Why not close GSAM down as a totally lost cause?"—McNulty was able to persuade others his team's bold ambitions were realistic. As he explained to anyone who cared to listen, the $3 \times 3 \times 10$ strategy boiled down to this: Three major markets would be addressed *simultaneously:* North America, Europe, and Asia. Three marketing channels would be developed *simultaneously* to reach three key customer groups: institutional investors, via direct selling and through investment consultants; other investment managers that had distribution and could offer third-party or subadvisory mandates to cover specialties like international investing, via direct selling and through consultants; and high-net-worth individuals, via Private Wealth Management. Ten investment products would be provided: money-market funds (through ILA), high-grade bonds, municipals, "quant" strategies, large-cap growth stocks, large-cap value stocks, small-cap stocks, international stocks, specialized funds subcontracted from other investment managers and, most important, hedge funds through a fund of funds.

Stunning as it is that it took the firm's management long decades to "get it" about investment management, GSAM's history provides a crucial illustration of Goldman Sachs's unrelenting "try and try and try again" approach to building each of its many business enterprises: Select one or two very able, very ambitious and promising, but not yet proven young stars. Point to a far hill and say, "Congratulations! You are the Chosen One who can find a way to capture that hill. It will be hard—maybe very hard—but the firm expects great things of you. We *know* you can do it. Now, get going and . . . take . . . that . . . hill!" When success is achieved, congratulations are given to the successful young stars—and so is another, even more challenging hill. If success is not achieved, the firm selects another one or two very able, very ambitious and promising, but not yet proven young stars. If success is *again* not achieved, the firm simply selects yet another one or two very able, very ambitious and promising young stars to take the hill. Eventually, the hill gets taken.

McNulty was searching for acquisitions, ideally of small firms with strong investment products and track records but needing help in selling, where the

Goldman Sachs organization was so clearly powerful. The search was bolstered by the M&A specialty that partner Milton Berlinski developed. He ran a seller-rep business as an active intermediary between small and midsize investment-management firms—where Goldman Sachs's institutional sales force had long-established, close working relationships—and large banks, insurers, and other institutions that were buying investment managers as "strategic partners." Goldman Sachs was in an ideal position on both sides of a lively new market to earn good fees by putting combinations together.

In 1995, Herb Ehlers's Tampa-based Liberty Asset Management, which had been spun out of retail broker Raymond James & Company, was in discussions with Berlinski about his seller-rep services when McNulty took Berlinski to lunch and asked: "Do you know any good little managers with superior investment people who are weak in marketing that GSAM should consider buying?" Apart from the obvious conflict-of-interest question of how Goldman Sachs, recently retained as an agent, could quickly change to act as a principal, it was the right question at the right time. Negotiations for another large financial-services organization to acquire Liberty had just recently broken down, so Liberty was "in heat," and GSAM could initiate discussions sure that Liberty was for sale and knowing all the particulars Berlinski had been learning in his work as Liberty's seller rep.

Merger discussions moved ahead quickly, and McNulty and Ehlers developed good personal chemistry. Ehlers recognized the asset-gathering strengths of Goldman Sachs while McNulty was impressed with Liberty's dedication to investing. As McNulty described the situation, "Liberty had a solid growth product, and they had a team who were absolutely devoted to investing. If you call them at home on a weekend morning, they're doing what they love most—reading annual reports! It's a passion, a personal passion. They're so dedicated to investing, you could call them addicted."

Adds Ford: "We brought good things to the party too. First, we had strong distribution and could raise a lot of money for Liberty, enabling their people to realize their personal dreams. Second, we had some pretty sophisticated expertise in risk analysis and risk management, and showed them how they could cut back any unnecessary risk in their portfolios.[3] Third, we would give them the security and confidence of having a major organization behind them, which enabled them to focus on their true passion: investing. Indirectly, we would also help them stay organizationally disciplined because we had a big stick in our hands. GSAM had the option, written right into the contract, to bring everybody at Liberty from Tampa to New York if things at Liberty didn't run smoothly."

But getting the final agreement signed was not easy. Herb Ehlers threatened to abort the deal after he saw draft legal documents. The lawyer working for Goldman Sachs may have known contracts and acquisition law very well, but he overplayed his hand in writing the terms because he didn't understand the key to successful mergers and acquisitions in a service business: trust between the key principals. Goldman Sachs's banker on the deal had let the lawyer take control of the contract, and the lawyer wrote every part of the merger agreement to GSAM's advantage. Item for item, the results were different from what Ehlers thought were accepted understandings. Thinking GSAM was trying to pull a fast one on him, Ehlers got angry and—at least as much in sadness as in anger—declared, "The deal is off."

After weeks of negotiations, McNulty had gotten to know Ehlers well and sensed there was something not yet settled. Somewhere, somehow, he just *knew* there was a way to save the deal. But what could it be? "Of course!" said McNulty to himself. "It's Yom Kippur." In drawing his line in the sand, Ehlers knew that Berlinski, the partner from the investment banking division who was supervising the deal, would be unavailable because he would be at temple, so GSAM wouldn't have its expert working in between the two principals. McNulty and Ehlers would be on their own. To McNulty, that showed how savvy Ehlers must be: "Since he's that smart, we *had* to win this deal because a guy that smart could be a control player for the future of GSAM." McNulty went to Corzine and explained the whole picture, but Corzine didn't get it. He tried to calm McNulty down, saying, "You win some and you lose some. We'll be okay." But McNulty couldn't calm down.

He quickly went to Paulson next and said, "Let's catch the seven a.m. flight out of Newark." Paulson agreed, and when they got to Tampa, they swung into action, making the strongest pitch they could. "Herb had the contract in front of him and we could see he had lots of marks on it—page after page. Our only hope was to go through it item by item." As Ehlers identified items he didn't like, McNulty would ask, "What *would* you like, Herb?" Item by item, Ehlers said what he wanted and thought had been agreed. Item by item, Paulson said one word: "Done!" Paulson said that one word a dozen different times. "Done!" "Done!" "Done!" After all the marked items were resolved, Ehlers said, "We'll go into another room and discuss among ourselves all you've said, and then we'll vote." After half an hour's discussion, Ehlers's colleagues came out smiling. They had voted yes.

The next priority was to make it clear to everyone at Liberty that while they all could remain in Florida, GSAM was in charge. McNulty recalled how he did this: "I told the guys at Liberty they could stay in Florida, but that I had a big inventory of warm winter coats in a big closet, and if performance ever went south and stayed there, I was going to send those coats to Tampa because they were *all* coming north—to stay. Naturally, this made it very clear to everyone that they better produce consistently good performance numbers. And the results of this enforced discipline were great for them—and great for us."

When the acquisition's final closing was only one week away, Ford called Ehlers to say, "It's important that we all agree on one thing. There's only one franchise or brand and only one vision for our future together. On the day after the closing, I'll call your office and there are only two possible ways for your folks to answer: 'Goldman Sachs' or 'Goldman Sachs Asset Management.' And you'll want to print some business cards—not many, but some—with 'Liberty' in big letters and 'Goldman Sachs' in smaller type right under it, and then we'll switch to some cards with 'Goldman Sachs' in the larger type and 'Liberty' under that in smaller type, and *then* we'll switch to new cards—and you'll want lots of these—with only 'Goldman Sachs Asset Management.' Always remember, Herb, *we* are the brand."

A few days later, when Ehlers was at Goldman Sachs's office in New York City, Ford walked him over to the large picture window with a great view of lower Manhattan looking south toward the outer harbor and said, "Look out this window and tell me what you see."

"The river, the ferry, the Statue of Liberty . . . and Brooklyn. Why?"

"Keep your eye on Brooklyn. *That's* the objective. I'll find a way to get you over there—ferry, tunnel, helicopter. You keep your focus entirely on Brooklyn, and don't even look at the river." The message was clear: Liberty should focus on investing while GSAM accumulated assets through selling.

A few years later, another round of negotiations developed over Liberty's five-year payouts. Ehlers called McNulty: "I've been looking again at the earn-out, and I realize it's not fair. We've done great work in recent years, but if our part of the market—growth stocks—suddenly goes against us, we'll come up short on performance, and our investors will disappear. We could be hurt badly by some fluke in the stock market."

"Sounds bad to me too. Tell you what, Herb. You're a proprietor. You've sold Liberty once before and then bought it back, so you study the whole situation and if you can come up with a fair rearrangement, we'll do it." In the end, Ehlers worked out a better buyback deal than McNulty ever could have proposed. McNulty returned the favor: "I did suggest that they take 50 percent in Goldman Sachs stock. They agreed and that worked *very* well." Goldman Sachs stock doubled and then doubled again by 2007.

The original deal for Goldman Sachs to buy Liberty was done in 1995, when Liberty had $4.5 billion in assets under management. Ten years later, assets under management were at $23 billion and rising, because GSAM had such strong distribution. GSAM had paid $80 million for Liberty. After a decade of strong asset buildup, the buyback by Ehlers's group valued it at over $2 billion.

G SAM was looking for more of the same and found a likely target in Rosenberg Capital Management (RCM), one of the finer investment firms on the West Coast. Claude Rosenberg was surprised when Berlinski, the Goldman Sachs banker managing the intended sale of his investment-management firm, suddenly went from being his agent to being a principal, saying, "We might be interested in buying your firm for Goldman Sachs." This again raised all the classic questions about conflicts of interest, but Rosenberg decided to go ahead with discussions with GSAM.

For GSAM, it soon developed, the underlying problem with acquiring RCM was business fit. RCM had a small international investment product that it really wanted to continue. But Goldman Sachs was already a well-established international investment bank with offices in every major country and significant research being done on all the major economies and most of the major corporations from its regional headquarters in London, New York, and Hong Kong. It would be hard for the firm to justify to clients or prospects having another international investment product headquartered in San Francisco. "A great city for living it may well be," says Ford, "but it's not considered a center of international investing compared to London or Hong Kong or New York." So keeping RCM's product separate would be a problem. "We'd be buying business we *knew* we were going to lose—and should lose. Not a smart move."

A larger problem was in bond management. GSAM had bond management and RCM had bond management, and the two bond operations were similar in investment style. The obvious answer was to bring RCM's bond assets and some of its key people to New York and combine them with GSAM's team into one major operation. But the RCM people, as settled San Franciscans, were not about to agree to that. And GSAM couldn't agree to pay a full price for a duplicate bond business when having two similar units would be confusing for clients, prospects, and the consultants who advise institutional investors on selecting managers. "We'd have had 'channel conflict' all over the place," says Ford. "And there were other problems. San Francisco is too far from New York, where GSAM had its headquarters. Claude Rosenberg had great stature in the pension market, but he had retired and nobody had filled his shoes. In addition, they had some interesting internal politics, and they had no new-business pipeline." So, after giving serious consideration to acquiring RCM, Ford and McNulty decided to take a pass—and kept looking for other firms to acquire.[4] It didn't take long.

"Did you guys see what I saw in today's *FT*?" It was still the spring of 1995, and George Walker had just come over to GSAM from Investment Banking. Highly regarded as a strategic thinker, Walker would effect three significant acquisitions in 1995–96—each valued not for the assets that were currently under management, but for its distinctive investment capabilities that could, with Goldman Sachs's prowess in sales and business development, lead to major increases in assets under management in five or ten years.

Walker was waving the *Financial Times* over his head and smiling. He saw an opportunity in the British government's decision to privatize the management of the British Coal Board's pension fund. "The auction for the right to manage the British Coal pension scheme has been declared a 'failed auction,' so there was no sale. But that doesn't necessarily mean that it's game over. I know I may sound crazy, but I'll bet we could negotiate to acquire the British Coal mandate if we act very quickly and make a decent offer." Would-be managers were expected to pay up front for the right to receive management fees for a fixed number of years, guaranteed by the British government.

"But, George, what in the world would we be buying? It's just a contract to manage two big pension funds—and for only seven or eight years. Not exactly hard assets, George."

"You're right—but you're wrong too. You're not looking at this for what it really is. Here's the way to see the value here: The UK pension business has long been closed to outsiders like us. Four big *British* investment firms—with four *British* consulting actuaries guarding the gates on new manager selections—control almost all the UK pension business. As things stand today, we'll never get in. But, if we can win the Coal, we'll suddenly be on the inside. We'll be able to show the consulting firms what we can really do—and they'll have to pay attention because we'll be out of the holding pen where they keep all the non-UK investment managers like GSAM. We'll have at least a toehold that we can then build on. If we produce decent investment performance and show we know how to build and manage a major investment organization, we can launch a total-immersion sales campaign to win over the consulting actuaries so they'll bring us more and more business. At the very least, they'll give us a decent chance to win business by including us in more of the beauty parades they now arrange when their clients are picking new managers."

The Coal Board had gone through two failed auctions. The senior investment managers were dead set against a UK acquirer because they knew they would all get made redundant and terminated because the acquiring manager would already have people in all the key positions. With five hundred thousand coal workers' pensions depending on it, the British government clearly wanted a strong buyer because the government had a contractual obligation to cover any shortfall due to poor investment performance by appropriating new money. This meant that good risk controls—a major strength of Goldman Sachs—would be particularly important.

Walker argued that if Goldman Sachs could get the mandate and be the Coal Board's manager, that would be the firm's ticket of admission—the key to open all those closed doors. "With £25 billion in assets, it brings us up to scale. We won't be really big, but we will clearly be a presence. With all the stockbrokerage commissions that the Coal generates, we can buy all the best investment research in the City of London. And we know from our brokerage work with them that the guys at the Coal [pension fund] have a pretty good portfolio team and pretty good research. But they don't do *any* marketing, so we'll do all the marketing and business development. And we can base our pitch on the truth; we bought this team because we believe in them—and that's why prospects should buy in too!"

GSAM had only twenty-five people in Europe, but decided it would bid for the multiyear contract, knowing that the Coal Board had problems with staff, problems with information technology, problems with operating procedures, and surely problems GSAM didn't yet know about. GSAM figured it had three two-year blocks of time to work within: two years to fix the problems, two more years to run the Coal Board funds and establish a good performance record, and two years after that to build assets through selling services to others.

"The Coal Board's senior people assured me in our first meeting that we would be getting a great team," recalls Ford, "so I said to them, 'Great! If they're as good as you say they are, this is the best deal in the world for them because with our marketing organization, we're really going to grow this business.'"

GSAM had an interesting proposition to sell to the investment consultants. They knew Goldman Sachs had staying power and would see this acquisition as a solid commitment to the UK market. The consultants were worried that the investment business was consolidating so much that it was virtually imploding. Only four important UK investment managers were still standing—down from six two years before and way down from twenty important managers fifteen years earlier. With only four investment firms left, the consultants were afraid of losing any more. As Blood said, "The whole market was really ready for strong, new managers like us." Ford quickly saw the opportunity and gave his strong support: "It was like a free option. If we have an up stock market, and we perform at least decently, we'll have had a big win. If there's a down market, we'll get our purchase price back through management fees and we've lost nothing." GSAM paid $75 million for the contract and, over the next six years, received $95 million in fees.

"We made lots of mistakes with that acquisition," remembers Blood. "But one after another they were corrected during the integration process. We made major investments in IT and in people, and it took us five years to reach breakeven, but when we did, we had a big, strong business base in the UK and a platform for all of Europe." Some in the firm judged that while McNulty cleared the land, laid the foundations, and built the ground floor, all the upper floors of GSAM were built by David Blood.

British Coal was an acquisition that became a real marriage because it gave GSAM market visibility and showed GSAM the best practices in client services. The Coal Board acquisition obliged GSAM to produce written definitions of several different portfolio-management capabilities. Over the next several years, this formalization developed into a major competitive advantage because large accounts increasingly wanted one or two managers with broad investment capabilities who could take responsibility for as much as half of their total fund—and then have a few smaller managers as outriggers to keep the major managers on their toes. GSAM focused its marketing efforts on the consulting actuaries as powerful gatekeepers. The best new-business opportunity was as a specialist manager, rather than a generalist managing all kinds of investments, as had been the British tradition—and GSAM was all about multiple specialties. McNulty's team set out to build the major business they now envisioned for GSAM.

Over the next decade, the business growing out of the Coal Board acquisition grew fortyfold—from $2.5 billion to $100 billion of assets under management—because GSAM's distribution was so powerful. Two major external changes played directly to GSAM's advantage: The United Kingdom's leading fund managers—Mercury Asset Management, Gartmore, Schroders, and Phillips & Drew—all suffered either poor investment performance or major internal organizational problems while GSAM's Coal Board acquisition did well. And the UK pension funds and manager-selection consultants, or consulting actuaries, shifted their focus from "balanced" managers to specialist managers—which was what GSAM had become as it demonstrated its capabilities to perform. The selection consultants—which most UK money managers disdained professionally—were the center of GSAM's attention. After two years of observation and intensive courtship, the consulting actuaries became convinced. Given their influence at most major funds, GSAM's focus paid off handsomely.

Internal changes were made too. GSAM compensation was separated from firm results and based much more than before on each individual's contribution. Each investment unit got incentive compensation based on its own investment performance. Blood and Donnahoe hired in a team of strong sales executives, set up an incentive compensation plan, and made it clear to all that bringing in the business was *the* priority. By 1998, GSAM's assets under management had grown enough for it to add effective salespeople to cover the Continent—where the same manager-selection consulting firms were powerful, specialist managers were becoming important, and the local competition was caught napping. After that, expansion in Asia was almost simple: replication of a strong sales and service organization to gather assets to be managed by the proven investment teams in London and New York.

The implementation of the 3 × 3 × 10 strategy was described with obvious satisfaction by McNulty: "Each product is a separate focus of energy. Centralized 'manufacturing' (managing investments) and local distribution make for the best business. We want to have the best team in each product. And in marketing, GSAM is like a Roach Motel: more assets come in than go out every day. We have balance without conflicts, and the operating units are small enough for each team to have real ownership commitment."

As Paulson and Corzine were quickly learning, the underlying economics of investment management as a business are marvelous: Assets grow almost automatically at an average annual rate of nearly 7 or 8 percent compounded because the stock market averages that kind of growth; since new assets can be added onto that base, annual growth averaging around 15 percent seems surely sustainable— which doubles assets in less than five years. Even 20 percent annual growth is not unusual, and *that* doubles assets every three and a half years.

GSAM continued to get better and bigger at gathering assets, which, from the owners' perspective, is the surest way to maximize profits and wealth. When investment management flourishes as a business, commitments to client service, investment professionalism, and quality control often fade. What's right for an owner is not necessarily what's right for a client, particularly when business incentives trump professional disciplines and conflicts of interest develop. For example, GSAM had explosive early success in Japan, raising $10 billion in mutual funds whose performance was enhanced with a winning dollar-yen play. But a little later, that extra foreign-exchange lift got reversed and assets melted away as Japanese brokers urged disappointed retail customers to sell and move on to their next "opportunity." Fees were high. In a global bond fund, it cost 5 percent to buy in plus 1 percent annually for management *plus* 0.5 percent for custody and 3 percent to terminate. There was no way investors could profit: Fees were too high, even relative to an optimistic estimate of value added.

Financially the Japanese failure had a silver lining, at least for GSAM. Profits in Japan on that first fund's introduction paid for the worldwide buildup of infrastructure for GSAM. "We knew that if we didn't globalize GSAM," explained McNulty, "other divisions or the firm's local offices would set up asset-management business units in any decent market we left uncovered. So we had to move quickly and preempt internal competition from our own colleagues. Every business should stick to its real strengths; Goldman Sachs's strength is selling. And we wanted to sell captive GSAM investment capabilities because raising capital for other investment-management organizations is a lose-lose proposition for GSAM. If the manager does well, they'll drop GSAM and use their performance record to raise future funds on their own, so GSAM loses. If their performance is poor, GSAM loses, period. The much better business model is to organize a fund-of-funds business with GSAM in control of the client relationships."

McNulty became convinced that "alternatives"—including private equity and hedge funds of all sorts—would be important, but he says, "You can't mix long-only investing and hedge funds in the same organization because the fee structures and profitability are so different; they are almost contradictory, and the requisite people skills and disciplines all differ. The economics and profitability are too different, the management styles are too different, and the internal glory is too different. How can you help but know that the hedge-fund business is so lucrative that it *has* to be your first priority? Besides, with hedge funds in a large organization, the incentives for hot managers to go out on their own are way too big."

The answer was to acquire an "alternatives" manager—ideally in a different city—and run that business separately in "production" but as part of a coordinated combination in marketing. Goldman Sachs did that in 1997 by acquiring Commodities Corporation, a $3 billion manager of managers or, to use the current term, a fund of funds.[5] During the 1970s, Commodities Corporation's returns had been superb, but the company "knew" that performance was everything, didn't believe in marketing, and culturally couldn't accept salespeople. As a result, it couldn't raise the money it could have managed, so revenues from fees covered costs only if and when investment returns were over 20 percent per annum and large incentive fees were earned. In 1998–99, investment performance was dreadful, and the company had to find a white knight quickly to take it over. The fit with GSAM was obvious. Anne McNulty, with consulting experience at McKinsey, was working as a consultant on information technology and human resources for Commodities Corporation. Her husband turned to Ford and grinned, "David, you always wanted to hire Anne. So now you'll have your cake and eat it too."

Operationally, Commodities Corporation broke up its total portfolio into many different subportfolios, and each manager ran his own piece. The returns were additive, but owing to the structured diversification, the risks were *not* additive: They offset each other, so total risk was significantly lower—the investor's holy grail. In a fund-of-funds business, returns are worth much more from the business owner's perspective because the risks are diversified down to a very low overall risk level. McNulty had known Commodity Corporation's CEO, Rick Hillenbrand, for years, and the two men liked and trusted each other.

Late in 1998, Commodities Corporation organized a series of "boutique" specialist investment units—across ten different asset classes—pursuing four common objectives: Know the risks in the portfolio and in the markets and then take only "on-purpose" risks—and reward investment managers explicitly for success. Diversify the portfolio widely to get a hundred different risk-reward decisions rather than having a portfolio driven by just one or two dominating decisions. In research, avoid stale old models and invest in developing the best models for the future. Take a global perspective. Since the world has many, many markets, understand and use their differences to capture true diversification.

"Commodities Corp gave us a big platform for entry into hedge funds and private equity," recalled McNulty with a smile, "and it had zero marketing capability, which was *our* great strength. One other thing: It was losing money when we bought it, so we bought them for just the value of their office building and the land around it—$11 million." Ten years later, Commodity Corporation's fund of funds had assets under management of many billions.

Organizationally, having co-heads of structural units like GSAM is strongly supported by the Goldman Sachs culture. It certainly costs more to have two leaders, but it's worth the money because the value is increased even more than the costs. While one unit head is at the firm developing alpha (superior investment results not directly correlated with beta, or market risk), the other head is out meeting with clients and prospects. As Ford says, "Teamwork can work *very* well if you truly believe in it."[6]

In 1999 and 2000, GSAM lost money. In 2001, it made $25 million, a laughably tiny amount within Goldman Sachs. But then in 2002 profits jumped to $120 million, and in 2003 they surged to $250 million. And in 2004 everybody noticed as profits kept soaring to nearly $1 billion, making GSAM a major contributor of repetitive rising earnings.

As McNulty had mused, "The pioneers get all the arrows." Even as his strategy was proving itself, McNulty got more than his share. GSAM's profit progress before he retired in 2001 was simply not fast enough for the traders, who were increasingly impatient and increasingly powerful within the firm. Nor was McNulty moving forward fast enough with his missionary educational campaign to teach everyone how to understand what it had and what it was getting. And while most senior people made articulate declarations about the importance of international experience and urged their best young people to develop experience in several different areas of the firm, most of the members of the management committee spent most of their careers in New York City and concentrated all their careers in one part of the firm's business. It was a classic case of "Don't do as I do, do as I say."

The earning power of GSAM is now quite formidable. The burgeoning profitability was invisible until it was already too late to change basic strategies and came after all the most important concepts had been proven by superb execution. Results were excellent in 2006. Its long-short quantitatively disciplined funds were up over 20 percent net of fees while many hedge funds faltered; most competitor funds were down somewhat or were up by only single digits. Given client demand, the firm estimated it could add another $2 billion in assets under management over eighteen months. In terms of absorbing a manager's capacity to add value, however, adding $2 billion to a hedge fund, because of its intense trading, could be like adding $30 billion to a long-only portfolio. To be sure of getting paid for the scarcity of capacity in its hedge funds, GSAM raised its fees from 1 percent base plus 20 percent of returns above a low hurdle to 1.5 percent plus

GETTING INVESTMENT MANAGEMENT RIGHT · 635

20 percent. GSAM had $100 billion in quantitatively disciplined portfolios—$50 billion in global tactical asset allocation, in which a manager makes frequent price-sensitive adjustments in a worldwide investment portfolio, and $50 billion in "enhanced index" funds—and believed it had capacity for another $100 billion. As partner Bob Litterman explained, "The firm tracks the trading cost, which now runs about 10 percent of our alpha, or value added. As this creeps up, we'll have to decide where and when to close this unit to new business."

A hot seller in the market is a product with a guaranteed return of principal, usually with a seven- or eight-year life to maturity. As with a zero-coupon bond, the investor can be guaranteed the $100 "par value" principal with $70 invested in available securities, and can then invest the other $30 opportunistically. People in other parts of the firm wanted to sell this product but insisted they needed to see GSAM's actual positions to price the product properly. But GSAM leaders didn't want to show them everything, knowing their own colleagues would trade against GSAM, particularly if there was a market crisis. That's why Goldman Sachs's leadership will be challenged again and again to manage an aggressive dealer organization and an asset-management business in the same firm. Asset management is a profession full of fiduciary responsibilities, not a caveat emptor business.

With the surge in business during the first half-dozen years of this century, the firm had to be careful not to maximize reported profits rather than reinvesting to build an even larger, stronger business. "To build a great asset-management business, the key decision makers have to love the business," says Blood. "That secret ingredient is crucial." With scale come challenges. The importance of person-to-person bonds of friendship that have been so important to the strength of GSAM are hard to sustain in a truly global business with ten categories of investment products and thousands of customers with many different needs in hundreds of cities.

While building a large global business, GSAM had a surprisingly personal touch in its nature, particularly among those who joined the firm under the Two Johns. When John McNulty's father died of a sudden heart attack at seventy-two in the late 1990s, McNulty turned to David Ford: "We never had much money when I was growing up. My dad was orphaned at thirteen and got little education. He worked hard for what little he got paid. He never once saw Easy Street. So I want to go all out for my father and give him a truly special burial. He was from Philadelphia, and I'd like to arrange it at what has to be the finest country club in the area. You're a member at the Merion golf club. Could you arrange it for me—for my dad?"

"Great idea! I'd be very glad to arrange it."

"David, that would be wonderful."

"And it *was* wonderful," recalls Ford. "Merion is really such a special place. And it was a beautiful day. John hired Ronan Tynan, the great Irish tenor, to sing Irish songs. Flowers were *everywhere*. Nice food. Lots of people came and they all had a *very* good time."

Only later, after it was all over, did McNulty tell Ford something he'd never told anyone at the firm because it had never mattered. His dad had worked for many years as a groundskeeper—at the Merion golf club.

35

PAULSON'S DISCIPLINES

S ome of the most difficult and important decisions for individuals and for leaders of organizations are "not" decisions. Decisions not to marry Alice or Sam, decisions not to take a job offer or, in a business, decisions not to acquire or merge. So it was for Hank Paulson and his decision not to combine with J.P. Morgan. At the time of decision, Paulson was classically alone at the top.

One strategy advanced by some at Goldman Sachs had been to achieve public ownership without going through the stress, uncertainty, and distraction of an IPO by combining the firm into a publicly owned bank. Chase Manhattan was mentioned most frequently. But after some initial exploration by Jon Corzine, that idea had not been pursued. At the Arrowwood meeting, John Thornton had protested that doing an IPO without a clear strategic vision of the organization's future and of how going public would advance that vision was like only one hand clapping. He went on to say that the firm's going public would almost inevitably lead to a merger . . . with a big bank. Then, to illustrate his point and give it specificity, he had said . . . with J.P. Morgan.

Later, after Goldman Sachs went public in 1999, the firm gave serious consideration to combining with J.P. Morgan. The prevailing view was that all the leading investment banking firms would have to have big balance sheets to succeed—or even to survive. Advocates of the merger pointed to how commercial banks had bought control of securities firms in London after Big Bang and how Citibank, having recently combined with Travelers, had acquired Smith Barney and Salomon Brothers. In most countries, commercial banks owned or were buying into investment banking firms and using their big balance sheets and price cutting to force their way into the business. The trends, many believed, were irreversible, and the mistake would be to stay romantically attached to the old separation of investment and commercial banking and try to compete without the strategic imperative of the future: a big balance sheet.

Corzine and J.P. Morgan's chairman and CEO, Douglas "Sandy" Warner, had had preliminary conversations and one meeting to explore a possible merger and had developed an easy rapport. After the IPO, Paulson followed up on Corzine's conversations by accepting an invitation to a private luncheon hosted by Warner at J.P. Morgan, where they talked about reviving those conversations. The two men were cordial to each other, but the luncheon led nowhere. After several months passed, Paulson invited Warner to breakfast at Goldman Sachs, after which they went to Paulson's office. As usual, Paulson went directly to the point: "We've done a lot of thinking about the future of finance and would like to talk very seriously about the merits of a combination. If, after serious consideration, it looks desirable, we would make a very specific offer."

Discussions were conducted during July and August by two teams of three: Paulson, Thain, and Thornton for Goldman Sachs and Warner, Walter Gubert, and Roberto Mendoza for Morgan. Others from both organizations joined in some of the division-by-division discussions. No numbers and no papers were exchanged. At Warner's insistence, it was agreed that poaching each other's employees was strictly forbidden. He worried that Goldman Sachs might pick off some of Morgan's best people and was particularly anxious to protect the bank's derivatives specialists.

Both groups had learned a lot about each other and their organizations' strategic fit. As Warner recalls, "The joint examination found—for both organizations—an even greater combined strength than had been expected or even imagined. Thain and Thornton seemed most keen, saying the combination was in their judgments a home run." To Warner, Goldman Sachs seemed particularly interested in his bank's derivatives capabilities, its international stature with both corporations and governments, its great strength in Latin America, and its large, prestigious investment-management business. While Warner's team was hearing clearly the expressions of interest from Paulson's team, they should have been better tuned in to their reservations.

Looking back, the consensus at Goldman Sachs was that Warner was wrong to be his own expert adviser and to put all his cards on the table at the start of the negotiations. More specifically, Paulson's team was surprised to learn that J.P. Morgan was spending as much as Goldman Sachs in M&A and in securities dealing—both in bonds and in equities—but could not generate half as much in revenues. They were also concerned to learn how much of J.P. Morgan's business depended on derivatives and proprietary trading, and they were particularly concerned about having to go through large layoffs after a combination.

Both organizations had regular board of directors meetings scheduled for the same week, and that week was fast approaching, so if a deal was to be done, the time for decision was coming up soon. "It's time now to be specific," said Warner. Given what he felt was the strong business case for Goldman Sachs's acquiring J.P. Morgan, it was time to set a price. To represent full fair value for J.P. Morgan's shareholders, that price would have to be a premium over the current market price for Morgan shares.

While the two organizations were exploring each other as businesses, Paulson and Warner and the others were learning more about each other as people and as business leaders. Warner was particularly anxious to settle on the management roles. He called Paulson and asked if he could come over to Goldman Sachs's offices. There he proposed that he and Paulson become co-chairmen of the new company. Paulson wasn't ready to get specific about titles until a decision had been made on a combination, but he wanted to avoid any misunderstanding about the senior management structure. Acknowledging the possibility of becoming co-chairmen with Thain and Thornton as co-presidents, he was clear on one specific: "I'll be CEO." Warner replied, "I do know the difference between a merger and an acquisition." Paulson recalls, "Sandy understood that as CEO I would select the leadership team and said, 'Hopefully, you will pick some of our guys for your top team.'"

Then Warner asked, "Why not be co-nonexecutive chairmen? We do the deal and then appoint Thain and Thornton co-CEOs, to address all the tough implementation issues and do all the reorganization work—work that will involve large redundancies in both organizations over three or four years of difficult integration." To make the acquisition work, there was sure to be lots of redundancy and many layoffs. For example, Goldman Sachs had 1,500 people in Tokyo and J.P. Morgan had 1,500 people in Tokyo.

Paulson brushed the proposal aside: "I'm not ready for that and our firm is not ready for that."

On Monday of the week when both organizations had board meetings, where presumably the combination would be ratified, Paulson told Warner, "I'm going to my apartment now—by myself—to give this whole proposition a deep think. Let me sleep on it and I'll call you in the morning."

Looking back years later, Paulson recalls, "I kept asking myself: In what business are they better than we are? In five years, where will they be stronger than we will be? At the very end, with board meetings coming up for both of us, I met early in the morning with Thain and Thornton and told them I had decided we were not going to do this deal—and hoped I wasn't disappointing them too much. Legally, we would be acquiring Morgan, but J.P. Morgan was so much bigger than Goldman Sachs that in reality *they* would be taking *us* over, and they would bury us. I also knew that somehow we'd figure out how to do everything they could do." Early that morning, Paulson called the members of Goldman Sachs's management committee and then all his directors. "There was no great push from our board. I had kept them close enough to my thinking all along so they would stick with me if I went either way on the decision."

At nine o'clock, Paulson called Warner. They had been planning to meet and discuss specific numbers so Warner was startled to hear, "Sandy, I've decided not to proceed. All I can tell you is that I went home to consider all our options and asked myself: Is this best for Goldman Sachs and what I really want to do? And the answer to that core question is no. And that's final." Paulson never called again.

Warner, in Paulson's view, could not have been more gracious as he thanked Paulson for calling. But after hanging up, Warner, who had been under increasing pressure from his board to do a deal, was understandably upset. He felt Paulson had never been serious and had just been asking all sorts of questions—"getting into bed for some sex with no intention of ever getting married." In frustration,

Warner protested, "At each stage along the way, their guys said the combination looked better and better and used terms like 'home run.' What has changed, for Christ's sake?"

The frustration Warner felt is still evident in his summation: "It's really something when one man takes something that important that far—with over a hundred people involved on each side—and then, overnight, decides 'No.'" The gulf between the two men spilled over into the press. A story appeared in the *Wall Street Journal* that Goldman Sachs had agreed to a merger and then reneged. Warner explains how that story originated: "Paulson had really spun it when he told the press that we went to them offering ourselves. This forced us to say something ourselves to set the record straight." Paulson denied this account: "Any leak came from J.P. Morgan and we responded."

Paulson was virtually alone when he made his decision, and he was profoundly alone when he told Thain and Thornton, "I hope I haven't disappointed you guys too much." Thain and Thornton, who had both favored doing the deal, each called their opposite numbers at J.P. Morgan to say they were surprised and that they would try to turn it around. But they couldn't change Paulson's decision.

Looking back, Paulson says, "Only a few people on the management committee were *not* bulls on J.P. Morgan." But as the years passed and J.P. Morgan merged into Chase Manhattan Bank, each observer, including Warner, came around to the conclusion that Paulson's decision had probably been right for Goldman Sachs. Balance-sheet assets, which would have been huge in a Goldman Sachs–Morgan merger, are a powerful store of value; they show the strength of past achievements and can be used to create new revenues and absorb risks and losses. But the real strength of a modern-day financial intermediary is not balance-sheet capital nearly so much as it is reliable, ready, large-volume access to the capital markets. And that depends on the creativity and connectedness of people with superior talent, drive, and strategic dynamism. These assets were far greater at Goldman Sachs and were increasing.

With the discipline and focus that Paulson had always lived by as a leader and talent finder, Goldman Sachs was almost certain to continue accumulating and compounding its competitive advantage. The firm's access to the open capital markets of the world meant that it could obtain assets and lay off risks at times of its own choosing. It did not need to own huge balance-sheet assets because it could always find institutions that would rent them to the firm. Meanwhile, the firm's own comparative advantages—unusually talented, motivated individuals interconnected through shared values, teamwork, Whitehead's Principles, and the high financial rewards of effectiveness—would lift Goldman Sachs to higher and higher levels of power and profit. Even though many able people believed that merger was the right way to go at the time Paulson was making his crucial decision, these competitive strengths could have been overwhelmed and dissipated by a combination with a bank—even with the best big bank.

Pragmatic, hard working, disciplined, and determined, Hank "Hammer" Paulson had been formidable as a guard at Dartmouth, where he was ranked as one of the college's twenty-four all-time best football players *and* made Phi Beta Kappa. He was formidable in government service, working at the Pentagon under David Packard and in the Nixon White House as liaison to Treasury and Commerce; formidable as a business developer in Investment Banking Services at Goldman Sachs's important Chicago regional office, where he went after earning his MBA (with distinction) at Harvard Business School; and formidable in his pursuit of business in China and Japan and with every corporation on his domestic call list.

Investment bankers had traditionally been expected to focus their relationship calls on corporate treasurers and financial VPs, not chief executive officers or presidents, because Wall Street's principal function was raising capital, a specialized finance function. But when Paulson was getting started in the late seventies, the takeover boom was changing all that. Investment bankers were no longer just talking about money; they were now taking about a company's very survival—and the CEO's own career—with new services like tender defense. Suddenly, the established relationships based on standard financings were eclipsed by new, more strategic relationships with CEOs. As a new man with no prior relationships that he had to spend most of his time maintaining, Paulson could focus all his energy on developing long-term client relationships and on the best opportunities for significant new business. And so he did. Government service had given him confidence in dealing with very senior people like cabinet officers, and his access to insider stories about the top people in government gave him a special advantage in his drive to link up with corporate CEOs. He made the most of his advantage, positioning himself as a confidant—not just another young investment banker—to CEOs at companies like Caterpillar, Kellogg, and Sears.

"Hank Paulson *is* tenacity," observes Lee Cooperman. Persistently forceful in expressing his ideas, Paulson was competitively aggressive without being abrasive. He regularly called client executives late at home and would go to the mat if he thought they were taking the wrong action in any deal. Similarly, says partner Peter Fahey, "He would not hesitate to block other firms if he thought something was 'not fair or not right for me and Goldman Sachs.' He's intensely competitive. Hank was a lot more than a bull in the china shop; he was a force of nature, very smart, and a huge producer."

Paulson's self-discipline served him well as a high-volume, high-value relationship banker. Still, it must have been surprising for client CEOs to be forced into a corner by Paulson's sincere, unrelenting logic as he worked to advocate a corporate action he knew was for the client company's own good. Over time, Paulson's persistence in doing what was right won him the respect and admiration of the Chicago business leadership, a group that prizes trustworthy directness and feels uncomfortable with the too-smooth ways it often associates with people from the coasts.

One of Paulson's great advantages in life is that he is always learning—partly through continuous observation of others, partly because he takes criticism easily with no defenses and no resistance, and never personally. A weakness is that he is almost oblivious to office politics and for years had to fight the urge to speak his mind immediately, without caution or consideration.

In developing relationships with client-company CEOs, Paulson was unconventional. He worked on nonbanking matters like the composition of boards of directors or investor relations—always looking for ways to demonstrate Goldman Sachs's value and win more business. Years later, Brian Griffiths, the Goldman Sachs international adviser who had been in Margaret Thatcher's cabinet and later became a lord, introduced Paulson to China's vice premier, Zhu Rhongji, and Paulson escorted Zhu to a rating-agency meeting after briefing him on how to respond to questions. After the meeting, the vice premier asked, "How did I do?" As always, Paulson was direct: "You did okay on the first and third questions but did not do well on three others." Chinese securities did not get the desired rating. Point made.

The Q&A was carefully rehearsed before they went back again—and got the rating they had hoped for. An important relationship was soon developing. In the firm's vernacular, Paulson was both highly professional and very commercial.

He made partner in 1982, and Steve Friedman appointed him and John Thain to co-head strategic planning for the banking division. As young, ambitious guys, their job was to think "new"—new markets, new services, and new ways of doing things on the simple theory that Goldman Sachs had "the attacker's advantage" versus Morgan Stanley and its traditional "white shoe" ways and established corporate clientele.

Paulson was a serious student of leaders, seeking to understand why some were so much more effective than others: "The more I observed the most effective leaders, the more I became convinced that the key is to have the right people in your own organization working for you and with you." Within Goldman Sachs, he soon earned a reputation for having the best people working with him to serve his clients, and for identifying outstanding talent early.

In 1990, Paulson chaired a firmwide strategic planning committee as John Weinberg was preparing to step down. Asked if he would become co-head of investment banking and go on the management committee, Paulson had serious doubts, because he didn't want to live in New York City. Steve Friedman quickly cut through that ambivalence: "Bob Hurst and Mike Overlock will be asked to be co-heads. We're offering you the opportunity to be the first of the equal co-heads. Would you like to be working *for* them or *with* them?" Paulson quickly accepted and went on the management committee.

Starting with a suite in New York's Pierre Hotel that he used each week from Sunday to Thursday, Paulson began commuting and teleconferencing regularly from Chicago. (He eventually bought an apartment in Manhattan when he became COO and moved to New York.) Since Chicago was closer to Asia, he took Asia while Hurst took the Americas and Overlock took Europe. Paulson was soon making the first of what would accumulate to seventy-five trips to China. Goldman Sachs had only five people in Hong Kong when he started; five years later it had 1,500.

Day after day, Paulson took, as his first priority, completing whatever loomed as the one most difficult or unpleasant task on his to-do list. And year after year his initiatives and discipline added strength and momentum to his career. "He has a bias for action," says Bob Steel. "You start by looking at what people want to accomplish, look for areas of agreement and then work toward achieving that." Armed with a few long-term principles—unrelenting client service and always asking for business, powerful work ethic, and a consistent commitment to identifying and developing future leaders—Paulson was free of prejudice or precommitments and open to finding the best way forward, which made it feasible for him to work effectively with many different people. Obviously sincere, he was seldom thought of as a pal, a charmer, or particularly charismatic. He was unconventional and unpolished. His clothes didn't fit well and his shirt tail was often hanging out, but he was connected with clients and built strong relationships. He gave unvarnished advice and was aggressive in getting the business.

Paulson found an ideal mentor in Jim Gorter, one of the firm's great relationship bankers and talent developers. When assigned to Chicago, Paulson was told, "Normally we don't assign men as young as you are to important client relationships, but you're bald enough to look older than you are so you'll be okay." Gorter took Paulson under his wing and counseled: "It's not how quickly you start completing transactions, but how well you do your work. Do everything the right way—always. Don't chase near-term transactions. Go long-term. Do it right and you'll get the really big business. Relationship banking is not a sprint; it's a marathon." Gorter taught Paulson a great lesson: "Secure people give all the credit they can to the other people on the team." The strength of this advice was amplified for Paulson by comparison to partners who took credit—sometimes more than they deserved—and seriously hurt their careers over the longer term.

Gorter would continue to counsel Paulson even when Paulson was CEO and Gorter had retired. Gorter would modestly say, "Of course, I'm no longer directly involved and can't be sure, but my instinct would be . . ." and then go on to give his wise advice. He gave Paulson the benefit of the best detailed thinking of a shrewd "firm patriot" who spoke in private and with candor.

Paulson also got advice from Steve Friedman on organizational and strategic decisions, particularly the buildup of principal investing. Eventually, despite the strong feelings Weinberg and others still held, Paulson would bring Friedman onto the board of directors.

. . . .

Paulson and the mergers group believed the firm's "no hostiles" policy tradition was holding Goldman Sachs back from lucrative business it could easily have had by advising large, ambitious, serial-aggressor corporations on takeovers. They believed the traditional policy did not reflect developments in global capital markets and that it had been designed for a clientele of smaller companies that were likely targets. In another of their personal policy clashes, Corzine had opposed any change that conflicted with the firm's "good guy" image as corporate management's most reliable friend. Paulson was determined to move ahead and said that what he called the "PR factor" was being way overblown. As a compromise, it was agreed to conduct an experiment. The firm *would* advise on a hostile takeover on two conditions: the experiment would be conducted outside the United States and would not involve any U.S. corporations; and, to be certain the payoff would be worth the reputation risk, the deal *and* the fee must be really big. As always, the quality of the client company, the probability of success, and the competition would also be criteria.

The chosen deal was Krupp's 1997 hostile acquisition of Thyssen—a multibillion-dollar deal in terms of market capitalization that would produce nearly $10 million in fees to Goldman Sachs. While some clients "wondered," the overall reaction was neutral in the European corporate community; there was little or no surprise because "everybody did it." In the long run, Krupp's move was truly brilliant. It originated with Ulrich Middelmann, who was then in charge of corporate strategy at Krupp and is now vice chairman. Middelmann recognized that Krupp's prospects were declining and would continue to decline unless a major change was made—and that merger with Thyssen would bring the combination up to a scale of operation that would create a durable giant.

Paulson and others at Goldman Sachs saw this as an unusual and compelling opportunity. Germany was both a strategic priority for the firm and a difficult market to break into. This takeover would give Goldman Sachs an opportunity to outflank the dominant national competitor in Germany: Deutsche Bank.

With detailed advice from Goldman Sachs, Krupp's execution of the surprise attack was timed perfectly. In Germany, Easter weekend is a four-day tradition that includes both Good Friday and Easter Monday as holidays. Most senior executives make this weekend a special event for their families by leaving instructions not to bother them with calls, and many travel considerable distances to one or another of Germany's numerous resorts—usually departing early Thursday afternoon. Their assistants "disappear" with their families too. So by announcing the tender offer late that Thursday afternoon, Krupp caught Thyssen completely unprepared. And for four straight days, Thyssen executives, widely dispersed to "unknown" locations and with no assistants on duty at headquarters, were unable to contact or communicate effectively with one another.

Blitzkrieg! No defense was possible to organize until well after all the newspapers, magazines, broadcasters, and financial news services had reported the story just the way Krupp wanted it defined. For a firm so long identified with being on the defensive, Goldman Sachs's performance on the attack was remarkable—and Paulson's point proven.

After Paulson took over as sole CEO, the process of completing Goldman Sachs's IPO was, after all the angst and anticipation that had built up, almost routine. Corzine performed his role as chairman with dignity and discipline. The roadshows were well organized and the reception constructive. Analysts did have various concerns. They worried about the disruption of changing from partnership compensation to corporate salaries and stock options. They worried about a diaspora of "IPO partners" once partners had completed three more years' service to achieve full vesting; analysts noted that the *average* partner would be worth $66 million—or, assuming an early run-up in share price, even more—and they doubted many would stay and continue to shoulder the burdens of working long, intense hours. Given the larger role of trading in its profit mix, the main and most persistent rap on Goldman Sachs was that it was really a giant hedge fund with a sideline in investment banking. The firm resisted this summary at first. But the comparisons to other investment banks were incontrovertible, and it wisely changed from rebuttal to a much more credible proposition: if you're looking for smooth earnings growth, you'll want other firms; our earnings will be more lumpy and less predictable because our focus will always be on long-term earnings growth. This more realistic positioning was well received.

The IPO succeeded brilliantly, raising $3.6 billion, making it the second-largest ever and creating more centimillionaires than any other.[1] On the first day, Goldman Sachs's newly public shares zoomed from $53 to $76 a share before closing the day at 70 ⅜. Best of all from the standpoint of Paulson and his colleagues, it left the partners and the management committee still in charge: 87.4 percent of the stock stayed in the hands of partners, retired partners, other Goldman Sachs employees, Sumitomo, and the Bishop Estate organization.[2] In spirit, the partnership persisted.

The concept of leadership at Goldman Sachs has changed completely over the past fifty years. Sidney Weinberg was a leader, but in many ways his firm was a proprietorship. While Gus Levy insistently expected many people to do all they could to build the business, there was no question that he was *the* leader—in overall pace and direction and on dozens of transactions every day. Whitehead and Weinberg pushed decision responsibility and accountability out to the unit heads. Rubin and Friedman matched even more widely distributed authority and responsibility with centralized accountability to the management committee. Paulson continued the multiplication of decision-making leaders and increased the coordination of operating units through centralized disciplines: risk controls, business planning, and performance measurement at increasing numbers of smaller and smaller, more agile units that were closer to particular markets.

"When I joined Goldman Sachs's senior management team," says Paulson, "John Whitehead told me that the most important thing we did as senior management was recruiting. If we had high-quality people, then all that senior management needed to do was figure out the firm's strategy and put dollars behind resources appropriately."

The number of leaders needed rose by a factor of ten in the years between Sidney Weinberg and the Two Johns; then by another factor of ten under Rubin and Friedman; and on upward by yet another factor of ten under Corzine and Paulson as the firm and its business became increasingly competitive and specialized. The firm had grown from 300 to 30,000, and the need for leadership had grown even more rapidly with the distribution of authority that comes with rapidly advancing technology, multiplying geographic and customer market segmentation, increasing competition, and the firm's own intensifying determination to prevail.

Paulson emphasizes the lessons learned from his observations of successful leaders. "The things that make a good leader are being open-minded, having a willingness to really ask for and accept advice, showing a sense of humility—and putting the right people in the right seats." He developed considerable confidence in his ability to evaluate people and match them with the responsibilities best suited to their development. "Business failures are always linked to people failures. I work hard to find outstanding people and try to match them with a job where they can succeed. Often, I'll say to them—and they always appreciate the candor—'I'm not sure you're in the right job for you. Let's repot you and see how you do.'"

Paulson stressed the importance of leadership. Everyone, no matter how junior, was expected to lead. As Paulson put it, "We're global and multicultural like other professional service firms, but we also have huge capital commitments and risks to manage. It takes many, many leaders. Goldman Sachs is leaders working with leaders." The firm had become too large and diverse, markets were changing too much and too fast, and consistently skillful leadership at all levels was too important to depend on the firm's traditional apprentice process to learning and development. In 1999, urged on by John Thornton and John Thain, Paulson appointed a development advisory committee to assess the firm's needs for a more systematic approach to developing the leadership effectiveness of its more than 1,000 managing directors.

Over six months, the committee gathered data in different ways. Internet surveys and interviews sought opinions within the firm on management and leadership development: how much was going on, how effective was it, and were the firm's changing needs being met? "Best practitioners" were visited around the world to study what they did and how well it worked. Finally, experts and consultants were interviewed to learn about the latest concepts in management development. During its study, the committee grew increasingly concerned about the need for many more well-developed leader-managers as a result of the firm's increasing complexity and global size. Each division was as large as the whole firm had been just ten years before.

Pine Street, as the program would be called, expanded its focus to include what was identified as "leadership acceleration" for a group of nearly 100 fast-rising VPs. The message was the same message the Two Johns had given new partners thirty years ago: Congratulations on your well-deserved promotion. We expect even more of you now, so take the pace up even higher and be a real leader.

Formal training was a foreign concept for Goldman Sachs. The firm had traditionally relied on one-on-one coaching. The committee recognized a major problem: the firm's culture, work ethic, and reward system were notoriously commercial, so something as soft and abstract as a program of management development would be consistently overshadowed by real transactions, particularly when the program was new and unproven. Leadership for the new leadership program would be crucial. Who better than Steven Kerr, the head of GE's fabled Crotonville leadership-development center? Thain and Thornton courted him for nearly a year, and he joined in March 2001. Even before officially arriving and even though somewhat mystified by the time and effort being invested in developing the program, he was soon joining in 6 a.m. planning sessions.

Bob Steel offered an explanation: "We talk about Goldman Sachs being a culture, but let's face it, it's also an economic relationship that we have. If Goldman Sachs doesn't earn any money, we're not going to end the day singing songs around the campfire and come back the next day with a warm glow. In the end, people need to believe that this training will help them do better at the firm and with their career or as individuals. They have to believe that. It's got to be about doing better at your job and being recognized as being better." To ensure the program would be embedded and accepted as an integral part of Goldman Sachs, a separate campus was rejected in favor of conducting all Pine Street activities in the firm's regular facilities and engaging firm leaders with strong internal credibility and strong connections to the firm's business success.

In 2005, the firm introduced small-unit workshops for two to twenty people at a time. Topics included how to jump-start your leadership in a new business, pragmatic guidelines on vision and strategy development to make a business unit more effective, how to convert vision and strategy into action steps, individual roles and specific task responsibilities, and how to resolve process or people problems that might limit business performance.

Paulson always was serious: serious about discipline, serious about getting business, serious about serving clients unusually well and developing people and making decisions—so consistently serious that it must have been a bit much for others. His partners did not resist teasing him or giving him a hard time—particularly if they thought he was encroaching on their territory and responsibilities, which they were not about to concede. In his early years as COO, Paulson wanted to examine the profitability of the firm's stockbrokerage business in London, so he called for a meeting with the co-heads of that business, partners Wiet Pot and Pat Ward. Paulson, who had a reputation as a commanding leader who liked to take charge of a meeting, had signaled ahead that he was dissatisfied with London's profitability. Pot and Ward had zero interest in being raked over the coals, so they agreed in advance to seize the initiative and ask Paulson all the questions—partly for fun and partly to control the session. Pot, a tough Dutch Catholic who is never intimidated, began asking questions right away to put Paulson on the defensive: "Why did you call this meeting?"

"I wanted to know how you are managing this particular business."

"I see, you had some sort of concern, perhaps a real worry. Okay, what exactly concerns you?" Paulson, who had expected to be asking the questions, was caught off guard. His first response was a bit uncertain. Pot quickly poured it on: "Which business is larger in London, Hank, equities or Private Client Services?"

"I'm not sure."

"You're not sure. Okay, how big are we taken together as a business?"

"I don't have an exact revenue number."

"So you don't know the revenues. Okay, how many analysts, traders, or salesmen do we have?"

The barrage of questions kept coming and coming at Paulson until Pot paused to say: "So, let me summarize. As the firm's COO, you've called a meeting—apparently because someone whispered to you that we may have a problem—but you don't know the size and mix of our business, our revenues versus competitors' revenues, the number of our people, or any other particular about our competitive situation or even why we run our business the way we do. So in brief you've called a meeting for which you are not prepared." Paulson retreated. He took it as a lesson learned and never again had a similar challenge in a meeting.

Goldman Sachs was looking for acquisitions that could give it strategic balance by adding strength among retail investors to its traditional strengths in the wholesale or institutional markets. Morgan Stanley had merged with

Dean Witter, and Merrill Lynch, the firm's other major competitor for corporate and institutional business, had, of course, built its strength in retail and then expanded into the corporate and institutional markets. Lehman Brothers, having acquired Shearson's retail system, was gaining strength and momentum. Acquiring Charles Schwab, advocated by John Thain and John Thornton as one way to gain access to the retail market, was seriously considered.

Aiming to increase its access to order flow and to get closer to the center of "price discovery" (finding the price that clears the market by balancing supply and demand), the firm in 2000 paid $6.5 billion—$4.4 billion in stock and $2.1 billion in cash—to acquire Spear Leeds & Kellogg, a large NYSE specialist firm, and agreed to set aside another $900 million to help retain Spear Leeds employees. Paulson was clearly the driving force in executing the decision and made several persuasive calls to key people in support of the equities division's strategy. That division had been struggling with weak profits and feared not having retail business would put it at a serious strategic disadvantage versus competition. He thought Spear Leeds was a close cultural fit with Goldman Sachs. Others worried that it had a history of securities violations, including a 1998 NASD fine of $950,000 for intentionally delaying reports of trades to get a profitable competitive advantage. Spear Leeds had responded that it was "not surprising that we have fallen short of perfection" given its trading volume. Paulson insisted at the time of the acquisition, "We feel very comfortable with their people and their standards."[3]

Within Goldman Sachs, views on the acquisition differed strongly. Skeptics argued that at $6.5 billion, it was far too expensive, that the specialist business was yesterday's business and sure to be headed for disruptive change, and that the two cultures were not complementary. Advocates saw the acquisition as a way to get closer to retail order flow, which was important to underwriting in the new dot-com era. Today the consensus would confirm that acquiring Spear Leeds was strategically wrong and not a good deal.

Spear Leeds & Kellogg had three different businesses. It was the largest specialist on the New York and American Stock Exchanges; it did a major clearing business, processing transactions for local brokers around the country; and it made markets in over 3,000 stocks on NASDAQ—which compared to just 380 stocks for Goldman Sachs. Spear Leeds served 20,000 accounts[4] so there were possibilities of cross-selling Goldman Sachs's services to those accounts. There were clear pluses and minuses to the transaction.

As Paulson said, "We were concerned that we didn't have access to retail business and retail distribution. This transaction was important to our people in the equities business. In a time of fast change, we wanted to expand our strategic options." The problem was that Goldman Sachs bought Spear Leeds before it had a clear understanding of the direction the market was moving in. The structure of the equity markets was in a state of flux and uncertainty. Spreads were under pressure.

Looking back, Paulson takes a rather optimistic view even while recognizing that the acquisition tarnished the firm's reputation: "While the specialist business deteriorated more quickly than we anticipated and the NASDAQ or over-the-counter business was very disappointing, we got a great technological trading platform in the clearing business that has worked out well and is today the backbone of one of the largest electronic trading networks in the world. So while that acquisition didn't enhance our reputation, net-net, it was probably okay." Others would be less sanguine. Some have groused about "vaporizing several billion." Whatever its merits in the clearing business, Spear Leeds executives were surprised to learn how badly inferior their technology for risk control was to what Goldman Sachs already had. Some called the acquisition the revenge of the dummies.

A sharper blow to the firm's reputation came from the IPO market. In 1999 and the first half of 2000, as the dot-com bubble market was peaking, Goldman Sachs had been the leading underwriter, with fifty-six new issues. However, this was no triumph in quality: 40 percent of those issues fell from their offering price, including Flowers .com, which came out at $21 and fell below $5, and PlanetRX.com, which fell from its $16 offering price to less than $4. Even excluding "e-tailers," 42 percent of the firm's Internet IPOs were down from their IPO prices, versus only 11 percent for rival Morgan Stanley.[5] Goldman Sachs and other firms were subsequently found guilty in federal court of breaking the industry's accepted rules of conduct and the securities laws in the notorious "analysts case." In what became known as the "global settlement," Goldman Sachs paid out $150 million.

Paulson led a major repositioning of Goldman Sachs's strategy and its franchise in the world's financial markets. The conceptual frame for this change traced back to the problems—and what was hidden by the problems—of Goldman Sachs's Water Street "vulture" fund. By the time the Water Street Recovery Fund was shut down, Paulson, Friedman, and Peter Sacerdote had become convinced that private-equity investing could have major attractions for Goldman Sachs. If properly designed and managed, it could fit strategically with the firm's commitment to agency corporate relationships.

Paulson was determined to establish a major business for Goldman Sachs in private equity and real estate—not as an agent, but as a principal investor. While Morgan Stanley separated its principal business geographically as its way of solving the problem of conflicts of interest, Paulson rejected that sort of action: "You could locate principal investing at the South Pole, but if you do something wrong or if an action is perceived as a conflict, that will hurt you with the same clients just as much."

During an era in which other banking firms were dropping out of private-equity investing and saying, "We don't want to compete with our clients," Paulson went the other way. Typical of his direct style and thoroughness, he visited with every significant private-equity firm and made his case: "We'll be smarter, better bankers and more effective in our work with you if we do this and gain the experience. We are going to do both principal investing for our own account—often, we hope co-investing with you as partners—and, as advisers, helping you accomplish your objectives. We believe we know how to manage the differences and avoid direct conflicts of interest. We want you to understand and certainly hope you will understand that from time to time, we are going to be investing for our own account, regularly and in size." There was no need to say that Goldman Sachs would not be asking for permission.

Paulson's drive met resistance within Goldman Sachs as well as outside. Senior Goldman Sachs people—particularly partners who had gone limited—would go to Paulson and say, "Hank, you're destroying the culture of Goldman Sachs," and follow on with an explanation like, "We cannot compete with our clients!" Paulson wasn't buying it. "What they really mean is that they don't know how or are unwilling to adapt to change. The facts are that our clients' expectations for capital commitments and sharing the risks are forcing us to be principals. The business is changing because our clients want us to change. If you don't or won't change, you *will* wind up with less than the best strategies, practices, and plans. The market—the world—does change, and as intermediaries, we must change."

Paulson—with help from John McNulty, Peter Sacerdote, and other partners—moved the firm to a new strategic proposition: it was committed to being both explicitly principal *and* agent. No longer could or should clients expect the firm to be just an agent or expect it to subordinate its interests in the principal investments it might make on its own account with its own capital, expertise, and access to information. If the firm had a client relationship, the people working for that client or that assignment would, of course, strive mightily to do all they could properly do to excel in completing that mission, including committing capital as a principal. But Goldman Sachs would also be working just as hard and just as cleverly and imaginatively for its own account.

"I saw that if we, as always, managed business selection and conflicts effectively and avoided direct conflicts, we could do both investment banking and principal investing," says Paulson. "If you deal openly with clients, this should serve all interests well and make us a stronger, more experienced firm able to do even better for clients in the future." Goldman Sachs leadership would be responsible for managing the differences so they would not be—and would not be seen to be—in conflict. Of course, a major challenge with such a position is that Goldman Sachs was holding itself responsible for deciding what was right and how others should perceive the firm's decisions, policies, and practices.

The change in strategic positioning would involve educating clients about the meaning of being a client. After Goldman Sachs invested—entirely for its own account—in Sumitomo Bank via a 4 percent convertible preferred bond with twenty years to maturity at a large conversion discount, the firm offered Singapore's Government Investment Corporation, one of the world's largest and most sophisticated investors, an opportunity to invest in a very different preferred issue: a 2 percent convertible with only two years of convertibility offered at a slight premium. The senior investment officer, Ng Kok Song, called John Thain to protest: "Is this the way you want to treat an important client?"

"You were offered what the firm is offering. If you don't wish to participate in this deal, that will, of course, be entirely your decision. Our responsibility is to offer you the same terms we offer all other major clients. What the firm does for its own account is separate." Goldman Sachs was redefining its role in a client relationship and redefining the role of a major client.

"Full disclosure of your strategy and your objectives—in advance—so clients know what they can or should expect is vitally important," says Paulson. "No surprises: full disclosure and full discussability. The firm's strategy must include not putting client X in harm's way. This is a lot easier to describe in general terms than to execute in specific situations. Co-heads and tri-heads [of business units] really help with decision complexities by providing a different perspective or opinion."

Paulson had been a believer in technology and its impact on the securities business since the seventies, when he first saw continuously updated bond prices displayed on a computer screen at a client's office. Goldman Sachs was certainly no technology leader in the early years. Senior management got its first briefing on the impact of the Internet in 1996, including answers to the basic question: What is the Internet?

That changed a lot. Paulson believed the firm was in a race to exploit the revolution in digital technology. "For people who can embrace change, there's great opportunity to grow. Others soon just won't be here." After the firm spent $5 billion in five years, by the middle of this decade proprietary trading algorithms handled twenty thousand derivative trades a day and 70 percent of the firm's Treasury bond trades—updating prices two hundred times a second and executing all trades up to $100 million automatically.

"The best protection is to continually reinvent ourselves so someone else doesn't do it to us," Paulson said. "What keeps me up at night isn't what our traditional competitors are doing, but that someone we didn't foresee will use technology to emerge as a significant rival." Paulson's strategy was to cover all the bases, enabling the firm to keep in close touch with changing technology and able to move quickly in any direction as developments clarified. "We have two dozen electronic trading ventures going on, and they're a sideshow compared to what we're doing in-house." Hull Group, for example, which traded derivatives through complex quantitative pricing models and algorithms, was acquired for $550 million and promptly expanded into equity-options trading. The greater the market volatility, the more Hull's trading speed and precise pricing increased profitability and market share. In Tokyo, Hull's know-how resulted in its controlling nearly half of all options trading.

Paulson pursued the same general goals through difficult times as a director of the New York Stock Exchange. In 2003, he was told by the exchange's CEO, Richard Grasso, "My compensation package is not on the agenda," so Paulson felt no need to change his plan to go birding in Argentina and missed the crucial meeting on Grasso's outsize compensation package. "He lied to you, Hank," advised an experienced senior colleague, "so you can and should resign with a clear conscience." But others insisted he should stay: It was his public responsibility. So Paulson, at considerable cost to himself, stayed on and worked through the problems. It was good for the exchange that he did stay. Over the next few years, the old, obsolete business model of the NYSE was revolutionized with the central limit order book, which consolidated limit orders received from all sources, and the merger with the Archipelago electronic stock exchange, which transformed operations and produced major gains in valuation for both sides.

Paulson's decision not to combine with a major bank left him with a major unanswered question: How would Goldman Sachs compete with the world's leading "universal" banks? All the universal banks were pushing their way into investment banking by lending capital. They were substantially increasing their lending capacity by syndicating term loans, but their main competitive weapons were speed to commitment, flexibility on terms that they could custom-tailor to the specific borrower, and price. If those who had advocated Goldman Sachs's combining with a big bank had foreseen these developments, they would have insisted on a merger.

In 2002, Paulson found an opportunity to obtain comparable capacity to provide capital without having to absorb a large commercial bank. The opportunity came from the firm's big friend in Japan: Sumitomo. Sumitomo had merged with Mitsui and was once again determined to expand, particularly in America. Paulson worked out an agreement in which Goldman Sachs made a substantial investment in the bank, and Sumitomo-Mitsui would provide a backup guarantee behind commercial paper issued by Goldman Sachs. With this innovation, the firm could deliver low-cost credit quickly and in large amounts—up to $1 billion—through an entity called William Street. Now Paulson had an enormous balance sheet that

Goldman Sachs could call on at any time. This arrangement also offered a major opportunity to develop investment banking business in Japan.

A round this time, Paulson gave one of his most important speeches as CEO. At the National Press Club, he discussed the state of corporate America and the lessons learned from the breakdown in financial reporting and corporate ethics and the resulting scandals involving Enron, WorldCom, and others. In a highly charged environment and against the counsel of some in the firm, Paulson laid out a comprehensive examination of accounting, corporate governance, and ethical issues that had coalesced to cause a crisis of confidence. "In my lifetime, American business has never been under such scrutiny. To be blunt, much of it is deserved." He went on to say, "I see this as an opportunity to reassess our practices, renew our principles, and rebuild the trust that is so fundamental to our markets and their vitality."

Initial reactions from some corporate executives caused Paulson to worry that he may have made a mistake to speak out so forcefully, but he was soon getting a broad and strong positive response. Senator Paul Sarbanes credited Paulson's statements with playing a key role in getting support for the Sarbanes-Oxley reform legislation.

As Enron, WorldCom, and the Wall Street research settlement began to fade in the public's eye, Paulson still wrestled with his disappointment that he and the firm hadn't done enough to positively differentiate Goldman Sachs during the bubble. What ensued was a year-long program called the chairman's forum, embodying Paulson's determination to get all the managing directors to show strong leadership and be personally accountable for good business judgment and advancing the firm's reputation. Paulson's personal engagement was typical of his discipline and commitment: During the first six months of 2005, he spoke at twenty-six chairman's-forum sessions around the world. Paulson maintained that the firm had not been truly distinguished in its own behavior, as it should have been, and led each group in discussion of what should be done.

E go management has been a continuing priority at Goldman Sachs since the days of Sidney Weinberg's saying to those he thought prideful, "You're so smart . . ." and proffering another Phi Beta Kappa pin from his collection. Later John Weinberg admonished colleagues: "Clients are simply in your custody. Somebody before you established the relationships, and somebody after you will carry them on."

If someone new to the firm says "I just did so and so," a partner will say, "Excuse me?"

"I just did a big trade," the newcomer repeats.

"Stop. Wrong pronoun. *We* just did a big trade. Try again."

As Bob Steel explains, "First-person singular is only used to describe a mistake, not an accomplishment. It may sound silly but little things like that are quite significant. I've never heard a boss at Goldman Sachs say, 'I just did this.' If I ever did, I'd be embarrassed."

Paulson remembers getting his first Goldman Sachs memo back from Jim Gorter. "Good memo!" was written at the top—and every "I" was crossed out in favor of "we."

The most visible test of Paulson's capability in matching people and positions—a capability that was certain to be watched closely by his board of directors—was in establishing his senior leadership team and his successors. He had become CEO with the explicit objective of stabilizing the firm's senior management.

Paulson had come to the top job with the support of his chosen co-COOs, Thain and Thornton, and an understanding among them that he would serve only two years. They had worked well together in the early years. But now he was having second thoughts on how long he should stay—and on his successors, which added to the question of his own appropriate tenure. Some partners did not react well to Thornton and Thain as co-COOs, feeling that they projected a sense of entitlement. John McNulty captured the problem that Thain and Thornton were developing for themselves: "They act like the owner's sons!" At the same time, Paulson came to the conclusion that he should stay: "I was naïve to think I could do my part in only two years. And I couldn't leave once we decided on the IPO."

Doubts were spreading about Thornton's becoming CEO. He was recognized as one of the most creative strategists and relationship builders the firm had ever had. As one partner summarizes, however, "Great charm and amazing macro-vision, he was superb on the big picture, but he had no long-lived or deep friendships with other partners. When he was co-COO, he didn't do the work. After he and Thain carved up the world and divided up the business units of the firm, Thornton seemed to lose interest and just didn't go to some of the areas he was responsible for. Just didn't go. Period." While some felt he might have been a great nonexecutive chairman, he didn't show the necessary interest in the nuts and bolts of implementation, control of costs, or organizational discipline.

Thornton would have picked up signals of a change in Paulson's feelings toward him as a co-successor and knew he had generated resentments within the firm. His ability to conceptualize remarkable strategies for the firm or for clients could be applied, of course, to his own career. Recognizing that Paulson was increasingly thinking of staying on, he asked only, "Stay if that's what you'd like to do, Hank, but please tell us so we can make our own plans." As Paulson gradually extended his estimated term and then stopped talking about leaving, Thornton did not wait. He had "conversations" with a few major U.S. companies about becoming CEO and continued to build up his personal franchise in China, where he had been rapidly expanding the firm's investment banking business.

For Paulson, as CEO, it would have been troublesome to have chosen a successor who did not give priority attention to careful implementation. He may also have been concerned that Thornton's brilliant conceptualizing and articulating could someday surprise him with the sort of surprise that had stunned Corzine in the management committee. Whatever the reason, Paulson told Thornton he would be staying. This began the conversation that led to the announcement that Thornton would be leaving. Paulson called directors one at a time to inform them and be sure they were comfortable with his thinking. John Browne of BP saw right away that Thornton was going down and couldn't be saved, so he stood back and let him go—but a year later, got him a seat on the board of directors at Intel.

Thornton would see the process of separation quite differently. Academic institutions are considered more central and prestigious in China than in America, so close observers may not have been surprised, at least in retrospect, to learn that Thornton accepted an appointment as a professor at Tsinghua University's business school, where he would teach an advanced course on leadership. What few would have known or appreciated was the importance attached to such an appointment by the Chinese government. Full professors must be endorsed by the State Council, a process closer to the way federal judges are confirmed in America. It takes time: at least six months. And Thornton would be the first non-Chinese elevated to such stature. The result was that while Paulson came to the conclusion that he would stay and lose Thornton in January—announcing it in March, with an effective date in July 2003—that separation process had already been quietly initiated by Thornton the previous October.

After leaving, Thornton had dinner with Thain and advised him to give fresh consideration to the situation, particularly if Lloyd Blankfein were advanced to equal status. While Thain had been working almost exclusively on internal operations and organization, Blankfein had been accumulating the power of profits. Starting with J. Aron, which had expanded boldly in oil trading and foreign exchange, he had then taken over and integrated fixed income and then added equities. His units now accounted for 80 percent of the profits of Goldman Sachs, and historically he who controlled the profits controlled the firm. Blankfein was increasingly popular—and he was smart. He and Thornton were not close.

Paulson had a plan. With Thornton out, he would appoint Blankfein, already a member of the board of directors, to be co-COO. Paulson recalls that when they worked together in 1994 on the operations committee, "I saw that Lloyd had great ability." Late on a December morning of 2003, Paulson completed the changes that he had planned so carefully and, as always on organizational matters, had talked over with his board of directors.

Paulson had discussed the co-presidency with Thain for several weeks, but Thain had been vigorously resisting that approach. That may be why Paulson decided to ask Thain to co-sign the memo to the firm announcing that Blankfein would be elevated to co-president. Paulson may have thought he had evidence that Thain would see that his best decision would be to stay, accept reality, and adapt—and continue earning large rewards in his already remarkable career. Realistically, he would have no comparably appealing alternatives.

But Thain did have an alternative. He knew John Reed from their service together on the MIT Corporation, equivalent to its board of trustees. Thain had been approached by Reed to be the new "reform" head of the New York Stock Exchange.

Major changes at the NYSE were certain and they played to Thain's strengths. The public-service integrity of the exchange had been severely questioned when Richard Grasso's prodigious compensation package became public, and the NYSE was falling behind in two major areas—automation and globalization—that were areas of strength for Thain. In addition, Thain felt more than ready to be a CEO and had always had a Boy Scout's instinct for public service. Thain and Reed had been having serious and advanced discussions, and Reed was ready to make a formal offer. So shortly after his heads-up, Thain closed his door, picked up his phone, and called Reed to say: "The mission at the exchange is right for me and the timing is good. If you can make a definitive offer now, we have an agreement."

Reed could and within hours did. Thain went to tell Paulson. Paulson knew Thain well enough to know he had no chance of getting him to change his mind—so he didn't try. Quickly recovering from the surprise, he took the line he would continue with: great pride that another leader from Goldman Sachs was responding to a major public need.

With all the changes, a casual observer could have seen the realities this way: Paulson picked Thornton and he's gone. He picked Thain and he's gone. Paulson won't want to lose any more carefully considered and carefully selected key lieutenants. He won't want to lose Blankfein. But Blankfein understood that only so long as he kept Paulson's confidence did he have leeway to continue making changes. Despite some initial disagreements, senior positions at the firm were soon filled by people both men wanted. Operationally, Goldman Sachs was becoming Lloyd Blankfein's firm, but Blankfein knew he would have to measure up. Paulson had already proved he was ready to make tough decisions—including decisions on management succession.

With Blankfein on the board and installed as COO, Paulson had his succession in place. He and his board had rigorously reviewed each of the firm's twenty-five top leaders and agreed on how and why each senior seat would be filled. He was confident that Blankfein would prove that he could handle being CEO of a very complicated but now publicly owned, globalized, and stabilized Goldman Sachs. And as the environment changed, he believed Blankfein would be able to adapt well. As Paulson expressed it, "Lloyd is a unique talent. For a dozen years, I've watched him develop as a leader."

· · ·

I n May 2006, Henry M. Paulson got a call, not the first, from the White House to discuss his becoming Secretary of the Treasury. He told partners he wasn't going to take the job, and John Whitehead advised against considering it: "This is a failed administration. You'll have a hard time getting anything accomplished."

On Saturday, May 20, Paulson met more than once with White House chief of staff Josh Bolten—who had worked at Goldman Sachs—to discuss the basis upon which Paulson would agree to serve.[6] Bolten had begun the conversation: "Let's discuss for a few minutes what you would want to know this job was going to be—on the hypothetical assumption that you had accepted because those understandings were the way you wanted to work." The two men worked out an e-mail memorandum of understandings that would include "regular, direct access to the president; equal stature with Defense and State; principal spokesman on all economic and fiscal policies—even those not normally reporting to Treasury; chair the economic policy luncheons in the White House, and ability to choose his own staff." With that understanding, Paulson went into a meeting with the president.

Their conversation centered on family—Paulson's family and Bush's family—and on other personal matters before turning to what Paulson calls "philosophies and objectives" and agreement on having regular, direct access, chairing the weekly policy luncheon, and being spokesman for the administration on all fiscal matters. As the conversation continued into its next hour, the president invited Paulson to join the cabinet. Knowing that "no agreement means anything unless real trust is earned," Paulson would sleep on it. Next morning, he called to accept.

Paulson's priorities when he became CEO eight years before had been to effect a smooth transition from private to public ownership with the completion of the long-anticipated IPO, to operate Goldman Sachs as a disciplined public company with an effective board of directors, to build the international business, particularly in China, to expand GSAM and private-equity investing substantially, to develop capable leadership succession, and to position the firm's overall strategy so its evolving policies and objectives would be understood and well accepted. When he left, Goldman Sachs was recognized as the premier "solutions provider." It had the best working relationships with the largest number of major corporations, governments, institutional investors, banks and private-equity investors; the best knowledge and understanding of companies, industries, economies, and markets; the largest appetite and capacity for taking risks of all sorts, with the ability to commit substantial capital; the strongest recruiting program; the highest compensation—and a well-accepted overall strategy for the future. Paulson had led the transformation of Goldman Sachs, and the experience in leadership had equally transformed him.

"The ultimate test of a CEO," Paulson says, "is that he worries about being sure no bad things happen, that he leaves the outfit in better shape and with a smooth leadership succession. I believe I left Goldman Sachs in materially better shape than it was in when I became CEO, both internally and externally." Even better, his colleagues at Goldman Sachs and his customers and competitors would agree.

While it would not have changed his decision to serve his nation and risk his reputation by joining the Bush administration, the irony, as some saw it, was that the financial benefit to Paulson of accepting the call of duty is surely greater than that enjoyed by any other public servant in U.S. history. Goldman Sachs has long had a policy that all deferred compensation becomes payable promptly to any partner who accepts a senior position in the federal government. Congress passed a law a quarter-century ago that people taking senior appointed federal positions who convert their investments into either an index fund or a blind trust can do so upon assuming office with zero taxable capital gain until such investments are later sold. If Paulson took advantage of these provisions, they enabled him to sell his shares in Goldman Sachs without raising any public questions and without tax and to diversify his large personal investments in a single stroke. For just over two years' service, the savings in Paulson's personal income taxes could have been as large as $200 million. Paulson had no interest in diversifying his investments and had never sold a share of Goldman Sachs stock. So these "benefits" were purely hypothetical.

There's another large irony. Paulson, who had encouraged others to diversify and stay at the firm, had never previously sold a share of Goldman Sachs stock. He sold his shares at $150, a price he believed deeply—and accurately—was low because 2006 was a very strong year, and he estimates that the timing of the sale cost him $200 million. He also had to liquidate his large private-equity holdings—including a substantial position in the Industrial and Commercial Bank of China, which has since multiplied fourfold. The tax break was no great boon to Paulson: He plans to give most of his wealth to his charitable foundation.

Philanthropy and public service are more important to Goldman Sachs people—particularly its alumni—than to any comparable group. This makes sense because they earn substantial wealth and have been beneficiaries of cultural, educational, and medical institutions. Still, it is impressive to recognize that no other organization spawns so many trustees of colleges and universities, art museums, foundations, libraries, and hospitals. At Goldman Sachs, service and serious giving are expected, and leaders are expected to set the pace.

36

❧

BEFORE THE STORM

While some of his partners still saw balancing Goldman Sachs's agency business with its principal investing as a worrisome choice, Lloyd Blankfein was sure it was instead a momentous strategic opportunity. At an internal meeting in London in 2005 he laid out his argument. It was a powerful extension of the strategic thinking that had originated with Friedman and Rubin and gathered force under Paulson—and could be traced all the way back to Gus Levy's business in arbitrage and block trading. For many years, Goldman Sachs had been able to do both—act on behalf of clients and invest aggressively for its own account—and keep them in acceptable balance. It accomplished that by emphasizing, particularly to clients and in public, the still-dominant agency business, particularly investment banking for corporations, research-based stockbrokerage, and investment management. The coexistence of agency and proprietary businesses had been feasible because proprietary activities were relatively small and incidental, and not in conflict most of the time with agency work for clients. So the choice between proprietary and agency had been deferrable, and deferring a choice had been profit-maximizing.

But both kinds of business were changing. No agency business had rising profit margins, and most were requiring more capital and more risk-taking just to maintain market share. Brokerage commissions were being squeezed harder and harder by institutional investors, particularly mutual funds and pension funds, where managers argued that both fiduciary duties and competitive necessity compelled them to negotiate lower rates. Commercial banks were increasingly competing with loans they then securitized and sold to investors, and cutting prices to get more business in M&A advice and underwritings, particularly debt underwritings. The adverse trends had been developing for some years and could no longer be offset by increasing volume.

Meanwhile, principal businesses were growing, and profit margins were high and holding up because only a relatively few firms could seriously compete—and all the major competitors were smart enough not to ruin the party by competing on price. Real estate, a huge market, had moved away from a business of negotiated private deals into a business of transactions on both private and public markets. That played to Goldman Sachs's dual strengths in both private transactions and public-market transactions. Private transactions could be either principal deals employing the firm's own capital or controlled deals for the big funds the firm managed with capital raised from individual and institutional clients. Either way, the profit margins were much wider, competition was much less keen, and the scale of operation was now much larger thanks to Goldman Sachs's going public.

Goldman Sachs's competitors, notably the giant "universal" banks like Citigroup, JPMorgan Chase, Deutsche Bank, and UBS, increasingly used their balance sheets not only to extend credit but also to underwrite stock and bond offerings, and they used their credit relationships as leverage to get M&A mandates. Blankfein felt Goldman Sachs would either make a definite choice to go its own chosen way in this new world or it would lose the freedom to make its own choice and sooner or later—probably sooner—would have a clearly inferior choice imposed upon it. "How can Goldman Sachs survive in a world of the big balance-sheet firms of Citigroup and JPMorgan Chase?" was the question analysts asked year after year. Few believed Goldman Sachs could succeed as a stand-alone investment bank basing its business strategy on the agency business of giving advice.

Not only did the firm need to make a serious choice, it needed to make that choice soon.[1] Given the pace of change in the world of finance, if Goldman Sachs was going to make that choice from a position of strength, it was probably now or never.

Blankfein made his case: Goldman Sachs's strategic opportunity—and, as he saw it, the firm's strategic imperative—was to integrate the roles of adviser, financier, and investor: giving astute advice and committing capital. The investment banking industry was reconverging after the repeal of Glass-Steagall: The merchant banking model of J. Pierpont Morgan, based on integrating lending with advice, was coming back. Goldman Sachs had the best advisory franchise in the world, but giving advice was not enough. Clients increasingly expected investment banks to help finance the transactions they recommended. The firm now had to be more willing to use its own capital on behalf of client transactions and for its own account.

As Blankfein asserted that day in London, Goldman Sachs had come of age and was no longer dependent on anyone or anything. With its worldwide operations *plus* its diversity of businesses *plus* its knowledge of economics, industries, companies, and markets *plus* its client relationships *plus* its capacity to embrace risks, the firm had developed for itself a unique strategic position. Each of those strengths was unequaled, and in aggregate they were unbeatable and unmatchable. Goldman Sachs was now free to capitalize on all the years of hard work and steady business development done by predecessors.

But it could all be lost.

Of course, it *would* be lost if the firm squandered its reputation or failed to anticipate, understand, and manage the many potential conflicts or failed to excel in its important agency businesses. It could be lost if the firm made the easy, obvious, familiar strategic blunder of designing its future strategy to replay old movies of its past success and staying too committed to the old agency business like stockbrokerege. Even Goldman Sachs could stabilize, stiffen, and lose bit by bit its vitality and its most valuable asset, the freedom to choose its own course. Shrinking profit margins would translate into inability to continue being Wall Street's most rewarding employer. And over time that would mean losing the unmatched ability to attract and keep the very best people. Already, the firm was losing a few star performers to hedge funds and private-equity firms. Everyone knew that Goldman Sachs did great recruiting and excellent training, so it was every recruiter's favorite fishing ground—and not every great employee would love forever the long hours and the intensity of working at Goldman Sachs. Take away the remarkable rewards and then have two or three so-so years—or worse—and the war for talent would be in full force against Goldman Sachs.

But that bleak future needn't come to pass, Blankfein told his colleagues. There was an alternative—a better, more profitable alternative. "We have the capital and investment prowess; we have one of the fastest growing asset-management operations in the world; we have the risk-management skills; we have the proprietary research; we have the originating deal-flow through our thousands of corporate relationships and our dozens of major relationships with private-equity firms; we have the knowledge of all the major financial markets around the world; we have the creative, driven people; and so we have every opportunity to reorient our business around both the needs of our clients and the traditional strengths of our firm." The proposition had one *if*—and really only one: *If* the firm had the wit to recognize that the strategic choice was not agency *or* principal. The best choice was and would be agency and principal combined together in an unbeatable whole.

As Blankfein explained, "We definitely need to continue nurturing major relationships with corporations, central banks, funds, and investors because they provide us with more and better deal-flow than anyone else, and we always need to preserve and build that great strength as much as possible. It is vital to our ability to be profitable and attract outstanding people to Goldman Sachs. Agency relationships are crucial to the firm. But never forget: When combined with being a principal, this strategy of being an adviser, financier, and co-investor allows us to recruit and keep the best people and keep building our reputation as the preeminent investment bank in the world. But if we insist on anchoring our firm only to the pure agency service strategy of the past, we will surely, gradually at first but inevitably with acceleration, cease to be leaders and even lose our relevance."

The crucial differentiating advantage of Goldman Sachs would be one that outsiders might find surprising: Its complex variety of many businesses was sure to have lots of conflicts. Goldman Sachs, Blankfein said, should embrace the challenge of those conflicts. Like market risk, the risk of conflicts would keep most competitors away—but by engaging actively with clients, Goldman Sachs would understand these conflicts better and could manage them better. Blankfein (who spends a significant part of his time managing real or perceived conflicts) said, "If major clients—governments, institutional investors, corporations, and wealthy families—believe they can trust our judgment, we can invite them to partner with us and share in their success."

By the time he gave this speech, Blankfein was well on his way to the top of Goldman Sachs. It had been a long, circuitous journey. Coming out of Harvard Law School in 1978 after Harvard College—both on scholarship, since his father was a Brooklyn postal clerk—he had tried for a job at Goldman Sachs but was turned down. He worked for a while at Donovan & Leisure but left that law firm (where his supervising partner said he was the only departing associate he truly missed) when a headhunter called him up and suggested he might be a fit with J. Aron. Blankfein wanted great success and was already perceiving that even with two Harvard degrees, his career in corporate law would be constrained and he would probably never create a fortune.

He wanted to manage a business and was intrigued with markets. He signed on at J. Aron when Herb Coyne was hiring people with law school training to solve complex problems and explain the solutions to clients. Where Donovan & Leisure was formal and uptight, J. Aron was informal—almost Wild West. With his delightful sense of humor and understanding of people, Blankfein soon became an unusually successful customer's man. He matched his obvious brainpower with unusual emotional intelligence and quickly developed acute numeracy to go with his verbal fluency. Unusually for anyone as bright as he was, Blankfein showed none of the frequently associated arrogance. Instead, he was accessible to others, so they too benefited from his perceptions, analysis, and judgment. And he was funny.

When J. Aron was acquired, Blankfein got into Goldman Sachs by the back door—and just barely. Fortunately, Mark Winkelman decided not to include him in the major layoffs and, against Bob Rubin's advice, encouraged Blankfein to switch from sales to trading. J. Aron expanded into risk-embracing trading in currencies as well as in oil and other commodities, and Blankfein flourished and rode the expansion to increasing authority.

Recognizing earlier than most that the major institutional investors were sure to continue squeezing the commission-based agency business, he concentrated on doing business with hedge funds. Their focus was on making money, not on saving costs; they acted quickly and paid full fare, so they were more profitable and, while much smaller in assets than the major institutions, their high turnover made them more profitable accounts for Goldman Sachs. Far better than most securities firms, Goldman Sachs knew how to meet their needs in a win-win working relationship.

Principal, risk-embracing trading in currencies was extended into derivatives and on into fixed income where embedded options increasingly mattered. Simultaneously, competition—particularly from large commercial banks—drove the profits from investment banking lower and the need to deploy large capital commitments higher. As a result, the traditional strategic priority of Goldman Sachs and its core profitability declined persistently and substantially. Risk-embracing trading grew more and more important in scale and profitability while the old pure agency service businesses faded. Blankfein was gaining strength within the businesses that were getting steadily stronger.

As one after another rival got outmaneuvered, his power compounded, and he had the political prowess, the ruthless objectivity, the capacity to learn and adapt quickly, and the driving ambition to go all the way to the top. His standing, particularly with Hank Paulson, continued to rise as their articulated visions for the future Goldman Sachs came into closer alignment. Blankfein was always looking ahead at least several moves and understood what was really important to the organization and to his seniors. He was skillful at managing upward. "His seniors *all* thought he was just terrific," says a colleague from his early years. When unit heads at J. Aron were all asked to produce quarterly reviews of their units' operations, Blankfein somehow knew this was a major request. While other unit heads treated it lightly, he did a superb job and broke out of the pack.

"We all knew that in our crowd of bright, committed fast-track young professionals, Lloyd was the exception," says the former colleague. "So very smart. So very quick. What a wonderful, nice sense of humor. And so original in his perceptions and analysis. He had great perspective: time and again he was seeing things very differently, way outside the box. Mark Winkelman picked it up right away too. Mark never laughed, never smiled, and always seemed *so* serious, while Lloyd was always seeing the comic side. But the minds of those two had an amazing understanding and bonding right from the start."

Blankfein's detached rationality generated fear and respect—and cut out costs that were not producing profits. When he visited one of the international offices, he asked, "What are all these guys doing?" First the flowers and the big bowls of fresh fruit were gone. Then the free soda. Then 20 percent of the staff was gone. Then another 20 percent was gone. Costs were coming down and people were cut out—almost as easily as the fruit and soda. They were costs too.

Blankfein surrounds himself with unusually bright people he has learned to trust over years of working together. His past as a lawyer comes out as he questions and questions until satisfied. Those who know him well say he wants to be challenged—not to be proven right, but to get to the right answer. Others are not so sure. "Lloyd is really smart—and he knows it," said a former partner. "He wants really smart people who will anticipate market trends and client needs and anticipate what he'll want even before he decides. Lloyd is usually right, but his centralized way of making decisions means Goldman Sachs is not *my* firm anymore."

Seemingly always in a state of anxiety, Blankfein says, "If I weren't afraid to assert anything with any kind of confidence, I would tell you that I'm the most insecure person in the world."[2] He is certainly not alone. Even with the powers and successes of today's Goldman Sachs, those old-time anxieties and insecurities that characterized the firm when it was striving for acceptance decades ago— or entering the established markets of Europe or Asia as outsiders or launching new businesses that nobody had yet mastered—continue to lurk at the core of the firm. Blankfein muses that Goldman Sachs's culture is "an interesting blend of confidence and commitment to excellence, and an inbred insecurity that drives people to keep working and producing long after they need to. We cringe at the prospect of not being liked by a client. People who go on to other commercial pursuits frequently self-identify as a former Goldman Sachs employee long after they have left the firm. Alumni take a lot of pride in having worked here."[3]

The number of alumni grows even in good times. "We just made ninety people partners—and caused real distress for three hundred very capable people, which will lead to one-third of those people deciding they just cannot stay and have to leave the firm in a year or so," Blankfein reflected in 2009. "Another third will hope to make partner the next time—in two years—and if they don't make it, they'll decide to leave or will be recruited away. The rest will adjust to reality and decide to stay. We cull the herd regularly, keeping the people we most want to keep, selecting our preferred choices, and making Goldman Sachs stronger and stronger." He adds: "While our primary focus is on developing our own people, lateral hires have been and will always be important to us. We'll add three to five stellar senior people this year."

Blankfein observes the Darwinian process as a means to the end of making Goldman Sachs a stronger competitor. He does not get confused by the personal stories and dreams of the talented individuals who do or do not advance. As important as the firm is to him—and every other partner—Blankfein believes commitment to the firm should never be everything. "If your obituary has nine paragraphs, the firm's tradition is that only two or three should be about your being a partner at Goldman Sachs. The rest should tell what else you have accomplished."

His rationality enables Blankfein to see opportunities for useful "soft" moves away from habitual "tribal" mistakes like the long history of treating retiring partners as almost instant outsiders—with abruptly downgraded ratings of their formerly admired capabilities. While this may have been an understandable reflection of both ambitions and insecurities, it was also an enormous waste of opportunity. With most partners going limited in their late forties—with twenty high-productivity years still ahead of them and with experience, expertise, and vibrant network relationships that would and did enable them to do great things elsewhere—it was a head-shaking wonder to see them feeling jettisoned by the firm they had served so well and were so committed to for so many years.

Blankfein is taking Hank Paulson's first steps—annual dinners for former partners with candid briefings on progress and a Web site—to a whole new level. "We organize twenty events a year for alumni. One recent one was specifically for those alumni on managing hedge funds."

A former partner has been meeting with all interested prior partners to learn firsthand what they would like the firm to do for them and what they would be interested in doing for the firm. The response has been positive, and the prospects for significant, profitable business are encouraging. "Alumni with high levels of good judgment are asked to serve on the board of directors of our mutual funds or business subsidiaries. Alumni love to come in to teach two or three sessions at our very large in-house educational program, Pine Street. We had a panel discussion of M&A—given by such alums as Steve Friedman, Geoff Boisi, and Mike

Overook—explaining some of the most interesting transactions they worked on at Goldman Sachs." Blankfein continues to increase the firm's commitment, and his own, to the Pine Street leadership development program. Notorious for asking questions, he seems to thrive on being interrogated by well-informed institutional investors. Where other organizations' leaders offer a set-piece presentation and give stock answers to a few questions, Blankfein likes to go directly to Q&A and often responds best to the toughest challenges.

Risk is complex and deceptive. There are known risks and unknown risks. And risk is not entirely quantitative. At the margin, managing risk is closer to an art than to a science and depends on experience and judgment. That's why the original J. P. Morgan so wisely emphasized character as the basis for extending credit.

Modern finance is based on one great simplifying assumption—that markets are efficient and that market prices reflect almost all that is known or knowable. So, if diversified to absorb imperfections, the aggregate portfolio will be "market efficient." Of course, for every rule there will be exceptions—exceptions that prove the rule—so when dealing with new or unusual securities, investors should diversify even more widely, adding a margin of safety so their portfolios will be protected against risks—except for the unusual and unexpected anomalies called black swans.

Too much faith in the rationality of the efficient market is *not* rational. In the vernacular, stuff happens. As chair of Goldman Sachs's audit committee, John Browne, the celebrated leader of BP, focused on risk management. Browne was pleased to see that discussions of risk—always complex and arcane in the securities business—were open, candid, and comprehensive at Goldman Sachs. Browne's challenge after the IPO was to transform risk management from the "family style" of a partnership to the procedural formality appropriate to a corporation—without losing the advantages of individuals taking personal responsibility for vigilance and accountability. One risk in auditing or in risk management is for a leader to stay too long in the responsible position, getting to know and like people as people, and developing perhaps too much trust or tolerance. There is a risk of going from not knowing enough to knowing enough and then on to thinking you know more than you do. Those with substantial experience knew that analytical models like value at risk (VaR), however widely celebrated as the latest thing in risk controls, would catch all the normal risks, but not the "killer" risks—the toxic black swans that reside in the six-sigma "fat tails" of a normal bell-curve distribution of probable events.

Almost every element of risk—toxic or rewarding—was on display in the mortgage crisis that rocked the United States and the world in 2007. At Goldman Sachs, the structured-products group of sixteen traders is responsible for making a market for clients trading a variety of securities based on residential mortgages. Simultaneously but quite separately, members of this group trade or invest the firm's own capital or take the other side of a client's transaction, either because they see a good opportunity or to fulfill their role as a market maker. Because those businesses are separate, it's well understood by all parties that Goldman Sachs has no obligation to tell trading clients what it is doing in its proprietary activities—even when it is handling buy orders for clients' accounts and selling for its own account, as was the situation in 2007.

A year earlier, in yet another line of business, Goldman Sachs had been a major underwriter of securities backed by subprime mortgages. Because subprime mortgage-backed bonds traded only occasionally and only privately, a new family of indexes, called ABX, was created to reflect these bonds' values based on instruments called credit-default swaps. These are derivatives that pay the buyer if borrowers default on their mortgages and the mortgage-backed securities fall in price. The derivatives actually trade more often than the bonds themselves, with their prices rising or falling as investors' views of the risk of subprime defaults rise and fall. As expected within the firm's mortgage department, the introduction of the ABX was great for traders: The firm made $1 million on the first day, but volume was thin and the firm had to use its own capital on most trades.

In December 2006, David Viniar, the firm's highly respected, long-serving, and unflappable CFO, pressed for a more negative posture on subprime mortgages.[4] He wanted the firm to offset its long position in collateralized debt obligations (CDOs) and other arcane securities that it had underwritten and was holding in inventory to trade for customers, and to do so by shorting parts of the ABX or buying credit-default swaps. When traders complained they did not know how to price their portfolios, Blankfein ordered them to sell 10 percent of every position: "*That's* the market price. Mark to that." Since the market was so thin, it took months to complete hedging the firm's exposure. By February 2007, the firm had a large short position, focused on the riskiest part of the ABX.[5] That index would drop rapidly from about 90 to nearly 60.

In late April, Dan Sparks, head of mortgages, and two traders, Josh Birnbaum and Michael Swenson, met with a small group of senior executives and warned of a major problem with the firm's inventory of $10 billion in CDOs: It was heading south. Sparks wanted the firm to cancel underwriting any pending CDO issues, sell all the inventory it could, and make major bets against the ABX index. Sparks's recommendation was accepted and implemented. By midsummer, with its change in position, Goldman Sachs was making large profits for its own account—while two Bear Stearns hedge funds vaporized and rumors were rife of major CDO losses at other firms. During the third quarter, this one unit reportedly made $1 billion.[6]

The separation between business units—and, dramatically, between their results—was made starkly explicit by the firm's response to stunning losses in the Global Opportunities Fund and Global Alpha. The first was a pure "quantitative equity strategies" fund; the second was a "macro strategies" fund. Global Alpha was considered the flagship of Goldman Sachs Asset Management, and both were quantitative funds—committed to following computer-generated trading signals. They combined the firm's vaunted expertise in risk management with its leadership in the world's markets for stocks, bonds, currencies, and commodities. Regularly described as rigorously risk-averse and asset-protective, Global Alpha was designed to have volatility or risk similar to the S&P 500 with returns that were advantageously uncorrelated with the S&P. The fund had produced a series of strong results and, being highly salable, was gathering assets at such a rapid clip that its managers spoke solemnly about limiting cash inflows to protect its ability to generate superior returns. Suddenly, in a single week in the third quarter of 2007, Global Alpha lost 30 percent of its value and Global Opportunities lost even more. The total loss in Global Alpha for the year was 37 percent.

During the same quarter, Goldman Sachs's reported profits increased 79 percent. While certainly not identical, the causes of the sharp loss and the strong gain were both connected to market reactions to the crisis in subprime mortgage-backed securities, whose roots traced back to years of sloppiness by credit providers and regulators.[7]

Global Alpha was highly liquid and could sell investments to reduce debt as assets fell. Global Opportunities was not liquid, so to prevent a highly visible failure, large amounts of new money were needed immediately, and there was too little time to raise the necessary capital from investors in the fund. Goldman Sachs injected $2 billion and raised another $1 billion from wealthy individuals like Eli Broad, in part to have an arm's-length validation of the terms for its own investment. CFO Viniar explained, "This is not a rescue. We believe this is a good investment." And so it would prove to be—from the depressed level at which it was made—for Goldman Sachs. The profit on the capital infusion was reported as $370 million in the first month.

As a partner reflects, "Only looking back could we see the real risk—the risk of arrogance. We didn't see it then, but it was there and it was growing because the outsiders of Goldman Sachs were no longer the outsiders. The firm was at the top. We had always been the best—always the top students and the best athletes and the class leaders. And now we were at the best firm—in our own self-appraisal. But that was the first step toward arrogance." Blankfein drew a similar lesson: "We're not that much smarter than the guys who got hurt so badly this time around, so we certainly can't be complacent."

While Global Alpha and its investors suffered major losses, and investors in securities underwritten by the firm experienced seriously disappointing performance, the firm and its own investors enjoyed the substantial profits Goldman Sachs produced by taking an astute and almost unique short position in the subprime mortgage market. While some would question whether the firm did not have an overarching fiduciary responsibility to all clients and customers to share its expertise across all three areas, senior management was and is clear: Each business unit is responsible and accountable for doing its best to complete the mission of that particular business—period. No business is its brother's keeper. Each tub on its own bottom.

The firm presents itself as a problem-solving provider of solutions. As an organization of skillful, smart, experienced people connected to corporations, governments, institutions, and expertise all over the world—an organization with its own capital, access to all the major markets, and a formidable appetite for risk—it has the ability to draw reliably, repetitively, and rapidly on all these strengths to create solutions of its own design that address customers' problems in ways no other firm in the world can match. The firm's strategic objective is to be recognized widely as the world's best solutions provider so that it will get the first call and will always have the freshest information, the most traffic, and the best opportunity to innovate—at the highest profits.

As an intermediary's service becomes a commodity or gets automated, the importance of being capable and committed to acting as a risk-assuming, capital-based, multimarket solutions provider goes up a lot—and so do the profits. If General Electric had a complex problem ten years ago, Goldman Sachs might have earned a $10 million fee for working out the best available agency solution. Today, with more precise knowledge of the various demands in specific markets, the firm may divide the problem into a variety of new, specialized components and work out a series of actions component by component—some pure agency, some principal, some a blend of both—with a variety of risk characteristics and a range of counterparties that would have been unheard of ten years ago and may still be unknown to most competitors.

Goldman Sachs has again reinvented itself into a new kind of financial organization that is profoundly independent—no longer dependent on one or two lines of business, no longer dependent on any particular market, no longer dependent on the goodwill of any corporation or institution, and no longer dependent on any single technology.

As a past partner explains, "In the blend of agency and principal-with-risk business, it's the principal business that really rings the cash register. I loved old Goldman Sachs and respect new Goldman Sachs. Respect is more important than a favorable regard to Goldman Sachs today." But another partner says, "Today Goldman Sachs is number one with clients and has arguably the best reputation and the dominant market share, and is best positioned to attract the brightest recruits. The firm has never been more focused on clients."

Yet Blankfein's self-professed insecurity, and even the traditional touch of paranoia, still very much has a place. The partnership, more than any private company, perhaps in the world, is free to choose its own future—unless, perhaps in a period of poorly performing global markets or because of catastrophic losses, the ultimate imperative of making larger and larger profits becomes too difficult. That would erode the edge that has enabled Goldman Sachs to attract, develop, motivate, and keep most of the financial industry's best people, always its strategic constraint.

The partnership is creating more successes than ever before, in more ways and places for more people, but it must always do better and better. That's why so many remarkable, capable, and ambitious people join the firm. And that's why Blankfein may have the toughest job ever as the leader of Goldman Sachs. And his successor's job will be harder still.

Blankfein knows that nothing is permanent or even particularly predictable for a giant financial intermediary—or for its CEO. Recognizing that Steve Friedman handled his leaving badly when the firm faced severe threats, Blankfein says Hank Paulson's leaving was optimal, adding: "When times are good, I wouldn't want to leave—and when they're bad, I couldn't leave."

THE PERFECT STORM

On Sunday, March 15, 2008, Lloyd Blankfein and David Viniar, both at home, were conversing on the phone while watching the business news on television. They had been concerned that Bear Stearns was having increasing problems getting funding for its balance sheet. The firm had appeared to both men to be on the brink of a high-profile failure, a failure that could be seriously disruptive to the markets and so could potentially cause problems for every global financial institution, including Goldman Sachs. So they were pleased to see the announcement that Bear Stearns—with a $25 billion commitment from the U.S. government—was being absorbed by JPMorgan Chase, moving the badly destabilized firm into strong hands: Morgan CEO Jamie Dimon ran a smart, strong bank. For half a minute, both men agreed that Monday would see a robust market based on relief that Bear Stearns would not cause major problems.

Then the price of the takeover came on the TV screen: $2 a share.

"No!" one of them exclaimed. "This *has* to be a mistake. It must be $20."

Then the low price was confirmed. "Wow! It really *is* just $2." Six months before, Bear Stearns shares had traded at over $100. Some Sunday!

Dimon had been ready to pay $10, but Treasury secretary Hank Paulson—starting at $1—had insisted on $2 to prevent "moral hazard," the concept that risk-taking must not be made risk free. Later, in the hands of JPMorgan and after Bear Stearns's executives—who were also major shareholders—revolted, the price was reset at $10.

The following Tuesday, Goldman Sachs and Lehman Brothers both reported their quarterly earnings. Encouragingly, both reports were slightly ahead of expectations. The markets rallied nicely. From March to June, the markets were firm and quiet. The credit markets particularly seemed to be opening up with good volumes of activity.

Then suddenly, in the summer, credit markets seized up and virtually stopped operating, the problems beginning in London. "There were no particular events," recalls Viniar. "The markets just stopped." With so many past assurances by CEOs giving way so swiftly to massive losses, the consensus in Wall Street and around the financial world suddenly became *We can't trust any of the banks.*

Rumors started to circulate about individual firms having difficulties with liquidity. The rumors concentrated on Lehman Brothers, followed by Merrill Lynch and then Morgan Stanley and—well after those three—Goldman Sachs.

Every major securities firm is deliberately exposed to many and varied risks taken to grow its business and meet the needs of its clients. But as risk premiums narrowed unprecedentedly, more and more investors were in search of yield. As the business shifted more and more to risk-taking on behalf of clients—most dealers were leveraged 25 or 30 to 1 on their balance sheets. So the importance of risk management had grown rapidly. The acknowledged leader in risk management is Goldman Sachs.

One of the tools used is Value at Risk, or VaR, which is designed for and works well for all but the most unusual market events. But it does not work well when markets behave extremely unusually—the now famous black swan—although this is when risk management is most needed. The unlikely events at the farthest reaches of estimated probability—the unexpected risks—can and do happen much more frequently than indicated by the classic bell curve, and those are the risks that most need monitoring. At most banks, the risk that the *measurement of risk* might be inadequate got forgotten—or was never learned—by those senior executives who were not traders and so did not have deep personal experience with the realities of market risk. At Goldman Sachs, many senior executives had come up through trading.

Goldman Sachs's contemporary risk management system was designed in 1994. In that year, the firm—greatly exposed to an overoptimistic expectation of low interest rates—got caught by surprise when the Fed raised interest rates seven times—from 3 percent to 6 percent. This threw the firm's bullish bets on bonds into a disastrous tailspin and imposed stunning losses. From this and other painful experiences, the firm developed a series of stress and scenario tests that goes well beyond VaR. For instance, in one test called WoW—Worst of the Worst—the firm assumes that the market events of 1987, 1994, 1998, and 2001 all happen at the same time and are 30 percent worse. (This test still fell short of the events of 2008.)

The rigorous system of checks and balances that overlays the metrics, models and tests that still differentiate the firm evolved from decisions made in late 1994. At Goldman Sachs, the controllers who monitor risks in each business unit do not report to the head of that business unit. They report directly to the CFO. The search for risk at Goldman Sachs is extensive, systematic, and assertive not—as at many banks—passive. The firm's open, flat organizational culture and assertive risk management work well with each other. "Open discussion" groups focus on each division's risks; other groups focus on units within each division. At Goldman Sachs, risk management is like the central nervous system in an animal: pervasive, independent, and constantly on the alert looking for potential trouble. Since Gus Levy's days in arbitrage, risk management has been central to Goldman Sachs's culture and its way of doing business. Rigorous risk management is in the firm's DNA.

A firm-wide risk committee of two dozen line executives meets each week to share recent market experiences, evaluate the many different risk management metrics and tests, and consider every large position. The firm believes that one of the most effective tools for effective risk management is mark-to-market accounting. All positions are marked to market every day at prices a buyer will pay. When Goldman reported third-quarter 2008 earnings that had been hurt by losses on leveraged loans, Viniar commented, "We recognize concentrated exposures early, and we move aggressively to reduce them. This risk reduction was painful. It caused us to have losses of over $3 billion. But daily marks [to market prices] actually strengthened our resolve to continue to reduce our exposures."

· · · ·

The other tool was strong institutional training and judgment—almost instinct—and was most apparent in September 2006. The decisions taken then would further help position Goldman Sachs to later navigate the financial crisis. When rivals Merrill Lynch and Morgan Stanley were boldly acquiring mortgage lenders, Viniar had told analysts why Goldman was hesitant to follow: "We have two primary concerns. One is a timing concern: Is this the right point in the cycle to do it? And the second is a retail concern. Goldman Sachs is largely an institutional business."

Three months later, Viniar, having observed that the U.S. housing market was weakening, met with Goldman Sachs's mortgage-trading department to advise that they offset their trading-inventory holdings of mortgage-backed collateralized-debt obligations and related securities. The firm developed a substantial hedge position against subprime products by buying up credit default swaps and other securities throughout 2007. Goldman Sachs won twice. First, unlike its major rivals that had large exposures to subprime mortgage-backed securities and took heavy losses, the firm largely avoided that level of exposure. Second, Goldman Sachs benefitted from its well-timed hedge.

Lloyd Blankfein, who jokes easily about his unimposing appearance ("I look better over the phone"), is remarkably engaging, a fanatical worker, and quick to make decisions. Comfortable while poking fun at his himself and at his colleagues, he has great respect for the value of the team, recalling, "Viniar said no on subprime. Personally I was excited about the trading opportunities, but David said no, and we are a team. So no it was."

Identifying the exact origin of the global financial crisis is as hopeless and pointless as defining the precise origin of Victoria Falls or Niagara Falls. Both are huge, powerful, unrelenting forces of nature. But just as obscure rivulets become named streams which join into small, only locally known rivers that flow together to make large rivers that are more widely known, the same combining took place in the contributing factors of the global crisis—but with crucial differences. Water is water, but the financial factors were varied by politics, by technology, and by contractual characteristics. Hardly anybody saw that they would come together in new, interactive combinations that were unpredictably toxic; that the global networks that fed them were often dominated by inexperienced, profit-hungry participants; that the scale to which some of the new combinations were growing would transform them from dangerously difficult to what Warren Buffett aptly called "financial weapons of mass destruction."

Like Niagara and Victoria Falls, the global financial crisis fell on the financial world with great force. The millions of micro-level personal pains were acute: sudden loss of job, loss of home, surprising obligation to pay down credit card debt. Companies—even gigantic corporations like GE—could not borrow as they always had to finance current operations or make routine investments. State and municipal governments, with revenues down and expenses surging, faced large deficits. As individuals, families, companies, corporations, and governments tried to brace themselves for hard times, gnawing questions included: How it had gone so badly wrong? Why had so few realized what fearsome troubles were brewing? What had caused this conflagration?

The obvious cause was subprime mortgages, but as H. L. Mencken warned many years ago, "There is always an easy solution to every human problem—neat, plausible, and wrong." Subprime mortgages were central to the conflagration, but other factors were central too, and by the time an inventory was taken it would seem that almost everybody was guilty of having had a hand in the toxic cookie jar. Indeed, the crisis was the culmination of brilliant innovations and calamitous mistakes stretching back over five decades.

One of the origins was a series of seminars led by Ayn Rand, author of *Atlas Shrugged* and other paeans to empowering individuals. One of her devotees was Alan Greenspan, who, as chairman of the Federal Reserve many years later, would champion deregulation of financial services.

In the 1960s, a "skunk works" of intense, creative mathematicians working in the bowels of J. P. Morgan & Co. developed a series of innovative derivatives. One was a form of insurance against bad things happening to bank loans. They became known as credit default swaps, in which a small annual premium is paid for a guarantee that if the borrower ever defaults, the writer of the guarantee will make good on whatever was in default. The obvious guarantor was AIG, America's most creative and entrepreneurial insurance company, so consistently the innovator in a generally sleepy industry that it had grown rapidly over the years to become the world's largest insurance company. AIG saw an opportunity to create a highly specialized, niche market business with almost monopoly pricing power and near monopoly profit margins. Ultimately, while only eleven industrial companies in the whole world have AAA credit ratings, 611,000 structured investment vehicles with credit default swaps got AAA ratings.

In 1966, DataCard Corporation perfected the mechanics required for bank credit cards, and by 1970 the predecessors of Visa and MasterCard had been formed. In 1971, two professors at the University of Chicago, Myron Scholes and Fischer Black, figured out the Black-Scholes options pricing model. In 1973, the Chicago Board of Trade launched the Chicago Board Options Exchange to trade standardized listed options. In 1975, interest rate futures and Ginnie Mae futures began trading. In 1977, Professor Richard Sandor developed Treasury futures contracts. The tools were now available to hedge and manage financial risk. Derivatives mutated and proliferated in many, many ways and some, taken to extremes, would become the primary engines driving the global crisis years later.

In the late 1980s the early Market Masters—later called Bloombergs—were the tech sensation of Wall Street. Almost miraculously, they could provide all the software and hardware needed to price and clear derivatives. About the same time, hedge funds began to proliferate. They—and the leading dealers on Wall Street—hired, advertised, and relied upon their "genius quants" with their amazing proprietary algorithmic computer models and their Bloombergs to create a seemingly perpetual explosion in creativity and innovation. As more and more market participants gained experience and skills in using these innovative financial instruments, their volume expanded geometrically. Credit default swaps were one of the fastest growing innovations. Ultimately, their total market value was estimated by the *Wall Street Journal* at $27 trillion.

AIG's corporate general counsel made an enquiry to the superintendent of the New York State Insurance Department, Neil Levin: Did he want to regulate AIG Financial Products? Levin said no. While his successor Eric Dinello has said, "I don't agree with his answer," it's not possible to learn now why Levin made his decision—he was at the top of the World Trade Center on 9/11. If Levin had answered as Dinello says he would have, most of the global financial crisis might have been avoided.

A broader stab at regulating derivatives came in Washington in 1998. The head of the federal Commodity Futures Trading Commission, Brooksley Born, sought to overturn a thirty-five-year-old ruling of the commission that exempted from regulation complex over-the-counter derivatives that were tailored between two parties; the theory was that sophisticated traders would take care of themselves. Her initiative was thwarted when she hit a stone wall of resistance by the top financial officials of the Clinton administration: Treasury secretary Robert Rubin, SEC chairman Arthur Levitt, Treasury undersecretary Lawrence Summers, and Fed chairman Greenspan, who Born says once admonished her: "I guess you and I will never agree about fraud. . . . You probably will always believe there should be laws against fraud, while I don't think there is any need for a law against fraud."[1]

About all that was lacking to feed the trading frenzy in derivatives was the imprimatur of the bond-rating companies. The basis for that was provided by David X. Li, a Canadian-educated Chinese actuary working for the RiskMetrics Group at JPMorgan Chase. In 2003 Li published a seminal paper on the correlation of default risk—how default of one bond linked to default of another bond. It was a key element in the conversion of risk to a tradable factor. On August 10, 2004, Moody's incorporated Li's formula on default risk into its ratings and substantially reduced its previous requirement that collateralized debt obligations (CDOs) meet a portfolio diversification hurdle. Standard & Poor's promptly followed. The number of AAA-rated CDOs exploded, and they were sold all over the world. But the models used by the rating agencies were not nearly as reliable as CDO investors assumed. Cheap money, volume-driven transactions, and anomalously rising house prices were all different than they had been in the prior decade when the models were constructed. David Li was about to become unintentionally the most powerful actuary in history.

In Congress, conservative Republicans and liberal Democrats found common cause for wholly different reasons to expand access to mortgage credit for marginal borrowers. Conservative Republicans wanted less regulation and freer markets, so they worked to reduce regulatory controls over the terms of mortgages and other kinds of consumer loans. At the same time, liberal Democrats pressed for fewer restrictions so mortgages would be easier to get and the middle-class benefits of home ownership would be extended to more families.

The stage was set for the perfect storm.

. . .

For a while after JPMorgan Chase's shotgun takeover of Bear Stearns, the markets seemed calmer. Then, in June, troubled Lehman Brothers reported another poor quarter. Paulson said later, "If [CEO Richard] Fuld had not found a solution by the end of the third quarter, he needed to have found a buyer." In fact, Fuld had been looking widely for a buyer. Over two years, he had held talks with AIG, GE, HSBC, Abu Dhabi Investment Authority, and Nomura. During the summer of 2008, Lehman Brothers was the primary focus of concern on Wall Street and the particular focus of the Fed and SEC. Meanwhile, Merrill Lynch had inked a deal with Qatar. Citigroup had raised money from the GIC, Singapore's sophisticated sovereign wealth fund, and Morgan Stanley had held talks about a major investment being made by China's sovereign wealth fund China Investment Corporation.

The general assumption was that action would be taken to protect Lehman Brothers from a run on the bank and from aggressive short selling by hedge funds that had formed themselves into a wolf pack and gone in for the kill when Bear Stearns seemed vulnerable. Lehman Brothers really seemed too big and too integral to the global financial system—interconnected through an enormous number of complex derivative contracts with financial institutions all over the world—to allow it to fail. And if it was allowed to fail its many connections would cause the credit markets to freeze up. If Lehman Brothers could not solve its own funding problems, a merger with another major bank or another major infusion of capital from the government would have to be worked out. The accepted assumption was the obvious: Lehman Brothers would be "repositioned," probably through a government supported merger, with severe penalties imposed on shareholders to prevent moral hazard.

Everyone underestimated Lehman Brothers' problem because everyone thought the real problem was how to settle that firm's large book of derivative contracts to prevent serious market disruption. Actually, with every major bank ready to cooperate, the derivatives problem could have been managed. But the derivatives contracts were *not* Lehman Brothers' biggest problem. Its biggest problem was a commercial real estate portfolio carried on its books at $53 billion. Selling such a large portfolio might have been feasible *if* the firm had plenty of time to sell specific properties in an orderly process. But with properties all over the world, all carried at high appraised values, there was no chance of selling them all at appraised values in thirty days or even ninety days. Another more immediate problem: Lehman Brothers' London-based broker-dealer was caught in a severe liquidity trap and needed swift, substantial support from headquarters. On Friday, September 12, Lehman Brothers' shares continued falling.

With the urging of Treasury and the Fed, a group of firms explored a private market solution, as had been arranged a decade before with Long Term Capital Management. Ten major Wall Street banks tentatively agreed on the Saturday night to try to create a thirty- or thirty-five-billion-dollar "bad bank" that would acquire Lehman Brothers' real estate assets. One Wall Streeter—making the obvious assumption that the Treasury and Fed would "reposition" Lehman Brothers—said with confidence: "Thinking logically and knowing that it will be Armageddon if they do nothing, a deal will be announced by 6:00 p.m. Sunday."[2] But Lehman Brothers was way too large and way too complex. It couldn't be done without major government financial support.

At the New York Federal Reserve that September weekend, regulators told over one hundred bankers that Lehman Brothers must merge or pray for a bailout—or declare bankruptcy. Treasury secretary Paulson eliminated one of those options, telling potential acquirers, "There's no government money here." Several argued he couldn't let Lehman Brothers fail. He insisted, "No . . . government . . . money." Paulson pressed for a private-sector solution: "It can't be just every man for himself." Still, the Fed believed that in the end Paulson would relent. The Fed was ready to help—if an appropriate buyer came forward. But Paulson insisted that federal law prohibited the Treasury from lending money or guaranteeing assets without congressional approval and that the Fed could not lend against Lehman Brothers' assets if it had reason to think such a loan could result a loss.

The systemic shock coming from a Lehman Brothers bankruptcy would put Merrill Lynch in immediate jeopardy. It was the third major dealer—after Goldman Sachs and Lehman Brothers—in commercial paper and the other money market instruments that had become central to financing the operations of most major industrial corporations. Serious trouble in the money markets almost immediately meant serious trouble for industrial America and for "Main Street" America. The real economy would be hurt—badly—in just a few days.

Greg Fleming, the president of Merrill Lynch, had recognized the strategic risk to his firm of trouble at Lehman Brothers months earlier and had outlined them to John Thain, the CEO, during the early summer. He had argued for a top-level meeting with Fuld and others of Lehman, but Thain had rejected that. Fleming pushed back, "If Lehman Brothers goes, Merrill Lynch will be next. The wolf pack will turn on *us*. But if we can find a way to save Lehman Brothers, the pressure will be off us." Thain wasn't receptive.

Now, on Friday, September 12, Fleming urged Thain: "We cannot wait to see what happens between now and Monday. There are too many unknown variables. We could be outmaneuvered. We know Lehman Brothers has talked with Bank of America. Knowing Dick Fuld, he's probably calling [Bank of America CEO] Ken Lewis right now. Let's talk to Bank of America ourselves *now*."

Fuld *was* calling Lewis—at his home in Charlotte—but he got nowhere. Donna Lewis, her tone of voice conveying exasperation, curtly told Fuld, "If he wants to speak with you, he will call you." Fuld understood. There would be no call from Lewis. His hopes of a deal with Bank of America had gone to zero. In a way that was out-of-character for Fuld, he retreated apologetically: "I am so sorry."

Barclays was soon identified as a major player. For years, it had been striving to become an international investment bank. Taking over Lehman Brothers would make it a major immediately. Lehman Brothers and Barclays had a "handshake" until Paulson's Sunday announcement that the government would not participate; that caused the British Treasury to say it could not go forward with its support plans without a U.S. backup during the few days it would take to get the shareholder approval required by British law.

Thain went to see Tim Geithner, president of the New York Fed, who made it clear: There would be no rescue for Lehman Brothers. This greatly increased the risk of failure for Merrill Lynch. Thain, as a strategist, searched for options. One option might be his old firm. Goldman Sachs might buy a minority position of, say, 10 percent in Merrill Lynch. He and Peter Kraus spent half a day negotiating with Goldman Sachs. Kraus had favored doing a deal with Bank of America, but shifted quickly to the possibility of a deal with Goldman Sachs.

Fleming called Edward Herlihy, a partner at Wachtell Lipton and long the lawyer for Bank of America: "You have to talk to us." He was told Thain would have to make the first call. "I know," replied Fleming. "I'm going to try."

Fleming urged Thain, "Tell the guys at Goldman Sachs that something's come up and you'll call them in a week." He thought Thain's and Kraus's interest in going to their old firm was too close to being a prejudiced "inside job." More important, he believed Goldman Sachs was itself in trouble or close to being in trouble, so where would it get the billions to buy 10 percent of Merrill Lynch? Thain, Fleming felt, was not a serious strategist if he would divert the team from working on a deal with Bank of America. Fleming was also angry with Thain's indecisive jumping from one possibility to another and was sure that a 10 percent equity stake was nothing like the strong, permanent solution Merrill Lynch so badly needed now.

Back at the Fed, Thain learned that Goldman Sachs was considering taking a 9.9 percent equity stake and providing a $10 billion line of credit. Just then, John Mack of Morgan Stanley went to him to say, "We should talk." That evening, Thain, Kraus, and Thomas Montag, head of the trading division, met with Mack to explore a possible deal, but by Sunday morning Thain had ruled out that option. He didn't think Mack and Morgan Stanley were acting with enough urgency. Greg Fleming continued to champion a Bank of America combination, hoping for a price in the high $20s to low $30s—far above the $17 at which Merrill Lynch's shares had been trading on Friday.

At noon, Thain called Lewis, who flew to New York for a 2:30 meeting with him. Acquiring Merrill Lynch would catapult Bank of America ahead of Lewis's major rivals, JPMorgan Chase and Citigroup. Thain was prepared to sell a large minority stake in Merrill Lynch. Lewis wanted the whole. Thain said, "I didn't come here to sell the whole company." But as they continued to talk through the strategic fit, Thain could see it too. Merrill was weak in corporate banking where Bank of America was strong. Bank of America was weak in wealth management, capital market trading, underwriting, and M&A, where Merrill Lynch was strong. Still, Thain didn't like the idea of a merger.

Sunday morning, Paulson was blunt: Make a deal or Merrill Lynch is finished. Lehman Brothers was going down, and to keep Merrill Lynch from following it into bankruptcy, Thain had no choice but to cut a deal—*now*. Badly shaken, Thain got an offer he could not refuse: Bank of America offered $29. At 6:00 p.m., Thain held a telephonic Merrill Lynch board meeting. At eight that evening he went to Wachtell Lipton to sign papers. Resolving final details took until nearly midnight Sunday night, so the champagne intended for toasting a deal at nine just had to wait. The merger would be made formal on December 31.

In the very last stages of discussion, Bank of America's lawyers at Wachtell Lipton had wanted specificity on one more item: executive bonuses. Tearing a page out of a notebook, a Merrill Lynch lawyer had written numbers for each of its top five executives. The number beside Thain's initials, JAT, read: "$40M." Thain believed he had earned a bonus of $40 million, but was warned by the Bank of America's chief administrative officer not to ask for so much. He would never be forgiven by Bank of America directors. Thain saw $40 million as appropriately large for the brilliant way he had taken control of Merrill Lynch and, most partic- ularly, engineered a great deal with Bank of America. As blockbuster deal-maker bonuses were then going on Wall Street, Thain's number was high but not outside the prevailing pattern. Others would strongly disagree. "That's ridiculous!" said John D. Finnegan, CEO of the Chubb Group of Insurance Companies and chair of the Merrill Lynch compensation committee. Thain later proposed a bonus of $10 million—slightly less than Lewis was to receive. Later, after a negative *Wall Street Journal* article, Thain suggested there be no bonus.

On Monday, September 15, after the whirl of meetings at the New York Fed, Thain and Lewis shook hands for photographers in front of a screen that had been swiftly decorated over and over again with the names Bank of America and Merrill Lynch. Thain spoke of the progress he had been making: "We have been consistently cleaning up the balance sheet, repairing the damage that was done over the last few years"—placing the blame clearly with his predecessor CEO, Stanley O'Neal. Merrill Lynch had increased its CDO volume from nearly nil in 2002 to a position as the world's largest in just four years. Then AIG refused to insure more of the firm's CDOs, so Merrill Lynch self-insured its huge volume of CDOs. As the mortgage business deteriorated in 2007, it announced a $7.9 billion write-down and a $2.3 billion loss, its largest ever. This led to ousting O'Neal, who received a departure package of $161 million.[3]

Monday morning, Lehman Brothers filed for bankruptcy. That set off a chain reaction that would severely disrupt credit markets, accelerate AIG's downward spiral, spread losses around the financial world, and scare Congress into approving the $700 billion government rescue plan. Bank of America announced its acquisition of Merrill Lynch for $50 billion. That afternoon, Thain held a "town meeting" at Merrill Lynch that was dominated by protracted standing applause for him. He was a hero. Thain's enthusiastic audience understood that he had rushed Merrill Lynch into a swift marriage with Bank of America barely ahead, it would turn out, of an accelerating series of gigantic losses on subprime mortgages that would surely have flattened "the thundering herd."*

Lehman Brothers, the world's fourth largest investment banking and securities firm, was gone—and Paulson had made the decision to let it go. Protests from the heads of other firms were angry, strong, and personal. Paulson, they said, had screwed up badly. Paulson, some said, let Lehman Brothers fail in order to take out a competitor of his old firm, Goldman Sachs. Others, more realistically, said Paulson could not incur the risk of moral hazard or the political risk of saving another mismanaged, overleveraged Wall Street firm when Congress and the public were already upset over what was being called the "Wall Street bailout." While at Goldman Sachs, Paulson would have been delighted to beat Lehman Brothers—or any other competitor. But at Treasury, Paulson's focus on public service and his place in history centered his thoughts on what was best for the nation. He couldn't keep saving big Wall Street firms. Congress would explode in outrage. Lehman Brothers put itself in such serious trouble that Paulson believed he had no real choice: It had to go. Others would disagree but Paulson had decided.

Monday opened to widespread chaos in the securities and credit markets around the world and to near panic on Wall Street. Spreads between bid and asked prices on credit default swaps quickly widened to near record amounts. Creditors knew that while the firm might have a serious liquidity problem, they

---

* Bank of America's Lewis was startled weeks later—as was Thain—when he got early reports of large losses accumulating at Merrill Lynch. He wanted to call off the whole deal, but Paulson, implicitly backed by the powers of government, was adamant: There would be no backing out.

would eventually get paid as Lehman Brothers' securities and properties were liquidated. Not so the stockholders. They would, in a bankruptcy, get nothing, or nearly nothing. This created a haves versus have-nots separation of interests and motivation. Another division of haves versus have-nots came quickly into view for every financial organization. Were they or were they not regulated by the Federal Reserve? There was the perception that those with Fed regulation could get all the liquidity they wanted at the Fed "window" any time they wanted it, but only those that had Fed regulation.

Taking Lehman out provoked more than angry voices and accusations by those directly involved. The dominoes were falling faster and faster. With sharp losses on Lehman Brothers' commercial paper, money market funds—the major buyers—lost confidence in the creditworthiness of corporate commercial paper, the way many major companies funded their operations and inventories. Banks lost the ability to trust other banks. If mighty Lehman Brothers could so swiftly be vaporized, why not *any* other large, medium, or small financial organization? Then AIG came under severe pressure. Then GE could not roll over its commercial paper. The whole market mechanism of global money flows froze. Credit was suddenly withheld from regular borrowers. The financial crisis was rapidly becoming a major negative force in the real economy. America and the nations of the world were being pulled into a global recession—an increasingly severe global recession—by the financial markets failing to function.

The Fed and the Treasury had a plan—ironically, the plan that had first been proposed to them by Lehman Brothers as a way it could have saved itself when the money markets refused to accept the commercial paper that had become essential to its funding. The government's plan: Make Goldman Sachs and Morgan Stanley regulated bank holding companies. While Lehman Brothers had been denied this opportunity just days before, the concept was now looking increasingly appealing. The plan had another step. Commercial banks, funded with demand deposits, were far less exposed to short-term, mark-to-market risks and problems with liquidity. Since the 1999 removal of the old Glass-Steagall separation of commercial banking from investment banking, the two kinds of businesses could be combined. Citigroup had acquired Salomon Brothers and Smith Barney, JPMorgan Chase had acquired Bear Stearns, and Bank of America had just acquired Merrill Lynch. Bernanke and Geithner were clear: Goldman Sachs must not fail and Morgan Stanley must not fail. Both

Paulson at Treasury and Geithner at the New York Fed were prepared to commit $10 or $25 billion to every major firm.

The next step: Pair each Wall Street firm with an appropriate bank. For this, Paulson had a lucky break. The CEO of Wachovia was Bob Steel. They had been together at Goldman Sachs for nearly thirty years. When Paulson was chairman of Goldman Sachs, Steel had been vice chairman. When Paulson went to Treasury, Steel joined him in a senior position from 2006 until he took over Wachovia in July 2008. They worked well together and understood each other. Wachovia could be combined into Goldman Sachs. Steel went to discuss this combination with Blankfein, but after an hour's discussion they concluded that neither institution was a solution for the other. (Soon, in a series of urgent late-night and pre-dawn moves, Wachovia would first agree to merge into Citigroup, then switch to a better merger into Wells Fargo.)

Geithner called Blankfein to say, "You should call Vikram Pandit," CEO of Citigroup. He had already told Pandit to be ready to receive such a call. Told to call by the Federal Reserve, Blankfein, of course, made his call. What followed was an awkward conversation because Pandit wasn't prepared for the call and had no interest in pursuing the matter. Geithner had also called John Mack at Morgan Stanley—who was in the midst of what appeared to be a desperate scramble to raise permanent capital from Japan's Mitsubishi UFJ Financial Group—to tell him he should be talking to Jamie Dimon at JPMorgan Chase. Mack was clearly on a speaker phone, presumably so others could listen in on Geithner's call. Mack said he would like to caucus with his colleagues for fifteen minutes and then call back. Geithner agreed.

When Mack called back, his voice tone was different. It was more formal—as though he were speaking to a sizable audience. He announced that Morgan Stanley would continue its discussions with Mitsubishi, thanked Geithner for his interest, and hung up. Meanwhile, market pressures threatened to overwhelm Morgan Stanley. Like wolves in a pack jumping up on a moose, hedge funds went on attack. They knew how to keep attacking: Short the stock and cause creditors to decide they had better pull back a bit; and then other creditors would pull back somewhat more, causing still others to pull back even more. In almost no time, a firm that relies on the money market, with thousands of lenders who all have many alternatives and no need to lend to any one particular borrower, could suddenly experience an accelerating run on the bank—even Morgan Stanley.

Near midnight on Saturday, September 20, Paulson's Treasury e-mailed a three-page legislative proposal to offices on Capitol Hill requesting authority to buy up to $700 billion of assets from financial institutions. Paulson wanted an open authorization—only weeks before a major election and within memory for some of Lyndon Johnson's rushing through the Gulf of Tonkin resolution to escalate and expand the war in Vietnam. Paulson's late request seemed an absurd misreading of Congress. Congress first rejected it but soon accepted that the global crisis was accelerating and passed the bill on October 3. Money market turmoil continued, however, until European governments—led by the U.K.—agreed to commit capital directly into their banks and Paulson reversed himself and his basic strategy to follow their lead. Only then did stability begin slowly returning to the money market.

In the week after Lehman Brothers filed for bankruptcy, Viniar and Blankfein spent most of their time explaining to everyone—employees, shareholders, journalists, institutional investors, counterparties—that Goldman Sachs had more than enough capital and more than enough liquidity. The Fed put out a press release confirming the financial strength of Goldman Sachs. It didn't matter. Nobody was listening. The facts, even important facts, had become irrelevant.

Word swirled through the stock market that the hedge funds that had mauled Lehman Brothers were again snarling and snapping at Morgan Stanley, shorting its stock, determined to bring the blue blood to its knees. Day after day, the bear raid got stronger. It looked increasingly likely that the hedge funds could destroy a great American firm. That's why Morgan Stanley, in what some saw as desperation, had been having exploratory talks with the Chinese government's sovereign wealth fund and with Mitsubishi UFJ. At Goldman Sachs, after years of intense and sometimes bitter rivalry, seeing Morgan Stanley struggling as Lehman Brothers had struggled provoked one reaction. As Viniar recalls, "We were *all* doing everything we could to be supportive of Morgan Stanley!"*

* Mitsubishi UFJ ultimately agreed to pay $8.4 billion for 20 percent of Morgan Stanley.

Then Goldman Sachs announced its quarterly earnings—again slightly higher than had been expected. Only a little later, Morgan Stanley announced its earnings—also higher than expected. Then the government announced specific terms for an AIG bailout (and installed Edward M. Liddy, then a member of the Goldman Sachs board of directors, as CEO). That seemed to signal that all three of the major rumor-surrounded organizations would be seen as OK and the markets could be expected to respond favorably. Not so. The market continued roiling and rumors flew, and dark rumors flew fastest. The market was down Thursday and down again on Friday.

Markets, in the long run, are based on hard facts and realities, but in the short run—even for several weeks and months—markets can be driven by perceptions and even substantial misunderstandings. If everyone somehow believes something is true—even if it isn't—that "truth" can become more real than reality. As always, it's hard to prove a negative, particularly when everybody "knows" a false positive.

One example of the collective refusal to listen was so inexplicable it would have been comical if it were not so important. Fed regulations have one objective as their highest priority: Ensure the safety of consumer demand deposits, period. That's why the Fed has never allowed banks to use the funding linked with demand deposits to support trading, underwriting, or investing—the core activities of investment banking. And that meant if Goldman Sachs or Morgan Stanley or any other investment bank acquired or merged with a Fed-regulated commercial bank, the investment bank would have no access to funding from its demand-deposit business. When a commercial bank engages in investment banking activities, the capital needed to support that business must be raised separately and segregated from the capital used to undergird the deposit-taking business. Putting it the other way around, Goldman Sachs's becoming a bank holding company did not and could not mean that it could ever use demand deposits to fund its investment banking activities.

Despite this "carved in stone" reality and despite the fact that bank stocks are among the most widely owned and are extensively researched by a small army of financial analysts, a basic misunderstanding became somehow accepted as holy writ. The tight consensus on the Street that fall was that the best way out of any liquidity or capital solvency problem for Goldman Sachs or Morgan Stanley would be to combine with a large commercial bank to get the stabilizing strength of demand deposits. In a rare showing of frustration, Viniar recalls, "The facts were *irrelevant*. Those four days were unbelievable. If we had combined on November 1 with *any* bank with substantial demand deposits, the financial world would have burst into cheers—but it would have been horribly wrong."

Over 8,000 American banking institutions were now regulated by the Federal Reserve Board of Governors. Only two major ones were not: Goldman Sachs and Morgan Stanley. Goldman Sachs had from time to time considered the possibility of acquiring or organizing or even becoming a bank holding company and being subject to Fed regulation in order to have ready access to the assured liquidity of the Fed window. But such a move had never seemed sufficiently advantageous, and adding another set of unfamiliar regulations held no attraction. Moreover, the established arrangement with Sumitomo Bank in Japan gave Goldman Sachs access to all the credit capacity it could use.

But now, with financial markets in severe disarray and major competitors already forced out of business, the importance of public assurance and the convenience of ready access to the Fed window for instant, virtually unlimited liquidity both loomed large as attractions. Blankfein and his leadership team huddled and agreed: The least bad strategy was to join the crowd and become a regulated bank holding company. They would try to complete all the necessary work over that weekend.

"That was one of Goldman Sachs's proudest moments," recalls Viniar. "We had over five hundred people in New York and London all working together to find qualified 'bank' assets we could put into our Utah industrial bank subsidiary. We were looking for a *lot* of assets: $150 billion." The search was intensive and rigorously analytical and was typical of Goldman Sachs teamwork.

While most people worked that weekend on finding and gathering bankable assets, others worked on the complex application for bank holding company status. Some slept in the office so they could continue straight through those forty-eight hours. Some worked eighteen hours, went home for a few hours' sleep and then logged in another eighteen hours. "Our group overdosed on Adrienne's

Pizza!" laughs Viniar. "By Sunday night, Goldman Sachs was a bank holding company and that was it."

Fed regulation was not really new to Goldman Sachs. For six months—ever since two days after Bear Stearns had been acquired by JPMorgan Chase, skilled regulators from the Fed had been continuously stationed at Goldman Sachs. Viniar recalls, "We had had lots of open conversations and had developed a good understanding of each other's interests and objectives."

In Wall Street, an important part of a firm's credibility is based on the stature and sophistication of those from whom or with whom that firm gets its capital. If Wall Street's major firms were turning overseas to what some arrogantly called "dumb money" sources, that must mean that all the "smart" money sources had to be sitting on the sidelines, refusing to participate. If the other major firms were all being turned down by their traditional or conventional sources of capital, would Goldman Sachs get turned away too?

Blankfein, Viniar, Cohn, and Winkelried met again and again to consider their strategy. They were explicit about one rule: *all* options were on the table for frank discussion. After intense discussion, this group made an important strategic decision: Despite clear indications of real interest—from the most sophisticated sovereign wealth funds, they decided that Goldman Sachs would not raise capital from those funds.

At his office in Chicago, Goldman Sachs banker Byron Trott got the critical call from Omaha. Warren Buffett had been using Goldman Sachs more and more frequently for stock and bond trading and, far more important, for deals. The firm had become Berkshire Hathaway's most important Wall Street firm. When he was chairman, Hank Paulson had assigned Trott to work with—realistically, *for*—Buffett, who always made his own decisions quite independently. Trott understood, and the relationship between the two men worked well. (When Chicago's Pritzker family wanted to sell part of their Marmon Group, Trott had arranged an unusual phased sale to Berkshire Hathaway.) Trott had taken the idea of a major equity investment in Goldman Sachs to Buffett. Buffett indicated that, on appropriate terms, Berkshire Hathaway could be interested in making a sizable equity investment in Goldman Sachs.

Buffett, the most respected investor in the world, was at the absolute opposite end of the spectrum from the so-called dumb money that other firms had been recently turning to. Berkshire Hathaway was the ultimate blue chip with one of the world's few AAA credit ratings. An investment by this American icon at this crucial time would be magical. A significant equity investment when everyone was scrambling for any kind of capital would send a clear and powerful message to the world: Goldman Sachs was going to be just fine!

Viniar knew exactly how to negotiate deals with Buffett. Don't. Buffett would make one offer. As Viniar explains, "You either took it or you didn't. He wouldn't love you more if you took it or love you less if you didn't, but there would be no bargaining, negotiating, or haggling over *any* of the terms."

Buffett made his offer: "Berkshire is ready to invest $5 billion today in a 10 percent preferred stock convertible at $110 with warrants to buy an additional $5 billion of common stock at $115 per share." Buffett knew how important his investment would be and, having had real difficulties with his prior investment in Salomon Brothers, knew what terms he wanted. Those terms included a unique provision. Each of the four senior executives of Goldman Sachs must sign a pledge that they and their families would not sell any shares of Goldman Sachs stock before Buffett sold his. The details were spelled out to Viniar in a late morning half-hour phone call that ended at noon. Buffett's offer was firm until four that afternoon. So Goldman Sachs's leadership had just four hours to decide.

They didn't need four hours. Even with the personal lock-in provision, the answer was clear to everyone by three. Viniar called Buffett. "Sorry, Mr. Buffett is not available. He is away from the office and cannot be disturbed." It was two o'clock in Omaha—and Buffett was still at lunch with his grandchildren.

At 3:30 Eastern Standard Time, Buffett called Viniar back. Goldman Sachs, without question, accepted Berkshire Hathaway's terms. Done deal.

Berkshire Hathaway's investment stabilized the situation, and the market seemed to settle down. On the back of Berkshire Hathaway's investment, Goldman Sachs sold another $6 billion of common stock, mostly to institutional investors, bringing in more "smart" money. While other banks and firms were scrambling to raise money—even on onerous terms from unusual sources— Goldman Sachs had raised substantial money from blue-ribbon sources on acceptable terms. The message was clear: Goldman Sachs was proving itself to be different—very favorably different. It had been accepting capital infusions opportunistically and was now *over* capitalized.

The governments of the major industrialized nations around the world were all lining up to guarantee their countries' banks. Unless the U.S. government made similar guarantees, American banks would be at a serious disadvantage, particularly in funding their operations in the global capital markets.

On October 23, the Tuesday after Columbus Day weekend, more money came in—this time from the United States Treasury and the Federal Reserve. Although Goldman Sachs did not need the additional capital it had little choice but to accept the funds. TARP, the federal rescue fund, would invest $10 billion in the firm.

As he looks ahead, Blankfein understands that government regulation and changes in regulation will be a major part of the competitive landscape. Blankfein recognizes that his firm has "gone public" not only financially, but also politically. As treacherous as markets can be, politics and public opinion can be even more difficult to work with—particularly now. As usual, he sees the subject from several sides simultaneously. "Sarbanes-Oxley cost us $100 million, but has also made our processes stronger. Regulatory limits can be good for Goldman Sachs because the tighter they are, the closer everyone will have to come to where we already are on risk management, mark-to-market valuations, and reduced leverage." On the other hand, "The world will be poorer if legislation and regulation constrict the ability of capital markets to allocate risk capital effectively." Blankfein's love of history and his interest in strategy may be behind his broader assessment: "America was the epicenter of the global financial crisis, but we're coping with the problems better than many countries and, ironically, will probably come out of all this stronger—relatively—than we were before the crisis."

The big risk for Goldman Sachs is that the government—with politics being so important—could make some bad decisions. For example, former Fed chairman Paul Volcker has recommended not allowing *any* banks to take on market risks. "If all trading converts to riskless accommodation and mere matching-orders facilitation," argues Blankfein, "trading in the global financial system will be far less flexible and dynamic. Buyers and sellers don't always meet unless a dealer is willing to take risk at a price in between. That is the value added in our capital markets."

"The vitriol toward Wall Street casts a pall over our industry, including Goldman Sachs." observes Blankfein. "It's ironic that our longstanding tradition of public service is now so misunderstood in Washington and in the media. It's almost been turned on its head—a virtue turned into a vice. That weighs heavily on the people of Goldman Sachs, who care deeply about the quality of their work and contributions and how those are perceived. Reputation counts for a lot in this business."

Goldman Sachs wanted to get away from TARP as quickly as possible, but did not want to get away from being regulated by the Federal Reserve with ready access to the Fed window and the assured, immediate liquidity that provides—if and when needed. As a last resort, that access can be crucial (with it, for example, Lehman Brothers would not have gone bankrupt). But while continuing to be Fed regulated, Goldman Sachs would prefer to convert from a bank holding company into a financial holding company. This structure is already being used by General Electric Credit, American Express, and General Motors Acceptance Corporation—organizations that have more leeway in the way they conduct their business than bank holding companies and a somewhat different approval process. For now and the next two years, however, Goldman Sachs has a waiver: It can continue to conduct its business very nearly as it had done before Fed regulation.

Explains Blankfein, "The big risk for the capital markets—and for the national and global economies—is that decisions on regulation may be made solely for political reasons, not for economic reasons as they should be." Under TARP, the Fed can essentially set any rules at any time. To repay TARP, Goldman Sachs needed permission from Treasury and the Fed, so it waited until after the "stress tests" were completed in the spring of 2009 and showed the firm had substantial excess capital. In the spring, institutional investors were already signaling that they would be interested in investing substantial equity money in Goldman Sachs so it could repay TARP, but at the then current market prices of Goldman Sachs stock that would entail significant dilution for current stockholders.

Goldman Sachs made it clear that it wanted to repay the $10 billion it got from the Treasury in October *if* that could be done with the blessing of the Fed and Treasury. "Operating our business without the government capital would be an easier thing to do," Viniar told a conference in Naples, Florida, in early February. "It would send a very good signal."

As Blankfein and his colleagues looked around at the carnage on Wall Street, a few remarkable realities came into focus: Goldman Sachs was strong. It had more capital than it needed—and even more than it could put to use—and it had great liquidity. Even more important for Goldman Sachs's longer-term strategy, every one of its competitors would be significantly less powerful. Lehman Brothers had been broken up and parts had gone into Barclays Bank. This would make Barclays stronger, but would it ever be as strong as Lehman Brothers had been? Merrill Lynch's organization had been damaged and it had surely lost or would lose some of its best customers and its best businesspeople. Citigroup (including Salomon Brothers and Smith Barney) would mostly do "commodity" investment banking now. Its aspiration to be a formidable investment bank was, for now, just that—an aspiration. UBS, Credit Suisse, and Deutsche Bank would all refocus on their commercial banking business. Even Morgan Stanley was unsettled. Did it really intend to make a major commitment, as announced, to retail banking? Its leadership seemed uncertain about its basic strategy, which was surely not a good thing in such challenging times. Blankfein sees Goldman Sachs in good position to compete with commercial banks in providing credit.

Not only were its competitors now somewhere between destabilized and damaged, but Goldman Sachs now had surplus capital while most competitors were "capital constricted." Goldman Sachs was actively recruiting stellar senior "rainmakers"—increasing its competitive strengths for the future—with little competition for these recognized stars coming from *any* of the other major firms. On the other hand, smaller firms, unencumbered by FDIC or Fed regulation, were actively competing for top bankers and for corporate clients, particularly where raising capital was not of primary importance and advice on financial strategy was.

"The financial world *is* more complex, and government is now a greater strategic risk factor than the markets." Groups that are not experts on the securities business but that have or will have a great deal of influence and even control over his industry and his firm: "Impressions and perceptions today are so volatile. While they can come and go very quickly, we need to recognize that public mistrust and skepticism will shadow our industry for some time to come." The dramatic failures of the financial world; the inexplicable complexities of the arcane world of CDOs, asset-backed securities, and derivatives; the sudden controversial prominence of Goldman Sachs alumni—Rubin, Paulson, Thain, Corzine, Steel, Friedman—all these have been combining into a cacophony of suspicion and resentment. Still, while refusing to agree that Goldman Sachs is in a truly dominant competitive position, Blankfein allows, "I wouldn't change places with any of our competitors. We are in a good position at this time."

AFTERWORD

Friendship has been a vital factor in enlisting more than one hundred partners of Goldman Sachs to share with me their own recollections and stories about the firm. Our meetings, interviews, and critique-review sessions have renewed and enriched the many associations I so enjoyed developing while serving over three decades as a strategy consultant to the leaders of various parts of the firm in Asia, Europe, and North America. Readers should know that most of the conversations reported here are best-effort re-creations. In many cases I was not there, and those who were there are subject to all the familiar difficulties of precise recollection. That's why each conversation has been reviewed with those who know best what was said and how it was said. Not surprisingly, these reviews have reduced the amount of slang and the frequency of conventional expletives while increasing the substance.

Accuracy about names, dates, and facts is a strong habit—even a compulsion—for investment bankers generally and particularly for the partners of Goldman Sachs. Whenever possible, facts and perceptions have been verified by those partners of the firm who lived the experience. An example is telling: To check for accuracy and objectivity, I sent a draft of one chapter to one former partner. Several errors of fact and one misunderstanding—or misrepresentation, depending on your own perspective—were identified. Within a week, to be certain the story was factually accurate, four senior partners who had been out of the firm for fifteen years, all still very busy people, had offered to meet with me. Three current partners also agreed to help get the story told as accurately as possible. Six other former partners were helpful via telephone.

The same kind of generosity—born out of caring for the Goldman Sachs they knew or know—was shown by Treasury secretary Hank Paulson's spending nearly two hours with me the day after he returned from an important negotiating trip to China; former Treasury secretary Robert Rubin's spending three hours in two meetings; Governor Jon Corzine spending a long Saturday morning with me in Manhattan for candid, private discussion; former undersecretary of state John Whitehead's meeting six times (most recently between calls to UN secretary general Kofi Annan and New York mayor Michael Bloomberg); John Weinberg's inviting me to his home several times for three-hour sessions; or Geoff Boisi, Frank Brosens, John Browne, Lee Cooperman, Eric Dobkin, George Doty, Gene Fife, Bob Freeman, Steve Friedman, Jim Gorter, Steve Hendel, Bob Hurst, Steve Kay, Fred Krimendahl, Bill Landreth, John McNulty, Bob Menschel, Richard Menschel, Robin Neustein, John Rogers, Peter Sachs, David Silfen, Frank Smeal, Roy Smith, Bob Steel, L. Jay Tenenbaum, Barry Volpert, Pat Ward, Peter Weinberg, Mark Winkelman, Richard Worley, Ray Young, and Roy Zuckerberg each meeting with me numerous times.

Spacious as this book has become, the story of Goldman Sachs is more spacious still. A few of the firm's landmark adventures have been squeezed out of these pages by compassion for the reader. Primary among them is the long series of wildly complex deals in which Goldman Sachs was involved in selling and buying New York's Rockefeller Center, and then selling it again, more than doubling the firm's investment in five years to $1.85 billion. For similar reasons, dozens of lesser fascinating or amazing stories have been relegated to the end notes that follow these pages.

As my interest in researching and writing a study of America's great professional firms increased, that interest had to remain an abstraction. I was totally immersed in a thirty-year all-out drive to lead Greenwich Associates in developing a worldwide franchise of research-based strategy consulting with senior management at professional financial services organizations. Our dream was to

serve the leaders in all of the world's 135 financial markets. Developing collegial relationships with each of these complex client organizations absorbed all the
time and energy my partners and I had. All of us put aside other interests to focus
on our own firm's immediate challenges.

By the mid-1990s, the demands on time had crested and other activities were
permissible. Appointed to the Overseers' Visiting Committee at the Harvard
Business School, I was delighted to note that John Whitehead would chair our
group. I admired him as the finest strategist and organization leader-builder on
Wall Street and as my most rigorous, through, and effective client. On a personal
level, I liked him and found his high expectations inspiring. Besides, I had an idea
for a book and would need John's cooperation.

Working with the clients of Greenwich Associates, I'd gotten acquainted
with many of Wall Street's most interesting people and had heard stories of many
others. My plan was to write insightful profiles of the most interesting contemporaries and collect the best available profiles of prior heroes—and villains—into
an enjoyable weekend reader. I couldn't imagine such a collection without Whitehead. So, much as I intended to serve Harvard Business School in our two-day
meeting, I also hoped to persuade John to let me write a profile of him. It wouldn't
be easy: As a firm, Goldman Sachs has a near fetish about no publicity, particularly for individuals—which is why there had never been a profile on John Whitehead or John Weinberg—and Whitehead had already deflected me when I had
first raised the subject. "That's not really our way here." But he had not said no.

Lucky me. During the social hour at the end of the first day of meetings at HBS,
I noticed a slim, stylish woman I'd never met but everyone knew: the first woman
to became a star television reporter—the young, assertive woman who reported on
the Kennedy administration, Nancy Dickerson—Nancy Dickerson Whitehead.

Knowing she would understand the merits of visibility and recognition as a
leader, I introduced myself: "I need your help. I'm writing a book about the great
leaders in the world of finance, and your husband should be one of the people
featured most prominently. Several others have already agreed to participate, and
John Wiley & Sons will publish the book next year. Can you help me persuade
your reluctant husband?"

"Sounds interesting, but I'll have to talk with John. He would have to
decide."

Lucky again. After our meetings, I caught the early Sunday morning shuttle from Boston to LaGuardia. The plane was nearly empty—but John and Nancy Whitehead were already on it. With a quiet smile Nancy said, "Call John on Monday."

When I called and made an appointment for an interview, I knew that the "weekend reader" book of profiles would make it.* More important, that interview with John Whitehead would be the first step taken toward the present book. The second was when John Weinberg decided that if his friend and partner was participating, he probably should too. We met several times on Sundays at the Weinberg home. I became sure that an objective study of Goldman Sachs could and should be done. I was determined to do it.

Over the next few years, I met with and interviewed the partners and former partners I had known best. The more I learned, the more I was sure that a serious book about Goldman Sachs would be interesting to do and very interesting to read, and that to be accurate it had to be an up-close and personal study. However, at Goldman Sachs—perhaps because the firm was going public, perhaps because firm leadership had changed, perhaps due to a resurgence of the firm's traditional reluctance to have any outsiders write anything that the firm does not control—willingness to see a candid study done as a book slowed way down. This came to me in the person of the firm's longtime public relations specialist, Ed Novotny, who called to say he understood I was interviewing various Goldman Sachs alumni for a possible book and that he would like to meet me. We met for lunch at the Yale Club across from Grand Central Terminal, and Ed explained that senior management had asked him or one of his people to accompany me on all my interviews; if that condition was not accepted, the firm would pass the word to everyone not to cooperate with me in any way. He hoped I would understand.

Having no alternative, I agreed to give it a try, but it soon proved hopeless. A "chaperone" from Public Relations would come to each interview. While everyone was polite, the character of the interviews changed from candid and interesting to cautious and dull. The difference was decisive—and depressing. I was getting pablum. I would have to give up on something for which I had had such high hopes.

---

* It was published by Wiley in two volumes as *Wall Street People* in 1996.

Coincidentally, I happened to have lunch at Michael's Restaurant on Fifty-fifth Street in Manhattan with two old friends. After a while, one of them, Gershon Kekst, the preeminent public relations consultant to corporations, asked me, "So, Charley, what's important in your life these days?"

"You're a week too late with that question, Gershon. Last week I could have told you, but not this week."

"What happened?"

"Last week I was all excited about writing a serious book about Goldman Sachs and how it became the leading securities firm in the world, but that's now over. They've started sending chaperones to sit in on my interviews, so I'm not getting the spontaneous candor or insights you really need to tell the story accurately, and I'm only going to do such a book if I can do it right—and that means 100 percent objectivity, warts and all, which is never going to happen with those chaperones."

Kekst reflected on this lament briefly and, looking straight at me, said quietly, "Call my office—after four." He then explained that he was a public relations consultant to the firm and would be glad to speak on behalf of the project.

At 4:01 that afternoon, I called Gershon, who mentioned a name at Goldman Sachs and added, "He's expecting your call. He'll work it out with you." While I'll never know for sure, Gershon must have said something like "A book on Goldman Sachs is inevitable, so why not cooperate with someone the firm knows who will produce a serious book?" The simplicity of the arrangement was all I could ask for: I would have access to the firm's archives and could interview all the alumni I wanted, come back with a draft of several chapters, and work from there together. Word would be passed that anyone interested should participate; that Goldman Sachs would help with factual accuracy; that one executive would read drafts for warts-and-all objectivity; and that final decisions on content, style, and evaluations would be entirely mine to make.

The previous time this book nearly never got written was in 1973, the second year in the early torturous struggle to bring Greenwich Associates into being. With just $3,000 of capital, a one-room walk-up office, no clients, no experience in consulting, one employee, and just enough savings to go for a year without any income, Greenwich Associates and I began the scramble to make it. The early seventies were not a great time in financial services: As the stock market fell and interest rates increased again and again, investment banks, commercial banks, and bond dealers were all cutting costs; they had no compelling need for a new, untried kind of research-based consulting service from a new, untested firm.

In this grim environment, I was surprised to receive a call from Inez Sollami, secretary to Gustave Levy, the senior partner of Goldman Sachs: "Mr. Levy wants to see you Wednesday morning." For weeks I'd been trying to see someone— anyone—at Goldman Sachs, the leading institutional stockbroker, so this was a real break. As I reached for my appointment calendar, she continued, "At seven thirty sharp." I'd never heard of anybody having a business meeting in the office that early in the morning and didn't know what train might get me there, but I certainly didn't care. "Thank you. I'll be there."

On arrival at Goldman Sachs, I was taken to Levy's curious and unique office in the middle of the trading room.

"I understand you have a report on Goldman Sachs and Company."

"Yes, Mr. Levy."

"Call me Gus."

"Yes, sir. We do have such a report, but—"

"I'd like to see it."

"I'm sorry, but I was about to say we cannot offer it to you. Like an underwriting, we offered our service starting nearly two months ago and couldn't get anybody at Goldman Sachs interested before the offering period closed for this year—over a week ago. So I'm sorry to say it's no longer available this year."

"We both know it can't cost you more than $20 to make another copy. And I think you do know I can get what I want on Wall Street."

"Yes, I know. But we promised our clients."

Levy must have thought I was the dumbest guy he'd ever met. He waved his hand in dismissal and turned his attention quickly to other things.

As I left, it dawned on me that I now would have to tell my friend and partner, Allan Munro, that I had not only turned down a fee we desperately needed but also surely jinxed for all time any chance of ever working with Goldman Sachs by offending its legendary senior partner. As it happened, Allan was in California and we had no chance to talk together for two days. By the time we did, I had seen Goldman Sachs partner Bob Menschel while walking along Wall Street: "Hear you saw Gus yesterday." My heart sank: Was Levy so offended by my declining his offer that he had actually discussed it with his partner? Warmly, Bob continued, "Gus thought you were okay."

I was so relieved—and elated—that as soon as I was far enough along the sidewalk that Bob would not notice, I jumped into the air and clicked my heels, thinking, "Just wait until next year!" We were almost certain to have Goldman Sachs as our client then, because our research on the performance of all the major firms showed good news for Goldman Sachs: It was one of the best.

In the decades since then, one of my great pleasures has been to witness the remarkably consistent, gracious, and professional way that staff members bring to life every day the Principles of Goldman Sachs.

The last time this book was nearly never written is now. Given the remarkable talents and the driving ambitions of the many people of Goldman Sachs, it cannot be surprising that strong differences are experienced at all levels. Some differences are philosophical, some are personal. In the urgency to get on with the business, many hurt feelings and mistakes were never addressed or resolved. Many are revealed here for the first time. If a vote of the partnership were taken today, this book would surely be scuttled.

ACKNOWLEDGMENTS

William S. Rukeyser, as editor extraordinaire, has been my partner, mentor, and friend in the multidimensional challenge of converting draft chapters into a finished book. Sometimes admonishing, always genial, and superbly skillful, he has worked his magic on many levels—therapist, teacher, coach, trainer, cheerleader, and chaplain. We met and worked together when he was establishing *Money* as the best consumer magazine in personal finance and investing. I wrote a short piece, which he edited with a combination of grace, skill, and impact that astonished me over thirty years ago. We lost touch, but when I met another Rukeyser, I asked, "Do you know Bill Rukeyser?" and learned I was speaking with one of his brothers. Getting contact information, I reached out hoping Bill could, perhaps, nominate a capable editor for me to work with. Mercifully, he agreed to edit a book on Goldman Sachs himself. He is a master. Over more than a year of intense work, our relationship continues to be increasingly effective and fun.

Working with deadlines—by taking on too many commitments—has always been part of my career, beginning with sprints across the Harvard Business School campus to slip my written analysis of a case, or WAC, into the slot that would shut tight on the ninth bell for 9:00 on Saturday night, and at least once only making it by the eighth bell. Even though work on this book began twenty-five years ago and has been a priority commitment for most of the past ten years, as we zoomed toward the final few days when no extensions could possibly be granted, I was precommitted to working in Seoul and Singapore and, despite substantial jet lag, requested a wake-up call at 2 a.m. to keep up with Bill in an hour-long, last-minute final rewrite of a particularly complicated chapter. Even that was fun.

John Gaddis, one of Yale's most popular professors and a superb historian and friend, introduced me to Andrew Wylie, my literary agent, who took a précis for this book to dinner on Shelter Island with John Makinson of Penguin. After discussing several book ideas, Makinson said, "What I really want is a book on Goldman Sachs." Smiling, Andrew pulled out my précis and, before he left the table, a deal was done. Ann Godoff and Vanessa Mobley have made the challenge of meeting submission deadlines—adjusted mercifully three times—more than stimulating and quite inspiring. As our main editor, Vanessa beautifully balanced personal grace and decisive good judgment.

Catharine Fortin and Kimberly Breed have joined with patience and good-will in the numerous challenges of typing longhand drafts in illegibly small writing with imperfect pens and crotchety facsimiles. Ed Canaday of Goldman Sachs graciously took charge of fact-checking all dates, names, and amounts, but all remaining errors are clearly mine alone.

Linda Koch Lorimer—my beloved wife and best friend—reviewed and critiqued an early draft with her usual unusual ability to provide perceptive insight and advice. Eli Jacobs and David Darst both improved the final text significantly by tightening up the story and the telling.

More than one hundred partners of Goldman Sachs and the nearly as many competitors who have helped me understand the achievements of Goldman Sachs and the world in which they were accomplished have individually and collectively made writing this book one of my most treasured experiences in a very fortunate life. I am forever grateful.

My one regret is that most of the people who make Goldman Sachs the great firm that it is, and most of the work that they do, must go unreported in this necessarily selective sampling of their wide, deep, and continuous collective determination to excel. That's the irony of selfless dedication to teamwork in an organization where exceptional talent, skill, and drive are so consistently "usual." And that's what makes Goldman Sachs the greatest financial institution in the world today.

NOTES

CHAPTER ONE   BEGINNINGS

1. DeCoppet & Doremus, Charles M. Schott, and John H. Jacqueline.

2. Paul Sachs retired from the business in 1914 and joined the faculty of fine arts at Harvard, where, years later, he and his wife entertained Sidney's son, John Weinberg, for regular Sunday luncheons during his student years at Harvard Business School. Weinberg continued his learning in later life by reading books, particularly on Abraham Lincoln, and collecting Lincolniana. He eventually received honorary degrees from Harvard and Yale.

3. *New York Times*, July 24, 1969.

4. Paul Cabot.

5. Walter Sachs.

6. Joseph, born in Wurzburg, Bavaria, in 1817, had served as tutor to the daughter of a well-off goldsmith named Baer; he eventually fell in love and eloped with the girl, Sophia Baer, and sailed in 1848 to Baltimore, where they raised five children. Just before the Civil War, Joseph moved his family to New York City, where he established a school for boys.

7. Walter joined the firm actively in 1908 and stayed involved until his death at ninety-six in 1980.

8. Walter E. Sachs, Memoirs from Columbia University Oral History Collection, p. 46.

9. Sachs, p. 50. Their New York agent then was Winter & Smillie.

10. Sachs p. 53. The business was run by Siegfried Bieber for many years until he returned to Germany to be a director of Berliner Handelgesellschaf.

11. Sachs, pp. 60–62.

12. A combination of three cigar manufacturers: Wertheim & Schiffer, Hirschorn Mack & Co., and Straiton & Storm.

13. Father of Maurice Wertheim, founder of Wertheim & Co., now part of Schroders.

14. Stephen Birmingham, *Our Crowd* (New York: Harper & Row, 1967).

15. Sachs, p. 79.

16. Her husband, Samuel Hammerslough, who sold men's haberdashery, was Rosenwald's uncle. Reputedly, one of his customers in Illinois, who could never find trousers long enough to fit, was Abraham Lincoln.

17. Kleinwort & Sons had little or no distribution

capability—selling was considered crude and was socially disdained—so they simply held the stocks they had underwritten until World War II. They made a paper fortune, but it didn't last. During the war the British government expropriated all foreign investments of British subjects, and the Kleinworts patriotically put the money into "Daltons"—low-interest government bonds with no fixed maturity date. A decade later, the bonds' market value had dropped by 85 percent.

18. Sachs, p. 111.

19. Ibid., p. 113.

20. Ibid.

21. Ibid.

22. Ibid., p.118.

23. Ibid.

24. Ibid.

25. *Our Crowd*, pp. 334–35.

26. *New York Times*, July 24, 1969.

CHAPTER TWO   DISASTER: GOLDMAN SACHS TRADING CORPORATION

1. Stephen Birmingham, *Our Crowd* (New York: Harper & Row, 1967), p. 336.

2. Hard feelings continued to exist between the two firms until 1956, when Sears Roebuck decided to set up a sales-acceptance (financing) subsidiary and Sidney Weinberg called on Robert Lehman, Philip Lehman's son, to invite Lehman Brothers to resume its historical place in Sears's financings. Even then, there was continuing rivalry over which name would go first. When Gimbel's department store was brought to market, Bobby Lehman said he wanted to honor his father by listing Lehman Brothers in the preferred position. Sidney Weinberg protested: "We can't honor my father—he was a tailor!" Weinberg prevailed, as usual: Goldman Sachs stayed first.

3. Albert Gordon, in discussion with the author, November 2000.

4. Written in collaboration with William T. Foster.

5. In 1923, for example, Thomas McInnerney, president of Hydrox Ice Cream in Chicago, merged his company with Rieck-McJunkin Dairy Co. of Pittsburgh to form the nucleus of National Dairy Products, which then acquired a series of other dairy companies. Postum went public

with an issue led by Goldman Sachs, Lehman Brothers, and E.F. Hutton; with acquisitions of such brands as Maxwell House and Jell-O, it eventually became General Foods. Goldman Sachs financed Warner Brothers's conversion to the "talkies."

6. Birmingham, *Our Crowd*, p. 335.

7. Vincent P. Carosso, *Investment Banking in America* (Cambridge: Harvard University Press, 1920), p. 290.

8. By comparison, Lehman Brothers got 12.5 percent of the Lehman investment trust's net earnings. John J. Flynn, *Investment Trusts Gone Wrong* (New York: New Republic Inc., 1931), p. 97.

9. Sachs, p. 144.

10. Including, for a while, 50 percent of Frosted Foods. When Frosted needed substantial infusions of capital to finance growth, Goldman Sachs Trading sold that stake to the other 50 percent owner, General Foods.

11. Flynn, *Investment Trusts*, p. 184.

12. Gordon, discussion.

13. Barrie Wigmore, *The Crash and Its Aftermath: Securities Markets in the United States, 1929–1933* (Greenwood Press, 1986), p. 436.

14. Lisa Endlich, *Goldman Sachs: The Culture of Success* (Little, Brown, UK, 1999), p. 46.

15. Winston Churchill was in the Visitors Gallery that day.

16. Sachs, p. 164.

17. Catchings subsequently went to California and became a radio producer. His son, a classmate of Sidney Weinberg's older son at Deerfield Academy (class of '41), died of leukemia in his senior year.

18. Wigmore, p. 141.

19. Endlich, p. 48.

20. Other Wall Street firms did the same.

21. Endlich, p. 49.

22. Flynn, *Investment Trusts*, p. 111.

23. Harvey D. Gibson of Bankers Trust. See Wigmore, p. 254.

24. Wigmore, p. 465.

CHAPTER THREE   THE LONG ROAD BACK

1. Al Feld, November 17, 1996.

2. The firm had only three hundred to four hundred employees during Weinberg's years.

In 2007 Goldman Sachs employed nearly thirty thousand.

3. *Time*, August 1, 1969, p. 69a.

4. At his peak, Whitney had borrowed over five million dollars in unsecured loans from friends and business associates, plus $2,897,000 from his brother George Whitney and $474,000 from J.P. Morgan & Company. He pledged $657,000 in bonds from the New York Stock Exchange's Employee Gratuity Fund, as well as several clients' securities, to collateralize the large personal loans with which he raised money to meet margin calls. In 111 different transactions, he borrowed money to repay loans that totaled nearly twenty-five million dollars.

5. Leslie Gould, *New York Journal-American*, May 11, 1938.

6. E. J. Kahn Jr., "Profile: Director's Director," *New Yorker*, September 15, 1956.

7. *Fortune*, June 1937.

8. Sachs, p. 175.

9. Arranged through a Goldman Sachs partner, Ernest Loveman, who had developed longstanding friendships with the principals.

10. Kahn.

11. *Fortune*, August 2, 1989, p. 84.

12. Musica had been in and out of trouble with the police and had been in prison twice—once for bribing customs officials and once for grand larceny—but he was charming. When a detective sighted him at Grand Central Terminal and called out, "Hello, Phil!" Musica, who was well into his years of impersonating F. Donald Coster, didn't miss a beat. Explaining confidently that he had gone straight and had a new business in Greenwich Village, he urged the policeman to "come on down for a visit."

13. *Fortune*, August 2, 1989, p.84. Musica, the deputy treasurer, and an agent of McKesson were found, when fingerprinted, to be brothers who had executed a carefully planned scheme to embezzle the funds.

14. *Harper's Monthly*, 1937, p. 586.

15. *Newsweek*, August 4, 1969.

16. *Journal-American*, October 22, 1937.

17. The invitation came through retiring Ambassador Joseph E. Davies. In August 1939, Weinberg crossed the Atlantic on Davies's luxury yacht, *Sea Cloud*. "You were the life of the whole party and

with your wit and humor you kept us all in a good frame of mind and made the trip enjoyable and full of interest," wrote another passenger, Richard S. Whaley, chief justice of the U.S. Court of Claims.

18. Weinberg had another reason: His wife and sons would not have gone because it would require taking the boys out of school.

19. *New York Post*, April 26, 1938.

20. *Time*, December 8, 1958, p. 91.

21. Told by Charles Wilson, *New York Herald Tribune*, January 6, 1950.

22. *BusinessWeek*, January 27, 1951.

23. Kahn.

24. Walter Sachs.

25. Kahn.

26. Sachs, p. 203.

27. The sixteen other banking houses named as defendants were Morgan Stanley & Co., Kuhn Loeb & Co., Smith Barney & Co., Lehman Bros., Glore Forgan & Co., Kidder Peabody & Co., White Weld & Co., Eastman Dillon & Co., Drexel & Co., First Boston Corp., Dillon Read & Co., Blyth & Co., Inc., Harriman Ripley & Co., Stone & Webster Securities Corp., Harris Hall & Co., and the Union Securities Corp. Attorneys from ten eminent law firms represented the various defendants, spearheaded by Arthur Dean of Sullivan & Cromwell, Ralph Carson of Davis Polk Wardwell Sunderland & Kiendl, and William Dwight Whitney of Cravath, Swaine & Moore.

28. Continental Can, B.F. Goodrich, McKesson & Robbins, Lambert Co., and Madison Square Garden (for all of which he also served on the executive committee), plus General Foods, Sears Roebuck, National Dairy, Cluett Peabody, and General Cigar. Weinberg averaged 250 meetings a year for twenty years.

29. Revered as the man to see even two decades later, Sidney Weinberg was called on by Dan Lufkin in 1959; Lufkin wanted to tell him about his plan to form a new firm—Donaldson Lufkin & Jenrette—and sought Weinberg's advice. "I won't say you can't do it. And I won't say you won't make it. But getting people to change the firm they rely upon for the money they need is at least as hard as getting people to change their religion. You'll have a long, long road ahead of you and you will have to do everything right to earn the reputation you'll need to have with each organization you want to

be a client." Then he added knowingly: "And the competition on Wall Street is tough."

30. Kahn.

31. Mrs. Weinberg died in 1967. Treasury Secretary Henry Fowler flew from Greece to attend her funeral, and then flew back to Greece.

32. *New York Times,* August 1, 1969.

CHAPTER FOUR
FORD: THE LARGEST IPO

1. E. J. Kahn Jr., "Profile: Director's Director," *New Yorker,* September 8, 1956, pp. 50–54.

2. Ibid.

3. The work of Ted Yntema, the CFO, and his successor, Ed Lundy. The complete—and completely private—practice annual reports were produced for several years.

4. Blyth later merged with Eastman Dillon, which merged into PaineWebber, which sold out to UBS.

CHAPTER FIVE
TRANSITION YEARS

1. Whitehead tells this charming story about an experience while stationed in Scotland for D-day training: "On my first night off, I stopped at a little store near the boat landing to buy a newspaper, always a scarce luxury aboard the ship. There was a very pretty girl behind the counter. Her name was Nanette MacGregor. She was seventeen and I was twenty-one. We struck up a conversation and she invited me home for dinner. She had a wonderful family: parents and two younger brothers. A little home cooking was very welcome after several months of navy fare. And so for about a month, I spent my liberty evenings with Nanette. She was very sweet. We'd talk about the war and what we hoped to do with our lives. I grew very fond of her, but it was a pure and platonic relationship. I continued to feel committed to Anne Burnett [whom he had begun dating in college], whose picture was on my bureau on the ship.

"Al MacIntyre had a very different experience on his shift. He met up with a girl who couldn't wait to get to the hotel room in Glasgow. According to Al's reports at breakfast, she was quite insatiable. He said that he'd never before seen anything quite like it, even though he'd gone to

Princeton. He actually lost weight because they never got around to dinner. One day, after about a month, Al arrived at breakfast looking particularly badly. I asked him what was wrong. He replied, 'Nanette got drunk and passed out, and I finally had to leave her in the hotel room to get back to the ship on time.'

"'Who did you say?' I asked. 'Nanette,' he replied. 'That's the name of the girl I've been seeing." My heart sank. 'What's her last name?' I asked, and he replied, 'MacGregor.' I could not believe we'd both been seeing the same girl, but as we exchanged more information, we both knew it was true. That night was my last liberty night and I caught the train to Glasgow. Neither of us ever saw her again."

2. Coming out of HBS, Whitehead had two choices on Wall Street: joining Goldman Sachs or joining Equity Corporation with David Milton, who was married to the Rockefeller brothers' sister, Mary.

3. John C. Whitehead.

CHAPTER SIX   GUS LEVY

1. His widowed mother failed in her hope of marrying one of the daughters to a wealthy European and felt she couldn't face staying in New Orleans, so she moved to the Bronx, where she worked as a seamstress and depended in later years on her son for support.

2. A cousin of Bernard Baruch who adopted a different spelling.

3. Walter Sachs.

4. Janet Wolf Levy's father was a limited partner in Goldman Sachs from 1935 to 1945.

5. Sachs, p. 59.

6. Ibid.

7. Menschel began in 1952 by joining his uncle, who was a floor specialist. "My parents were very pleased: Here I was, twenty-three years old, fresh out of Syracuse University and already a member of the New York Stock Exchange! And my uncle, who had no sons, was also pleased. He taught me the business."

8. Members of the committee included John Whitehead, John Weinberg, George Doty, Ray Young, and Ed Schrader.

9. Michael C. Jensen, *The Financiers* (New York: Weybright & Talley, 1976).

10. Carl H. Tiedemann of DLJ.

11. Among his many other philanthropic commitments, he was treasurer of American Friends of Canada, president of Jewish Philanthropy of New York, treasurer of the International Synagogue at JFK Airport, trustee of the Jewish Museum, trustee of Fordham University and Reed College, and on the Board of Visitors of Tulane University. He received honorary degrees from Syracuse, Tulane, and Mount Sinai School of Medicine.

12. Levy was also chairman of Mount Sinai Medical Center and the Mount Sinai School of Medicine.

CHAPTER SEVEN THE WRECK OF THE PENN CENTRAL

1. At the time of Penn Central's bankruptcy, total commercial paper outstanding by all issuers was nearly forty billion dollars. Commercial paper came in two types. The larger part was issued directly to investors by giant finance companies like GE Credit, GMAC, and Ford Motor Credit, and $17.8 billion was issued by industrial corporations through commercial paper dealers, of which Goldman Sachs was the leader.

2. Goldman Sachs filed a creditor claim with its insurance company for $87.5 million.

3. Jonathan O'Herron, who had been at the Buckeye Pipe Line subsidiary. *Forbes*, December 15, 1973, p. 22.

4. Robert E. Bedingfield, "SEC's Study of Pennsy," *New York Times*, August 8, 1972, p. 41.

5. Paul A. Gorman.

6. "High Cost Money Hurts the Penn Central," *BusinessWeek*, June 6, 1970. By December 31, 1969, on a consolidated basis Penn Central's long-term debt (including obligations due within one year) was $2.6 billion. Of this, almost one billion dollars was due as payments of principal during the next five years. Payouts of $228 million were due in 1970, $156 million in 1971, $172 million in 1972, a staggering $270 million in 1973, and $160 million in 1974. Making this future even bleaker was the Penn Central's increasing difficulty in borrowing more money to refloat this debt, because there was so little unencumbered collateral left. As the Penn Central prospectus noted: "Substantially all investments and properties included in the balance sheet and substantially

all properties of the transportation company . . . have been pledged as security for loans."

7. Actually a subsidiary called Pennsylvania Company.

8. It was hardly normal for a railroad whose chief predecessor companies at one time were gilt-edged investments to borrow short-term Eurodollars and Swiss francs or borrow by issuing commercial paper. Even more unusual, neither the Pennsy nor the Central—unlike a majority of U.S. railroads—had ever before been through the wringer of bankruptcy proceedings. One result was that the Penn Central had never simplified its complex debt structure. It was, instead, a maze of bonds issued by some sixty subsidiary railroads, leased lines, affiliates, and other properties.

9. "The Penn Central's Misguided Gamble," *BusinessWeek*, June 27, 1970.

10. Michael C. Jensen, *The Financiers* (New York: Weybright & Talley, 1976).

11. On February 4, 1970, Goldman Sachs officials were "shocked . . . into immediate action," according to "Goldman Sachs Ordered to Pay," *Wall Street Journal*, December 30, 1970, p. 11.

12. H. Eric Heinemann, "Goldman Sachs Is Sued," *New York Times*, November 17, 1970, p. 63.

13. Including one brought by American Express, which had declined to participate in the November 1970 lawsuit, for $4.8 million, and one by Fireman's Fund for $1.9 million.

14. Peat Marwick Mitchell, the accounting firm named in the action, said in its statement that "the commission has before it no credible evidence which justifies action against the firm" and asserted, "The commission, once again, has seen fit to include auditors in its apparent program to offer scapegoats to the public."

15. In general, a consent agreement is an administrative decision expediting the disposition of cases involving alleged violation of federal securities laws. Although binding on the defendant because of the court's participation, it is not an adjudication because nothing has to be proved or disproved. It is similar to, but not the equivalent of, a plea of nolo contendere, since no admission or denial of charges is made, but usually grows out of an offer by the defendant to settle.

16. "Fraud at Penn Central?" *Newsweek*, May 13, 1974.

17. "Heavy, Heavy," *Forbes*, August 15, 1971.

18. Deposition read in Southern District Court of New York on September 12, 1974.

19. Southern District Court Reporter's transcript, p. 1459 for September 23, 1974.

20. Dun & Bradstreet won dismissal of a suit by Mallinckrodt Chemical charging fraud and negligence in NCO's giving Penn Central a prime rating. The court concluded that NCO had acted in good faith and had sent copies of Penn Central's poor earnings reports at year-end 1969.

21. Robert J. Cole, "Goldman Sachs Loses Case," *New York Times*, October 10, 1974, p. 69.

22. "Goldman Sachs Is Said to Pay," *Wall Street Journal*, March 20, 1975, p. 20.

23. "A Suit Is Averted," *New York Times*, March 22, 1975, p. 41.

24. "Goldman Sachs Ordered to Pay $500,000 in Suit Tied to Penn Central Collapse," *Wall Street Journal*, December 30, 1975, p. 4.

25. "Goldman Sachs Wins Suit," *Wall Street Journal*, June 14, 1976, p. 10.

26. "U.S. Appeals Court Overturns Ruling," *Wall Street Journal*, August 12, 1976, p. D-7.

27. The other 15 percent of the stock would be owned by Conrail employees through an employee stock ownership plan (ESOP).

CHAPTER EIGHT   GETTING GREAT AT SELLING

1. After graduating from the University of Pittsburgh, where he studied finance and accounting, Young had gone to Harvard Business School with 240 others in the accelerated program run for the navy. Derwood "Dee" Algar headed sales before Young became a partner in 1958.

2. In 1960, when the firm had 550 people, sales had seventy-four, with thirty-six of them over fifty.

3. Dick Menschel graduated from Syracuse, where he managed the humor magazine; joined the air force; then, with polio, spent eight months at Walter Reed Hospital and Warm Springs, Georgia, before going off to Harvard Business School and eventually joining Goldman Sachs in 1959. He held management roles thereafter. "My first assignment was a real break: working on the issuance of the Federal Street Fund under Mr. Weinberg." The "deal book" for that offering

half a century ago sits on the credenza in Menschel's office. In 1968 Menschel became partner in charge of the institutional sales department, selling both stocks and bonds.

4. Mnuchin had joined Goldman Sachs in 1957, straight out of Yale and the army. A champion bridge player with superb card sense, he was almost predestined for Levy's trading desk. "I always knew I wanted to be a trader," he recalled, "even though I didn't know anybody in Wall Street or anything about trading. After Yale and two years in the army as the most undecorated soldier in history, I went to Goldman Sachs, where Gus hired me." (Levy knew Mnuchin's father, a lawyer, through philanthropic work.) Told to report a few weeks later on a specific day at 8 a.m., Mnuchin went in at seven thirty hoping to get off to a good start and make a favorable impression. No such luck. "Gus had forgotten all about hiring me. But he was quick on his feet and said, 'You'll work in bonds for now.'" Mnuchin quickly figured out the real reason he was assigned to bonds: "That had to be because all the seats in equity trading—seven on one side and seven on the other side of the trading desk—were already assigned." After thirty-three years at Goldman Sachs (and earning $8.7 million in his final year), Bob Mnuchin left in 1990 and with his wife, Adriana, renovated and opened the luxurious Mayflower Inn in rural Connecticut. In addition, he built a major art dealership and she developed two retailing chains—Tennis Lady and Cashmere, Cashmere.

CHAPTER NINE   BLOCK TRADING: THE RISKY BUSINESS THAT ROARED

1. Managed by Jack Meyer, who went on to head investments at the Rockefeller Foundation and then to head investments at Harvard before establishing his own investment firm, Convexity Capital.

2. At the same time, the New York City pension fund, which had a disproportionate holding in the "Big Mac" bonds created to deal with the city's fiscal crisis—tax-exempt bonds in a tax-free portfolio—was selling those bonds in a wonderfully imaginative way. It conducted highly visible competitive-bid sales of fifty-million-dollar tranches of the bonds to the best bidder among a

group of major banks. All these sales were well covered by the press. Then, using that "fair pricing," the fund sold billions of those same bonds in strict secrecy to large insurance companies.

3. Two firms specialized in odd-lot retail transactions of less than one hundred shares to accommodate smaller trades made by numerous small retail accounts, packaging orders of fewer than one hundred shares into one-hundred-share round lots.

4. Truman Bidwell, a day trader at the NYSE, encouraged both Goldman Sachs and Donaldson Lufkin & Jenrette to engage in block trading. Dick Jenrette recalls, "Biddie came to me because we were both members of Chi Psi fraternity and explained how we at DLJ could do a very good business—at the old fixed-rate commissions—if we would commit a moderate amount of capital to 'inventory' or 'position' blocks of stock or, more often, parts of blocks when the other side was not fully available at that time and at that price." DLJ, Bear Stearns, and Shields & Co. joined in the business, but Goldman Sachs was always the clear leader.

5. Reciprocal business—called "recip" in the jargon of Wall Street—soon resolved into semiformal arrangements at understood rates, such as the equivalent of 8 percent interest for demand deposits maintained at banks or 6 percent of the value of mutual fund shares sold—with both sides keeping close track of the amounts of commission business promised and paid.

6. Sam Stayman, inventor of the Stayman Convention in bridge and one of the managing partners at Strand & Company, a hedge fund, and a friend and bridge partner of Mnuchin's, agrees: "There's a great similarity between trading and duplicate bridge tournaments. In tournaments, you have to imagine what's happening at the other tables, have a feel for the psychology of the situation at the moment, and Bob can do the same with markets."

7. *Institutional Investor*, October 1971, p. 53.

8. Ibid.

9. Ibid.

10. Who went on to be the powerful treasurer of the World Bank.

CHAPTER TEN REVOLUTION IN INVESTMENT BANKING

1. Admission to partnership required Whitehead to put up five thousand dollars, which, as the firm knew, was all the capital Whitehead had.

2. Weintz recalls that after serving in the air force, "I knew from my years at Norwich Academy, an all-boys school in Vermont, that college for me had to be two things: coed and in a warm climate. So I went to Stanford. Then into sales with Vicks VapoRub. I was very good at it, but it wasn't the career for me. Still, it was great training before going on to the Harvard Business School. Coming out of HBS, I wasn't sure what to do next, but a classmate, George Strong, urged me to interview with Goldman Sachs, saying, 'It'll be great practice for you because they're *very* thorough.' So I did and met [partner] Vern Horton, who had a great personality, and we hit it off well. This was even after he asked me if I'd taken any finance courses and, when I told him which ones, he'd asked, 'They're required, aren't they?' and I'd sheepishly said yes. Anyway, they invited me down, and I agreed because at the very least it was a free trip home. One Saturday morning, I was told, 'General Doriot wants to see you!' I ran right over with no shave and no tie. [Georges Doriot, an austere Frenchman, had served in U.S. Army procurement during World War II and, while a popular and influential professor at Harvard Business School, continued to use his military title.] "Doriot hit the roof when he saw me so disheveled and promptly sent me back to my dorm to get shaved and dressed. He'd been called by Goldman Sachs to ask what he thought of me. Doriot was not at all keen on Wall Street but acknowledged it would be useful to 'have a few of my boys down there' and encouraged me to go. During the next few weeks of job interviewing, Goldman Sachs was *everywhere*. I interviewed at Owens-Corning Fiberglas—with Jim Weinberg. At U.S. Steel, I interviewed with Bay Estes, who had been at Goldman Sachs. And it was the same at another place. I called my father and said, 'Dad, this Goldman Sachs is really wired in. They're really in on what's going on.' So I joined Goldman Sachs in 1954 at $4,200."

3. *Institutional Investor*, June 1987, p. 29.

~~R TWELVE~~
~~WO JOHNS~~

Institutional Investor, November 1977, pp. 21–27.

2. John Weinberg and John Whitehead, Memorandum to partners, October 27, 1976.

3. *Euromoney*, June 1990, p. 33.

4. *Euromoney*, January 1990, p. 38.

5. *Euromoney*, November 1992, p. 59.

6. Irwin Ross, "How Goldman Sachs Grew and Grew," *Fortune*, July 9, 1984, p. 158.

7. Roy C. Smith, *The Money Wars* (Truman Talley Books, 1990), p. 329.

8. Richard House, "Why Goldman Sachs Rankles Its European Rivals," *Institutional Investor*, December 1992, p. 71.

9. *Euromoney*, June 1990, p. 34.

10. *Forbes*, November 23, 1992, p. 115.

11. Doty had graduated from Fordham and Columbia Business School, worked at Price Waterhouse, and then switched to Lybrand.

12. Doty was not the first partner in charge of administration: Levy had called investment banker Myles Cruickshank back from retirement to do the job, and Cruickshank was proving that the concept of having a full-time administrative manager was effective when he died suddenly of a heart attack.

13. When new partners were being named, if you were not going to get "the call," one of the partners you worked with would take you aside the day before the announcements: "Don't come in tomorrow, okay?"

14. *Forbes*, November 23, 1992, p. 115.

15. *New York*, November 14, 1983, p. 14.

16. Paul Ferris, *The Master Bankers* (New York: William Morrow & Company, 1984).

17. *BusinessWeek*, "How Playing the Tortoise Paid Off for Goldman Sachs," May 7, 1990, p. 130.

18. *Financial Times*, January 18, 1993, p. 31.

CHAPTER THIRTEEN
BONDS: THE EARLY YEARS

1. And father-in-law of partner Roy Smith.

2. With Jim Gorter, Henry Fowler, Richard Menschel, Ray Young, and Levy.

3. Simon was offered the same 5 percent of the partnership that Weinberg and Whitehead then had.

4. After graduating from Dartmouth in 1961, Downey went into the army and then joined Liberty Mutual in sales before moving to R.W. Pressprich.

5. Not all niches were created equal: There was a strong negative public reaction against large corporations getting a tax break by doing huge industrial revenue bond financings—U.S. Steel had a one-billion-dollar issue—and in 1968, such financing was prohibited except for pollution-control projects. However, as Whitehead correctly anticipated, "There will be other types of municipal financing."

6. Michael Mortara in mortgages was a stellar exception: He accepted and was accepted by Goldman Sachs and became a major contributor until his premature death in 2000.

7. The Black-Derman-Toy model used the binomial tree framework of the Cox-Ross-Robertson model for valuing equity options.

8. Emanuel Derman, *My Life as Quant: Reflections on Physics and Finance* (Wiley, 2004), p. 285.

CHAPTER FOURTEEN   FIGURING OUT PRIVATE CLIENT SERVICES

1. Goldman Sachs had been in the individual or retail brokerage business since the late 1940s—but with little volume. In those days, one hundred thousand dollars of gross annual commissions with a payout to the salesman of thirty thousand dollars was considered good business.

2. Compensation was changed from a share in commissions generated—which had encouraged transactions and turnover—and linked to asset-management fees. While it would take time to build a base of business large enough to generate comparable income for the individual salesman, the rearrangement aligned individual incentives with the firm's business objectives. Personal incomes and firm profits both rose. Private wealth advisers, as they were now called, could concentrate on the core decision—setting the right asset mix—for each investor and leave the complexities of continuous implementation to investment specialists. This division between marketers and execution specialists, so reminiscent of John Whitehead's revolutionary restructuring of investment banking, converted PCS from an

"eat what you kill" hunter business to a sustained "agricultural" business that contributed steady, highly valued fee-based earnings in time to make an important positive contribution to the success of the firm's IPO.

3. Born into a lower-middle-class family in Buffalo, Dan Stanton lost his father when he was four years old. His mother became a high school teacher and put herself through law school, became a state attorney general and a judge, and eventually served on the New York State Supreme Court. Dan went to a Jesuit college, sold encyclopedias for Britannica, earned an MBA at Columbia, and got a job at Goldman Sachs in 1981.

CHAPTER FIFTEEN
J. ARON: UGLY DUCKLING

1. Trading in interest-rate futures began in 1975 and developed slowly in the first few years.

2. Tom Israel of A.C. Israel & Co., a commodities firm.

3. Customers were given code names or account numbers because the central banks of major countries insisted on privacy and everyone knew that an employee might, intentionally or unintentionally, tell somebody something somehow about a major country's monetary secrets.

4. The imperfection in the hedge was that London gold bars weighed four hundred ounces, while New York or Comex bars weighed one hundred ounces, so there was a small specific risk of having to pay a premium price to convert from one size to the other.

5. Metallurgy Hobshen of Belgium.

6. ACLI, a successor firm to A.C. Israel, was acquired by Donaldson Lufkin & Jenrette during this same period. Salomon Brothers's first major experience with commodities had come in the late 1960s when it went to A.C. Israel to get help deferring partners' taxable income. The technique arranged was to go long September "old crop" cocoa and short December "new crop" cocoa. This arrangement worked far better than expected: Not only were taxes deferred, but September cocoa went to unanticipated high prices, making a memorable profit for the partners of Salomon Brothers—and creating a very favorable view of commodities.

7. Endlich, p. 95.

8. *New York*, November 14, 1983, p. 16.

CHAPTER SIXTEEN   TENDER
DEFENSE, A MAGIC CARPET

1. After earning his MBA at Wharton in 1969, Bob Hurst joined Merrill Lynch, built up his clientele over the next five years, and became that firm's youngest vice president. In 1974, when a senior Merrill Lynch executive was transferred into investment banking and started calling Hurst's clients and acting as though he was their main banker, Hurst called Bob Conway at Goldman Sachs to say that he might be interested in a switch. Interviews were arranged with Ross Traphagen and Jim Weinberg in IBS. They went well, so Hurst met with John Whitehead. "He gave me the best 'negative' sale you can imagine, saying things—one right after another—like: 'You're doing so very well at Merrill Lynch, surely you wouldn't want to have to start all over from the bottom of the ladder at Goldman Sachs'; 'We are very reluctant to bring people in laterally, and you would be seen as an outsider'; 'You must recognize that it will take considerable time for you to prove yourself externally with the companies you'll be assigned and even harder to prove yourself internally at Goldman Sachs.' By the time Whitehead had put down all these negatives—which, of course, I assured him, challenging as they might be, I was sure I could overcome—he had me selling myself on a switch to Goldman Sachs in the most effective way!"

CHAPTER SEVENTEEN   THE USES
AND ABUSES OF RESEARCH

1. Bowen was an early president of the New York Society of Security Analysts.

2. After four years as an undergraduate at Columbia University and one unhappy year at Columbia Business School, Ellis got a job in research at Bank of New York under Carter Bacot, who went on to become CEO. Ellis's father was a retailer, and Joe had worked in the store, so he became a retailing analyst at BoNY. After five years at the bank and a second recruiting invitation, he joined Goldman Sachs, where he became the first analyst without managerial responsibility to become a partner. He stayed twenty-eight years.

3. Einhorn went to Rutgers and the University

of Illinois for its PhD program, but his plans for an academic career got aborted by a phone call. "I was teaching a course in investments using the textbook written by Cohen, Zinbarg, and Zeikel and was looking for a summer job. My dad knew an HR manager at Prudential and found there might be an opening in economics. One evening, I was startled by a phone call—from Ed Zinbarg, one of our textbook's authors. He was chief investment officer at Prudential. I started there and then went on to Goldman Sachs."

4. Patrick McGeehan, "Goldman Sachs Releases Stock Analyst," *Wall Street Journal*, May 28, 1999.

5. The fifty million dollars intended for investor education ran into a political squall within the SEC and got stymied. The professionals who had volunteered to serve the public interest all resigned in protest.

6. Patrick McGeehan, "Goldman Sachs Moves to Tighten Stock Analysts' Independence," *New York Times*, February 20, 2002.

Chapter Eighteen
John Weinberg

1. The IRS guidelines, structured to prevent individual investors in small companies from unfairly getting capital-gains tax treatment on distributions that were really dividends, specified exactly what constituted maintaining an investor's percentage ownership and therefore what constituted a dividend rather than the proceeds of a sale. The arrangement between DuPont and Seagram followed the guidelines precisely but achieved a result directly opposite to the IRS's expectation. Using derivatives and a time-structured agreement, the payment from DuPont to Seagram was clearly a dividend as defined by IRS guidelines. (Under Canadian tax law, which affected Seagram, the dividend was also tax-free at the Canadian corporate level.) Specifically, Seagram was paid one billion dollars in cash and $7.3 billion in ninety-day notes with equity warrants worth $440 million, and it retained 8.2 million shares. The warrants would allow Seagram to purchase forty-eight million shares of DuPont at $89 for a period of sixty days in 1997, fifty-four million shares for sixty days in 1998, and fifty-four million at $114 in 1999. Because Seagram got warrants to buy 156 million

shares—exactly equal to the 156 million shares it sold—it was deemed to have maintained exactly the same beneficial equity interest in DuPont. The reality that the warrants would never be exercised simply didn't matter. Soon after the repurchase, Congress introduced legislation to change the law governing this type of transaction.

2. *American Lawyer*, November 1981. Weinberg's serving on Seagram's board of directors also precluded Goldman Sachs from engaging in lucrative arbitrage.

3. *New York Times*, August 16, 1984.

4. John Weinberg's other directorships included Knight-Ridder, Witco Chemical, McKesson & Robbins, Cluett Peabody, Cowles Communications, Bulova, General Development, Van Ralte, Capital Holding—as well as Seagram and DuPont. Weinberg also served as a charter trustee of Princeton and on the boards of Deerfield, Teachers College, New York Hospital, the Japan Society, the China Medical Board, the Economic Club of New York, and the American Arbitration Association. He was the only investment banker on the Business Council, the prestigious group organized by his father at FDR's request.

5. One cheery paternal invitation to "come for dinner and stay the night" was given without concern that the room and board would be proffered at J. P. Morgan's stately home in Washington, D.C., being used during the Korean War by Sidney Weinberg and his two senior colleagues on the War Production Board, General Lucius D. Clay and Charles E. "Electric Charlie" Wilson—or concern that the younger Weinberg was then a very junior officer in the Marines.

6. *New York Times*, August 16, 1984.

7. Robert J. Cole, "Low-Profile Leader Takes Charge," *New York Times*, August 16, 1984, p. D5.

8. Dorothy Rabinowitz, "A Cautionary Tale," *New York*, January 8, 1990, p. 35.

9. "Goldman Suffers Some Blemishes," *Wall Street Journal*, January 18, 1990, p. C-1.

10. Weinberg and his wife, Sue Anne, who studied for a doctorate at Columbia Teachers College, were married for over forty years.

11. Managing director of Sumitomo Capital Markets Inc., Kondoh was a brilliant maverick, fluent in English, and a high-ranking graduate of the elite University of Tokyo. Assigned to interna-

tional planning, he performed a key role in a two-million-dollar 1985 strategic planning exercise for Sumitomo by McKinsey & Company.

12. Morgan Stanley's market value at the time was a little higher—three and a half times book.

13. Roy Smith and Michael Coles were both on Gant's negotiating team. After going limited, Coles served as an adviser to Sumitomo's New York branch. (He gave his retainer fee to charity.)

14. Voting rights were never offered and never requested.

15. Before the first five years were up, Bob Rubin wanted to press for an extension. Don Gant would have waited longer, knowing that Sumitomo wouldn't want to lose face by having the deal come apart and believing that waiting could create time pressures that might enable Goldman Sachs to obtain more favorable terms, such as reducing the 12.5 percent to 10 percent. Rubin, Gant, and Weinberg went to Tokyo for a spectacular ceremonial dinner with Sumitomo executives, at which Rubin said Goldman Sachs would like to extend the relationship ahead of schedule. The Japanese were more than pleased.

16. Gant was well advised by Rodger Cohen, who had had an office in Japan and who later became managing partner of Sullivan & Cromwell.

17. Fifty years after the war, Weinberg recalled how harsh combat had made both sides: "The Japanese never signed the Geneva Convention on war conduct, which covered taking and holding prisoners. If you took a pillbox or something, Japanese soldiers would come out with their hands up—holding grenades behind each hand—until they got close enough that you might see the grenades and then they would throw them at your unit. The battalion commander came around saying, 'This will not be in writing, but we are not accepting any more surrenders.' We captured a group of Japanese soldiers in an old copper-mine tunnel. I went over thinking I'd sit in the shade in the tunnel. My sergeant suggested I go elsewhere. I said I'd planned to sit in the shade. I was eighteen then, too young for what they planned to do. So my sergeant says, 'Sir, get the fuck away from here!' And off I went. My gunnery sergeant was a real old-corps Marine who asked me one day if I'd ever killed a guy. "Not that I know of." So my sergeant tells me that won't do and sets up to change

it. I was a pretty good shot in those days . . . so it didn't take very long."

18. Weinberg joined the Marines in World War II as a private, rising to second lieutenant. Called back to service in the Korean War, he mustered out as a captain. At his funeral, the honor guard folded the American flag into the traditional perfect triangle for presentation to Sue Anne Weinberg. The recessional was the "Marines' Hymn."

19. Weinberg's home was in the nearby town of Greenwich.

20. *Economist*, September 29, 1990, p. 93.

CHAPTER NINETEEN
INNOCENTS ABROAD

1. Brown's father had been in the Occupation forces, so he grew up speaking Japanese. He joined the Jesuits, who sent him to teach and learn economics at Harvard Business School, but in Boston he met a Japanese woman who was studying at the New England Conservatory of Music, fell in love with her, left the church, and joined Citicorp, where he worked in a joint-venture consulting company with McKinsey.

2. Coles was born in England, skipped college, flew in combat in Korea for the Royal Navy, fell in love with an American, and applied to and was accepted by Harvard Business School before joining Goldman Sachs.

3. Four years later, the firm had three times as many people—180—and was moving into offices in the Old Bailey office complex.

4. Established as First International Bank Ltd. in 1973 by the First National Bank in Dallas, the unit had been one of the more aggressive UK merchant banking subsidiaries of a U.S. commercial bank until reined in by its parent in 1979, which caused several senior people to quit. When acquired by Goldman Sachs, it had a dozen employees and loans outstanding of only forty million dollars.

5. After Big Bang, J.P. Morgan nearly acquired Wood Mackenzie but called off their deal at the altar. Wood Mackenzie subsequently merged with the merchant-banking firm Hill Samuel & Company, and the merged firm was later combined into NatWest Securities, the stockbroking arm of National Westminster Bank.

6. Another strategic opening not taken can be

traced back to Whitehead's experience at Haverford College. Edmund Stennis left Germany in the early thirties because he was so opposed to Hitler and taught at Haverford College, where his students included Whitehead, who recalls that Stennis rebuilt his family fortune through astute investing while teaching. As Whitehead explains, "Stennis had contributed about one-third of the capital Siegmund Warburg needed to launch New Trading Company—which fledgling firm later became S.G. Warburg & Company—so it was not surprising that Stennis introduced me to Siegmund Warburg. We became good friends and I visited him several times at his home in Switzerland. Siegmund maintained in public that he'd retired from Warburg's, but he actually kept very tight control with telex instructions on very specific operational matters—three times every day."

Goldman Sachs might have combined with S.G. Warburg: One firm was the leader in the United States but not significant in the UK; the other firm was powerful in the United Kingdom but not in America; Neither was strong on the European Continent—and both needed to become strong in each other's market to be truly "international." Whitehead explained why that didn't happen: the subject "had never been even considered because we just don't believe in expanding through acquisitions. Besides, we would have had problems with their having several quite powerful but much, much older partners. Also, they have a tendency, as we saw it, toward what might be patrician to some, but to others could seem like arrogance. Slow and cautious we may well be, but we always want to build up our own, one step at a time."

7. Mulvihill was the same "uncle" who advised younger stars: "Weddings, bar mitzvahs, and funerals are all once-in-a lifetime events in the employee's life. Go to every one you possibly can—and always get there at least fifteen minutes early, so you'll have plenty of time to make friendly small talk with the other people who care too."

8. Ward and Mayhew later became friends. Mayhew's son got a job at Goldman Sachs and Ward spent weekends at Mayhew's country home. Knowing Mayhew was an old Etonian but not a college graduate, Ward decided on another occasion to have some fun with him. "What did you study at Cambridge, David?"

"I didn't go to Cambridge," came the quick, quiet reply.

"Oh, not Cambridge. Well then, what was Oxford really like?"

"I didn't go to Oxford," came a still quieter reply, and then, in a combination of apology and drawing a "do not cross it" line in the sand, Mayhew went on: "In my day, most young boys did not bother going to university."

9. Peter Spira, who had joined from S.G. Warburg, saved the firm from losing the mandate by deleting an excessive *force majeure* provision that would surely have been rejected by HM Treasury if noticed and probably the firm would have lost the mandate which proved crucial to its success in Europe.

CHAPTER TWENTY-ONE   HOW BP ALMOST BECAME A DRY HOLE

1. The market fell 12.8 percent on October 28, 1929, "Black Monday," the worst single day of the 1929 crash.

2. James Hanson, chairman of Hanson Trust, had secretly called on Chancellor of the Exchequer Nigel Lawson at No. 11 Downing Street in May 1985, offering to buy the whole block of BP. Lawson declined, explaining that a wide shareholding would be sought, not a single buyer.

3. Nigel Lawson, *The View from No. 11*, p. 758.

4. Two smaller government companies had already been privatized: Amersham for seventy-one million pounds, followed by Britoil for £549 million.

5. Clement Attlee's Labour government gave five reasons for nationalization in 1945: improve labor relations; promote full employment; increase productivity; make regulation of monopoly more efficient; and replace short-term expediency with broader national priorities.

6. Most British underwriters kept 5 percent of their total participation; BP's advisers—Rothschild and S.G. Warburg—kept 10 percent. Schroders's loss on its £10 million underwriting was only a very tolerable £1.5 million.

7. Lawson, *View from No. 11*, pp. 774–75.

8. The Labour Party's spokesman had apparently resolved in advance to attack Lawson's decision;

he evidently had been led to believe Lawson would simply defer the matter. Surprised by Lawson's announcement, he immediately reversed his own argument, saying the issue should have been postponed and opening himself up for a classic parliamentary putdown as Lawson, who knew Gavyn Davies had worked in the past for Labour, mocked him in swift reply: "The Labour Party today is simply the friend of Goldman Sachs!"

9. The same accounting treatment was used for the Maxwell settlement and for the fine in the so-called Analysts settlement.

10. Lawson, *View from No. 11*, p. 275.

CHAPTER TWENTY-TWO
CHANGING THE GUARD

1. Rubin had a subtle, graceful style and a quirky sense of humor that had special meaning for the brilliant young people who worked with him. Some of the most treasured stories were trivial in substance but not in their meaning to the insiders. For example, Rubin and Brosens often shared a cab uptown. Rubin always got out first and always paid the fare, tipping generously. One night, Brosens protested that he should at least split the fare. Rubin shook his head. Smiling, Brosens reached into his pocket and pulled out a quarter, which he ceremoniously presented to Rubin, who looked at it solemnly, paused, and then observed quietly with exaggerated ceremony, "You're overpaying me," and then paused again before saying, "Let me think about that." After a still longer pause, he came to his considered, final conclusion: "No. that wasn't really right. You wouldn't be overpaying me. You'd be *way* overpaying me"—and smilingly piled out of the cab.

2. Linda Sadler, "Goldman Is Being Aggressive," *Wall Street Journal*, January 9, 1985, p. 4. The market-share numbers came from Securities Data.

3. Rich Friedman (no relation) was the operating head of the unit.

CHAPTER TWENTY-THREE
TRANSFORMATION

1. Fischer Black had understood the power of technology in trading securities early, and in 1971

wrote a prescient paper: "Toward a Fully Automated Exchange."

2. Black and Scholes wrote a paper in 1973 showing both their derivation and Merton's, but it was so arcane that professional journals repeatedly rejected it until, after several years, Merton helped them get it published.

3. Partly at the suggestion of Jack Treynor, who had known him at Arthur D. Little.

4. Perry Mehrling, *Fischer Black and the Revolutionary Idea of Finance* (John Wiley & Sons), p. 219.

5. Mehrling, *Fischer Black*, p. 12: Svi Bodi interviews with Fischer Black in July 1989.

6. Stanley Diller, former professor at Columbia Business School, made a similar contribution in fixed income.

7. In February 1990, Black moved over to the fixed-income management group in GSAM, and in late 1992 he moved to fixed-income research.

8. Mehrling, *Fischer Black*, p. 241.

9. Ibid., p. 284.

10. Ibid., p. 97.

11. The arithmetic average of 1 and 3 is $(1 + 3)/2$, or 2, while the geometric average of 1 and 3 is $(1 \times 3)/2$, or $1\frac{1}{2}$.

CHAPTER TWENTY-FOUR
FALSE STARTS IN INVESTMENT
MANAGEMENT

1. Capital Group Companies manages the American Funds group of mutual funds for individual investors, Capital Guardian Trust for institutional accounts, and Personal Investment Management Services for wealthy-family funds. Capital Group Companies is one of the world's largest and most capable investment-management organizations. (See my book, *Capital*, published by John Wiley & Sons, 2004.)

2. Later, in the 1980s and 1990s, Merrill Lynch, Morgan Stanley, and Credit Suisse First Boston each built a large investment management business.

3. Later James Coxon came over from London to head up sales. He did do some successful selling.

4. Anise Wallace, "New Division Is Planned by Goldman," *New York Times*, May 9, 1989, p. D5.

5. Michael Siconolf, "For Just $1,200, You Too Can Be Goldman Client," *New York Times*, April 6, 1990, p. C-1.

6. Barbara Donnelly, "Goldman Offers Fund of Its 'Top 50' Picks," *Wall Street Journal*, June 21, 1991, p. C-1.

7. McNulty nearly went to another firm when he came out of Wharton. "Do you have any plans?" asked George Ross, head of Goldman Sachs's office in Philadelphia and a repetitively successful recruiter of Wharton's best MBAs. It was a Sunday afternoon. "Yes, I'll be joining Salomon Brothers on Monday," said McNulty. Stormed Ross in reply: "I'll be goddamned! No way! You be near your phone tonight, ready for a call!" Later that evening Ross called to say he had talked with Richard Menschel and he was now making a firm offer. McNulty accepted and joined PCS to work in Florida. "Goldman Sachs had a very special feeling about it. Joining was like coming home. The work was a true vocation."

8. Smirlock paid the SEC a fifty-thousand-dollar fine to settle the charges.

Chapter Twenty-five Robert Maxwell, the Client from Hell

1. Maxwell had a twenty-million-pound life insurance policy underwritten by several Lloyd's of London syndicates. The policy would not pay off if death were due to natural causes, such as a heart attack, but would be triggered if death were due to an accident or murder. Dr. Iain West, head of forensic medicine at a London hospital, prepared the British pathologist's report.

2. Gordon Thomas, *Gideon's Spies: The Secret History of the Mossad* (New York: St. Martin's Press, 1999), p. 219.

3. Nick Davies, *Death of a Tycoon* (New York: St. Martin's Press, 1992), p. 339.

4. The terminology used by British regulators.

5. In late 1985, Maxwell acquired a substantial stake in Britannia Arrow (previously called Slater Walker Securities), which had acquired the investment firm MIM from Aetna. Britannia Arrow later acquired Invesco Capital Management. The investment firms were combined and took the name Invesco MIM PLC in early 1990.

6. Department of Trade and Industry, Report, 1974, p. 7. Under British law, the pension funds were not required to have trustees.

7. Ibid.

8. Ibid., p. ix.

9. Maxwell organized Bishopsgate Investment Management, whose sole business was managing the MCC and Mirror Group pension funds. All but one of BIM's directors were directors of Maxwell's private companies. Inexplicably, Britain's Investment Management Regulatory Organisation licensed Bishopsgate under the Financial Services Act of 1986, which is why Maxwell had access to the funds' assets. As a result, the British government arguably had a moral responsibility to recover the funds lost or purloined.

10. Ibid., p. xv.

11. Ibid., p. xvi.

12. Only arm's-length transaction business was to be done. Goldman Sachs was not to act as an agent for Maxwell, and he was not to be a client of the firm.

13. Peter J. R. Spira, *Ladder and Snakes* (privately printed, 2005), p. 280.

14. His talent as a trader was real. In 1991, when the Vuitton family wanted to sell a $320 million block of LVMH shares, their traditional banker, Banque Paribas, offered to buy the shares at a discount, but Sheinberg won the trade by bidding at the market. He then outmaneuvered short-sellers by buying two hundred million dollars more shares and then, as the shorts bid up the price to cover their short positions, reselling to institutions on the basis that a premium was justified by the unique company, its unique value, and a unique opportunity to obtain good-size positions. Sheinberg played his cards skillfully—and, as a trader, made a profit of over ten million dollars.

15. Department of Trade and Industry, Report, 1991, p. 25.

16. John Mason, "Maxwell Trial," *Financial Times*, September 23, 1995, p. 6.

17. Fife's personal share of the settlement was four million dollars. Reserves—at a larger amount—had been taken in 1991, 1992, and 1993, so charges would have to be shifted back and changed to the correct amount now that the settlement had been set at $254 million.

18. Anita Raghavan, "Goldman Sticks to Plan on Allocating Settlement Lost," *Wall Street Journal*, April 14, 1995.

19. Norma Cohen, "Sheinberg Steps Down," *Financial Times*, November 29, 1994, p. 30. Mirror Group Newspapers's pension fund trustees

filed lawsuits in New York seeking fifty-seven million dollars from both Sheinberg and Goldman Sachs. As the *Wall Street Journal* reported: "Despite the fine, Goldman tried to distance itself from the Maxwell matter. 'The regulatory glitches have nothing to do with Robert Maxwell,' said Gregory Palm, a Goldman partner and co-general counsel. 'They really aren't Maxwell related,' he said. 'They were back-office accounting and computational errors that had nothing to do with who was on the other side of the trade.' He added: 'In any transaction of the same type, the same problem could have arisen.'" The Financial Services Authority's disciplinary order specified that "SFA did not conclude that Goldman Sachs or any of its personnel participated in any illicit conduct with, or were aware of illicit conduct by, Maxwell or any entity controlled by or associated with him."

20. Michael Siconolfi and Nicholas Bray, "Britain Orders Goldman Sachs to Pay a Penalty," *Wall Street Journal*, June 17, 1993, p. A-6.

21. DTI Report, p. 28.

22. G. Rascal Zachary, "Goldman, Coopers Are Cited in Report on Maxwell Collapse," *Financial Times*, April 2, 2001.

23. "Maxwell Trial: Goldman Sachs May Have Wrecked Deal," *Financial Times*, October 19, 1995, p. 11.

CHAPTER TWENTY-SIX MAKING ARBITRAGE A BUSINESS

1. Calm and smooth as he usually was, Tenenbaum was not *always* detached. On occasion, Tenenbaum's frustrations reached overload and he showed a terrific temper—once pulling the telephone out of the wall and throwing it across the trading room.

2. Robert Rubin grew up in Miami, Florida, and came to Goldman Sachs after Harvard College, London School of Economics, Yale Law School, and two years of practicing law at Cleary Gottlieb.

3. During the 1970s—as the stock market averages fell, inflation rose to record highs, underwriting volume plunged, and profitability on Wall Street dried up—most of the other firms cut back on arbitrage, but Goldman Sachs got even more active. With almost no real competitors, it nearly had the market—and the profit opportunities—to itself.

CHAPTER TWENTY-SEVEN J'ACCUSE

1. Lisa Endlich, *Goldman Sachs: The Culture of Success* (New York: Little Brown, 1999), p. 113.

2. James Buchan, "Handcuffs on Wall Street," *Financial Times*, February 16, 1987.

3. "Suspicious Trading," *Wall Street Journal*, February 12, 1988, p. 1.

4. By selling and promptly rebuying, Freeman effectively deferred settlement by a few days while maintaining his position. The "financing" cost him one-eighth of a point in price change and would lead to a massive change in his life.

5. Siegel was the first in his family to go to college, determined to advance as far and as fast as possible and not repeat his father's going bankrupt at forty-seven. Robert Siegel and his brother had owned three shoe stores serving a middle-class market near Boston. They struggled to survive as retailers of American-made shoes in competition with low-cost imports and efficient chain operations.

6. Siegel was close with Ivan Boesky, investigators found. He had invited Boesky to play tennis in the spring of 1982. Boesky arrived in a pink Rolls-Royce. When Siegel, then thirty-four, expressed concern about the future of his firm and said he was sure it was cramping his own business, Boesky offered a position in his firm, Ivan F. Boesky & Company. Boesky called that summer and invited Siegel to meet at New York City's Harvard Club for a drink. Guiding the conversation to personal finances, Boesky renewed his job offer. Siegel demurred but had an alternative: He could consult to Boesky on possible takeover situations and earn consulting fees on the side or a year-end bonus. Both men knew just what they were saying, without being explicit. Since Boesky was such an active trader in so many stocks, Siegel's tips would be easily mixed in with Boesky's other trading and go unnoticed, particularly if the trades were done well in advance of any specific deal. "Let's have coffee" became their telephone signal for a personal meeting.

7. Other call holders in the arbitrage department agreed and sold too. One arbitrageur was away that day and did not sell: Bob Rubin.

8. Sarah Bartlett, "A Top Trader at Goldman

Sachs Pleads Guilty," *New York Times,* August, 1987, p. 1.

9. In a case involving Equity Funding and an analyst named Ray Dirks, who first identified a massive fraud, the SEC argued that when an expert got an apparently innocuous piece of data that he could fit with other pieces to form a decisive insight, he had made himself an insider. The Supreme Court rejected this approach for outsiders with no fiduciary responsibility to the corporation.

10. James B. Stewart, *Den of Thieves* (Simon & Schuster, 1991).

11. Levine was, in fact, typical of the people who lie, cheat, and steal in various fields: counterfeiters of papal bulls in the Middle Ages, scientists who falsify data on experiments to get publishable results, housewives who cheat on their husbands, and citizens who play games on expense reports or on income taxes. Deceivers typically focus on their own immediate gain and deny or discount the penalties and percentages of getting caught, wrapping themselves and their thoughts in private delusions. While each delusion is singular in its details, they follow an intriguingly consistent pattern. Most get involved gradually, never quite recognizing or admitting to themselves that they have broken their own promises or have broken the norms of the community in which they live. Most deceivers are new to their community—which is partly why most feel so little loss in flouting community rules. They have little invested in their connections with the established norms, the reasons the norms were established, or the reasons for adhering to them.

12. *New York Times,* January 10, 1986.

13. James Sterngold, "Goldman Aide Tied to Insiders," *New York Times,* October 9, 1986.

14. *The Economist,* February 21, 1987, p. 81.

15. Endlich, *Goldman Sachs,* p. 118.

16. Confirmed recently directly to the author by the then head of investment banking at Kidder Peabody and the then CEO of Drexel Burnham.

17. *Den of Thieves,* p. 155.

18. Boesky's total position of 1.8 million shares worth $42 million was four times the peak position at Goldman Sachs.

19. Christopher Byron, *New York* magazine, September 1989.

20. Edward Oakley Thorp, *Beat the Dealer* (New York: Blaisdell, 1962).

21. "Small Securities Firm Links Drexel's Milken, Goldman's Freeman," *Wall Street Journal,* April 6, 1988, p. 1.

22. Thorp was never involved in or even aware of the activities that were questioned. His office was in Newport Beach, two thousand miles away from Princeton. Thorp was engaged in quantitative research and the development of sophisticated investment ideas.

23. "Freeman's Attorney's Battle," *Wall Street Journal,* November 28, 1989, p. B14.

24. Laurie P. Cohen and Milo Geyelin, "Freeman Sentenced," *Wall Street Journal,* April 18, 1990.

25. Freeman tutored and coached basketball at Boys Harbor Inc., a social-service agency in East Harlem, New York. He was free to act as an unregistered investment adviser and, after three years, to act as a registered investment adviser.

Chapter Twenty-eight
Building a Global Business

1. Fife had offered to go two years before, but Bob Conway got chosen. Then Fife's first wife died after a long struggle with a virulent cancer. Jim Gorter raised the question of Fife's going to London as the two men were driving away from the meeting at which they had arranged the sale of Bank of America's headquarters building for $555 million—a price chosen because the building was at 555 California Street—to Shorenstein Properties. That price was much higher than any other bid, but real estate prices were low and soon to rise substantially, so the investment was a great success. Fife had started his career at Blyth & Company and transferred to Goldman Sachs's San Francisco office as a vice president in investment banking.

2. In the equities division, language fluency was more common than in investment banking. Partner Bill Landreth spoke French.

3. When Fife arrived, Goldman Sachs had three hundred people in London; a decade later, it had two thousand—a nearly sevenfold increase.

4. Exceptional leaders already building business in London included Bill Landreth in security sales and James MacLaren in investment banking.

5. Philip Rosen was retained to identify Goldman Sachs's public relations weakness and produced a list of twenty-five things wrong about Goldman Sachs.

6. Originally leased by Bob Wilson, who was exiled to London after presiding over the Penn Central commercial-paper fiasco, and later used by Roy Smith and Bob Conway.

7. De la Dehesa was Secretary of State for Economy and Finance. Sheinberg knew him because he covered central banks.

8. By 1991, "country adviser" was replaced by "international adviser" to reflect the reality that many advisers were actively involved across the world in the firm's activities and sometimes only a little in their home countries. The vice-chairman title was dropped.

9. Mayoux graduated from Ecole des Hautes Etudes Commerciales (HEC) and Ecole Nationale d'Administration (ENA), was appointed Inspecteur de Finances, and served as a special adviser to the minister of Finance. For twelve years, he was CEO of Crédit Agricole, Europe's largest retail bank, chaired various reform commissions, and reorganized the steel industry as CEO of Sacilor. He then served as CEO of Société Générale, the bank where he is now honorary chairman. He is a commander of both the Légion d'Honneur and l'Ordre National de Mérite. Despite his many distinctions, Mayoux was not an immediate success when he first met senior people in New York. Bob Rubin, Steve Friedman, and Geoff Boisi did not go for him. But nobody said Fife could not hire Mayoux, so he went ahead.

10. Prodi defeated Silvio Berlusconi, who defeated Prodi in the next election and then lost to Prodi again a few years later. Berlusconi won reelection in April 2008.

11. When the telephone system of Greece announced its intention to privatize, Goldman Sachs couldn't find a way to avoid paying a bribe. So the firm opted out. The mandate was won by Morgan Stanley—but years later the deal had still not come to fruition.

12. Sutherland had also been attorney general of Ireland and commissioner of Competition for the European Community in Brussels.

13. After Telefónica, privatizations of other big Spanish concerns—Repsol and Endesa—and ADR offerings for giant private banks—Bilbao Vizcaya and Banco Santander—followed, and Goldman Sachs was regularly earning fees of $20 million every year for its work in Spain. Success in Spain helped open opportunities in Latin America, as well as across Europe. And success with Telefónica soon led to a series of telecom privatizations in Holland, Denmark, and Mexico, where Goldman Sachs was chosen to manage the massive privatization underwriting for Telefonos de Mexico (Telmex)—with a $20 million fee. The grand finale was the privatization of Deutsche Telekom with a fee close to $40 million.

14. Goldman Sachs had not developed the giant BP privatization transaction into a business relationship.

15. Plaut took over from Paul Achleitner, who led Goldman Sachs's German business for five years before he left to be finance director of Allianz, the giant insurer based in Munich.

16. Siemens was also the first major German corporation to use management consultants. In the 1980s, it retained both McKinsey and Boston Consulting Group to do studies and to have a direct comparison to see which firm did the best work—at the best fee.

17. In February 1999—right at the peak of the Internet bubble—Goldman Sachs helped Siemens spin off its semiconductor business in an €8 billion IPO. At €35 per share, demand was so strong—retail customers oversubscribed the issue an incredible 250 times—that follow-on investor bidding took the price up nearly threefold to €100. A few years later, the share price was at €8. "I should have known we were in a bubble," says Plaut sheepishly. "Capital Group took zero shares and Fidelity simply flipped it."

18. Klaus Luft also arranged an "impossible" mandate as a German working with Bob Rubin: NCR's defense against AT&T.

19. ICBC has 20,000 branches and 100 million retail customers, and is about twice as large in assets as the next largest bank in China.

CHAPTER TWENTY-NINE
STEVE QUIT!

1. The Bishop Estate had been a customer of bond salesmen Fred Stack, who developed a close relationship that led to discussion of a possible

investment similar to Sumitomo's. Corzine met the Estate's key people at a Marriott near Dulles Airport for a preliminary discussion and then flew to Hawaii for a brief closing session.

2. Anita Raghaven and Michael Sicondolfi, "Friedman Steps Down as Goldman Chairman," *Wall Street Journal*, September 14, 2004, p. C1.

3. Ibid.

4. Michael Carroll, "Inside Goldman's College of Cardinals," *Institutional Investor*, October 1994.

CHAPTER THIRTY
COLLECTING THE BEST

1. Goldman Sachs was the first to recruit Harvard MBAs in the 1920s. The Depression ended that practice.

2. Robert Levering, Milton Moskowitz, and Michael Katz, *The 100 Best Companies to Work For in America* (Reading, Mass.: Addison-Wesley, 1993).

CHAPTER THIRTY-ONE
JON CORZINE

1. Corzine grew up in Wilkie Station, Illinois (population 500), and earned an MBA at the University of Chicago. He met his future wife, Joanne, in kindergarten. They grew up together and were married for thirty-three years, but divorced when he went into politics.

2. Don Gant led the 1987 negotiations and Jon Corzine led the 1989 negotiations.

3. Corzine asked partner Bob Litterman, a stellar "quant," to study risk management and develop one overall risk management system to replace the two-inch-thick daily computer printout he was then getting with reports of positions in each of dozens of separate trading units. Applying VaR (value at risk) metrics, Litterman made it possible to establish risk limits for each trade. Previously, as most traders accumulated trading profits, their self-confidence rose and their risk taking grew geometrically. Surprisingly, once VaR was established, most traders preferred knowing their limits.

4. Boris Groysberg, Sarah Mathews, Ashish Nanda, and Malcolm Salter, "The Goldman Sachs IPO," Harvard Business School Case 9-800-016, revised April 14, 2006, p. 11.

5. Laura M. Holson and Andrew Ross Sorkin, "Tel-ecommunications Powerhouse; Goldman Sachs Rules as Industry Is Transformed in Europe," *New York Times*, December 13, 1999, p. C1.

6. A major dinner meeting with AIG that included Corzine was organized by others.

7. Corzine says he wasn't entirely alone. He recalls taking with him Chris Flowers, the banker in charge of financial institutions, who went on to a spectacular success in private equity after leaving Goldman Sachs.

CHAPTER THIRTY-TWO   LONG-
TERM CAPITAL MANAGEMENT

1. Sandy Weill had comparably great motivation for ordering his traders to unwind all their "perfect arbitrage" positions: The merger of Salomon Smith Barney and Travelers with Citibank was scheduled for completion that same October.

2. The main role of the Fed was to protect the group from charges of illegal collusion.

3. Corzine's recollection differs: He says the discussions with Buffett were fully disclosed to the entire group of bankers.

4. Today Corzine says the management committee knew—or at least Roy Zuckerberg knew, with the implication that he must have told all the others. This is the kind of explication that earned Corzine the nickname "Uncle Approximate" and so upset his senior partners.

CHAPTER THIRTY-THREE   COUP

1. It was determined at the executive committee meeting that Paulson would immediately be made co-chairman and then, at the June partners meeting, would additionally be made co–senior partner by vote of the partnership.

2. "Chief Resigns from Shared Post, at Goldman" *New York Times*, January 12, 1999, p. C1.

CHAPTER THIRTY-FOUR
GETTING INVESTMENT
MANAGEMENT RIGHT

1. In Investment Banking, Suzanne Donnahoe had worked with Milton Berlinski on sales and acquisitions of investment-management firms. In the mid-1980s, David Blood went directly from Har-

vard Business School into the investment banking division. Soon, even before being made a vice president, he was heading the debt capital markets division with David George and Jon Corzine. Because Blood had lived in Brazil and spoke both Spanish and Portuguese, he was assigned to cover Latin America in 1989–90 from New York City. In 1992, he joined John Thain in the bond division for four years and transferred to London.

2. Their first strategy was actually "2 × 2 × 2"—$200 billion in assets with $200 million in profits by the year 2000.

3. In 1995, investment manager Cliff Asness got a $5 million bonus—the largest paid to any nonpartner—but he knew it was just a small fraction of the profit he had made for the firm, so he quit to launch his own hedge fund and took three credit analysts with him. There was a silver lining to the storm clouds: partner Bob Litterman, the firm's risk manager for trading, transferred over to develop a global risk-management capability for GSAM called PACS. It matched portfolio construction to each client's specific investment goals, using rigorous product specifications with "risk budgets" of "tracking error" and risk measurement based on the concept that 100 percent of the risk accepted by each client should be used to achieve superior long-term performance.

4. Later Berlinski negotiated the ultimate purchase of RCM by Germany's Dresdner Bank—which also bought Kleinwort Benson, the distinguished London merchant bank with a sizable asset-management business that had participated in Kleinwort Benson McCowan.

5. Commodities Corporation was based on Helmut Wyman's theories of profits in speculative markets.

6. GSAM was managed by Ford and Blood until Ford went limited, after which Blood managed the organization for four years from London.

CHAPTER THIRTY-FIVE
PAULSON'S DISCIPLINES

1. After William Clay Ford Jr., CEO of Ford, got an allocation of 400,000 shares of Goldman Sachs in the IPO—the largest allocation to an individual—a Ford shareholder sued, alleging the allocation was a reward for Ford Motor's business with Goldman Sachs and claiming that

any gain on the shares belonged to the company. While a Ford committee concluded that Mr. Ford had not acted improperly, the company agreed to settle in November 2004, and Goldman Sachs agreed to pay $13.4 million—$10 million to a Ford charitable trust (relieving Ford of a prior commitment) plus legal expenses. The firm, denying any wrongdoing, said that Mr. Ford was the kind of long-term investor it most wanted. Ford sold his shares immediately and gave the $4.5 million profit to charity. John Thornton is a Ford director and had befriended Ford at Hotchkiss School. (Jenny Anderson, "Ford Settles Investors' Suit Over IPO of Goldman," *New York Times*, November 4, 2004, C-4.)

2. *BusinessWeek*, May 17, 1999.

3. Patrick McGeehan, "Goldman Sachs to Acquire Top Firm on Trading Floors," *New York Times*, September 12, 2000, p. C2.

4. "Lex Column: Goldman Sachs," *Financial Times*, September 12, 2000, p. 26.

5. Neil Weinberg, "Fear, Greed and Technology," *Forbes* 165, no. 11 (May 15, 2000), p. 170.

6. President George H. W. Bush and his wife, Barbara, were in the residence, so Paulson got a chance to renew his acquaintance with "41."

CHAPTER THIRTY-SIX
BEFORE THE STORM

1. While Blankfein did not use the term, his presentation is described by others as "Lloyd's 'fork in the road' speech." Blankfein's unorthodox persistence was adumbrated early in life by his strategy in dating a Wellesley College student who lived in Kansas City: He took a summer job at Hallmark to be near her. They did not marry.

2. Bethany McLean, "The Man Who Must Keep Goldman Growing," *Fortune*, March 17, 2008, p. 131.

3. Ibid.

4. David Viniar went to Bronx High School of Science and Union College, graduated from Harvard Business School in 1980, joined Goldman Sachs, and made partner in 1992. He served under John Thain and became CFO in 1999.

5. Specifically, the focus was on ABX 06-2 and a subindex of it linked to the lowest-quality credit.

6. Kate Kelley, "How Goldman Won Big on

Mortgage Meltdown," *Financial Times,* December 17, 2007.

7. The creation and collapse of the subprime mortgage securities market and the harm done to many marginal borrowers and the enormous losses taken by financial institutions were malign examples of how wrongly financial markets can behave when free of well-established internal disciplines or regulation by industry umpires or governments. The impact of the collapse was enormous. The hurt to leading institutions—Citigroup, UBS, Merrill Lynch, Morgan Stanley, and many others—was large, swift, and visible. The hurt done to individual families will be largely private, personal, and invisible—but dream-destructive.

Traditionally, a mortgage lender's loan officer was trained in credit judgment and, while rewarded for making loans, was penalized for bad loans. His or her career depended on doing good conservative work to build profitable volume while not making mistakes. The mortgage lending institution acted as principal, lending its own money and keeping the loan on its own books.

All this changed with the securitization of mortgages, particularly the subprime mortgage loans most colorfully defined as "ninja" loans, made to individuals—usually young, first-time home-buyers—with *no income, no job,* and *no assets.* Many of these borrowers saw house prices rising steadily, knew interest rates were low, and could borrow on interest-only (IO) terms, with no principal payments due for the first five years. Since house prices were rising faster than the rate of interest, increasing numbers of borrowers appeared to make money on the expanding differential—so, increasingly, houses got bought on speculation. Meanwhile, mortgage bankers who originate mortgages sold off their loan portfolios as securitized assets through Wall Street firms that competed for the lucrative underwriting business. Competing for volume, mortgage banks gave their officers incentives to drive for volume and made it easier to produce volume by cutting the traditionally required down payment from 20–25 percent of the purchase price to just 5 percent—or even less.

Wall Street underwriters made large profits selling securitized mortgages. They competed for market share, paying large bonuses to those who won the most volume. Credit agencies, competing with each other for the fees they got paid by the issuers, gave high ratings to mortgage-backed securities. As the underwriters eased into mortgages of lower and lower quality, nobody called out "The emperor had no clothes!" and the volume increased—increasing profits and incentives to originating lenders, profits and bonuses to underwriters, and profits and market share to rating agencies, while borrowers appeared to profit on the ever-expanding speed between the interest cost of the mortgage and the rising price of the house.

Mortgage securities, collateralized by larger, diversified portfolios of mortgages, were then "sliced and diced" into several different tranches, each with its own creditworthiness and its own credit rating. When individual mortgages in that portfolio went into default—as some were sure to do—the highest-quality tranche was fully protected because the portfolio of collateral was larger than the volume of securities sold. In addition, insurance against loss was purchased in order to obtain the best possible interest rates. Not surprisingly, a few insurance companies specialized in this type of insurance and competed with each other for more business.

The different tranches—with credit ratings ranging from AAA to BBB—offered different rates of interest and were sold to different groups of buyers. Since the lowest-quality tranche could not be sold, banks had to keep the worst "junk"— but could, according to the banks' permissive accountants, off-load them to Cayman Islands companies created for that very purpose and thus called Special Purpose Vehicles.

Meanwhile, all over the world, investment managers, banks, insurance companies, pension funds, and others reaching for higher-interest securities with high credit ratings, bought more and more securities backed by mortgages of lower and lower quality taken out by ninja borrowers.

Thirty years ago, the median down payment required of a first-time buyer was 18 percent. In 2005–2006, the median payment was only 2 percent—and half the buyers put nothing down. The tiny equity could be okay if house prices always rose, but in 2007 the average house price dropped nearly 9 percent. As a result, some fifteen million homeowners owed more on their mortgage than their houses were worth in the market.

Several factors combined to appear to justify AAA ratings, which were, in retrospect, miscalculations of several risks: relying on historical loss experience without adjusting for real changes in the whole system of mortgage origination; taking too much comfort in geographical diversification when other factors had become more powerful and were not diversified; taking too much comfort in the history that house prices in the United States had never, on average, declined year-to-year; and an inability to model or predict borrower behavior—including fraud—in a declining market for house prices.

Then house prices, instead of rising at record rates, began to fall—for the first time since the Depression—because the ratio of house prices to rental rates had gotten way above trend; because mortgage terms could not get even easier and had already attracted marginal house buyers and speculators; because overbuilding was flooding the market (leaving numerous vacant houses with overgrown lawns and FOR SALE signs), which pulled prices downward; and because borrowers had zero or even negative equity in their houses, making it more rational to walk away than to keep paying on the now-too-large loans. While no one or two of these problems would have had serious consequences, the confluence of adversities created combinations that were cataclysmic, particularly in California.

CHAPTER THIRTY-SEVEN
THE PERFECT STORM

1. Rick Schmitt, "Prophet and Loss," *Stanford Magazine*, March/April 2009.
2. Charles Gasparino, "Feds, Street Draft Deal," CNBC, September 13, 2008.
3. "Thundering Herd Faltered and Fell," *New York Times*, November 9, 2008, p. 1.

INDEX